Proportional Representation in Presidential Nominating Politics

Also published for the Institute of Government, University of Virginia:

Chester W. Bain, *Annexation in Virginia: The Use of the Judicial Process for Readjusting City-County Boundaries.* 1966. xiv, 258 pp.

Chester W. Bain, *"A Body Incorporate": The Evolution of City-County Separation in Virginia.* 1967. xii, 142 pp.

David G. Temple, *Merger Politics: Local Government Consolidation in Tidewater Virginia.* 1972. xii, 225 pp.

Thomas R. Morris, *The Virginia Supreme Court: An Institutional and Political Analysis.* 1975. xvi, 188 pp.

Weldon Cooper and Thomas R. Morris, *Virginia Government and Politics: Readings and Comments.* 1976. xviii, 438 pp.

Larry Sabato, *The Democratic Party Primary in Virginia: Tantamount to Election No Longer.* 1977. ix, 169 pp.

Proportional Representation in Presidential Nominating Politics

Paul T. David and James W. Ceaser

with

Edmund Beard

Samuel K. Gove

Jean G. McDonald

Richard Murray

Howard L. Reiter

Published for
The Institute of Government, University of Virginia
University Press of Virginia
Charlottesville

4804637

THE UNIVERSITY PRESS OF VIRGINIA
Copyright © 1980 by the Rector and Visitors
of the University of Virginia

First published 1980

Library of Congress Cataloging in Publication Data

David, Paul Theodore, 1906–
   Proportional representation in presidential nominating
politics.
   Includes index.
   1. Presidents—United States—Nomination.   2. Pro
portional representation—United States.   3. Political
conventions.   I. Ceaser, James W., joint author.
II. Title.
JK521.D36   329'.022'0973   79-4387
ISBN 0-8139-0787-X

Printed in the United States of America

Foreword

This is the seventh volume in a series of publications issued jointly by the Institute of Government and the University Press of Virginia and dealing with politics and public affairs in Virginia. This examination of proportional representation in presidential nominating politics, although it includes a case study of Virginia's experience in 1976, ranges beyond the boundaries of the Commonwealth to give us a more comprehensive view of one important aspect of state and national politics. Few observers today would deny that the past decade has brought tremendous change to American politics, including modifications of the basic rules of the game. The nature and consequences of those rules changes are questions well worth our attention, and professors David and Ceaser here contribute importantly to an understanding of them.

CLIFTON MCCLESKEY, Director
Institute of Government

Charlottesville, Virginia

Preface

This study was conceived in the fall of 1975, when many political analysts were predicting a "brokered" or multiballoted convention in the Democratic party in 1976. The belief that a nominee would not be chosen on the first ballot rested on two premises: first, that none of the candidates possessed sufficient appeal or political strength to emerge from the primaries as a clear and undisputed front-runner; and second, that the new party selection rules requiring the use of a proportional division of the delegates in many states would tend to disperse the delegate totals among a large number of candidates and thus make it more difficult for any one candidate to obtain a majority. Under the original conception of this study, each state was to be assigned an observer who would follow the state's delegate selection process, paying particular attention to its method of dividing the delegates. The observer would then study the behavior of the state delegation at the convention under the anticipated situation of a bargained decision. No comprehensive study of the nominating process had been done for over twenty years, and it seemed clear to us that many of the earlier generalizations about delegation behavior would need revision in light of both the different rules under which delegates are now chosen and the changed character of state and local party organizations.[1]

The second part of the project, the study of delegation behavior at the convention, was canceled when it became apparent that the

[1] For the last comprehensive study of the nominating process, see Paul T. David, Malcolm Moos, and Ralph M. Goldman. *Presidential Nominating Politics in 1952*, 5 vols. (Baltimore: Johns Hopkins Press, 1954).

Democrats' decision would in fact be made on the first ballot. In light of the earlier expectations, this outcome itself demanded explanation. In part, it was due to unexpected developments at the political level: Jimmy Carter proved to be a much more formidable candidate, and his opponents much weaker candidates, than virtually anyone had supposed. But this was not the entire story. As we turned to a closer study of the delegate selection rules, we discovered that they were not nearly so hostile to a first-ballot victory as most initially believed. There was first the obvious fact that proportional representation was not universally required in 1976; as it happened, over one-third of the delegates were chosen under sanctioned "loophole" (i.e., nonproportional) systems. But even where proportional rules were employed, their tendency to produce a bargained decision was not nearly so pronounced as we had expected. The shift to proportional systems had two major effects that tended to offset each other. On the one hand, proportional representation as a method of apportioning delegates did indeed possess the anticipated dispersing or fragmenting result. On the other hand, however, as one integral part of a set of rules emphasizing the concept of representation of national candidates rather than party organizations or interest groups, proportional systems allowed a leading contender to pick up committed delegates in states that, under previous rules, would most likely have chosen a much larger number of uncommitted delegates.

Beyond this, our study revealed the importance that variations in the rules can have on the balance of political forces within both parties. For example, had proportional rules been used in all of the Republican primaries in 1976, it would almost certainly have helped the conservative wing of the party and given the nomination to Ronald Reagan. The significance of these and other findings about the effects of the rules served as a partial consolation for the necessity of reducing the scope of the original project.

The book is divided into two general parts. The first analyzes the selection process as a whole, describing the various selection systems now being used and tracing the origin, growth, and potential future consequences of the new principle of proportional representation. The second part looks at the operation of selected state systems; it consists of six independently written state reports chosen to represent a cross section of the different kinds of selection procedures and to provide some indication of the variety of political contests in 1976. Apart from being asked to cover a few general questions relating to the effects of the rules on the division of delegates, the authors were left to develop their case studies on their own. This "decentralized" approach reflected our conviction that, despite the increased standardization in selection procedures that has taken place over the past decade (especially in the Democratic party), each state nomination race remains in many respects unique, colored by its own laws, party rules, traditions, and political culture.

As in most joint projects, there was some division of labor between the authors. Professor David conceived the project and handled most of the administrative chores, including the voluminous correspondence with the many state collaborators. Chapter 1 was jointly written, Professor David had primary responsibility for chapters 2 and 3, and Professor Ceaser for chapters 4, 5, and 6.

In connection with this project we would like to thank the Institute of Government at the University of Virginia, which sponsored the study from the beginning. The Institute's director, Clifton Mc-Cleskey, and its editor, Sandra H. Wilkinson, both read the manuscript in its entirety and offered many valuable suggestions. Also, the Institute's executive secretary, Elizabeth Hull, very capably supervised all of the secretarial work required during the course of the project. The Earhart Foundation provided financial assistance for travel and materials, for which we are very grateful. Carol Casey of the Congressional Research Service kindly provided copies of official election returns and other data for a considerable number of states. The data were analyzed with the help of B. Nelson Ong, Gale Mattox, and John Epperson, all graduate students at the University of Virginia.

Other institutes of government and departments of political science throughout the country were helpful in recruiting state directors who assisted in the national project by providing information about their states. We would like in particular to acknowledge the contributions of the following:

William H. Steward, Jr., University of Alabama; Bruce E. Keith, University of California, Berkeley; Howard L. Reiter, University of Connecticut; Catherine Rudder, University of Georgia; Roger F. Snider, University of Idaho; Samuel K. Gove, University of Illinois; Edmund Beard, University of Massachusetts, Boston; Ronald J. Hy, University of Mississippi; Thomas Payne, University of Montana; Don W. Driggs, University of Nevada; Robert U. Anderson, University of New Mexico; Louise S. Brennan, University of North Carolina; Boyd L. Wright, University of North Dakota; John H. Kessel, Ohio State University; Jean McDonald, University of Oklahoma; Christine Howells, University of Rhode Island; Alan L. Clem, University of South Dakota; Ross E. Dobson, Russell L. Smith, and Larry W. Thomas, University of Tennessee; Richard Murray, University of Houston, Texas; Hugh Bone, University of Washington; Allan S. Hammock and Robert DiClerico, West Virginia University; James R. Donoghue, University of Wisconsin; and Oliver Walter, University of Wyoming.

Contents

Contents

Tables

Tables

PART I

National Events and Analysis

CHAPTER 1 / Proportional Representation in the Democratic Party

THE Democratic party in recent years has been engaged in a continuing effort to reform its party rules and practices. The objective of the reformers has been to open the party's nominating process to participation by all Democrats in a manner that will be "full, meaningful and timely." This general reform effort was accelerated by the unhappy experience of the 1968 Democratic National Convention, which was considered by many observers to be unfairly constituted, closed off from rank-and-file influence, and subject to manipulation at critical moments. The movement toward proportional representation of each presidential candidate's strength in delegate selection also seems to have begun after the 1968 election, in the work of the Democratic party's Commission on Party Structure and Delegate Selection, generally known as the McGovern Commission. That commission set forth the results of its work in the well-known report *Mandate for Reform*, published in 1970.[1]

The McGovern Commission report established eighteen guidelines that were presented to the state parties as legal requirements and eventually were enforced in nearly all of the states. The new rules asserted the supremacy of the national party in legislating the character of the selection process. That supremacy subsequently received the implicit backing of the Supreme Court in the case of *Cousins* v. *Wigoda*,[2] and the principle now seems firmly established.

[1] Commission on Party Structure and Delegate Selection (Senator George S. McGovern, chairman), *Mandate for Reform* (Washington, D.C.: Democratic National Committee, 1970).

[2] 419 U.S. 477; 42 L.Ed. 2d 595; 95 S. Ct. 541 (1975).

The guidelines of 1970 were divided into three main groups. The first of these dealt with "rules or practices which inhibit access to the delegate selection process." Here the McGovern Commission began its work with a renewed attack upon the problems of discrimination based on race, color, creed, or national origin. Previous action on this subject had been taken by the 1964 convention, by a Special Equal Rights Committee that followed, and by the 1968 convention. The McGovern Commission reiterated the standards that had previously been proposed and required their incorporation into the written rules of each state party. The state parties were also required to take affirmative action to overcome the effects of past discrimination, but with the understanding "that this is not to be accomplished by the mandatory imposition of quotas."[3] Despite this disclaimer, the operation of the new rules in 1972 resulted in many parts of the country in something approaching quotas for black delegates. The same was true of a related guideline on full representation of women and young people, since quotas based on population were widely calculated and frequently enforced in 1972. These requirements were the most controversial clauses in the new rules, and the problem of how to enforce affirmative action without requiring quotas has been much argued ever since. Other provisions in the first group of guidelines dealt with voter registration, costs and fees for participation, and a requirement for individual state party adoptions of written rules covering essential aspects of the delegate selection process.

The second group of guidelines focused on "rules or practices which dilute the influence of a Democrat in the delegate selection process, after he has exercised all available resources to effect such influence." Under this heading, proxy voting was forbidden in party meetings at all levels; a quorum of not less than 40 percent was required for all official party committee meetings taking part in the delegate selection process; and the unit rule was forbidden "in any stage of the delegate selection process" (repeating a rule adopted by the 1968 convention). Further, states were required to select at least 75 percent of their delegates at the congressional district level or lower, and the apportionment of delegates among the districts was regulated. Also included in this section, although

[3] *Mandate for Reform*, p. 40.

no formal requirement was set forth, was the guideline recommending adequate representation of support for lesser presidential candidates (to be discussed at length later).

The third group of guidelines was more miscellaneous, dealing with rules and practices that did not fit neatly into either of the previous groups. Here adequate public notice of party meetings was required; ex officio delegates were prohibited; and all processes related to delegate selection were required to take place within the presidential year. Also, a strenuous effort was made to provide safeguards for the slate-making processes that tend to control the outcome of caucuses, conventions, and primaries.

Taken as a whole, these new rules were a call for more democracy in party affairs and an open door for participation in the presidential nominating process by any Democrat so minded. In commenting specifically on the problems of fair representation of minority views on presidential candidates, the McGovern Commission concluded the opening section of its report concerning the issues it had sought to address with the following statement:

One issue of special concern to the Commission was the fair representation of supporters of each presidential candidate on the state's delegation. Many witnesses at our hearings believed that the unrestrained application of majority rule in primary, convention and committee systems, produced much of the bitterness and divisiveness characteristic of 1968.

In California, a "winner-take-all" primary state, Senator Robert Kennedy received 46 percent of the vote (compared to 42 percent for Senator Eugene McCarthy and 12 percent for the slate ultimately committed to Vice President Hubert H. Humphrey). The delegation pledged to Senator Kennedy became the sole representatives of California Democrats to the National Convention. In New Hampshire, on the other hand, McCarthy received only 42 percent of the vote in the presidential preference primary, yet 83 percent of the delegates to the National Convention from New Hampshire cast their ballots for him.

In Minnesota, a caucus-convention system, the supporters of Senator McCarthy comprised 42 percent of the delegates to the state convention, but, by majority vote, were denied any of the 20 at-large delegates elected by that body. In New York, where the at-large segment of the delegation is appointed by the State Committee after the delegate primary, the delegates chosen by a majority of that committee bore scant resemblance in their presidential preferences to the results of the primary election, causing a serious rift among Democrats in the state.[4]

In view of these considerations, the commission adopted Guideline B-6, which urged "adequate representation of minority views on presidential candidates at each stage in the delegate selection process." This was not one of the guidelines that state parties were "required" to accept; rather, it fell into a group of guidelines which the commission considered desirable but about which there were doubts concerning the immediate feasibility of universal compliance. The commission's commentary on the guideline was as follows:

The Commission believes that a full and meaningful opportunity to participate in the delegate selection process is precluded unless the presidential preference of each Democrat is fairly represented at all levels of the process. Therefore, the Commission urges each State Party to adopt procedures which will provide fair representation of minority views on presidential candidates and recommends that the 1972 Convention adopt a rule requiring State Parties to provide for the representation of minority views to the highest level of the nominating process.

The Commission believes that there are at least two different methods by which a State Party can provide for such representation. First, in at-large elections it can divide delegate votes among presidential candidates in proportion to their demonstrated strength. Second, it can choose delegates from fairly apportioned districts no larger than congressional districts.

The Commission recognizes that there may be other methods to provide for fair representation of minority views. Therefore, the Commission will make every effort to stimulate public discussion of the issue of representation of minority views on presidential candidates between now and the 1972 Democratic National Convention.[5]

In urging this guideline upon the states, the commission recognized proportional representation as one means of achieving fair representation, but it gave equal recognition to the commonly used pattern of plurality elections at the congressional district level or lower.

[4] Ibid., p. 32.
[5] Ibid., pp. 44-45.

The commission noted with approval that New Mexico had become the first state to provide for proportional representation in a presidential primary.[6]

Some observations should be made here about the view, reflected in the commission's call for "adequate representation of minority views on presidential candidates," regarding the kind of representative role the delegate should play. The focus in representation is placed on directly reproducing the candidate preference of the participants, rather than the interests of the organization or of the party as seen by the convention delegates. This view follows that of the earlier Hughes Commission, from which the McGovern Commission borrowed most of its argument. The Hughes Commission report implicitly identified two different theories of representation in the existing "mixed" nominating system. According to the first theory, delegates represented above all the interests of their respective state and local party organizations and, through them, the interests of many of the organized groups that comprised the Democratic party following. According to the second, the delegates represented the choice of the party's mass constituency—"the people"—in their expressed choice of a nominee. These two theories existed side by side. The party-oriented element, having its origins in nineteenth-century theories of the role of parties, found its institutional expression both in the caucus states and in those primary states which by legal arrangements or tradition had sought to isolate themselves from the intrusion of national candidates; the candidate-oriented or plebiscitory element, having its origins in the selection theory of the Progressives, found its institutional expression in those primaries which allowed contests among the national contenders.

The Hughes Commission in its 1968 report made perfectly clear which of these theories the reformers favored: "A confluence of historical forces has made the 1968 Democratic National Convention an occasion of great moment in the inexorable movement of Presidential politics in America toward direct democracy." The commission report continued: "The fact that many states declined to provide for delegate selection entirely by primary was acceptable to the nation—but only because the system did not override or frustrate the national commitment to direct democracy

[6] Ibid., p. 50.

in the naming of presidential nominees."[7] The preference for a direct candidate focus in the selection of delegates was justified on the grounds that party organizations, even if changed, could no longer correctly represent the will of the party's following. This change in the 1960s from group or pluralist politics to mass movement politics rendered the organizations' claim invalid and meant that the only way to represent accurately the constituency of the party was by a formal process in which each citizen could express a candidate preference: "Whereas bargaining among representatives of party organizations once could be said to represent the interests and views of the mass constituency of the party, the decline of the interest groups behind the bosses has undercut that rationale."[8]

During the two years preceding the 1972 convention, most of the Democratic state parties moved to bring their practices into line with the requirements and recommendations of the McGovern Commission, which were further reinforced in the language of the official call for the 1972 convention. Michigan and North Carolina joined New Mexico in providing for primaries with proportional representation. Among the caucus states, Minnesota and Colorado moved to install proportional representation. In any case, all of the caucus states were required to elect at least 75 percent of their delegates at the congressional district level or lower.[9]

In California persistent efforts to change the winner-take-all primary were defeated by Republican opposition led by the Re-

---

[7] Commission on the Democratic Selection of Presidential Nominees (Harold Hughes, chairman), *The Democratic Choice: A Report of the Commission on the Democratic Selection of Presidential Nominees* (published by the Commission, 1968, at the Democratic National Convention, Chicago), pp. 9, 11-12 (reprinted in 90th Cong., 2d Sess., 1968, 114 *Congressional Record* 31546).

[8] Ibid., p. 14. According to Austin Ranney, the McGovern Commission did not favor extending direct democracy in the form of more primaries, but instead by opening up the caucus and convention procedures. See Ranney, "Changing the Rules of the Nominating Game," in James David Barber, ed., *Choosing the President* (Englewood Cliffs, N.J.: Prentice Hall, 1974), pp. 73-74. Still, there is the same emphasis in the McGovern Commission report on the representation of the participants' candidate preferences; and Ranney concedes that the effect of the reforms has been to increase dramatically the number of primaries.

[9] *Mandate for Reform*, p. 45.

publican governor, Ronald Reagan. Thus, at the 1972 Democratic National Convention, California became the foremost illustration of the problems surrounding fair representation of voters. Senator George McGovern had won the statewide vote and under California law was entitled to all of the California delegation. Supporters of Senator Hubert H. Humphrey, who had been only narrowly defeated, mounted a challenge to the McGovern delegation, on grounds that it was selected in violation of Guideline B-6. They claimed a proportionate share of the delegation for Humphrey. Eventually the issue was settled on the floor of the convention by a vote favorable to the McGovern delegation, which led to McGovern's victory in the nominating contest. But the entire problem had been dramatized in such a way that further action was inevitable. Consequently, the Rules Committee of the 1972 convention proposed as one of its recommendations "that delegates to the 1976 Democratic Convention shall be chosen in a manner which fairly reflects the division of preference expressed by those who participate in the presidential nominating process."[10]

Some members of the Rules Committee believed that the full achievement of this recommendation would require proportional representation. Congressman Donald M. Fraser of Minnesota, who had proposed the language just quoted, declared: "In my opinion this would require a candidate that had 40% of the vote to have approximately . . . 40% of the delegates. This would be true no matter how the vote might be subdivided within a state."[11] But the Rules Committee, in its report to the convention, made no specific reference to proportional representation, and this aspect of the matter did not come up in floor debate. The convention approved the recommendation for yet another commission to review the guidelines of 1972 and to adopt such additional guidelines as might be necessary to implement fully the call for the 1976 convention.

This authorization brought forth the work of what became known as the Mikulski Commission, after its chairwoman, Barbara Mikulski of Baltimore. In considering the McGovern Guideline B-6,

[10] *Report of the Committee on Rules,* Democratic National Convention, 1972, Article XVIII, Section 4, available at the Democratic National Committee Headquarters, Washington, D.C.

[11] Record of proceedings, Committee on Rules, Democratic National Convention, 1972, available at Democratic National Committee.

Mikulski referred to it as a guideline on "proportional representation," and the debate that followed centered on the extent to which proportional representation was feasible and desirable, either statewide or at the congressional district level. The Mikulski Commission assumed that any decision would involve interpretation of the convention mandate, quoted above, and that it had authority to impose or not to impose proportional representation at the congressional district level, as long as it avoided winner-take-all at the statewide level.

Reservations about the dangers of proportional representation were expressed. For example, Governor John J. Gilligan of Ohio commented, "The more you talk about giving proportional representation to losers, the more you guarantee that no one is ever going to be able to come into that Convention with enough votes to carry it on an early ballot."[12] Nevertheless, the Mikulski Commission in its recommendations agreed that, at all stages of the delegate selection process in the caucus states, proportionality should be required for candidates who received at least 10 percent of the votes at any level. Candidates receiving less than 10 percent could be eliminated if the states so desired. (This was an increase from the figure of 5 percent that had been used previously in the commission's discussions.) For the primary states, the commission also favored proportional representation at both district and at-large levels, again with a possible cutoff of minor candidates who received no higher than 10 percent of the votes; however, it was prepared to accept primaries in which 75 percent or more of the delegates were elected on a plurality basis at the congressional district level or lower. Such primaries became known as "loophole" primaries.[13]

The Mikulski Commission report was considered by the Democratic National Committee on January 11 and 12, 1974, and most of it was approved without change. But the recommendations for proportional representation, including the cutoff provision, were among those most hotly debated. Opponents claimed that they would lead to frivolous candidacies and to fragmentation of

[12] Transcript of Mikulski Commission deliberations, Sept. 21, 1973, p. 230, available at Democratic National Committee.

[13] Commission on Delegate Selection and Party Structure (Mikulski Commission), *Democrats All*, Dec. 6, 1973, p. 18, available at Democratic National Committee.

delegate strength. Penn Kimble, director of the Coalition for a Democratic Majority (a group representing the more conservative Democrats), went even further and challenged the representational theory of proportional representation, at least as it applied to the caucus states. He argued that the use of proportional representation with its "candidate preference" provision would encourage local party leaders to commit themselves earlier than they had done under previous arrangements, thus losing the flexibility that was the chief advantage of the caucus method. The uncommitted status, he argued, would face an "insurmountable disadvantage" in the face of the pressure from candidate campaigns.[14]

Kimble then shifted ground and, in an intriguing suggestion that will be developed at greater length later, argued that, to the extent that the uncommitted status is employed by candidates for delegates, such a status might serve as a vehicle for the direct representation of organized constituency blocs. Unable to find representation through the party organizations, these groups would seek to select their own delegates. One would then see the formation of the kind of national constituency blocs that some of the old Progressive reformers favoring proportional representation had supported. As Kimble expressed his view, "One likely result of the imposition of declarations of Presidential preference and proportional representation on basic levels of the delegate selection system is that those who feel a justified need to keep their presidential options open will organize themselves as constituency blocs. A black caucus, labor caucus, conservative caucus or pro-abortion caucus could elect its representatives more readily than an 'uncommitted' . . . caucus."[15]

The Democratic National Committee ultimately approved the Mikulski Commission recommendation for proportional representation, but the cutoff provision was revised from 10 to 15 percent as a further safeguard against minor candidates. The provision for "loophole" primaries remained unchanged.[16]

---

[14] Written statement delivered at the meeting of the Democratic National Committee, Feb. 29-Mar. 1, 1974, available at Democratic National Committee.
[15] Ibid.
[16] *Report of Commission on Delegate Selection and Party Structure, as Amended* (Washington, D.C.: Democratic National Committee, 1974).

11

The next forum at the national level to consider these issues was the December 1974 midterm conference of the Democratic party in Kansas City. The object of that conference was the adoption of a party charter which would come into effect after the 1976 convention. One question was whether to include any kind of fair representation clause on delegate selection. The Coalition for a Democratic Majority, representing the more conservative Democrats, was opposed to including such a clause. The so-called New Politics group insisted on inclusion of something similar to the language of the McGovern Commission report, and it won on this issue. Article Two, Section 4, of the Democratic party charter provides that "the national convention shall be composed of delegates who are chosen through processes which . . . assure that delegations fairly reflect the division of preferences expressed by those who participate in the presidential nominating process."[17]

Meanwhile, the Democratic National Committee had established a Compliance Review Commission to monitor and advise the state parties regarding compliance with the revised rules for delegate selection. Most of the states with long-established loophole primaries, including New York, New Jersey, Pennsylvania, Ohio, and Illinois, elected to retain them. California revised its primary law to permit each party to follow a system of its own choice: The Democrats opted for a combination of district and at-large elections, while the Republicans chose to retain statewide winner-take-all, as favored by then governor Ronald Reagan. Many other states enacted new presidential primary laws, and most of these seem to have opted for some form of proportional representation, either for both parties or for Democrats at the party's choice. In some of these states, this action was the beginning of the Republican party's involvement in questions of proportional representation in delegate selection.

The resulting mixture of delegate selection systems employed in 1976 on the Democratic side can be categorized as follows:

a. Thirteen states used the so-called loophole primaries, in which delegates could be selected at the congressional district level or lower without the requirement of proportional representation, as long as 75 percent of the delegates were selected at those

[17] The full text of the charter, as adopted, was reprinted in *Congressional Quarterly Weekly Report,* Dec. 14, 1974, p. 3334.

levels. Two of the states selected all of their delegates at the congressional district level. In the other states, the statewide at-large delegates, usually picked by a state committee or convention, had to be mandated in their candidate preferences according to some kind of proportional scheme.

b.　　Sixteen states and the District of Columbia used proportional representation primaries. In these, the delegates selected in the districts (at least 75 percent of each delegation under national rules) were assigned on a proportional basis according to the vote within each district. Thirteen of the states in this category had part of their delegations chosen statewide, with eleven states mandating these delegates proportionally on the basis of a statewide vote and two states mandating them in the same proportion as the delegates chosen in the districts. The proportional primary systems varied greatly in respect to the cutoff point that was used to qualify for delegate representation and to eliminate minor candidates. Fifteen percent was the highest cutoff point that could be used under national rules, but a state was free to choose a smaller percentage or simply to provide for absolute proportionality, i.e., any percentage of the popular vote that was high enough to elect at least one delegate. Ten of the sixteen proportional primary states used the 15 percent cutoff, while the others chose either 5 percent or absolute proportionality.

c.　　Twenty-one states used the caucus-convention method. Proportional representation was in effect in all these states and had to be employed at all levels, beginning generally with mass meetings at the lowest level. In contrast to previous years, participants were required either to specify their candidate preference or to state that they were uncommitted, in order that proportionality could be computed; and delegates to be elected for the next higher level of meetings were apportioned on this basis. Nearly all of the caucus states used the 15 percent cutoff point for eliminating minor candidates, the highest permitted under national party rules.

On the Republican side, no national party rule sanctioned proportional representation, and so the picture was very different. The Republican party's delegate selection systems, as summarized next, remained largely unchanged from previous years, except as they were affected by changes in state laws that had been made under Democratic influence.

a.   Sixteen states used variants of a plurality or winner-take-all primary system (what would have been called a loophole primary on the Democratic side); however, in almost all of these states, most of the delegates were elected at the congressional district level, with a minority elected statewide. In one state, California, it was winner-take-all on a statewide basis. The district delegates were chosen sometimes on slates with a formal requirement of winner-take-all and sometimes as individuals on a plurality basis, which in effect usually operated to promote winner-take-all. The statewide portions of the delegations were chosen by a variety of methods: formal winner-take-all; individually by plurality; or at the discretion of state committees or conventions.

b.   Eleven states used proportional representation primaries. These primaries were characterized by a greater variety than those of the Democratic party because of the absence of national party specifications. Two states, for example, elected all of their delegates statewide. Two states used 20 percent as a cutoff point, while six others either used 5 percent or an absolute proportional system. Overall, the Republican proportional primaries were somewhat more "proportional" in character than the Democratic ones.

c.   Twenty-three states and the District of Columbia used the caucus-convention method. The Republican caucus method differed from that of the Democrats in three important respects. First, there was no requirement in the national rules for participants or delegates to specify their candidate preferences; as a consequence, most of the delegates were chosen on an uncommitted basis, regardless of whether they had a candidate preference at the time. Second, there was no requirement for proportional representation. The principle was used informally to promote party harmony in some areas; but as the presidential race intensified, winner-take-all was increasingly pressed by both the Ford and Reagan forces. Finally, a large proportion of the delegates were selected statewide by state conventions. This meant that there were slates of substantial size at stake, and the tendency as the race progressed was to press the narrowest majorities to assert full control of these slates.

A state-by-state presentation of the systems by which delegates of both parties were selected is provided in Appendix A. Also, the

Table 1.1. Numbers of delegates chosen under each system of representation in 1976

Selection system	Democratic party		Republican party	
	Number of delegates	Percentage of total	Number of delegates	Percentage of total
Plurality				
Primary	989	32.9	1,151	50.9
Nonprimary [a]	2	0.1	711	31.5
Quasi-proportional [b]	226	7.5	5	0.2
Proportional				
Primary	1,100	36.5	392	17.4
Caucus	691	23.0	—	—
Total	3,008	100.0	2,259	100.0

SOURCE: Computed from the data assembled in Appendix A.

[a] Includes delegates selected in caucus states and those in primary states mandated at discretion of state conventions or committees.

[b] Includes statewide delegates that reflect proportionally the candidate preferences of delegates elected at district levels under plurality systems. (Statewide delegates reflecting candidate preferences of district delegates elected under proportional methods are counted under proportional.)

numbers of delegates selected under each system are summarized in Table 1.1.

With so many states already committed to the use of proportional representation in the Democratic party, it is not surprising that the issue of making it universal came up for consideration in the proceedings of the 1976 Democratic National Convention. After a vigorous debate at a meeting of the convention's Rules Committee on June 20, 1976, the committee voted by 58½ to 58¼ to propose the following resolution for convention adoption.

Section 9. Resolved further that in reviewing and modifying the Delegate Selection Rules, the Commission on Presidential Primaries shall construe Article II, Section 4, clause (ii) of the Charter to bar the use of delegate selection systems in primary states which permit a plurality of votes at any level to elect all of the delegates from that level. This provision shall not be amendable as a Bylaw.[18]

[18] Report of the Rules Committee, Democratic National Convention, 1976, available at Democratic National Committee.

This action occasioned a minority report from the Rules Committee, proposing that the following substitution be made for section 9:

Resolved that the Commission on the Role and Future of Presidential Primaries in reviewing delegate selection rules shall analyze and review the use of the so-called "loophole" primaries as provided in the Delegate Selection Rules of the Democratic Party (Rule 11) and, if appropriate, recommend changes.[19]

The issue in turn came up on the floor of the convention for action on July 15, 1976. The minority report was said to be favored by both the party chairman, Robert S. Strauss, and the presidential nominee, Jimmy Carter; however, the labor coalition of liberal unions had been mobilizing against it, and Carter's floor managers failed even to secure a roll call vote. The minority report was defeated on a voice vote and the majority recommendation was approved.

Supporters of both sides of the issue were looking ahead to 1980 and 1984. Carter's forces, expecting an easy victory in 1980, wished to have the advantages of plurality choice wherever possible and did not wish a possible insurgent opponent, such as California Governor Edmund G. Brown, Jr., to have the aid of proportional representation. The labor and liberal groups who favored proportional representation were continuing in a well-established ideological position, but they were also considering their own interests as identifiable minorities.[20]

The action of the 1976 convention to abolish loophole primaries is not self-executing and could encounter considerable difficulty. Taken at face value, the action requires the thirteen states that had loophole primaries in 1976 to reconsider their systems and fundamentally change them. New York, New Jersey, Pennsylvania, Ohio, and Illinois are among the states that presumably will be required to adopt new state legislation. Meanwhile, the subject has been under consideration, as the convention directed, by the

[19] Minority Report No. 5, Rules Committee, Democratic National Convention, 1976, available at Democratic National Committee.

[20] *Congressional Quarterly Weekly Report,* July 17, 1976, p. 1938; see also the syndicated column by Rowland Evans and Robert Novak, *Washington Post,* July 19, 1976.

Democratic party's Commission on Presidential Nomination and Party Structure, generally known as the Winograd Commission. This body has fifty-eight members, including a number of representatives from the Carter administration as well as many former members of the McGovern and Mikulski commissions. The Winograd Commission met on January 22 and 23, 1978, to make its final recommendations in time for action by the Democratic National Committee in the spring of 1978. The loophole primary was one of its major concerns.[21] Its recommendations are discussed in chapter 6.

[21] *Congressional Quarterly Weekly Report*, Jan. 28, 1978, pp. 199-200; David S. Broder, "Shorter Primary Season Is Planned by Democrats," *Washington Post*, Jan. 22, 1978.

CHAPTER 2 / The 1976
Democratic Nomination Contest

THE presidential election year of 1976 opened with a wide field of candidates for the Democratic presidential nomination. The list of actual or potential candidates who were serious enough to have been raising campaign funds in 1975 included thirteen names:[1]

Candidate	Campaign Fund Receipts in 1975
George C. Wallace	$3,131,627
Henry M. Jackson	2,221,323
Lloyd Bentsen	1,000,036
Jimmy Carter	989,125
Morris K. Udall	943,206
Fred R. Harris	426,522
Sargent Shriver	388,956
Birch Bayh	337,347
Terry Sanford	327,283
Milton J. Shapp	283,878
Ellen McCormack	106,700
Frank Church	26,832
Robert C. Byrd	20,000

Notably absent from this list were Senator Edward M. Kennedy, the popular choice of many Democrats, who had repeatedly declared that he would not run in 1976; Senator Hubert H. Humphrey, the candidate of 1968; and Senator George S. McGovern,

[1] From reports to the Federal Election Commission, as reported by *Congressional Quarterly Weekly Report*, Feb. 14, 1976, p. 319.

the candidate of 1972. McGovern had been beaten so badly in 1972 that he was never a serious contender for 1976, but Humphrey was still potentially a candidate of great strength. Humphrey had decided early on a waiting game. With so many candidates, none of whom looked particularly strong, Humphrey anticipated a convention deadlock, after which it might turn to him as a compromise choice. Meanwhile, he was highly available but not officially campaigning.

As 1976 approached, most of the better known candidates were pursuing strategies based on previous experience. George Wallace had every intention of pursuing again the tactics that had given him so much prominence in both 1968 and 1972, despite the physical handicaps resulting from his near assassination in 1972. Henry M. Jackson, national committee chairman in 1960, was mindful of the strategy pursued by John F. Kennedy in that year, while also trying to overcome some of his obvious limitations as a campaigner in 1972. Jackson proposed to concentrate on New York and the big industrial states, cultivating his relationships in those states with strong party organizations and with organized labor. Morris Udall was seeking to inherit George McGovern's following and proposed to follow his strategy of early campaigning in almost all states. Similar ideas were entertained, at least initially, by Birch Bayh and Fred Harris; it could be expected that the two of them, together with Udall, would divide the liberal vote.

The eventual winner, Jimmy Carter, was virtually unknown at the beginning of 1976 as far as the national electorate was concerned. More than any other candidate, however, Carter was free of commitments to past strategies and thus could adapt as fully as possible to the emerging conditions of the party and the electorate in 1976. According to Gerald Pomper, he was the only candidate who was not essentially fighting some previous war.[2] Carter had left office as governor of Georgia in January 1975, and he was thereafter free to give his entire time to campaign travel and to efforts to build an organization throughout the United States, with particular concentration on states of early importance such as Iowa, New Hampshire, and Florida. His basic strategy was to achieve successes in the critical early states, to defeat George

[2] Gerald M. Pomper et al., *The Election of 1976* (New York: David McKay Company, 1977), pp. 7-10.

Wallace in the early southern primaries, and to run thereafter with recognition as a national candidate in all parts of the country. By southern standards Carter was a liberal; he started with strong black support, yet could still hope to defeat Wallace. For the rest of the country he was a centrist candidate, his appeal spanning a wide spectrum of issue positions and focusing on his image as a fresh, honest personality with no commitments to the establishment in Washington. Carter expected to enter almost all of the primaries and to work actively in most of the caucus states.

Iowa, a caucus state, was the first test. On January 19, 1976, caucus meetings were held throughout the state in 2,530 precincts and were attended by some 45,000 Democrats. These meetings were much more thoroughly covered by the media than ever before, partly because of the national Democratic party rules changes in effect for the first time in 1976 under which every caucus participant either had to state a candidate preference or had to declare himself uncommitted. The results for the major contestants, based on early unofficial returns from 88 percent of the precincts, were:[3]

Uncommitted	37.1%	Udall	6.0%
Carter	27.6	Shriver	3.3
Bayh	13.2	Jackson	1.1
Harris	9.9		

The media announced these results as an early triumph for Carter, as indeed they were in view of the previously inflated expectations of several of his competitors. Carter had worked early and hard in the state; but Bayh, Harris, Udall, and Shriver had also campaigned extensively. The votes for all except Carter probably were minimized by the 15 percent rule; no one was credited with votes in any precinct caucus unless he had at least 15 percent of that caucus. In caucuses where they did not have that much strength, presumably most of the supporters of the minor candidates switched to uncommitted status in the hope of combining with enough similarly situated persons to reach the 15 percent level.

The Iowa results were not immediately convertible into numbers of delegates won, because the precinct meetings were merely

[3] *Congressional Quarterly Weekly Report,* Jan. 24, 1976, p. 189.

the first step in a process that would not end until the state party convention on May 29. But, as in all caucus systems, it could be expected that the frontrunner in the precinct meetings would increase his lead as the process worked its way through the higher levels of meetings.

Mississippi, another caucus state, was the second test; it was important as the first confrontation between Carter and George Wallace. Early results on January 24 were:[4]

Wallace	43.9%	Shriver	12.3%
Uncommitted	27.5	Bentsen	1.6
Carter	14.0	Harris	1.1

Carter had made much less of a commitment of resources in Mississippi than in Iowa. Carter and Wallace were both looking forward to the Florida primary as their most important early battleground. Also, based on these results, Bentsen and Harris clearly looked weak as southern competitors.

The third set of results came from Maine, another caucus state. Caucuses that began on February 1 produced these early returns:[5]

Uncommitted	47.3%	Bayh	1.4%
Carter	39.6	Shriver	1.4
Harris	7.2	Humphrey	0.5
Udall	2.7		

Another set of results came from precinct caucusses in Oklahoma on February 7:[6]

Uncommitted	35.7%	Bentsen	12.0%
Harris	19.89	Wallace	11.5
Carter	19.87		

These results were thought to spare candidate Harris embarrassment in his home state, but they also left Carter in a good position. The real loser, as the media unanimously agreed, was Bentsen, who had made a massive effort. On February 10 Bentsen announced that he was withdrawing from national campaign efforts, even though still in the race as a Texas favorite son.

[4] Ibid., Jan. 31, 1976, p. 243.
[5] Ibid., Feb. 7, 1976, p. 275.
[6] Ibid., Feb. 14, 1976, p. 321.

Finally, some inconclusive results from Alaska on February 10 ended the early season of caucus results before primaries.

New Hampshire, first as usual among the primary states, held its election on Febrary 24. Complete but unofficial returns both in the preference vote and in delegates won were:[7]

	Votes	Delegates		Votes
Carter	29.4%	14	Humphrey (write-ins)	5.6%
Udall	23.9	3	Wallace (write-ins)	1.4
Bayh	16.2		Jackson (write-ins)	1.4
Harris	11.4		McCormack	1.3
Shriver	8.7			

Udall, Bayh, and Harris had all devoted major efforts to New Hampshire; therefore, the results were a severe disappointment for them. Carter had not attracted much press attention in New Hampshire before his Iowa victory, but he had been working hard there at the voter level for a year. New Hampshire made him the acknowledged front-runner for at least the moment. Its plurality system of voting also gave him most of the delegates in the first actual election of delegates.

Close on the heels of New Hampshire came the Massachusetts primary on March 2. Nearly complete early returns, under a completely proportional representation system of voting, were:[8]

	Votes	Delegates		Votes	Delegates
Jackson	22.7%	30	Shriver	7.5%	7
Udall	18.0	21	Bayh	4.9	1
Wallace	17.1	21	McCormack	3.5	1
Carter	14.2	16	Shapp	3.0	1
Harris	7.7	6	No preference	1.4	

The Massachusetts results were considered a major victory for Jackson—his first presidential primary victory at any time and a sharp contrast to his floundering results in 1972. Udall and Wallace were reasonably content with their showings. Carter's results, from his point of view, were disastrous and did nothing to help in the oncoming struggle against Wallace in Florida. Birch Bayh announced shortly afterwards that he was suspending his national

[7] Ibid., Feb. 28, 1976, p. 459.
[8] Ibid., Mar. 6, 1976, p. 503.

campaign, while Shriver stayed in to await the later results in Illinois.

The Florida proportional primary of March 9 was the next major event of the season. The results, for those polling more than 3 percent, were:[9]

	Votes	Delegates
Carter	34.3%	34
Wallace	30.6	26
Jackson	23.9	21

Carter thus had won a clear victory over Wallace in a large southern state in which Wallace had won in 1972 with 41.6 percent. Thereafter, the Wallace campaign was downhill all the way except in Alabama, and Carter's strength as a national candidate was reaffirmed. Milton Shapp, who polled 2.4 percent in Florida, subsequently canceled his campaign and withdrew from the race even in his home state of Pennsylvania.

The Illinois primary on March 16 was next. In the preference vote, which had no effect on delegate selection, the results were:[10]

Carter	48.4%
Wallace	27.8
Shriver	16.2
Harris	7.6

This was another defeat for Wallace and a blow to Shriver, who had expected to do much better in Illinois. He suspended his active campaign. Senator Adlai E. Stevenson III was the announced preference of delegate candidates in most districts and won 85 of the 155 delegates, mainly in the Chicago districts controlled by the Daley organization. Carter won most of the other delegates, 53, winning most of the contests in districts where both Carter and Stevenson delegates were on the ballot. The total showing was considered a major boost for Carter, from a state in which he had been careful not to antagonize the regular party organization. The results in Illinois left him well ahead in the national delegate count, as he had in fact been almost from the beginning.

The North Carolina primary on March 23 was Carter's third substantial victory over Wallace, and the first primary in which

[9] Ibid., Mar. 13, 1976, p. 547.
[10] Ibid., Mar. 20, 1976, p. 605.

Carter polled over 50 percent of the vote. The results for principal candidates were:[11]

	Votes	Delegates
Carter	53.6%	36
Wallace	34.7	25
Jackson	4.3	

Wallace had carried the state in 1972 with 50.3 percent of the vote. Under North Carolina's proportional representation system, only candidates receiving more than 5 percent of the vote received delegates; thus Carter and Wallace split the delegation.

The New York primary was held on April 6. Although this primary included no direct preference vote on presidential candidates, it was held under a revision of state law in March 1976 whereby delegate candidates could be identified on the ballot with their presidential candidate or as uncommitted. Of the 274 delegates, 206 were chosen by the voters in congressional district elections, with the at-large delegates to be selected later in proportion to the district election results. The total outcome in terms of delegates was:[12]

Jackson	104
Udall	70
Uncommitted	65
Carter	35

The showing was obviously a significant win for Jackson, his second, but far short of the landslide he had hoped for. Carter had made only a limited commitment in the state but had collected some delegates. Udall had done better than expected.

In the Wisconsin primary, also held on April 6, Udall was initially predicted as the winner by two of the television networks. However, by the morning of April 7, it was clear that Carter had another victory. The returns for the principal candidates were:[13]

	Votes	Delegates			Votes	Delegates
Carter	37.3%	26		Jackson	6.5%	6
Udall	36.3	25		McCormack	3.7	1
Wallace	12.7	10				

[11] Ibid., Mar. 27, 1976, p. 678.

[12] Ibid., Apr. 10, 1976, p. 810.

[13] Ibid., p. 813.

All of the candidates listed won delegates proportionately; there was no cutoff percentage in this primary other than the share of the votes necessary to elect one delegate.

After a lull of three weeks, the Pennsylvania primary occurred on April 27. Widely heralded as a decisive test in a big industrial state, and one in which Jackson expected to do well, this primary proved to be clearly a victory for Carter in the preference vote—and even more so in the delegate elections. Early returns for leading candidates were:[14]

	Votes	Delegates		Votes	Delegates
Carter	37.2%	64	McCormack	2.9%	
Jackson	24.7	19	Shapp	2.6	17
Udall	18.8	22	Uncommitted		46
Wallace	11.4	3			

Texas held its delegate election primary on May 1, under legislation that had been passed in 1975 in an effort to help Bentsen. Delegates were elected on a plurality basis in thirty-one state senatorial districts; Carter won ninety-two delegates to Bentsen's six, while Wallace elected none. The actual voting was less lopsided; it could be calculated that it was divided approximately as follows:[15]

Carter	47.6%
Bentsen	22.2
Wallace	17.5
Others	12.7

Four primaries were held on May 4—in Indiana, Georgia, Alabama, and the District of Columbia. Carter won heavily in Indiana, with 68.0 percent of the vote, and in Georgia, his home state, with 83.9 percent. In Alabama, Wallace was the early winner in delegate elections in seventeen of the twenty-seven districts; runoffs between Wallace and Carter delegates were necessary in most of the other districts. In the District of Columbia, Carter ran well ahead of Udall and two uncommitted slates. After these four elections, Carter's lead in delegate strength stood at 548 delegates, or 36.9 percent of those thus far elected. Jackson was second with 200 delegates, Udall third with 162, and Wallace fourth with 140. Car-

[14] Ibid., May 1, 1976, p.1052.
[15] Ibid., May 8, 1976, p. 1080.

ter had been steadily picking up votes in caucus states as well as in the primaries.[16]

Nebraska and West Virginia held their primaries on May 11. By this time Senator Frank Church and Governor Jerry Brown had entered the race and were compaigning actively, Church in Nebraska and Brown in Maryland. Church succeeded in upsetting Carter in Nebraska, where Brown was not on the ballot, with the following results:[17]

	Votes	*Delegates*
Church	38.8%	15
Carter	37.8	8
Others	23.4	

Church's victory, although it made an eventual Carter nomination seem a little less inevitable, made only a small dent in Carter's strong lead in delegates accumulated nationwide. In West Virginia the state's favorite son, Senator Robert C. Byrd, won an easy victory with opposition only from supporters of Governor Wallace. West Virginia held the only Democratic primary in which Carter's name was not on the ballot.

The Maryland primary on May 18 was noteworthy as the scene of a stunning victory by Governor Brown after his remarkable but late-starting campaign. The early results were:[18]

	Votes	*Delegates*
Brown	48.3%	
Carter	36.9	32
Others	14.8	21

Even given Brown's impressive victory in the preference vote, he had started too late to enter a delegate slate in the delegate election, and Carter thus won most of the delegates.

More important was the Michigan proportional primary, also on May 18. It was the scene of Udall's last major effort, although he remained in the contest in other states until the end. The results were:[19]

---

[16] Ibid.

[17] Ibid., May 15, 1976, p. 1209.

[18] Ibid., May 22, 1976, p. 1245.

[19] Ibid., p. 1243.

	Votes	Delegates
Carter	43.5%	69
Udall	43.2	58
Others	13.3	2
Uncommitted		4

What were billed as two regional primaries occurred on May 25: (1) Tennessee, Kentucky, and Arkansas in the South and (2) Oregon, Nevada, and Idaho in the Northwest. Carter heavily defeated Wallace and other candidates in the three southern states and picked up most of the delegates. Brown won heavily in Nevada and Church in Idaho, his home state. In Oregon's newly proportional primary, the results were:[20]

	Votes	Delegates
Church	34.6%	15
Carter	27.4	12
Brown		
(write-ins)	23.3	7
Others	14.7	

Rhode Island, South Dakota, and Montana held their primaries on June 1. Carter was the winner on a plurality basis in both Rhode Island and South Dakota; in Montana, Church ran ahead of Carter by about two to one. After these elections Carter's lead in delegate strength stood at 869 delegates, or 38.6 percent of those elected thus far, with Udall at 291, Jackson at 237, Wallace at 168, others at 293, and uncommitted at 395. At this point, a total of 2,353 delegates had been selected, with 755 still to be chosen.[21]

The primary season reached its final climax on June 8, when Ohio, New Jersey, and California were voting. Ohio's loophole primary proved to be an important closing victory for Carter, with the unofficial results as follows:[22]

	Votes	Delegates		Votes	Delegates
Carter	52.2%	126	Wallace	5.7%	
Udall	21.0	20	Others	7.2	6
Church	13.9				

[20] Ibid., May 29, 1976, p. 1328.

[21] Ibid., June 5, 1976, p. 1423.

[22] Ibid., June 12, 1976, p. 1472.

The New Jersey results were ambiguous; in a preference poll that omitted Jerry Brown, Carter ran heavily ahead of Church and Wallace. But in statewide voting on delegates at large, the uncommitted led all the rest, followed by Carter, Udall, and Church, in that order. California went for Brown as expected, with the following results in this proportional primary:[23]

	Votes	*Delegates*		*Votes*	*Delegates*
Brown	59.0%	204	Udall	5.0%	2
Carter	20.5	67	Wallace	3.0	
Church	7.4	7	Others	5.1	

Carter picked up 218 delegates in these three primaries to increase his nationwide total to about 1,091, with Udall running second at 313, and the uncommitted delegates standing at 490.5.[24]

Mayor Daley of Chicago had predicted that if Carter carried Ohio, he would win the nomination; and the day after the Ohio election, Daley declared his support for Carter. Governor Wallace also announced his support for Carter and urged his delegates to transfer their allegiance. Senator Jackson likewise did the same. On June 9 the media generally concluded that Carter had won the nomination. His delegate count exceeded the required 1,505 some weeks before the convention opened on July 12.

The actual balloting at the convention on July 14 was an anticlimax. Carter was nominated with 2,238.5 votes on the first ballot before delegates began switching votes. The corresponding vote for Udall was 329.5 and for Brown 300.5.[25] Senator Walter F. Mondale of Minnesota was nominated for vice-president, thus completing the Democratic ticket.

[23] Ibid., p. 1474.
[24] Ibid., pp. 1471, 1473.
[25] Ibid., July 17, 1976, p. 1873.

CHAPTER 3 / The 1976 Republican Nomination Contest

REPUBLICAN presidential politics began in 1976 with two announced candidates: President Gerald R. Ford and former governor
Ronald Reagan. Both had begun organizing their campaigns during
1975. As an incumbent president, Ford was generally favored to
win, but Reagan had strong support, particularly in the South and
the West. Reagan had raised $1,925,571 in campaign funds by the
end of 1975, and Ford, $1,688,256.[1] There were no other con-
tenders for the Republican presidential nomination.

In the caucus states Republican activity began later than on the
Democratic side and was conducted under looser rules that tended
much more toward the selection of uncommitted delegates. As a
result, the Republican caucuses received much less attention from
the national media during the early stages of the campaign. In contrast to Carter's accomplishment in Iowa, neither Ford nor Reagan
could develop any early "momentum" from the caucus contests.
As far as the Republican race was concerned, the attention of the
nation was focused initially on the primaries. Both Ford and
Reagan were entered in most of the primaries, although Reagan
was more selective in the concentration of his early efforts.

As usual, the New Hampshire primary on February 24 was regarded as a critical opening test, and the Ford managers viewed its
approach with much trepidation. However, Ford did win a clear
but narrow victory in the preference vote, with 50.6 percent of
the vote to Reagan's 49.4 percent. Ford gained seventeen delegates
to Reagan's four.[2]

[1] *Congressional Quarterly Weekly Report,* Feb. 14, 1976, p. 319.
[2] Ibid., Feb. 28, 1976, p. 459.

In Massachusetts the following week, Ford won heavily with 62.3 percent of the vote to Reagan's 34.3 percent. Unlike the plurality system in New Hampshire, delegates in Massachusetts were awarded proportionately; Ford won twenty-seven delegates, Reagan won fifteen, and one was elected as uncommitted.[3]

As the March 9 Florida primary approached, some of Reagan's managers were predicting a two-to-one victory. The results came as a shock. Ford won the statewide vote by a margin of 6 percent and captured forty-three of the state's sixty-six delegates. Pressure was then put on Reagan to withdraw from the race, and most analysts assumed that his candidacy was doomed. Reagan refused to concede, however. One week later in Illinois, Ford again bested the challenger, with 58.9 percent of the vote to Reagan's 40.1 percent and Lar Daly's 1.0 percent. Early returns gave Ford thirty-one of the delegates and Reagan twelve delegates, with thirteen delegates uncommitted.[5]

Reagan recovered in the North Carolina primary on March 23. Although Ford had expected to win easily, he lost by 46 percent of the vote to Reagan's 52 percent, with the delegates awarded proportionately.[6] Thereafter, it seemed clear that Reagan would stay in the race with substantially improved prospects.

In New York on April 6 the Republican primary was traditional, with no presidential candidate identification on the ballot. An uncommitted organization slate won 114 of the 117 delegate places; Reagan won the other 3 delegates although he had not attempted a campaign in the state.[7] In the Wisconsin primary, also on April 6, Ford won by 55.3 percent of the votes to Reagan's 44.4 percent. Ford carried each of the congressional districts there and won all of the delegates on a plurality basis.[8] In Pennsylvania, on April 27, another traditional outcome resulted. Under state party rules, the delegation was elected as uncommitted but was assumed to be mainly favorable to Ford. Reagan had made no effort to campaign in the state.[9]

[3] Ibid., Mar. 6, 1976, p. 503.
[4] Ibid., Mar. 13, 1976, pp. 547-48.
[5] Ibid., Mar. 20, 1976, p. 605.
[6] Ibid., Mar. 27, 1976, p. 678.
[7] Ibid., Apr. 10, 1976, p. 812.
[8] Ibid., p. 813.
[9] Ibid., May 1, 1976, p. 1054.

The Reagan campaign received a major boost in Texas on May 1 and in Indiana on May 4. Reagan swept the delegate elections in Texas, winning all ninety-six district delegates and carrying the popular vote by about a two-to-one margin. As if to demonstrate that his appeal was not confined to Sun Belt states, in Indiana Reagan won in the popular vote by 51.3 percent to Ford's 48.7 percent and took forty-five delegates to Ford's nine on a plurality basis.[10]

In other primaries on May 4, Reagan defeated Ford by 68.4 percent to 31.6 percent in Georgia, carried every congressional district in that state, and won all of the delegates on a plurality basis. A nearly identical result occurred in Alabama, where Reagan also won every delegate.[11] Suddenly, Reagan was ahead of Ford in the national delegate count by 366 to Ford's 292, with another 292 delegates uncommitted.[12]

Primaries were held on May 11 in Nebraska and West Virginia. In Nebraska, where Ford had campaigned vigorously, Reagan won by 54.6 percent to Ford's 45.4 percent. In West Virginia, however, Ford won by 56.6 percent to Reagan's 43.4 percent.[13]

The Michigan test on May 18 was more important than either the Nebraska or West Virginia primary. It was widely conceded that Ford could not withstand a loss in his home state, and he had campaigned hard to prevent such an occurrence. Ford did win there by 65.0 percent to Reagan's 34.3 percent, restoring vitality to his national campaign. Ford also won in Maryland on the same day, by 57.9 percent to Reagan's 42.1 percent.[14]

Primaries were held in six states on May 25. Ford won in Oregon, by 52.4 percent to Reagan's 47.6 percent; he also won somewhat unexpectedly by narrow margins in Tennessee and Kentucky. However, Ford lost heavily to Reagan in Nevada, Idaho, and Arkansas.[15] After these primaries, Ford was again ahead in the national delegate count by 769 to Reagan's 620, with 169 delegates uncommitted.[16] In the June 1 primaries in three states, Ford won

[10] Ibid., May 8, 1976, pp. 1079-81.
[11] Ibid., pp. 1082-83.
[12] Ibid., p. 1080.
[13] Ibid., May 15, 1976, pp. 1209-11.
[14] Ibid., May 22, 1976, pp. 1243-45.
[15] Ibid., May 29, 1976, pp. 1327-30.
[16] Ibid., p. 1327.

by about two to one in Rhode Island, lost narrowly in South Dakota, and lost heavily in Montana.[17]

In the final big-state primaries on June 8, Ford won in Ohio by 56.6 percent to Reagan's 43.4 percent, while losing in California by 34.3 percent to Reagan's 65.7 percent. Ford won 91 of the 97 delegates in the Ohio district elections; Reagan won all of the 167 California delegates under winner-take-all rules. In New Jersey, only Ford was entered in the preference vote; but there was a contest between two nominally uncommitted delegate slates, an organization slate favoring Ford and another slate pledged to Reagan. The organization slate won all of the delegate positions and was expected to favor Ford by about 60 to 7 delegates. On June 10 the national delegate count showed Ford to be ahead by 889 delegates to Reagan's 839, with 244 delegates uncommitted and a total of 1,130 needed to secure the nomination.[18]

Another month of action was still ahead in about a dozen caucus states, either to elect complete state delegations or to elect delegates at large. Reagan won most of the delegates in Missouri, Washington, Colorado, Idaho, Montana, and New Mexico; Ford won most of the delegates in Delaware, Iowa, and Minnesota. In North Dakota on July 10 something of a turning point may have occurred. Previously it had been anticipated that the North Dakota delegation would be evenly split; however, Ford won twelve delegates, Reagan two, and four were elected as uncommitted. On the final day of caucus action, July 17, Reagan won all twenty delegates in Utah while Ford won all thirty-five in Connecticut. The result left Ford ahead of Reagan in the national delegate count, even though both were still within striking distance of the nomination.

With delegate selection concluded, Ford and Reagan both concentrated their efforts on renewed attempts to win over the uncommitted delegates. Within a few days, each was claiming that he had won enough delegates to ensure nomination, but this claim was not confirmed either way by any of the several unofficial agencies that were keeping score. After Reagan announced the selection of Senator Richard S. Schweiker of Pennsylvania as his proposed running mate, however, there was a noticeable weakening of Reagan's support.

[17] Ibid., June 5, 1976, pp. 1422-24.
[18] Ibid., June 12, 1976, pp. 1471-75.

At the Republican National Convention in August, the Reagan forces were defeated on a proposal for a rules amendment, by 1,068 to 1,180 delegate votes. The proposed new rule would have required each presidential candidate to announce his choice for a vice-presidential running mate in advance of the presidential balloting—a move that was clearly intended to embarrass President Ford. On the roll call for the actual nomination the next day, August 18, Ford won by 1,187 votes to Reagan's 1,070.[19] However, the conservative forces were allowed to control much of the platform drafting, as well as the choice of a vice-presidential nominee, who proved to be Senator Robert Dole of Kansas.

[19] Ibid., Aug. 21, 1976, pp. 2253-54.

CHAPTER 4 / The Effect of Alternative Selection Systems on the 1976 Nomination Race

MOST studies of nomination races focus on the political factors that favor one candidate over another and ignore the influence of the rules. This approach is understandable in view of the fact that the electoral system is normally constant, while it is the candidates, issues, and strategies that change. To question what the results of a race would have been under a different electoral system might seem to be an unnecessary exercise in abstraction. Moreover, any such analysis can never produce definitive conclusions, for the subject is no longer what actually occurred, but rather what might have occurred under a hypothetical set of circumstances.

Yet no complete account of the nomination races since 1968 can afford to neglect the impact of the rules. This issue must be considered because the rules have undergone such extensive changes in each of the past two elections. The candidates in 1976 faced a very different selection system from those who ran in 1968 or even in 1972; furthermore, the aspirants in 1980 will almost certainly encounter a system that is substantially different from the one in 1976. This continual change naturally alters the usual perspective on the rules. They can no longer be considered by the political analyst as a given but necessarily appear as a variable whose consequences are as unpredictable as those of most other political factors.

One of the principal objectives of this research project was to consider the various consequences of alternative delegate selection systems. In particular, we wanted to investigate the possible differences arising from the two methods of apportioning delegates that are now most frequently used and that constitute the realistic options for current policymakers: (1) proportional representation and (2) plurality systems, mostly at the substate level.[1] One way to explore the differences between these systems is to look at the results in a particular election year and to ask how a change in the rules might have affected the outcomes among the candidates. Data for the 1976 nomination were collected and analyzed for this purpose.

The method to be followed in discussing this question is quite simple. The delegate totals for each party from the 1976 race are broken down into the three basic system categories identified in chapter 1: (1) proportional representation primaries, (2) plurality and loophole primaries, and (3) caucus arrangements (which were conducted under proportional rules in the Democratic party and plurality rules in the Republican party). In order to calculate the results under a universal system of proportional primaries, the totals in the plurality primaries must be converted on the basis of proportional rules and the results then added to the totals of the actual proportional primaries. The conversion is done by returning to the raw data of the electoral returns and, after making a few minor assumptions, applying proportional rules. To determine the results under a system of plurality rules, the process is reversed: the proportional primary totals are converted on the basis of plurality rules, and the results are then added to the totals of the

[1] By the substate level, we are referring to the election of delegates in districts that are smaller than the state as a whole. Most plurality and loophole primary states used the congressional district as the basic electoral unit. Exceptions in the Republican primaries were in California, which used a statewide winner-take-all primary; and in Alabama and West Virginia, which had more delegates elected at the statewide level than in the districts. On the Democratic side, the exceptions were in the direction of smaller units: Texas, Pennsylvania, and New Jersey used state senatorial districts, while Alabama created twenty-seven specially drawn districts.

The analysis of alternative election arrangements that follows does not include an inquiry into the winner-take-all system at the statewide level. Not only is this system a highly unlikely option in the future, but also it was used in only a limited number of cases in the past. The emphasis given to it by James Lengle and Byron Shafer in a recent article seems to us largely misplaced. See Lengle and Shafer, "Primary Rules, Political Power, and Social Change," 70 *American Political Science Review* 25-40 (March 1976).

actual plurality primaries. Because of their special status, the caucus states are treated separately and in a less systematic fashion.

As a methodological note, it is necessary to point out that the process of converting delegate totals can only provide an indication of what the results might have been. Had the rules been different, the strategies of the candidates would also have differed in certain respects. Behavior cannot be expected to be constant under different institutional arrangements. Mindful of this difficulty, the converted totals are employed with a certain caution. Where it is evident on the basis of a commonsense view that a different set of rules might noticeably have influenced the strategies of the candidates, the analysis will attempt to take this into account. Our goal is not to be strictly rigorous, but rather to introduce as much rigor as possible into the questions that are being explored.

THE DEMOCRATIC NOMINATION RACE

As a beginning point for analyzing the impact of the rules on the contest in the Democratic party, Table 4.1 lists by system categories the actual results of the delegate selection races. (A state-by-state breakdown of these and all other results discussed in this chapter is provided in Appendix B.) The figures provided in Table 4.1 are based on the delegates' original mandate from the state selection contests, not on the vote at the national convention. (The final vote total is not used because it would include the large shift to Carter after most of the other candidates had freed their delegates to vote as they wanted.) It is worthwhile to note that the Democratic race in 1976 is the first one for which a reliable official total of this kind can be given for the caucus states. In previous years the commitments in the caucus states were informal. However, under the new proportional representation rule for the caucus states, the national party requires that delegates be chosen on the basis of an explicitly declared candidate preference.

The system categories in Table 4.1 obviously cannot be used to explain the basic levels of support for the candidates. How well the candidates did was determined mostly by their political strength and by their decisions about where to run—not by the system under which they competed. The succeeding analysis seeks

Table 4.1. Actual results of the Democratic selection process by system categories

System category	Total	Carter	Brown	Udall	Wallace	Jackson	Church	Others	Uncommitted
1. Loophole primaries	1,263	541	85	126	43	137	15	167	149
2. Proportional representation primaries	1,037	430	225	116	106	57	54	17	32
Subtotal primary states	2,300	971	310	242	149	194	69	184	181
3. Caucus states	657	203	9	88	20	43	8	62	224
Total, all states	2,957	1,174	319	330	169	237	77	246	405

SOURCE: Delegate Selection Project, 1976.
NOTE: Includes state totals only. Excluded are totals from territories and District of Columbia.

to understand not the basic level of support for each candidate, but rather the marginal impact of hypothetical changes in the rules. Even so, one result in Table 4.1 is probably attributable to the system categories—and that is the degree of strength of the uncommitteds. In the caucus states, the uncommitteds won 224 out of a possible 657 delegates, or 34 percent; in the primary states, on the other hand, uncommitteds captured only 181 of a possible 2,300 delegates, or 8 percent. Since uncommitted slates could have been fielded in every state, the better showing of this preference in the caucus states cannot be explained by the accidental cause of a national stragegy not to enter certain races; nor does it seem plausible that the political character of the states in each category can account for the difference. If the results of the 1976 race can be considered typical on this point, a more probable explanation is that under the current laws and rules governing the Democratic selection process, the caucus states are likely to produce a lower percentage of delegates bound directly to a national candidate than the primary states. In making this point, it is crucial to observe that we are speaking only of a relative trend within each of the categories. In fact, since 1968 the reform rules have encouraged a greater candidate focus in all categories of selection systems.[2]

A difference also exists between the relative strength of the uncommitteds in the loophole primaries (12 percent) and in the proportional representation primaries (3 percent). Although this more modest difference might well be the result of the character of the states in each of the categories, it is the kind of difference that one would expect, given the theory of representation implicit in each system.[3] In the loophole primaries, the delegates must be voted on individually, though their candidate preference is now

[2] In addition to the requirement of identification of candidate preferences in the caucus states, the national party asked its state party affiliates to publicize the presidential candidate preferences of candidates for delegates where state law prohibited listing them on the ballot. In 1976 only West Virginia did not allow such identification. New York changed its state law at the last minute to bring it in line with the "spirit" of the national party rules.

[3] Nearly three-quarters of the uncommitted delegates elected in loophole primaries came from New York and Pennsylvania, where powerful local party organizations in certain districts backed uncommitted delegates. The greater

stated on the ballot. By contrast, in nearly all of the proportional primaries (and in some of the plurality races in the Republican party) the delegates are listed under the names of the national candidates. Under the loophole primary, the voters' attention is directed to the individual delegate as well as to the candidate status he or she has adopted; under the proportional primary, the voters' attention is directed to the national candidate alone. Given this difference, one can see why prominent individuals or party organizations might be more inclined to use—and succeed with—an uncommitted status under a loophole system.

The points discussed above may seem rather technical, but they relate ultimately to a fundamental question about the nature of representation in the selection process. Uncommitted delegates, one is apt to find, are not selected because they have no candidate preference, but rather because they represent a dimension other than a specific candidate preference; e.g., the interests of the local party or of some particular group. Thus, the defined representational role of the uncommitted delegate is likely to be quite different from the committted and instructed delegate, whose chief function is to translate a predetermined preference into a share of the decision-making power.

Hypothetical Results of Different Primary Selection Systems

To obtain the results of the Democratic primaries under proportional rules, the delegate totals in the loophole primaries must first be converted to hypothetical totals under proportional rules. Unfortunately, this conversion cannot be done for two of the major loophole states—New York and Pennsylvania—because official election returns in these states did not indicate the candidate preferences of the defeated delegates. Thus, the totals from these two states are omitted from the following analysis.

The results of the conversion are shown in Table 4.2. Line 1 gives the actual results of the loophole primary contests, while line

strength of the party organizations in these states, when compared with that of the organizations in the proportional primary states, might account for most of the difference in the number of uncommitteds between the two system categories.

2 shows the conversion. In calculating this conversion, we assumed a 15 percent cutoff rule, which was the figure most commonly used in the Democratic proportional primaries. To obtain the total of a race under a system using proportional rules in all states, we merely add the total on line 2 to the actual results of the proportional primaries on line 3. Also, because some of the states using proportional primaries had a cutoff different from 15 percent, an alternative calculation is provided under which the proportional primary results are all first standardized to the 15 percent rule.

A comparison of the actual results of the loophole primaries in line 1 with the conversion in line 2 shows a significant loss of delegates for the front-runner, Jimmy Carter, and a gain for many of the weaker candidates, chiefly Udall, Wallace, and "others" (principally Bentsen in Texas). These results confirm one prediction made in many of the early analyses of proportional rules: proportional systems, when compared to plurality systems, tend to spread or fragment the vote in any multicandidate race, giving a larger percentage of the total delegates to the weaker candidates.

Even if New York and Pennsylvania had been included in this analysis, it does not appear that the basic direction of the results in Table 4.2 would have changed. Some of the weaker candidates who won pluralities in none or only a few of the districts in these two states would have obtained a larger share of the delegates under proportional rules. Wallace, for example, would have done considerably better in Pennsylvania. Regarding the relative strength of Carter and Jackson, the results in these two states would have tended to cancel each other out. Although Carter would have lost many delegates to Jackson (and others) in Pennsylvania, he (as well as other candidates) would have gained some delegates at Jackson's expense in New York.

Turning next to the results of a Democratic race under a loophole primary format, the beginning step again, as shown in Table 4.3, is to convert the actual totals of the proportional primaries (line 1) to hypothetical totals under a loophole system (line 2). The standard loophole procedure for perfoming this conversion was to award the district delegates to the winner of the district race and then divide the at-large delegates in each state in proportion to the share of each candidate in the district races. To obtain the complete results of a race under loophole rules, the actual total of

Table 4.2. Results of Democratic primaries under proportional representation

System category	Total	Carter	Brown	Udall	Wallace	Jackson	Church	Others	Uncommitted
1. Actual total of loophole primaries	811	443	85	29	40	10	15	150	39
2. Loophole primaries converted to proportional representation	811	360	53	60	71	9	17	177	64
3. Actual total of proportional representation primaries	1,037	430	225	116	106	57	54	17	32
Total (line 2 plus line 3)	1,848	790	278	176	177	66	71	194	96
4. Proportional primaries standardized to 15 percent cutoff	1,037	442	246	132	97	68	48	—	4
Total (line 2 plus line 4)	1,848	802	299	192	168	77	65	177	68

SOURCE: Delegate Selection Project, 1976.
NOTE: Omits totals from New York, Pennsylvania, and District of Columbia.

Table 4.3. Results of Democratic primaries under a loophole system

System category	Total	Carter	Brown	Udall	Wallace	Jackson	Church	Others	Uncommitted
1. Actual total of proportional representation primaries	1,037	430	225	116	106	57	54	17	32
2. Proportional representation converted to loophole	1,037	445	302	111	36	84	59	—	—
3. Actual total of loophole primaries	811	443	85	29	40	10	15	150	39
Total (line 2 plus line 3)	1,848	888	387	140	76	94	74	150	39
4. Loophole primaries on a standardized basis	811	450	75	35	37	15	16	150	33
Total (line 2 plus line 4)	1,848	895	377	146	73	99	75	150	33

SOURCE: Delegate Selection Project, 1976.
NOTE: Omits totals from New York, Pennsylvania, and District of Columbia.

the loophole primaries (line 3) is added to this converted sum. An alternative calculation is also provided in line 4 that standardizes the existing loophole results to the formula defined above. This standardization is necessary because some of the loophole primary states selected their at-large delegates in a different manner than that indicated above, and also because many of the district results in the loophole races yielded splits among candidate preferences—an outcome that reflects the fact that delegates were voted on individually in these races.[4]

Table 4.4 provides another basis for comparison in which the results of both the proportional representation primaries and the loophole primaries are converted to a pure plurality system; i.e., one in which all district delegates are given to the candidate winning the district vote, and all at-large delegates are given to the candidate winning the statewide vote.

A comparison of the actual results of the proportional primary states with both the hypothetical loophole results and the pure plurality results for these states shows in general a marked increase for the stronger candidates, Carter and Brown, and a decrease for the weaker candidates. Some deviations from this pattern exist, but the general direction of the trend is unmistakable. It confirms once again the general theoretical proposition about the "concentrating" effect of a plurality system relative to a proportional system.

A summary of the results of the Democratic primary races under each system is presented in Table 4.5. Because the actual results are a mixture of the plurality and proportional rules, they are listed in line 3 in order to see most clearly the effect of a successive movement away from proportional rules and toward plurality. The greater concentrating effect of plurality rules is well illustrated in this table. The combined share of the two front-runners, Carter and Brown, increases from 58 percent of the total under proportional rules to 72 percent under a pure plurality system. The movement for most candidates is monotonic, although

[4] The extent to which the loophole rules allowed for voting on the basis of the individual delegates rather than on the basis of national candidates alone is illustrated by the results in Pennsylvania. Of the fifty districts, only eighteen had all of the delegates pledged to the same candidate; in the remaining thirty-two, the delegates were split among two or more candidate preferences.

Table 4.4. Results of Democratic primaries under a plurality system

System category	Total	Carter	Brown	Udall	Wallace	Jackson	Church	Others	Uncommitted
1. Proportional represen- tation primaries converted to plurality	1,037	472	304	86	21	89	59	—	—
2. Loophole primaries converted to plur- ality	811	452	94	13	37	11	16	160	28
Total	1,848	924	398	99	64	100	75	160	28

SOURCE: Delegate Selection Project, 1976.
NOTE: Omits totals from New York, Pennsylvania, and District of Columbia.

Table 4.5. Summary results of outcomes in the Democratic primaries under alternative systems

System category	Total	Carter	Brown	Udall	Wallace	Jackson	Church	Others	Uncommitted
1. All primaries proportional	1,848	790	278	176	177	66	71	194	96
2. All primaries proportional, standardized to 15 percent cutoff	1,848	802	299	192	168	77	65	177	68
3. Actual results of primaries	1,848	873	310	145	146	67	69	167	71
4. All primaries loophole	1,848	888	387	140	76	94	74	150	39
5. All primaries loophole on standardized basis	1,848	895	377	146	73	99	75	150	33
6. All primaries plurality	1,848	924	398	99	64	100	75	160	28

SOURCE: Delegate Selection Project, 1976.
NOTE: Omits totals from New York, Pennsylvania, and District of Columbia.

variations due to such factors as regional support do exist in certain cases.

The Caucus States

In the Democratic party the caucus states were all required by national party rules to use proportional representation at every stage in the selection process. This requirement changed the traditional practice in most of the caucus states in two important respects. First, delegates within each district were rewarded according to the proportional share of support for each candidate rather than on a winner-take-all basis, as frequently had occurred in the past. In some caucus states, of course, a rough kind of proportionality previously had been employed informally in order to reduce conflict and maintain party harmony. But this practice had been far from universal, as was evident in 1972, for example, when supporters of Senator McGovern managed in many areas to use narrow pluralities to obtain full slates of delegate support.[5] Second, the participants at all stages were required by national rules to cast their votes for delegates by specifying a candidate preference (uncommitted being one such preference). Proportional rules made this specification necessary because some standard was needed by which to define a proportional share. Previously, the selection of delegates to the district and state conventions in the caucus states had been conducted under practices in which most of the delegates were technically uncommitted, leading in turn to the selection of many uncommitted national convention delegates. In practice, these delegates often made commitments to national candidates but the delegates were not bound or mandated in the same sense as under the current rules.

What was the effect of the changes to proportional representation in the caucus states? One could attempt to answer this question by following the same method of conversion as in the primary states; i.e., changing the delegate totals from the final selection stage to what they would have been under plurality rules. When this is done (see Table 4.6), Carter emerges as the chief beneficiary of the

[5] See the discussion of William R. Keech and Donald R. Matthews, *The Party's Choice* (Washington, D.C.: Brookings Institution, 1976), pp. 208-10.

change, gaining at the expense of Udall and the uncommitteds; the totals of the other candidates are only slightly altered, because each had a base of support in a particular geographic area and managed to pick up delegates under plurality that were lost elsewhere under proportional rules.

However, the conversion in Table 4.6 obscures more than clarifies the total effect of proportional representation in the caucus states. The problem results from the inability to consider the consequences of proportional representation in the first stages of the process—the mass meeting and intermediary conventions. To calculate the overall effect of proportionality, one would have to begin at these earlier stages and determine their impact on the composition of the delegates at the district and state conventions, from which the national delegates were chosen. The data for any such exercise are not available, and it is impossible as well to know how various forces would have coalesced and bargained under plurality rules. The closest piece of empirical information bearing on this question is a listing on a statewide basis of the candidate preferences of all participants. These results, though not apportioned by districts, nevertheless provide a rough indication of what the situation was in the localities at the first stage in the process. In only two of the twenty-one caucus states (Connecticut and Delaware) is it clear that Carter received a statewide plurality. More importantly—and in spite of the apparent intention of the rule requiring a candidate designation—the uncommitteds held the edge in fifteen states, often by a very substantial margin.[6] Had plurality rules been in effect, it seems very likely that a much larger share of the delegates at the district and state conventions would have been at least technically uncommitted.

The large committed Carter delegate bloc from the caucus states resulted from two sources: (1) the delegates to the district and state conventions who were already pledged to him and (2) a significant number of uncommitted delegates at these levels who shifted to him before the selection of national delegates. In the case of the first component, Carter seems to have benefited directly from the proportional rules. Under a plurality system, the

[6] *Congressional Quarterly Weekly Report,* July 10, 1977, pp. 1809-11. This source gives a comprehensive table of available results at all levels of the process in the caucus states.

Table 4.6. Results of Democratic caucus states under plurality rules

System Category	Total	Carter	Brown	Udall	Wallace	Jackson	Church	Others	Uncommitted
1. Actual results of caucus states	622	191	3	83	20	43	5	62	215
2. Caucus states converted to plurality	622	232	0	54.5	20	49	0	63	203.5

SOURCE: Delegate Selection Project, 1976.
NOTE: Omits totals from the territories and from Colorado, where no official totals could be obtained.

Table 4.7. Actual results of the Republican delegate selection process by system categories

System category	Total	Ford	Reagan	Uncommitted
1. Plurality primaries	1,156	398	458	300
2. Proportional representation primaries	396	211	184	1
Subtotal, primary states	1,552	609	642	301
3. Caucus states (Est. as of July 17)	677	237	354	86
(Final convention vote)	677	295	382	—
Total all states (using caucus state est.)	2,229	846	996	387

SOURCE: Delegate Selection Project, 1976, and *Congressional Quarterly Weekly Report*, Aug. 14, 1976.
NOTE: Includes state totals only. Excluded are totals from territories and the District of Columbia.

uncommitteds could have used their advantage to prevent selection of Carter delegates to the next level. Undoubtedly, many of the uncommitted delegates would have moved to support Carter under plurality rules; but without the large contingent of committed delegates available to Carter at the first stage, his national total might have dwindled. This, in turn, could have minimized one of the most powerful influences leading many of the uncommitted delegates to the state and district conventions to switch to his column—viz., the impression that he would be a certain winner.

There is another reason why the conversion process in Table 4.6 cannot reveal the full picture. Caucus states traditionally have differed from primaries in that the participants have not operated under the same constraints as the "single commitment" imposed by a ballot. Instead, participants in mass meetings and conventions could alter their strategy in light of the behavior of other participants. Moreover, in the search for a plurality, they would engage in extensive bargaining. The proportional rules changed this aspect of the caucus procedures. Because each candidate received a proportional share, there was no need to bargain in the search for a plurality, for nothing was gained by any such coalition of forces. Indeed, the participants who opted for a particular candidate were not allowed to shift their preference unless they happened to vote for a candidate receiving less than 15 percent. Consequently, a "stop Carter" movement comprised of all those who might gain from an open convention became a virtual impossibility. Under plurality rules, enough of the candidates could have banded together (or given their support to the uncommitteds) to obtain a plurality, after which they could have denied Carter any delegates. Under proportional rules, however, Carter could not be prevented from keeping his fair share, regardless of the alliances formed among the other candidates.

The effect of the change to proportional representation in the caucus states in 1976 is thus very difficult to determine. There are too many imponderables to predict with confidence exactly what might have occurred. The evidence that is available suggests that the change probably assisted Carter and penalized the uncommitteds. Proportional representation allowed Carter to make inroads in a large number of states where the uncommitteds, often led by party regulars, might otherwise have been able to dominate the selection process. Once Carter gained national momentum, the proportional rules negated any potential gain that could have been made by a "stop Carter" movement in the caucus states.

The Democratic Experience: Conclusions

For Jimmy Carter's candidacy, there were opposite and, to some extent, offsetting effects deriving from proportional representation. In the primary states, where Carter led all candidates, the existence of proportional rules clearly lowered his delegate total; and the extension of proportional rules to the plurality states would have reduced it still further. On the other hand, in the caucus states, where Carter trailed the uncommitteds, he probably benefited from proportional rules.

Besides the effect of the new rules on Carter's absolute total, one must also consider its consequence on the relative standing of the candidates. Looking only at the existing proportional primaries in 1976, we find that, while Carter would have gained slightly by a change to plurality, Brown would have gained considerably, largely because of his victory in California (see Table 4.3). Indeed, if the focus is shifted from individual candidates to ideological tendencies, a very different conclusion begins to emerge regarding the effects of proportional representation on Carter's candidacy. What might be called the center-right of the party (Carter and Wallace) did better with proportional rules than without; the center-left (Jackson, Brown, Udall, and Church) did more poorly. The reason for this is that in the proportional primaries Wallace and Carter together were taking more delegates from the liberals because of proportional rules than the liberals were taking from both of them (see Table 4.3). The damage to Carter under proportional representation was inflicted more by Wallace than by any other candidate; but Wallace's delegates had no place to go except to Carter.[7]

[7] In the process of converting the totals from one system to another, it is possible to determine how many delegates each of the candidates won—and at which candidates' expense—because of proportional representation (as compared with the hypothetical existence of a plurality system). Each candidate gains delegates in some districts (where he does not finish first) and

Alternative Selection Systems and the 1976 Nomination Race

Before the 1976 race, analysts who discussed the effects of proportional representation asked two basic questions: (1) how would it affect the relationship between stronger and weaker candidates, all things being equal; and (2) how would it affect the balance of power within the party among its various ideological positions. On the first question, we have seen that the existence of proportional representation tended to disperse the delegates, taking away from the strong and giving to the weak—although this dispersion did not go so far as to create a brokered convention in 1976. A number of factors help to explain this result: (1) proportional representation was not universally implemented; (2) one candidate (Carter) proved so much stronger than the others that a brokered convention became doubtful no matter what selection system was in existence: (3) proportional representation in the caucus states actually helped the leading candidate against the uncommitteds; and (4) the use of the 15 percent cutoff rule in most Democratic primaries served to reduce by a substantial margin the amount of fragmentation.[8]

The second question, how proportional representation would affect the permanent balance of forces in the party, is almost impossible to answer on the basis of the 1976 experience. Before the race got under way, there seemed to be a rather clear division

loses them in others (where he is the plurality winner). With Carter, one finds that, overall, proportional representation allowed him to win delegates at the expense of Brown (mostly in California), Jackson, and Church. He lost delegates because of proportional representation to Wallace (mostly in the South) and to Udall.

[8] The significance of the level at which the cutoff point is set, in terms of how it affects the degree of dispersal and concentration, is discussed in chapters 5 and 6. Here we may merely observe that in Massachusetts, under what was nearly a "pure" system of proportional representation, the distribution of delegates was:

Jackson	30	Harris	6
Udall	21	Bayh	1
Wallace	21	Shapp	1
Carter	16	McCormack	1
Shriver	7		

Total: 104

Under a 15 percent cutoff rule in the districts and with the at-large delegates divided in proportion to the district delegates, Jackson would have received 47 delegates in Massachusetts, with Udall receiving 29, Wallace 21, and Carter 7.

between the conservative wing of the party, represented by Wallace, and the liberal wing, represented by Udall, Bayh, or Harris. The center, as it then was conceived, was occupied by such traditional liberals as Jackson and Humphrey. When the question of proportional representation was posed, conservatives wondered whether in fact they would be able to gain more delegates in districts with liberal or centrist majorities than they would lose in districts with conservative majorities. Many of Wallace's supporters believed the answer to this question was yes, and so they favored proportional representation. On the other side, certain liberals reached the opposite conclusion, believing that they could cut into districts with a centrist or conservative plurality and gain more from these than they would lose from their own strongholds.

These various positions could not really be tested fully in 1976 because of the emergence of Carter, who shunned any ideological position in favor of a more direct personal appeal. To the extent that Carter could be placed on an ideological spectrum, he was on the center-right for most white voters, but paradoxically a liberal to most black voters.[9] Thus Carter and Wallace were both able to win their expected shares of conservative sentiment in the Democratic party in the North. Liberals, on the other hand, attempted little and failed miserably in the South, even in proportional races.[10] Carter was able to capture the moderate support as well as the support of black voters. Whether in the future a more clear division of forces will emerge and allow a test of the ideological effect of proportional representation remains uncertain. For the

[9] See, for example, the "New York Times/CBS Poll," *New York Times,* Apr. 29, 1976.

[10] In the southern primaries (Ala., Ark., Fla., Ga., Ky., La., N.C., Tenn., and Texas), the only liberal candidates to receive any support were Brown (two delegates) and Udall (three delegates). Jackson, a centrist, won twenty-one delegates in Florida. Clearly this failure was in part strategic: liberals may have thought that Carter or Terry Sanford would siphon off the moderate and liberal sentiment in the South without either one of them posing any real danger for the nomination. Their delegates would then have to turn to one of the nonsouthern liberal candidates. Nonetheless, the very weak showing of Udall, even in the proportional representation primaries, must be a cause for some concern among liberal candidates seeking to mount a serious campaign in the South.

present, however, it seems that the liberal wing has the most cause for concern.[11]

THE REPUBLICAN NOMINATION RACE

The actual results of the Republican contests, presented by system categories, are shown in Table 4.7. Because of differences in the political situation and the rules, this table is not fully parallel with that for the Democratic party in Table 4.1. The caucus totals in the table are not official since Republican delegates in the caucus states are not required to specify a candidate preference, and the commitments that delegates do make are in no sense binding. The first set of figures given for the caucus states is the totals reported by the *Congressional Quarterly* as of the end of July—figures that, in many instances, were based on informed guesses.[12] Because there is no official mandating of the caucus delegates, the only truly reliable count is the actual vote of the delegates at the convention, which is also provided in Table 4.7.

A word must also be said about the uncommitteds. In one respect, the number of uncommitteds shown in Table 4.7 in the caucus states is underestimated since some of the committed delegates were considering changing their status. Further, in the primary states the large number of uncommitteds is partly fictitious. All but fifteen of these delegates came from the states of New York, Pennsylvania, and West Virginia. After Reagan bypassed an active challenge in these three states, President Ford also decided not to compete directly, thereby leaving the field to an uncommitted slate devised by the party organizations. However, it was understood by nearly everyone that the uncommitted slates in New York and Pennsylvania would be predominantly for Ford. In addition to this,

[11] A solid, but limited, basis for support for liberals in the South would seem to exist among black voters. These voters favored Carter overwhelmingly in 1976, usually in contests in which none of the liberal candidates were active. Still, poll data suggest southern blacks are one of the most liberal groups in the nation. See Philip E. Converse, "Change in the American Electorate" in Angus Campbell and Philip Converse, eds., *The Human Meaning of Social Change* (New York: Russell Sage, 1972).

[12] Adapted from the state-by-state discussion of delegate selection results in *Congressional Quarterly Weekly Report*, Aug. 14, 1976.

the laws governing Republican primaries in Pennsylvania and West Virginia bar the listing of the delegates' candidate preference on the ballot.

Hypothetical Results of Different Primary Selection Systems

To calculate the results of the Republican primary races under the proportional rules, we follow the same basic procedure as in the Democratic contests. The results of the plurality races are converted to hypothetical proportional totals based on a 15 percent cutoff rule. Omitted from the analysis (as shown in Table 4.8) are the states of New York, Pennsylvania, and West Virginia because of their previously discussed uncommitted status.

The results of the conversion of the plurality primaries show a slight overall net gain for President Ford of seventeen votes. Under proportional representation Ford would have made substantial gains at Reagan's expense in California and in Texas, Georgia, and Alabama—three bastions of conservative Republicanism. Reagan would have cut into Ford's total in Ohio, Illinois, Wisconsin, and New Jersey—states in which the moderate wing of the Republican party is dominant.

These results seem to contradict the claim made by Reagan on several occasions that he would have been the nominee if proportional representation had been used in all of the primary states. But in assessing Reagan's claim, it is necessary to go beyond the numbers and to take into account strategic options. Table 4.8 omits the three states of New York, Pennsylvania, and West Virginia—states in which, as already mentioned, Reagan made an early decision not to offer a contest, no doubt because they were plurality races. Although Ford also did not compete, the party slates in Pennsylvania and New York were known to be moderate in outlook. Ford ultimately received 226 delegate votes from these two states, while Reagan received only 30. In West Virginia, Ford won 20 of the state's 28 delegates.[13]

---

[13] West Virginia held a candidate preference or "beauty contest" primary. On the basis of the results, Reagan would have won 11 delegate votes under a proportional system, 3 more than he actually received at the convention.

Table 4.8. Results of Republican primaries under proportional representation

System category	Total	Ford	Reagan	Uncommitted
1. Actual totals of plurality primaries	871	398	458	15
2. Plurality primaries converted to proportional representation	871	415	439	17
3. Actual totals of proportional representation primaries	396	211	184	1
Total (line 2 plus line 3)	1,267	626	623	18
4. Proportional primaries standardized to 15 percent cutoff	396	200	196	—
Total (line 2 plus line 4)	1,267	615	635	17

SOURCE: Delegate Selection Project, 1976.
NOTE: Omits totals from New York, Pennsylvania, and West Virginia.

Table 4.7 illustrates graphically the importance to Ford of the support of the nominally uncomitted delegates from New York and Pennsylvania. When the votes from these two states are omitted Reagan runs well ahead. Reagan, in fact, received a mere 11 percent of their delegate total, even after his bold—or, more accurately, desperate—effort to shake loose some of the delegates by naming Senator Schweiker as his would-be vice-presidential candidate. Clearly, proportional rules would have netted Reagan more than 11 percent, even without an active campaign. Under proportional rules in Massachusetts, where Reagan did not campaign, he nevertheless picked up fifteen delegates, or 35 percent of the total delegation. If Reagan had received a share as small as 24 percent in New York and Pennsylvania—and if all other things had remained the same—he would have been the nominee. These, of course, are very big "ifs," but they are merely intended to indicate that there are grounds for Reagan's assertion that proportional representation would have assisted his candidacy. More generally, one can perhaps conclude that if the plurality states were to adopt proportional rules, the number of delegates going to a conservative candidate would increase significantly. Conservatives, it appears, are currently "penalized" by plurality rules, in that they constitute a larger minority in states with a moderate majority than do moderates in states with a conservative majority.

To ascertain the results of delegate selection under a plurality system (see Table 4.9), the totals in the proportional primaries are first converted to plurality results and then added to the totals of the actual plurality races. The plurality rule employed in this calculation is the one most frequently used in the existing Republican plurality states: all of the district delegates are given to the winner of the district races, and all of the at-large delegates to the winner of the statewide race. An alternative calculation also is provided under which the results in the plurality primaries are standardized to the formula just defined.

Ford would have been the slight beneficiary of this change, as his gains in Michigan, Massachusetts, Kentucky, and Tennessee would have more than offset his losses in North Carolina, Arkansas, South Dakota, and Idaho. Yet this difference is so slight and the contest in many districts was so close that there is no basis for concluding that a shift of the proportional states to plurality rules would have benefited the moderate wing of the party.

Table 4.9. Results of Republican primaries under a plurality system

System category	Total	Ford	Reagan	Uncommitted
1. Actual totals of proportional representation primaries	396	211	184	1
2. Proportional representation primaries converted to plurality	396	244	172	—
3. Actual totals of plurality primaries	871	398	458	15
Total (line 2 plus line 3)	1,267	622	630	15
4. Plurality primaries on a standardized basis	871	403	452	16
Total (line 2 plus line 4)	1,267	627	624	16

SOURCE: Delegate Selection Project, 1976.
NOTE: Omits totals from New York, Pennsylvania, and West Virginia.

The summary results of the outcome for the Republican races under the different systems are presented in Table 4.10. These figures show that, in the case of either change, Ford would have improved over his actual totals. Yet it is also important to remember that, if proportional rules had been employed, Reagan might well have entered the New York and Pennsylvania primaries. In this case, some very significant changes would probably have occurred. Reagan would have benefited considerably from a proportional system and Ford, from a plurality system. Although such results apply only to the particular candidates in 1976, they are at least suggestive of the major consequences that may be in store for the Republican party if there is a further movement to proportional representation.

The Republican Caucus States

Delegate selection in the Republican caucus states in 1976 was conducted in the traditional way: by plurality voting, with the delegates not being officially committed. Because of this system, no totals are available for the candidate preferences of the participants at the lower levels. Furthermore, because of the different rules, candidate preference was not always the guiding consideration in the selection of delegates. All of this makes it impossible to calculate the results under a proportional system. From a practical standpoint, however, this is no loss. The caucus procedures are governed by party rules, state and national; and at this time there is no sentiment in the Republican party to change to proportional representation in the caucus proceedings.

A number of features about the Republican caucus contests nevertheless merit consideration. First, the plurality system, while it operated in many cases as a winner-take-all race between Ford and Reagan, was not exclusively focused on a direct choice between the national candidates. Many delegates to the district and state conventions were chosen as a matter of prerogative, because of their position in the party organization. In many instances this was true even for the selection of national delegates.

Second, the absence of a formal commitment by the delegates was of some significance. Because the delgates were formally uncommitted (even when they may have been chosen by a majority

Table 4.10. Summary results of outcomes in the Republican primaries under alternative systems

System category	Total	Ford	Reagan	Uncommitted
1. All primaries proportional	1,267	626	623	18
2. All primaries proportional, standardized to 15 percent cutoff	1,267	615	635	17
3. Actual results of primaries	1,267	609	642	16
4. All primaries plurality	1,267	622	630	15
5. All primaries plurality on standardized basis	1,267	627	624	16

SOURCE: Delegate Selection Project, 1976.
NOTE: Omits totals from New York, Pennsylvania, and West Virginia.

for one or another of the candidates), some of them continued to think of their role as that of "trustee," able to change their preference at their own discretion. For this reason, as will be seen in the chapter on Virginia in Part II, competition for the loyalties of the various caucus state delegates continued up until the convention, despite their earlier tentative commitments.

Finally, the totals for most of the Republican caucus states show a great deal of concentration for a particular candidate, rather than a close division. In fifteen of the twenty-three caucus states, one candidate received more than 80 percent of the delegations's support (see Appendix B, Table 5). This concentration was due in part to the regional strengths of the two candidates, with Ford running very strongly in the East and Midwest and Reagan in the West and South. Given these geographical strengths, the plurality rules accentuated the differences. Moreover, one must consider the level at which the delegates were chosen. In preparing for 1976, the Republicans increased the size of the convention from 1972 and assigned most of the new delegates to the states on a statewide at-large basis, rather than within the districts. This meant that a larger share of the delegates were selected at state conventions, where the national candidate focus tended to be strongest and where a plurality could net a candidate a large slate of delegates. The large number of delegates selected at this level contributed to the concentration of delegate support behind a given candidate within each state, as well as reinforcing the strong state or federal character of the caucus delegations at the Republican National Convention.

CHAPTER 5 / Theoretical Considerations of Proportional Representation in Delegate Selection

THE selection process in 1976 offers no more than a partial test of the potential effects of proportional representation on the selecttion of convention delegates. Many delegate contests were still conducted under plurality rules, and the novelty of the principle meant that the candidates and other participants could only begin to calculate its influence and to experiment with its possible strategic implications. Part of the potential influence of proportional representation may also have been obscured by the particular political forces that operated in 1976. For proportional representation to have had the immediate visible impact that many analysts predicted—viz., the creation of a multiballoted convention—it would have been necessary to have a reasonably close race between two (or more) front-runners, with other candidates in a position to siphon off at least some of the delegates. Only then could the anticipated fragmenting of delegate support have taken place. In the Republican race, this condition was not met because only two candidates competed. On the Democratic side, Jimmy Carter unexpectedly emerged as a powerful front-runner, quickly rolling over the opposition of such hopefuls as senators Jackson and Bayh and Governor Wallace. Meanwhile, two of Carter's strongest potential opponents, Hubert Humphrey and Edward Kennedy, decided not to compete for delegates—decisions that initially may have been made in the expectation that the political factors and the new proportional rules would result in an "open" convention. Accordingly, many contingent factors produced Carter's single-ballot victory, and it is easy to conceive of some slight changes in the political situation such as a Udall victory in New Hampshire, where the liberal vote was split among four candidates, or an earlier start by Governor Jerry Brown—that would have altered the character of the race and magnified the effects of proportional representation.

The "failure" of proportional representation to produce a bargained convention decision in 1976 should not, therefore, be taken as conclusive proof of its insignificance. Indeed, contrary to the general view, there is one sense, as we shall see, in which proportional representation actually helps to produce single-ballot victories. On the other hand, it is also clear that proportional representation does possess the potential under certain circumstances for a strong fragmenting effect—and hence for the encouragement of a multiballoted convention. What seems clear above all is that the full implementation of proportional representation is certain to have a significant impact on the selection process, not only on the outcome of nomination races but also on the strategies of the candidates and the activities of the various groups within each of the parties. Some of these possibilities were already evident in embryonic form in 1976. Others may take longer to materialize and can only be deduced from an analysis of the structure of the new arrangements. The exact consequences cannot be stated with certainty, in part because we do not yet know the full extent to which proportional representation will be adopted or the particular forms it may assume. But the significance of the change makes it desirable to explore its possible effects as far as insight may permit.

ORIGINS AND THEORY OF PROPORTIONAL REPRESENTATION

Proportional representation is a relatively modern idea that arose in the middle of the nineteenth century in England, western Europe, and the United States. In England the first major proposal for the system was made in 1859 by Thomas Hare.[1] It was later given wider currency after receiving the endorsement of John

---

[1] Thomas Hare, *The Election of Representatives*, 4th ed. (London: Longmans, Green, 1873).

Stuart Mill in his classic work, *Considerations on Representative Government*. The Hare-Mill plan is sometimes referred to today as a "personal" system because it awards legislative seats directly to the individual candidates rather than giving them first to the political party and then to the candidates within that party. This individualistic element of the plan was designed to secure representation in Parliament for members of "the instructed majority" who would serve as a "competing corrective to the instincts of a democratic majority."[2] Although a fair representation of the political sentiments of the nation was one objective mentioned by Hare and Mill, their primary emphasis was on improving the quality of representation.

In the United States, by contrast, the idea of proportional representation has been advocated chiefly for the purpose of securing what some have considered to be a just representation of political forces in the nation. The first American proposal, devised in 1844 by historian Thomas Gilpin, was offered during the general debate on the nature of congressional representation in the 1840s.[3] This debate arose in reaction to the spread of the general ticket system in the states—the system of electing all House members from the state at large on a plurality basis, which by 1842 was in use in six states and threatening to spread. Like the use of a similar scheme for the election of presidential electors, this system originated in the attempts of certain state parties, temporarily in the majority, to maximize their influence. Gilpin's plan would have maintained the multimembered districts within the states but divided the representation according to the proportions of the vote given to each party, with the party itself setting the order of the names on the list. Fairness in representation, according to this view, required that each vote for a particular party be given its due weight in the choice of congressmen. In this way no votes would be lost, as they allegedly were under the existing system. However, in response to the same problem of statewide districts, Congress adopted a different solution: a

[2] John Stuart Mill, *Considerations on Representative Government* (Indianapolis: Bobbs-Merrill Company, 1958), pp. 117-18.

[3] Thomas Gilpin, "On the Representation of Minorities of Electors to Act with the Majority in Elected Assemblies," in J. R. Commons, *Proportional Representation* (Philadelphia: John C. Clark, 1844), pp. 110-11, 237-39.

uniform national requirement of representation by single-member districts. This solution was in accord with the traditional theory of representation in America, as outlined in *The Federalist Papers*, under which an individual congressman was understood to represent his district as a whole and not merely that portion of the electorate that had provided him with a plurality.[4] Schemes for multimember districts with proportional representation were again brought before Congress just after the Civil War, in attempts by white southerners to obtain representation in states dominated by a black voting majority. But these schemes made little progress, and since then proportional representation has been a dead issue as far as Congress is concerned.[5]

Municipal reformers were the only group to achieve any success with proportional representation before the recent period of national convention reform. Approximately twenty-five cities adopted proportional systems for election of their city councils in the early years of this century. Reformers advocating proportional representation argued that it was inherently a fairer system, that it would help to reduce the control of party organizations over the electoral process, and that it would change the focus of representation from territory to the more rational basis of political belief. The experience of these cities with proportional representation, however, was anything but positive. All but one of the cities has abandoned the system, a fact which led the most well-known

[4] James Madison, Alexander Hamilton, and John Jay, *The Federalist Papers*, no. 57, ed. Clinton Rossiter (New York: New American Library, 1961), pp. 350-56. The Founders naturally expected that representatives would consider the national interest, which in part would be discovered from the deliberations within Congress. Representation by territorial unit would tend to give Congress some discretion since members could appeal to different groups within their constituencies to support various stands.

[5] The idea of proportional representation has appeared in Congress from time to time in connection with electoral college reform. Since the disputed election of 1876, the proposal has been made repeatedly that each state retain its constitutional weight in the electoral college, but that its assigned numbers of electors be divided among the presidential candidates in proportion to their shares of the popular vote in the state. This plan received active attention during the 1950's, when it was known as the Lodge-Gossett plan. The primary impetus for this reform was always the alleged unfairness of the winner-take-all system, especially when it was applied at a level as high as the entire state. But the plan was ultimately opposed and defeated. The current proposal for electoral college reform favored by most reformers—and by President Carter—relies on a direct popular vote.

textbook on local government to conclude that while "various kinds of proportional representation systems have been used in American local cities, none has had any enduring popularity."[6] The most frequently cited evils of the system were unstable majorities and recalcitrant, and sometimes extremist, minorities.

In recent years American political scientists have given little attention to proportional representation except as they have been concerned with its effects in European nations and with its general theoretical properties as an electoral system. The major issues addressed by these scholars have related to the possible influence of proportional representation on the number of parties within a nation and the character of its underlying electoral cleavages. One well-known student of proportional representation, F. A. Hermens, has stressed the independent influence exerted by electoral arrangements, arguing that the adoption of proportional representation can lead to a proliferation of political parties and to the kinds of parties that appeal to a narrow base of ideology or interest.[7] Others have denied that the electoral system can exert so much influence, stressing instead the causal importance of the underlying cleavage structure in society. According to this argument, whenever the divisions in society are such that they cannot be contained by two parties, a multiparty system will emerge, the character of the electoral arrangements notwithstanding. In this view, the electoral system usually is a reflection of the preexisting party system rather than a cause of it. A multiparty system will exert strong pressure to implement proportional representation, whereas a system in which two parties predominate will tend to adopt elections by the plurality method.[8]

The correct position probably lies somewhere between the two views just identified.[9] Unless aided and abetted by underlying

---

[6] Edward Banfield and James Q. Wilson, *City Politics* (New York: Random House, 1963), pp. 96-97.

[7] F. A. Hermens, *The Representative Republic* (Notre Dame, Ind.: University of Notre Dame Press, 1958).

[8] See, for example, John G. Crumm, "Theories of Electoral Systems," 2 *Midwest Journal of Political Science* 357-76 (November 1958).

[9] See Seymour Martin Lipset, *The First New Nation* (New York: Doubleday and Company, 1967), p. 353. For a general discussion of the effects of proportional representation, see Douglas W. Rae, *The Political Consequences of Electoral Laws* (New Haven: Yale University Press. 1967).

cleavages in society capable of sustaining a multiparty system, proportional representation by itself might be unable to cause a proliferation of parties. But where there is a range of possible outcomes, proportional representation can facilitate a multiplication of parties, both by making it easier for new parties to get started and by preserving older parties that under a plurality system might fade out of existence. And, of course, proportional representation always maximizes the influence of nonsectional minor parties by giving them representation in proportion to their vote. In explaining the existence of a particular electoral system, the number of existing parties is obviously an important factor. But there is no absolute correlation between the electoral system and the number of parties. Legislators and constitution makers may thus have discretion in fashioning the kind of electoral arrangements they think best. To sum up, one probably should not speak of inevitable consequences deriving from proportional representation, but rather of certain tendencies that it promotes, the most important being an increase in the number of nonsectional parties. (The qualification relating to sectionalism is necessary because a potential party with a strong base of support in a given territorial unit may receive a greater incentive for its formation from a plurality system than from proportional representation.)

In what way does this analysis of proportional representation for general elections to a legislative body relate to its possible effects in the selection of delegates to national party conventions? The answer is not immediately obvious, for the situations clearly are very different. Proportional representation for seats in legislative bodies gives actual representative power to parties or individuals unable to win a plurality. Proportional representation in the selection of convention delegates, on the other hand, seems in one respect to be merely a different way of collecting popular preferences for a single decision—the selection of a nominee. Despite this very important difference, however, one suspects that there may be at least some relationship between the electoral effects of proportional representation in each instance. Nor is the delegate selection process simply a way of registering popular preferences; the conventions retain the prerogative of deliberating on the decision of a nominee as well as on a number of other significant matters. Thus, the possibility of certain analogous effects between proportional representation for legislative elections and such representation for delegate selection deserves our consideration.

EFFECTS OF PROPORTIONAL
REPRESENTATION ON DELEGATE SELECTION

Critics of proportional representation contend that it promotes a fragmenting of delegate support among a number of candidates, and perhaps constituency blocs, and thus increases the chance of a multiballoted convention. But if fragmentation is in fact one effect of proportional representation (as discussed), it is by no means the only effect. The recent reforms, proportional representation included, also produce a countervailing tendency that in some ways reduces the chance of a bargained convention decision. Such an effect results from the ways in which the reforms have diminished the influence of the party organizations, which formerly were the chief source of delegates, with their capacity and incentive to hold out and deal independently with the candidates. Even when in recent years, such as 1960, party power brokers used this independence to create first-ballot victories, the nominations were still in a sense the result of a bargaining process. The candidates had to come to terms with party leaders and delegates who were not bound by the selection process to any particular candidate. The recent reforms, by opening up the delegate selection process to the direct solicitation of national candidates, have made it easier for a strong candidate to capture the nomination outright, without the need to bargain with independent power sources.

Proportional representation contributes to this plebiscitary character of the nominating process both in the caucus proceedings and in primaries. In the Democratic party's caucus states, the division of delegates according to candidate preference encourages participants to make commitments to national candidates and accustoms the participants to regard direct activity by the candidates as fully legitimate. An uncommitted preference is still an available choice and was used extensively in 1976; however, it is now an option that must be deliberately chosen, rather than the norm for all delegates, as it was in the past. Moreover, with the delegates being awarded proportionally by candidate preference, there is now an official breakdown of the results, much as in a primary. This means that the media could—and in 1976 did—focus on the caucus states as races in which a candidate can be declared a winner.[10]

The tendency of the mass media to report elections as if they were horse races creates the need for a candidate "winner"; a slate of uncommitted delegates does not serve that need very well. If one assumes that the party organizations still have a good chance of winning pluralities in caucus states, then the effect of proportional representation is to cut into the number of delegates that these organizations control and to award minor shares to delegates chosen by the various candidate organizations. In the case of 1972, many caucus proceedings were captured by grassroots candidate organizations, which under a plurality system actually tended to inflate the number of candidate-oriented delegates when compared with the likely effects of a proportional system. But such dominance by candidate organizations probably should still be considered more the exception than the rule. One can see this from the results of the caucus states in the Democratic race in 1976: even with the rule requiring the designation of candidate preference, the uncommitteds finished first in the initial stage of the proceedings in fifteen of twenty-one states. Under the previous rules, party regulars would probably have controlled a much larger share of the delegates from these states.

In primary states, proportional representation contributes marginally to a more direct candidate focus on the part of the delegates when contrasted with the loophole primaries, in which the delegates are voted on individually. The latter arrangement allows voters to choose delegates because of their own personal status or position, with the result that many delegates are chosen "against the grain" of the candidate plurality within the district. Such delegates can reasonably consider themselves to have a certain degree of independence—to have been chosen as "trustees" rather than as bound agents. In proportional representation primaries, by contrast, the delegates are chosen by the slates and are thus likely to consider themselves bound by a direct popular

[10] See *Congressional Quarterly Weekly Report*, July 10, 1976, p. 1809.

mandate. There are, therefore, some very important influences deriving from proportional representation that strengthen the candidate focus of the selection process and enable strong national candidates to win committed delegates in instances where they previously could not do so.

When one turns to the influence of proportional representation in apportioning the delegates, however, it becomes clear that proportional representation has a very different effect. As related literature suggests, proportional representation tends to splinter the delegates among a number of candidates, provided more than two are in the race. (When only two contestants are involved, as in the Republican race in 1976, proportional representation can alter the outcome between the two candidates but obviously cannot produce any fragmentation.)

The splintering effect promoted by proportional representation is likely to be greatest during the initial stage of a campaign in which, as in the Democratic races of 1972 and 1976, there are several candidates in the field. Table 5.1 gives hypothetical delegate selection plans. The results have one "accidental" element, in that Stevenson emerges as a leading candidate because of his success as a favorite son in Illinois. In this case Stevenson profited from the advantage that a plurality system gives to a candidate (or party) with a concentrated regional appeal. Notwithstanding this one aberration, the general tendency of the different systems seems clear enough. The plurality system would give the seven minor candidates only six delegates, or a mere 1.6 percent of the total delegates in the four races; in contrast, the Massachusetts system (nearly an absolute proportional system) would give them fifty-three delegates, or 14.3 percent of the total. If the New York and Pennsylvania primaries (which took place rather early in the campaign) were also included, the number of delegates "wasted" on minority candidates under a proportional system would have been much greater. Table 5.1 also illustrates the significance of the 15 percent cutoff, which can cut down dramatically on the amount of fragmentation.

After the initial phase of the campaign, when the number of active candidates is certain to decline, the fragmenting effect of proportional representation can continue from two possible sources: (1) an occasional marginal favorite son and (2) the contin-

Table 5.1. Delegate outcomes under alternative selection systems, first four Democratic primaries in 1976 (New Hampshire, Massachusetts, Florida, Illinois)

	Major candidate preferences						Uncom-mitted	Total for major preferences	Total for seven minor candidates
System category	Carter	Jackson	Wallace	Stevenson	Udall				
Actual systems in the four states [a]	124	51	50	87	23		16	351	20
Proportional on the Massachusetts plan	80	54	69	62	26		27	318	53
Proportional with 15 percent cutoff	90	68	62	73	36		16	345	26
Plurality similar to loophole [b]	111	84	36	85	28		21	365	6
Pure plurality [c]	117	83	36	92	21		19	365	6

[a] New Hampshire and Illinois had loophole primaries; Massachusetts had a proportional system with no cutoff at either district or statewide levels; Florida had a proportional system with 15 percent cutoff.

[b] Plurality elections in the congressional districts; statewide delegates, if any, alloted in proportion to the district delegates.

[c] Plurality elections in the congressional districts; statewide delegates governed by plurality in the statewide vote.

uance in the campaign of weak national candidates. The first effect is illustrated by the results in 1976 in Texas. Even though Senator Bentsen had already withdrawn as a national candidate by the time of the Texas primary, he still obtained about 21 percent of the vote. Under the existing plurality system in small districts, he received six delegates; under a proportional system, he would have captured thirty-seven (see chapter 11, on Texas).

The second effect can be seen in Table 5.2, which gives the delegate totals under alternative systems for the three primaries taking place on the final primary day, June 8. Even at this point, after the field had been considerably narrowed, proportional representation would have enabled the weaker national candidates (Church and Udall) to siphon off a larger number of delegates from the two front-runners.

It is impossible to make any abstract determinations about the extent of the fragmenting effect of proportional representation, for such an effect clearly depends upon the level of any cutoff point that is established, as well as on the number of candidates and their relative strength in any particular race. Nor can one say whether the fragmenting effect is more powerful than the offsetting advantage that proportional representation provides to the national candidates in the form of being able to capture a large number of committed delegates. It does seem clear, however, that in any future race having two formidable national candidates and a number of minor ones, the universal application of proportional representation will increase the chances of a bargained convention decision.

Perhaps the most interesting possible results of proportional representation will develop only when and if candidates and participants begin to anticipate a bargained decision-making process. If a bargained result was expected, then proportional representation would provide an added incentive to hesitant minor candidates to enter the race, as well as perhaps encouraging more constituency blocs such as labor unions, women's groups, and blacks to participate directly in the selection of delegates. Minor candidates would choose to run in the hope of becoming a "dark horse" choice in the event of a stalemate, or perhaps to bargain their votes for some possible tangible reward, the most important being the vice-presidential nomination. Constituency blocs would participate in order to maximize their influence at the point closest to the final

Table 5.2. Delegate outcomes under alternative selection systems, final Democratic primary day in 1976 (Ohio, New Jersey, California)

System category	Brown	Carter	Udall & Church	Others	Total
Actual systems in the three states [a]	287	218	29	6	540
Proportional with 15 percent cutoff	257	212	63	8	540
Plurality similar to loophole [b]	363	160	9	8	540
Pure plurality [c]	374	153	7	6	540

[a] California used a proportional system with a 15 percent cutoff; Ohio and New Jersey had loophole primaries.

[b] Plurality elections in the districts; statewide delegates alloted in proportion to the district delegates.

[c] Plurality elections in the districts; statewide delegates governed by plurality in the statewide vote.

decision; i.e., at the convention, rather than at the delegate selection stage. Proportional representation makes participation logical in both of these cases because minor candidates and constituency blocs alike can win a share of the decision-making power by emphasizing their particular appeal to some groups or ideological tendency rather than by appealing to a broad electoral base. The results in the case of such appeals seem to parallel the fears expressed by many critics who oppose proportional representation in general elections for legislative bodies.

Although both of the possibilities noted—fragmentation among candidates and among constituency blocs—could occur simultaneously, either one, if dominant, would impart a very different character to the selection process. Under a candidate-oriented system, the national candidates would be the focal points in the race. They would build their own organizations and would attempt, when not merely seeking bargaining power, to win enough support to obtain the nomination. Under a constituency-oriented process, there would be strong national organizations working to promote their own particular interests by capturing delegates who would function in the decision-making process as delegate blocs, negotiating with potential nominees in return for specific commitments. In the former case, the voters and participants would choose their delegates to represent their choice of a specific candidate; in the latter case, they would identify with a group and choose their delegates to select a candidate to represent their interest and viewpoint.

Thus far, the trend under reform clearly has been in the direction of establishing a candidate-oriented process. It is the candidates who receive the attention of the media and who are in a position to offer to prospective workers and supporters the promise of direct benefits. Moreover, with most of the delegates selected in primaries, candidates appeal to a "mass" electorate that is often beyond the control of intermediary groups or their leaders. Yet the possibility that constituency blocs might come to play a crucial role should not be overlooked, especially since the adoption of proportional representation provides new opportunities for these blocs to win direct control over convention delegates.

Some groups, in fact, began to act or to contemplate national action in 1976, and it is probably no mere coincidence that organized labor became the strongest supporter of the universal application of proportional representation. Labor pursued a strategy of getting labor delegates added to delegations of various Democratic candidates, negotiating in various states to obtain representation within a candidate's contingent. The strategy of its leaders was to form a labor bloc at the convention in the event of a deadlock.[11] Many black leaders and some liberal organizational leaders planned concerted group action in 1976, although both attempts failed in the face of strong candidate appeals to their mass constituencies— something which could change under different political circumstances.[12] Finally, Ellen McCormack's antiabortion campaign indicated a possible course of action for an issue-oriented group under a system in which an intense but small segment of the party could capture a modest number of delegates.

A variety of strategies would be available to these constituency blocs. The plan followed by labor in 1976 is perhaps the most likely to net delegates, as it does not directly challenge the primacy of national candidates in the process. At the same time, such a strategy does not by itself pull delegates away from any of the candidates and thus does not contribute to the possibility of a bargained decision. An alternative which would contribute to this result and which was briefly considered by some black leaders in 1976 is to field a "holding candidate" who could attempt directly to win delegates for the group but who would not be a bona fide challenger for the nomination.

As with its effect on the number of parties in a regime, proportional representation can lead to a proliferation of intraparty factions only when there is the potential for multiple divisions within the party's electoral base. In the Republican party two distinct factions currently exist, thus providing little stimulus for the creation of a multifactional system. In the event of a close contest between these two factions, one can imagine a candidate's using proportional representation to win a balance of power, but a multiplication of more or less permanently organized constituency groups seems highly unlikely. In the Democratic party, on the other hand, there is a wide diversity of interest groups and ideological tendencies which could under a proportional system develop

[11] Ibid., Mar. 17, 1976, pp. 680-81.

[12] *New York Times*, Mar. 21, 1976, p. 42.

into formal electoral agencies, holding preconvention conferences and acting as permanent intraparty factions.

THE EFFECT OF PROPORTIONAL
REPRESENTATION ON CONVENTION DECISION MAKING

Not since 1952 has the nation witnessed a multiballoted convention—the longest such unbroken series of first-ballot victories since the convention system began. Consequently, it is difficult to predict how a decision would be made in a modern deadlocked convention. Past examples can provide little guidance because the method of selecting delegates has changed completely. The units that formerly exercised control in such conventions, the organization-controlled delegate blocs, have largely disappeared. The new units likely to emerge are candidate blocs and national constituency blocs. It is far from certain, however, whether either of these can function as a bargaining group in a sense comparable to the old organization-controlled blocs. Neither one, it appears, possesses anything like the same means to constrain or "discipline" its membership. Each candidate bloc collectively will share a commitment to its candidate, but can this collective commitment be transformed into concerted action when a candidate no longer appears to have a chance of becoming the nominee? The national constituency blocs may share an apparent common interest, but what is to ensure that leadership squabbles and splinter factions will not develop?

It would seem, then, that there are at least three basic models for future decision-making processes if bargaining is required. First, the decision could be made at the top by the national candidates. Such a result would give an ironic outcome to the reform movement, which was publicly justified on the grounds that it would make the decision-making process more open and democratic. This contrast between promise and performance could lead in turn to a challenge of the legitimacy of the convention system, especially if the candidate with the largest contingent of delegates was ever denied the nomination. One could then easily imagine the disappointed partisans of the defeated favorite attacking the convention system for being undemocratic.

Second, the decision could be negotiated among the various constituency blocs that might emerge. The obvious danger of this method is that the nominee would become too greatly beholden to one or more of these groups. Formerly, interest groups were represented in the nominating process though the party organizations, which gave these groups access but also maintained a buffer between the candidates and the groups. If constituency blocs should ever become the principal arbiters of the nomination, it would contradict both the preference of the reformers and the grounds on which they declared the old system obsolete. The "new politics" was founded on the assumption (or hope) that pluralistic influences were declining in favor of the activities of independent, issue-oriented individuals.

The final possibility is that of an open convention in which the above-mentioned blocs do not form or maintain cohesiveness. The decision would then be left either to individual delegates acting independently or to ad hoc groups and leaders that would form at the convention and about which very little could be known in advance. Indeed, the very unpredictability of such an outcome was the chief worry of many of the party leaders who opposed proportional representation. Although such a convention would seem to be democratic in form, one might well wonder about the quality of its deliberations. Democracy in so large an assembly could turn out to be dangerous if the delegates acting individually were unable to bargain effectively or to communicate with each other, or to be a sham if a few ad hoc spokesmen emerged temporarily and controlled the direction of the proceedings.

Over the long period of single-ballot victories, many have come to consider both the selection process and the convention in a new light. The nomination decision, it is now often thought, is made not by a deliberative process among the delegates as in the past, but instead by the voters and participants in the caucuses. Given this fact, the way to achieve fairness is to have the delegates represent the people's expressed candidate preferences. The capacity of the delegates to deliberate or to bargain for their constituents is irrelevant; the delegate serves, much like the presidential electors, to represent a share of the people's expressed will.

Proportional representation was adopted under the influence of this general view and constitutes the most vigorous or "radical" attempt thus far to secure a perfect reflection of the participants' will. The central paradox of proportional representation is that, while it derives from a general view of selection that tends to deny or undermine the right of the convention to make an independent choice, it also increases the chances that the conventions will in fact be called upon to do so.

In principle, of course, there is no reason why a bargained result or "brokered convention" should result in an undesirable outcome. It could be argued, in fact, that the process of negotiation would produce a nominee more likely to represent a consensus within the party—in contrast to the divisive results of the plurality system that in 1972 rammed through the choice of a factional candidate. Indeed, one Democratic party official was heard to rejoice at the adoption of proportional representation: "What the reformers have done is to put the nomination back into the back room—where it belongs."[13] The problem with this view—and with its quaint optimism—is that the actors in the back room will now be quite different than before, if in fact they can all manage even to fit into one room. And given the democratic rhetoric that accompanied reform, it is questionable whether the new decision makers will have enough freedom to make a wise or even a politic choice.

[13] *Washington Post*, Mar. 31, 1974.

CHAPTER 6 / The Outlook for 1980

IF THE opinion of most activists in the Democratic party can be accepted, the decade-long task of revising the party's rules for delegate selection is now almost completed.[1] The final action was taken by the Democratic National Committee in June 1978, when it adopted in revised form a set of recommendations proposed by the Commission on Presidential Nomination and Party Structure, commonly known as the Winograd Commission. The most important item in the new rules is the provision on proportional representation. In accordance with the resolution on proportional representation passed at the 1976 Democratic convention, the national committee decided to require a proportional division in all multidelegate districts. The committee postponed a decision on the controversial question of whether to permit single-member delegate districts, which could have created another kind of loophole system. The matter was finally resolved a year later in the "call" to the 1980 convention, which banned the use of single-member districts. As a result, the rules now call for all delegate races to take place in multimember districts using proportional representation. In addition, the new rules contain provisions that would:

Expand each state's delegation by 10 percent to provide for greater representation of party leaders and elected officials. Those selected would have to reflect the same division on candidate preference as the other delegates in the state.

[1] *Congressional Quarterly Weekly Report*, June 3, 1978, p. 1393. Background for this chapter was obtained through interviews with Austin Ranney and Ken Bode, both members of the Winograd Commission, and with Elaine Kamark, the research director of the commissions's staff.

Shorten the delegate selection process to a three-month period. This provision will not become fully operative until 1984.

Ban, without the possibility of exemption, all "open" primaries; i.e., primaries in which crossover voting by registered Republicans or independents is allowed, as in Wisconsin, If a state insists on such a primary, the state party will be asked to conduct its selection of delegates by the caucus method.[2]

The conclusion of the Democratic party's revision of its delegate selection rules does not necessarily mark an end to the extensive process of change in the nominating system. One of the most important factors affecting the character of the nominating process is the ratio of primary to caucus systems, and the decision on this matter rests entirely with the state governments, not the national parties. Moreover, the states possess additional powers in relation to the national parties. Those states which currently have loophole primaries may refuse to adopt proportional rules; and even those currently using proportional rules conceivably might decide to shift to a loophole format. Faced with a problem of this kind, the Democratic party would have to choose between acquiescing in the states' decisions and requiring their state affiliates to ignore state law and proceed with a party-run caucus system.[3] Thus, action by the states could still force a significant revision of the selection system independent of any further rule making by the Democratic party.

[2] In practice, the distinction between "open" and "closed" primaries is often blurred. A truly closed primary would restrict voting to preregistered members of a party, with the preregistration being declared well in advance. Most primaries, however, are only nominally closed; voters are asked at the time they cast their primary vote whether they are Democrats or Republicans, with no further obligations being incurred. This last requirement is all the Democratic party rules insist upon. The type of primary that the rules ban is one in which the voter is not even asked to make the minimal acknowledgment of Democratic identification.

[3] Under the new rules, the state party organization is required to take "provable positive steps" to help secure passage of legislation that meets national party rules (Rule 20). However, when even these steps have been taken but the legislation has not been secured, the national party may require state parties to adopt alternative caucus procedures that are in conformity with national rules. It is conceivable also that the national party might attempt to convert delegate totals from loophole to proportional results and then award the delegates on a proportional basis.

However, barring any widespread resistance by the states to the Democratic party's new rules or any movement to abandon presidential primaries, one can look forward to the following general characteristics for the delegate selection process in 1980 and beyond. First, the process will be dominated, as it was in 1976, by presidential primaries, which will continue to be overwhelmingly oriented toward selecting or mandating delegates on the basis of their declared candidate preferences. Second, most, if not all, of the Democratic primaries probably will be conducted under proportional systems. In addition, if the states adopting proportional systems decide to require it of both parties, the Republican primaries also will become predominantly proportional. Finally, Democratic caucus procedures will all be conducted under proportional rules based on the criterion of national candidate preferences. The Republican caucuses will probably retain their current form, i.e., plurality rules based on the criterion of national candidate preferences.

THE EVOLUTION OF THE
DEMOCRATIC PARTY RULES OF 1978

The Winograd Commission was established by the Democratic National Committee in October 1975 with the limited mandate to study the effects of the growing number of presidential primaries. The convention subsequently gave it the additional task of examining the delegate selection rules and making recommendations to the national committee.[4] The commission operated under circumstances very different from those of either of its predecessors. When it began its major work following the 1976 election, there was relative harmony within the party and obviously no belief that extensive changes were required to "save" the party. There was also a Democratic presidential incumbent who had considerable influence over the appointment of new commission members when the size of the commission was expanded following the 1976 election. Accordingly, it was inevitable that the decisions of the commission would be influenced by those considerations which promoted the

[4] *Congressional Quarterly Weekly Report,* July 2, 1977, p. 1375.

president's interest. Even before the commission began its deliberations, this prospect began to worry reform-minded members of the party. "My big fear," said Rick Scott, chairman of Minnesota's Democratic Farmer Labor party, "is now that we have an incumbent, the changes may be for less open participation. Can we resist what happened in other times, when the White House was the dog and the party became the tail?"[5] For the minority of self-proclaimed reformers, the answer to this question increasingly became no. As the deliberations of the commission proceeded, the reformers continually charged that the rules were being rigged to minimize the risks of a challenge to the president in 1980. In making this criticism, reformers were forced to acknowledge one highly undesirable effect of the entire process of party reform, at least from their viewpoint. Over the past decade, the reform movement had succeeded in establishing the principle that the national party had the chief legislative power over the delegate selection rules. With a Democrat as the incumbent, this power came partly under his control. The irony of this situation could not be overlooked: a process that was designed to help the "outsiders" was now (claimed) to be under the dominance of an "insider."

It is important, however, not to exaggerate the significance of this influence. The president, who had been elected under a refomed system, had no desire to alter dramatically the character of the nominating process. The chairman of the commission, Morley Winograd, claimed that a consensus existed in the party about the reforms and that all the commission was doing was "fine tuning the process."[6] Reformers, of course, claimed that some of the contemplated changes went much further than "fine tuning"; however, when judged from the perspective of the general evolution of the system, the major disagreements over the cutoff for proportional representation and the advance time for filing to enter the primaries were marginal (though certainly not inconsequential). In addition, for political reasons the White House could not afford to ignore entirely the reformers' objections. After the outcry against some of the original commission proposals, the president's advisers agreed to a number of concessions, though reformers still remained highly dissatisfied with the results.

[5] Ibid.
[6] Ibid.

Actually, it is too simplistic to speak of a single division within the commission between the president's contingent and the reformers. A third group, the academics, also played an important role. This group, which included Austin Ranney, Jeane Jordan Kirkpatrick, and some members of the commission staff, had certain theoretical objections to the dismantling of the parties that had taken place since 1968 and sought, as far as possible, both to enhance the role of the state party organizations and to improve the prospects that the selection process would reach a consensual choice.[7] A working alliance developed within the commission between the president's contingent and the academics, the former supplying most of the votes and the latter many of the arguments. Even though the interests of these two groups were not identical, it quickly became clear that there was a common ground between them, for those proposed revisions which promoted a consensual choice also could be seen as advancing the interests of the president. Both of these groups could agree on the need to avoid a set of rules that tended to encourage a large number of challengers with small blocs of delegates who could perhaps force a brokered convention. The reformers, on the other hand, wanted to keep the process as "open" as possible, meaning that there should be no artificial attempt to disenfranchise any segment of opinion or to discourage the quick entrance of any candidate into the competition.

Although the dispute between the alliance and the reformers took place at the margins, in fact each position reflected a different conception of how the selection process should operate. The alliance wanted a system that tended to narrow the choice to those with a genuine potential for being nominated. As one proponent of this view put it, "you're trying to create the situation where winners win and losers lose."[8] In all likelihood, the winner would become apparent before the convention; but in the event of a deadlock, the bargaining would take place among delegates chosen to represent serious candidates, not factional groups. In calling for a cutoff higher than 15 percent, the commission report, re-

[7] The thesis of party decline was developed recently by Jeane Kirkpatrick in *Dismantling the Parties* (Washington, D.C.: American Enterprise Institute, 1978).

[8] *Congressional Quarterly Weekly Report*, June 3, 1978, p. 1394.

flecting the views of the alliance, argued that "if all states use proportional representation the chances diminish that a front-runner will emerge by [the time of] the convention."[9] Although it may seem paradoxical that a "pro-party" position would want to avoid a convention decision, it must be recalled that the type of convention likely to take place would bear little resemblance to the managed affairs of previous times.

The reformers, though not explicitly favoring an open convention, were unwilling to include in the rules any institutional mechanisms to avoid it. Any such bias was thought to violate the norm of democratic fairness and, more importantly, to give an edge to the established groups within the party. The reformers argued that the 15 percent cutoff rule should be mandated for all the primaries and that no lengthy filing period should be required.

Throughout this debate, there was a certain disproportion between the modesty of the actual differences over the proposed changes and the depth of the theoretical disagreement. One is reminded of the debates over many welfare state issues today, in which the concrete differences between the parties are often quite narrow, but in which the supporting arguments, when extended logically, reflect fundamental differences. A similar phenomenon can be seen in the report of the Winograd Commission, which, in arguing for the less "radical" of the possible changes, actually raised questions about many of the principles of the entire reform movement.

In fulfilling its first assignment to "study" the growth of primaries, the commission indirectly seemed to challenge the entire development of the primary-dominated system. At the very least, one finds none of the fulsome praise for democratic participation that marked the McGovern Commission's approving citation of the adage that "the cure for the ills of democracy is more democracy."[10] Instead, the reader is offered a sober and objective treatment of the causes of the recent movement to primaries. Three factors are cited: (1) the general mistrust of party organiza-

[9] Commission on Presidential Nomination and Party Structure (Morley A. Winograd, chairman), *Openness, Participation, and Party Building: Reforms for a Stronger Democratic Party*, submitted February 17, 1978, available through the Democratic National Committee.

[10] *Mandate for Reform*, p. 14.

tions in the American political tradition, which can be traced back to the Progressives and even to the Founders; (2) the great tensions in the Democratic party during the period from 1968 to 1972, which were expressed in the demand for some form of the institutional change; and (3) the attempt by many state party leaders to avoid the complications of the caucus rules imposed by the national party, as well as perhaps a desire on their part to avoid the more "radical" results of many of the caucuses in 1972. (Given the choice between reformed caucuses and primaries, many leaders apparently thought that primaries were more likely to produce a moderate result.) Of these three reasons, the second might appear to offer the best justification for the primary movement. Yet the commission in no way suggests that the increased number of primaries actually helped to reduce the tensions within the party. If anything, one is left with the impression that the strains were inherent in the political situation and that the call for more primaries was seized upon by those dissatisfied with the 1968 party nominee in the erroneous belief that institutions, not political differences, were the cause of these strains.

The commission continues its report by surveying the data on the characteristics of the delegates. One interesting finding here is that, in 1976, the caucus system selected slightly more delegates who had held party offices in their career than either the loophole or the proportional primary system did.[11] This finding is of some significance, as it raises the general issue of the character of the reformed caucus procedures. Although no data are available for 1972, the general impression of most observers is that the caucuses were the most vulnerable to a takeover by amateurs. In 1976, however, the case was quite different; the party regulars exerted a great deal of influence in many of the caucus states, as indicated in chapter 5. Thus, the final verdict on the reformed caucus procedures remains open. The situation in 1972 may prove to be an exception rather than the rule; and the caucuses, even when operating under reform rules, may still be the best system for maximizing the influence of state party organizations in the presidential process.

Another noteworthy finding of the commission was that the loophole primaries are more likely to send public officials to the

[11] *Openness, Participation, and Party Building*, p. 21.

convention than either of the other systems.[12] This once again corroborates the general theoretical argument of chapter 5 that the loophole arrangement continued to reflect something of the trustee theory of representation. Because delegates were voted on individually, it was still possible for the voters to choose delegates on the basis of their personal standing, rather than on the basis of which candidate they supported. This fact might explain why more public officials were selected under this system.

Clearly, then, the movement to universal proportional representation is likely to diminish the number of elected officials at the convention. But this tendency will be partly counterbalanced under the new rules by the expansion of each state delegation by 10 percent, with preference in the selection to be given to party leaders and elected officials. Still, unlike the loophole arrangement, these delegates must be selected so as to have the same proportional breakdown of candidate preferences as the other delegates. If no uncommitteds are chosen, then none of the party leaders or elected officials can hold this status.

In discussing the role of the state party organizations, the commission frankly acknowledges the inconsequential role played by the regular party organizations under the current selection process. The state parties "have more of an administrative than an active, decision-making role in presidential elections."[13] This is true, according to the commission, regardless of whether a state uses a caucus or a primary system. Although one might dispute this last claim, by and large the overall assessment is correct. The party organizations have virtually no power under the present system.

Overall, the arguments and the tone of the commission report suggest a certain dissatisfaction with some of the current arrangements. Yet the case that the commission builds is not developed to make a direct assault on any of the previous reforms, but rather to justify a more limited extension of reform than some expected. The three most controversial proposals of the commission were the following:

1.   A filing deadline for primaries of no less than fifty-five and no more than seventy-five days in advance of the primaries. Reformers objected vigorously to this provision, declaring that it

[12] Ibid.
[13] Ibid., p. 27.

was designed to close out late challengers, such as Governor Brown in 1976. Their counterproposal was for a filing deadline of no more than sixty days in advance.

2. A cutoff point on proportional representation that would grow increasingly larger in three stages as the campaign advanced. States holding primaries or scheduling the first step of their caucus proceedings before the second Tuesday in April would have a 15 percent cutoff (with no option to go any lower). During the second stage, until the second Tuesday in May, the cutoff would be 20 percent; and in the final stage, 25 percent. Reformers objected to this "consensus-building mechanism" and countered with a number of proposals for a lower cutoff point.

3. A provision that would allow a state to adopt single-member delegate districts in which the winner would be determined by a single plurality. Reformers objected to this provision on the grounds that it would create another "loophole" system. They proposed to include in the rules an outright ban on single-member districts.

In the period following the issuance of the commission report, reformers stepped up their attack on these three provisions. Sensing, perhaps, the strength of the opposition, the White House agreed to make some concessions. As Mark Siegel, a former Carter aide on the commission, observed: "Clearly the White House goal was to help the president as much as possible. They wanted three or four significant changes which would have been far more than fine tuning. But they have conceded, and what comes to the floor [of the Democratic National Committee] will not be a radical change in the rules."[14]

The final compromises drawn up before the Democratic National Committee meeting changed two of the three proposals cited above. The filing deadline was expanded in both directions to allow for a period of no less than thirty to no more than ninety days before the election. The change from fifty-five to thirty days was the more important of the two and represented a distinct victory for the reformers. The proportional representation cutoff point was changed by a rather complicated provision that dropped entirely the idea of an increasing threshold as the campaign proceeded. Under the new rules, the cutoff point both for the selection of

[14] *Congressional Quarterly Weekly Report,* June 3, 1978, p. 1393.

delegates at the final stage in the caucus states and for the selection
of at-large delegates in the primary states may be set by the states
at no lower than 15 percent and no higher than 20 percent. (At
earlier stages in the caucus proceedings, state parties may establish
whatever cutoff point they desire.) In the election of delegates at
the district level in primary states, the cutoff point would be fixed
on the basis of dividing the number of delegates elected by 100.
Thus, in a district with four delegates, the cutoff point would be
25 percent. In no case, however, can a cutoff point be set any
higher than 25 percent.

What, then, are the possible implications of the new proportional representation rule for the character of the nominating process? Nothing definitive can be said, of course, until the states
actually begin to revise their laws and the national party decides
how it will enforce the new rules. But two opposite tendencies
seem to be at work under the new rules when compared with
those in existence in 1976. On the one hand, the extension of
proportional representation to all Democratic primaries increases
the chances of an open convention by adding systems that produce
a greater degree of fragmentation among the delegate totals. More
than one-third of all the delegates in the Democratic party in 1976
were chosen in loophole systems, making the potential shift to
proportionality something more than an incremental change. (In
the Republican party, the effects cannot yet be determined, for
it is not known whether the new state laws will require proportional
representation for Republican primaries as well.) On the other
hand, however, this potential for greater fragmentation is to some
extent offset by the higher cutoff points mandated by the Democratic party rules. In 1976 the maximum cutoff point for all systems using proportional representation was 15 percent, and a considerable number of states used a lower figure for part of all of
their delegate selection process. (For a listing of the state provisions,
see Appendix A.) Under the new rules, the minimum in these cases
is 15 percent, and the maximum is increased to 20 percent. The
more important change comes in the districts. In 1976 a 15 percent
maximum cutoff point was in effect for the districts in states using
proportional representation. The new formula introduces a cutoff
point which varies according to the number of delegates in the district, and which may go as high as 25 percent. The actual average

cutoff for the districts will only become known after the states have determined how they will apportion their delegates. But if apportionment formulas similar to those of 1976 are used in 1980, only a modest number of districts will have cutoff points lower than 15 percent, and most will have to be at 20 percent or above.[15] Since most of the delegates are likely to be selected at the district level, this change marks a considerable diminution of the fragmenting potential of proportional systems.

Proportional representation was established as a general principle in the Democratic party after the 1972 election. The chief cause for the switch to this new system was not the self-interest of a dominant candidate, but a certain understanding of "fairness" which demanded a more explicit focus in the selection process both on the expression of national candidate preferences and on an exact replication of those preferences. Observers who concentrated on studying the possible effects of this new principle initially thought that it would produce a brokered convention under conditions in which the establishment of a harmonious party coalition would be difficult, if not impossible. But the effects of the system were not quite so simple as was first supposed. While the principle of exact replication of candidate preferences tended to increase fragmentation, the principle of candidate representation left more delegates to be captured directly by a front-runner. In 1976 these two effects tended to offset each other, and nominees of both parties were chosen on the first ballot. The latest rules create two additional, and once again countervailing, effects. Proportional representation will be extended, encouraging more fragmentation; but, through higher cutoffs, it will become less proportional, which will discourage additional fragmentation. Which of these two tendencies will prove the stronger over a period of several years cannot yet be determined. But if it is the first, we may yet see the transformation to open conventions widely predicted when the principle of proportional representation was first adopted.

[15] In order for the cutoff point under this system to fall lower than 15 percent, more than six delegates must be assigned to a district. In 1976 most congressional districts had fewer than six delegates, which under the new rules would have meant cutoffs varying between 20 and 25 percent. Moreover, a number of states—New Jersey, Texas, and Pennsylvania—used state legislative districts in which no more than four delegates were assigned to each district.

PART II

Studies in Selected States

CHAPTER 7 / Massachusetts
A Primary State

EDMUND BEARD University of
Massachusetts at Boston

MASSACHUSETTS is a state of many contrasts. Neal Peirce has called Massachusetts "perhaps the most liberal state, politically, in the Union."[1] It was the only state to vote for George McGovern in 1972. Earlier, its legislature had passed the "Vietnam Bill," stating that Massachusetts residents did not have to fight abroad in the absence of a congressional declaration of war and instructing the state attorney general to file a complaint in the Supreme Court. (The Court refused to hear the case.) Massachusetts also passed the nation's first "no fault" insurance law, and the state has one of the most rigorous gun registration laws in the country. The state's Republican senator, Edward Brooke, was the only black in the Senate.

Author's Note: Many people generously provided information and insight for this study. They include Chester Atkins, Frank Conway, Paul Counihan, John Eller, Charles Flaherty, Barney Frank, George Goodwin, Jr., Jerome Grossman, Xandra Kayden, Jack Kenny, Gordon Nelson, Francis Sargent, Alan Sisitsky, John Sears, and many of the delegates to the 1976 national conventions.

[1] Neal R. Peirce, *The New England States* (New York: W.W. Norton, 1976), p. 63. In addition to Peirce, other good introductions to Massachusetts politics are Edgar Litt, *The Political Cultures of Massachusetts* (Cambridge: MIT Press, 1965); Murray Levin, *The Compleat Politician* (New York: Bobbs Merrill, 1962); and Alec Barbrook, *God Save the Commonwealth* (Amherst: University of Massachusetts Press, 1973). Of course, the best guide to Boston politics may still be Edwin O'Connor's *The Last Hurrah* (Boston: Little, Brown, 1956).

Yet there is another side to this story. Boston, Massachusett's largest city and also its state capital and cultural center, has often been served by some of the least responsible and most demagogic local officials in the country, particularly on its city council and school committee. A finding of intentional, continued official policies of school segregation led a federal court to order the busing of Boston school children; since then, Boston's racial climate has improved little. The passage of the "Vietnam Bill" described above was, at least in part, the result of an attempt by the Democratic legislature to embarrass the liberal Republican governor, Francis Sargent—who in turn thwarted the effort by signing the bill. The possession of handguns may be tightly controlled, but auto theft is epidemic; the progressiveness of "no fault" auto insurance is counterbalanced by the fact that Boston's traffic laws are hardly enforced at all. Of the twelve counties nationwide with the longest delay between initial entry of a civil case and a trial in superior court, six are in Massachusetts. The state is next to last in the nation in the ratio of superior court judges to population. [2] Ethnic identification plays a major role in Massachusetts politics. Its state legislature is basically a case of two-man rule, exercised by the house speaker and senate president.

Massachusetts elected its first Democratic speaker of the state house of representatives, Tip O'Neill, in 1949. The house has had only one two-year period of Republican leadership since. Currently, the Democrats hold more than 80 percent of the house seats and thirty-three of the forty senate seats. Only 16 percent of the state's electorate is registered as Republican, and what remains of the party is bitterly split between a moderate and a conservative wing. But the Democrats' lead is not so overwhelming as it might appear. At least one of the state's national senators has long been a Republican; and the two predecessors of the present Democratic governor, Michael Dukakis, were both Republicans (Francis Sargent and John Volpe). In addition, two of the Republican party's more renowned national cabinet officers in recent years, Eliot Richardson and Christian Herter, came to national attention after winning statewide offices under the Republican label. Reflecting certain Yankee traditions and the party's origins in abolitionist

[2] Nick King, *Boston Globe*, Apr. 24, 1977.

sentiment, the GOP has often been the more liberal party in the state.

The Democratic party is also split into two wings: one blue collar and socially conservative, the other liberal, academic, professional, and technological. The first is in control of the legislature. The second, with a strong suburban coloration, votes in presidential primaries but is not so active in local politics. The Boston area's famed academic community, in particular, devotes much more time to Washington or New York politics than to those of Boston; this specialized participation strongly contributes to Massachusetts's national rather than local image as a very liberal state. (The McGovern victory, in addition to being strongly influenced by suburban voters, also undoubtedly reflected a considerable statewide anti-Nixon bias based in part on the Kennedy connection.)

Dukakis, Massachusett's current young Greek American governor, was originally a strong liberal who now prefers to define his goals as "realistic," somewhat in the mold of California's Jerry Brown. Neal Peirce has pointed out that "many national experts consider Massachusetts civil service the most ossified, rigid, and unresponsive system in the entire United States."[3] The state has perhaps the most impressive concentration of academic resources to be found in the world, but most are in private rather than public institutions; the substantial gains made by the University of Massachusetts system have been a recent, and perhaps temporary, phenomenon.[4]

Peirce calls Massachusetts "a remarkable civilization at once dying and being born anew." Daniel Webster was more careful: "Massachusetts—there she is; Behold her and judge for yourself."[5]

BACKGROUND OF THE MASSACHUSETTS PRIMARY

Massachusetts has had a presidential primary since 1912, with the exception of the years 1932 to 1938, when delegates were selected

[3] Peirce, *The New England States*, p. 90.

[4] For a harsh criticism of the state's approach to public higher education, see Nina C. McCain, *Boston Globe*, Apr. 24, 1977, p. A4.

[5] I am indebted to Professor George Goodwin for calling this quotation to my attention.

by state convention.[6] The 1912 statute provided for the direct election of delegates by congressional districts; also, the names of presidential and vice-presidential candidates could appear on the ballot for preferential voting. An amendment in 1916 eliminated this latter provision, while at the same time allowing delegate candidates to indicate on the ballot their presidential preference if the presidential candidate had given prior written consent. For the next few years, apparently, "the split caused in Republican ranks by the Bull Moose Party and the inability to muster strong primary support for the 'regular' Republican nominees in 1912 and 1916 made the Republican leaders in the state wary of changing the pre-primary statutes."[7] Whatever the reason, no further revisions were forthcoming until 1932 when, as noted above, the primary was temporarily abandoned. However, in 1938 the law was once again made similar to that of 1916—with delegates (not including those at large) being selected by direct plurality vote in primaries, including at least one from each congressional district, and delegate candidates being given the opportunity to indicate a presidential preference. No additional changes were made until 1951, when another intra-Republican party struggle similar to that of 1912 led to action. In the view of the Massachusetts Legislative Research Council, Republicans supporting Eisenhower as the presidential nominee at that time, "fearing that General Dwight D. Eisenhower would not assent to the use of his name on the ballot," felt that a change allowing space on the ballot to write in the choice for president, although not to be binding, would presumably reflect a strong preference for Eisenhower. The Research Council further notes that "Democrats generally opposed the bill, and, it is reported, Governor Paul A. Dever signed the measure reluctantly. He along with Democratic legislators who opposed it viewed it as an attempt to limit party control of the presidential pre-primary process."[8]

In 1966 a significant change was made when the presidential candidates' names were placed on the ballot and the entire delega-

[6] The following account draws heavily on Legislative Research Council, *Report relative to Presidential Pre-Primary Practices*, The Commonwealth of Massachusetts, Jan. 27, 1969.

[7] Ibid., p. 34.

[8] Ibid., pp. 35-36.

tion was required to vote on the national convention's first ballot for the winner of the statewide preference vote, regardless of the candidate preferences of the individual delegates. Only that statewide winner could release the delegation from the obligation. An accompanying provision stated that, if the slates of delegates and alternates at large which had been submitted by the state committee faced no opposition, they were then automatically elected and their names would not appear on the ballot. This could preclude an election and therefore the possibility of sticker or write-in candidates in the contest for delegates at large. Since it took a considerable organizing effort to muster the signatures needed by law to qualify a slate of at-large delegates, it was expected that this provision would often assure the success of the state party's selected group. The 1966 changes also required that at least two delegates (rather than just one) be elected from each district.

Apparently, among the pressures behind the 1966 revisions was the feeling of Robert Kennedy's supporters in the state that a Kennedy candidacy in 1968 might win the preference vote but not fare well in the selection of at-large delegates. As it happened, Eugene McCarthy was the only name on the Massachusetts Democratic ballot in 1968, and he accordingly received Massachusetts's seventy-two votes at the Chicago convention. In 1972 George McGovern's supporters managed to field an at-large slate of delegates which won while McGovern was also winning the statewide preference vote and all but one of the district votes. Thus, the 1972 Massachusetts delegation voted for McGovern out of conviction—an action unlike that of 1968, when Humphrey supporters in the delegation grudgingly voted, as legally required, for McCarthy. McGovern's success, incidentally, forced Boston Mayor Kevin White, Congressman Tip O'Neill, and the state's treasurer, senate president, house speaker, and attorney general (all of whom were Muskie delegate candidates) to watch the convention on television. This exclusion of party officials and officeholders from the delegation was one of the reasons for dissatisfaction with the 1966 law that led to changes again in 1975. Other relevant factors were the new Democratic national party rules and a movement to create an early regional primary in New England.

The move for a regional primary was led in Massachusetts by widely respected state Representative Barney Frank, political consultant Mark Shields, and Lieutenant Governor Thomas O'Neill, Jr. On May 29, 1975, representatives from Maine, Massachusetts, Rhode Island, and Vermont met at the Massachusetts State House in Senate President Kevin Harrington's office to discuss the proposed regional primary. Representatives from the other states seemed uncertain about the idea, but Vermont eventually did decide to hold its primary on the same date as Massachusetts (and Maine may yet decide to do so in 1980). The main attack on a regional primary, however, was led by New Hampshire, which was determined that its primary would continue to be held earlier than any other state—no matter when that might be. On the same day as the meeting in Boston, New Hampshire Governor Meldrim Thompson signed into law a provision for holding the New Hampshire primary on March 2 or "on any Tuesday a week before the primary in any other state." In amending its statutes on the presidential primary, Massachusetts went ahead with the selection of March 2 as the new date of its primary, despite opposition in the state. This opposition came mainly from the Citizens for Participation in Political Action (CPPAX) and other liberal "reform" groups; they all preferred the previous date in late April, believing that the March 2 date would not provide enough time for organization and the sorting out of alternatives.

Also, under the 1975 revision of the law, the secretary of state was required to list on the primary ballot the names of all persons who were generally recognized as presidential candidates, the names of candidates supported by nomination papers signed by 2,500 voters, and the names of candidates submitted by the chairmen of the state party committees. A presidential candidate who did not want his name on the ballot could have it withdrawn by filing an affidavit with the secretary of state by the second Friday in January. Under these provisions, the names of twelve candidates appeared on the 1976 Democratic primary ballot (Bayh, Bentsen, Carter, Harris, Jackson, Kelleher, McCormack, Sanford, Shapp, Shriver, Wallace, and Udall) and two on the Republican ballot (Ford and Reagan). Ballot position was determined by lot, and there was space on the ballot for write-in votes and votes for "no preference." By a previous law, voters in a party primary had to be registered either with that party or as independents. The section of the law calling for direct election of delegates was repealed, and each party was given the task of actually selecting the delegates. Pledged delegates, selected at party caucuses, were bound to their candidate on the first ballot unless released. The law, incidentally, did not specify proportional representation in delegate selection, although both parties decided to practice it.

All other aspects of delegate selection were left to the state parties. Massachusetts sent 104 delegates and 76 alternates to the 1976 Democratic convention and 43 delegates and 43 alternates to the Republican convention. The Democrats selected 78 delegates and 61 alternates by congressional districts, while the remainder were chosen at large by the state committee. Thirty-six Republican delegates and alternates were chosen by districts, and 7 of each at large.

THE DEMOCRATIC DELEGATION

The Democrats scheduled caucuses on Sunday, February 15, 1976, in each congressional district for each presidential candidate and for uncommitteds. Before these caucuses, each presidential candidate had to file with the Democratic State Committee chairman by no later than January 2 the names, addresses, and telephone numbers of two persons from each congressional district who were authorized to conduct that candidate's district caucus. Also, the locations of the caucuses had to be submitted to the state committee before January 16. It was the responsibility of the presidential candidates and their representatives to publicize their caucuses adequately.

To participate in a caucus (including being chosen as a delegate or alternate), a person had to be a registered Democrat residing in that district, although others could attend as observers. Persons had to be present to vote or to be selected as a delegate or alternate; no proxy voting was permitted. All of the presidential candidates could and did require participants in the caucuses to sign statements of support to the candidates. Slate making was allowed, but no slate of delegates or alternates could, by virtue of endorsement, receive preferential treatment.

Only one uncommitted caucus could be held in each congressional district. The first group of ten registered Democrats from each congressional district that filed formal intention with the chairman of the Democratic State Committee was empowered to organize the uncommitted caucus for that district. The uncommitted caucuses were held simultaneously with those for presidential candidates, and all aspects of the delegate selection plan, the affirmative action plan, and the time schedule applied equally to them. Candidates for no-preference delegates and alternates had to sign a statement that they were registered Democrats and were not committed to a presidential candidate. They could not participate in any other caucuses, nor could they subsequently become part of a presidential candidate's approved list of delegates and alternates.

The caucuses were called to order at 2:00 p.m. on Sunday, February 15. A nomination had to be seconded by two persons present and eligible to vote. Nominations had to remain open at least thirty minutes, after which they could be closed by two-thirds of those present and eligible to vote. Each candidate for delegate was allowed one two-minute speech and could distribute one sheet of paper on his or her behalf. Voting was by secret ballot and the use of tellers appointed by the caucus chairperson. There were no printed ballots. Election was by a majority of those present and voting. (There was no quorum requirement for any caucus.) Those eligible to vote could vote for as many persons as they wished, up to the maximum number of persons to be elected. This number varied from six to seven delegates and three to four alternates, according to a formula giving equal weight to (a) the total population of the district and (b) the number of votes in the congressional district for the Democratic presidential candidates in 1968 and 1972.

Separate ballots were used for male and female candidates, and each slate of delegates and alternates had to be composed of 50 percent men and 50 percent women. After the first ballot, the person receiving less than 15 percent of the total votes cast or the fewest votes was dropped. The same occurred on subsequent ballots. The caucus chairperson forwarded the list of elected delegates and alternates to the presidential candidate and to the Democratic State Committee. The presidential candidates had the right to approve delegates and alternates pledged to them, as well as to determine the final rank order listing. Although this power was used sparingly, there were some shifts in the rank ordering that had resulted from the caucuses, sometimes because of local political rivalries. A presidential candidate (other than a write-in) who failed to hold congressional district caucuses or to file slates of delegates and alternates was not entitled to receive delegate or alternate allocation. However, this eventuality did not, in fact, occur.

Allocation of Delegates among Presidential Candidates

The state Democratic party in Massachusetts did not use the 15 percent cutoff rule suggested by the national party; with twelve candidates in this early primary, there were fears that in some, if not all, of the districts no candidate would receive over 15 percent of the vote. Thus, there might have been the anomalous situation of no "winners," with the state committee naming uncommitted delegates.

Only the votes for presidential nominees, write-in candidates, and those expressing no preference were used in calculating delegate distribution; blanks were dropped. The percentage of the presidential vote in each congressional district (minus blanks) was multiplied by either six or seven delegates (depending on the allocation formula) to determine the number of delegates to be awarded. Any presidential candidate receiving less than 0.4955 of a delegate by this process was simply dropped. The allocation of delegates and alternates then began with the candidate receiving the largest percentage of votes and proceeded downward until all delegates and alternates were allocated. Whole delegates were allocated first; then any unallocated delegates were awarded, in order, to the highest unused percentages of a delegate. This process allowed Sargent Shriver to receive one delegate in the Sixth Congressional District with 7.36 percent of the vote, while receiving no delegates in the Ninth Congressional District with 7.35 percent of the vote. (This also meant that the district cutoff point in Massachusetts proved to be 7.36 percent.)

In the event that sufficient votes were cast for write-in candidates to warrant the allocation of delegates and alternates, the Democratic State Committee would have held caucuses in the affected congressional districts to select them. The candidates once again would have had the right to approve or disapprove the caucus lists, and the candidates could also have provided the caucuses with approved lists from which to choose. No write-in candidate did in fact receive sufficient votes to necessitate this process, although Hubert Humphrey won 2.1 percent of the vote in the Third Congressional District and 1.6 percent in the Twelfth District. Likewise, no "no-preference" delegates were awarded at the district level, although 2.1 percent of the voters in the First Congressional District chose no preference, and 1.5 percent did so in the Eleventh District.

The criticism that the early primary and even earlier caucus dates would be harmful to organization and participation had some merit. The caucuses were underpublicized and consequently poorly attended. Perhaps because it had never been tried before, the caucus system in practice was best described as chaotic. Organized groups or people who had personal organizations that could be brought out fared quite well in the absence of large general public participation. In Massachusetts this meant that organized labor in particular gained a decided advantage; in fact, all of the major candidates negotiated about delegate spots with labor representatives (including the teachers, especially) before the caucus dates. The labor groups in turn, and on a somewhat free-lance basis, spread their support (or pledges of support) broadly. In this respect, the caucus system in Massachusetts encouraged labor to hedge its bets, or at the least gave it the opportunity to do so (To a certain extent, women's groups tried the same tactic.) The result was that labor, especially if the teachers are included, was quite heavily represented in the delegation.

At-Large Delegates

Twenty-five percent of the Massachusetts Democratic delegation (twenty-six delegates and fifteen alternates) was chosen at large by the new Democratic State Committee (elected in the March 2 primary) at its meeting of June 1, 1976. A quorum of 40 percent of those eligible to vote (which included the newly elected state committee and those members of the national committee elected after January 1, 1974) had to be present. The at-large delegates and alternates were allocated on the basis of the percentage of votes received statewide by each presidential candidate, no-preference, or write-in candidate. The same apportionment process was used as in the districts, except in this case the candidate's percentage of the total state vote (minus blanks) was determined and then multiplied by twenty-six. The figure of 0.4955 of a delegate was still used, with those candidates below that figure receiving no delegates. This approach at the at-large level allowed Milton Shapp to receive one at-large delegate for his 2.95 percent of the statewide vote; while the antiabortion candidate, Ellen McCormack, with 3.5 percent of the vote, and Birch Bayh, with 4.75 percent, also received one delegate each. Hence, the actual statewide at-large cutoff was 2.95 percent of the vote.

Again, the presidential candidates had the right to approve or disapprove candidates for delegate or alternate at large. Presidential candidates could submit to the Democratic State Committee approved lists containing the names of twice as many proposed delegates and alternates as they were eligible to receive. The lists were expected to be composed of 50 percent men and 50 percent women. Nominations for at-large delegates and alternates could also be made by members of the Democratic State Committee, and the chairman could also open nominations from the floor, which he did. All candidates for delegate or alternate at large, except those who were uncommitted, had to have the approval of the presidential candidate whom they sought to represent.

In the event that a presidential candidate eligible for at-large delegates was no longer an active candidate at the time of the selection of the at-large delegation, national rule 12-5 provided that his allocation of delegates either could be given to a remaining candidate of his choice or could become uncommitted. Before the June 1 meeting, the Massachusetts state committee polled all of the candidates by letter and phone to learn if they were still active. All replied in the affirmative (including Bayh, Shapp, Harris, and Wallace) except Sargent Shriver, who did not respond. Shriver had been eligible for two of the twenty-six at-large delegates. His two at-large delegates were accordingly changed to uncommitted by the state committee. The slots were then filled by state Representative Charles Flaherty, the chairman of the state committee, and Doris Bunte, a black state representative.

As shown in Table 7.1, the entire selection process resulted in a national convention delegation consisting of thirty Jackson sup-

Table 7.1. Massachusetts Democratic primary, 1976
(Actual makeup of delegation to 1976 Democratic National Convention)

Congressional district	Jackson	Udall	Wallace	Carter	Harris	Shriver[a]	McCormack	Shapp	Bayh	Uncommitted[a]
First	1	1	2	1	1					
Second	2	1	2	1						
Third	2	1	1	1		1				
Fourth	2	2	1	1	1					
Fifth	2	2	1	1		1				
Sixth	2	1	1	1	1	1				
Seventh	2	2	2	1	1					
Eighth	2	2	1	1						
Ninth	2	1	2	1						
Tenth	2	1	1	1		1				
Eleventh	3	1	2	1						
Twelfth	2	1	1	1		1				
At large	6	5	4	4	2	0[a]	1	1	1	2[a]
Total	30	21	21	16	6	5	1	1	1	2

SOURCE: Massachusetts Democratic Party State Committee.

[a] By virtue of his percentage of the primary vote, Sargent Shriver should have received two at-large delegates. When he withdrew from the race, the state committee changed their status to uncommitted.

porters; twenty-one each for Udall and Wallace; sixteen for Carter; six for Fred Harris; five for Sargent Shriver (who would have had seven had he not lost his two at-large spots); one each for McCormack, Shapp, and Bayh; and two uncommitted (from Shriver's at-large allocation). Had Massachusetts used the 15 percent cutoff rule, only four presidential candidates, and not the actual nine, would have received delegates: Jackson would have received forty-seven delegates; Udall, twenty-nine; Wallace, twenty-one; and Carter, seven delegates. A plurality system would have concentrated the delegates even more, with Jackson getting seventy-one delegates, Udall twenty-one, and Wallace twelve. Use of this last approach would have shut out Carter in Massachusetts.

Affirmative Action

On December 7, 1974, at the Kansas City miniconvention, the Democratic party adopted a national party charter which included an absolute requirement for affirmative action programs at the state level to "encourage full participation by all Democrats, with particular concern for minority groups, native Americans, women and youth in the Delegate Selection Process and in all party affairs." The Massachusetts State Democratic party identified ten "designated target groups": blacks, Puerto Ricans (and other Spanish-speaking people), native Americans, women, student youth, nonstudent youth, senior citizens, Portugese-speaking people, French-speaking people, and other non-English-speaking people.

To implement an affirmative action program at the state level, the chairman of the Democratic State Committee first appointed an affirmative action committee consisting of two persons from each of the twelve congressional districts, plus the constitutional officers in Massachusetts. Then this committee, together with the state chairman, appointed ten members to represent the ten target groups, who were not yet represented on the committee. Membership on the affirmative action committee without vote, but with all other privileges, was also open to all other Democrats. A five-member compliance review committee was likewise appointed by the state committee. The affirmative action committee was headed by Jerome Grossman, a self-described "left liberal" and a longtime McCarthy/McGovern activist in the state.

Next, each ward and town committee was instructed to appoint no later than May 15, 1975, a local affirmative action committee, to include representation from designated target groups residing in the community. An analysis of recent participation and party enrollment of each target group was supposed to be conducted by each local unit to identify target groups requiring concentrated efforts. In each congressional district an affirmative action committee with open membership was also formed. This committee was to work with the local units to stimulate implementation of the plan.

Under the heading of services, each local unit was encouraged to make transportation available, if requested, to all party meetings and functions to reach those who might otherwise not attend and to provide child care services when requested at the same gatherings. Finally, each local unit was encouraged to schedule meetings at times and places that would actively encourage participation, rather than inhibiting it. The state affirmative action committee, in cooperation with the Democratic State Committee, undertook a fund-raising program of direct mail, personal solicitation, and special events to fund the affirmative action plan.

The chairman of the committee, Jerome Grossman, was deeply committed to affirmative action. He considered the Massachusetts plan the "best in the country"; and despite his interested perspective, his assessment may be correct, since the plan met with consistent applause from the Democratic National Committee. Yet Grossman was not happy with the results of affirmative action in 1976. Table 7.2 shows the number of members of the ten target groups included in the Massachusetts Democratic delegation, while Table 7.3 permits a comparison of this result with that of the 1972 delegation.

In 1976, with proportional representation being applied at the district level, the most common result was that the top one or two delegates in the rank ordering of each candidate's slate were the only ones elected. Yet when the district caucuses and/or the presidential candidates were setting the rank order, the most likely persons to receive the highest rankings were the district notables, such as well-known activists or labor representatives, most of whom

Table 7.2. 1976 Massachusetts Democratic National Convention delegation (by affirmative action target group)

Target group	Uncommitted	Bayh	Carter	Harris	Jackson	McCormack	Shapp	Udall	Shriver	Wallace	Total
Women	0	1	13	3	24	1	1	18	2	7	69
Noncollege youth	0	0	9	0	2	0	1	8	0	1	21
College youth	0	0	2	0	3	0	0	2	0	2	9
Blacks	1	0	2	0	1	0	0	3	0	0	7
French-speaking	0	0	1	0	0	0	0	0	1	2	4
Portugese	0	0	1	0	2	0	0	0	0	0	3
Spanish-speaking	0	0	0	0	1	0	0	2	0	0	3
Elderly	0	0	0	0	1	0	0	0	0	1	2
Native American	0	0	0	0	1	0	0	0	0	0	1
Other non-English-speaking	0	0	0	0	1	0	0	0	0	0	1
Others	0	1	7	4	21	0	0	12	3	23	73

SOURCE: Affirmative Action Committee of the Massachusetts Democratic Party.
NOTE: The figures on this chart represent a combination of delegates and alternates. Twenty-four persons were counted twice or more under the ten target groups as a result of multiple classification.

Table 7.3. Massachusetts Democratic National Convention Delegations of 1972 and 1976 (by affirmative action target group)

Target group	1972		1976	
	Delegates	Alternates	Delegates	Alternates
Women	50	27	43	26
Youth	27	21	18	12
Blacks	11	1	4	3
French-speaking	4	0	3	1
Portugese	not identifiable		2	1
Spanish-speaking	1	2	2	1
Elderly	1	0	1	1
Native American	1	0	0	1
Non-English-speaking	not identifiable		0	1
Total	95	51	73	47
Others (white men over thirty)	approximately 20% of the delegation		49	24

SOURCE: Affirmative Action Committee of the Massachusetts Democratic Party.
NOTE: The totals for affirmative action target groups in the delegations are somewhat misleading due to overcounting because of multiple classification (for example, a young, black woman). In the case of the 1976 delegation, twenty-seven of the affirmative action target group delegates and alternates were counted twice or more as a result of multiple classification. The exact figures are not available for 1972, but it seems reasonable to suggest a somewhat higher percentage of overcounting.

were white males. Thus, a conflict developed between affirmative action and proportional representation. Using proportional representation and, accordingly, usually selecting only one or two persons from the top of each slate, the tendency is to choose well-known persons with power and clout in the district who can mobilize support. Almost by definition, such persons are not those who are targeted by affirmative action.

In 1972 in Massachusetts, all of the names of candidates for delegate positions were on the ballot, including at-large candidates. The presidential candidate who won the statewide preference vote was to receive all of the delegate votes on the first convention ballot, but the delegates themselves had been selected by the voters at the district level, from slates, on a winner-take-all basis. The McGovern slates were heavily populated by affirmative action target groups, and by selecting the entire slate on a winner-take-all basis, the minorities and women were swept in. In 1976 the presidential candidates' slates of delegates in most cases still included many women and minorities. However, when the rank ordering took place, there was a tendency for the minorities to have lower listings and for well-known white men and women to appear at the top. Then after the primary, when the one or two highest ranked delegates were in fact elected according to their candidate's percentage of the vote, the minorities were eliminated.

One solution to this problem is to establish quotas to ensure affirmative action. This approach holds that political parties should be representative of their constituent elements. By this reasoning, if blacks provide 25 percent of the Democratic vote in an area, they should have 25 percent of the authority, responsibility, and rewards of the party. This argument also raises the specter of Miami in 1972, and it ignores the substantial question of "preferential" versus "demographic" representation. Another solution would be to defer the delegate selection caucuses until after the primary. Then each presidential candidate would know the number of delegates to which he was entitled and could arrange his lists to give effect to affirmative action. The Democrats in Massachusetts were not required to hold their caucuses before the primary, and the Republicans in Massachusetts did not do so. Still another answer is merely to stress broad programs like the Massachusetts affirmative action plan and then simply to hope for the best. This is, of course, a long-term and potentially frustrating process, and one which the media will not necessarily promote. Grossman found, for example, that the media representatives whom he contacted were often much more interested in writing stories about a wealthy, white, male, Jewish businessman who was doing all this work to pull blacks and Puerto Ricans into the political process than they were in the substance of the affirmative action plan or in giving it free publicity.

All this having been said, it should be pointed out that Grossman is not a reticent man, that he was interested in becoming national committeeman (he has since succeeded), and that publicity for such a good cause could hardly hurt that ambition. Finally, Grossman's plan was just that—a plan; there is considerable doubt as to whether much of it ever was undertaken seriously at a local level. One well-informed active Democrat in the state commented: "Grossman's plan counted for zilch. I'd be surprised if eight people read it. It was a joke; it never happened." This may be exaggerated. But whatever the cause, blacks and Puerto Ricans did not turn out at the caucuses, were not strenuously promoted for the at-large seats, and consequently did not go in large numbers to New York. Of course, it should also be remembered that affirmative action may sometimes be cosmetic. One major state Democrat called some of the delegates so selected "affirmative action submarines," persons who were really filling the "U.A.W.'s slot" or the "teachers' slot" and were in fact responsive to those interests, and not to some demographic subdivision. This was particularly true of the at-large delegates.

Organizing the Delegation

The Democratic delegation gathered at Framingham in mid-June. Jimmy Carter, who had finished fourth in the primary but was now the acknowledged national front-runner, was not popular there. There was a pervasive feeling that Carter was going to win, but no consequent rush to join him; instead, the delegates pursued their own objectives. The Carter supporters recognized this sentiment, understood it, and accepted the probable result. They simply held back, secure in their impending victory in New York.

Charles Flaherty of Cambridge, the Democratic state party chairman and an uncommitted at-large delegate, was selected as delegation chairman. Recognizing the merits of discretion, the Carter group deferred to Flaherty and the Jackson delegates (whose candidate had, after all, won the primary). The result was that no one was nominated to oppose either Flaherty as chairman or Jackson delegate Lisa Simonetti, a twenty-year-old employee in the Massachusetts house, as secretary. The Carter and Udall groups got one seat each on the convention committees, while Jackson got most of them.

Flaherty had become state chairman in 1973 as a compromise candidate in an agreement between Edward Kennedy, state Senate President Kevin Harrington, and state House Speaker David Bartley. Prior to that time, Kennedy had tended to designate the party chairman by himself; but in 1973, with busing and Chappaquidick, Kennedy had lost some maneuverability in the state.

By this time, the state Democratic party chairmanship was not exactly a political plum. Before 1959 the office had had some independent influence. But then senator John F. Kennedy and his allies decided that state chairman "Onions" Burke (actually a potato farmer) was too independent and too "old school" (to be delicate) to be identified with Kennedy's home state. Burke was consequently purged.[9] From that point on, the state party was a function of the Kennedy operation, first for John F. and then for Edward. Furthermore, the state legislature, the congressional delegation, the governor, and the other statewide elected officials did not necessarily want the state party office to become a potential rival power center. With Edward Kennedy secure in the U.S. Senate, his own interest in the state party also waned. In certain ways the party was similar to any organization that only gets geared up every six years, and the aging process had taken its toll. This is the situation that Flaherty inherited.

One interesting passing story concerns Boston Mayor Kevin White's apparent desire for the delegation chairmanship in 1976. Before the final selection of at-large delegates, two meetings were held between White, Flaherty, state Senate President Harrington,

[9] One of the best, and most readily accessible, accounts of this event can be found in Larry O'Brien, *No Final Victories* (Garden City, N.Y.: Doubleday, 1974).

and state House Speaker Thomas McGee (who had recently succeeded Bartley) to discuss the convention. At one of these meetings, White asked for both an at-large seat and the chairmanship.
Harrington and McGee remained neutral, but Flaherty expressed
his own desire for the position. Jackson's effort in the primary had
received considerable help from members of White's organization,
and White may have expected some rewards from that quarter.
Flaherty was a well-positioned neutral choice, however, and he
easily prevailed. (Jackson himself reportedly deleted the names of
Harrington and McGee from his list of at-large candidates on the
grounds that, because he had asked for their endorsements early
and they were not forthcoming, now there were others more deserving.)[10] Without the chairmanship, White did not wish to be a
delegate, and he consequently had no official role in New York.
This was quite a comedown from the heady days of 1972, when
White was actively considered for the vice-presidential nomination,
and of 1973-74, when he had launched a serious, carefully planned
early campaign for the presidency itself. Of course, these events
occurred before Boston's busing trauma. In 1975 White barely defeated state Senator Joseph Timilty in a bitter mayoral election;
Timilty proceeded to play a substantial role in the Carter campaign.

At the Democratic Convention

The Massachusetts delegation cast votes for seven different presidential candidates at the national convention. Sixteen votes went
to candidates other than Carter, Udall, Brown, or McCormack—the
largest number of "other" votes cast by any state delegation.
(Minnesota cast fourteen such votes and Wisconsin, thirteen.)
These sixteen votes included eleven for Wallace, two of the ten total votes cast for Jackson, two of the nine total votes for Harris,
and one of the two votes for Milton Shapp. The delegation gave
eighty-three vice-presidential votes to Walter Mondale, eleven to
Henry Jackson, nine to Gary Benoit (about whom more later), and
one to Allard Lowenstein.

The Carter group was generally kept well informed by Carter
headquarters and voted the "conservative" position on the three

[10] Ken Hartnett, *Boston Globe*, July 30, 1976, p. 23.

rules roll calls. The Jackson group was quite hostile to anything pertaining to Carter but was less likely to be available on the floor to cast its votes. Absenteeism also marked the Wallace contingent. The Udall group tended to vote the "reform" position and stayed on the floor to do so.

There were some moments of tension, but only in the context of a placid convention. Twenty-seven of Jackson's thirty delegates switched to Carter (two stayed with Jackson and one went to Mc-Cormack), but only after Carter operative Landon Butler had personally apologized to the Jackson caucus for an earlier threat by Carter aide Mark Zweicker that Massachusetts might be "blacklisted" if it did not join the Carter forces. The Jackson group for a while pushed for an open convention choice of the vice-presidential candidate, but it never got the idea off the ground. (It was this effort that had aroused Zweicker's ire.)

Carter also received substantial support from the Wallace and Shriver delegations. Wallace met with his Massachusetts supporters twice in two days to recommend support of Carter. In previous weeks the group had had little success in trying to contact Wallace's national organization and had received no instructions. These meetings only partially defused what had been considerable and deeply felt resentment of Carter as a "traitor" who had "hurt our best friend." This position was most emphatically stated by Alfred Farese of Everett, who had been a college roommate of Wallace. Along with other complaints, Farese disliked Carter's Southern Baptist style; he spoke heatedly in the Wallace caucus, noting that, among other virtues, Wallace had not exhibited the anti-Catholic bigotry Farese had encountered years earlier as a student at the University of Alabama. Farese spoke of shifting support to Jerry Brown or anyone else who would oppose Carter. He and ten others voted for Wallace throughout.

Carter did not do as well with the Harris and Udall supporters. Five weeks before the convention, the six Harris delegates had received a telegram releasing them and urging that Carter's nomination be made unanimous. The delegates were "very unhappy" with this directive. Otherwise, there was no contact with Harris; they received no instructions or suggestions on the vice-presidential choice, the platform, or the rules questions. Three Harris delegates finally voted for Carter. Morris Udall received twenty-one votes, the same as the number of delegates he had won in the March 2 primary, but this resulted from some minor shifts. Congressman Michael Harrington, for example, switched from Harris to Udall at the final tally.

Overall, the Carter group was satisfied with Massachusetts's showing. Carter had come in fourth in the primary. The Carter group's leaders, Joseph Timilty of Mattapan and Joyce Alexander of Cambridge, had set as their goal fifty-three votes, a majority of the delegation. They were pleased with the sixty-five votes they ultimately received.

The Massachusetts delegation provided a major part of what little controversy existed at the relatively bland "unified" convention. James Killilea's speech nominating the antiabortion candidate, Ellen McCormack, was openly hostile to Jimmy Carter. He denounced Carter (throughout referring to him as "Mr. X") as a liar, a Pontius Pilate, and a greedy abuser of power. Despite its passion, the speech was generally ignored by a restless, noisy audience. In addition, on the convention's last afternoon, Massachusetts delegate Gary Benoit, a twenty-three-year-old student from Northampton, was nominated for vice-president despite his ineligibility due to age. Benoit had earlier observed that there "isn't a single plank in the Democratic platform I can support." The nominating and seconding speeches emphasized opposition to busing and federal gun control. Of the twelve votes Benoit received, nine came from Massachusetts and three from North Carolina. Two of the speeches for Gary Benoit were given by City Councilman Albert "Dapper" O'Neil, one of Boston's most colorful and less coherent public officials, and Robert 'Whitey" McGrail, proprietor of Whitey's Place, a tavern on D Street and Broadway, South Boston. Two days earlier, McGrail had beaten delegations from Alabama and Kentucky in the U.S. Beer Drinking Championship at Maude's Tavern in the Summit Hotel. By his own admission, McGrail prepared for his nationwide television appearance by consuming fifteen more beers. The *Boston Globe* reported, "It wasn't a great speech, but . . . he didn't stutter."

Massachusetts also provided moments of high ideals, as when Archibald Cox (who was not a delegate) nominated Morris Udall for president, as well as others of modest humor. During the presidential roll call, Massachusetts passed when it was first called and cast its votes at the end of the ballot. It was later revealed that the pass was necessitated because the original poll of the delegation totaled 107, 3 more than the state's allocated 104. As the secretary of the delegation, Lisa Simonetti, observed, "This could only happen in Massachusetts. That's what makes us adorable." Before passing, Charles Flaherty, the delegation's chairperson, had taken the opportunity to refer to Massachusetts as "the one and only" in reference to its lonely 1972 vote for McGovern. When Lindy Boggs at the podium accepted a motion to have Carter's nomination declared by acclamation before Massachusetts had been called a second time, Flaherty added, "how soon they forget."

THE REPUBLICAN DELEGATION

Delegate selection in the Republican party in Massachusetts was somewhat simpler than for the Democrats—both because there were only two Republican candidates and because all delegates were selected after the primary, when it was clear precisely how many delegates would be awarded to each candidate. It also helped that President Ford carried the state by almost two to one (64.5 percent of the adjusted two-candidate vote to 35.5 percent for Ronald Reagan) and that this proportion held up consistently through every congressional district.

In the face of the newly revised primary law, the Republican State Committee (then headed by John Winthrop Sears, not to be confused with the Reagan campaign manager) appointed a delegate selection committee to draw up appropriate procedures. The committee consisted of three Reagan supporters—William Barnstead, a former state chairman who was to be defeated soundly by Tip O'Neill in the 1976 congressional race in the Eighth District, Edward King, and Roy Richardson; and four Ford backers—Sears, Frank Conway, Nancy Sinnot, and Josiah Spaulding, another former state chairman. The major issue of contention was proportional representation. The Ford supporters had been in contact with Ford headquarters in Washington and had been instructed to push for a "winner-take-all" system. The state law simply provides that delegation selection "shall be by that system adopted by the state committee . . . provided . . . that the distribution of delegates under any such system shall reflect the preference expressed by the voters on the presidential preference portion of the ballot at the presidential primary." Faced with the ambiguity of this law, the Ford supporters on the delegate selection committee sought an opinion from the Supreme Judicial Court of Massachusetts. The response was that the law was unclear and that either proportional representation or winner-take-all could well satisfy it. Sears then pushed for winner-take-all at the congressional district level (the so-called loophole primary).

This view did not prevail, however, and the committee voted four to three for a proportional representation system. Frank Conway, the current state party treasurer and a Ford delegate to Kansas City, believes that the Ford group was simply not "tough enough" and that they were worn down by the "aggressive, almost obstructionist tactics" of the Reagan supporters. Conway admits that this was not the only factor, however. At the decisive meeting of the committee, Josiah Spaulding, who had not attended all previous committee sessions and had not been explicitly instructed by Sears, provided the deciding vote. His position was that proportional representation was obviously "fairer," and therefore he should not oppose it.

In the March 2 primary, President Ford won two delegates in each district to Reagan's one. The congressional district caucuses were held on Sunday, May 23, 1976, and all registered Republicans living in the district could participate. Any participant, after stating a presidential preference, could place his or her name in nomination for delegate. Each nomination required one second, and each nominee could speak for three minutes. Three delegates and three alternates were to be selected in each congressional district. Voting in the caucuses was by written ballot, and nominees for delegates were listed under the names of the presidential candidates they supported. (Both Ford and Reagan delegates were chosen at the same time and location—in the same hall.) Each participant could vote for six nominees, but all had to be of the same presidential preference. Those receiving the highest number of votes, equal to the number of delegates to be awarded to that candidate, were elected. Those receiving the next highest number of votes, were elected as the alternates, providing that each delegate and alternate pair consisted of one man and one woman. The list of elected delegates and alternates was forwarded to each presidential candidate committee by May 26. Such a committee could veto any delegate on the list by writing to the state chairman by June 1, 1976. If a delegate was vetoed, the replacement would have been the next highest vote getter of the same sex meeting the committee's approval; however, no delegate was thus vetoed.

At-Large Delegates

The Republican State Committee met on June 12 to select at-large delegates and alternates. Nominations (of two men and two women) could be made by each of the eight state committee divisions and by special task forces for affirmative action established under national party rules. In addition, a nomination could be secured by petition among the state committee members, with six signatures required. A total of forty candidates stood for election for seven at-large delegate and seven alternate positions.

Ford received four of the at-large delegates and Reagan, three delegates, as a result of the Massachusetts State Republican party's decision to apply proportional representation to the entire state delegation on the basis of the statewide vote. Hence, Ford's adjusted statewide vote of 65.5 percent merited twenty-eight of the forty-three state delegates, and Reagan's 35.5 percent deserved fifteen. Had those proportions been applied simply to the seven at-large delegates alone, Ford would have received five delegates and Reagan, two.

Voting was by written ballot. Each member could vote for fourteen nominees. Those persons receiving the highest number of votes, equal to the number of delegates to be elected for that presidential candidate, were elected. Those persons of the opposite sex receiving the next highest number of votes were elected alternates. It might be noted that this process could have resulted in a Massachusetts Republican delegation composed of 100 percent male delegates and 100 percent female alternates, or vice versa. (The Democrats required that the delegate and alternate groups be considered separately in this respect.) As it happened, however, the total Ford delegation had fifteen females and thirteen males, while the Reagan forces included seven females and eight males. Presidential candidate approval of the at-large delegates was also required. The President Ford committee had a room at Framingham State College, where the state committee was meeting; and Richard Mastrangelo, northeast regional director of the President Ford committee, was in attendance and approved delegates. The Reagan forces had picked their chosen delegates in advance and knew precisely who would be elected, although Diane Bronsdon, the state chairwoman of Citizens for Reagan, was in attendance to watch the proceedings. The at-large delegates for Ford were Senator Edward Brooke, Paula Logan, state Representative Andrew Card (who recently had narrowly missed election as state chairman), and Henry Cabot Lodge; the at-large delegates for Reagan were Roy Richardson, Diane Bronsdon, and Otto Wahlrab. The Ford forces had offered a delegate position to former governor and U.S. senator Leverett Saltonstall, who continues to be active on the town committee in his home of Dover, but he declined it.

One issue that arose concerning the at-large delegate allocation was whether an uncommitted delegate should be assigned. Besides Reagan and Ford, Republican voters had the choice of voting no preference, writing in a third candidate, or simply leaving the choice blank. A debate ensued within the Republican delegate selection committee about whether to combine the statewide votes for "no preference," all other candidates, and blanks—a total which would have merited one at-large delegate—and then appoint such a delegate, or whether to ignore the blanks, thereby leaving the total votes for no preference and all others too low to qualify for a delegate. Sears favored naming one uncommitted delegate, but the majoity of the committee voted the other way. This delegate position ultimately was assigned to Reagan. This question arose again at the national convention in a somewhat different form, as will be discussed later.

As noted, the delegation was composed of twenty-eight delegates for Ford and fifteen for Reagan. If Massachusetts had used the 15 percent cutoff rule, the district results would have been identical, but Ford would have received five of the at-large delegates and Reagan, only two—thus giving Ford a total of twenty-nine delegates and Reagan, fourteen. If a plurality system had been used, Ford would have received all forty-three delegates.

Affirmative Action

There was no effort at the district level to impose any sort of affirmative action plan, other than the requirement that delegates and alternates be of opposite sexes. Under Rule 29 of the national convention rules adopted in Miami Beach in 1972, a committee was set up to review Republican national rules. The result of this effort was that each state Republican chairman was to establish task forces for women, youth, heritage groups, seniors, and blacks. Between May 25 and June 5, 1976, one caucus was held for each of these task forces within the state. All of them met in eastern Massachusetts—three in Boston, one in Saugus, and one in Lexington. (The women's caucus charged a one-dollar membership fee.) If eighty or more persons attended the caucus, it could nominate one man and one woman as candidates for delegate or alternate at large. The only one of these task force caucuses that managed to attract eighty members was the heritage group, but the other four task forces also forwarded names of candidates to the state committee. They were always considered somewhat suspect, however, as the products of rump sessions; and although the names were never formally rejected, none was elected, either. (It should be noted that each of the eight state party divisions could also nominate two men and two women, and that nominations could be made by circulating petitions throughout the state party committee.)

The only at-large delegate or alternate selected who actually came from one of the five task forces was Dr. Geza Jako of Melrose, from the heritage group, who was the alternate to Mrs. Paula Logan. Frank Hatch originally had been elected to this alternate seat, but he withdrew. Twenty-year-old Jamie Gillman was then nominated for this position. He had been a candidate of the youth task force; but since that caucus had not been attended by the required minimum number of people, he had not been legitimately nominated. However, Gillman had proceeded to secure a nomination by getting six members of the GOP state committee to sign a petition. He was also in effect considered the youth nominee. The Ford supporters were interested in rewarding Dr. Jako, a long-term contributor to the GOP who had worked hard for President Ford and for the GOP in the past and who was the only person actually nominated by a task force caucus of the proper size. Therefore, the state GOP discussed the situation with Jamie Gillman and found that all he wanted was to go to the convention; he did not care if he got to vote or not. So they made him a page for the convention (which gave him access to the floor) and made Dr. Jako the alternate.

Organizing the Delegation

On Sunday, June 13, a caucus of delegates to the Republican National Convention was held at the Marriott Inn in Newton, just west of Boston. Prior to this date, however, a change had occurred in the state party chairmanship. Gordon Nelson, a self-described "libertarian" and a strong Reagan supporter, had been elected as state chairman to replace John Sears.

Sears did not run for reelection. He apparently had lost the support both of key members of the Massachusetts Federation of Republican Women, one of the largest and most effective political organizations in the state, and of party conservatives. This in turn seems to have disenchanted Senator Brooke. Also, for the 1974 Senate nomination against Edward Kennedy, Sears had supported Mike Robinson, a young furniture factory owner and a "new face," over Brooke's choice, Carroll Sheehan. Sears had earlier received Brooke's support for the chairmanship when William Barnstead had been removed after the 1974 election, in which Barnstead had actively contributed to the loss of incumbent liberal Republican Governor Francis Sargent. The Sheehan/Robinson matter, together with Sear's liberal (by Republican standards), Yankee, Beacon Hill, intellectual manner, had soured the party's conservatives. Therefore, Brooke appears to have agreed that it was time for him to be replaced.

As a delegate who was also state chairman, Nelson presided over the delegation caucus. This temporary position proved to be one without influence as the Ford majority took every available position for themselves—including delegation chairman, secretary, and treasurer, national committeeman and woman, and every convention committee seat. There was no real opposition to Brooke as delegation chairman. The Reagan forces were, however, very angry at getting none of the key committee posts (two seats each on the Rules, Resolutions/Platform, Credentials, and Permanent Organiztion committees). Their heated protests about "democracy," "fairness," "equity," and even "good sportsmanship" were in vain.

The Ford forces controlled each election, and their twenty-eight votes took all the spoils.

At the Republican Convention

There were no vote switches in Kansas City. The delegation voted twenty-eight to fifteen against requiring Ford to disclose his vice-presidential choice before the ballot (the 16C issue), and again twenty-eight to fifteen for Ford for the nomination. Robert Dole was generally accepted throughout the delegation, although with considerably more enthusiasm by the Reagan element. Senator Brooke stated that he had hoped for "a more moderate candidate"; and Eliot Richardson, Ford delegate from the Fourth Congressional District, admitted that he was "puzzled" by the selection. Gordon Nelson, on the other hand, strongly praised it. In the vice-presidential balloting, two Massachusetts votes were actually cast for Richardson (not including his own, and against his wishes), and two others were not cast at all because the delegates were away from their seats. The remaining thirty-nine votes, however, went more or less readily to Dole. John Sears, one of those voting for Richardson, proceeded to resign as head of the Ford effort in Massachusetts, while claiming that the selection of Dole had nothing to do with his act. Brooke readily accepted the resignation, publicly noting that Sears had alienated some of the party conservatives: "John has not been the most tactful person during all of this. He has alienated certain segments of the party, and there was some feeling that we should not go into this campaign with this type of leadership."

Frank Conway and Congresswoman Heckler, on the Rules Committee, voted the straight Ford position. On the floor the Ford contigent was careful to have the alternates to Richardson and Henry Cabot Lodge readily available, in light of media and other demands on those two individuals.

The only interesting skirmish in the delegation came when the Reagan forces tried to prevent four delegates from voting on the first presidential ballot (three to come from the Ford column and one from Reagan). This resulted from a ruling by Republican National Committee counsel William Cramer on the "Justice" rule that the North Carolina delegation should be divided twenty-eight for Reagan, twenty-five for Ford, and one to represent the voters who marked no preference in the North Carolina primary. This move was designed to help President Ford, since Reagan would lose a delegate on the first ballot; however, Nelson and other Massachusetts Reagan strategists used the ruling to argue that, since 7.2 percent of the voters in the Massachusetts Republican primary had chosen either no preference, a third write-in candidate, or to leave that part of the ballot blank, Cramer's ruling should also disenfranchise four Massachusetts delegates. Cramer later modified his North Carolina stand, and the Massachusetts challenge was dropped.

Finally, it should be noted that the Republican party in Massachusetts has long been much better organized than the Democrats. The secretary of the delegation to the Democratic convention kept no records of the rules roll call votes. The Republicans, on the other hand, produced an attractive Kansas City convention booklet listing not only the officers, delegates, and alternates but also the media representatives in Kansas City from Massachusetts and other information. The Republicans also maintain a well-staffed full-time state party headquarters in Boston. The Democratic office was run from Flaherty's State House desk. The state Republicans have long been the best (and often the only) source of formal and informal information on both parties. However, this disparity may be changing. The state Democratic party recently chose as its new chairman thirty-year-old state Senator Chester Atkins, an able, widely respected figure with strong views about a viable, effective party organization.[11]

CONCLUSIONS

Proportional representation as practiced in Massachusetts produced some interesting effects. Under its nearly "pure" system,

[11] Atkins inherited a party organization without an office, a telephone number, or a staff, and with a $40,000 debt. Within a few months he had organized a party fund-raising dinner—featuring Vice-President Mondale and every major Democratic officeholder in the state—which drew over one thousand party faithful, wiped out the debt, and left enough money to rent an office and hire a staff. Whether this new energy will overcome the inherent weakness of the state committee position, however, is unclear.

the Democratic party in Massachusetts sent delegates pledged to nine different presidential candidates, as well as two uncommitteds, to the convention in New York. Use of the 15 percent cutoff rule suggested by the national party would have given delegates to only four candidates: Jackson, Udall, Wallace, and Carter (a distant fourth). A plurality system would have shut out Carter completely, leaving seventy-one delegates for Jackson, twenty-one for Udall, and twelve for Wallace. The Massachusetts Democratic delegation ultimately cast its votes for seven presidential candidates. Also, one-fifth of the delegation did not vote for Walter Mondale as vice-presidential nominee, instead spreading twenty votes among three other persons.

The Republicans had less trouble, primarily because they had only two candidates and because Ford carried every congressional district in the state by a consistent two-to-one margin. The Republicans had some interesting early squabbles, however, over ambiguities in the Massachusetts presidential primary law as amended in 1975. The Republican State Committee sought an opinion from the state's Supreme Judicial Court and was told that either proportional representation or winner-take-all could satisfy the law. Some of the Ford supporters then pushed for winner-take-all at the district level; and although this view did not prevail, it apparently would have been legal.

The Democrats in Massachusetts held caucuses before the primary for each presidential candidate in each congressional district to select slates of delegates. These were then rank ordered, although the candidate had the opportunity to alter the ordering if he wished. After the primary, votes were totaled in each district and delegates were awarded proportionally, starting at the top of the slate. In only one instance did any candidate receive as many as three delegates in one district. In all other cases, two was the maximum and one was very common.

One unforeseen result of this process was that affirmative action objectives were badly served. At the preprimary caucuses there was a strong tendency for well-known white men and women to fill the top slots on the slate, since they were in fact well known, were organized, and had "clout." Blacks, other minorities, and youth tended to fill slots further down the slate. Then, when only one or two delegates were awarded to a presidential candidate in each district, the white men and women at the top of the slate were chosen while the minorities were not.

There was no effort by the Republicans to impose an affirmative action plan at the district level, other than the requirement that delegates and alternates be of opposite sexes. The state committee did establish task forces for women, youth, heritage groups, seniors, and blacks to nominate candidates for at-large delegates. However, the only visible result of this effort was one alternate seat awarded to a person from the heritage group.

In 1975 changes had been made in the Massachusetts presidential primary law to take the names of delegate candidates off the ballot and to move the primary date from late April to March 2. As noted, delegate selection was left to the state committees, with few statutory limitations. There was a strong sense among the proponents of the ballot changes that the use of a caucus system at the district level tends to build a stronger party organization, which they applauded. In addition, there was recognition of the practical problem of getting all those delegate names on the ballot when there may be as many as a dozen presidential candidates. In 1972 this had often necessitated use of a paper ballot, and the constraints of printing and counting such ballots had been considerable. The date change resulted both from an attempt to create a regional primary and from the belief that an early primary would have more national impact on the race. However, there is a general feeling around the state that the latter did not happen, and that somehow Massachusetts got lost in the shuffle between New Hampshire and Florida.

The decision of the Democratic State Committee to select 25 percent of the delegates at large was strongly opposed by many "grassroots participation" groups who disliked giving such power to the state party. Many of these same people also disliked the change in the primary date, expressing concerns about the possible restrictive effects of Massachusetts weather in early March as well as the lessened time for people to get involved or to be organized. As it resulted, this criticism was not without merit.

The future of the Massachusetts primary is not entirely clear. There is still support for a regional primary, and people are not wedded to the present date. The secretary of state's office in 1977 began a study of the presidential primary, in conjunction with

Harvard's Kennedy Institute of Politics. Its intent is to evaluate the Massachusetts primary system in terms of costs to the state and to the candidates and as a mechanism of party building; the study will also compare the system to the processes in the other New England states. Whether this will result in changes in the law is uncertain. What is clear is that each time the primary law in Massachusetts has been altered in the past, it has been in response to a particular political situation, either before or after the fact, and in the hope of newfound political advantage for the sponsors of such a change. Massachusetts politics is ethnic, feudal, personalized, and undisciplined. There is no reason to expect any of these patterns soon to shift drastically.

At the party level, certain changes probably will be made by the Democrats to improve the outcome of affirmative action efforts, but there is little indication that the Republicans are rushing to follow suit. The Democrats are also likely to revise their relatively "pure" proportional representation process by instituting some cutoff level, perhaps the 15 percent suggested by the national committee. Beyond that, the Democrats in the state seem to be waiting for the results of the secretary of state's study and for further direction from the national committee. The Republicans continue to fight among themselves while wondering if the Democrats will leave them any room at all to maneuver.

CHAPTER 8 / Oklahoma
A Caucus State

JEAN G. McDONALD University of Oklahoma

FROM the time of its statehood, Oklahoma was dominated by the Democratic party, but the Republican party possessed the potential for serious political competition. This potential arose from the regional strength of Republicans in the northern tier Oklahoma counties, which were originally settled by northern Republicans. As the Republican party expanded its appeals to residents of the two largest Oklahoma cities (first the oil capital of Tulsa and then Oklahoma City), Republicans appeared to be on the threshold of success. Finally, candidates attractive both to Republicans and to the more conservative Democrats sparked a winning combination for the Republican party. Thus, the state was led into an era of party competition in national elections and, to a more limited extent, in state elections.

Republican strength was first manifested in presidential elections. Beginning in 1952, Oklahoma has favored Republican presidential candidates in every following presidential election with the exception of 1964. The gubernatorial office was the next important position to be won by a Republican, when the former Republican state chairman, Henry Bellmon, was elected governor in 1962. He was succeeded by another Republican, Dewey Bartlett, in 1966. Although Republicans subsequently have not been able to repeat their gubernatorial victories, they remain a potential threat in the governor's race. Further Repub-

Author's Note: The author is indebted to Steve Schiff for his assistance and also wishes to thank Republican and Democratic leaders in Oklahoma for their ready cooperation.

lican success occurred in the U.S. Senate races of 1968 and 1972 in the elections of proven "winners" Bellmon and Bartlett. Thus, as the delegate selection process began in 1976, Oklahoma had two Republican U.S. senators, a high probability of success in carrying the state for the Republican presidential candidate, and an increasingly confident, competition-oriented Republican party.

The Democratic party's response to competition was analogous to the proverbial ostrich—sticking its head in the sand. The weak Democratic party organization has not been able to obtain the necessary support from Democratic candidates and officeholders to build a strong, viable organization. Rural Democrats appear threatened by any potential changes in the party, apparently fearful of losing what control they perceive they have. The working rule of some Democratic senators and governors has been to keep the party in debt and, thus, under their control. State party chairmen, usually the choice of either the governor or another elected official, have lacked the independence to build the party into a strong organization. Consequently, the party has resisted reforms of almost any sort, and any state chairman who attempted to introduce progressive change was hard pressed to survive.

Changes in the Democrats' 1972 delegate selection process would not have been accomplished without the mandate from the national party. The 1972 delegate selection process was particularly threatening to the rural element and the traditional party power brokers who had always been able to influence past delegate selection, and resentments arose from the fact that the process greatly weakened the influence of those people who had worked in the party for many years. Rather than cultivate the infusion of new blood into the party as a way to build a stronger organization, the "old-timers" became bitter, viewing the new system as a denial of rewards to the party faithful. Delegate slots had always been regarded as earned through years of service, and the McGovern reforms flew in the face of that notion. In 1976 some party workers wanted to create time or service requirements for delegates, but this was not approved. However, party leadership has not been convinced of the importance of maintaining the credibility of the delegate selection process, particularly at a time of increasing party competition. They accept the present system only because they have had no other option.

The Republican party, on the other hand, has shown increasing organization at the state level. In spite of occasional dissension between the moderate and conservative branches of the party, it has been a model of cohesion compared to the Democrats. The state chairman is salaried, and the office of the state head-quarters is well staffed and financed. The Republican organization is trained and efficient, relying heavily during campaigns on media usage and extensive telephone banks. Bellmon's gubernatorial victory in 1962 convinced the Republicans that they could win important offices and marked the beginning of an era of partisan fervor. That fervor is conservative at the grassroots and, generally, at the party leadership levels. Thus, support for conservative candidates such as Ronald Reagan is predictable if one is familiar with the nature of the Republican party in Oklahoma.

THE DEMOCRATIC DELEGATION

Oklahoma Democrats retained the caucus system of selecting delegates in 1976 and followed the national party's guidelines of proportional representation, a reform which was welcomed by most even though scorned by some. However, the use of proportional representation did bring to fruition the changes that had been occurring in the Democratic party and helped to quell the frustrations felt by losing minorities in previous years.

Background for 1976

In describing the Oklahoma parties' delegate selection process of 1952, Cortez Ewing and June Benson concluded: "The impression seems justified that there could be improvement in the manner in which Oklahoma participates in the presidential nominating process."[1] If improvement is defined as the opportunity for a

---

[1] Paul T. David et al., *Presidential Nominating Politics in 1952*, 5 vols. (Baltimore: Johns Hopkins Press, 1954), 3: 312.

more open, representative, uniform process of selecting delegates, then Oklahoma Democrats have improved, especially since 1968. However, strength of party leadership in the recent convention system has been diluted, further weakening an already weak party system.

Through 1968, selection of convention delegates was primarily a process of party chieftains' rewarding the party faithful and "bigwigs." Few of those chosen as delegates were women, and almost none were minorities or students. As Otis Sullivant, veteran news observer, remarked before the 1964 state convention, "After the party takes care of various leaders and big contributors on the delegation, there won't be many places left." And there was no process to ensure otherwise.

Also, through 1964, party organization meetings took place the same year as delegate selection meetings, a procedure quite confusing to the rank and file. Elections of precinct, county, district, and state officers occurred early in the year; then in the spring or early summer, delegate selection began. Precinct delegates might be selected to attend county conventions, and county conventions sometimes met within a week of the state convention. Congressional district conventions, as such, were not held. Instead, the district central committee met a day or so before the state convention, and this select group chose the apportioned number of district delegates. Each district was granted an equal number of delegates; and since several more delegates usually were chosen than were granted the right to vote at the national convention, most delegates could cast only a fractional vote. However, the national committeeman and committeewoman always had one full vote each.

The unit rule was usually invoked by the Oklahoma delegation to the national convention and also was often used by county delegations to state conventions. This rule bound the entire group to vote as a bloc, according to the majority of the group. In years when harmony reigned, the rule presented no problem. But if conflict arose over candidates, as was especially true in 1968, the losing candidate's supporters were most unhappy. When, in 1968, the level of discontent with the system reached its height in both Oklahoma and elsewhere, many people were ready to embrace the reforms of the McGovern guidelines—they were ready to eliminate the unit rule and proxies and to open up the system. But this number did not necessarily include the party stalwarts, who were to play a lesser although continuing role in the new system.

In 1972 precinct, county, and district conventions were all held on uniform dates. Also, district delegates were elected by convention rather than by the district central committee. Overall, the system was opened up considerably, especially to women and minority groups. However, even though the unit rule was outlawed, the plurality system was still in effect. In three district conventions, walkouts were staged by either Humphrey or McGovern supporters who believed they had been denied representation under plurality rules. Thus, the state was set for acceptance of a system in 1976 which would grant representation to supporters of all major candidates, those who could garner 15 percent of the support of any party meeting. Proportional representation had come to Oklahoma.

The Delegate Selection Process, 1976

When Democrats gathered in precinct meetings across Oklahoma the afternoon of February 7, 1976, they came to cast their votes in the long line of decisions that would lead to selection of national convention delegates. The votes cast at the grassroots level would eventually help to select the Democratic presidential candidate. Further, those attending met within the framework of a new set of party ground rules which "forced" them to come prepared to declare their personal preferences for president.

The new ground rules, the Democratic Party of Oklahoma 1976 Delegate Selection Plan, which were distributed to party leaders at all levels in the fall of 1975, established the proportional representation method of selecting delegates in line with national party reforms. The plan explained how proportional representation was to work in practice, including exact procedures to be followed (e.g., what to do in case of a tie, how to round off figures when necessary).[2]   Consequently, it was hoped that all precinct chairpersons would enter their meetings with a clear

[2] *Democratic Party of Oklahoma 1976 Delegate Selection Plan,* p. 4, available from the Oklahoma State Democratic Party.

understanding of the rules and procedures. The plan covered other areas of concern in the selection process as well. For example, it explained how and why each congressional district was to receive its number of delegates, following the Democratic National Committee guideline that 75 percent of the delegates were to be chosen at the district level. (A district's apportioned share was based on Democratic vote cast in the previous general election.) Additionally, affirmative action was included in several portions of the plan. The first of six basic elements of the Democratic party rules stated that the party was to be open to all "regardless of race, sex, age, color, creed, national origin, religion, ethnic identity, economic status, or philosophical persuasion."[3] However, in a reaction to 1972, quotas for various groups were prohibited, except for females. Delegate and committee selection was to be equally representative of both sexes, insofar as possible, and no more than 60 percent of the delegates could be of the same sex. Rule 36 was the formal affirmative action rule. This rule declared that discrimination "in the conduct of Democratic Party affairs is prohibited."

Precinct Meetings. Those attending the precinct meetings on February 7, 1976, were influenced, to an extent, by Democratic actions in other states and by the status of contending candidates. Since the Oklahoma Democrats met early in the election year, the original slate of thirteen presidential candidates had not as yet been narrowed down.[4] However, results in other states pointed to the strength of Jimmy Carter and the desire of many grassroots Democrats to remain uncommitted.

The choices of Oklahoma Democrats attending precinct meetings reflected the strength both of Carter and of uncommitted segments. However, Oklahomans also expressed their own special preferences. Fred Harris, a native Oklahoman, previously had served a term as U.S. senator from the state. Although Harris had proved too liberal for the majority of Oklahomans (he retired from his Senate seat in 1972 when his chances for winning appeared bleak), a certain amount of loyalty could be exepcted for a native son. As Table 8.1 demonstrates, Harris finished third in precinct balloting. Another interesting aspect of Oklahoma Demo-

[3] Ibid., p. 3.
[4] See chapter 2.

crats' choices involved Texan Lloyd Bentsen. Bentsen had ranked third among candidates able to raise money in 1975, but he had fared poorly in early caucuses, including those in Mississippi. If Bentsen could not make an adequate showing in a conservative state bordering his home state, then his chances of obtaining the nomination would be slim. He failed to garner the necessary support in Oklahome precinct meetings and subsequently announced his withdrawal from the campaign on February 10.

However, barring the above two examples, Oklahoma Democrats demonstrated a strong affinity for the choices in other states—uncommitteds and Carter. As Table 8.1 shows, uncommitteds ran first in every district but the Fifth (Oklahoma City), where more liberal Democrats demonstrated their strength and Harris came in first. Carter ranked third in every district but the Fourth and Sixth. However, he so overwhelmed Harris in the Sixth District that Carter led Harris in the statewide tally.

The strategy of the various candidates and the uncommitted leadership was to "get out the ranks." Because numbers become very important in proportional representation systems, a major goal of each organizing group was to provide 15 percent of the total in attendance at each precinct meeting. Also, bargaining with uncommitteds became a matter of importance, as did discouraging the opposition from attending. Both aspects of proportional representation were to remain evident through each level of the selection process.

County Conventions. By February 28, when county convention delegates assembled, the field of national candidates had narrowed slightly. And, as Table 8.2 shows, most counties selected as delegates to the district and state conventions those who either supported one of the prominent candidates at the time—Carter, Wallace, and Harris—or remained uncommitted. County conventions adhered to the same rules and delegate selection plan as had the precinct meetings. Delegates selected by county conventions were to attend both the district and state conventions.

In 1972 seven counties had been the scenes of heated battles between pro-McGovern forces and other candidates' supporters. A contrast was seen in these same counties in 1976. In four of these counties—Tulsa, Oklahoma, Comanche, and Cleveland—McGovern forces had won all of the delegate slots in 1972 when

Table 8.1. Democratic presidential preferences in Oklahoma as indicated by selection of delegates at the precinct level in precinct meetings, February 7, 1976

Candidate	Congressional district numbers						Total	Percent
	1	2	3	4	5	6		
Uncommitted	387	744	626	364	248	439	2,808	40.0
Carter	159	134	144	314	236	317	1,304	18.5
Harris	231	166	191	239	277	98	1,202	17.0
Bentsen	105	127	290	114	88	179	903	12.8
Wallace	84	113	189	114	148	90	738	10.4
Other	11	7	20	6	20	28	92	1.3
Total	977	1,291	1,460	1,151	1,017	1,151	7,047	100.0

SOURCE: Copied from chart on the wall of Oklahoma State Democratic Headquarters. These figures were compiled for the press on Saturday night, February 7.

Table 8.2. Democratic presidential preferences in Oklahoma by district after county conventions, February 28, 1976

| | Delegate selection on basis of county conventions | | | | |
	Uncommitted	Carter	Harris	Wallace	Total
First District (Tulsa, surround.)	49	29	25	—	103
Second District (eastern)	90	27	17	7	141
Third District (southeastern/south central)	84	38	20	22	164
Fourth District (southwest/south central)	48	44	29	9	130
Fifth District (Oklahoma City)	36	33	40	—	109
Sixth District (western Oklahoma)	65	51	6	7	129
Total	372	222	137	45	776
Total, percent	47.9%	28.6%	17.7%	5.8%	100.0%

SOURCE: Based on county convention records.

the plurality rules were in effect. In 1976 only two of these same counties had a majority of Harris supporters; even so, Harris was able to gain some district and state delegates in the other two counties because of proportional representation. In the remaining three counties, the McGovern supporters had battled and lost completely in 1972 under the plurality plan. In 1976 the Harris forces fared well in only one case, Grady County, where Harris backers were able to win three of the ten delegate slots. If the plurality system had been in effect in 1976, Harris apparently would not have received the support that McGovern had received. On the other hand, the proportional representation system guaranteed Harris a rather firm base of support, albeit a small one.

The Tulsa County convention offered an interesting study in coalition building and in the increasingly active role of educators in the delegate selection process. Within the uncommitted bloc in Tulsa, a coalition of classroom teachers, labor representatives, and university liberals or progressives met together to select an "uncommitted slate" which would be representative of all members of the coalition. Wallace forces were offered but declined six slots on the slate, and consequently they ended up with nothing when the coalition held together, despite some bitterness. Labor and teachers were also important in the Harris bloc at the same convention.

Democrats came out of the county conventions with overwhelming support for electing uncommitted delegates to the national convention. However, it appeared that Carter could still make a good showing at the district and state conventions, especially if many of those attending could be convinced to switch their support to him.

District Meetings. After the county conventions, the various blocs looked to the district conventions on March 20. It was there that, according to national rules, 75 percent of the state's Democratic delegates—or a total of twenty-eight delegates—were to be chosen. Thus, the stakes were rising as "real" delegates to the national convention were chosen. Switches were occurring in and out of the uncommitted blocs and from the candidate blocs that lacked the numbers necessary under the 15 percent rule to select delegates at the district level. Bargaining and trade-offs attempted to attract people from one bloc to another; and. within blocs, some individuals began overt campaigning for delegate positions.

In the week before the district conventions, Governor David Boren publicly endorsed Jimmy Carter, becoming the first governor to do so. In a press conference, the governor said he had favored Carter for some months but wanted to maintain an uncommitted posture until March 15.[5] Moreover, Boren hoped that district delegates would consider Carter's positive qualities as they entered the convention period. This move by the governor, calculated to boost the number of Carter delegates, did not have the intended impact. The Carter forces gained only one more delegate to the national convention than they had expected. Some speculation existed that the governor's announcement may have solidified the opposition, particularly among the activist teacher groups who were unhappy at the time with what they perceived to be the governor's lack of support for education.

Basically, the strength of the various factions at the county convention level was maintained through the district meetings; exceptions occurred only in the Second and Third districts (see tables 8.2 and 8.3). Table 8.3 permits a comparison of the actual results of the district conventions with those which might have obtained had the plurality system been in effect. This table makes it obvious that Carter was aided by proportional representation in Oklahoma. All other things being equal, Carter would not have obtained any delegates at the district level under the plurality system, but he was able to gain eight delegates under proportional representation. Interestingly, Harris's delegate strength, which remained quite stable through all levels of the selection process, would have been almost identical under either system. Uncommitteds would have greatly increased their lead under the plurality system.

In the First District (Tulsa County), the uncommitted delegates were influenced by the actions within the uncommitted bloc at the county convention. The coalition described above, consisting of teachers, union members, and progressives, continued at the district level. At a caucus before the district meeting, coalition members agreed that labor would obtain one and progressives the other of the two uncommitted delegate positions. Although teachers participated in the coalition, they did not have enough votes within the uncommitted bloc to bargain for a delegate. At the district

[5] *Norman Transcript*, Mar. 19, 1976.

Table 8.3. Apportionment of Oklahoma Democratic National Convention delegates at district conventions

District	District convention delegates			No. of national delegates	Actual apportionment under proportional representation		Apportionment under plurality	
	Carter	Harris	Uncommitted					
First	31 (28%)	25 (23%)	54 (49%)	4	Carter	1	Uncom.	4
					Harris	1		
					Uncom.	2		
Second	26 (19.5%)	—	107 (80.5%)	5	Carter	1	Uncom.	5
					Uncom.	4		
Third	54 (31.8%)	26 (15.3%)	90 (52.9%)	6	Carter	2	Uncom.	6
					Harris	1		
					Uncom.	3		
Fourth	45 (36.3%)	29 (23.4%)	50 (40.3%)	4	Carter	1	Uncom.	4
					Harris	1		
					Uncom.	2		
Fifth	33 (30.3%)	41 (37.6%)	35 (32.1%)	4	Carter	1	Harris	4
					Harris	2		
					Uncom.	1		
Sixth	52 (39.7%)	—	79 (60.3%)	5	Carter	2	Uncom.	5
					Uncom.	3		
Total				28	Carter	8	Uncom.	24
					Harris	5	Harris	4
					Uncom.	15		

SOURCE: Based on district convention records and computations by the author.
NOTE: Wallace does not appear in this table because he had not qualified for a single national convention delegate, and his supporters therefore had been released to go elsewhere.

meeting itself, the nominating process within the uncommitted faction was perfunctory. Also, within the Harris bloc the delegate preference was relatively unanimous, and Maynard Ungerman, Harris's Tulsa coordinator, was selected without much opposition. The Carter camp experienced some difficulty agreeing on delegate candidates, however, for they tended to be organized around personalities.

In the Second District, Carter was the only presidential candidate to qualify for a national convention delegate, and the uncommitted bloc was increased by the addition of Harris and Wallace supporters. The uncommitteds won four national convention delegates, more than in any other district.

The Third District was the governor's home district as well as the home of the speaker of the House of Representatives, Carl Albert. Both of these officials were virtually assured delegate slots. The state cochairperson was also a Third District resident and ran successfully as an uncommitted delegate. Several uncommitted delegates switched their preferences to either Carter or Harris before the district meeting, and at the convention itself an attempt was made to convince Wallace supporters to leave the uncommitteds (whom they had joined) and join the Carter camp. Two alternate slots were promised the Wallace group should they support Carter. However, the uncommitted leadership convinced the Wallace supporters that they would have more flexibility at the national convention if they stayed within this faction, and that was the course they chose to take.

The Fourth District meeting was particularly important for Carter supporters. Carter had forty-four district delegates as that convention opened and needed only two more to obtain two national delegates. The additional two would almost certainly have had to come from the uncommitted faction since here, as in all other districts, the Harris group stood firmly together. When the uncommitteds were polled, only one of them switched to the Carter camp; thus, the Carter people lost an additional delegate to the national convention by only one vote. The uncommitteds subsequently stood firm and voted overwhelmingly not to reopen the polling of their group.

In the Fifth District, on the basis of precinct and county convention activity, it was no surprise that Harris should have a good base of support. Very little switching of preferences occurred at this district meeting; only one uncommitted switched, and that was to Harris. That same individual then became a Harris delegate, the only black chosen as a national delegate in the six district conventions. Wallace supporters switched to uncommitted because they had missed the 15 percent cutoff point at the county convention. They tried to secure an uncommitted delegate slot at the district level but were defeated by a person who had been uncommitted from the start.

The Sixth District convention held no special surprises, and the uncommitteds retained their majority. Teachers, especially prominent at this meeting, were able to elect two of the three uncommitted delegates.

The State Convention. The state convention, held April 3 and 4 in Oklahoma City to select the remaining nine delegates, was different from most ot those in the history of Oklahoma Democrats; it might have been considered a "free-for-all" by some, an open convention by others. Although bargaining and enticements were used in attempts to attract uncommitteds to candidate blocs, delegate slots were relatively open within each bloc.

One explanation for the openness of delegate selection may have been the rule requiring equitable representation of the sexes. District convention selections had underrepresented females; consequently, this inequity had to be resolved at the state level. Seven of the nine delegates were to be female; all of the Carter and Harris delegates and one uncommitted delegate had to be women. It appears that party leaders were more willing to allow women to battle among themselves for delegate spots than they would have been for men to do so. One Carter worker interviewed at the convention noted that several women would be running against each other and that the Carter leaders would just "let them fight it out."

An essential element for each of the caucuses was to maintain a cohesive group and to instill in those attending the importance of being present when the presidential preference poll was taken. This appeared to be an easier task for the candidate groups than for the uncommitteds, since loyalty to a particular candidate could be a compelling reason for being present. Attendance of uncommitted delegates dropped in the afternoon of the first day; consequently, at the crucial polling of delegates to determine numbers, the uncommitted faction lost a national delegate. The count of uncommitteds at polling time was 283; Carter people had 300 in attendance and gained an extra delegate over what they had expected. On Sunday afternoon, the second day, when national convention delegates were selected, 305 uncommitteds were present. The uncommitteds were granted three delegates; the Carter forces, four; and the Harris bloc, which had remained stable, two.

Within the various caucuses, the battles for delegate positions varied in intensity, with the bloodiest occurring in the uncommitted camp. The labor-teacher-progressive coalition prominent in the First District attempted to have its slate of delegates selected. The coalition won the first two slots but then lost support and was unable to capture the third position. Regardless of faction, a great deal of campaigning for delegate positions was evident. Posters, placards, and handout sheets were abundant proof that this convention was different from earlier ones. A few party leaders were bitter over the delegate choices. Evidently some believed that too many new, non-party workers were selected and that the party faithful had been ignored. Neither member of the national committee was selected as a delegate, and the state chairman bowed out so that a black delegate could be seated. Although it is true that many delegates were not party old-timers, some of them were well-known names in the Democratic party. Furthermore, several of the women had given years of service to the party, and a few were the wives of public officials. Still, only three incumbent public officials were included in the delegation—the governor, Carl Albert, and a black state representative.

Had a plurality system rather than a proportional representation system been in effect, the final tally for delegates would have been different, as illustrated in Table 8.4. Uncommitted forces would definitely have been strengthened under plurality rules, impressively so had they attended the polling session at the state convention in full strength.

Organizing the Delegation

Proportional representation apparently caused no organizational problems for the Oklahoma Democratic delegation. The delegates met at the governor's mansion three weeks after the state convention. State Democratic chairman Bob Funston, who had given up a delegate seat so that more blacks could be elected at the state convention, was unanimously elected chairman of the delegation. Funston, whose presidential preference was uncommitted, was nominated as delegation chairman by a Harris delegate and was seconded by a Carter delegate.

Various logistical problems were also handled at the meeting. A leading Carter organizer observed that uncommitted delegates had refrained from switching to Carter before the meeting in order to bargain for more passes to the convention floor and gallery. A second meeting to iron out details of housing and travel was held several weeks before the national convention.

Table 8.4. Plurality versus proportional representation in selection of delegates in Oklahoma

| | Democrats | | |
	Carter	Harris	Uncommitted
Hypothetical, plurality	9	4	24
Proportional representation			
(actual)	12	7	18
	Republicans		
	Ford	Reagan	
Plurality (actual)	0	36	
Hypothetical, propor-			
tional representation	4	32	

SOURCE: Actual results obtained from party sources; hypothetical alternative results computed by the author.

National Convention Voting Record

Other than the roll call votes for presidential and vice-presidential candidates, there were only three other roll call votes at the national convention. Only on one of these occasions did the Carter forces make a major effort to try to influence the vote. The first roll call vote of the convention concerned the minority report that would have permitted debate on the party platform. Carter delegates lobbied against the change, arguing that the lengthened proceedings would bring disharmony and disorder. The minority report failed by a vote of 1,595½ to 730½, with the Oklahoma delegation voting with the majority, 29 to 3. All three dissenting votes were cast by Harris delegates.

Two other minority reports to the Rules Committee report were defeated on July 15, 1976. The first would have elaborated the rules for the 1978 midterm party conference by requiring that at least two-thirds of the 2,000 delegates be elected from units no larger than a congressional district. The report won a majority of those voting but not the 1,505 votes required for passage. The Oklahoma delegation cast 11 votes for the minority report, 24 against, and 2 abstentions. The other roll call vote concerned a minority report changing the rules on minority reports. It failed to gain a majority; but Oklahoma voted 22, yes; 13, no; and 2 abstentions.

Oklahoma's vote for the Democratic party's nominee for president was thirty-two for Jimmy Carter, three for Fred Harris, one for Morris Udall, and one for Barbara Jordan. All of the Carter delegates were committed to vote for Carter, and they did support him. All of the eighteen uncommitted delegates also voted for Carter. One uncommitted delegate explained that he switched "because he [Carter] already had the nomination and at this point I felt unity was important to win in November." Several other uncommitted delegates commented that Carter was not their first choice but was an acceptable alternative. One uncommitted delegate voted for Carter "because Hubert Humphrey was not a candidate for the nomination." In a more negative tone, two uncommitted delegates suggested that they were not happy with Carter but went with him anyway; as one of them stated, "I had no other choice by convention time because of coalitions. Your vote did not mean much."

Of the seven Harris delegates, three voted for Harris, two switched to Carter, one changed to Udall, and one voted for Barbara Jordan. Before the convention Harris had publicly released his delegates and suggested that they vote for Carter. A Harris delegate emphasized the point: "The reason I switched had to do with my original candidate's wishes. While in New York I contacted Fred Harris asking his advice. My original intention was to remain loyal to Fred for I had exerted a considerable amount of energy and spent much time working in Harris's behalf. However, as Fred explained, our party represented an alternative to the present status quo and it was going to take a unified party to do such." Another Harris delegate, however, had a different attitude: "I was originally a Harris delegate. When Harris withdrew he told his delegates to vote for Jimmy Carter. Morris Udall, on the other hand, simply released the delegates pledged to him to vote as they saw fit. Because Udall had basically the same philosophy as Harris and he did not insult my intelligence by telling me how to vote, I switched to him."

Senator Walter Mondale was expected to receive all of Oklahoma's thirty-seven votes for vice-president. However, the delegation had secretly agreed to vote for Carl Albert if Mondale had secured the nomination before Oklahoma was called in the roll call. When Oklahoma was called, Mondale had in fact won enough votes, so Albert received thirty-six votes for vice-president. The sole vote for Mondale was cast by the surprised Albert.

Delegate Perceptions of Proportional Representation

After the national convention, a short questionnaire was mailed to all Democratic delegates and alternates soliciting their opinions of porportional representation. Sixteen of the thirty-seven delegates and seventeen of the twenty-nine alternates responded to the questionnaire. Of the thirty-three total respondents, sixteen rated proportional representation as a "very good" method of selecting delegates; twelve rated it as "good"; one as "not so good"; and four as "poor." Those who perceived the system as "very good" felt that it provided a voice and representation for supporters of all the major candidates. Those rating the method as "good" felt some improvements could be made on a basically sound system. Those who rated it as either "not so good" or "poor" believed it was too complicated and divided the party at all levels.

Twenty-eight of the respondents were in favor of using proportional representation in delegate selection in future years. As expected, there was a direct correlation between how the respondents rated the system and whether they were in favor of using it in the future. All five who disliked the system were against its future use. Those who felt modifications were needed if the system were retained made various suggestions for future improvement. One group of suggestions involved the 15 percent minimum vote requirement to secure delegates at each level of the process. Some thought that the 15 percent requirement should be lowered; others, that it be raised; and another believed that those participants who switch preferences after not gaining 15 percent should not be ostracized by their new group. Several who were questioned suggested modifications not directly related to proportional representation, but rather to the delegate selection process as a whole. These ideas included elimination of such items as precinct caucuses, national conventions, and uncommitted delegates. Also mentioned was the adoption of a state primary.

The five respondents not in favor of continuing proportional representation argued that the system allowed the rank and file to have too much control over the selection process, that the plurality system used in 1972 was better, and that proportional representation created factionalism within the party that will be difficult to overcome. One delegate wrote, "It was the worst possible situation. I still get cold chills thinking about it. I absolutely hated everything about it."

The majority of delegates and alternates were pleased with proportional representation when it was compared to the plurality system of 1972. By large majorities, the respondents felt proportional representation fostered more open conventions (25 to 4) and afforded all candidates better representation (27 to 4) than the plurality system. A majority of delegates and alternates also disagreed with the statement that proportional representation causes more bitterness than the plurality system (21 to 8). A slightly smaller majority disagreed with the comments that proportional representation was more divisive than the plurality system (18 to 9) and made obtaining support for the Democratic nominee more difficult (19 to 10). One respondent stated, "There is obvious division before any selection process. The process per se is never the cause in my opinion."

Also, the respondents believed that proportional representation, when compared to plurality, provided better opportunities for minorities and females to be delegates. However, a majority of respondents agreed that proportional representation was much more complicated than the plurality system (20 to 10). Some typical comments were that "it was confusing to many at precinct caucuses because they didn't understand it," and that it was "too complicated [so that] by the time most people comprehended the plan, it was too late for their participation." The group was almost evenly divided concerning the matter of whether proportional representation lessened factional fighting (15 to 14) and discouraged bitterness (16 to 12) when compared to the 1972 plurality method. On this point one delegate replied, "Both systems are equal, neither is perfect."

Leadership Perceptions of Proportional Representation

Despite the generally laudatory comments given proportional representation by the Democratic National Convention delegates and alternates, a number of Democratic party leaders were much more negative about the system. Commenting on the 1976 procedure, two leaders complained that loyal party workers were not rewarded with national convention seats. One remarked, "Proportional representation is unfair to dedicated supportive party leaders that keep the party alive in off-election years." Another leader went further in saying, "It's not fair to send little Mary Smith to the national convention and you don't hear from her till four years later. Party workers are entitled to go to the conventions." The bitterness among some party leaders was apparently detected by at least a few of the delegates to the convention. Several made comments that they were treated as second-class citizens by the longtime political veterans.

At the same time, another top party leader was enthusiastic about proportional representation, claiming that proportional representation worked "one hundred times better than plurality system . . . . It contributed as much as any one thing to the fact we won the presidency." He also believed increased participation in the precinct meetings was the result of the new system. A mixed reaction to proportional representation was voiced by still another leader who said, "it was horrible . . . the mechanics and mathematics. It wasn't very workable, and I agree totally with the concept, too."

THE REPUBLICAN DELEGATION

Republicans maintained their traditional system of delegate selection in 1976; namely, the plurality or winner-take-all system. And, as events evolved, this was also a year in which a Republican minority—supporters of President Ford—experienced some dissatisfaction with the system because of their inability to achieve representation in their national delegation. Thus, the contrast between the systems of nomination used by the two political parties could clearly be observed in Oklahoma in 1976.

Background for 1976

The Oklahoma Republican party followed traditional procedures in electing its national convention delegates in 1964, 1968, and 1972, and the state was allotted twenty-two national delegates in each of these years. Precinct meetings selected delegates to county conventions, which, in turn, selected representatives to congressional district and state conventions. Two national convention delegates and alternates were elected at each district convention, while the remaining ten at-large delegates and alternates were chosen at the state convention. The State Republican Executive Committee served as the nominating committee for the state convention, submitting its recommendations to the convention. In each year, the entire slate was approved by the convention majority. This system of selecting national delegates continued essentially unchanged in 1976.

In 1964 Oklahoma was the first state in the nation to elect a Republican national delegation pledged to Senator Barry Goldwater, and all of Oklahoma's twenty-two votes at the national convention in San Francisco supported Senator Goldwater.

The slate of at-large delegates nominated in 1968 included several Republican public officials, the governor, the attorney general, and two congressmen. Alternates included Tulsa's mayor, the state party chairperson and vice-chairperson, the national committeewoman, and the district chairmen. Obviously, the delegation had a strong public official component. Delegates were not officially committed to vote for a specific candidate in 1968; but, initially, seventeen backed Nixon, while five supported Reagan. However, the state convention also passed a resolution calling for the "favorite son" nomination of Governor Bartlett. Bartlett withdrew before the convention opened, endorsing Richard Nixon; and the delegation eventually split with fourteen for Nixon, seven for

Reagan, and one for Rockefeller. Oklahoma's sympathy for Ronald Reagan appeared early.

As was to be expected, all twenty-two national delegates supported the incumbent president in 1972, for Republicans have retained a certain stability in their selection process over the years. Their system has always been relatively uniform and somewhat more open than that of the Democrats, even though in past years women and minorities were not represented on delegations in the Republican party any more than in the Democratic party.

The Delegate Selection Process, 1976

National Republican party rules leave the state party relatively free in its delegate selection process; thus, Oklahoma Republicans essentially followed the procedures they had used in the past. The Republican rules do encourage openness and prohibit proxies, and they also place restrictions on the number of delegates who can be chosen at the district level versus those chosen at the state level. Thus, in 1976 one-half of the delegates were to be selected at the district meetings (three per district) and the other half at the state level, with a total of thirty-six national delegates.

Republican state rules do not specify the method for selection of convention delegates. Apportionment of county delegates to be selected at the precinct level is based on the precinct's Republican presidential or gubernatorial vote in the previous election. The county executive committee determines this apportionment; however, each precinct is guaranteed at least one delegate. County apportionment is also defined accordingly.

Votes at country, district, and state conventions may be cast in whole votes or in fractions of one-half votes. Open delegations are permitted if approved by county convention vote. In such a case, persons may sign up to attend the district or state convention, and the sheet for such signatures must be located in a place where everyone has access to it. Such a list is to be submitted to the Republican district or state convention chairman seven days before the convention.[6]

[6] Oklahoma Republic Party, *Rules of the Republican Party of the State of Oklahoma*, p. 23, available from the Oklahoma State Republican Party.

Oklahoma Republican rules do not contain an affirmative action section. Party leaders do not feel it is necessary at the present time, preferring to select the individuals who are most deserving of delegate positions. As one Republican leader stated: "We have no quotas. We don't call it affirmative action. We look at people as individuals. Women are looked at the same as men. We elected more women than men [as national convention delegates] without any attempt to choose a certain percent of women." (Nineteen of the thirty-six delegates in 1976 were women.)

The difference between the use of a plurality system and of proportional representation to select delegates is evident in observing the Republican and Democratic parties in Oklahoma in 1976. Regardless of the operating rules in effect, however, Reagan forces in the Republican party and uncommitted forces in the Democratic party would have been strong and would have achieved the bulk of the votes. Even so, the proportional representation system did encourage and result in a diversity of candidate representation in the Democratic party that was almost impossible in the Republican party, given the plurality system. Consequently, Ford supporters in 1976 found themselves in a position similar to the McGovern supporters in 1972; both groups found it nearly impossible to gain delegate spots. The following description of the Republican nominating procedure illustrates this fact.[7]

Precinct Meetings. Precinct meetings held by the Republicans on April 6, 1976, evidenced not only the strong sentiment in the state for Ronald Reagan but also the hard work of the Reagan campaign staff. Precincts in all but one of the counties in the state registered a preference for Reagan. In Garfield County (Enid), precincts were split evenly between Ford and Reagan. In Oklahoma County, Reagan's margin over Ford was almost four to one, with 1,601 pro-Reagan votes and 422 pro-Ford votes cast.[8] Tulsa, the traditionally Republican stronghold of urban Oklahoma, was somewhat more sympathetic to the president, as Reagan defeated Ford by only three to two. Another potential presidential candidate, John Connally fared well in the southeastern counties of the

[7] Collection of data for Republicans was difficult because they have no centralized record keeping. Consequently, the following account relies on interviews and newspaper articles.

[8] *Daily Oklahoman,* Apr. 7, 1976, p. 1.

state. Thus, even though Reagan support was strong at the precinct level, it was not unanimous. Had a proportional representation system been used, supporters of the other candidates might have been able to pick up a few county delegate positions.

Caucusing before precinct meetings occurred for Republicans as it did for Democrats. Reagan forces appeared better organized than Ford people throughout the campaign; and this applied at the precinct level as well, as one case illustrates. In a precinct in Comanche County (Lawton), Reagan workers called registered Republicans and asked about their presidential preference. Pro-Reagan persons and those leaning toward Reagan were then called a second time, reminded of the precinct meeting and informed of its time and place. As Republicans entered the precinct meeting, they were asked their presidential preference, and almost everyone attending was a Reagan supporter. The precinct leaders asked for volunteers to attend the county convention and then reminded the volunteers to be sure to stay for the entire convention.

County Conventions. At the county conventions on April 24, Reagan continued to maintain a strong lead over Ford. However, theoretically all delegates chosen were uncommitted, so that exact estimates of strength are difficult. The Oklahoma County chairman believed Reagan was holding a four-to-one lead. Reagan slates were elected in Comanche and Tulsa counties, and thus Reagan's strength was evident in the urban areas. A few counties conducted straw polls, and Reagan's lead held in those counties, as the following tabulation illustrates.[9]

	Reagan	Ford	Uncommitted
Woods County	37	17	6
Okfuskee County	13	7	1
Ottawa County	13	13	2
Wagoner County	22	3	5

While Reagan's grassroots appeal made the work of his campaign staff easier, the staff was still quite organized. The state cochairperson for Reagan commented that the overwhelming feeling for Reagan among the state party's activists aided their task.

District Meetings. The Reagan momentum continued to build as Republicans gathered at their district conventions on May 8. No

[9] *Sunday Oklahoman,* Apr. 25, 1976, pp. 1-2.

doubt could be left in the minds of observers that Reagan was dominating the delegate selection process, as all six districts chose pro-Reagan delegates by large majorities. The *Daily Oklahoman* reported that Ford supporters were not even able to elect alternates.[10]

In three districts—the Third, Fourth, and Sixth—no opposition to Reagan nominees emerged. At the Fifth District convention in Oklahoma County, however, pleas were made for Ford. The Ford supporter who was nominated as a delegate received 137 of the 564 votes cast; had proportional representation been in effect, 24 percent of the delegates would have supported Ford and 76 percent, Reagan. Thus, Reagan would have received two delegates and Ford, one. The defeated Ford delegate nominee stood before the convention to object and said, with some feeling, "But fairness would also require representation on the delegation for those Oklahoma Republicans that favor President Ford."[11]

In the First District, a Tulsa University student nominated as a Ford delegate received 29 votes, while the Reagan totals ranged from 155 to 163. In this case, Ford's strength of approximately 16 percent would not have been sufficient to elect a delegate had proportional representation been in effect. In the Second District 350 delegates attended the convention. One person who announced as a Ford delegate did not even receive a seconding speech. Three uncommitted individuals were nominated and defeated; one of them appeared to the district chairman to be truly uncommitted, while two of them seemed to favor Ford. Certainly the latter two were perceived by the convention as pro-Ford; otherwise, they would have had nothing to lose by openly stating their allegiance to Reagan.

According to the *Tulsa World*, turnout at the Third District convention was unusually high.[12] Attendees numbered 250, as compared to 80 in 1972. Ford again was overwhelmed, and no Ford delegate candidates were even nominated. Attendance was also high at the Fourth District meeting, and the chairman estimated Ford strength was, at most, 15 percent. However, once again, no Ford supporter was even nominated for a delegate

[10] Ibid., May 9, 1976, pp. 1-2.

[11] Ibid.

[12] *Tulsa World*, May 9, 1976, p. 1.

position; the district chairperson attributed this to the lack of organization within the Ford camp. In the Sixth District the same story was repeated at a well-attended convention.

The State Convention. By the time the Republican state convention was held on May 15, Reagan's strength had increased rather than decreased. Furthermore, Reagan's appearance as the convention's keynote speaker did not hurt his chances. Nationally, it was apparent that Reagan's hopes for the presidential nomination were more than a dream, and Oklahoma Republicans would do their part to help the dream become a reality.

Traditionally, the State Republican Executive Committee is most important in the delegate selection process at the state level, and 1976 was no exception. Composed of approximately thirty members, the committee meets a day or so before the convention to interview those persons wishing to be national convention delegates. Each delegate candidate has to submit a written application to the committee, which, in turn, interviews potential choices. Subsequently, the committee decides which ones should be recommended to the state convention. Not in the previous twelve years had the state convention failed to accept the nominees of the state executive committee. In 1976 the recommended slate, all pro-Reagan, was accepted by a most substantial majority.

Approximately 120 people applied for delegate positions, and 36 candidates—18 delegates and 18 alternates—were selected by the committee. The time-consuming task of narrowing the list of applicants to 36 was aided by the fact that the executive committee was strongly pro-Reagan and wanted to ensure a Reagan delegation. According to a Reagan leader, the pro-Reagan members of the executive committee met before the official meeting. Applicants were discussed with a representative of the Reagan campaign, and they were then ranked according to their commitment to Ford or Reagan or their lack of commitment. Of course, strong Reagan sympathizers rated most highly. Ultimately, the Reagan segment of the executive committee decided on a slate, and these persons were nominated at the state convention.

Nominations are open from the floor at the Republican state convention, and the Ford forces were not to be denied on this point. They believed, since state polls showed one-third of Oklahoma's Republicans for Ford and two-thirds for Reagan, that

Ford deserved one-third of the delegates to the national convention. Since the Ford supporters had not been able to convince the executive committee to apportion the delegate slots, they nominated six individuals, all pro-Ford, on the floor of the convention. The votes received by these pro-Ford candidates ranged from 225 to 269, whereas the votes for the persons on the Reagan slate ranged from 1,207 to 1,296. It was an obvious mismatch. However, had proportional representation been in effect, the Ford delegates, whose supporters comprised 16 percent of the state convention delegates, would have been allowed three delegates, and the Reagan bloc would have been assigned fifteen. Counting the one delegate that the Ford faction might have been able to win at the Fifth District meeting, proportional representation would have resulted in four Ford delegates and thirty-two Reagan delegates being sent to the national convention. Thus, it appears that the use of the plurality system in the Oklahoma Republican party denied representation to a minority of its members who, under proportional representation, would have achieved some, albeit limited, success.

Organizing the Delegation

Republican delegates and alternates met for a short time immediately after the state convention in Oklahoma City. They subsequently reconvened in early summer in Tulsa to elect a chairman of the delegation, as well as the national committeeman and committeewoman. Skip Healey, the outgoing national committeeman, was elected chairman of the delegation. Also at this meeting, national convention committee assignments were made and various details worked out.

National Convention Voting Record

Oklahoma and Texas were the only two states at the Republican National Convention consistently producing a majority that voted against Gerald Ford and his positions. As discussed above, Oklahoma delegation was fiercely pro-Reagan. The delegates voted unanimously in favor of proposed rule 16C, the Reagan-sponsored amendment to the Rules Committee report regarding vice-presidential selection. One delegate originally had balked at voting for the proposal, but she was asked to consider leaving the floor and letting her alternate cast a favorable Reagan vote. The delegate then changed her mind and supported the amendment.

Despite the delegation's 100 percent vote for Reagan as presidential nominee, the Oklahoma delegates were not pleased with Ford's choice of the more conservative Dole as his running mate. Although Dole gained a plurality, the majority of the Oklahoma delegates voted for other candidates. Dole received seventeen votes, compared to fifteen for Representative Philip Crane of Illinois and four for Senator Jesse Helms of North Carolina.

CONCLUSIONS

The 1976 national convention delegate selection process brought some real changes to the Oklahoma Democratic party—changes that met with mixed, though mainly positive, reactions. For the Republican party, 1976 was a year of continuation of past customs and traditions in delegate selection, and the process encountered only a small degree of dissatisfaction among those who were on the losing side.

Proportional representation in the Democratic party meant that several Democratic presidential candidates gained some representation at the national convention, at the expense of those whose strength was not enough to garner 15 percent support at meetings. Bitterness between factions appeared lessened; all apparently could accept the fact that they would get the representation to which they were entitled. Any fighting that may have occurred took place within factions and, by and large, was not bitter. Certainly the system seemed to result in a more open and democratic selection process, a far cry from the closed conventions of pre-1972 days.

CHAPTER 9 / Illinois
A Primary State

SAMUEL K. GOVE   University of Illinois

NOT only because it is a large state but also because of its political structure, Illinois ranks high in the national political scene. It has a large number of convention votes in each party as well as a large number of electoral votes (twenty-six). It is a very competitive state (a "swing state," in fact) and receives much attention both in national elections and in primaries electing delegates to national political conventions. The events of 1976 proved to be no execption to these generalizations.

Perhaps Illinois's most striking political distinction is the existence of the last well-organized political machine. The Democratic party in Chicago, long headed by the late Chicago Mayor Richard J. Daley, is unique in its ability to deliver the vote. Although its main bailiwick is the city, it is also very important in statewide politics.

In 1976 the Chicago organization returned to national Democratic circles, where it was accepted in good standing. The 1968 and 1972 conventions had been disastrous for Mayor Daley. In 1968 the Democratic convention was held in Chicago, and the antiwar demonstrations held there resulted in adverse national attention, with many charges of police brutality. In 1972 Mayor Daley and his colleagues were "kicked out" of the Miami convention. They were unseated by McGovern forces who charged they had not followed the national party rules in delegate selection. This unseating was upheld on the basic federal question by the courts, which ruled that national party rules prevail over state election laws.

In the 1976 spring primary, the organization Democrats accomplished one of their major objectives by defeating incumbent Democratic Governor Dan Walker. The Democratic organization also did fairly well in selecting its delegates in the primary (and controlling the Illinois delegation at the convention), but it had a disastrous fall election. Most of the statewide (and some local) Democratic candidates lost to Republicans; included in this number was Jimmy Carter, who lost the state electoral vote to Gerald Ford. Despite the statewide losses in November, however, Mayor Daley remained Mr. Democrat in Illinois until his death on December 20 at age seventy-four.

Neither in Chicago and Cook County nor statewide have Illinois Republicans had an organization comparable to that of the Democrats. But they do have some pockets of strength where they annihilate the nearly nonexistent other party. This is particularly true in the "collar" counties around Cook. In 1976 Illinois was Ford Country. The Ford forces, led by former governor Richard B. Ogilvie, had clear control of the state delegation to the Kansas City convention; but more important, as mentioned previously, they carried the state for Ford in November.

A swing state, Illinois has been considered a microcosm of the nation. Since 1860, the historical pattern in presidential elections has been for Illinois to cast its votes with the winner. Only in 1884, 1916, and 1976 has this not occurred. Likewise, since 1928 the percentage of each party's vote nationally in presidential elections has been very close to that of the state. Usually, the Illinois vote is only a percentage point or two different from the national percentage. In 1976, however, state results did not mirror the national trend completely—Illinois went for Ford, although the percentage difference was, similar to previous years, only 2.1 percent away from the national split.

THE 1972 DEMOCRATIC CONVENTION

At the 1972 Democratic National Convention in Miami, the Chicago organization delegates chosen in the March primary were challenged and unseated by the McGovern forces. Included among those forced to leave the convention was Mayor Richard J. Daley.

This was an affront to the mayor and had a serious impact on party unity.

The Chicago organization delegates (Wigoda delegates) were challenged before the party's Credentials Committee by a group of independent delegates (Singer delegates).[1] The charge was that the procedures under which the Wigoda delegates had been selected violated party guidelines incorporated in the call of the convention. The Wigoda delegates had been selected at the March primary under Illinois statutory procedures.

The challenge by the Singer forces was on the grounds that the delegates elected in March were unrepresentative of various groups (blacks, Chicanos, females, youth), contrary to the party rules.[2] It was also charged that the delegates were "slated" in closed meetings, again in violation of party rules. In fact, slate making in Democratic primaries in Illinois had been the practice for many years.

In response to the challenge, the acting chairperson of the Credentials Committee, Patricia Roberts Harris, appointed a hearing

[1] The Chicago organization delegates were known as Wigoda delegates, after Chicago Alderman Paul Wigoda, who filed the suit in Illinois courts on behalf of himself and his fellow organization delegates, after they had been challenged by the independent delegates. The challenging delegates were known as Singer delegates, after Chicago Alderman William Singer, who headed the challenging delegation and had been in opposition to Mayor Daley.

[2] Subsequently, in February 1975, then alderman William Singer challenged Mayor Daley for renomination in the Chicago primary. He was defeated overwhelmingly. Mayor Daley, in the Singer challenge, received support from the unlikely source of political columnist Mike Royko, who wrote in an open letter to Alderman Singer:

"Your people ran—and they should get credit for it—but they lost. The only way they could have won would have been if none of Daley's people were on the ticket in the first place. And it is asking an awful lot, even in the name of reform, for Richard J. Daley to step aside for Reggie William.

"It makes even less sense to me that some of your other delegates are people who didn't try to run in the primary. Your co-leader Jesse the Jetstream [Jackson] didn't make it to his local polling place. He's being hailed as a new political powerhouse and he couldn't deliver his own vote" (*Chicago Daily News*, July 5, 1972).

For a full account of the Illinois credentials contest in 1972, see William J. Crotty, "Anatomy of a Challenge," in Robert L. Peabody, ed., *Cases in American Politics* (New York: Praeger Publishers, 1976), pp. 111-58.

officer, Cecil F. Poole, to review the case. The officer's proceedings were extensive, resulting in 2,000 pages of transcript and 500 exhibits. On June 25, 1972, Poole's hearing concluded that the party guidelines had been violated "in letter and in spirit." The Credentials Committee, and subsequently the full convention, upheld the hearing officer, and the fifty-nine regular delegates were unseated. (Not unexpectedly, party chief Daley did not go out of his way to "deliver" the vote for McGovern in the November election, although the city did go for the Democratic nominee.)

The actions of both the Credentials Committee and the convention resulted in much litigation in both state and federal courts. On the eve of the Miami convention, the Daley forces obtained an Illinois court injunction prohibiting the anti-Daley delegates from taking their seats. When this order was ignored, Daley supporters began contempt proceedings, which were upheld by the Illinois courts. In a landmark decision, the U.S. Supreme Court ultimately ruled in *Cousins* v. *Wigoda*[3] that Illinois could not send the fifty-nine Cousins insurgents to jail. (Chicago Alderman William Cousins led the petitions in federal court for the Singer forces.) The Court reversed an Illinois appellate court decision that state law, and not the national party rules, exclusively controlled the selection of delegates to the presidential nominating convention. Writing for the Supreme Court majority, which ruled against the Daley organization, Justice William Brennan remarked: "Delegates perform a task of supreme importance to every citizen of the Nation regardless of their state of residence. . . . The States themselves have no constitutionally mandated role in the great task of the selection of the Presidential and Vice-Presidential candidates. . . . The Convention serves the pervasive national interest in the selection of candidates for national office, and this national interest is greater than any interest of an individual State."[4]

This far-reaching decision has great potential impact on our federal system. However, it did not prevent Mayor Daley from being seated at the 1976 convention in New York. In fact, Daley was referred to as the convention's "super star," and one reporter wrote that the "canonization of Daley" had begun. Daley seemed to

[3] 319 U.S. 477; 42 L.Ed. 2d 595; 95 S. Ct. 541 (1975).

[4] Ibid. Justice Rehnquist, joined by Chief Justice Berger and Justice Stewart, filed a concurring opinion. Justice Powell dissented.

enjoy the limelight in 1976; but he did feel the need for dinner when George McGovern spoke and with several colleagues left the convention floor, seeming to hold the upper hand against the former insurgents.

THE ILLINOIS STATUTES

The Illinois election statutes were an important factor in *Cousins* v. *Wigoda* and subsequent litigation. Several efforts to change the statutes have been made since the actions of the national parties regarding delegate selection, but few have been successful. This is not surprising—any proposed changes have strong political overtones. Getting political parties to agree is most difficult, and getting the factions within a party to agree is even more difficult. Thus, the election laws have not been significantly amended in recent years.

The Illinois election laws set the time of the primary for national delegate selection (March), provide two formulas for delegate selection in plurality primaries, and provide for a nonbinding presidential preference primary. The presidential preference primary in Illinois, in essence a popularity contest, is clearly advisory only. Specifically, the law states, "The vote for President . . . shall be for the sole purpose of securing an expression of the sentiment and will of the party voters with respect to candidates for nomination for said office, and the vote of the state at large shall be taken and considered as advisory to the delegates and alternates." Likewise, delegate candidates are not bound by their preference for president, although a candidate must file with his statements of candidacy "a statement declaring the name of his preference for President of the United States or that he is uncommitted." There is no provision in the law requiring the elected delegate to vote for his preferred candidate at the party convention.

For this study, however, the most significant part of the election law is found in the two options that the state parties have for allocating convention delegates. These options do not include selection by proportional representation, nor has this method been proposed in amendments to the election laws.

There are two statutory alternatives. Under Alternative A, the total number of delegates and alternates is divided equally among the congressional districts, to the highest whole number possible. The delegates not to be elected from congressional districts (that is, the remainder not equally divisible among the congressional districts) shall be elected at large in the primary, by state convention, or by a combination of the two. Alternative B provides that the total number of delegates and alternates are apportioned among the congressional districts, to the highest whole number possible, on the basis of a formula which gives equal weight both to population and to the party's presidential vote in the previous election. Delegates not allocated to districts are selected at large in the primary or by state convention. At the time that each state central committee certifies to the state board of elections the specific alternative to be used by the party, it must also certify the method to be used for electing at-large delegates. In recent years, Alternative A has been used by the Illinois Republicans; Alternative B, by the Democrats. In 1976 both parties provided that their at-large delegates would be selected by state conventions.[5]

The alternative plans of delegation selection were in litigation before the 1976 conventions. The Democratic State Central Committee certified a plan to the state board of elections that was in variance with the two alternatives, but in compliance with national party regulations. (It had been approved by the Compliance Review Commission of the Democratic National Committee.) This formula provided that

Equal weight shall be given to the average of the vote for the Democratic candidates in the two most recent presidential elections and to Democratic Party enrollment as measured by the Democratic Party vote in the primary election of March 19, 1974.

Fractions shall be placed in rank order, highest first, and delegates shall be allocated thereby until the full complement is reached.

[5] On June 27, 1977, the General Assembly passed House Bill 365; it was approved on September 22, 1977. This bill changed Alternative A for the selection of delegates to national conventions. The major change in the option is that at least ten of the delegates to which the state is entitled are selected at large (elected in the primary on an at-large basis, selected by the state convention, or chosen by a combination of these two methods). Additional at-large delegates are those remaining unallocated after equal division among the state congressional districts.

A bill to permit this option was introduced in the General Assembly but did not pass. The political realities of the plan were that it would increase the number of delegates to be selected from congressional districts within the city of Chicago and would result in a corresponding decrease in the number of delegates selected from elsewhere in the state.

The state board of elections refused to accept the new plan, and the state central committee filed a petition for mandamus in the state supreme court. A divided court in a *per curiam* decision denied the writ of mandamus. The court said, "We are reluctant to assume, for example, as the plaintiff seems to assume, that the General Assembly could validly delegate to any and every national political party the authority to formulate such delegate appointment plans as it saw fit, to be implemented at state expense."[6] The court did not interpret the *Cousins* decision as providing for this. Alternative B was then used by the Democrats.

THE 1976 PRESIDENTIAL PREFERENCE PRIMARY

The Illinois presidential preference primary on March 16 attracted seven candidates, four on the Democratic ballot and three on the Republican. The Democrats were George Wallace, Jimmy Carter, Fred Harris, and Sargent Shriver (Shriver at one time had been an active businessman in Chicago). The two serious Republican candidates were President Ford and Ronald Reagan, with the third being perennial local candidate Lar ("America First") Daly.

On the Democratic side, Jimmy Carter received 48.4 percent of the vote, followed by Wallace (27.8 percent), Shriver (16.2 percent), and Harris (7.6 percent). Carter did well in Cook County and Chicago, leading Wallace overall there by 235,000 to 130,000 votes. Surprisingly, however, Wallace carried Mayor Daley's ward (the 11th) by a 5,150 to 5,032 margin. The political pundits did not consider this worth mentioning. The results of the Illinois preference primary continued Carter's national momentum, although he did not do as well in securing convention delegates. On

[6] *Touhy* v. *State Board of Elections* (62 Ill. 2d 303), opinion filed Jan. 26, 1976. Interestingly, Governor Dan Walker was given permission as an individual citizen and a member of the Democratic party to file an amicus curiae brief.

the other hand, the primary was another blow to Wallace's campaign, while Shriver suspended his candidacy after the Illinois campaign.

On the Republican side, President Ford, with the support of most of the party's leadership, received 58.9 percent of the popular vote to Reagan's 40.1 percent. Lar Daly, as usual, finished a distant third.

THE DELEGATE SELECTION PRIMARY

The delegate selection contests in the March 1976 primary received much attention from the media. The primary was marked by an unusually large number of candidates—both those pledged to various presidential candidates and those who were uncommitted.

The Democrats, using Alternative B, varied the number of delegates to be selected from district to district, depending on relative local party strength. Numbers varied from nine delegates in the very strongly Democratic First District to five delegates in each of three strongly Republican districts. The number of alternates was generally half the number of regular delegates.[7] The total number of delegates elected in the Democratic primary was 155, plus 72 alternates.

The state Republican party decided, in accord with Illinois statutes, to use Alternative A, selecting four delegates and four alternates from each congressional district. Republicans elected ninety-six delegates and ninety-six alternates in the primary.

The Democrats

The Democratic delegate primary, in contrast to the Republican primary, was a noisy affair. There were over eight hundred candidates for delegate seats, and nearly full slates of candidates were filed as being committed to Senator Stevenson, Governor Carter, Senator Humphrey, Governor Walker, Governor Wallace, and former senator Harris. Other candidates were pledged to Congressman

[7] Districts with an odd number of delegates (9, 7, 5) received the next lower number of alternate delegates (for example, 4 instead of 4.5).

Udall, Sargent Shriver, and senators Kennedy, Jackson, Bayh, Bentsen, and Mondale. Governor Walker had a full slate in each district, and Governor Wallace almost accomplished the same. Senator Stevenson had candidates in all but one district; however, in some districts he had more candidates than seats to be filled, while in other districts he had fewer candidates. Jimmy Carter had virtually no delegate candidates in Chicago, but elsewhere in the state he had nearly full slates. Carter obviously was not challenging Mayor Daley at that stage of the presidential primary sweepstakes.

The average number of delegate candidates per congressional district was over thirty, with a high in the Tenth (sixty candidates) and a low in the Third (eighteen). The Tenth District (Evanston) had eleven candidates for Stevenson (although only seven were to be elected), plus full slates for Carter, Humphrey, Udall, Walker, and Wallace, and a six-man slate for Harris. (There were also three uncommitted candidates, three candidates for Shriver, and one for Bayh.) The organized slate for Stevenson, composed primarily of independent Democrats, won the delegate seats. The Chicago North Shore district (the Ninth), with forty-seven candidates, had a voting pattern similar to the Tenth. Here the Chicago organization slate won handily. The downstate district, which includes the University of Illinois Urbana-Champaign campus, also had forty-seven candidates. In this district the Carter slate won rather easily.

The strategy of the Chicago organization in the primary was to elect delegates committed to favorite son Adlai Stevenson III. This strategy proved to be successful, and Stevenson gained 79 of the 155 delegates elected from districts. Jimmy Carter was second, with 54 delegates. Fourteen of the delegates elected were uncommitted, 3 each were pledged to Humphrey and Wallace, and 2 to Governor Walker. That the organization in Chicago supported Stevenson is attested by a reporter who wrote that "the list of Stevenson-pledged delegates from most Cook County Congressional districts reads like a Who's Who of the regular Democratic organization, led by the mayor himself who topped the ticket in the 5th district." Sixty-five of the 79 Stevenson delegates were labeled Daley loyalists.

In the same primary, Governor Walker was defeated for renomination by Daley candidate Michael Howlett, a defeat which had top priority with Mayor Daley. The rout of Walker was nearly complete when only 2 of his 156 delegate candidates were elected. A Daley spokesman even tried to have the governor banned from the Democratic convention floor in New York, but the convention arrangements committee did not support such a maneuver. Walker toyed with the idea of running in November for reelection as a third-party candidate. However, he ruled out this possibility when he sent a telegram to the state Democratic convention saying, "I am a Democrat and I believe strongly in the two-party system."

There is no purpose in attempting to relate the results of the Democratic delegate election to those of the presidential preference primary. Only Carter, Wallace, Shriver, and Harris entered the preference primary. Although Carter finished first in the preference primary, with 48.4 percent of the vote, he received only 34.8 percent of the total delegate vote. Stevenson led the delegate vote on a percentage basis with nearly 51 percent of the total. These results again highlight the meaninglessness of the preferential primary in 1976 except as a media show and a "momentum" exercise for candidates.

If a proportional representation method of delegate election had been used, it would have decreased the number of delegates for Stevenson and Carter and would have distributed a number of votes to the also-rans. A straight plurality method of election would have changed the distribution of delegates between Stevenson and Carter only slightly. But the political realities of the state are relevant to any consideration of these hypothetical election devices. In particular, the popularity and voter appeal of some delegate candidates as politicians themselves often overshadow voter attachments to the presidential candidates to whom these delegate candidates are committed. Thus, it is not surprising to find that Stevenson delegate Richard J. Daley exceeded all other delegates in the state in total votes, receiving a substantial 76,000 votes. (At the same time, each of the other delegates from Daley's Fifth District received over 60,000 votes, with one receiving nearly 73,000.) No Democrat came close to doing as poorly as the Republican low man, who polled only 1,000 votes. Also, several Democratic congressman ran (and won) as delegate candidates in their districts, thereby in effect testing their own reputations and abilities to draw voter support.

Proportional Representation in Presidential Nominating Politics

The Republicans

The Republican contest was primarily between Ford and Reagan, both of whom had delegate candidates in most districts. Lar Daly had a handful of candidates (3), as did right-winger Donald Du-Mont (6), and Senator Charles Percy (2). Of the remaining 241 total candidates, 58 were uncommitted, while the others were pledged to either Ford or Reagan.

Reagan had approximately the same total number of candidates as Ford, and they were distributed throughout the state. However, the election results were a rout by the well-organized Ford forces. Ford gained seventy-two of the ninety-six seats, while Reagan secured only eleven. Thirteen uncommitted delegates were also elected.

Ford's success in delegate election (he won 75 percent of the slots) was disproportionate to his success in the presidential preference popularity primary, in which he received 59 percent of the vote. If a proportional representation selection process had been used, it is estimated that Ford would have received only forty-nine of the ninety-six delegates, while Reagan would have had thirty-five delegates; seventeen would have been uncommitted. On a straight plurality basis, Ford would have received seventy-seven delegates, with Reagan's number reduced from eleven to eight.

Given the realities of Illinois politics, these hypothetical calculations present problems. First, in 1976 the slate-making system did not work—in some districts more delegate candidates for either Ford or Reagan filed than there were delegates to be elected (four in each congressional district). In each of six districts, six Ford delegate candidates filed, while the same situation was found in three districts with Reagan candidates. Second, as mentioned previously, many candidates for delegates are themselves popular political figures, and the votes they receive are more often personal endorsements than indicators of voter attachments to a presidential candidate. Several Republican congressmen ran for delegates in their districts, thus testing their own reputations to draw voter support. For example, the delegate drawing the most votes statewide was Congressman John N. Erlenborn of strongly Republican DuPage County, who received 46,000 votes. (He was committed to Ford.) Erlenborn outdistanced his fellow Ford slate-mate by over 7,000 votes. The number of votes that elected delegates received, of course, varied tremendously. The delegate receiving the fewest votes statewide was Ford delegate Robert Holloway of the strongly Democratic First District. He needed only 1,035 votes to win a seat at the Kansas City convention.

THE STATE PARTY CONVENTIONS

Next on the Illinois presidential agenda were the state conventions of the two political parties. The Democratic convention was held in the state capital of Springfield in April, followed by the Republican convention in Oak Brook in June. State conventions in Illinois are rather loose affairs and usually there is little floor action—at least when compared to the national conventions. The only significant business for the state conventions is the selection of nominees for the Board of Trustees of the Univeristy of Illinois, the adoption of party platforms, and, in presidential years, the selection of presidential electors and at-large delegates for the national convention. In 1976, the Repbulicans also had some national party offices to be filled.

At their 1976 state conventions, the Democrats selected fourteen at-large delegates and the Republicans, five. Under party rules, the Democrats allocated their at-large delegates according to the percentage distribution of delegates selected in district primaries. Thus, Stevenson received seven of the fourteen delegates, Carter received five, one was uncommitted, and the last seat was given to a Humphrey supporter.[8] The Democratic convention also selected eleven at-large alternates. The convention action brought the total Illinois Democratic delegation to 169 delegates and 83 alternates.

The at-large delegates were selected without significant conflict, and harmony was the rule of the Democratic convention. The Stevenson delegates included the candidates for statewide office in the fall. The Carter delegates were led by Carter's Illinois campaign manager, the Reverend James Wall. The other Carter delegates were campaign workers, but not well known statewide. With both

[8] Humphrey supporters won the seat in a toss with Wallace supporters, since the two of them were tied with three district delegates apiece.

slates, there was an obvious attempt to provide a balance for women and minorities.

The Republicans had more controversy at their convention. Reagan forces were striving to obtain some of the at-large delegates from a convention dominated by Ford supporters, led by former governor Richard B. Ogilvie. Specifically, Reagan's supporters wanted two of the five at-large delegates. They claimed they were entitled to these seats because of the 40 percent vote Reagan had received in the presidential preference primary. (This was about the only time that the results of the popularity contest were mentioned after the March primary.) When the Reagan spokesman argued in committee that Reagan was entitled to two delegates through "proportional representation," Ogilvie replied that Reagan had "gained all of the California delegates under a 'winner-take-all' rule." Another Ford delegate said, "When the Reagan people are willing to give Ford fifty delegates in California, we will think about proportional representation in Illinois." The Reagan forces subsequently modified their demand to one seat, but they were defeated by a vote of 867 to 523. The Ford forces thus prevailed, and the seats were assigned—five to Ford, none to Reagan. The total Illinois delegation included 101 delegates and 101 alternates.

As expected, the Republicans, after an uneventful contest, selected Ogilvie as the delegation chairman. Other offices were actively contested, however, and this produced a lively convention. Underlying all of the various contests was the Ford-Reagan issue.

THE DEMOCRATIC NATIONAL CONVENTION

By the time the elected district and at-large delegates arrived at the July Democratic convention in New York, all but the shouting was over. Mayor Daley had predicted that if Carter carried Ohio in the June 9 primary, he would win the nomination. Carter did win that contest, and Daley then declared his support—a move which started a landslide of endorsements. For all intents and purposes, the convention's work was resolved.

At their state convention in Springfield, the Democrats had delayed selecting a delegation chairman because of the possibility of an open fight for vice-chairman. That selection was made in New York before the opening of the national convention, and Daley was chosen unanimously as chairman. He was nominated by Carter's state manager, the Reverend James Wall, and seconded by colorful Chicago Alderman Vito Marzullo. There was a slight conflict for the vice-chairmanship, but eventually a Carter delegate, Suellyn Johnson of Wheaton, was selected over an Urbana Carter delegate. At the same caucus, 165 of the 169 delegates voted to support Carter, although only 58 had been elected as Carter delegates.

Mayor Daley was a center of attraction on the convention floor. As an Associated Press story said, "Proud politicians, tittering girls, men bent with age and almost everyone else at the Democratic National Convention paid a visit to Mayor . . . Daley's chair. . . . People stood in line in the aisle next to his chair, seeking a few words, an autograph, an interview and probably in some cases, a favor." Daley addressed the convention on the urban affairs section of the party platform, and generally the reception was warm. He appealed for a "progressive" platform and a party that "in its finest moments" was never restrictive. Daley did not mention the 1968 or 1972 national conventions. The mayor had come full circle since those conventions. As Max Frankel wrote in the *New York Times*, "Though he did not express it, he must have felt a touch of parental pride as Mr. Carter stage-managed his triumph and suppressed trouble with an effective contribution of charm and muscle."

The voting for the presidential nomination was anticlimactic. Along with most of the other delegations, the Illinois delegation voted for Carter. On the roll call, Carter received 164 of the state's 169 votes. The remaining votes were scattered among Jerry Brown, Morris Udall, and Ellen McCormack.

The next item of business was the selection of the vice-presidential candidate, a matter in which Illinois had a particular interest since favorite son Adlai Stevenson III was one of seven included in Carter's final considerations. He was interviewed by Carter but then eliminated. Newspaper comments blamed Stevenson's lack of success on his "dullness" as a speaker and campaigner. Illinois supported Carter's choice of Senator Mondale as the vice-presidential nominee, casting all but four of the state's votes for the Minnesota senator.

THE REPUBLICAN NATIONAL CONVENTION

Unlike the Democratic nomination, the Republican nomination was still unsettled when delegates arrived in Kansas City. The Illinois delegation was strong in support for Ford; but Reagan supporters seemed solid, and some delegates were still undecided. At a press conference in Chicago before the convention, Ogilvie claimed that there were only two truly "undecideds." Additionally, he said, two Reagan delegates were wavering because of the selection of Senator Schweiker of Pennsylvania as Reagan's vice-presidential running mate. Ogilvie's count showed eighty-one delegates for Ford, twelve for Reagan, two delegates leaning toward Ford, four leaning toward Reagan, and two truly uncommitted. The *New York Times* reported the same estimate.

The search for delegates by both camps continued at the convention. Illinois received a little notoriety when Ogilvie announced that Ford delegates had been offered a bribe to switch to Reagan. Charges and countercharges were made by both sides, but the incident was soon forgotten.

The first convention test of the respective strengths of the two camps came on the proposed party rule change to require a presidential candidate (Ford) to name his choice for vice-president before the balloting on the presidential nomination. The Illinois delegation voted with the majority to defeat the proposed rule. The Illinois vote showed twenty in favor of the change, seventy-nine opposed, and two abstentions. Several observers did not classify those results as a clear Reagan-Ford vote, since some Ford delegates were for the proposed rule as a matter of principle.

On the roll call for the presidential nomination, the Illinois delegation voted eighty-six for Ford and fourteen for Reagan, with one abstention.[9] Only New York, Pennsylvania, and Ohio gave Ford a larger number of votes. Ogilvie had delivered the vote for Ford, as he was to do again in November.

The only remaining business was selecting a vice-presidential candidate. Illinois Senator Charles Percy had been mentioned in many circles as a possible candidate, and the Illinois delegates passed a resolution urging Ford to give him "serious considera-

[9] The abstention was cast by an alternate delegate. His principal, who was absent, was an uncommitted delegate and the alternate, although for Ford, felt he should vote as his principal wished.

tion" for the vice-presidency. According to newspaper accounts, there were a scattering of negative votes when that resolution was considered. However, Ford's choice proved to be Senator Robert Dole of Kansas. When the floor vote came on Senator Dole, divisions between the Ford and Reagan supporters were absent, and Illinois cast a unanimous 101 votes for Dole.

THE NOVEMBER ELECTION

Illinois was the scene of intense campaigning in the fall of 1976. Although the Ford-Carter contest received much attention, state and local elections were also highlighted—particularly the campaign of the Republican gubernatorial candidate, Jim Thompson. Polls early in the fall, later to be substantiated, showed Thompson far ahead of Daley's candidate, Secretary of State Mike Howlett. Republican incumbent Attorney General William Scott appeared to be a sure winner, as did Democratic state Treasurer Alan Dixon as the candidate for secretary of state. The voters showed much independence—splitting their tickets for state candidates for both parties. In fact, there appeared to be more ticket splitting in 1976 than in earlier years, even though this trend has been accelerating recently.

Jim Thompson won with the largest plurality in Illinois history—1.390 million votes. Republican Attorney General Scott also won with a large plurality of 1.116 million votes, and Secretary of State-elect Dixon, a Democrat, had an even larger plurality of 1.344 million. The only close race was for comptroller, with Democrat Michael Bakalis defeating incumbent George Lindberg by 180,000 votes.

Usually presidential and gubernatorial candidates of the same party are the winners in Illinois (1972 was the most recent exception). It is widely believed that in 1948 Adlai Stevenson, running for governor, carried in Harry Truman in the presidential election in this crucial state. In 1976 it might well be argued that, with his huge plurality for governor, Jim Thompson carried in Gerald Ford, who won the state's presidential election with a slender plurality of 113,000 votes. Ford received only 50.3 percent of the vote, and Carter, 48 percent.

The Ford-Carter contest did not follow typical Illinois voting patterns. Carter carried 35 of the state's 102 counties, including Cook, but his main geographic strength was in southern Illinois in the "Bible belt." Mayor Daley's organization won the Chicago vote heavily for Carter, with 814,000 votes to Ford's 389,000. Daley also carried his own ward for Carter by 19,000 to 9,000. The total vote in Cook County (Chicago and suburbs) was relatively close—1,180,000 for Carter to 987,000 for Ford. It was the vote downstate that won the day for Ford in the state. In the process of electing Ford while the nation elected Carter, Illinois lost its claim to be a barometer state. Did the method of selection of convention delegates have anything to do with this outcome? That is very unlikely, but Jim Thompson certainly did have a lot to do with it.

CONCLUSION

The 1976 election was a departure from Illinois's previous political history. Most notably, Illinois did not vote with the nation in the November presidential election. As usual, the state did play an important role in the national conventions. The early primary results helped mobilize support for President Ford but had little impact on the ultimate Democratic outcome. However, Mayor Daley later jumped on the Carter bandwagon, and this action may have been the push needed to secure the nomination for Jimmy Carter.

Given the delegate selection process in the primary and the subsequent delegate behavior in New York and Kansas City, it is difficult to imagine that a change in that selection process would have affected the outcome in Illinois. As Keech and Matthews say, "Delegate selection procedures have little effect on who wins and who loses at national party conventions."[10] The political leadership, at least in Illinois, seems quite able to adjust to new ground rules. Even without Mayor Daley, the Chicago Democratic organization will undoubtedly be able to remain in charge, delivering the votes and electing convention delegates in Chicago under any system. The political leadership has shown, especially in the Demo-

[10] William R. Keech and Donald R. Matthews, *The Party's Choice* (Washington, D.C.: Brookings Institution, 1976), p. 237.

cratic party, that it can adjust to the new ground rules brought about by the McGovern and Mikulski commissions. The only way those opposed to the regular organization seem to be able to get into office is by action of the national party leadership or through support in the courts, as was the case for the Miami convention delegates in 1972.

If the aim of changing the ground rules is to bring about fundamental change in the system, then more changes must be made in the delegate selection process. Those intent on bringing about change—independents and reformers—must secure party leadership. But tinkering with one small part of the overall system—here, delegate selection—will not cause significant change. The political world of Illinois is too complex for minor adjustments to make much difference.

CHAPTER 10 / Connecticut
A Primary-Caucus State

HOWARD L. REITER   University of Connecticut

WHAT do professional politicians in a state want from the presidential nominating process? Their aims can be divided into internal and external goals. The former are those which involve the power struggle within the state party, and which presumably have effects beyond the presidential campaign year. The latter are those which involve the national party and the outcome of the presidential nominating convention.

Internal goals depend upon the degree of factionalism within the party, and whether existing conflict can be accommodated peacefully. If two or more factions are seeking total victory over each other, then the state organization will seek absolute control over the delegation and the elimination of factional rivals from the national convention slate. On the other hand, a leadership that desires to keep all factions at least minimally happy will ensure representation to each in the delegation. Moreover, this will be done in a manner calculated to persuade each faction that it is getting as many delegates as its true strength merits. We might call these mutually exclusive internal goals *factional victory* and *balance*.

Author's Note: This study was made possible by a grant from the University of Connecticut Research Foundation and the assistance of four capable young assistants, Frank DiBlasi, Richard Handelman, James Kelman, and Peter Miecznikowski. Numerous party activists provided valuable information, and five deserve mention here: Democrats Donald Meikle and Donald DeFronzo and Republicans Frederick Biebel, Nancy Owen, and Donald Schmidt. Michael Millican of the Associated Press was also generous with his help.

Externally, the state party organization wants a presidential candidate who will help the state ticket and who owes his nomination in part to the state party. This implies at least four conditions. The first is *unity*, a delegation controlled by the state party leaders. This need not be inconsistent with the goal of balance, for the leaders may be willing to tolerate a factionally diverse delegation as long as the delegates vote the way the leaders desire. Second is *flexibility*, the ability of the leaders to swing the delegation to an appropriate candidate should their first choice prove weaker or otherwise less desirable than another. The third is *timing*, which can work in one of two ways. Either the delegates are early on the winner's bandwagon—"for Roosevelt before Chicago" or "for Kennedy before West Virginia"—and thus are able to tell the candidate that they were with him all the way; or they lend their support at the last moment before victory, like the New Jerseyites for Nixon in 1968 or the Mississippians for Ford in 1976, and are able to claim that they provided the crucial votes. Either one is difficult to achieve, for in a competitive situation it takes keen foresight to spot the winner early, and it takes shrewdness and luck to provide the critical votes before other delegates do. Finally, one wants an *acceptable candidate*, one who will be popular in one's state, ideologically compatible, and not anathema to important groups of voters back home. Ultimately, one wants either to be on the winner's bandwagon early or to lead an uncommitted, negotiable slate to the convention.[1]

Connecticut in 1976 provides a useful case study of the ability or inability of state party leaders to achieve these goals. The state and the year are especially noteworthy for three reasons: (1) party leadership has traditionally been strong in the Constitution State; (2) 1976 was a year of keen competition for the presidential nomination in both parties; and (3) the Democrats adopted an entirely new procedure for selecting delegates, while the Republicans retained the system previously used by both parties. The following discussion will first review the delegate selection process in both parties and then evaluate which goals were met, and why.

---

[1] This model of convention politics was suggested by Nelson W. Polsby, "Decision-Making at the National Conventions," 13 *Western Political Quarterly* 609-19 (1960).

THE STATE AND ITS POLITICS

Prosperity and diversity describe Connecticut's population of three million. The state is highly urbanized, including five cities whose populations exceed 100,000, and ranks first in per capita income. A majority of Connecticut's workers are in white-collar occupations, and the economy is heavily industrial—notably defense plants—with a concentration of insurance companies as well. Besides the big cities, the state includes numerous smaller cities, sprawling suburbs, and small towns and farms. Its population is more than 40 percent Roman Catholic; 6 percent are blacks, and Jews and Puerto Ricans each comprise about 3 percent. Moreover, Connecticut has one of the nation's highest concentrations of foreign-born and their children.[2]

This population diversity gives rise to a competitive two-party system, and the patterns of voting behavior will contain no surprises for those familiar with party politics throughout the North. Democrats are strongest in the cities, among ethnic groups (especially Catholics), and with organized labor. The relationship with labor is sometimes difficult, for as Duane Lockard wrote years ago, it is "at once a blessing and a curse. . . . As with the business groups supporting the Republicans, there is an implied *quid pro quo* attached to their support." This became especially significant in the presidential jockeying in 1976. Republicans are strongest among the wealthy and Protestants, and in small towns and suburbs. In a state so heavily ethnic, the Republican party has more Italian-Americans and other ethnics than its counterparts elsewhere and frequently nominates them for high office (although usually not for governor).[3]

The presidential nominating process is based to a great extent on the state's six congressional districts. Although Connecticut is

[2] See the *Pocket Data Book* (Washington, D.C.: Bureau of the Census, 1973) and various volumes of the Census of 1970; Michael Barone, Grant Ujifusa, and Douglas Matthews, *The Almanac of American Politics 1976* (New York: E. P. Dutton & Co., 1975), pp. 145-54; and Neal R. Peirce, *The New England States* (New York: W. W. Norton & Co., 1976), pp. 188, 222-25, 228.

[3] Duane Lockard, *New England State Politics* (Chicago: Henry Regnery Co., 1968), pp. 234-43; and Peirce, *The New England States*, p. 201. The quotation is from Lockard, p. 263.

not marked by the regional or upstate-downstate rivalries that are found in so many other states, some generalizations can be made about these districts. The First (Hartford) and Third (New Haven) are the most Democratic; the Fourth and Fifth (Fairfield County area) are the most Republican; and the Second (eastern Connecticut) and Sixth (northwest) are the most rural, and although they vote Democratic, it is by a lesser margin than the First and Third.[4]

Since the end of World War II, Connecticut has gone through two distinct periods, the first ending with the 1958 elections. In that period, the Republicans carried the state's electoral votes in all three presidential elections, elected two of four governors, four of six U.S. senators, twenty-nine of thirty-six U.S. representatives, seventeen of twenty state officials, and controlled the state senate half the time and the state house of representatives all the time. This period was followed by an era of Democratic rule. From 1958 through 1974, Republicans won Connecticut's electoral votes only once, the governorship once in five attempts, a Senate seat once in six attempts, thirteen of fifty-four House seats, state official positions three out of twenty-six times, the state senate once in nine tries, and the state house four times out of nine. Statewide party registration figures a year before the 1976 election gave the Democrats 37 percent, Republicans 27 percent, and independents 36 percent.[5]

The Democratic ascendancy has been attributed to numerous factors. These include the recession of 1958, John Kennedy's nomination in 1960, attractive Democratic candidates, the national Republican party's rightward turn in the 1960s, reapportionment of the legislature, and the relative liberalism of the Northeast in national politics. But the cause most often mentioned has been the skill of the Democratic party leadership, personified by John Bailey, who served as state chairman from 1946 until his death in 1975. Bailey's ability, which gave him the national chairmanship

[4] Lockard, *New England State Politics*, p. 234; also see the *Congressional District Data Book*, 93d Congress (Washington, D.C.: Bureau of the Census, 1973), and Barone et al., *Almanac*.

[5] Murray S. Steadman, Jr., "Connecticut: The Politics of Urbanization," in George Goodwin, Jr., and Victoria Schuck, eds., *Party Politics in the New England States* (Durham, N.H.: New England Center for Continuing Education, 1968), pp. 31, 21; and registration data from Oct. 11, 1975, from the Office of the Secretary of the State of Connecticut.

in the Kennedy and Johnson years, put him in a long line of strong party leaders in Connecticut's history. His strength consisted in part of shrewd bargaining among the many fiefdoms that make up Connecticut's Democratic party, of agreements with labor, and of the promotion of attractive moderate condidates. For a long time it seemed that the state would withstand the weakening of party organization in evidence elsewhere.

But signs of organizational weakness began to appear as early as 1955, when Connecticut became the last state to adopt any kind of primary, a "challenge primary" held after the party caucus or convention had made its designation; then in 1966 the mandatory party lever in the voting booth was made optional. The insurgency of Senator Eugene McCarthy in 1968 was a more direct threat to Bailey's control, for it produced the state's first divided delegation at a Democratic National Convention in forty-four years. That insurgency led to the victory of Joseph Duffey in the 1970 senatorial primary, followed by the Democrats' loss of both the Senate seat and the governorship, and to the organization of a liberal pressure group, the Caucus of Connecticut Democrats. In 1972 the delegation was again split, and in 1974 another blow was dealt to party harmony as two organization stalwarts fought vigorously for the gubernatorial nomination. Bailey's last major act of unity was to persuade Attorney General Robert Killian not to challenge U.S. Representative Ella Grasso in a gubernatorial primary.[6]

Republicans have similarly had a long tradition of centralized leadership in Connecticut. Observers have noted a rivalry between the Hartford area and wealthy Fairfield County, with conservatives traditionally concentrated in the latter. In national Republican politics, however, the party stands to the left; and since 1964 the delegations to the national convention have voted for William Scranton, Nelson Rockefeller, and the liberals' apportionment formula in 1972. Not until 1976, however, were conservatives excluded from the slate.[7]

[6] Lockard, *New England State Politics*, p. 244; and Peirce, *The New England States*, pp. 196-97.

[7] Peirce, *The New England States*, p. 20. For national convention votes before 1976, see Richard C. Bain and Judith H. Parris, *Convention Decisions and Voting Records*, 2d ed. (Washington, D.C.: Brookings Institution, 1973).

The 1974 elections marked a climax of Democratic rule in Connecticut. Representative Grasso recaptured the governorship for her party by a landslide; Senator Abraham Ribicoff was even more decisively reelected; the Democrats won all statewide races and gained a congressional seat; and both houses of the legislature went from comfortable Republican majorities to better than three-to-one Democratic control. As landslides so often do in American politics, this one left Connecticut Democrats disunited. Governor Grasso was soon locking horns with Democratic leaders of the legislature and the Hartford machine, as well as with public employees' unions, over her fiscal austerity program and matters of patronage. If 1974 left the Democrats in power but disunited, however, it had the opposite effect among Republicans. In June 1975 a vigorous businessman from Stratford, Frederick Biebel, became state chairman, and the dearth of major Republican officeholders gave him little competition. Senator Lowell Weicker, the most visible Republican, had never been deeply involved in party affairs. Both the Democratic fissures and the Republican harmony would play a role in the 1976 presidential nominating process.

THE DEMOCRATS

As a machine-oriented state, Connecticut for many years had a delegate selection process designed to guarantee control by the party leadership and the attainment of the goals mentioned in the introductory part of this chapter. State law provides for a state party convention whose delegates are selected by the 169 town and city party committees, and which in turn can select national convention delegates. Not only is the convention an easier vehicle for leadership control than a primary, but party leaders also benefited from the fact that delegates to the state convention had to be designated by local organizations or defeat organization slates in challenge primaries, an unlikely event.

However, in preparation for 1972 and even more for 1976, rules emanating from the Democratic National Committee upset the system in Connecticut as far as the state party was concerned. Although affirmative action requirements need not have changed the system (malleable delegates might now have to include more women, minority group members, and young people, but they could still be organization stalwarts), the requirements to ensure proportional representation of presidential candidates' supporters destroyed any chance of achieving either factional victory or any of the external goals. Now the delegation would be a grabbag of different candidates' supporters, controlled by nobody; only the goal of balance could be achieved. And to make matters worse, the rules governing the state convention failed to comply with national guidelines. The problem was that state law allowed town committees to endorse a state convention delegate slate as the "official" slate, and this preferential treatment conflicted with national party guidelines.

Faced with the possibility of having his delegation excluded from the 1976 national convention, state chairman Bailey took action in January 1975. He appointed a forty-member committee under the chairmanship of Danbury attorney Norman Buzaid to produce new procedures in conformity with national guidelines. One of its tasks was to adopt an affirmative action plan, and by the end of the year another committee of eighty-one members had been appointed to publicize the selection process among women, minority groups, and others. The more difficult job was to adopt new delegate selection procedures, and it was a long and conflict-ridden process.[8]

The system that was eventually adopted began to take shape fairly early. The drafters rejected a statewide primary, which would have been less amenable than other methods to organization influence, and which would also have required state legislation. Instead, they decided in favor of party-operated primaries to be held in each town and city. Each town and city would then send delegates to one of six congressional district conventions; those delegates would be divided among the supporters of various

---

[8] To obtain the rules and the process that produced them, the author relied on four sources: *Rules for Selecting Connecticut Delegates to the 1976 Democratic Convention* and *Regulations for Implementation of Connecticut Delegate Selection Plan,* both publications of the Democratic State Central Committee, available from the Connecticut State Democratic Party; numerous articles in the *Hartford Courant;* and telephone interviews with Donald Meikle, publicist for the state central committee, on Aug. 25 and 31, 1976.

presidential candidates, depending on how well the candidates had run in the town. Each of the six congressional district conventions would elect several national convention delegates, based on proportional representation of candidates' supporters at the congressional district convention. No delegates would be chosen at large. The whole process would be run and financed by the Democratic party, not by the state. Even though simple in outline, the system was complicated enough to make it difficult for many citizens to understand. Indeed, much of the press commentary on the process stressed how confusing it was.

This confusion was one of several features of the plan that served the interests of the state organization, which wanted an uncommitted slate sent to Madison Square Garden. After all, the fewer the citizens who understood the process, the lower the turnout would be. The party organization was probably confident that it could get its stalwarts to the polls, and they would outnumber other voters. The decentralized nature of the primaries would also contribute to the low turnout by minimizing the amount of attention given to the process by the mass media. Chances of an uncommitted slate's going to New York City would be further enhanced by provisions that an uncommitted slate was to appear automatically on all town ballots (in contrast to presidential candidates, who had to show minimal strength in a town to appear on its ballot), and that the votes of any candidate securing less than 15 percent of the total vote in any town were to be added to that town's uncommitted vote. Moreover, the process was timed late in the spring, enabling the state party to help break a possible deadlock at the national convention. Among the features favored by the state organization but rejected by the Legal Advisory Council of the Democratic National Committee were requirements that the uncommitted slate appear first on the ballot; that the names of delegate candidates rather than presidential candidates be listed on the ballot, thereby further confusing the voter; and that towns be allowed to opt for a caucus instead of a primary. The final result was a process satisfactory to nobody. Liberals were upset about the ways in which the organization had influenced the rules, and the state chairman was concerned about the lack of guarantees for representation of women or minority groups. The attitude of many party professionals was summarized by Frank Santaguida, the state labor commissioner, who asked, "Why are you wasting our time with all this democracy?"[9]

On March 5, 1976, the state chairman published a list of all active presidential candidates, each of whom could qualify for the primary by naming a state coordinator and paying a filing fee of $1,000. The state chairman determined by lot the order in which the candidates would appear on the ballot, but the presidential candidates were not guaranteed a spot on every town's ballot. Only if they had enough supporters to form a full slate in that town would they appear on its ballot. Each town was allotted a number of delegates equal to its number of delegates to the state convention.

Only the presidential candidates' names would appear on the ballot. Elsewhere in the polling place there would be a list of supporters of each candidate who wished to be delegates to the congressional district convention. When the votes were cast, those of any candidate receiving less than 15 percent would be added to the votes for the uncommitted slate. If there were fewer delegates than presidential candidates who qualified for them, candidates would then receive fractional votes. If a candidate were entitled to, say, three of a town's five delegates, then only the top three names on his list would go to the congressional district convention.

Not all presidential candidates chose to enter the Connecticut primary. Some had organizational problems, and some had already dropped out of the race before the deadline. Those remaining appeared on the ballot in the following order: the uncommitted slate, Ellen McCormack, Jimmy Carter, Morris Udall, Henry Jackson, and Fred Harris. Besides the uncommitted slate, which automatically appeared everywhere, only Carter qualified for every town's ballot. Jackson and Udall came close, each qualifying in 162 out of 168 towns.[10] McCormack was listed in 68 towns, and Harris in 13.

[9] Jack Zaiman, "Democrats Prefer Own System," *Hartford Courant*, July 27, 1975.

[10] In one town, rural Franklin, only seven people attended candidate caucuses, and so the town chairman received the state chairman's permission to cancel the primary and appoint Franklin's lone delegate to the Second District convention (*Willimantic Chronicle*, May 11, 1976).

Preprimary jockeying revealed the embarrassing degree of disunity within the party. The state organization was headed by William O'Neill of East Hampton, who was both majority leader of the state house of representatives and, after Bailey's death, state chairman. He and the state party stalwarts backed the uncommitted slate. Governor Grasso broke with O'Neill and endorsed Jackson, as did numerous relatively conservative politicians and labor leaders. Udall was supported by leading liberals and was overwhelmingly endorsed by their Caucus of Connecticut Democrats. The governor's alienation of both the Hartford machine and the bulk of organized labor drove those power blocs away from Jackson and into the arms of Jimmy Carter, who normally had not been receiving such strong labor support that early in the campaign. Especially active in the state on Carter's behalf were officials of the United Auto Workers, the International Association of Machinists, the Connecticut Education Association, and the American Federation of State, County, and Municipal Employees. Their role was to have interesting effects at the national convention. Carter was also backed by a few noted liberals, including Joseph Duffey, former governor Chester Bowles, and Representative Toby Moffett.

Since the primaries were only the first step in the process, and because Michigan's primary would be held on the same day, the candidates spent little time in Connecticut. Jackson and Udall were both handicapped by a series of primary losses and delays in federal funding. Jackson engaged in some campaigning, perhaps to keep his flickering hopes alive and certainly to repay Governor Grasso for her support; a crushing Jackson defeat would prove even more humiliating for her than for him. Udall spent enough time in the state to hurt his campaign by announcing his opposition to a local industry, the Trident submarine program. He was not helped by his subsequent limited endorsement of the program, nor by Carter's consistent support for it.[11]

By the time of the Connecticut primary on May 11, Jimmy Carter was clearly the national front-runner, having crippled Jackson's chances in the Pennsylvania primary two weeks earlier

[11] This account of the preprimary activities is based on numerous articles in the *Hartford Courant* and UPI dispatches published in the *Willimantic Chronicle*, the *New York Times*, and the *Hartford Advocate*.

and having deprived Udall of any victories. The prospect that the Connecticut delegation would be a deciding factor in a split convention was looking less and less likely. On primary day, 106,604 Democrats voted, or fewer than 19 percent of the registered Democrats, and they gave Carter yet another close victory over "second-place Mo" Udall (see Table 10.1).[12] Organization endorsements helped in some areas, as in Hartford where Carter won more than half the vote, and in Bridgeport where Jackson won exactly half. But statewide, the two most potent party leaders, Governor Grasso and state chairman O'Neill, saw their favored slates run a poor third and fourth, respectively. The voters apparently were uninterested in supporting either a faltering candidate or a slate whose candidate preference was as yet unknown. To that extent the rules failed to give the organization what it wanted and revealed how uncontrollable even a low-turnout primary could be.

Carter carried four of Connecticut's six congressional districts, running best in the First District, the home of the Hartford machine. Udall carried the two others, with his best showing in the Fourth, where affluent suburban liberals were concentrated. Carter carried seventy-nine towns, Udall seventy-five, and they tied in one. The Carter vote was more evenly distributed across the state than that of any other major candidate, mirroring the across-the-board appeal he showed elsewhere. In Connecticut, such a showing enabled him to win more than 15 percent of the total vote in all but two towns, so that his votes were seldom taken from him and given to the uncommitted slate. As Table 10.1 shows, he was the only candidate to secure a greater proportion of the congressional district convention delegates than his proportion of the primary votes. As the organization had intended, the 15 percent rule also aided the uncommitted slate substantially.

On June 12 the congressional district conventions met, and by that time the nationwide race was virtually over. The primaries in other states had ended four days earlier; and although Carter's final primary showings were unimpressive, his delegate lead was so wide that his opposition collapsed. The day before the June 8 primaries, Carter had received the endorsement of Connecticut's

---

[12] Because the primary was run by the party, there are no official government figures for the outcome. These are from the *Hartford Courant*, May 12, 1976.

Table 10.1. Early outcomes of the Connecticut
Democratic party's nominating processes

Candidate	Percentage of votes won in the primary	Percentage of delegates won for district conventions
Jimmy Carter	33.2	34.4
Morris Udall	30.8	30.4
Henry Jackson	17.8	13.5
Uncommitted slate	12.8	21.4
Ellen McCormack	5.2	0.4
Fred Harris	0.2	0.0
Total	100.0	100.1

SOURCE: Data were obtained from the *Hartford Courant*, May 12, 1976.
NOTE: Second column total does not equal 100.0 due to rounding.

Senator Ribicoff; and once again, the late timing of Connecticut's delegate selection process reduced the state's Democrats to running to catch the bandwagon.

Each district convention was to select from eight to ten national convention delegates, depending on how many registered Democrats lived in the district and how many votes had been cast for the two most recent Democratic presidential nominees. At each convention, the delegates were polled as to their presidential preference. If any candidate received less than 15 percent of the delegates' votes, his or her supporters could switch to another candidate on a subsequent ballot. Once the balloting ceased—and it was not clear from the rules exactly when that would happen—the chairman and secretary of the district convention would determine how many national convention delegates each candidate merited. Then the supporters of each candidate would caucus and select the national convention delegates and alternates from that district.

The roll call votes available for five of the six district conventions, and newspaper accounts of the sessions, make it clear that there was plenty of jockeying at these conventions. However, it is difficult to generalize about the patterns of vote switching, except to say that uncommitted delegates tended to switch to the candidate who was strongest in their district. Perhaps this reflects their desire to jump on the winner's bandwagon. The most interesting district was the Sixth, the home of Governor

Grasso. Since her candidate, Jackson, won fewer than 15 percent of the votes there, she was in danger of failing to attend the national convention as a delegate! Such a fate would have been unheard of if the organization were still in control. To avoid this embarrassment, she persuaded some of the uncommitted delegates to switch their votes to Jackson, giving him a delegate from the district. However, at the same time, some of the uncommitted delegates switched to Udall; as a result, the uncommitted slate fell below 15 percent and lost its representation from the district at the national convention. The remaining uncommitteds then switched, and when the smoke had cleared, Jackson had two national convention delegates from a district in which he had started with none. As the fourth and fifth colums of Table 10.2 show, Jackson ended the day with four more delegates than he would have received without vote switching; and he was no longer even a candidate!

Table 10.2 also shows the number of national convention delegates that would have resulted from various types of selection procedures. Udall would seem to be least affected by the procedure used. Carter would have benefited tremendously from a winner-take-all system; but other than that, his delegate totals do not vary much from one method to another. It seems ironic that, of all the possibilities, the actual outcome (the last column) was closer than any of the others to the most democratic (the first column).

In any event, the district convention outcome was academic, for Jimmy Carter had already secured the nomination. Within a few days, all of Connecticut's uncommitted and Jackson delegates, including the governor, had swung their support to Carter. Only the sixteen Udall delegates held firm. Politically, the delegates were representative of the forces that supported their respective candidates. The Carter delegates tended to be tied either to the Hartford machine or to the labor unions. Udall delegates tended to be veterans of liberal campaigns such as the McCarthy, McGovern, and Duffey efforts and included a number of state legislators. Jackson (now Carter) delegates tended to be moderate-to-conservative officeholders like the governor. Among the uncommitted (also now Carter) delegates were the state chairman and members of the Democratic National Committee. Demographi-

Table 10.2. Numbers of Connecticut Democratic National Convention delegates who would have been won under various selection procedures

Candidate	Statewide popular vote, proportional no cutoff	Statewide popular vote, proportional 15% cutoff	Winner-take-all by cong. district	1976 system, without vote switches	As it was
Jimmy Carter	17	21	35	20	19
Morris Udall	16	19	16	17	16
Henry Jackson	9	11	0	4	8
Uncommitted slate	6	0	0	10	8
Ellen McCormack	3	0	0	0	0
Total	51	51	51	51	51

SOURCE: Data for the last column were obtained from reports in the press generally available in the state. Data for the other columns were computed by the author.

cally, these delegates were a more heterogeneous group than their Republican counterparts, but they were far from a cross section of Connecticut's population, having more men and being wealthier and more educated. Women comprised a smaller proportion of the Democratic delegates than of the Republican, perhaps reflecting the relaxation of affirmative action requirements (see Table 10.3).[13]

At the national convention, Governor Grasso was chosen to head the delegation, but real control was exercised by a coalition of Carter and Udall backers headed by the vice-chairmen of the delegation, Hartford City Councilman Nicholas Carbone (Carterite) and the majority leader of the state senate, Joseph Lieberman of New Haven (Udallite). The bloc of thirty-five delegates that supported Carter was divided between organization stalwarts and labor union leaders. In keeping with a national trend toward the increased power of constituency groups at Democratic national conventions, the labor delegates for Carter formed their own caucus and kept in close touch with their national unions.[14] They voted against the Carter position, and with the liberals, on some procedural votes on the convention floor. Clearly, their first priority was their constituency and not the candidate. (It must be noted, however, that none of those procedural votes was vital to Carter's nomination.) The Udall delegates all voted for the Arizonan on the presidential roll call, resisting appeals for unanimity, and kept in touch with their counterparts in other delegations. Several days after the convention, the delegation reconvened to select Connecticut's three members of the national committee. Again, the Carter-Udall coalition exerted its leverage, and chosen as members were the party chairman from Hartford, a United Auto Workers official, and the leader of the Caucus of Connecticut Democrats. Frozen out of the process were state

[13] Delegates' names appeared in the *Hartford Courant*, June 13, 1976. Information on delegation activities was provided by Donald DeFronzo, a Udall delegate who kept a detailed record and conveyed it in telephone interviews on July 20 and 22 and Aug. 24, 1976; and the *Willimantic Chronicle*, June 23, 1976.

[14] On this trend, see Denis G. Sullivan, Jeffrey L. Pressman, Benjamin I. Page, and John J. Lyons, *The Politics of Representation* (New York: St. Martin's Press, 1974), ch. 3.

chairman O'Neill and Governor Grasso, whose slates had fared so poorly in the primary.

What did the delegates think of the system that had chosen then? To find out, we polled them by telephone after the national convention and obtained comments from forty-eight of the fifty-one delegates in unstructured, open-ended interviews. The general direction of the reforms proposed by these delegates seemed in keeping with the old saw that the best cure for the shortcomings of democracy is more democracy; the most commonly cited specific reform, mentioned by fourteen delegates, was a direct primary to select delegates. Other frequently mentioned reforms included simplification of the rules, a regional primary, lowering the 15 percent cutoff, and having the state run the primary. All in all, twenty-four delegates suggested further democratizing reforms such as the direct primary; ten of them proposed restoring the old system or making the new system less reflective of mass preferences; and eleven delegates proposed reforms that would shift the system neither toward democratization nor away from it. Of the various blocs of delegates, only the uncommitteds stood apart from the others; they were more likely to advocate making the system less democratic, which may be because so many were professional politicians. All in all, however, if the delegates polled represent the party's elite, their views may explain why in 1977 Connecticut was to adopt a new system for 1980, one less cumbersome and more democratic.

THE REPUBLICANS

Connecticut's Republicans, not faced with pressure from their national committee to reform their delegate selection process, were free to retain the state convention system abandoned by the Democrats. Like the Democrats, the Republicans chose their delegates late—along with Utah, the last state to select them.

The Republicans' selection process began on March 23, 24, and 25, when town and city organizations met to choose most of the 1,004 delegates to the state convention.[15] Except for 72

[15] The rules are summarized in *How to Become a Delegate to the Republican National Convention,* a publication of the Republican State Central Committee.

Table 10.3. Demographic background of Connecticut national convention delegates

	Democrat	Republican
Sex		
Male	76.5%	68.6%
Female	23.5	31.4
(Number of cases)	(51)	(35)
Race		
White	90.2	97.1
Black	9.8	2.9
(Number of cases)	(51)	(35)
Family income		
Under $10,000	4.2	0.0
$10,000-$25,000	47.9	20.6
$25,000 plus	47.9	79.4
(Number of cases)	(48)	(34)
Education		
Under 12 years	2.1	0.0
12 years	14.6	11.4
Some college	18.8	8.6
College graduate	12.5	45.7
Graduate school	52.1	34.3
(Number of cases)	(48)	(35)
Age		
18-29	8.3	0.0
30-39	27.1	8.6
40-49	35.4	48.6
50-59	16.7	28.6
60-69	8.3	14.3
70-79	4.2	0.0
(Number of cases)	(58)	(35)
Mean	45.3	48.6

SOURCE: Data were provided by Michael Millican of the Associated Press. It was not possible to obtain data for all delegates in all cases.
NOTE: Percentages do not always total 100.0 due to rounding.

delegates chosen by party leaders to represent state senatorial districts, the delegates were divided among the towns according to their Republican vote in the most recent gubernatorial election. Each town was guaranteed at least 2 delegates, and could choose them by caucus, town committee, or convention, as local rules designated. All delegates could be challenged in a primary to be held on May 4, but a town's delegates would have to be opposed by an entire slate of opponents; individual delegates could not be challenged.

The state convention was to meet on July 16 and 17 in Hartford. Friday evening, July 16, would be a business meeting; on Saturday, July 17, a candidate for U.S. senator would be nominated, seventeen at-large national convention delegates would be chosen, and then delegates would reassemble into six congressional district conventions, each to select three national convention delegates.

Compare this process to that of the Democrats and notice how much more conservative it is. There is much local autonomy, a kind of federalism resulting from the minimum of two state convention delegates per town, and, above all, no presidential preference primary. The party leadership also benefits from the requirement that primary challenges require a full slate of opponents. For example, if a resident of Hartford wanted to challenge one delegate, he or she would have to find fifteen others with whom to form a slate, and that entire slate would have to defeat the organization slate.

Using a mail questionnaire and subsequent telephone calls to nonrespondents, we asked Republican town chairpersons exactly what process had been used to select state convention delegates. Of our 162 total respondents, 86 reported that the caucus had been used, 63 had used the town committee, 4 had used a convention, and 9 had used miscellaneous methods. Further questions to the chairpersons about the candidate preferences of both the participants at those meetings and the state convention delegates (acknowledging that the perceptions of the chairpersons are not always reliable) elicited overwhelming majorities for Gerald Ford among those with a specific preference. Above all, these chairpersons reported that the process had been consensual, with few clashes and no challenge primaries. If these reports are accurate, the domination of the state convention by the Ford forces may simply have reflected the proclivities of the grassroots party leadership as well as the masses.

The preference for Ford is easily explained in a state that is in the party's liberal, northeastern wing and most of whose voters would presumably find Ronald Reagan anathema. For most of the campaign, state chairman Frederick Biebel maintained public neutrality, even resisting an effort by the New York state chairman to get all state chairmen in the Northeast to endorse Ford. But on June 29, Biebel gave Ford that endorsement; and by that time the Ford chairman in Connecticut, party budget chairman Joseph Burns, was predicting a unanimous delegation: "If at the present moment, Mr. Ford was 300 or 400 delegates ahead, it would be a different story. But I don't think the state party can be magnanimous about it. I think the situation indicates we must have 35 firm Ford votes; Connecticut's votes could be the ones that give the nomination to Ford."[16] This was apparently the rationale for the events that followed.

There was a fledgling Reagan movement, but it lacked well-known leaders. Some of the older conservative leaders declined involvement for personal or political reasons, and Reagan's coordinator was a young lawyer and former congressional candidate, James Altham of Hamden. Altham characterized the Reagan campaign as a rightwing populist effort to draw blue-collar workers and Roman Catholics into the party around social issues. A survey commissioned by the state central committee and conducted by Cambridge Opinion Studies did include some Ford-Reagan demographic comparisons. That survey is not ideal for our purposes, since it included Democrats and independents as well as Republicans and compared those who favored Ford over Carter with those with those who favored Reagan over Carter. Consequently, some respondents fell into both categories. Nevertheless, it appears that Reagan backers were indeed more blue-collar, less educated, and

[16] UPI dispatch published in the *Willimantic Chronicle*, June 17, 1976. On preconvention activities, see also ibid., May 24 and 25 and June 29, 1976. According to one scholar, it was indeed Connecticut's votes that made it rational for uncommitted delegates to join the Ford camp; see Philip D. Straffin, Jr., "The Bandwagon Curve," 31 *American Journal of Political Science* 702 (November 1977).

more Roman Catholic than Ford supporters, suggesting some support for the Reagan leader's perceptions.[17]

By the time the convention met, the state leaders had opted for an all-Ford delegation. In effect, they preferred the internal goal of factional victory to that of balance (although the Reaganites did not represent an ongoing faction). The leaders apparently regarded the Reagan forces as too few in number to require representation, and they did not take seriously the argument that the Reagan supporters were party workhorses who would sit on their hands in the fall if kept off the delegation. As for external goals, a unanimous delegation would clearly be unified, and perhaps flexible if Ford faltered. Likewise, timing was in Connecticut's favor, as the race went down to the wire and the state was able to give Ford thirty-five delegates. But the most important criterion was the clear-cut preference for Ford over Reagan in the state.

In light of that, the state convention was run with a heavy hand by leaders who wished to leave nothing to chance.[18] So confident were the state leaders of victory that they invited Ford to address the convention and staged a private meeting between the president and the national delegates-to-be before they were formally chosen. On Friday evening, there was an acrimonious debate over the rules. The leaders wanted all national convention delegates to be chosen by slate; the Reaganites, hoping to win some delegates here and there, wanted each congressional district caucus to decide whether it would choose the delegates by slate or individually. Representative Stewart McKinney, the permanent chairman of the convention, angered the Reagan forces by citing obscure procedural rules from the manual of the state house of representative to defeat their mo-

[17] Telephone interview with James Altham, July 26, 1976; see also Kevin P. Phillips, *The Emerging Republican Majority* (New Rochelle, N.Y.: Arlington House, 1969). Survey data were generously provided by Donald Schmidt, deputy chairman of the state central committee. An Associated Press survey of all Republican delegates found Ford delegates to be more educated and wealthier than Reagan delegates; see the *New York Times*, Aug. 8, 1976.

[18] This account of the state convention events was based on personal observation and that of research assistants, as well as accounts in the *Hartford Courant* and *Hartford Times* on July 17 and 18, 1976. Accounts of how the Ford slate was assembled came from telephone interviews with the state chairman and the six congressional district convention chairpersons in July 1976, shortly after the national convention.

tion that a presidential preference poll be conducted among the state convention delegates, and that the at-large delegates be divided between Ford and Reagan proportionally—roughly the same procedure the Democrats had used. That motion was killed when a voice vote shouted it down, and McKinney ruled on another voice vote that the requisite 20 percent of the delegates had not voted to take a roll call vote on the motion.

Saturday morning saw the nomination for U.S. senator, in which the incumbent, Lowell Weicker, handily defeated a state senator, George Gunther of Stratford. In some respects the Weicker-Gunther race may have paralleled the Ford-Reagan contest. Since Weicker was regarded as more liberal than a Republican should be, and less loyal to his party, he faced a great deal of resentment from conservative Republicans. His role in the Watergate hearings and his public criticism of the campaign tactics of the 1974 Republican gubernatorial candidate only fed the anti-Weicker flames. After the vote, Weicker made a brief acceptance speech, followed by an address by Gerald Ford. The president spoke forcefully, in a manner to be duplicated later in his Kansas City acceptance speech, and he was enthusiastically received.

After lunch, the convention reconvened in a slightly more mellow mood. McKinney apologized to anyone who thought he had been unfair the night before, and a Reagan spokesman then announced that the Californian's supporters would offer no opposition to the at-large Ford slate. This was done in the hope that party leaders would respond to the gesture by allowing Reagan some delegates from the congressional districts. The Ford at-large slate was then approved by voice vote.

The delegates then divided into the six congressional district conventions. In all but the Fifth District, where the Reaganites failed to produce a slate, a Ford slate was opposed by a Reagan slate, and in all of them the Ford slate won overwhelmingly. The closest vote was in the Fourth, where the vote was ninety-eight to thirty. As a result, Gerald Ford won all thirty-five of Connecticut's national convention delegates.

At this point one might ask to what degree this unanimous Ford slate was unrepresentative of party sentiment. What was the Reagan strength in the Connecticut party? To answer this question, six estimates were used: (1) the Cambridge Opinion Studies survey for the state central committee, which asked 1,200 Republicans in late June and early July which candidate would be stronger (at best an indirect measure of personal preference); (2) the town chairpersons' estimates of the preferences of participants in state convention delegate selection meetings (subject to chairpersons' misperceptions); (3) the same chairpersons' estimates of the preferences of state convention delegates (again subject to misperceptions); (4) a nonrandom but systematic aisle poll of the delegates at the state convention taken by this author and an assistant (subject to the possible reluctance of some delegates to state to a stranger a preference so much at odds with that of the state leadership); (5) the Weicker-Gunther vote (which may or may not have correlated with Ford-Reagan preferences); and (6) the votes in the congressional district conventions. This last measure may be the most direct test of state delegate sentiment, but it is hampered by the fact that complete votes were taken in only three districts. In the First District, a voice vote was taken, and this author, who was in attendance, estimated the result; in the Fifth, as noted, the Reaganites did not offer a slate; and in the Sixth, the voting was terminated before the end of the roll, and the district chairman estimated that the Ford slate was getting 85 percent of the vote. It is unfortunate for our purposes that the Reagan forces offered no slate in the Fifth District, for that is known as a relatively conservative district. Our statewide estimate of the district convention vote was based on an aggregate of the other five districts. The results of these estimates are presented in Table 10.4, and they show a general consensus when uncommitteds are excluded. These figures also suggest that, if the state central committee's poll conducted by Cambridge Opinion Studies was accurate, the Reaganites were slightly underrepresented at the state convention. If the Republicans had been using a system involving a primary with proportional representation and a 15 percent cutoff, the Reagan supporters might well have barely made the cutoff and won six delegates.

How were the Ford slates chosen? At large and in the congressional districts, party leaders publicized the openings and solicited requests from any interested persons. Among the criteria for delegates, according to the leaders, were support for Ford, party service, geographic balance, and the inclusion of women. The

Table 10.4. Various estimates of Ford and Reagan strength in Connecticut

Estimate	With uncommitted			Without uncommitted	
	Ford	Reagan	Uncom.	Ford	Reagan
1. Cambridge Opinion Studies survey of Republican voters	75%	15%	10%	83%	17%
2. Town chairpersons' estimates of local party activists	80	12	8	87	13
3. Town chairpersons' estimates of state convention delegates	40	4	56	90	10
4. Aisle poll of state convention delegates	85	12	4	88	12
5. Vote for U.S. senator at state convention	87	13		87	13
6. Vote for national convention delegates in congressional district conventions	87	13		87	13

SOURCE: See text.
NOTE: Percentages do not always total 100 due to rounding.

resulting delegation was a veritable Who's Who of Connecticut Republicanism. The at-large slate included, among others, the state chairman and vice-chairwoman, both National Committee members, all three Republican members of Congress, both minority leaders of the state legislature, and the women's federation president. District delegations were top-heavy with town chairpersons, state central committee members, and local public office holders. Table 10.3 demonstrates how demographically homogeneous the delegation was. The typical Republican delegate was white (all but one), had an income of over $25,000 a year (all but seven or eight), held a college degree (all but seven), and was between forty and fifty-nine years old (all but eight). This may reflect the party's base, and also the emphasis on including party notables in the delegation. As noted above, the Republicans were more successful than the Democrats at including women. This may give some credence to the claim of professional politicians that the way to affirmative action is through centralized leadership. Such leadership is also the way to ensure that party notables are included; recall the Democrats' problems in including even the governor on their delegation.

The delegates chose Senator Weicker and state chairman Biebel as cochairmen of the delegation.[19] Weicker soon announced that he would not be going to Kansas City, preferring instead to campaign for reelection. There was speculation in the press that he was disappointed not to have been chosen sole chairman. In Kansas City, the delegation functioned as a well-oiled cog in the Ford machine. Connecticut was one of nine delegations to vote unanimously not to require Ford to name his vice-president before the presidential roll call vote, and again one of nine to vote unanimously for Ford for the nomination. Delegate Joan Rader of Greenwich was one of the leaders of an effort to remove the antiabortion plank from the platform, a move opposed by some of Connecticut's delegates lest it endanger the Ford nomination. That proposal never came to a vote on the floor. One delegate, William Menna of Ansonia, temporarily abstained on the vice-presidential ballot as a protest to the way in which Biebel had been running the delegation. Otherwise, the delegation unanimously supported Robert Dole on that vote.

On the Republican side, then, Connecticut played a more pivotal role in 1976 than a small state usually does. By selecting its delegates late in the game and by bringing in a unanimous delegation, the state maximized its impact; Biebel was one of those asked to advise Ford on his choice of a running mate. In a larger sense, however, Connecticut and other comparatively liberal states came away from Kansas City with little other than their preferred nominee. Both the platform and the choice of Dole for vice-president were responses to conservative pressure, and the failure of the party's liberal wing to extract more of a price from Ford for their loyalty is one of the most interesting aspects of Republican politics in 1976.

[19] Information on delegation activities was obtained from telephone interviews with delegates Frederick Biebel, Lilliam Ludlam, William Menna, and Joan Rader, and alternate Jeffrey Ossen, Aug. 23 through 25, 1976; UPI dispatches printed in the *Willimantic Chronicle*, Aug. 10 through 20, 1976; *New York Times*, Aug. 20, 1976; and *Hartford Courant*, Aug. 20, 1976. For a list of delegates, see the *Hartford Courant*, July 17, 1976.

POSTSCRIPT: NOVEMBER 1976 AND BEYOND

November 2, 1976, was a day of comeback for Connecticut's Republicans. Gerald Ford won 719,261 votes to Jimmy Carter's 647,895, and for the first time in twenty years, the Republican standard-bearer ran better in Connecticut than in the rest of the nation. Factors commonly cited for Ford's capture of the state's eight electoral votes were Democratic divisions, Governor Grasso's unpopularity, Roman Catholic discontent with Jimmy Carter, and the landslide reelection of Senator Weicker. Although the congressional delegation retained its four-to-two Democratic majority, the Republican victory in the presidential race may have helped the party to make gains in both houses of the state legislature. In each house they raised their share to more than one-third of the seats but failed to win control.

On December 6 Connecticut's closed primary statue was upheld by the U.S. Supreme Court, which affirmed a three-judge federal court's ruling without hearing arguments on the matter and without issuing an opinion. Two independent voters, one of them the father of consumer activist Ralph Nader, had challenged the provision that someone had to be registered as either a Democrat or Republican to vote in that party's primary. The lower court had held that there was a valid state interest in preventing distortion of primary contests.

On June 3, 1977, the state legislature, with bipartisan support, established a new presidential primary system for both of Connecticut's parties. Presidential candidates identified as such by the secretary of the state or qualifying by petition would appear on every town's ballot, the uncommitted slate would appear last, and there would be no 15 percent cutoff. Each candidate would receive a number of delegates according to his or her proportion of the popular vote, and the individual delegates would be designated at candidate caucuses two weeks before the primary. Delegates would pledge to support their candidates, if still active, on two national convention ballots; broken pledges would be punished by loss of party registration for four years. These delegates would be chosen at large or by congressional district according to national party rules. The primary would be held on the Tuesday after the first Monday in March, raising the possiblility of a regional primary with Massachusetts and Vermont. The process begun by Connecticut's Democrats in 1975 appears to have resulted in a full-fledged presidential preference primary, complete with proportional representation, for both parties in the state.[20]

EVALUATING THE SYSTEMS

Did the Democrats make a mistake in changing from the old system to the new? The answer, of course, depends on the values one brings to the comparison. An exponent of the traditional system of professional politics, adhering to the goals outlined at the beginning of this chapter, might make the following argument:

The Democrats made a big mistake in abandoning the state convention. The process of producing a new system proved divisive and left nobody very happy. Even the delegates whom the system eventually sent to Madison Square Garden are dissatisfied with it. By adopting the system, Connecticut sacrificed any chance of playing a major role in choosing the Democratic presidential nominee. The delegation sent to New York City was divided into at least four blocs, and the fact that most of the delegates were committed to candidates before the primary reduced their flexibility. Those sixteen Udall delegates, for example, held out for their candidate and kept Connecticut from uniting behind Carter. The state's timing was off, for its Democrats were not with Carter all the way, nor did they give him help at a decisive moment. And finally, the delegation could not make a united choice regarding which candidate would be best for Connecticut in the fall. In fact, Carter did rather poorly (for a Democrat) in November, and perhaps some of that can be attributed to divisions in the party which the selection process only exacerbated.

Even by the reformers' own standards, the system failed. Fewer than 19 percent voted in the primary; so much for participatory democracy. The delegation included only four young people, and fewer women than the Republicans had; so much for affirmative action. And it was only after some bizarre vote switching at con-

---

[20] All 1976 election data in this chapter were obtained from the *Statement of Vote*, published by the state as Public Document No. 26. On the lawsuit, see the *New York Times*, Dec. 7, 1976. On the new primary law, sources were Public Act No. 77-535 and articles in the *Hartford Courant* and *New York Times*, June 4, 1977.

gressional district conventions that the political makeup of the delegation approximated the primary returns; so much for proportional representation, the raison d'être of the system!

Our professional politician might have contrasted this situation with that of the Republicans:

The GOP leaders were able to run a party the way it should be run. They chose their best—or least worst—candidate, they united behind him, and they were able to give him a boost when it really counted. And despite the threats of the Reagan minority, they carried their ticket to victory in November.

In response, a party reformer might make an argument similar to the following:

The only serious problem with the Democrats' new system was that it did not go far enough. If the system were not so new and complicated, more voters would have cast their ballots in the primary; and had the district conventions been eliminated, the problem of vote switching would never have arisen. While affirmative action is not as easily achieved under this system as others, the party's record is not so bad: there was a greater proportion of black delegates than there are blacks in the state at large, and there was a decent economic and age mix. In the future, candidates can make a greater effort to include women and young people.

Why did Connecticut fail to carry more weight with Carter? Bad luck. The late timing of the process hurt, but only because Carter was so strong from the beginning; the late timing of the Republican state convention helped, but only because Ford failed to secure *his* nomination early. It was the timing of the process, and not its mechanics, that made the Democrats look worse than the Republicans. And Ford won the state in November for many reasons, of which the delegate selection processes were probably rather tangential. After all, the delegate selection system did not create the Democrats' divisions.

At any rate, the above considerations are less important than the rationale for the new system, which is equity for all elements of the party. Who can doubt that the Democratic delegates were a fairer representation of their party's sentiment than the Republican delegates? What the GOP may have gained in efficiency, they lost by forming a socioeconomically overprivileged delegation that offers little encouragement to newcomers to try to become delegates; and the disaffection of the Reaganites is another problem.

Different values are served by each system, and it ultimately becomes a question of priorities. One inescapable conclusion is that our reformer is right about one point: the greater influence of the Republicans at their national conveniton can be attributed to their luck in timing. They faced a down-to-the-wire battle between Ford and Reagan, and their system contributed nothing to the fortunate timing.

Ultimately, however, one's preference ought to depend upon one's concept of democratic government and the capabilities of the electorate.[21] One such concept suggests that the electorate is quite limited in its ability to decide among candidates on the basis of important questions of public policy. As a consequence, the party system is under no obligation under this concept to present a "real choice" to the voters, and the requirements of an election are met by nothing more than having politicians nominate candidates who they believe are most likely to win. The public will then have a choice among credible candidates, and the winner will not be bound by numerous campaign pledges that will limit his or her discretion. Under this concept, party politicians are not only expected to try to win, but they absolutely must try to do so, lest they nominate unlikely candidates (a Goldwater or a McGovern) who deprive the voters of a choice by driving them into the arms of their more credible opponents (a Johnson or a Nixon).

An alternative concept of democracy begins with greater faith in the electorate's ability to cope with great issues of public policy. Such a public will be frustrated if it is always confronted with a "meaningless choice" of candidates, such as Ford and Carter, who represent the same moderate patch of ground. A nation of responsible voters will want a greater choice among candidates and, more

[21] For articulate expositions of what is referred to as the first concept of democracy, see Joseph A. Schumpeter, *Capitalism, Socialism, and Democracy*, 2d ed. (New York and London: Harper & Bros., 1947), ch. 22-23; Edward C. Banfield, "In Defense of the American Party System," in Robert A. Goldwin, ed., *Political Parties, U.S.A.* (Chicago: Rand McNally & Co., 1961); and James Q. Wilson, *The Amateur Democrat* (Chicago: University of Chicago Press, 1962), ch. 12. For equally well-stated versions of the second concept, see E.E. Schattschneider, *Party Government* (New York: Rinehart & Co., 1942); "Toward a More Responsible Two-Party System," supplement to 44 *American Political Science Review* (1950); and David S. Broder, *The Party's Over* (New York: Harper & Row, 1972).

importantly, among platforms. It is thus incumbent upon politicians to nominate the most credible candidates that represent the party philosophy.

The implications of these conflicting concepts for party reform become clear. The first concept, having little faith in the policy-making function of the electorate, does not require that voters play a major role in the nominating process; nor does it put any limits, except ethical and legal ones, on practical politicians' pursuit of self-interest. The system used by Connecticut's Republicans in the 1976 fits into the first concept.

The second concept, having great faith in the policymaking role of the electorate, justifies a great deal of participation by party masses in the nominating process and looks with favor upon the role of issues in that process as well. If the system used in 1976 by Connecticut's Democrats were further democratized by removing the congressional district conventions, it would fulfill the requirement of citizen participation and give issue-oriented groups and candidates an even greater possibility of influence. Under 1976 rules, the more conservative Republican candidate, Reagan, received no national convention delegates from Connecticut, while the most liberal Democrat, Udall, garnered nearly one-third.

Compared to the American people as a whole, the citizens of Connecticut rank high in wealth and education, and their level of voting participation is consequently also quite high. In 1976, for example, 84 percent of the state's registered voters went to the polls in the general election. It may be that Connecticut's electorate, by virtue of this high interest, may be especially equipped to fulfill the expectations of the second concept of democracy. But the reader should judge which of the two models makes more sense for the parties, the voters, and ultimately the future of public policy in America.

CHAPTER 11 / Texas
A Primary State

RICHARD MURRAY University of Houston

THE May 1 Texas presidential primary was one of the four or five most important contests that occurred during the 1976 campaign. On the Democratic side, Jimmy Carter emerged from the Texas primary and subsequent state convention with the largest bloc of committed delegates he would win outright in any state. Coming right after his breakthrough victory in the Pennsylvania primary just four days earlier, Carter's Texas success went a long way toward providing him with a delegate base sufficient to ride out a string of defeats in the final month of the primary season.

But if Texas was important for the Democrats, it was a critical battleground for the Republicans. Ronald Reagan's campaign had limped into the state, the former California governor having lost five of six previous match ups with President Ford, including two that he was expected to win. Reagan was running out of money, the press and electronic media were speculating on how long he could keep his campaign afloat, and the morale of his staff was sagging. President Ford was confident that the momentum of the campaign remained with him, despite a close loss to Reagan in North Carolina. With the strong support of U.S. Senator John Tower (the leader of the Texas Republican establishment) and with ample funds in hand, Gerald Ford seemed to have a great opportunity to dispose finally of the most serious intraparty challenge an incumbent president had faced since 1912. Ford chose to make an all-out effort. The president personally campaigned in Texas for five days, thus spending more time there than in any other primary state in the nation; and his organization spent nearly a tenth of its prenomination funds in the state. However, the president's best efforts were for naught. Ronald Reagan won a smashing victory in Texas, and his revived campaign contested Gerald Ford from that point forward to the convention on virtually an equal footing. The GOP had lost its last chance to avoid a bruising intraparty battle that would ultimately go down to the last vote at the convention.

Before examining the context and consequences of the delegate selection process in Texas, one point is in order. Despite the critical timing and large number of delegates at stake, the Texas primary attracted only modest national attention. Three factors account for this. First, the primary was new to Texas, the state having previously used the caucus-convention system to select national party delegates. This meant that the primary had no "traditional" significance of the sort that veteran political observers seem to appreciate. Second, prior assessments of the likely outcome of the primary tended to minimize the election's significance. It was widely reported, for example, that Reagan and Ford would probably each win a number of delegates and that the Californian's inevitable withdrawal from the presidential quest would be postponed a bit. Third, but not least in importance, the Texas polls closed at 7:00 p.m. on a Saturday, a time and day when the television networks are not eager to provide political coverage. So while Tuesday primaries in smaller states like North Carolina, Indiana, and Michigan were covered in detail by television news, Texas was conveniently omitted from the networks' coverage schedule.

THE CONTEXT OF DELEGATE SELECTION

Before 1976 Texas selected delegates to the national party conventions by a caucus-convention system. A three-tiered system was utilized in which voters in the respective party primaries, held the first Saturday in May, were eligible to attend mass meetings at the precinct level on the day or evening of the election. Attendance at these precinct conventions was usually less than 10 percent of the primary voters. These local meetings in some 5,000 precincts considered various resolutions and selected delegates to county conventions (or state senate district conventions in populous counties), which were held the second Saturday in May. Precincts sent delegates to these meetings on the basis of 1 per 25 votes cast for the party's nominee for governor in the last general election. The county-senatorial district meetings in turn selected delegates (on a 1 per 300 votes for governor basis) to the state conventions held in June of presidential years. The state conventions then designated the Texas delegates to the national party gatherings.

Historically, Texas delegations to both party conventions were homogeneous in their makeup. In the case of the Republicans, such homogenity reflected the fact that only a tiny fraction (3 to 5 percent) of the Texas electorate voted in the GOP primary or took part in party affairs. This small group was made up almost entirely of conservative, middle-class Anglos. (In Texas usage, an Anglo is almost any person who is neither black nor Mexican American.) Except for the well-known case in 1952 when a surge of Eisenhower supporters flooded the Republican precinct meetings and overwhelmed the establishment party elements that favored Taft,[1] little controversy or conflict has been present either in the Republican delegate selection process or within the delegations at the national conventions.

The Texas Democratic party, on the other hand, has long been an umbrella association that covers a number of groups in conflict with each other. Over the last thirty years, much of this conflict has been expressed through a rather well-defined liberal-conservative split within the state party, with the conservatives maintaining effective control of the party mechanisms. In view of this factionalism, the homogeneity traditional to Texas's Democratic delegations was achieved primarily by imposing the unit rule at the various levels of delegate selection. The usual result of this practice was that liberals were systematically eliminated by the conservatives and resorted to "walking out" and holding rump meetings to protest their exclusion from meaningful participation in the presidential process.

In light of this pattern, the Democratic party's elimination of the unit rule for voting at the Chicago national convention in 1968 and the subsequent prohibition of its use at lower party levels in 1972 were of great consequence to the conservative Democratic establishment in Texas. The additional requirements that groups consistuting as much as 15 percent of the participants in party

---

[1] The dispute was resolved in a crucial floor fight at the convention. The Eisenhower forces won the fight, seated their delegation, and went on to victory.

meetings must be proportionally represented and that categoric groups like women, blacks, and Mexican Americans must also be fairly represented in the delegate selection process further undermined the conservative faction's control of the presidential nomination process in Texas.

The collapse of conservative control was dramatically evident in 1972. The Texas delegation selected under the new party rules was one of the most heterogeneous at the Miami Beach national convention. Liberals committed to McGovern constituted about a third of the group; a hodgepodge of conservatives and moderates led by Democratic gubernatorial nominee Dolph Briscoe made up another third; the remainder consisted of ardent Wallace supporters. The great hostilities within the delegation surfaced on virtually every roll call. On many votes the nominal delegation leader, Briscoe, was unable to announce the Texas tally in turn and had to pass several times before an agreed-upon count could be given.

The Miami Beach experience left the caucus-convention system in bad favor among establishment Texas Democrats. Dolph Briscoe, whose leadership difficulties at the convention helped his Republican opponent mount the strongest challenge to a Democratic gubernatorial candidate in a century, was understandably willing to try alternative procedures for 1976. The conditions for change were also enhanced by a national movement from the caucus-convention to the primary system of selection. The specific catalyst for switching to a primary, however, was the emergence of Texas's Democratic senator, Lloyd Bentsen, as a serious presidential aspirant. Bentsen knew that if his bid for the Democratic nomination was to have any chance of success, he had to have a secure base of support in Texas. The senator also knew that, given the continuing divisions within the Texas Democratic party, he would have great difficulty securing this base if delegates were chosen under the 1972 procedures. Accordingly, Bentsen began building political support in the state for a primary system of selecting national party delegates. When the Texas legislature met in January 1975, Bentsen's staff had a primary bill introduced. This bill, with modest changes, was enacted into law in May 1975, just before the legislature adjourned for the biennium.

As might be expected, the Texas primary law represented a finely honed effort to advance Lloyd Bentsen's presidential ambitions within the guidelines set forth by the national Democratic party. The law took advantage of the "loophole primary" feature that the national party had allowed in 1972 and 1976. This loophole permitted slates of candidates to run in "winner-take-all" primaries if the electoral units were no larger than congressional districts. This type of primary had enabled George Wallace to capture over 90 percent of the Florida delegation to the Democratic convention in 1972 with only about 44 percent of the statewide primary vote. Bentsen hoped to benefit similarly in his home state in 1976.

The Texas primary law gave the major parties discretion in deciding whether they wanted to hold primaries at the congressional district level or at the state senate district level. In either case, at least three-fourths of the delegates had to be elected in the primaries, with the remainder chosen via the traditional convention system. Alternates were also to be chosen by the June party conventions.

The Republican party decided to use congressional districts, of which there are twenty-four in the state, and assigned four national party delegates to be elected from each. Since the state was apportioned only 100 Republican delegates, this meant that 96 percent would be elected in the party primary. The Democrats opted for the thirty-one state senate districts as election units. They assigned three delegates to be elected in each of twenty-six districts, giving the five other districts a bonus fourth delegate each because of strong support for the party's presidential nominee in 1972. This meant that, out of a total of 130 delegates allocated to the state, 98 would be directly elected in the primary. With 32 delegates remaining to be picked at the June Democratic convention, this second phase was still of moderate importance for the Democrats.

Candidate access to the Texas ballot was made difficult. This reflected Senator Bentsen's desire to keep most other Democratic contenders out of the state so he could have a head-on contest with George Wallace, a match he felt sure he could win. Presidential candidates or groups wishing to sponsor uncommitted slates had to file with the secretary of state an application and petition containing signatures of registered voters equal in number to at least 1 percent of the votes cast for the relevant party's candidate for governor in the last general election. Filings had to be made for each district in which the candidate or group was to be placed on the ballot. All materials had to be sent to the secretary of state by February 2, 1976, a full three months before primary election day and far in advance of most other states' cutoff dates. Control of the slates filed in each district was given to the presidential candidate, who would designate a delegate selection committee in each district. Delegates elected on a candidate's slate were bound to that person for three ballots at the national convention unless the candidate withdrew, released the delegates, or received less than 20 percent of the total vote on the second ballot.

Texas does not have registration by party; therefore, the only requirement for voting in either party's primary was to register at least thirty-one days before May 1, 1976. Votes would be cast for individual delegates, whose names would appear on the ballot. However, delegate candidates organized as a slate would be grouped together and their affiliation clearly designated.

One important change was made in the "Bentsen Bill" as it worked its way through the Texas legislature in the spring of 1975. As if to emphasize the narrow and special purpose of this particular bill, lawmakers added a "self-destruct" clause which eliminated the primary law in 1977. Thereafter, Texas would revert back to the caucus-convention system of selecting presidential delegates unless a future legislature otherwise directed.

THE DEMOCRATIC DELEGATION

Despite the careful calibrations of the Bentsen forces, things began to go awry for the senator as soon as the primary bill became operative. For one thing, competition was greater than Bentsen had anticipated. He and George Wallace qualified slates in all districts, as expected; but former Georgia governor Jimmy Carter, who began to emerge in late 1975 as Bentsen's major rival for moderate southern support, also got slates on the ballot in all thirty-one districts. Liberal elements in the state, with the assistance of Bentsen's old enemy Ralph Yarborough,[2] qualified uncommitted slates

[2] Yarborough, a thirteen-year veteran of the U.S. Senate, was defeated by Bentsen for renomination in the 1970 Democratic primary. Bentsen ran a very hard-hitting campaign against the incumbent, and the bitterness between the two men has not faded.

in eighteen districts. Fred Harris got on the ballot in fourteen districts, Sargent Shriver in five, and antiabortion candidate Ellen McCormack qualified in another five districts.

The Primary

The Bentsen camp began organizing its delegate slates months before the required filing date. Advisory committees were constituted in the districts, and efforts were made to recruit prominent individuals as candidates for the delegate positions. A conscious effort also was made to balance slates along sexual and racial lines. One woman was typically slated in three-person districts, for example, while two were sought in four-person areas. Additionally, minority candidates were fielded in districts with sizable black and Mexican American populations. Table 11.1 summarizes the sexual and ethnic composition of the five major contending groups in the primarly. This table shows that, although Bentsen failed to slate women in proportion to their numbers in the state, he did provide a close ethnic balance in his ninety-eight delegate candidates. The senator also slated a half dozen labor leaders in blue-collar districts, along with a number of local officeholders.

George Wallace, in composing his delegate slates, drew on a strong state organizational base he had retained from his campaigns in 1968 and 1972. The Wallace organization made some effort to have females on its slates, but all ninety-eight of the Wallace candidates were Anglos. Unlike the Bentsen and Wallace organizations, which started with strong bases in Texas, the Carter campaign assembled its slates in haste, using whoever was available and willing or could be persuaded to run as a delegate. In Houston, for example, four of the fourteen Carter candidates came from a small firefighters' union that had assisted in the petition drive to qualify the Carter slates. Table 11.1 shows that Carter's slates were comparable to Bentsen's in sexual and racial makeup. The ninety-eight candidates included thirty-eight women and twenty blacks or Mexican Americans. As one might expect, the partial slates supported by Texas liberals (the Harris and uncommitted delegates) included higher proportions of both women and minorities.

While the crowded primary field in Texas was worrisome to the Bentsen forces, their problems in other states also became paramount early in 1976. The senator had hoped that early successes in the caucus states of Mississippi and Oklahoma would establish him as a serious contender for the nomination. Instead, Bentsen drew virtually no support in the Mississippi meetings and was badly beaten by Carter in Oklahoma. After some reflection, Bentsen withdrew from the national campaign. The Texan continued his state presidential effort, however, since it was thought that a late withdrawal might damage his prospects for reelection to the Senate in November 1976.[3]

By April, the Wallace effort was not faring much better. George Wallace's defeats by Jimmy Carter in the Florida and North Carolina primaries made it obvious, weeks before the Texas election was held, that his presidential effort was not going to succeed. Similarly, the candidacies of Fred Harris and Sargent Shriver had not taken hold as their Texas backers might have hoped, and Ellen McCormack's "right to life" effort was demonstrating little strength in the state. Therefore, Jimmy Carter remained as the only viable presidential prospect in the state Democratic field.

Carter, however, was not in a position to exploit this opportunity. The Pennsylvania primary was the Tuesday before the Texas election on Saturday, and Carter needed a clear cut victory in a large northern industrial state more than he needed another triumph, albeit a vote-rich one, in another southern state. Accordingly, most of the money raised within Texas by the Carter campaign was sent to Pennsylvania, where Carter faced Senator Henry Jackson and Congressman Morris Udall, the last important survivors of Carter's dozen or so original opponents in the nomination struggle. The national Carter organization felt that if Carter did well in Pennsylvania, he would reap a large share of the Texas delegates due to the absence of strong competition in the state. Of course, Carter's solid victory over Udall and Jackson in Pennsylvania on April 27 put him in a position to do just that.

Turnout in the Texas Democratic primary was moderate, with about 1.4 million voting. This number was far below the more than 2 million participants in the 1972 Democratic primary when a spirited governor's contest had drawn voters to the polls. Never-

---

[3] Bentsen was the second person to take advantage of the "Johnson Law" which was passed by the Texas legislature allowing Lyndon Johnson to run for the presidency or vice-presidency and his U.S. Senate seat at the same time.

Table 11.1. Sexual and ethnic composition of delegate candidate slates in 1976 Texas Democratic primary

Category	Approximate percentage of Texas electorate	Slate affiliation				
		Bentsen	Carter	Wallace	Uncommitted	Harris
Men	49	62	60	67	34	25
Women	51	36	38	31	23	20
Anglos	76	76	78	98	42	33
Blacks	12	11	9	0	11	8
Mex. Americans	12	11	11	0	4	4
Total candidates	—	98	98	98	57	45

SOURCE: Prepared from newspaper accounts as corrected by Democratic party sources.

theless, the Democratic vote was more than three times that of the Republicans' record vote. Carter, as one might have expected, won a strong victory. What was not expected was his almost complete sweep of the delegates at stake. Carter's slates took about 49 percent of the vote cast for presidential delegates, but he won ninety-two of ninety-eight delegates. Senator Bentsen got about 21 percent of the vote and won six delegates. Wallace ran third with 18 percent of the vote. Most of the remaining 12 percent was taken by the uncommitted slates. Table 11.2 presents the mean vote figures for the major delegate slates in the thirty-one senate districts. The figures in parentheses indicate the number of delegates won by each candidate in the various districts.

Carter's uniform strength throughout the state (his slates led in thirty of the thirty-one districts) enabled him to take virtually all the delegates. Minority candidates on Bentsen slates (one black and two Mexican Americans) edged out individual Carter candidates in three districts, and the senator carried the heavily Mexican American Twenty-Seventh District in South Texas. Bentsen ran second to Carter in most areas, although George Wallace was second in a number of East Texas districts and the uncommitted slate was strong in the Austin area. The data in Table 11.2 show that the "Bentsen Bill" worked in that it gave a great bonus to the candidate with good support in all regions of the state. Of course, the beneficiary of this in the Democratic primary turned out to be a man who had been virtually unknown in Texas when the law was fashioned.

The Precinct and Convention Meetings

As mentioned earlier, the Texas primary law retained the old caucus-convention process, but only to select delegates not designated in the May election and alternates to the national conventions. Since all but 4 of the 100 Republican delegates were elected on May 1, there was but modest interest in the GOP proceedings. The Democratic meetings, on the other hand, retained some significance since 32 national delegates remained to be chosen.

Democratic precinct, county, district, and state conventions have traditionally provided the stages on which bitter intraparty

Table 11.2. Democratic delegate voting in the May 1 Texas primary

Senate district	Bentsen	Carter	Wallace	Uncom.	Harris	Shriver	McCormack
			Mean vote for delegate slates				
1	14,052	37,712(3)[a]	16,669	—	—	—	—
2	6,764	27,071(3)	12,853	6,604	—	—	—
3	14,211	35,817(3)	21,796	—	—	—	—
4	8,015	20,732(3)	9,482	5,189	3,835	—	—
5	14,133	36,963(3)	18,076	—	—	—	—
6	6,380(1)	7,538(2)	3,260	5,183	498	—	—
7	5,851	12,248(4)	3,646	5,463	990	—	1,056
8	3,008	10,396(3)	2,846	2,884	1,337	—	—
9	4,032	19,166(3)	8,216	4,181	—	—	—
10	4,038	15,091(3)	2,861	2,870	1,048	—	—
11	5,047	8,536(4)	1,893	4,286	1,260	—	782
12	4,491	16,269(3)	3,277	4,072	—	599	965
13	5,478	12,826(3)	3,978	4,774	984	—	811
14	8,260	31,326(4)	6,963	25,803	2,478	—	—
15	4,016	8,743(3)	2,934	5,372	676	—	619
16	4,719	13,130(3)	3,554	3,284	1,454	—	—
17	10,291	21,275(3)	7,086	8,941	1,298	—	—
18	11,840	26,584(3)	11,456	—	1,995	—	—
19	7,884(1)	11,986(2)	3,661	—	—	5,451	—
20	17,445(1)	21,896(3)	10,262	—	—	4,645	—
21	16,944	24,292(3)	9,117	—	—	—	—
22	8,893	42,152(3)	11,815	8,623	—	—	—
23	4,931	8,324(3)	2,897	2,873	—	—	—
24	10,317	33,303(3)	10,078	—	2,096	—	—
25	9,862	27,109(3)	9,888	7,140	—	—	—
26	7,213	12,246(4)	3,333	—	—	4,489	—
27	26,141(3)	15,500	6,146	—	—	—	—
28	5,442	23,362(3)	6,920	5,559	—	—	—
29	10,721	15,043(3)	4,099	—	—	4,323	—
30	12,574	34,056(3)	9,938	—	—	—	—
31	11,098	27,311(3)	9,256	—	—	—	—
Total	284,091(6)	658,003(92)	238,256	113,101	19,949	19,507	4,233
Percentage	21.3	49.2	17.8	8.5	1.5	1.5	0.3

SOURCE: Data from the office of the Texas secretary of state.

[a] Delegates won in the district are in parentheses.

battles have been waged. At the beginning of the presidential campaign, there was little reason to believe 1976 would be any different. Conservative, party establishment elements began organizing early to get their supporters to attend the precinct conventions and sign in as Bentsen delegates. Their liberal opponents were working to turn out people to sign in as uncommitted at the meetings. And Wallace, who had gotten a third of the 1972 Texas delegates via a caucus procedure, also aimed a major effort at getting his voters to the local meetings. The Carter campaign, spread thin in Texas from the beginning, directed little effort to the precinct meetings.

Statewide figures on precinct attendance are not available, but there is evidence that the uncommitted liberal forces came out ahead in the initial mass meetings on May 1. Liberal leaders estimate that half the participants at the conventions signed in as uncommitted. One factor that helped the liberals was the light attendance at the meetings compared to past presidential years. Virtually no Wallace supporters bothered to attend the conventions, even though in 1972 they had accounted for fully a third of the participants. The absence of conservative activists who for the first time were voting in the Republican primary also undercut the normal opposition to the liberals. Finally, it is evident that Senator Bentsen had no greater ability to get people to the precinct meetings than he did to draw voters to the polls on election day.

Two important developments occurred in the week between the precinct meetings and the district/county conventions. First, Bentsen formally released his delegates to the district meetings, so that the support he had gained at the precinct level (between 15 and 20 percent) was not reflected in the next round of conventions. Second, the Carter campaign experienced a great deal of momentum due to events within and without Texas. At home Governor Briscoe strongly endorsed Carter, while nationally the candidate won primaries in Georgia and Indiana. Pressures began to build for delegates to sign in at the district/county conventions as committed to Carter. This shift to Carter was enhanced by the fact that very few delegates selected at the precinct meetings were pledged to another active candidate for the presidency; thus, they could change their preferences without conflict with earlier commitments.

Table 11.3. Delegate presidential preferences and national delegate apportionment at the Texas state Democratic convention, 1976

Preference	Percentage	Delegates received	Hypothetical distribution of all delegates [a]
Carter	62	20	87
Uncommitted	26	9	43
Brown	5	2	0
Wallace	3	1	0
Others	4	0	0
Total	100	32	130

SOURCE: Data from Democratic party sources; last column computed by author.

[a] The distribution that would have prevailed if all of the national convention delegates had been chosen by the state convention on a proportional basis with a 15 percent cutoff.

The results of the swing to Jimmy Carter were apparent in the choice of delegates sent to the Democratic state convention that convened in Houston on June 18, 1976. A straw poll was taken of all delegates to determine their presidential preferences, and the results were used to apportion the 32 at-large delegates to the national convention. Table 11.3 presents the results of that poll and the corresponding delegate assignments. This table also includes an estimate of the likely distribution of national delegates on a proportional basis had the June Democratic convention chosen all the delegates, as was traditional in Texas. The Carter forces probably would have still won a large majority of the delegates (87), but fewer than they won under the mixed system actually used (112). Also, it is likely that the delegates committed to Governor Brown, lacking the 15 percent required to ensure representation, would have formed an alliance with the uncommitted liberals and taken the remainder of the delegation (about 43 positions).

There was little dispute at the convention about the division of the delegates to the New York national convention. The Carter forces, looking ahead and hoping to unite the often divided Texas Democratic party for the November election, encouraged a spirit of tolerance and fair play. Consequently, delegates were given to candidates like Governor Jerry Brown of California and George Wallace, each of whom had considerably less than 15 percent of the support from the convention.

More serious problems at the convention arose in deciding which individuals would be added as at-large national delegates. Since most of the Carter delegates elected in the May primary were not established party leaders or office holders,[4] there was pressure to add a number of such persons at the June meeting. Additionally, women and ethnic minorities pressed for a large share of the thirty-two at-large positions on the grounds that they were underrepresented among the elected delegates. The convention, with Carter leaders managing negotiations behind the scenes, added Governor Briscoe, Land Commissioner Bob Armstrong, former U.S. senator Ralph Yarborough, and Houston Mayor Fred Hofheinz to the delegation. Fourteen of the thirty-two at-large delegates chosen were women, eight were black, and eight were Mexican American. With these additions, the total Texas delegation to New York included seventy-nine men and fifty-one women; ninety-one of the delegates were Anglos, eighteen blacks, and twenty-one Mexican Americans. Although neither women nor ethnics were represented in the delegation in proportion to their normal contribution to the Democratic presidential vote, both groups did improve their standing somewhat as compared to 1972.[5]

The National Convention

The Texas delegation to New York comprised one of the most enthusiastic "big state" groups supporting Jimmy Carter. A large majority came to the convention personally committed to Carter; most of the others accepted the inevitability of his nomination and were prepared to make the best of it. The presidential ballot-

[4] Some sense of the inexperience of the Carter delegation elected in the primary is gained from the fact that only one member of the group had previously served as a national Democratic delegate.

[5] Women comprised 39 percent of the Texas Democratic delegation in 1976, compared to 30 percent in 1972. Some 30 percent of the delegates in 1976 were black or Mexican American, compared to less than 20 percent in 1972.

ing on the evening of July 14, 1976, confirmed this general sentiment. Jimmy Carter received 124 of the 130 votes from Texas,
while Jerry Brown received 4 and George Wallace and Leon
Jaworski each received 1. The delegation was equally firm in supporting Carter's choice of Mondale for the vice-presidential nomination. The Minnesota senator received 126 votes from Texas,
Fritz Efaw received 2, Barbara Jordan received 1, and there was 1
abstention.

All in all, about the most exciting incident for the Texans in
New York occurred when delegate Hall Timanus was robbed of
several hundred dollars outside his hotel at four o'clock in the
morning. Timanus was the only Wallace delegate from Texas; the
robber was a black male.

THE REPUBLICAN DELEGATION

To a considerable extent, the Reagan-Ford contest in Texas reflected long-standing tensions within the state Republican party.
Although the Texas GOP is a demographically homogeneous party
(middle class, Anglo, mostly suburban), hostilities have built up
over the years between the "establishment" elements of the party,
headed by Senator John Tower, and an insurgent wing that includes the party's 1972 gubernatorial nominee. Henry "Hank"
Grover. Both groups are certainly conservative in their political
orientation, but the insurgent wing is more uncompromising in its
approach to politics. Led by hard-line leaders such as former Harris
County chairperson Nancy Palm (Napalm to her critics), the insurgents by 1975 had had enough of the Ford-Rockefeller administration and turned to Ronald Reagan with enthusiasm. Senator
Tower, meantime, had emerged as one of Gerald Ford's strongest
congressional allies. Thus, the battle lines in Texas were drawn
along a traditional fissure in the party, albeit one that had not
been evident in Republican presidential politics in recent elections.

The Primary

The Texas Ford and Reagan campaigns easily qualified slates in
the twenty-four congressional districts of the state. With the ex-

ception of four uncommitted individuals and one uncommitted slate in a Houston district, the Ford and Reagan delegate candidates had the field to themselves. The campaign started slowly but warmed up after it became apparent that Texas was a "must win" state for Reagan, and that Ford would make a maximum effort in the state to finish off his rival. Reagan visited Texas three times and spent about $400,000 from his depleted campaign funds in the state. Ford outspent Reagan by about two to one; however, the Californian was the beneficiary of sizable "private" expenditures by local supporters. For example, Hank Grover, arch-conservative former state senator and GOP gubernatorial nominee, spent over $35,000 of his own money buying newspaper ads in small towns and cities around the state urging conservatives to vote in the Republican primary.

In general, Reagan had the support of more party activists at the county and local levels, while Ford drew endorsements from "name" Republicans around the state. A number of elected Republicans, like Congressman Bill Archer from the western side of Houston, tried to avoid taking sides in a campaign that grew more bitter as the election approached. The Reagan camp relied heavily on both local organizational efforts and advertising targeted at conservatives. Ford depended on the extensive media coverage of his forays about the state and a major television-radio blitz in the closing weeks of the campaign.

Estimates of the likely outcome varied, but most news analysts took the position that Governor Reagan had started with a lead which the vigorous Ford campaign was steadily diminishing as the campaign progressed. Many of the president's supporters thought that they could repeat the Florida experience, in which Ford had overcome an initial Reagan lead and won the primary by a few points. One factor that created uncertainty was the question of who would actually vote in the Republican primary. Reagan's supporters (such as Grover) were making unabashed appeals for conservative Democrats and Wallace supporters to "cross over" and vote for Reagan. The Ford campaign tried to counter this by urging moderates and independents to vote for the president. Everyone was certain that the previous record vote of 147,000 in the 1964 Texas Republican primary would be surpassed, with estimates of the likely GOP vote ranging from 200,000 to 500,000.

Table 11.4. Republican delegate voting in the May 1
Texas primary

Congressional district	Mean vote for delegate slates		Reagan percentage
	Ford	Reagan	
1	1,467	5,726 (4) [a]	79.6
2	2,447	4,618 (4)	65.4
3	22,214	39,465 (4)	64.0
4	4,511	13,950 (4)	75.6
5	4,698	10,989 (4)	70.0
6	6,254	13,599 (4)	68.5
7	25,712	38,674 (4)	60.1
8	3,299	7,411 (4)	69.2
9	3,540	7,081 (4)	66.7
10	6,999	11,504 (4)	63.2
11	4,160	8,465 (4)	70.5
12	5,162	12,587 (4)	70.9
13	4,629	13,733 (4)	74.8
14	2,780	8,481 (4)	73.9
15	2,101	5,962 (4)	74.3
16	2,108	6,088 (4)	74.3
17	2,713	7,317 (4)	73.0
18	2,604	3,378 (4)	56.5
19	6,527	17,708 (4)	73.1
20	2,359	3,858 (4)	62.1
21	12,075	24,666 (4)	67.1
22	7,805	14,779 (4)	65.4
23	2,986	5,987 (4)	66.7
24	5,440	12,954 (4)	70.4
Total	144,290	298,980 (96)	67.5

SOURCE: Data from the office of Texas secretary of state.

[a] Delegates won in the district are in parentheses.

From the moment that the tally of the votes began at 7:00
p.m. on May 1, it was clear that Ronald Reagan was going to win a
smashing primary victory and that the Republican contest for the
presidential nomination was far from over. Voting had been heavy
throughout the day, with about 445,000 balloting in the primary,
and Reagan swept all regions of the state. Table 11.4 presents the
mean vote figures for the Reagan and Ford slates in all twenty-
four congressional districts. As was the case in the Democratic primary, most voters cast a "straight ticket" for all delegates on one
of the slates, so the mean vote is a good measure of support for
the presidential candidates.

Table 11.4 shows that the number of votes cast varied tremendously among the various congressional districts. The Seventh District, for example, had about 64,000 voters, while the Eighteenth District had only 6,000. These disparities reflected the successful efforts of Democratic state legislators to draw boundary lines so as to concentrate most of the Texas Republican voters in a few congressional districts. Despite this variance in votes cast, however, the vote division was remarkably stable. Reagan's margin of victory ranged from 56.5 to 79.6 percent, but in twenty-two of the twenty-four districts his slates got between 60 and 76 percent of the votes. Under the winner-take-all provision in the state's primary law, Reagan's slates won all positions, giving him 96 of the state's 100 national delegates.

In the aftermath of Ford's electoral disaster, the Ford camp stressed that its defeat was attributable largely to Wallace supporters crossing over and voting for Reagan. While some previous Wallace supporters undoubtedly did vote in the Republican primary, it is not reasonable to credit them with the drubbing given the president. For one thing, most of the votes cast in the GOP primary came from such strongly Republican areas as the western part of Houston and the north side of Dallas County; in both 1968 and 1972 Governor Wallace had little electoral support in these areas. Second, one should keep in mind the consistent margin of victory that Reagan gained in all parts of the state. Reagan not only did well in areas of Wallace strength such as East Texas, but he also won, by comparable margins, counties in South Texas where Wallace was very weak.

The Precinct and Convention Meetings

The June Republican state convention merely put the finishing touches on Reagan's Texas sweep. To the surprise of no one, Reagan added the remaining 4 at-large delegates to his total, thereby securing all 100 Texas delegates.

There are some problems in analyzing the presidential delegate selection process within the Republican conventions. First, the GOP rules did not require a "sign in" procedure so there is no uniform record of presidential preference. Second, with few delegates at stake and the Reagan forces clearly in control, the Ford camp made little effort to contest the various party meetings. Consequently, there are virtually no recorded votes at the district or state meetings that measure relative support for the two contenders. The few recorded votes at the June convention, for example, usually occurred when there was a question as to whether a hard-line Reaganite or a more moderate Reagan supporter was to be included in the delegation.

In general, there is agreement that Reagan had at least as large a margin of support in the precinct mass meetings and subsequent conventions as he had in the primary voting. A good guess is that Reagan backers comprised about three-fourths of the participants in the precinct-district/county-state convention process. With this kind of strength and with no rules requiring proportional representation, Reagan was assured of gaining the four remaining national delegates and all alternate positions. These positions were carefully allocated to the faithful. Not only were Ford supporters like Senator Tower excluded, but also prominent neutral party leaders like John Connally (who eventually declared for Ford just before the convention) and Congressman Bill Archer were rejected for alternate positions.

Reagan's strength in these party meetings indicates that, had the state still been operating under the old caucus-convention system, the final result of the process would probably have been the same. Given the consistent majority support that Reagan had around the state and the lack of protection for minority blocs, it seems likely that the state convention would have chosen a solid Reagan delegation if the final selection of all delegates had remained in its hands.

The National Convention

The Texas Republicans who journeyed to Kansas City faced a very different situation from that of the Democrats in New York. Though they, too, were a unified delegation, the 100 delegates and 100 alternates came to the convention with the certain knowledge that they faced a hard, bruising, uphill battle for their champion.

Although Ronald Reagan had several delegations that were strongly committed to his candidacy, none was more loyal than that from Texas. Many in the group had been upset, if not chargrined, by Reagan's choice of Senator Richard Schweiker for the vice-presidential nomination; but they swallowed this bitter pill and rallied behind the challenger. The Texans were angered from the opening of the convention by the poor seats which they believed the Ford camp had arranged for them. Other incidents such as the dumping of toilet paper on their heads by Jack Ford during a floor demonstration for the president (the Ford family was seated directly above the Texans) increased their ire. As the convention progressed, the Texas Republicans proved to be the most raucous, anti-Ford group in the hall. They cheered, shouted, and hooted to the last breath before finally and tearfully acknowledging Ronald Reagan's defeat. Even then, most could not unite behind the party's nominee.

Votes on three different matters at the convention demonstrate the delegations's loyalty to Reagan and distaste for Ford. The first was on Rule 16c, which the Reagan forces proposed and which would have required all presidential candidates to name their vice-presidential choices before the balloting for the presidential nomination. Many Texans questioned the wisdom of making this issue the key vote, but still the delegation voted 100 to 0 for the rule, which was rejected by a total vote of 1,068 to 1,180. The second vote was for the presidential nomination, on which the group held for Reagan, again by 100 to 0. Perhaps the most interesting vote, however, was for the vice-presidential nomination. After President Ford announced his selection of Senator Robert Dole, most of the Reagan supporters rallied behind this choice and the nomination was approved with 1,921 votes for Dole, 235 for others, and 103 abstentions. The Texas vote was quite different. Robert Dole received just 26 votes from the Lone Star State, while Senator Jesse Helms from North Carolina, one of the most conservative members of Congress, received 43 votes and Ronald Reagan received 9 votes. Twenty other votes were scattered among a dozen individuals ranging from John Connally to Roger Stauback, with one delegate abstaining. The bitterness engendered at Kansas City among the Texans lingered well into the fall campaign and increased President Ford's problems in getting his campaign against Carter in Texas organized and into action in the state.

Table 11.5. Delegate selection in Texas in 1976: a comparison of results under four different plans

		Democrats			Republicans	
Plan	Carter	Bentsen	Wallace	Uncom.	Others	Ford	Reagan
Caucus-convention system used in 1972	87	0	0	43	0	0	100
Primary on a proportional basis with a 15 percent cutoff	64	37	21	8	0	28	72
Primary using a plurality	123	7	0	0	0	0	100
Actual results with mixed system	112	6	1	9	2	0	100

SOURCE: Actual results from the office of the Texas secretary of state and Democratic party sources; other data computed by the author.

REVIEW AND ASSESSMENT

In reviewing the 1976 delegate selection process in Texas, several pertinent questions arise. First, what difference did the particular method used make? Would the results have been decidedly different if another procedure had been utilized? Second, how did the state react to the experience of its first presidential primary? Is the system likely to be retained, and if not, what alternative might be instituted? Finally, what is the general significance, if any, of the 1976 Texas experience?

A definitive answer can be given to the first question—the combined primary-convention delegate selection system did produce distinctive results compared to several alternative methods that might have been used. Table 11.5 presents the results that would have obtained under four different methods of selecting national party delegates. The first alternative estimates the results if the 1972 caucus-convention system had been retained in 1976. The second shows delegate apportionment after the 1976 primary as it would have been if all delegates had been elected from districts on a proportional basis. The third assumes that all delegates would have been elected in a primary on a plurality basis. The fourth presents the actual results produced by the mixed primary-convention system.

Table 11.5 shows that Democratic leader Jimmy Carter's delegate totals would vary by almost a factor of two, depending on the plan used. Carter would have received just 64 delegates in a proportional primary with a 15 percent cutoff, but he would have obtained 123 delegates in a plurality primary. The plan actually used was rather favorable to Carter's candidacy since it yielded 112 delegates, or about 25 more than he would have likely won under the 1972 procedures. The results for the other Democrats would vary far more. The uncommitted liberals, for example, would have received about 43 delegates under the 1972 procedures (assuming that they allied with the Brown forces as suggested earlier); but they received just 9 under the system actually used and would have received none in a plurality primary system.

The impact of the various plans is less on the Republican side. This reflects the fact that there were only two GOP contenders, and one (Reagan) had a sizable advantage over the other throughout the state. One should note, however, that President Ford would have won twenty-eight delegates in the May 1 primary had a proportional rule with a 15 percent cutoff been used.

Despite the fact that the Texas primary did not boost favorite son Lloyd Bentsen's chances for national office, reaction to that method of electing delegates was generally favorable in Texas. Republicans were delighted to have so many new voters in their primary, and liberals were equally delighted with the Democratic primary. Conservative Democrats, and especially Governor Briscoe, were relieved to avoid the horrors of Miami Beach in 1972.

With just about everybody happy about the way the primary worked—although for different reasons—it seemed quite likely that the 1977 biennial session of the Texas legislature would restore the primary process. Primary bills were introduced in both houses early in the session, and differing versions were eventually approved in each chamber. However, the final primary bill did not come out of conference committee until late in the session, and a single conservative Democratic senator was able to kill it by threatening a filibuster. Consequently, Texas at present has reverted to the caucus-convention system which operates within the guidelines laid down by the national party organizations. There will be just one more legislative session before the next presidential year; however, some variant of a presidential primary probably will be approved in 1979. The most likely prospect is that a mixed primary-convention system will be re-enacted, with the majority of the delegates directly elected. Access to the ballot will probably be simplified, and voters should be able to vote for the presidential candidates directly. Given the action of the 1976 Democratic National Convention in killing winner-take-all primaries for 1980, it also seems probable that, if a new Texas primary law emerges, it will allocate delegates on a proportional basis with a 15 percent cutoff.

Finally, what generalizations are warranted from the delegate selection process in Texas? In the opinion of this observer, Texas is a perfect example of the incredible complexity, to the point of foolishness, that exists in the presidential nomination process. Most electoral contests in America occur under stable rules that are relatively simple and thus easily understood by those who wish to inform themselves. An exception of enormous significance to this practice occurs in the process whereby the number of major party presidential contenders is reduced to two. We now have fifty states and a half dozen other entities, each with their own political culture, traditional practices, and short-term interests, interacting with two national party structures to shape the constituencies that nominate presidential candidates. Since the makeup of these constituencies now usually predicts the ultimate nomination, the manner of selecting delegates has become of enormous import.

The Texas case illustrates how selection rules can be altered late in the game for a particular candidate's benefit, with consequences that are very difficult to predict. With similar instability in other states, we are approaching the point where no scholar and no candidate can hope to grasp the basic rules and their practical implications without the assistance of a computerized data bank that is regularly updated. Such a situation raises questions about the basic legitimacy of the nomination process.

Let us return to the Texas case. In 1980 this state, with such a large number of delegates that it cannot be ignored by seekers for a contested nomination, will operate under a different set of selection rules for the fourth time in twelve years. We may not know before May 1979 what these rules will be. Nor, given their newness, will one be able to forecast accurately what their practical effect will be in the Texas context which will then prevail.

CHAPTER 12 / Virginia
A Caucus State

JAMES W. CEASER   University of Virginia

VIRGINIA in 1976 was one of a diminishing number of states that still selected its national convention delegates by the caucus method. Between 1968 and 1976 the number of caucus states declined from thirty-four to twenty-one, and their collective share of the national delegates fell within each party from about one-half to one-quarter. This change resulted chiefly from the reform movement in the national Democratic party. Even though many reformers now insist that they never intended to increase the number of primaries, there can be little doubt that their rhetoric, which extolled the benefits of direct democracy, encouraged the change.[1] Moreover, the reform rules imposed by the national party in 1970 and then again in 1974 made substantial demands on the states in the way of changes in their traditional proceedings—changes that interfered with what party regulars considered to be their legitimate right to conduct local party business under the same caucus proceedings. Consequently, in many cases state party officials preferred to separate the management of party affairs from national delegate selection. Finally, as the shift to primaries began to gain its own momentum, some of the national Democratic candidates lent their support to establishing primaries in instances where they believed they could win a convincing popular victory.

[1] For a discussion of the reformers' intentions with respect to primaries, see Austin Ranney's "Changing the Rules of the Nominating Game" in James Barber, ed., *Choosing the President* (Englewood Cliffs: Prentice Hall, 1974).

Some of these same pressures were felt within the Democratic party in Virginia. Legislation for a primary was submitted to the state General Assembly in 1974, and one of the Democrats' best-known candidates, Henry Howell, favored the idea. In his characteristically colorful rhetoric, Howell decried the "Mysteries of caucus conclaves" and declared that caucuses were "for the Republicans and the Byrds, not for the people or the Democratic party."[2] But the primary proposal never made much headway in the state. The Republican governor, Mills Godwin, opposed it, as did other leading Republican officials. More than anything else, however, it was the absence of support from the Democrats, who control both houses of the state legislature by large majorities, that kept the bill from making any progress. The liberal element within the party had fared exceptionally well under the reform procedures in 1972 and could see no good reason to risk adopting a new system. The moderates had gained control of much of the party organization after 1972 and were hopeful that they could dominate the proceedings in 1976. Moreover, liberals and moderates alike feared a strong showing by George Wallace in any primary contest.

Virginia thus kept its caucus system and became the largest caucus delegation in the Republican party and the third largest, after Missouri and Minnesota, in the Democratic party. The state was the focal point of an intense struggle in the Republican party between President Ford and Ronald Reagan, a struggle that continued until the final vote at the national convention. The contest in the Democratic party settled down to a three-way affair among the candidacies of Jimmy Carter and Morris Udall and an uncommitted slate led by the state party regulars.

The size of the state's delegations, along with the presence in both parties of vigorous contests in 1976, make Virginia an excellent case for studying the general properties of the caucus

[2] *Richmond Times-Dispatch*, Mar. 23, 1976. For a general discussion of the Byrd machine and recent Virginia politics, see J. Harvie Wilkinson III, *Harry Byrd and the Changing Face of Virginia Politics* (Charlottesville: University Press of Virginia, 1968); Ralph Eisenberg, "Virginia: The Emergence of Two-Party Politics," in William Havard, ed., *The Changing Politics of the South* (Baton Rouge: Louisiana State University Press, 1969); and Larry Sabato's *The Democratic Party Primary in Virginia: Tantamount to Election No Longer* (Charlottesville: Published for the Institute of Government, University of Virginia, by the University Press of Virginia, 1977).

system. This chapter will consider briefly the evolution of Virginia's parties and caucus procedures over the past decade and then focus on the events of the 1976 selection process. A comparison will be offered between the selection procedures in the two parties, with a particular view toward discovering the consequences of employing proportional representation rather than a plurality system.

THE DEMOCRATIC PARTY

Before the recent party reforms, the selection process in most Democratic caucus states was dominated by the regular participants in party affairs. They participated not only to choose national delegates but also to select district and state party chairmen and national committee representatives. In Virginia, in fact, under state law the party committees still retain the option of nominating their candidates in conventions.

The reforms introduced by the national party encountered opposition from many party officials in the caucus states because of the increased focus they placed on national politics.[3] The McGovern Commission rules of 1970 were adopted to facilitate participation by the party's rank and file in the choice of a presidential nominee. Little attention was given to the effect that this focus might have on the conduct of state and local party business. What troubled the regulars was the prospect of a takeover of the state organizations by persons having little concern or interest for the well-being of the state party. Moreover, as of 1976 the caucus states were saddled with the additional burden, imposed by the Mikulski Commission rules, of conducting state party business with delegates chosen by proportional representation according to shares allotted to national candidate preference. As noted previously, these difficult demands prompted party regulars in many states to relinquish any influence they had in national delegate selection in exchange for maintaining control over internal party affairs. In states that retained the caucus system, the party organizations were faced with the task of

[3] Austin Ranney, *Curing the Mischiefs of Faction* (Berkeley: University of California Press, 1976), p. 206.

attempting to protect their own interests in the face of a set of hostile, or at least alien, rules. It is from the perspective of this problem that the 1976 Democratic delegate selection process in Virginia is best viewed.

Historical Background

From 1944 through 1964, the Democratic party in Virginia was firmly under the control of the powerful—and conservative—Byrd Organization. Participation in the caucuses was effectively restricted to regular party members. Little incentive existed for isolated local challenges, because all of the delegates were chosen at the state convention and because the unit rule was always in effect. From 1944 through 1960 the Virginia Democratic delegation cast its votes at the national convention as a unified bloc, and its support was always given to a candidate more conservative than the party's national choice. (In 1964, Johnson was nominated by acclamation, so no record exists of the state's vote.) The Virginia delegation's voting record during the period from 1944 through 1960 was:

Year	Party nominee	Candidate supported by Virginia delegation
1944	Roosevelt	Byrd
1948	Truman	Russell (before and after shift)
1952	Stevenson	Russell (all three ballots)
1956	Stevenson	John Battle
1960	Kennedy	Lyndon Johnson

The party began to undergo some fundamental changes in 1968. Most of the pressure for change came from forces within state; however, the national requirement for nondiscrimination in party affairs that was adopted at the 1964 convention also forced greater attention to the rights of blacks and resulted in the selection of the party's first black convention delegates. The opposition that had mounted within the state to the Byrd Organization very nearly succeeded that year in overthrowing the incumbent state party chairman. Clearly, the grip of the Byrd machine on the caucus proceedings had begun to slip; this decline was aided by the civil rights legislation of the 1960s, which removed many of the state's restrictions on suffrage, and by the continuing shift in the state's population from the rural areas to the Washington suburbs and the Tidewater urban corridor. As one close observer remarked in 1968, "The most unusual thing about the state convention is that the decisions were not decided somewhere else last month or last week."[4]

For the first time since 1944, the state convention in 1968 did not adopt the unit rule. The delegation split in its presidential preference, giving 42½ votes to Humphrey, 5½ to McCarthy, 3 to Governor Moore, and 2 to Channing Phillips, a black national committeeman from Washington, D.C. But despite the evident changes that had begun to take place within the state party, the delegation sent to the Chicago national convention was still very much a conservative one over which the Byrd Organization continued to exercise substantial influence. This was more apparent from the roll call votes than from the division on the presidential nominee. The minority platform report on Vietnam, which won 40 percent of the entire convention vote, received only 15 percent of the Virginia delegation's vote; and the motion to end the unit rule, which passed the convention with 52 percent of the vote, was supported by only 18 percent of Virginia's delegates.

The selection process in 1972 brought additional and more profound changes in Virginia's Democratic party. Added to the political forces seeking to overthrow the old order was the influence of the national party's new delegate selection guidelines. The rules mandated by the McGovern Commission included requirements for widespread publicity for mass meetings, all of which had to be held on the same day; de facto quotas in the selection of blacks, women, and young people as delegates— quotas that were supposed to be followed throughout the process and that in effect increased the influence of blacks, who acted with some of the characteristics of a unified group; and selection of at least 75 percent of the delegates at the district level or below. These rules enabled large numbers of people interested primarily in presidential politics to participate in caucuses for the first time. Many of those who took advantage of this opportunity were motivated by the anti-Vietnam war movement

[4] *Richmond Times-Dispatch,* July 29, 1968.

and were liberal in their political views. Under the new apportionment scheme, these participants could expect to win delegates in some areas, even if they should lose in the state as a whole.

The delegates to the district and state conventions were elected either directly at the mass meetings or in a two-stage process by city or country delegates who had been chosen at those meetings. It was at the mass meeting stage that the "amateurs," stimulated by their interest in national politics and urged on by the campaign organizations of the national candidates, showed up in force. The selection of delegates to the higher levels took place without a formal declaration of candidate preference. Even so, in many of the meetings slates were identifiable in terms either of candidate preference or ideological leanings. In most of the larger meetings, there were at least two such groupings, frequently referred to as "liberal" and "moderate." In many areas with large concentrations of black people, a third slate of blacks was also in evidence. The mass meetings were often long and protracted, and the contests bitter. In one meeting, former Democratic governor Mills Godwin was rejected as a delegate to the state convention, prompting him to begin his conversion to the GOP.[5] In another mass meeting in Norfolk, the liberal slate swept virtually all of the 145 state convention delegates and gave no places to conservative elected officials.

The district and state conventions convened in Roanoke. On the first evening the delegates split into their respective district meetings, conducting district party business and electing forty-one of the state's fifty-three national delegates. The next day the same delegates then met as one body to conduct the state party's business and to select the remaining twelve national delegates. Many of the district conventions had strong liberal majorities and elected slates of delegates informally pledged either to some liberal candidate or to Senator McGovern. A liberal majority also controlled the state convention and selected its own twelve-delegate "slate," nine of whom indicated at that time their support for Senator McGovern.

The liberal character of the 1972 delegation was evident from its voting record at the national convention. On the presidential balloting the delegation divided as follows (before vote shifts):

[5] The Democrats claim, however, that Godwin had already made pledges to support the national ticket of the Republican party (interview with Democratic state party chairman Joseph Fitzpatrick, June 22, 1976).

Candidate	Number of delegate votes
McGovern	33.5
Jackson	4
Chisholm	5.5
Sanford	9
Wallace	1

The liberalism of the delegation was equally evident from some of the other roll calls at the convention:

Issue	Percentage of convention in favor	Percentage of Va. deleg. in favor	Number of states more liberal than Va.
Minority report on guaranteed income	33.1	56.6	2
Minority report on women's rights	36.5	57.5	2

The state party organization also changed in 1972, since the liberal presidential-year participants naturally gave their support to the opponents of the Byrd Organization. The state convention elected George Rawlings, the leader of the antiwar forces, as a national committeeman; and Joseph Fitzpatrick, who had just missed unseating the conservative party chairman in 1968, was elected new party chairman. For Rawlings, the liberalism of the convention, including its support of a slate for Senator McGovern, represented "a new day" for the state party. But Fitzpatrick was more careful, sensing that the "new politics" majority was an artifact of the presidential politics of 1972 and not indicative of the views either of a majority within the state or of the party "regulars" who had been working since the early 1960s to overthrow the Byrd Organization. Fitzpatrick spoke not of a new day, but of "bringing Democrats together." After the 1972 election he emphasized a centrist position, disappointing some of the liberals who had backed him but winning the support of the moderate regulars. The latter group began to win control of the party organization in many areas of the state, as many of the liberal presidential-year participants ceased to take part in party affairs.

Among the regulars, there was no desire either to turn the clock back to the days of dominance by the Byrd Organization or to confine the selection process to regulars alone. They did fear, however, that if regular participants failed to agree on a common strategy, the attempt to build a stable organization could be undermined either by a mass movement from the left or by a Wallace challenge from the right. It was disruption of either sort that the organizational leaders hoped to avoid in 1976.

Delegate Selection in 1976

The Virginia Democratic party's selection procedures were changed once again in 1976 in response to a new set of national party rules. After 1972 the idea that state selection procedures could be regulated by the national party had become an accepted principle. Each state was required to submit its selection rules to the national party's Compliance Review Commission, which then scrutinized them to determine their compatibility with national regulations. Changes were frequently required by the commission—in Virginia's case, on no fewer than four occasions.

The major new national rules as they applied to the caucus states were as follows. First, the selection of delegates at all levels in the process had to take place according to explicit candidate preference, with "uncommitted" being one of the possible choices. In effect, people at the mass meetings were asked to ballot for presidential candidates. Second, the process had to make use of proportional representation of candidate strength at all levels. Thus, if a candidate received 20 percent of the votes at a mass meeting, he could receive 20 percent of the delegates allotted to that unit. If, however, a candidate received less than 15 percent support at any level, state rules could deny that candidate a share of the delegates—an option that Virginia and every other caucus state adopted. Third, at every level of the process, the participants supporting each candidate preference—and not the mass meeting or convention as a whole—were empowered to select their own delegates. Everyone would gather initially and express his preference; thereafter, the delegate share for each preference was determined, and the adherents of each candidate would then retire to make their own choice of delegates, without any intervention or review by the entire body. Fourth, in the selection of the national delegates, each presidential candidate had the right of approval of his delegates; thus, no delegate of which the candidate disapproved could be "forced" on him by his own supporters. Finally, the quota provision of 1972 was dropped and replaced by a series of affirmative action regulations which required each state party to publicize its selection process and make a special effort to involve minority groups.

The new rules oriented the caucus delegate selection process, more than ever before, around the choice of a national presidential candidate. This presented a formidable problem for the state party, as the party business was conducted by the same delegates elected to represent the national candidates. To safeguard the party's interest, state organizational regulars, led by Joe Fitzpatrick and Attorney General Andrew Miller, devised a two-pronged strategy designed to enable the regulars to dominate the selection process and to minimize the potentially divisive influences deriving from national politics. The first step was to write a set of party rules, consistent with the national requirements, that would do as much as possible to ensure control by the party regulars; the second was to agree on a preferred candidate who would allow regulars to stay united, at least initially, in order to control the delegates to the district and state conventions.

"Outsiders" in the party at the time, such as Henry Howell, naturally saw this strategy as a threat to their own influence. Howell sought to use Carter's popularity to embarrass the regulars. The struggle between the regulars and Howell's followers (which foreshadowed the division between Miller and Howell for the gubernatorial nomination race in 1977) was always just beneath the surface of presidential selection politics in 1976.

The Rules. The rules were formulated in a series of meetings by the party steering committee that ranged over a two-year period and that involved many revisions, often in response to the demands of the national Compliance Review Commission. The rules were modified and amended down to the very last moment—too late, in fact, for a final edition to be printed in time for the mass meetings. This procedural irregularity, combined with the great complexity of the new rules, created a good deal of dissatisfaction at many of the caucus meetings, and this dissatisfaction was not always dispelled by party leaders, who themselves resented the infringement of the national regulations on traditional local methods.

Following is a synopsis of some of the most important rules adopted by the state party, together with a discussion of their intended effect as seen by party leaders.

1. Separate district and state conventions by two weeks; assign the selection of all national delegates to the district conventions.

The intent of this rule was to free the state convention and state party business from the immediate influence of presidential politics. The two-week period between the district and state conventions would supposedly allow time for tempers to subside and for delegations to focus entirely on state party affairs. In addition, party officials may have believed that those delegates interested only in national politics would be content to play a minimal role at the state convention. (The same delegates were elected to serve in both the district and state conventions.)

Transferring the election of what had been the at-large delegates from the state to the district conventions completed the decentralization in the Democratic party that had begun in 1972. This change, along with certain changes in the Republican party, reversed the traditional roles of state and local leaders within the two parties. In 1968 all of the Democratic party delegates had been selected at the state convention, where state party leaders played a key role; in the Republican party, nearly all of the delegates that same year were selected in the districts in a highly decentralized system. By 1976 the Democrats had moved to a complete district system, whereas the Republicans, because of a new national apportionment formula, elected more than one-third of their delegates at the center.

2. Local option for the selection of district-state delegates by precincts and magisterial districts. The selection of delegates by the mass meetings might take place, at the option of the local unit party committees, either at the unit level (city or county) or by the smaller electoral districts that comprise that unit, i.e., by wards or magisterial districts.

According to party leaders, the use of smaller electoral districts could help regulars to win control of the selection of delegates. Since support for a particular presidential candidate within a locality was often concentrated in a few wards or magisterial districts, adopting the option of using the smaller unit would limit that candidate to the number of delegates from those districts, no matter how many devoted amateurs were brought out to pack the meetings. On the other hand, it was likely that the broader geographical distribution of party regulars would enable them to influence the election of delegates in all sparsely populated meetings. State chairman Joseph Fitzpatrick viewed this option in the early spring of 1976 as the best way to prevent a possible Wallace "coup." (Wallace had just finished well in the caucuses in Mississippi and South Carolina.) Fitzpatrick states, "I don't want George Wallace taking over the Democratic party of Virginia and I don't think the Democrats of Virginia want that either."[6] Part of the strategy to stop Wallace involved increasing the number of black delegates, which Fitzpatrick argued would be facilitated by the selection of delegates at the lowest level. This option, while not adopted universally, was used in many of the large cities—Norfolk and Richmond, among others—and though the feared "boom" for Wallace never materialized, the plan nevertheless probably served to increase the strength of regulars.

The adoption of this rule by state party leaders created some difficulties regarding the question of proportional representation. In small districts allotted only two or three delegates, the problem of determining proportionality—especially when national rules imply that any candidate receiving support of 15 percent or more of the participants must receive a delegate—becomes very difficult. Consider, for example, a three-delegate district, in which a total of 100 persons participated at the mass meeting. If candidate A received 60 votes, candidate B, 25 votes, and candidate C, 15 votes, should each candidate receive one delegate? The obvious unfairness of this result led state party officials to adopt a slight modification that was accepted by the Compliance Review Commission. The formula, employed throughout the entire delegate selection process, was:

$$\frac{\text{number of persons in candidate caucus} \times \text{number of delegates allotted}}{\text{total number of participants at the mass meeting}}$$

A resulting figure of more than 0.5 was rounded up to the next whole number, and the awarding of delegates took place sequenti-

[6] *Washington Post*, Mar. 15, 1976.

ally, beginning with the smallest whole number. Considering again the example cited above, use of the formula would yield the following results:

Number of delegates awarded

Candidate A $\dfrac{60 \times 3}{100} = 1.80$ 2

Candidate B $\dfrac{25 \times 3}{100} = 0.75$ 1

Candidate C $\dfrac{15 \times 3}{100} = 0.45$ 0

This solution was still not without difficulties of its own. If the division had been 60 persons for candidate A, 23 for candidate B, and 17 for candidate C, then each candidate would receive one delegate, despite the great disparity between the top and bottom candidates. In such situations, which occurred in a number of districts, there were complaints that the system was absurd; and, indeed, it would be difficult to argue that a winner-take-all system would have been less just.

3. Prefiling of candidates for delegate (at local option). This rule required anyone who wanted to be a delegate to the district and state conventions to prefile with a local party official at some specified time before the mass meeting.

Party regulars in many areas favored this provision as a means of determining a week or so before the mass meetings which candidate organizations were active. The rule could also, perhaps, increase the number of regulars selected as delegates, for they would be more likely to prefile than would supporters of presidential candidates with weak campaign organizations. Under this rule, a presidential candidate who was entitled to a certain share of the delegates but whose caucus had an insufficient number of persons who had prefiled would have to forgo part of its share. The benefit of this rule for regulars was diminished, however, by two changes demanded by the national party: (1) Candidates for delegate were not to specify a presidential candidate preference when they prefiled, and (2) in the event that a particular presidential preference was entitled to more delegates than the number of prefiled persons supporting that preference, the caucus for that group could fill its quota with other supporters.

4. Mandating of delegates. All delegates selected from a mass meeting to a candidate who received 15 percent or more of the delegates within that district were obliged to continue to support that candidate at the district convention (as they presumably would want to do). Those elected to a candidate who received less than 15 percent of the delegates in the district were free to switch. Uncommitteds could also switch at the district convention, regardless of the percentage of delegates they had won. In the selection of national delegates from the district conventions, delegates committed to an active candidate would be bound for three ballots at the national convention.

The latter provision of this rule was adopted after most party regulars had opted to follow an uncommitted policy in the initial stages of the selection process; it was designed ostensibly to be "fair" to the candidates who had spent so much effort in securing their delegates. But the provision also served to make the uncommitted status appear more appealing, since delegates chosen under that label would not be locked into a position from which they could not switch; an uncommitted delegate might run as "favorable" to a particular candidate, but he would have the option at the convention of changing his vote.

The preceding discussion of the Virginia party rules illustrates something about the tension that exists between the national Democratic party and some of its state parties. The national rules for caucus states were apparently designed to reduce the influence of party regulars and elevate that of the supporters of various presidential candidates. The Virginia state party was attempting, by working within the interstices of the national rules, to establish a system that gave as much weight as possible to the party regulars. In pursuing this strategy, the proposals of the state party were sometimes overruled by the national party. The state party, for example, had wanted delegates from the mass meetings to be chosen by the meeting as a whole rather than by the caucuses of the individual candidates. The national Compliance Review Commission refused. Such decisions often angered party officials, who believed the interference to be unwarranted and who resented the national party's unwillingness to appreciate the state party's interest in the caucus system.

Since the national party and the state party approached the question from a different perspective, some degree of conflict was probably inevitable. The national rules were written under the influence of a set of ideas that took little account of the claims of state parties. Those rules were designed to deal in a certain way with national delegate selection and ignored the fact that the same process used to select national delegates also was used to select the persons who conducted state party business. The state party, on the other hand, was concerned, as most organizations are, with organizational maintenance—with protecting the well-being of the organization and its mission and reducing as much as possible the uncertainties of an external environment. This tension is certain to remain as long as the national party emphasizes the representation of expressed candidate preferences of the individual participants, rather than the interests of the state party organizations.

Political Strategy. Long before the presidential campaign had begun in earnest, party leaders in Virginia began to look for a candidate whom they all could agree to support, at least in the initial stages of the selection process. Their objective focused as much on maintaining the unity of the state party as on deciding who should be the national nominee. If party regulars all supported the same candidate, then any split in their ranks could be avoided. Commitment to a candidate was also thought preferable to running as uncommitted, on the grounds that no support could be generated for a "noncandidate." But this strategy, whatever its merits, was upset by the regulars' choice of Lloyd Bentsen. Bentsen's poor showing in the early primaries and caucus states forced him to withdraw as an active candidate in March and thus left the Virginia regulars without a candidate.

The logical candidate choice for the regulars at this point would have been Jimmy Carter. But the organization Carter had established in the state was led by James Gibbs, a known ally of Henry Howell, and Howell himself was working actively on Carter's behalf. Supporting Carter would thus have meant that the regulars and Andrew Miller would be placing themselves in a sense "under" Henry Howell, a move that was clearly impossible. The selection process therefore became entangled with the ambitions of state politicians, and Jimmy Carter himself was soon embroiled in Virginia politics.

The majority of party regulars, led by Andrew Miller and Joseph Fitzpatrick, decided to adopt an uncommitted strategy, at least for the first phase of the mass meetings. This strategy turned out to be quite successful—probably more so, in fact, than any candidate strategy would have been. Party regulars could disagree among themselves on their national candidate preference yet still agree to back the same slate for the sake of protecting the state and local party organizations. Moreover, many within the party, as well as many of the potential participants in the caucus proceedings, had not yet made up their minds. Finally, the regulars could offer to the candidate organizations a share of the uncommitted delegates, a proposal that was tempting to those who feared that they would receive less than 15 percent support at the mass meetings or who wanted to maintain good relations with the regulars.

The organizational effort on behalf of the candidates varied in intensity. Carter clearly had the best organization; in addition to a statewide network of locally recruited helpers, staff members from the national organization arrived in every district two weeks prior to the mass meetings to assist in turning out supporters. Compared to this, Udall's effort was very limited; it focused on the Eighth and Tenth districts (the Washington suburbs) and on certain pockets of liberal support elsewhere in the state. The effort on behalf of Wallace was minimal, a surprise to many within the state. Whatever potential support he had within the electorate was not organized systematically, and by the time of the mass meetings, his national effort had begun to fail.

The Carter campaign was hampered, however, by the dispute between Carter's own original campaign forces and the state party regulars. While Carter wanted a strong showing in the state for his committed forces, he also did not wish to alienate Miller and Fitzpatrick, whose support he hoped to obtain at a later date. Miller sought assurances from Carter that Howell's support of Carter would not be reciprocated in the gubernatorial primary of 1977. Howell's forces, meanwhile, urged the Carter organization to make a vigorous effort on behalf of the committeds and to attack the opportunism of the regulars. Carter had a very delicate situation on his hands, and he handled it by attempting to give both sides part of what they wanted. In his one campaign appearance in the state, just before the April 3 mass meetings, Carter stated that "I have no intention of getting involved in the primary campaign for governor," an obvious bow to Miller. But then, in an equally obvious gesture to Howell, Carter declared that "the uncommitted slate will not be controlled by the people of Virginia but by the political leaders who will be free to support candidates who did not think enough of Virginia to come here and campaign."[7]

What struck one most about the maneuvering that took place before the mass meetings was the high degree of uncertainty under which most of the participants operated. Even as the mass meetings approached, there was concern that Wallace might score well; Carter, Udall, and uncommitted strategists often had little idea of how many of their supporters would turn out, and they were even more uncertain about how many to expect for the other candidates. The absence of polling data, the unfamiliarity with the reform rules, and the lack of experience of many of the local coordinators left many mystified about what would happen on April 3.

The Mass Meetings. When the delegates to the district conventions were chosen on April 3, the uncommitteds gained a decisive victory. Statewide they had won 59 percent of the delegates, compared with 30 percent for Carter, 9 percent for Udall, and only 2.5 percent for Wallace. They had a plurality in every district except the Tenth, where Udall finished first. If the uncommitteds chose to remain in that category at the district conventions, which of course they were not obliged to do, they would have been entitled to thirty of the state's fifty-four delegates, with Carter having seventeen, Udall four, and three yet to be determined (see Table 12.1).

The success of the uncommitteds was due chiefly to the work of the party regulars, who turned out with their supporters in large numbers. Their "neutrality" toward the national candidates was possible because the intensity of commitment to any of the candidates was not, in general, very great, and many within the state were at this time genuinely uncommitted. The uncommitteds also gained support in the mass meetings from participants voting for candidates receiving less than 15 percent of the total. These persons were permitted to join another group and usually chose the uncommitteds. (When it could make a difference, however, Harris and Udall forces tended to join together.) Finally, the large amateur turnout that had occurred in 1972 never materialzed in 1976. The number of participants declined from an estimated fifty thou-

[7] Ibid., Mar. 30, 31, 1976.

238

sand in 1972 to an estimated thirty thousand in 1976.[8] There was neither the enthusiasm toward the candidates nor the burning issues that had stimulated participation in 1972. Under these circumstances, the regulars constituted a much larger share of the total, and their steady participation in most geographic areas of the state added further to their advantage.

The long-range institutional question of whether the state party regulars can continue to protect their interests under the new caucus rules cannot be answered from the experience of 1976. Certainly the regulars did much better than even they had hoped by the use of an uncommitted strategy. Yet their success was based on a number of factors that one cannot yet say are normal. The relative absence of strong issues in the race, the lukewarm feeling toward the candidates, and the vivid memories of the bitter struggles of 1972—all of these circumstances helped the organization in their 1976 triumph, and they all might perhaps be considered unusual. It will take the experience of more presidential campaigns to see if the two functions of the caucus proceedings—selecting national delegates and conducting party affairs—can be effectively contained within the same process.

Carter forces could—and did—claim a victory since Carter received more delegates than any other candidate and triumphed over his closest rival, Udall, in eight of the state's ten congressional districts. But the seventeen delegates that Carter won outright fell far short of the twenty-five or thirty delegates that had been mentioned by some of his national campaign organizers. A major effort was then planned to win over some of the uncommitteds before the election of national delegates at the district convention seven weeks later.

How well did the new selection rules work at the mass meeting stage? As noted previously, there was a good deal of confusion about the procedures, and few understood—even after explanations were offered—the rationale for the mathematical formula by which the proportions were determined. The complexity of the rules evoked the astonishment and often the derision of many of the participants. It added to the length of the meetings and also created a situation in which the few who were knowledgeable about the rules would usually be asked to run the meetings. The pro-

[8] Interview with state party chairman Joseph Fitzpatrick, June 22, 1976.

Table 12.1. Virginia Democratic district convention delegates elected in mass meetings, April 3, 1976

District	Total number of district delegates	Uncommitted	Carter	Udall	Wallace	Other[a]	Estimated number of national delegates per candidate	
First	305	180	101	22		2	Uncom.	3
							Carter	2
Second	269	171	93		4	1	Uncom	3
							Carter	2
Third	289	167	95	12	14	1	Uncom.	3
							Carter	2
Fourth	308	179	86		38	5	Uncom.	3
							Carter	2
							?	1
Fifth	295	174	97	16	4	4	Uncom.	3
							Carter	2
Sixth	288	133	132	20		3	Uncom.	2
							Carter	2
							?	1
Seventh	304	217	44	30	13		Uncom.	4
							?	1
Eighth	207	180	41	49		7	Uncom.	3
							Udall	1
							Carter	1

Ninth	317	208	103	1		5	Uncom. 4 Carter 2
Tenth	396	113	98	115		—	Uncom. 2 Udall 3 Carter 2
Total	2,978	1,722	890	265	73	28	Uncom. 30 Carter 17 Udall 4 Undetermined 3

SOURCE: Figures provided by the Democratic State Party of Virginia.

[a]The total votes received by each of the candidates in this category were as follows: Humphrey, 11 votes; Harris, 8 votes; Brown, 2 votes; and Boothe, 7 votes.

cedures were designed to be democratic; but, ironically, many participants complained that the process seemed beyond their control.[9]

The supporters of the candidates winning minority shares were the most satisfied with the results. Proportional representation gave them their fair share; indeed, in some of the smaller meetings in which only three delegates were chosen, there were instances in which candidates with the support of 20 percent of the participants received the same share (one delegate) as a candidate receiving nearly 50 percent support. The 15 percent cutoff rule operated to reduce frivolous candidacies. Unfortunately, no data were available regarding the number of participants who initially voted for a candidate obtaining less than 15 percent support. However, even these participants were not completely shut out of the selection process, since they were given a second chance, after being informed of their initial failure to qualify, either to combine forces in an attempt to qualify or to give their support to another candidate.

Proportional representation brought a surface harmony to the meetings by reducing the stakes of the conflict. There was no bargaining that involved an all or nothing result as in a winner-take-all system. The proceedings were conducted so that as soon as the candidate preferences of the participants were declared (on a formal written "ballot"), the meetings split up into their respective candidate groupings. All then waited for the initial delegate shares to be declared, after which those persons backing a candidate receiving less than the votes required to win a delegate were given the opportunity to join another caucus. Only these persons could bargain or negotiate, their leverage stemming from their power to affect the delegate division by joining with others. After these participants made their final declarations, each candidate group was notified of the number of delegates to which it was entitled, and then proceeded independently to select its own delegates. The major candidate groupings were thus never required to confront or deal with one another.

It is difficult to determine exactly how proportional representation affected the outcome at this stage, for the candidate's strate-

[9] Evidence on these points was collected by a number of students who attended caucus meetings througout the state. The conclusions reached in this paragraph represent a consensus of these observers.

gies and even the participant's preferences might have been different under another set of rules. Under previous plurality rules, the various candidate groups would have had to bargain and to form coalitions in the search for plurality. The declaration of candidate preferences does, however, allow some educated guesses to be made about the influence of proportional representation.

Its most obvious effect is to give greater representation to those candidates who fail to obtain a plurality but who have widespread support. This "bonus" is drawn from the plurality winners. What this meant in Virginia is that Carter fared much better than he would have under a plurality system and that the uncommitteds fared worse. Udall's case is more difficult to analyze, as his strength was highly concentrated in the Tenth District, where he won a plurality. Though a minor candidate statewide, Udall had strong support in certain geographical areas, and a plurality system might have been more favorable to his final total than proportional rules. The general rule would seem to be that minor candidates with strong geographical concentrations benefit more from a plurality than from a proportional system; candidates with support dispersed throughout a state—but not having a plurality—do better under proportional rules. (Of course, it is quite possible that if plurality rules had been in effect, the Carter delegates and the uncommitteds would have joined together in the Tenth District to win a plurality; in general, it makes sense to assume that competitors would prefer the uncommitted to an actual opponent.) In Carter's case, he had relatively strong support throughout the state but he failed to win a plurality in any of the districts. Conceivably, under plurality rules, Carter could have been virtually shut out in Virginia. Indeed, he would have faced similar problems under plurality rules in many of the caucus states; in spite of the requirement of a formal designation of candidate preference, the uncommitteds finished first in the initial stage of the caucus proceedings in fifteen of the twenty-one caucus states. While Carter might well have been the candidate in the best position to gain the support of these uncommitteds at a later point, it is fair to say that his delegate total throughout the campaign would have appeared much less imposing had it not been for proportional representation in the caucus states.

The District Conventions. For the second stage of his Virginia campaign, Carter shifted his attention to winning the uncommitted delegates, while his opponents, to the extent that they were active, sought to maintain the status quo. The Carter organization was changed after the mass meetings, with state director James Gibbs, not a special favorite of the regulars, being shifted out of the state. After a considerable amount of discussion with the Carter organization, both Andrew Miller and Joseph Fitzpatrick announced their support for Carter's candidacy. This move signaled what many thought would be a major shift among the uncommitteds to Carter, and the figure of forty pledged Carter delegates from Virginia was frequently mentioned by officials in the Carter organization.

Carter in fact fell well short of this estimate. After the district conventions met on May 22, he had added only seven committed delegates to his total (see Table 12.2). Many of the uncommitteds continued to have strong doubts about Carter, and some were reluctant to lock themselves into an absolute commitment to support him for the first three ballots. Moreover, Carter's national momentum had been slowed somewhat earlier that same week by a defeat in Maryland and a narrow victory over Udall in Michigan. To many, the race was not yet over.

On the other hand, as Carter's supporters pointed out, as many as ten of the delegates chosen as uncommitted had announced their intention to vote for Carter. One reason that these delegates had not been chosen directly as official Carter representatives was the inability, in many cases, of the original supporters of Carter to reach an agreement with the uncommitteds who wished to join him. After the major uncommitted leaders had announced their support for Carter, a series of negotiations took place between the "new" Carter supporters and the original supporters. The former wanted to be assured that, if they joined the Carter group, they would obtain a share of the national delegates, if necessary by holding separate informal meetings within the Carter grouping at the district conventions. In some cases this agreement proved difficult to implement because of mistrust between the two groups. Moreover, some of the originally uncommitted who wished to be elected national delegates perceived that their chances would be better if they remained with the uncommitted caucus, as they had support from some who did not favor Carter's candidacy.

The operation of the district conventions repeated the basic proceedings used in the mass meetings. The meeting initially divided into different groups according to the candidate preferences. Those in groups with less than 15 percent were then permitted to join other groups, their objective being places as national delegates or alternates if a switch could affect the district delegate total.

The effect of proportional representation at this stage of the process, when compared to hypothetical plurality results based on a formula that gives all the district delegates to the plurality winner, was not substantial (see Table 12.2). The reason was that Carter and the uncommitteds would have traded advantages under a plurality system, as each was ahead in certain districts. Udall might have done as well or better under a plurality system because his support was concentrated in the Tenth District. However, these conclusions, it should be emphasized, are only estimated. Under a plurality system the different groups would have been able to bargain with one another; and the objective, no doubt, of those opposed to or unsure of the front-runner (Carter) would have been to prevent his acquisition of formally committed delegates.

Some brief comments should be made about the effect of the new rule allowing the presidential candidates the right of approval over their national delegates. This power was one that obviously had to be used carefully for fear of alienating local supporters. Udall, in fact, handled the matter by abrogating his right, declaring that whomever his caucuses chose would be acceptable to him. Carter appointed someone in each district to exercise the right of approval for him, and these persons in some instances played a role in working out the allotted shares between the "new" and the "old" Carter supporters. The number of delegates agreed upon for the new supporters could be guaranteed, if necessary, by the candidates's right of approval.

The National Convention. Little of note occurred at the national convention in New York. The uncommitteds all declared for Carter. Also, by releasing his delegates, Udall allowed those bound to him in Virginia to vote as they pleased. Six of the seven Udall delegates stayed with their candidate and one shifted to Carter, making the final delegate count forty-eight for Carter and six

Table 12.2. Virginia Democratic delegate distribution after district conventions, May 22, 1976

Congressional district	District convention delegates			National delegates as awarded under proportional representation	Hypothetical results on plurality basis [a]
	Uncom.	Carter	Udall		
First	170	134		2 Carter 3 uncom.	5 uncom.
Second	unavail.			2 Carter 3 uncom.	5 uncom.
Third	130	159		3 Carter 2 uncom.	5 Carter
Fourth	unavail.			2 Carter 4 uncom.	6 uncom.
Fifth	124	117	54	2 Carter 2 uncom. 1 Udall	5 uncom.
Sixth	124	164		3 Carter 2 uncom.	5 Carter
Seventh	unavail.			2 Carter 2 uncom. 1 Udall	2 ½ Carter 2 ½ uncom.
Eighth	unavail.			2 Carter 1 uncom. 2 Udall	2 ½ Carter 2 ½ Udall
Ninth	143	174		3 Carter 3 uncom.	6 Carter
Tenth	unavail.			2 Carter 2 uncom. 3 Udall	7 Udall
Total				23 Carter 24 uncom. 7 Udall — 54	21 Carter 23 ½ uncom. 9 ½ Udall

Source: *Richmond Times-Dispatch*, May 23, 1976.

[a]The hypothetical results on a plurality basis were estimated on the basis of the actual returns in national delegates awarded, supplemented by the voting results at the district level where available. Thus, in the Ninth District, Carter was credited with all of the delegates in view of his plurality in the voting returns. In the Seventh and Eighth districts, where voting returns were unavailable and Carter was tied on the number of national delegates awarded, the hypothetical results were split.

for Udall. The state party had found a candidate who represented very well its moderate position and behind whom it could unite in the upcoming campaign.

THE REPUBLICAN PARTY

The liberal takeover of the Democratic party in the caucuses of 1972 was matched that same year by a conservative triumph within the state's Republican party. Press reports of caucus activities were filled with reflections on the parallel developments taking place in each party; the Republicans' conservative victory masterminded by Richmond lawyer Richard Obenshain, in which the party's long-dominant moderate element was displaced by committed ideological proponents on the right, was likened to George Rawling's successful liberal strategy within the Democratic party that resulted in the replacement of the traditional Byrd Organization.

Yet one very crucial difference, besides the antithetical ideologies of the two groups, distinguished these two transformations. The Democratic change took place in the context of a heated presidential contest in which national political issues, along with the new reform rules, stimulated broad participation. It was the interest in the presidential race that brought out so many liberals and resulted in a liberal majority at the state convention. The conservative triumph in the Republican party, on the other hand, took place when there was no disputed presidential contest. By turning out for these meetings, the new Republican participants evidenced a much stronger commitment to long-term involvement in state party affairs than their liberal Democratic counterparts. As the strength of the "new politics" element in the Democratic party waned after 1972, that of the conservatives in the Republican party increased.

The retreat of the Democratic organization from its new politics stance of 1972 has not altered the basic direction of party realignment within the state. The Democratic organization, once to the right of the Republicans on many issues, is now clearly to the left, although this obviously does not hold true for all Democratic candidates. Meanwhile, the Republican party, which before 1972 was the state's "liberal" organization, now is dominated by conservatives. These new conservative regulars, though flexible

247

enough to back candidates slightly more moderate than them-selves, are very much moved by and committed to conservative principles. Although they control the party organization, they cannot be considered "regulars" in the traditional sense of being pragmatic power brokers; as one observer aptly put it at the 1976 Republican state convention, "the Democrats are a party of careerists; the Republicans are a party of ideologues."[10]

The Republican organization in Virginia is composed of three identifiable groups. First is the traditional moderate element whose geographical base is in the western part of the state. This area was long the core of Republican strength in Virginia, with its commitment to the party traceable back to the Civil War, when white farmers and workers strongly resisted fighting a war for the slaveholders of the east and south. Somewhat populist in character and having very few blacks, this area has not been as sensitive to the race issue as some of the "black belt" counties of the Southside or Tidewater. As a result, on the race issue and some other questions, the Republicans in the 1950s and 1960s served as the moderate alternative to the Democrats. An exemplar of this type of Republicanism—and still the unofficial leader of this wing of the party—is former governor Linwood Holton, who defeated Democrat William Battle in the 1969 gubernatorial race to become the state's first Republican governor in this century. Holton's control over the state party—and the brand of Republi-canism which he represents—came to an end in 1972 when the state party chairman whom Holton supported, Warren French, was soundly defeated by Richard Obenshain. Holton's subordinate role was also confirmed in the 1976 convention when his nominee for national committeewoman was replaced by a candidate backed by the conservative forces.

The second group, the conservatives, draws its support from businessmen and professionals in cities and suburbs in the eastern part of the state. Many of the conservatives were first brought into the party in 1964 in response to the Goldwater national campaign. Their ranks have since grown as the party has become more iden-tified with conservative principles. They are reenforced by a third group comprised of some of the recent converts from the old Byrd Organization—the most well known of whom is Mills Godwin, elected as governor both under the Democratic label in

[10] *Richmond Times-Dispatch,* June 6, 1976.

1965 and the Republican label in 1973. The leading survivor of the old Organization group, Senator Harry Byrd, has remained an independent since 1970, despite the blandishments of many Republican party leaders. Even so, the 1976 party convention in effect endorsed Byrd by refusing to nominate a Republican candidate to oppose him for the U.S. Senate in 1976. (This action, taken by the same convention that selected the state's at-large convention delegates, illustrates the interconnection that exists in Virginia between national and state party business.)

Despite the differences among these groups (in particular, that between some of the "mountain-valley boys" of the west and the eastern conservatives), the party has thus far been able to maintain a fragile outward unity. In this respect, the Virginia GOP stands in marked contrast to the Republican party in North Carolina, where roughly the same split exists and the feud between the two factions has bitterly divided and weakened the party. One factor favoring accommodation in Virginia is the party's leadership, which has appreciated the damage that a serious rift would entail for the party as a whole. In addition, the caucus system, while revealing the splits, has also kept conflicts from spreading by avoiding the divisiveness of primary campaigns.

National Rules on Delegate Selection

The Republican party's national delegate selection rules leave much more autonomy to the states than the rules of the Democratic party. There is no national requirement for proportional representation, no stipulation that candidate preferences be officially designated, and no provision for national candidate approval of the delegates. Nor is there any national party body in the Republican party comparable to the Democrat's national Compliance Review Commission, which checks state procedures before the convention to determine their conformity to national rules.

The 1972 Republican National Convention did, however, endorse some changes in procedures. Proxies were disallowed in the selection of national delegates, and a ban was placed on any ex officio delegates. Greater emphasis was also given to "openness" in the selection process, which meant, among other things, making generally available more information about the selection process in order to encourage citizen participation.

There is one area in which the Republican national rules traditionally have been more restrictive on their state counterparts than those of the Democratic party. This is on the matter of apportioning delegates between the districts and the state at large. In the Republican party, delegates are alloted to the states by a formula that allows a certain number of delegates per congressional district and a certain number to the state at large. The delegates must be chosen in this fashion unless otherwise specified by state law. In caucus states, where state law allows the parties to apportion the delegates, the state parties must thus follow the national rules.

The new apportionment formula that the Republicans adopted for 1976, which expanded the size of the convention from 1,348 to 2,249 delegates, assigned most of the additional delegates on an at-large basis. The proportion of delegates selected by the state conventions in the caucus states thus increased significantly from 1972; the following tabulation illustrates this increase in Virginia, as well as showing the comparative Democratic figures:

	Republican		Democratic	
	District	At-large	District	At-large
1972	20	10	41	12
	(66.7%)	(33.3%)	(77.4%)	(22.6%)
1976	30	21	54	0
	(58.8%)	(41.2%)	(100%)	(0%)

In Virginia and some of the other large caucus states, this change on the Republican side increased the relative significance of statewide majorities and consequently raised more complaints from minorities in 1976 about "steam rolling" tactics by the majority which deprived them of legitimate representation. In caucus state after caucus state in 1976, the statewide delegates were selected in intense contests based on a de facto winner-take-all system.

State Rules

The Virginia Republican party followed the example of the national party by giving a large degree of autonomy to its district and local unit committees in running the caucuses. In 1976, as in the past, each congressional district's party committee was permitted to determine the date of its own district convention, the size of the district convention, and the apportionment formula among the local units. Each local unit in turn fixed the date of its own mass meeting.

The district and state conventions are separate bodies and each devises its own apportionment plan. In practice, there is a considerable overlap in their composition, as many persons are selected to serve as delegates to both. For example, in the Seventh District, which had 320 delegates to its district convention and 213 delegates to the state convention, most mass meetings first selected a group that was to attend both conventions and then added another group that would participate in the district convention only.

The state convention in 1976 was enlarged by over 1,000 delegates from 1972 in an effort by the Republican organization to build more support for the party and involve a greater number of active participants in its affairs. Here one can see a function of the caucuses that is not performed by a primary: while a primary involves more participants in the casual act of casting a ballot, it cannot, like the caucuses, be used to recruit persons who will serve the organization on a long term basis.

The state Republican party makes use of an unusual practice known as the "full-vote" option. Under the party regulations, any unit (city or county) can empower its delegation to vote the full share of that unit's allotted delegates, and the vote will be counted in full. The unit's vote is distributed in the same proportion as the expressed views of the delegates in attendance at the convention. Thus, if only nine delegates of an eighteen-person delegation attend, each delegate's vote would count double. Most units chose to adopt this option, and it was also widely used at some of the district conventions in which attendance often fell short of the allotted total. This option is not the same as a proxy provision, for no delegate is entitled to give his vote to someone else. In a party which has yet to build a broad base of activists in many areas in the state, the option is important for maintaining geographical distribution in the convention's voting, although one might question whether it offers party leaders an incentive to stimulate participation in the local mass meetings.

While the use of the unit rule is illegal at all levels in the Republican party, a mass meeting or convention is permitted under state

party rules to "instruct its delegates on specific issues or candidates."[11] As the majority or plurality selects the delegates anyway, this rule is not frequently invoked. There is also a strong
reluctance on the part of many party members to bind national
convention delegates, many of whom are important party figures.
None of the national delegates were instructed in 1976; and this,
as we shall see, was important in supporting the view which many
of the delegates held that they were in a sense "trustees," entitled
to use their own discretion. The rule binding delegates was employed, however, at some of the mass meetings in the selection of
delegates to the district and state conventions. This occurred in
several instances in which a majority supporting Ronald Reagan's
candidacy wanted to make certain that the entire delegation chosen would support his candiacy. The general counsel for President
Ford's campaign committee contended that such a practice violated the national party regulation barring the unit rule, and he
threatened to challenge the Virginia delegation at the national
convention. The threat was dropped, however, after an agreement
was worked out between the Ford and Reagan national campaign
staffs to avoid all convention challenges. The practice accordingly
still remains permissible.

National party rules do not allow any delegates to be selected
ex officio. By custom, however, the at-large delegates include
high-ranking party officials and officers, including the governor,
U.S. senator, and state party chairman. State convention practices
allow an official nomination committee, consisting of the congressional district chairmen, to present a proposed slate of national delegates to the convention, although the state convention
is not bound either to vote on this slate or to conduct the election
of delegates by slates.

Events 1976

The mass meetings at the county and city levels all took place
in April and May. Although no estimates are available on statewide participation, it is clear that substantially fewer Republicans

[11] Plan of Organization for the Republican Party of Virginia, available from
the State Republican Party of Virginia.

than Democrats took party in the mass meetings. In Charlottesville, for example, 405 Democrats attended, but only 70 Republicans; in Albermarle County, 253 Democrats and 27 Republicans; and in Richmond, 900 Democrats and 200 Republicans. One reason for the Republicans' lower attendance was that the mass meetings were not all held on the same day throughout the state, thus making effective publicity about the dates of the meetings more difficult than in the Democratic party. But party rules alone cannot account for the entire difference. The Republican party in Virginia, though at least the equal of the Democratic party in terms of electoral strength, has not yet built up as large a cadre of regular participants.

The activities on behalf of Ford at the mass meeting stage varied from area to area within the state. Early in the campaign, Ford's state organization, headed by former congressman Stanford Parris, calculated that in some districts Ford's strength relative to Reagan was so weak that nothing but a token effort was merited. Such a decision reflects in part the character of a winner-take-all system; when the margin for a candidate seems safe in one area, it hardly makes sense for an opponent to waste scarce resources in a challenge that can win no delegates. (On the other hand, in areas calculated to be close, the incentive to allocate resources increases.) Ford's state campaign also faced difficulty in recruiting campaign organizers because most of the activists within the party, including most of the local party leaders, favored Reagan.

Reagan's organization was much stronger and was competitive throughout the state. Headed by Kenneth Klinge, a well-known conservative organizer, the staff managed to secure the endorsements of a slate of notable state Republicans in the General Assembly. In addition, by mid-May Reagan's staff had obtained the support of seven of the ten Republican district chairmen. Reagan himself visited the state twice, once at the end of March to deliver the guest speech at the Republican's Bicentennial Dinner and again in May, shortly after his North Carolina primary triumph.

The mass meetings within the Republican party were not, however, always contests between the two national candidates.

Although in some areas a division between the Ford and Reagan forces was clear-cut, in others the delegates to the district conventions were chosen because of their standing within the local party, regardless of their candidate commitments. In some meetings, moreover, the number of participants barely equaled or even fell short of the total number of district and state delegates to be elected, meaning that virtually any known Republican in attendance could be selected. Finally, in some instances the selection of delegates was influenced by local party considerations, by a delegate candidate's preference for district chairman, or, as in the First District, by a delegate candidate's preference for the party's congressional nomination.

Because of the fashion in which the delegates were selected at the mass meetings, their national candidate preferences often were not known until the district conventions convened. These conventions exhibited a much clearer alignment of forces on the basis of presidential candidate preference; but even at this stage, the penetration of the national race was not complete at every convention. In some instances, delegates were selected because of their personal stature within the party, such as Richard Obenshain in the Third District. In addition, because the national delegates were selected by the conventions as a whole, rather than within the candidate groupings as in the Democratic party, it was possible for forces other than candidate preferences to play a role. At the Eighth District's convention, many Reagan followers actually believed they had a narrow plurality favoring Reagan's candidacy; but they lost two of the three delegates because of personal feuds among their delegate candidates and because the two Ford delegates, Stanford Parris and state Senator Wiley Mitchell, possessed independent support. In the Ninth District, long known for its unique brand of politics, the three delegates were elected as uncommitted, reportedly in an effort to "persuade" President Ford to appoint a federal judge from their district. Overall, winner-take-all was the rule rather than the exception, but even in these cases, it must be remembered that the delegates were not formally bound to support any candidate. The results of the ten district conventions, as they were reported in the press just after the conventions were:

District	Leaning Ford	Leaning Reagan	Uncommitted
First	—	3	—
Second	—	2	1
Third	—	2	1
Fourth	—	3	0
Fifth	—	3	—
Sixth	3	—	—
Seventh	—	3	—
Eighth	2	1	—
Ninth	—	—	3
Tenth	—	3	—
	5	20	5
	(16.6%)	(66.6%)	(16.6%)

The state convention was known in advance to have more supporters for Reagan than for Ford. This, all Republicans agreed, entitled Reagan to a majority of the delegates, but just how far such support should be pushed was a matter of great dispute between the two candidate organizations. The convention's formal nominating committee, comprised of the state's district party chairmen, agreed weeks before the convention on a "protocol" portion of the twenty-one-member slate consisting of eight leading party officials. Of that number, five were known supporters of Reagan, Governor Godwin had declared for Ford, and both Lieutenant Governor John Dalton and state party chairman George McMath were uncommitted. This left thirteen delegates to be contested when the nominating committee met on the eve of the convention.

The nominating committee drew up a proposed slate consisting of twelve persons favorable to Reagan and one who was uncommitted but generally thought to be leaning toward the president. Leaders of the Reagan organization at first objected to the selection of an uncommitted delegate but finally announced that they would back the slate. The Ford forces argued before the committee that, for the sake of fairness and party unity, Ford should be given delegates proportional to his share of supporters at the convention, said to be about 35 percent. The committee rejected this appeal, contending that the Republican party had no requirement for proportional representation and that their job was to put together a slate "acceptable to the majority at the convention."[12]

Dissatisfied with this decision, Ford's campaign manager, Stan Parris, chose to fight the nominating committee's slate on the floor of the convention. As an alternative to the committee's slate, Parris proposed that the delegates be selected individually by the whole convention. This strategy was based on the hope that the convention majority might be more charitable to Ford than the nomination committee, and that certain of the proposed Ford delegates might be able to win on the basis of their personal stature. The leaders of Reagan's organization decided to accept the challenge, as it would give them the possibility of winning all of the contested delegates. The Reagan forces won the gamble and captured the thirteen-member slate. Thus, of the twenty-one at-large delegates, Reagan claimed (at that time) at least eighteen, with a chance for two others. Governor Godwin stood alone as a declared supporter of the president. The count for the Republican delegation as a whole stood as follows on June 6:

	Reagan	Ford	Uncommitted
District delegates	20	5	5
At-large delegates	18	1	2
Total	38	6	7
	(74.5%)	(11.8%)	(13.7%)

The use of a plurality system in the Republican party made both the race and the outcome very different than it would have been under proportional rules. At the district level, a de facto winner-take-all system prevailed (or so it was thought in early June) in seven of the ten districts. This worked to the advantage of the president in two instances (the Sixth and the Ninth, which was declared as uncommitted), while in five other cases it worked to Reagan's benefit. Because of the varying geographic strengths of the two candidates, the proportion of district delegates that each candidate won was probably not very different from what would have been obtained under a proportional system. The great deviation from proportionality occurred in the selection of at-large delegates, where Reagan captured far in excess of his proportional share.

[12] Comment of M. Patton Echols, chairman of the Convention Nominating Committee, Washington Post, June 8, 1976.

The conclusion of the delegate selection process did not, however, mark the end of the campaign. There were delegates selected as uncommitted whom both sides continued to pursue. Moreover, the delegates who had been selected by majorities favorable to either Reagan or Ford were not formally pledged, and some interpreted this to mean they were fully within their rights to change positions. Typical of the "trustee" attitude on the part of these delegates was the following statement of a delegate from the Seventh District, elected by a majority committed to Ronald Reagan: "I had always been basically for Mr. Ford. I was elected as a Reagan delegate, but many of the people who voted for me were Ford supporters. This was more of a personal vote for me rather than Mr. Reagan. Many of my closest political friends are Ford supporters. Right now I'm also still keeping an open mind."[13]

This attitude prompted officials from both of the national campaign organizations to probe for the "soft spots" in the Virginia delegation. By an intensive effort, which included selective invitations to the White House for some delegates, Ford managed to win the votes of at least three Reagan delegates as well as those of most of the uncommitteds. The contest for votes continued down to the balloting at the convention itself, in which thirty-five votes were cast for Reagan and sixteen for the president. The shift to the president by delegates thought to be elected to Reagan was resented by the other Reagan delegates, and one delegate asked that the delegation be polled individually so that Republicans in Virginia would be aware of who had changed their votes. Although shifts by informally committed delegates were not common within the Republican party as a whole, the experience in Virginia in 1976 indicates that the method employed to select delegates in the Republican caucus states still allows for a residual element of the trustee theory of representation that once was so common within the caucus states of both parties.

CONCLUSION

The contrast between the Republican and Democratic caucus procedures in Virginia reveals two significant characteristics of the

[13] *Charlottesville Daily Progress*, Aug. 8, 1976.

proportional representation rules in the Democratic party. First, and most obviously, proportional representation yields different results from a plurality basis for the apportionment of delegates; it gives more delegates to minority candidate preferences, except where these may have a strong base of support in particular geographic units. Moreover, by eliminating the winner-take-all element in each contest, proportional representation diminishes the stakes involved in any given conflict, particularly when compared with the selection of a large number of delegates on an at-large basis at the state level, such as occurred in the Republican party in 1976.

Whether the proportional system is fairer, and whether fairness in this sense should be the overruling consideration in determining selection rules, are questions that cannot be adequately addressed within the confines of a study of delegate selection in one state. What can be said, however, is that if proportional representation had the advantage of being fairer, this fairness comes at the expense of what, at least traditionally, has been considered the merit of flexibility in the caucus proceedings. The proportional system in the Democratic party precludes the kind of bargaining at the selection stage that in the past was typical of the caucus procedures in some states. Delegates at the district conventions, when they have been selected for a particular national candidate, cannot band together to oppose a strong front runner. In effect, this eliminates the capacity of the caucus states to register "second choice" preferences. Moreover there is little occasion, except in the case of the uncommitteds, for delegates to engage in the give-and-take that can foster new political alliances.

Second, proportional representation entails a different representational role for the national delegate. From the initial stages of the process, delegates are chosen on the basis of a particular candidate preference by the participants registering that preference. This procedure continues until the final selection of national delegates takes place, at which point the national candidates also are given the express right of approval. Virginia state party rules, following in the spirit of this candidate orientation, even bound the delegates committed to an active candiate for three ballots at the national convention. Reflected in these provisions is the idea that the delegate serves as a bound agent chosen to express the will of the participants, a theory of delegate representation that formerly applied only to the delegates chosen in certain of the primaries. The plurality rules in caucus states often produce the same result in practice; nevertheless, there is a sense in which the delegates, being formally uncommitted, retain the right to make decisions at their own discretion. The "delegate" as opposed to the "trustee" theory of representation entails a devaluation of the national convention as an independent deliberative body and shifts the locus of the nomination decision to the delegate selection process.

There is, finally, the vexing issue of whether caucus proceedings can and should perform the dual function of selecting national delegates and attending to the business of the state party. This issue is especially problematic in the Democratic party, since the national party rules place many constraints on the state parties. There is, for example, no good reason for supposing that state party business is best conducted by delegates chosen on the basis of proportional representation. Strong pressures will therefore continue for the caucus states to separate the national delegate selection process from the remainder of their proceedings. Yet, if one holds that the state parties have a right to be represented at the national convention and, further, that they can continue under the new rules to obtain modest representation, then the recommended policy would be a continuance of the caucus system.

Appendix Tables

Index

Information for the tables contained in appendixes A and B was derived from *Congressional Quarterly Weekly Reports,* from information supplied by the Democratic and Republican national committees, and from figures provided by state boards of elections and project volunteers. The categories into which the selection processes are grouped in Appendix A are defined in chapter 1, pp. 12-14.

APPENDIX A / State Delegate Selection Systems, 1976

Table A1. Delegate selection systems in the Democratic party. Group I: "Loophole" primaries

State	Number of delegates	Number selected at district level [a]	Number selected statewide	Division of statewide delegates
Alabama	35	27 (special dist.)	8	Reflects district division
Georgia	50	38	12	Reflects district division
Illinois	169	155	14	Reflects district division
Louisiana	41	32	9	Reflects district division
Maryland	53	40	13	Reflects district division
Nebraska	23	23	—	—
New Hampshire	17	17	—	—
New Jersey	108	81 (special dist.)	27	10 at large with 15% cutoff; 17 reflecting proportion of other 91
New York	274	205	69	Reflects district division
Ohio	152	114	38	Statewide proportional representation with 15% cutoff
Pennsylvania	178	134 (special dist.)	44	Reflects district division
Texas	130	98 (special dist.)	32	Reflects district division with 15% cutoff
West Virginia	33	25	8	Reflects district division
Total	1,263	989	274	

[a] Congressional district, except as noted.

Table A2. Delegate selection systems in the Democratic party. Group II: Proportional representation primaries

State	Number of delegates	Number selected at district level [a]	District cutoff	Number selected statewide	Division of statewide delegates
Arkansas	26	24	Enough for 1 delegate	2	Selected by state committee Without reference to district vote
California	280	210	15%	70	In proportion to district delegation
Florida	81	61	15%	20	In proportion to statewide vote, 15% cutoff
Idaho	16	13	5%	3	In proportion to statewide vote
Indiana	75	57	15%	18	In proportion to statewide vote, 15% cutoff
Kentucky	46	35	15%	11	In proportion to statewide vote, 15% cutoff
Massachusetts	104	78	Enough for 1 delegate	26	In proportion to statewide vote, enough for 1 delegate
Michigan	133	100	15%	33	In proportion to statewide vote, 5% cutoff

Montana	17	16	15%	1	—
Nevada	11	11 (special dist.)	5%	—	—
North Carolina	61	46	5%	15	In proportion to statewide vote, 5% cutoff
Oregon	34	34	Enough for 1 delegate	—	—
Rhode Island	22	18	15%	4	In proportion to statewide vote, 15% cutoff
South Dakota	17	13	15%	4	In proportion to statewide vote
Tennessee	46	37	15%	9	In proportion to statewide vote, 15% cutoff
Wisconsin	68	58	Enough for 1 delegate	10	Enough for 1 delegate
District of Columbia	17	13 (special dist.)	15%	4	In proportion to district delegates
Total	1,054	824		230	

a Congressional district, except as noted.

Appendix A

Table A3. Delegate selection systems in the Democratic party. Group III: Caucus states (proportional representation)

State	Number of delegates
Alaska	10
Arizona	25
Colorado	35
Connecticut	51
Delaware	12
Hawaii	17
Iowa	47
Kansas	34
Maine	20
Minnesota	65
Mississippi	24
Missouri	71
New Mexico	18
North Dakota	13
Oklahoma	37
South Carolina	31
Utah	18
Vermont [a]	12
Virginia	54
Washington	53
Wyoming	10
Subtotal	657
Territories	34
Total	691

[a] Also held primary which was not binding on delegates.

Table A4. Delegate selection systems in the Republican party. Group I: Plurality primaries

State	Number of delegates	Number selected at district level [a]	Number selected statewide	Selection of statewide delegates
Alabama	37	21	16	Winner-take-all (potential) [b]
California	167	—	167	Winner-take-all
Florida	66	45	21	Winner-take-all for 16; 5 reflect district results
Georgia	48	30	18	Winner-take-all
Illinois	101	96	5	At discretion of state convention
Indiana	54	33	21	Winner-take-all
Maryland	43	24	19	Winner-take-all
Nebraska	25	25	—	—
New Hampshire	21	15	6	Winner-take-all (potential)
New Jersey	67	45	22	Winner-take-all (potential)
New York	154	117	37	At discretion of state committee
Ohio	97	69	28	Winner-take-all
Pennsylvania	103	84[c]	19	Appointed by state committee
Texas	100	96	4	Appointed by state convention
West Virginia	28	12[c]	16[c]	Winner-take-all (potential)
Wisconsin	45	36	9	Winner-take-all
Total	1156	748	408	

[a] Depending on state law, delegates in districts were selected either individually or by slates on a winner-take-all basis.

[b] Potential winner-take-all refers to a situation in which voters elect delegates at large individually; winner-take-all refers to a situation in which state law gives entire at-large slate to winner of the statewide vote.

[c] Delegates not permitted to identify with national candidates on ballot.

Table A5. Delegate selection systems in the Republican party. Group II: Proportional representation primaries

State	Number of delegates	Number selected in district	District cutoff	Number selected statewide	Division of statewide delegates
Arkansas	27	12	Enough for 1 delegate	15	Statewide vote; enough for 1 delegate
Idaho	21	—	—	21	17 selected statewide with 5% cutoff; 4 delegates chosen by state convention
Kentucky	37	—	—	37	15% cutoff
Massachusetts	43	36	Enough for 1 delegate	7	Statewide vote; enough for 1 delegate
Michigan	84	—	—	84	5% cutoff
Nevada	18	—	—	18	5% cutoff
North Carolina	54	33	20%	21	20% cutoff
Oregon	30	30	Enough for 1 delegate	—	—
Rhode Island	19	19	33 1/3%	—	
South Dakota	20	6	20%	14	20% cutoff
Tennessee	43	24	15%	19	Statewide vote; enough for 1 delegate
Total	396	160		236	

Table A6. Delegate selection systems in the Republican party. Group III: Caucus states

State	Number of delegates
Alaska	19
Arizona	29
Colorado	31
Connecticut	35
Delaware	17
Hawaii	19
Iowa	36
Kansas	34
Louisiana	41
Maine	20
Minnesota	42
Mississippi	30
Missouri	49
Montana [a]	20
New Mexico	21
North Dakota	18
Oklahoma	36
South Carolina	36
Utah	20
Vermont	18
Virginia	51
Washington	38
Wyoming	17
District of Columbia [b]	14
Subtotal	691
Territories	16
Total	707

[a] Also held a primary that was nonbinding.

[b] Law allows for primary in the event of a contest; Reagan did not file.

APPENDIX B / Delegate Totals under Alternative Selection Systems

Table B1. Democratic delegate totals, actual results

	Carter	Brown	Udall	Wallace	Jackson	Church	Others	Uncommitted	Total
Group I: Loophole primaries									
Alabama	3			27				5	35
Georgia	50								50
Illinois	59			3			93	14	169
Louisiana	13			9			19		41
Maryland	32		7		10			4	53
Nebraska	8					15			23
New Hampshire	15		2						17
New Jersey	25	83[a]							108
Ohio	126		20				6		152
Texas	112	2		1			6	9	130
West Virginia							26	7	33
Subtotal	443	85	29	40	10	15	150	39	811
New York [b]	33		73		103			65	274
Pennsylvania [b]	65		24	3	24		17	45	178
Total, Group I	541	85	126	43	137	15	167	149	1263

Appendix B

Table B1 (cont.)

	Carter	Brown	Udall	Wallace	Jackson	Church	Others	Uncom-mitted	Total
Group II: Proportional primaries									
Arkansas	17		1	5				3	26
California	67	204	2						280
Florida	34			26	21	7			81
Idaho	2					14			16
Indiana	48			9				18	75
Kentucky	37		2	7					46
Massachusetts	16		21	21	30		16		104
Michigan	69		58	2				4	133
Montana	4					10		3	17
Nevada	3	6				1		1	11
North Carolina	36			25					61
Oregon	12	7				15			34
Rhode Island	7	8[a]				7			22
South Dakota	9		7						17
Tennessee	43			1				1	46
Wisconsin	26		25	10	6		1	2	68
Total, Group II	430	225	116	106	57	54	17	32	1,037
Total, Groups I and II (exclud-ing N.Y. and Pa.)[b]	873	310	145	146	67	69	167	71	1,848
Group III: Caucus states									
Alaska	5		19					10	10
Arizona				1					25

Table B1 (cont.)

	Carter	Brown	Udall	Wallace	Jackson	Church	Others	Uncommitted	Total
Connecticut	19		16		8			8	51
Delaware	10							2	12
Hawaii			1		1			15	17
Iowa	20		12				2	13	47
Kansas	16		3		1			14	34
Maine	9		5					6	20
Minnesota							48	17	65
Mississippi	5			11			4	4	24
Missouri	39		3		1		1	27	71
New Mexico	8		6					4	18
North Dakota	8							5	13
Oklahoma	12						7	18	37
South Carolina	9			8				14	31
Utah	4					5		9	18
Vermont	3	2	3					4	12
Virginia	23		7					24	54
Washington			7		32			14	53
Wyoming	1	1	1					7	10
Subtotal	191	3	83	20	43	5	62	215	622
Colorado [c]	12	6	5			3		9	35
Total, Group III	203	9	88	20	43	8	62	224	657
Total, all states (excluding N.Y., Pa., Colo.) [b, c]	1,064	313	228	166	110	74	229	286	2,470

[a] Uncommitted delegate slates in New Jersey and Rhode Island are credited to Governor Brown, as it was understood that most of these delegates would support him.

[b] See text, p. 39, for explanation of the omission of New York and Pennsylvania.

[c] Figures for Colorado at the district level were unattainable; therefore, the state's totals are omitted from the conversion to hypothetical results in tables B2 and B4.

Table B2. Democratic delegate totals, hypothetical results, proportional

	Carter	Brown	Udall	Wallace	Jackson	Church	Others	Uncommitted	Total
Group I: Loophole primaries									
Alabama	12			23					35
Georgia	49			1					50
Illinois	41			15			97	16	169
Louisiana	13			11			13	4	41
Maryland	17		4		7			25	53
Nebraska	11					12			23
New Hampshire	8		7				2		17
New Jersey	50	53 [a]	5						108
Ohio	95		44		2	5	6		152
Texas	64			21			37	8	130
West Virginia							22	11	33
Total, Group I	360	53	60	71	9	17	177	64	811
Group II: Proportional primaries									
Arkansas	23			3					26
California	57	223							280
Florida	34			26	21				81
Idaho						16			16
Indiana	63			12					75
Kentucky	37		2	7					46
Massachusetts	7		29	21	47				104
Michigan	72		61						133
Montana	4					10		3	17
Nevada	3	8							11
North Carolina	36			25					61
Oregon	12	7				15			34
Rhode Island	7	8 [a]				7			22
South Dakota	9		7					1	17
Tennessee	45			1					46
Wisconsin	33		33	2					68
Total, Group II	442	246	132	97	68	48		4	1,037
Total, Groups I and II	802	299	192	168	77	65	177	68	1,848

Table B2 (*cont.*)

	Carter	Brown	Udall	Wallace	Jackson	Church	Others	Uncommitted	Total
Group III: Caucus states									
Alaska								10	10
Arizona	5		19	1					25
Connecticut	19		16		8			8	51
Delaware	10							2	12
Hawaii			1		1			15	17
Iowa	20		12				2	13	47
Kansas	16		3		1			14	34
Maine	9		5					6	20
Minnesota							48	17	65
Mississippi	5			11			4	4	24
Missouri	39		3		1		1	27	71
New Mexico	8		6					4	18
North Dakota	8							5	13
Oklahoma	12						7	18	37
South Carolina	9			8				14	31
Utah	4					5		9	18
Vermont	3	2	3					4	12
Virginia	23		7					24	54
Washington			7		32			14	53
Wyoming								10	10
Total, Group III	190	2	82	20	43	5	62	218	622
Total, Groups I, II, and III	992	301	274	188	120	70	239	286	2,470

NOTE: The 15 percent cutoff rule is applied to the races in each district; statewide delegates are divided in proportion to the district delegates. New York, Pennsylvania, and Colorado have been omitted from this table because the election results were unavailable in a form that permits precise conversion.

[a] Uncommitted delegate slates in New Jersey and Rhode Island are credited to Governor Brown, as it was understood that most of these delegates would support him.

Table B3. Democratic primary delegate totals, hypothetical results, loophole rules

	Carter	Brown	Udall	Wallace	Jackson	Church	Others	Uncommitted	Total
Group I: Loophole primaries									
Alabama	3			27				5	35
Georgia	50								50
Illinois	57						91	21	169
Louisiana	10			10			21		41
Maryland	30		8		15				53
Nebraska	7					16			23
New Hampshire	17								17
New Jersey	33	75[a]							108
Ohio	117		27				8		152
Texas	126						4		130
West Virginia							26	7	33
Total, Group I	450	75	35	37	15	16	150	33	811
Group II: Proportional primaries									
Arkansas	26								26
California		280							280
Florida	37			20	24				81
Idaho						16			16
Indiana	75								75
Kentucky	46								46
Massachusetts			28	16	60				104
Michigan	73		60						133
Montana						17			17
Nevada		11							11
North Carolina	61								61
Oregon	8					26			34
Rhode Island	11	11[a]							22
South Dakota	17								17
Tennessee	46								46
Wisconsin	45		23						68
Total, Group II	445	302	111	36	84	59			1,037
Total, Groups I, and II	895	377	146	73	99	75	150	33	1,848

NOTE: Delegates within each district are credited to the candidate preference receiving highest district average; statewide delegates are assigned proportionally to reflect division of district delegates. New York and Pennsylvania have been omitted from this table because the election results were unavailable in a form that permits precise conversion.

[a] Uncommitted delegate slates in New Jersey and Rhode Island are credited to Governor Brown, as it was understood that most of these delegates would support him.

Table B4. Democratic delegate totals, hypothetical results, plurality

	Carter	Brown	Udall	Wallace	Jackson	Church	Others	Uncommitted	Total
Group I: Loophole primaries									
Alabama	2			29				4	35
Georgia	50								50
Illinois	52						98	19	169
Louisiana	8			8			25		41
Maryland	36		6		11				53
Nebraska	7					16			23
New Hampshire	17								17
New Jersey	14	94[a]							108
Ohio	139		7				6		152
Texas	127						3		130
West Virginia							28	5	33
Total, Group I	452	94	13	37	11	16	160	28	811
Group II: Proportional primaries									
Arkansas	26								26
California		280							280
Florida	48			15	18				81
Idaho						16			16
Indiana	75								75
Kentucky	46								46
Massachusetts			21	12	71				104
Michigan	88		45						133
Montana						17			17
Nevada		11							11
North Carolina	61								61
Oregon	8					26			34
Rhode Island	9	13[a]							22
South Dakota	17								17
Tennessee	46								46
Wisconsin	48		20						68
Total, Group II	472	304	86	27	89	59			1,037
Total, Groups I and II	924	398	99	64	100	75	160	28	1,848

Table B4 (*cont.*)

	Carter	Brown	Udall	Wallace	Jackson	Church	Others	Uncommitted	Total
Group III: Caucus states									
Alaska								10	10
Arizona			25						25
Connecticut	35		16						51
Delaware	12								12
Hawaii								17	17
Iowa	40							7	47
Kansas	26							8	34
Maine	15							5	20
Minnesota							59	6	65
Mississippi				20				4	24
Missouri	45½							25½	71
New Mexico	11½		2					4½	18
North Dakota	13								13
Oklahoma	9						4	24	37
South Carolina	4							27	31
Utah								18	18
Vermont								12	12
Virginia	21		9½					23½	54
Washington			2	49				2	53
Wyoming								10	10
Total, Group III	232		54½	20	49		63	203½	622
Total, Groups I, II, and III	1,156	398	153½	84	149	75	223	231½	2,470

NOTE: District delegates are credited to candidate preference receiving the highest district average; statewide delegates are credited to candidate preference with the highest statewide total. New York, Pennsylvania, and Colorado have been omitted from this table because the election results were unavailable in a form that permits precise conversion.

[a]Uncommitted delegate slates in New Jersey and Rhode Island are credited to Governor Brown, as it was understood that most of these delegates would support him.

Table B5. Republican delegate totals, actual results

	Ford	Reagan	Uncommitted	Total
Group I: Plurality primaries				
Alabama		37		37
California		167		167
Florida	43	23		66
Georgia		48		48
Illinois	75	11	15	101
Indiana	9	45		54
Maryland	43			43
Nebraska	7	18		25
New Hampshire	18	3		21
New Jersey	67			67
Ohio	91	6		97
Texas		100		100
Wisconsin	45			45
Total, Group I	398	458	15	871
Group II: Proportional representation primaries				
Arkansas	10	17		27
Idaho	4	17		21
Kentucky	19	18		37
Maine	28	15		43
Michigan	55	29		84
Nevada	5	13		18
North Carolina	25	28	1	54
Oregon	16	14		30
Rhode Island	19			19
South Dakota	9	11		20
Tennessee	21	22		43
Total, Group II	211	184	1	396
Total, Groups I and II	609	642	16	1,267

Table B5 (*cont.*)

	Ford	Reagan	Uncommitted	Total
Group III: Caucus states [a]				
Alaska	17	2		19
Arizona	2	27		29
Colorado	5	26		31
Connecticut	35			35
Delaware	15	2		17
Hawaii	18	1		19
Iowa	19	17		36
Kansas	30	4		34
Louisiana	5	36		41
Maine	15	5		20
Minnesota	32	10		42
Mississippi	16	14		30
Missouri	18	31		49
Montana		20		20
New Mexico		21		21
North Dakota	11	7		18
Oklahoma		36		36
South Carolina	9	27		36
Utah		20		20
Vermont	18			18
Virginia	16	35		51
Washington	7	31		38
Wyoming	7	10		17
Total, Group III	295	382		677
Total, all states excluding N.Y., Pa., and W.Va.)	904	1,024	16	1,944

NOTE: This table omits New York, Pennsylvania, and West Virginia, where delegates were chosen without formal commitment.

[a] Caucus state figures are based on national convention votes by the state delegation.

Table B6. Republican primary delegate totals, hypothetical results, proportional

	Ford	Reagan	Uncommitted	Total
Group I: Plurality primaries				
Alabama	13	24		37
California	57	110		167
Florida	34	32		66
Georgia	16	32		48
Illinois	49	35	17	101
Indiana	23	31		54
Maryland	33	10		43
Nebraska	9	16		25
New Hampshire	11	10		21
New Jersey	56	11		67
Ohio	62	35		97
Texas	28	72		100
Wisconsin	24	21		45
Total, Group I	415	439	17	871
Group II: Proportional representation primaries				
Arkansas	10	17		27
Idaho	4	17		21
Kentucky	19	18		37
Maine	29	14		43
Michigan	55	29		84
Nevada	5	13		18
North Carolina	20	34		54
Oregon	16	14		30
Rhode Island	13	6		19
South Dakota	9	11		20
Tennessee	20	23		43
Total, Group II	200	196		396
Total, Groups I and II	615	635	17	1,267

NOTE: The 15 percent cutoff rule is applied to the district races; statewide delegates are divided in proportion to the district delegates. This table omits New York, Pennsylvania, and West Virginia, where delegates were chosen without formal commitment.

Table B7. Republican primary delegate totals, hypothetical results, plurality

	Ford	Reagan	Uncommitted	Total
Group I: Plurality primaries				
Alabama		37		37
California		167		167
Florida	45	21		66
Georgia		48		48
Illinois	77	8	16	101
Indiana	9	45		54
Maryland	43			43
Nebraska	8	17		25
New Hampshire	18	3		21
New Jersey	67			67
Ohio	91	6		97
Texas		100		100
Wisconsin	45			45
Total, Group I	403	452	16	871
Group II: Proportional representation primaries				
Arkansas		27		27
Idaho		21		21
Kentucky	28	9		37
Maine	43			43
Michigan	84			84
Nevada		18		18
North Carolina	3	51		54
Oregon	16	14		30
Rhode Island	19			19
South Dakota	3	17		20
Tennessee	28	15		43
Total, Group II	224	172		396
Total, Groups I and II	627	624	16	1,267

NOTE: District delegates are credited to the candidate with the plurality in that district; statewide delegates are credited to candidate with a statewide plurality. This table omits New York, Pennsylvania, and West Virginia, where delegates were chosen without formal commitment.

Index

Page numbers followed by *t* refer to tables.

Close Calls

CLOSE
CALLS

Jan Reid's Texas

BY JAN REID

Texas A&M University Press : *College Station*

Copyright © 2000 by Jan Reid

Manufactured in the United States of America

All rights reserved

First edition

The paper used in this book meets the minimum requirements
of the American National Standard for Permanence
of Paper for Printed Library Materials, z39.48-1984.
Binding materials have been chosen for durability.

Library of Congress Cataloging-in-Publication Data

Reid, Jan.

      Close calls : Jan Reid's Texas / Jan Reid.—1st ed.

        p.   cm.

     ISBN 0-89096-965-5 (alk. paper)

     1. Texas—Description and travel. 2. Texas—Social conditions—
20th century. 3. Texas, South—Description and travel. 4. Texas,
South—Social conditions—20th century. 5. Texas—Relations—Mexico.
6. Mexico—Relations—Texas. I. Title.

  F391.2.R45   2000

  976.4'063—dc21   00-030242

FOR ROY HAMRIC

& JIM ANDERSON

CONTENTS

Acknowledgments

On May 9, 1998, a remarkable thing happened to me, my wife, Dorothy Browne, my stepdaughter, Lila Vance, and Greg Wilson, who was not yet her husband but was already a member of our family. They were in Austin, and I was in a rehabilitation hospital in Houston trying to recover from a bullet wound, suffered in a Mexico City robbery, that had left me paralyzed from the waist down. An old friend, whose name I won't disclose, paid me a visit that night. Two decades earlier, he had gotten busted holding some pot in Mexico, and he wound up not in prison but in a hellish municipal jail in Piedras Negras. He was one of the benefactors of a wild jailbreak that is described in these pages. He swam the Rio Grande and has since been a model citizen. Off the record he had helped me with that story, and he was appalled and driven to paranoid frenzy, some weeks later, when someone who looked like his twin brother was pictured fleeing a jail cell on the cover of *Texas Monthly*. Total coincidence, I insisted, and in time he learned to laugh about it.

Now he was dating a senior editor of that magazine, and he had stopped by to see me while visiting his mother in Houston. In Austin another friend, Gary Chapman, was knowing of high-tech ways, and he had rigged up a cybercast, I guess you would call it, that would allow me to witness an event in Austin on a computer screen in the hospital. Though he was anxious about his mother, my friend from the old days stayed with me; no one else was in the computer room, and I wouldn't have had the strength to get my wheelchair back to the elevator.

The video failed just as the event in Austin was getting started, and we caught only portions of the audio. But a remarkable group of friends had organized a literary evening and auction to raise money for our medical and living expenses. The people who read that night were all heroes of mine, in different ways. John Graves. Gary Cartwright. Darrell Royal. Larry L. King. Kinky Friedman. Molly Ivins. And Ann Richards. My wife had played bridge with Ann before she ran for elective office and then worked for her when she was Texas' treasurer and governor. But even in the company of such good friends, Dorothy had dreaded the occasion. She feared it would be downcast and somber. Instead it was rowdy and ribald—one of the best parties, many people told me, that Austin had seen in years. I wouldn't have had it any

other way. I wish I could have been there; but then there would have been no reason for it. "Wow," I heard Dorothy say when she was called to the micro-phone. She talked about friendship and community and, without much evidence, predicted: "He's gonna walk." And in time I did.

Turk Pipkin emceed that raucous occasion, and he wrote Ann Richards a draft of her remarks. Ann knew it had been twelve years since my last book was published, and that I'd been inching along on two novels while paying my bills writing magazine articles, almost all of them about some facet of Texas. In her remarks Ann said that it was time for a number of those articles to be gathered in a book, and that she knew people in the audience could make that happen. Molly Ivins and others seconded the proposal. Dave Hamrick of Barnes and Noble, a longtime friend and ally of Texas writers, told an editor of Texas A&M University Press that he would like to have a chance to sell such a book. And that editor made of one the kindest and warmest phone calls I've ever received. Later she helped select the articles and defined the book's broad themes. Mike Levy, the publisher of *Texas Monthly* who had been instrumental in getting me home from Mexico, waived several company rules, for the rights to most of my stories belonged to the magazine. Cathy Casey, a senior editor, gathered up everything I had written for the magazine. Readers made valuable suggestions and a faculty committee at Texas A&M gave the project a green light. Jane Newnham helped me put the articles into the form needed by the Press. With time running out, Bill Hauptman helped me identify the title.

All those people, and those who organized and attended the reading, are responsible for this book. As are a star-studded lineup of Texas musicians who performed The Jan Reid Rescue Concert organized by Mike Hall and Joe Nick Patoski a week after the literary event. Rescued indeed. To the doctors and therapists who got me on my feet, and to the hundreds of people who uplifted me with letters and calls and financial assistance—to all of them, with gratitude I have no way of adequately expressing, I offer this handful of stories.

CLOSE CALLS

INTRODUCTION

The Accidental Journalist

I'm an accidental journalist. I was a reader growing up in North Texas; it beat hoeing the flowerbeds. In the summers, between chores and baseball games, I would ride the city bus down to Wichita Falls' stately little library and fill my pack with juvenilia about animals and ball players, mostly. As adolescence burbled in my juices a best-selling novel appeared, *Harrison High*, written by an author, John Farris, when he was a teenager. Examined now, the book is a dreary endorsement of the mores of the 1950s, but in hallways and locker rooms then it was a sensation, full of thwarted sex and coiffured hoodlums. Inspired, I holed up in my room with a sheaf of note-book paper and scribbled three or four chapters about the lusty problems of a tailback and the cheerleader he most desired. When I started illustrating them I knew the plot had petered out.

I came to the notion of writing as a craft the first time I sat up all night reading a book. I was by then a college freshman, and the phrasing and dialogue that roused me to such uncharacteristic behavior was J. D. Salinger's novel *The Catcher in the Rye.* I had little more than the color of my skin in common with his protagonist, the runaway New York preppie Holden Caulfield. Yet I was moved to my bones. How did a writer *do* that?

A seed was sown, but I wasn't ready to cultivate it. I went through a sorry phase underwritten by my parents. He was a refinery worker, she the daughter of a tenant cotton farmer. The Depression had bitten a mean chunk out of their youths, and their concept of college was utilitarian. The point was to come out prepared to make a living. I thought they should have been able to send me off somewhere stylish. At the hometown university, now called Midwestern State, I started out to be a football coach, then an economist, then a lawyer, then an historian of Latin America or ancient Siam. I had no idea. On impulse I joined the Marine reserves to put on some muscle and get a glimpse of the 1960s promised land, California. I woke up with my head shaved in San Diego, hearing the warbling menace of drill instructors and the drumbeat of marching boots, and thought, pal, you're going to make some mis-

takes in life, but this one's a doozy. Yet it turned out to be my Vietnam draft dodge: Lyndon Johnson and his advisors decided that it hurt them less politically to draft poor kids with no connections than to call up the reserves. I'm not ashamed I sat out the war defending the shores of Abilene. I didn't get out of it by virtue of having a rich and powerful dad. But I still flinch at memories of my intellectual sloth and odd bouts of drunken thuggery. In those years I spent more time shooting pool than reading books or dreaming about writing.

One summer between shifts on a construction crew I started a short story that wandered and rambled nowhere close to an ending. Finally, in my last semester I signed up for a creative writing course. The teacher, James Hoggard, was a versatile and gifted writer; he wore tweeds and corduroys, smoked a pipe, and though he was just four years older, he possessed an erudition that intimidated me. But he encouraged me from the start, and we soon became close friends. Here at last was something I thought I could do. And wanted to do.

For a novice writer raised in that part of the state, a trailblazer loped far out front. Larry McMurtry had won regional acclaim with his early North Texas novels and essays; he was rattling cages in Archer County, just twenty miles away, and his books were being made into movies. My stock was rooted in the same red soil, though my elders were farmers and wildcat oilmen, not cattle ranchers. I didn't meet McMurtry for another twenty years and have never been able to say I know him. But it was impossible not to be influenced by him.

I was twenty-three when I left Wichita Falls. I lived in Dallas for a couple of years, working for an insurance company. I found the city stifling and strange. The sixties were grinding to an end, but here they were a televised mirage. Dallas was as fixed in the fifties as John Foster Dulles. I toyed with the idea of staying on as an advertising copywriter. A schoolteacher in Arlington broke my heart, and I spent the nights banging out a novel about an unhappy young man driven to political assassination. It excited one publisher but, thank God, never saw print. Writing it made me feel uneducated. I hadn't read enough to be a writer.

I arrived in Austin as a graduate student the summer of 1970. Some relatives had lived there when I was growing up, and I always looked forward to our trips to see them. The city and outlying Hill Country were the prettiest parts of Texas I'd seen, and as a boy I had been a breathless fan of Darrell Royal's University of Texas football teams. Now Royal and his employers were fixtures of a deeply resented establishment. The student tenements in

Austin were redolent with political unrest and wafts of smoked dope. Jimi Hendrix and Janis Joplin blared from the open windows.

But if reading was what I desired, the graduate program in American studies left time for little else. I worked hard and did all right for a while. One afternoon, following weeks of heavy slogging through the novels of Henry James, I hurled a tome the length of my apartment when he had a heroine daintily exclaim: "Oh! Oh! Oh!" The books firing my imagination were McMurtry's collection of essays, *In a Narrow Grave;* the Willie Morris memoir, *North Toward Home;* and John Graves' ruminations on nature, history, and neighbors, *Goodbye to a River.* I was determined to stay on long enough to finish a master's degree so I would have something to show my parents, but after just a year I was an academic burnout. For me the Ph.D. chase was a rat race that drew out all my fears of inferiority. Amid a swarm of comely women I was a lonesome mess.

The chairman of the department was William Goetzmann, a Pulitzer Prize-winning historian of the West. One night he invited the graduate students to his home. The star candidate for a job at UCLA or Cornell pulled me aside and said: "Get out of this while you still can." Instead of going home and quietly pondering his advice I stayed on at the party, knocking down shots of our professor's vodka. I was observed mumbling to myself in the kitchen. At the end of the evening, as our host amiably conversed and no doubt longed to clear the house of us, I found myself on a living room sofa with two or three others, arguing the merits of Texas fiction. Goetzmann held that aside from the few novels Paul Horgan had set in Texas, there was nothing of the first water. As I remember it, I made an impassioned case for McMurtry's *Leaving Cheyenne* and Bill Brammer's *The Gay Place.* Boy, I told him good. Then I flung open the door, planning a masterful exeunt, and walked into a closet.

Now I had two degrees and *still* no trade. When the oilfields around Wichita Falls played out, the refineries closed and my dad had been transferred to the East Texas town of Mount Pleasant. I stayed with them as the job search began. One day the mail brought a note of acceptance from the *Texas Observer* for a poem I'd submitted. It was my first published writing, and I savored the giddy rush of elation, but I had the good sense to retire at once from that fray. I'm no poet. Still, I took it as an omen. I was confident I could write, and I started applying for jobs with big-city newspapers. The *Fort Worth Press* was hanging on by a thread. I knew the prose and lore of exceptional Texas writers who had come out of there—Blackie Sherrod, Dan Jenkins, Bud Shrake, Gary Cartwright. When I made the appointment I thought they

would recognize the natural succession and be glad to get me. The weekend editor wore jeans and a T-shirt. Ignoring the file of unpublished manuscripts I offered him as evidence of my talent, he gave me a fact sheet about a corpse found in a Trinity River bottom, and told me to produce a story in fifteen minutes. The typewriter where he sat me down had no J—the key was broken. I choked: failed the test completely and slunk down the stairs, humiliated.

I came up dry with the large dailies because I couldn't convince anyone I was a reporter. I swallowed my pride, took my mom's advice, and answered an ad in the paper thrown on their lawn, the *Mount Pleasant Tribune.* The job included servicing a couple of advertising accounts, and I wore out a clutch on my car delivering papers on a rural route. Part of my pay was the nickels and dimes scraped from machines outside cafes and motels. But it was first-rate on-the-job training. I covered a city council, a school board, the "cop shop," rodeos, murder trials, cattle auctions, Friday night football. The meadows and pine forests in that country were beautiful and yet felt somewhat alien to me. Many before me have observed that the culture in those woodlands belongs to the South, not the West. I had begun to realize that Austin, San Antonio, and the surrounding hilly terrain were where I wanted to put down roots. I horrified my folks and quit one job to seek another, but I surprised them and landed well—the sports editor of the *New Braunfels Herald-Zeitung.* Half the people in the Hill Country town were Hispanic, but it was run by people whose first language was German. I found the Texas Germans gruff but affable. I made lasting friends in New Braunfels, held that job three years, and stayed in the area several more.

In the course of pounding the pavement that led me there, I was talking to the editor of *Texas Parks & Wildlife* magazine in Austin one day. He read a few of my clips and said he was sorry he had nothing for me. As I turned to leave, he said, "You know, some guys in town are starting a new magazine. I heard the publisher at a Chamber of Commerce luncheon the other day. You ought to go talk to him."

The editor directed me to an uncomely two-story building nearby. Up the dark and narrow stairs I arrived in an office and asked to see the publisher. A bald man about my age strode out with an air of tremendous agitation and haste. He wore a necktie and long-sleeved white shirt.

"No jobs, we got no jobs," he said, shaking my hand then snatching the folder of my clips. "But we're looking for writers. Ideas. Stories. But no bluebonnets." He vetoed that with a karate-like slash of his hand. "I don't want to see anything about bluebonnets." Then, just as abruptly, he was gone.

That was my first exposure to Mike Levy, the founder of *Texas Monthly*. The story of his obsessed and single-minded determination to put out a state-wide magazine has been well told elsewhere. Mike has always had a habit of working his marketing slogans into his everyday discourse. He's like an old-time sidewalk barker: say it often enough to enough people and eventually the message gets across. He was competing against Sunday supplements of papers in Houston, San Antonio, and his native Dallas. In content they were soft and safe, full of clichés. So his new marketing campaign promised no sacred cows or spreads of bluebonnets. (About fifteen years later, with quiet satisfaction I would slip into his pages a short piece about the state flower.)

As I was moving to New Braunfels, I received a short note from a *Texas Monthly* editor, Greg Curtis. He said my essay and book review were too dated to publish, but he liked the writing and urged me to send him ideas for other stories. In early 1973 I remember seeing their first issue on an Austin newsstand. As I stood browsing, a young woman asked me how it was. "Surprisingly good," I said.

Stumped for ideas to pitch them, I plunged into my new job, but within days the pursuits converged. A couple of losers robbed an ice house in San Antonio, ran a red light in front of a cop, and soon led a convoy of twenty-five to forty officers and reporters on a ninety-mile-per-hour chase up Interstate 35, guns blazing both ways. Shades of the old frontier—desperados running from the posse. The bandits' car tumbled off the road beside a New Braunfels high school, and they expired shortly and predictably, with 122 bullet holes in the driver's door alone. My twelve-hundred-word piece on the shootout and chase ran in May, 1973, *Texas Monthly*'s fourth issue. I kept a photocopy of the forty-dollar check for a long time. I thought it certified me as a writer.

All the rage in those days were books like Hunter S. Thompson's *Fear and Loathing in Las Vegas,* Michael Herr's *Dispatches,* and Tom Wolfe's *The Electric Kool-Aid Acid Test.* Themes of war, drugs, craziness. Wolfe codified the style of writing with a foreword to his anthology *The New Journalism.* The emphasis was on snappy dialogue, scene-by-scene construction, and brash inventiveness—Wolfe specialized in sound effects. In proclaiming a new art form he pronounced the novel dead. Nonsense, of course. If much of Wolfe's writing holds up today, it's probably his subsequent novels. But magazine journalism, long the pedestrian of American writing, became a force in the 1970s. A man named Clay Felker developed the publishing formula at *New York,* where Wolfe made his flashy debut. The city magazine aimed at hip, urbane, upscale consumers—what to do, where to eat, what to buy.

A lawyer who chose not to practice, Mike Levy absorbed every angle and

nuance of the formula while selling ads for *Philadelphia* magazine. The difference was that this true believer meant to apply it to a sprawling, wildly diverse state whose residents take great pride in their rural past and vast stretches of emptiness. Someone wisely talked him out of naming his magazine *Texas Cities*, but the lineage and self-image were clear. Bill Broyles, the first editor of *Texas Monthly*, gave me a copy of Wolfe's anthology when he asked to add my name to the masthead as a contributing editor.

Felker had carried down from the mount one commandment that always grated on me: No poetry or fiction. Why? It never diminished the quality and heft of the *New Yorker*. The prohibition was dismissive and estranging to writers any magazine could use. The literary quarterlies I had been wooing might pay half a penny a word. But these magazine folks were willing to publish me regularly and pay me hundreds of dollars for features. So I set my fiction on other burners and happily became a magazine journalist.

And I was in good company. Bill Broyles and Greg Curtis had been writing students of McMurtry at Rice University. Bill hired two more of their Rice colleagues, Griffin Smith, Jr. and Paul Burka, and enlisted two experienced freelance writers, Larry L. King and Gary Cartwright. Other originals, freelancer and staff, included Richard West, Ann Barnstone, Al Reinert, Stephen Harrigan, and Prudence Mackintosh. In time that crowd could boast more than a dozen first-rate collections of non-fiction, some fine novels, hair-raising true crime books, two Academy Award nominations, a hit Broadway musical, a presidential speechwriter, and a lodestone of Texas political commentary. But in those days you could look around the room and see we didn't know what we were doing.

Except one desk in that cramped Austin office was reserved for a writer we held in awe. While working on the senatorial staff of Lyndon Johnson, Bill Brammer had written his novel *The Gay Place*. Published in 1961, it was really a triplet of novellas, loosely strung together, and was set more in Austin than Washington. But his creation of a profane Texas governor named Arthur Fenstemaker was received as a telling inside look at Johnson's character; the book is still considered one of America's best political novels. Denied access when he got a contract to write a non-fiction book about Johnson's sudden presidency, Brammer found that the exotic vices of the sixties enticed him far more than the hard work of finishing another novel. Billie Lee, as everyone now called him, would die in 1977 from an amphetamine overdose when he was just forty-seven. It's a sad tale and yet he was a joyous little man. And for me and countless other writers who crossed his path, he was a gently coaxing mentor.

Texas Monthly got only a couple of stories out of him before he stopped coming to work and spared admirers the pain of letting him go. During those first months he didn't teach us so much as he opened the gate and told us to scat. In the tiny office his raconteuring could be quite a distraction to writers trying to push a paragraph along. Bill Broyles likes to tell the story of how Billie Lee came in one day strung so tight he hummed like a telephone wire. He sat down, leaned back, clasped his hands behind his head, and soon had the staffers hanging on every word. Suddenly he stopped and looked at his desk with real alarm. "My hands!" he cried. "What happened to my hands?"

After he quit the magazine I went to see him one day when I was in Austin. Prominent on a wall of his apartment was one of Mike Levy's famous memos. The publisher complained that the stack of *New York, Philadelphia,* and other exemplars of Clay Felker's genius had been put out for the writers' enjoyment and edification. Those were Mike's magazines, damn it, and following was a list of the issues he wanted back. Tacked around the memo on Billie Lee's wall was the cover of every one of the purloined classics.

Now I blink and find that twenty-five years have passed. During that time I've finished fewer books than I would have hoped and I've paid the bills some months and years as a government and political speechwriter. But for the most part I have made my way as a freelance magazine writer. That's not something you would wish on a grandchild. Financial security is not a characteristic of the trade. On the other hand, I have seldom been bored by my work, and I have come to know a great deal of Texas. I've complained at times that it's a double whammy—not only do I live in Texas, but it's all anybody ever wants me to write about. But for all my bitching, moaning, and foreign wanderlust, I love the place.

This book is a roadmap to a large part of my life. When I was younger I would carve mental notches of my conquests—*Esquire, Men's Journal, Mother Jones, The New York Times Magazine*—knowing that in most cases it would be a one-night stand. One of the articles in this book, the end piece, is an uncut version of an essay I wrote for *GQ*. All the rest first appeared in *Texas Monthly*—though I've taken the opportunity here to trim and smooth and change some things back the way I wanted them. The magazine has enjoyed national respect and prominence and a very long run. I take pride in its successes and admit to my part in its failings. A journal that started out rattling the establishment has become the establishment, and like a cat now it often sits preening, adoring its place in the world. It remains hidebound by Clay Felker's formula. But the most stinging criticism is that we, the writers and

editors, have been lily-white from the start. It's true, and no one knows exactly why and how that happened. It certainly wasn't the racism of which we've been accused. Yet while the magazine has addressed the state's diversity in its coverage, it has failed to encourage and enlist the talent within those ethnic communities. No wonder they're alienated and contemptuous.

It stings a bit when I'm characterized as "a *Texas Monthly* writer." From the start it has largely operated as a staff-written magazine, but the distance of a freelance relationship has worked best for both them and me. The one time I was employed there, after a few months I was "downsized" in a way that felt distinctly like a firing. We were like the couple who live together happily and so get married and screw it up. I was broke and bitter for a while. But in other years their press published my favorite book, the novel *Deerinwater,* and when I lay hurt and close to dying or paralysis in Mexico, they were the ones who got me home. They've been my friends half my life. And that friendship is the genesis of this book.

I wish the assignments had given me more chance to write about women— for that I've confided in my unprolific fiction. I've seldom written about religion or business, as such, and I'm about as low-tech as they come. But I've avoided the niches and specializations that some writers seek. I'm blessed with a restless curiosity and an appreciation of the ways that people and place shape each other. Range and versatility have been my long suits.

I've never been inclined to belabor my ancestors. The names—Reid, Shelton, Nichols—bolster my belief that they were part of the Scotch-Irish flood of people who came south then west across America in the nineteenth century. Where and when they came ashore as immigrants is lost in the generations, and Texas, I suspect, is just where they happened to stop. But sometimes I imagine a crowded wagon driven by a man, my great-great-grandfather Reid, who lost an arm fighting with the Confederates at Shiloh. His son, whom I remember as a tall, gentle, blind man in his nineties, rode on a cattle drive to New Mexico on a route that took him through the Lincoln County War, the killer's proving ground of Billy the Kid. That man, my great-grandfather, settled in the Central Texas hills that would beckon me. He loved to tell the story of living to see one of his sons land an army biplane in the litter of a grain field and stride up to the home place grinning, wearing a uniform of World War I. Home place. I didn't start out with an uncommon take on Texas. But in bits and pieces maybe I've ended up with one.

MARCH, 2000

PART I

THE TEXAS
CHARACTER
Legacy of Courage,
History of Violence

The last Comanche and Kiowa bands were whipped and banished and barbed wire etched its rectangles across the plains by the 1880s. Yet the ethos of the frontier continues to define us. I have trouble believing Texans are any more violent than comparably diverse and populous groups of people in the United States. Violence is a national problem and condition, not a provincial one. The hardiest vestige of the Texas frontier exists not in dusty little towns and wide open spaces—à la Hollywood—but in our inner cities. From the first query I mailed to an editor, I spent years chasing the tail of violence. I reflected on the fixation that Texans have with guns, and the article set off a furious storm of complaint. I rode in squad cars with Dallas street cops who ushered me into a world of pimps and junkies and bar fighters—a straitlaced city's raw, gritty, and humorous underside. A year later, one of the Dallas cops I had profiled got into a savage hand-to-hand fight with a nineteen-year-old black kid, and killed him. The shooting threatened to ignite Dallas race relations that had smoldered for decades, and I was the only reporter the beleaguered cop chose to talk to. Emotionally I couldn't take a constant diet of that. A time came when I felt I was dwelling too much on the dark side of human experience, so I withdrew from it.

Or so I thought.

Texans freed themselves from Mexican rule with acts of violence, and those whose homesteads pushed back the frontier lived with the knowledge that any day ferocious aborigines might come. The courage born of facing dire harm and peril is a large part of our legacy. But physical bravery is just one

kind of courage. It can sustain the faith and culture of a tiny, impoverished tribe of Kickapoo Indians in the borderlands of Texas and Mexico. It can drive the days and nights of sisters who try to save their historic family ranch from the might of real estate developers and the state's corps of road builders. And courage can distinguish a lonely, defeated old politician who with courtesy and grace hangs on to his principles in the face of a young, dismissive, and cocksure majority.

A Grand Canyon

I grew up in North Texas and am naturally drawn to that region's lore. The plains were the site of the Texans' and soldiers' last, furious wars against the Comanches and Kiowas, and the Indian wars corresponded with the first and bravest of the cattle drives. The names and adventures of Quanah Parker, Charles Goodnight, and Ranald Mackenzie have thrilled and fascinated me since I was a boy. The Comanches' pivotal defeat came in Palo Duro Canyon. And the plains' first great cattle ranch took root there just one year later.

When an editor asked in 1985 if I would write about Palo Duro, I jumped at the opportunity. But the question soon became, How? My wife, Dorothy Browne, who then worked for a civil liberties organization in Austin, said she knew an Amarillo lawyer who sometimes did pro bono work for them. He was kind of a cowboy, she said, and he rode mules in Palo Duro Canyon. My long friendship with Selden Hale was born—as was my admiration for the mule, a historically neglected but essential creature of our frontier past. I prefer not to inject myself into magazine stories, but on this assignment it was unavoidable. For the first time, Dorothy went with me on a story assignment. Our adventure was dwarfed by the awesome human events that once transpired in the canyon. Still, it was a mule ride to remember.

Nowadays the Nile-green plain of the Panhandle abounds with distant compass points: windmills, telephone poles, ranch houses with stands of cottonwoods and elms. But when Coronado's expedition wandered across that barren in 1541, the Spaniards were lost in a shortgrass sea. No hills, no trees, no shrubs, nothing but moving brown herds of shaggy bison. The only features of terrain were the dry, shallow lakebeds now called playas (the Spanish word for shores) and smaller depressions that came to be known as buffalo wallows. In those low spots rainwater gathered and stood, the theory goes, and over the ages the buffalo millions deepened them by rolling in the mud and

dust. Sweating under postfeudal armor and Panhandle heat, the conquistadors were, in modern vernacular, as spooked as they could be.

Francisco Vásquez de Coronado, the well-married colonial governor, led a mass migration of cavalry, infantry, priests, and Indians—fifteen hundred of them in all—along with thousands of horses, cattle, and sheep. In search of Quivira, the richest of the seven mythical Cities of Gold (an intoxicating myth, considering that the first had proven to be nothing more than a Zuñi pueblo), the Europeans were lured on by a captured Indian slave they called the Turk, because he looked like one. "Just ahead," he kept telling them. One of Coronado's officers, Don Rodrigo Maldonado, was dispatched eastward until he could find something—anything—to report. He tried to line his way back to camp with piles of rocks and buffalo chips. The land offered no inkling of what he was about to see. From a distance of three hundred to four hundred yards, the horizon of pale grass may have shown its first sign of parting, a glimpse of the underlying caliche. And then, suddenly, he was on the stunning brink of it—a vast chasm extending thousands of yards across, a subsoil mountain range snaking and broadening in the distance for miles, dropping off from the prairie five hundred feet and more. Straight down.

The rock cliffs were hued downward in beige and yellow, grays becoming olive and lavender, maroons approaching vermilion on the canyon's floor. On the walls boulders perched at precarious angles. The crags and mesas suggested the profiles of camels, humans, apes. The cheeks of the earth's rock face wore a stubble of clinging juniper; among glens of grass, trees grew thick trunked and tall on the canyon's floor. Mexican traders later named the canyon Palo Duro, which means hard wood. Coronado's scout gaped at a geological fluke that had begun as a simple erosion gully about a million years earlier. The rock formations tell anteceding stories of Ice Age horses, sabertoothed cats, dinosaurs, and the landlocked Permian Sea. Don Rodrigo Maldonado had no clear sense of that, of course. He was probably thinking that if they could just find a safe way down, here at last was shelter and water. But after seeing nothing but miles of the eerie uniform plains, standing on the rim of Palo Duro produces a vertigo that suggests the epochs and transcends mere centuries. How could this netherworld of utter contrast *be* here?

Four hundred forty-three years later, my wife and I sat on saddled mules and peered down over the canyon rim. Ordinarily, we embarked on camping trips with chilled asparagus, a marinated lamb, my stepdaughter, Lila, and the family car. Having left with apologies and a promise of souvenirs to the child, this morning we wore boots, thick shirts, leather work gloves, stylish trim-line

chaps called chinks, bandannas, and gimme caps (hers a *USS New Jersey*, mine a Bell Helicopter). We were dudes with a mildly daring recreational plan.

You can drive through a well-maintained state park at the mouth of Palo Duro, but to really appreciate the canyon you have to see the upper regions owned by private ranchers, one of whom had granted us access. I was a dilettante historian on muleback—not the most swashbuckling self-image—and Dorothy was along for the ride. Against the backdrop of Palo Duro's past, the cushy triviality of our little adventure had me feeling sheepish. But now the rock-hard fact of the place had my heart in my throat.

I do not wish to exaggerate the dimensions of Palo Duro Canyon. Seen from the air, it loses much of its mystery. Wrinkled with gullies, the plain deteriorates into a raw scrape of erosion, the brakes of the heavily silted and aptly named Red River. The headwater ravines sprawl 120 miles across four counties south of Amarillo. Geologically, Palo Duro's rock formations are said to approximate those along the rim of the Grand Canyon—a good mile above the massive Arizona canyon's floor. On the scale of comparison, that will do. But the schizophrenic dislocation and euphoria born of first seeing Palo Duro have not diminished since Coronado's discovery. The plain goes straight to the brink, then picks up and extends with the same monotony beyond the divide; it would not be a good place to stub one's toe in the dark.

While the dry creek and wooded meadows below were handsome, at the moment I couldn't call them inviting. Our host rancher, like most of his neighbors, had brought in bulldozers to grade crude roads down to the floor. Locally the Caterpillar operators have reputations and renown comparable to those of Alaskan bush pilots. Using the blades for brakes, they essentially skidded down the cliffs, prepared at all times to bail out. Some of that heavy machinery landed upside down on the canyon's floor. Safe and easy ways down are Palo Duro's scarcest feature.

Selden Hale, a laconic man with prematurely gray hair, had volunteered to be our guide and outfitter. Selden practices criminal law in Amarillo, but the inscription on his stationery, "Mules, Outlaws, Pistols, and Cynicism," suggests his avocation and preferred topics of conversation. His great-grandmother was one of the first Anglo-Saxon women to settle in the Panhandle, and he grew up on his family's ranch north of Borger. Raised on horseback, he now has a middle-aged devotion to mules that has both its romantic and practical sides. To someone of his troglodytic nature, it doesn't hurt mules' cause at all that population curves indicated mules should have been extinct in this country by 1958. Lots of times Selden feels practically extinct himself.

But he has also found that mules suit his needs better than horses. He likes to hunt elk high in the Rockies or ride for days through rugged sections of North and West Texas, seeking a sense of the lost frontier. And mules are the perfect vehicles. With tremendous power in their hindquarters, mules are disproportionately stronger than horses, and they can recover from exhaustion in a single night. Their narrow hooves, short step, and relatively long front legs enable them to traverse steep terrain that makes stumblebums of horses, which evolved, in all fairness, on the open plains. Also, mules keep their heads and concentrate better when rocks start to slide. Human observation of these rough-country traits go as far back as Homer, who wrote in the *Iliad:* "And before them went the mules; And ever upward, downward, and sideward they fared."

In preparing us for Palo Duro's steep terrain, however, Selden had warned that riding mules requires more patience than traveling on horseback does. Reins laid on the right side of a horse's neck signal a desired left turn. To communicate the same request to a mule, you have to extend your left arm far out and slowly pull its head around—the difference, roughly, between steering a power-everything Oldsmobile and steering a dump truck. Stopping a mule requires just as much effort. "Lean back in the saddle, pull back on the reins, then release," he briefed us. "Lean back, pull back, and release. All the time, you're saying, 'Whoa.' That's important. Say, '*Whooooa.*'"

Because of my weight and the length of my legs, Selden had lent me his own favorite mount, Stagger Lee, a big mule with an unusual white splash on his haunch. "Great name," I said, patting the mule's thick neck. "The old blues song."

"That," our guide mumbled vaguely, "and, uh, well, he does have a little stagger in his step."

After making sure the cinches were tight, Selden eyed the canyon floor and told us to follow the example of those bulldozer operators: "Kick your feet out of the stirrups and let the mules have their heads. If it looks like you're going to get some action, don't be afraid to jump off."

Noting the length and sobriety of our exchanged stares, he decided wisely that perhaps we weren't quite ready for that. Leaving the "scenic route" for another time, he led the strawberry-roan pack mule, Pumpkin, and disappeared around the switchbacks astride the sorrel, Reddy. Dorothy and I stumbled and slipped afoot and clung to our mules' reins. The best thing I can say about that hike is that it didn't take very long. At times I clawed at rocks with my gloved left hand and tried to fend off Stagger Lee's sixfold weight with my right. (Pulling rank on the chain of being, I let him have the ledge.) He huffed and puffed in chorus with me and staggered often,

misstepping with his right front foot. "He's going to step on me and crush me for sure," I kept thinking, though in fact his occasional pressure was as tentative and considerate as a cat's. Dorothy and her beast, Fat Mule, descended in the same heart-thumping fashion. I asked her later what she had been thinking. Her reply: "I am Lila's only mother."

My first impression of the floor was the extraordinary redness of the exposed bedrock and soil. Interlaced with shining white veins of gypsum, which suggest the evaporation of a landlocked sea, the dominant red-brick shale is characteristic of the Quartermaster formations that geologists place in the Permian Age, about 390 million years ago. A third of the way up the walls the bedrock shale variegates into maroon, gray, and lavender patterns called the Spanish Skirts. The multicolored bluffs belong to the Tecovas formation, which derived from sediments of jungle swamps and streams. The Tecovas shales contain much of Palo Duro's wealth of fossils. Toward the rim the blond quartz, sandstone, and caliche represent the Ogallala formation. These youngest rocks are often the most resistant to erosion, which accounts for all the long-necked buttes and balanced pedestal rocks that geologists call hoodoos.

Despite the jabbering excitement that marked our safe descent, as we rode across the canyon floor Dorothy and I both fell silent and simply stared. Palo Duro's geological trademark is a three hundred-foot pillar named the Lighthouse because of the shape. Always beyond some ridge, the Lighthouse vanished and reappeared as mysteriously as the moon.

Like the Grand Canyon, Palo Duro dug itself into being with the help of flowing water. Springs and red clay gullies make intermittent creeks and flood ravines that become a running stream, the Prairie Dog Town Fork; the Red River's two-thousand-mile trek toward the Mississippi is born. Over 90 million years the Panhandle's incessant wind has also played a part. But the erosion of Palo Duro is distinctive because so much of it works straight down. In a process called piping, surface water percolates downward, weakening and undercutting porous layers, removing grains of sand. Eventually the formations cave in on themselves. Boulders propped on the steep grades above the floor have the appearance of a stop-action landslide, and the effect is no illusion. In this form of erosion, the debris creeps, slips, and flows. The rapidity of the vertical erosion was apparent in the sad state of this ranch's fences. Long sections sagged and twisted into strands of barbed-wire rope because the supporting soil had fallen away from the cedar posts. Palo Duro is a giant hole in the ground, forever consuming itself.

Yet for all its alluvial origins and oasis-like flora, Palo Duro suffers the scarcity of water so obvious on the plains. Rainfall averages only twenty inches a year; rock hounds liken the canyon to the Painted Desert. Still, Palo Duro makes splendid use of what little moisture it has. Scrub oak, catclaw, and mountain mahogany were abundant enough in the draws that to keep Fat Mule moving, my wife had to bang him often with her heels—befitting his name, he had a keen eye for delectable nibbles along the way. Though mesquite and occasional willows thrive on the canyon floor, the dark jade of juniper dominates the woodland hue. And it's not just the pestilent growth that we call scrub cedar; that brush chokes the higher ravines and clings to the canyon walls. On the floor, Rocky Mountain junipers make splendid shade trees with trunks several feet thick. Palo Duro's water supply is meager, but the seep springs are easy to spot. Set above and against the dark juniper, the cottonwoods' green stands out as bright and cheery as clover. The cottonwood is the plains equivalent of its relative, the mountain aspen. If you find cottonwoods on the arid plains, you find water, the roosts of wild turkeys, the soothing clatter of waxen leaves in the evening breeze.

The floor produces a strangely inverted sense of well being. The ages of its habitations almost whisper. Coronado's men, after making their own harrowing descent, encountered Teyas Indians, who hunted buffalo on foot, used dogs as pack animals, and foraged plums, berries, and grapes on the canyon's floor. According to Coronado's chroniclers, the aborigines were neither hostile nor friendly. They stared a lot. On one of the first evenings, the Spaniards watched storm clouds turn the green of copper above the canyon walls. The storm destroyed equipment, stampeded horses, and sent hailstones, which one writer claimed were as large as bowls, bouncing off the men's plumed helmets. Still, the Spaniards never doubted that they were better off in the canyon than up there on the featureless plain. Running short of provisions during that fortnight, the bravest among them ventured out on the prairie and hunted buffalo. The Spaniards often crouched beside the carcasses until the sun's descent created shadow—and direction—from the slain forms. At night their colleagues blew trumpets and lit fires on the canyon's rim so the crazed hunters could find their way back. One of the friars with Coronado, Juan de Padilla, proposed a service thanking God for His mercy and bounty. He said the Palo Duro mass eighty years before the Pilgrims celebrated their Thanksgiving at Plymouth Rock.

The hunting shack that served as our base camp was nestled under cliffs in a thick grove of junipers and cottonwoods. Our mules approached a pool of

the rust-colored creek thirstily enough but soon confirmed their reputation as finicky drinkers, turning up their noses at the gypsum taste.

I helped Selden unload Pumpkin, whose initial performance as a pack mule had warmed her new owner's heart. Once the saddles, traces, and pack frames came off, mules always like to take a good roll in the dirt; even old United States Army manuals advised teamsters to indulge that whim. Because it wasn't possible to corral Pumpkin, Selden's fears of a fugitive mule weighed heavy on his mind, so he tied her to a tree. The prospect of an afternoon off wasn't enough to diminish her mulish pique, though, and she pitched a lunging, heel-kicking fit that succeeded only in making shackles of the halter rope. "Are you through now?" Selden yelled at her. "*Will that do?*"

Throughout our brief acquaintance, the mules had remained totally mute, except for the occasional, exerted snufflings of equine lips. But now, while we lunched on dried fruit and granola bars, Reddy extended his neck, bared his buck teeth, and voiced the cry that prompted Westerners to nickname mules Rocky Mountain canaries.

On the way out of the camp, Selden spurred Reddy across the shallows of the creek. "I wish I could have lived a hundred years ago," he said, then smiled at the quaintness of his remark. "As long as they'd let me keep penicillin."

We came upon a windmill that hadn't pumped water in a long time. The absence of moisture thinned and stunted the trees. As the canyon widened and the sky paled with midday heat, the desolation of the rock formations seemed almost lunar. Though a few Herefords chewed their cuds and stared, the apparent lack of animal life was unsettling. A lone buzzard lazed on the updraft. The wildlife was there, but in the presence of humans it tried to go unseen.

"Godamighty!" erupted Selden. "What an eye!"

He swung down off Reddy and snatched a fragment from the strew of rocks. It was an unfinished but well-crafted arrowhead that would have been used for large game. To the original inhabitants, much of Palo Duro's magic lay in its splendor as a hunting ground. Ice Age Paleo-Indians hunted mammoths and giant bison here more than twelve thousand years ago. Archaics established their culture about 5000 B.C., supplementing a diet of half-raw meat with vegetation foraged off the canyon floor. During the time of the early Christians, Neo-Americans hunted in Palo Duro but also made pottery and cultivated crops. As it often happened, the barbaric villagers lost the choice domain to more warlike nomads. Apaches claimed Palo Duro for three hundred years before losing it in turn to their blood enemies, the Comanches. Both tribes relied on buffalo—the Comanches more than the Apaches—but

hunting bison on foot was no easy task. The Indians were forever starting range fires, hoping to stampede the herds over cliffs. Palo Duro offered both a place to trap buffalo and a secure base camp for the hunts and warring sorties on the plains. The arrival of Spaniards on horseback revolutionized the lives of the Apaches and Comanches. In addition to making them even more war-like, the borrowed horse culture meant they could match the mobility of buffalo, deer, and other countless prey. They thought they would never have to go hungry again.

Our ride wore on with telling effects. The mules were lathered and gaunt. Dorothy's carriage in the saddle reflected ample hours of youthful riding experience, but she was up against the friction of her denim seams. Blue jeans are blue jeans, right? Wrong. She quickly discovered why the inside seams of Levi's are sewn outward and ride far back against her thighs. The more sightly, hidden seams of her Liz Claibornes rode precisely on the contact points of her saddle and knees, scraping two large and painful strawberries. My ouchy sacrum was batted like a Ping-Pong ball every time Stagger Lee broke a trot. Still, I was getting the hang of it. The mule's natural gait is a driving, long-stepping walk. The saddle rhythm is comfortable, almost sensual. Circling back toward the hunting shack, we rode through a broad dry creek with chopped rock walls. A characteristic formation of great intrigue to Palo Duro geologists, the exposed gypsum sagged and buckled like a worn-out mattress. We paused and commented on the prettiness of a salt cedar in frail lavender bloom. A songbird twittered.

I was thinking that it takes a long while to begin to hear the quiet. In the city your hearing throws up a selective barricade against the freeways and trucks and all intrusive sound. On the way to the airport the day before, I had come close to my first fistfight in about twenty years. My opponent was an earnest young man with all the right liberal causes on his bumper stickers, and the serious issue in question was whether I had any right to honk my horn at a van backing blindly out of a post office parking space. "Civilization!" I was thinking. "By golly, rural is better." As we came out of the creek bed, I slouched in the saddle, enjoying the mule's rhythm. Slow dance, Stagger Lee. I removed my gimme cap and wiped my brow, holding the reins loosely with the other hand. I was writing, as writers are wont to do—gone to the Bahamas, my wife puts it. I was writing this paragraph, without the least suspicion about how it was about to end.

It may have been a rattlesnake. Perhaps it was the urban vibes and prose style. But all at once the long black ears jumped erect, swung about, flared with alarm, and I was off to the races on a runaway mule. Stagger Lee's full-

tilt boogie caught me by such surprise that I lost one rein, which hardly enhanced pulling him up. I'm not sure how the gimme cap wound up back on my head. But leaning over his neck, trying to grab the flopping rein, I had mortal visions of how much this fall was going to hurt. The hard ground and pointed rocks may in fact have kept me aboard. I'm certain the adrenaline helped. For at least five seconds, I rode the hell out of that mule. All the time I was yelling, "Hyeeeaaah! Hyeeeaaah!"

"Try '*Whoooooa!*'" our guide suggested from afar.

With both reins finally in hand, I leaned back, pulled back, and released not much at all. "Whoa," I soothed Stagger Lee, who shuddered and rolled his eyes unhappily. "It's all right. Whoa."

"Hyeeeaaah," Selden chided, grinning at my wife. "I think that's Samurai for 'giddyup.'"

Long after the cottonwoods and hunting shack fell deep in shadow, the sun was resplendent on the blond cliffs. Dorothy and I dragged our chairs outside and eased our soreness with whiskey scavenged from hunters' trash. Watching the darkness gather, Selden told us about his great-grandparents, who settled in the Panhandle in the late 1870s. Preparing for bed one pleasant spring night, they laid an infant niece in her crib and cracked the door to let some air in. Attracted by the light, a rabid skunk ran inside and attacked the child. The shattered man wrapped his niece in a blanket and, using two horses, rode nearly two hundred miles without stopping to the nearest doctor, in Dodge City, Kansas. The doctor told him there was nothing to be done. He returned home but kept on riding, far south into Texas, to locate a madstone, a hairball found in the stomach of a buffalo. Plains Indians believed that the hairballs had magic medicinal properties. The child died, of course. It was a sad story, movingly told. Selden's point, I think, was that we have a rather petulant way of exaggerating our hardships now. Somewhere off in the woods a whippoorwill sang its blue cry. We propped our chairs back and admired the orange rise of a big moon, almost full. Little more than a hundred years ago, that benign romantic vision would have struck terror in our souls. A Comanche moon.

The Comanches started out as Shoshones—short, thick, broad-jawed people who lived in the Rocky Mountains and were despised for their crude tribal lore and pitiable dietary pursuits by their more lordly neighbors, like the Sioux. In 1705 the Spaniards first encountered some of these people, who had feuded with kinsmen and moved down onto the plains. That meeting of cultures

revised the status of Comanches almost overnight. They became the continent's elite horsemen. At the peak of the tribe's prestige and power, an ordinary Comanche male might own two hundred fifty horses, his war chief fifteen hundred. Because of their skill at breeding and stealing horses—and pack mules—their Shoshone dialect became the trade language of the aboriginal plains. Raiding deep into Texas and Mexico, they liked to ride in the warm months, when the grass was long and rich in nourishment. They timed their raids to coincide with the waxing moon; with plenty of light, they could attack the settlers when they slept and then be fifty miles away by dawn. Hence the chilling term, "Comanche moon." Comanches didn't just kill and scalp. They stole children, raped and mutilated women, slowly tortured men to death. Paramilitary bands of Texas Rangers fought back with blood and atrocity in their own eyes. Among other things, the Comanche wars perfected the new American art of proximate murder by handgun. Five national governments made various claims on the Southern plains, but savages on horseback blocked settlement for 150 years. The Spanish term stated reality in that 240,000-square-mile area—"Comanchería."

But by the summer of 1874 Comanchería had dwindled to a string of renegade encampments in Tule Canyon, a branch of Palo Duro. Quanah Parker, the young firebrand whose mother, Cynthia Ann Parker, was the most famous of the children stolen and raised in Comanche captivity, led one band of kinsmen, but there were Kiowas and Cheyennes as well. They were hiding out from United States cavalry led by a talented but bedeviled young colonel named Ranald Mackenzie. One of his commanding generals was William T. Sherman, best known for his Civil War march to the sea. On a Texas foray Sherman had almost ridden into the fate that would befall his peer George Armstrong Custer.

The Comanches and other southern plains tribes believed that the bluecoats had sworn, at an elaborate 1867 parley in Medicine Lodge, Kansas, that buffalo hunters would never be allowed south of the Arkansas River. But another well-known Civil War figure in the command, General Philip Sheridan, encouraged the hide men, as they called themselves with swagger, to kill bison wherever they found them. Even in the Texas Legislature, voices were raised against the slaughter, but Sheridan testified that the military principle here was to destroy the enemy's "commissary." The violence in Texas escalated wildly until 1874, when a large force of allied tribes attacked a party of hide men at a Canadian River compound called Adobe Walls. The besieged hunters included young Bat Masterson, and during that frantic battle Quanah emerged as the Comanches' last war chief. For all his valiance and

courage in that fight he was shot and disabled. The hunters' .50-caliber guns enabled them to hold off the Indians, whose morale and great alliance collapsed. After Adobe Walls Ranald Mackenzie received orders from Sherman to bring the tribes into submission once and for all. Palo Duro was the last stronghold of Quanah's beleaguered band, which understood commissary, too. Because of its sheer rock walls, Palo Duro was one of only three places on the Southern plains where buffalo survived in any numbers.

Comanches ruled Palo Duro for most of two centuries, but in the lore they left they had little to say about it. Comanche faith was individualistic; they had taboos but no dogma or respected priestly caste. Comanches invoked visions to discover their names and forever sought the magic that would bolster their natural strength. Particularly toward the end, warfare was their religion. However awed and stirred they may have been by the look of the place, it is unlikely that Comanches ever attached to Palo Duro the sort of totemic significance that, say, the Sioux ascribed to the Black Hills. Had Comanches discovered some of the mammoth fossils in Palo Duro, that surely would have inspired earnest mystical conversation. They believed that mammoth bones were the remains of their horrific tribal bogey, the Great Cannibal Owl. But Comanches were practical folks. They chose Palo Duro as the base camp for their last stand because of the military security that comes with inaccessibility.

Cavalry approached Palo Duro from the south. Mackenzie had ascertained the hostile bands' whereabouts from a Comanchero trader, after stretching him around a wagon wheel. The engagement came at the end of a twelve-hour forced march; tired soldiers peeked down over the rim at the Indian encampments just as dawn began to streak the sky. Over the centuries, first introductions to Palo Duro don't change much. "The whole command dismounted," Robert Carter wrote in his vivid frontier memoir, "and each officer and man, leading his horse in single file, took the narrow zigzag path, which was apparently used by nothing but Indian ponies and buffalo. Men and horses slipping down the steepest places, stumbling and sliding, one by one we reached the bottom."

Surprised warriors emerged from their teepees with wives and children in tow, grabbed what they could, and ran like mountain goats for higher ground. Though the battle lasted all day, the only verified casualties were three dead Indians and one wounded Army trumpeter. Mackenzie set the Indian teepees, belongings, and provisions on fire, and his men managed to herd more than fifteen hundred captured horses and mules out of Palo Duro. Several miles out on the plains, his infantry set about the gory task of shooting all animals that their Indian guides didn't want to keep. It took them all day to

kill eleven hundred head. (The vast pile of bones lay out there for years, until farmers finally hauled them off in wagons and sold them as fertilizer for twenty dollars a ton.) With the Panhandle winter coming on, for the de-horsed Indians it was over, just like that. Eating nuts, grubs, and rodents, Quanah Parker's band held out the longest, and that was little more than a year. Other Comanche warriors straggled on foot into Fort Sill, where they were locked in miserable compounds and thrown raw meat over a fence.

It was one of the choice ironies of Western United States history—with information procured by torture, the soldiers had sneaked up on the war's last major engagement under a Comanche moon and struck the telling blow by resorting to the horse-thieving ways of the enemy. Of course, Mackenzie's soldiers had no idea they had won the war. They were happy enough not to have broken their necks getting down to the fight. After camping one night in a buffalo wallow, they stayed their horses and mules under guard near Palo Duro's rim. The Indians had vanished. Admiring the scenic vistas below, the soldiers spread along the rim and consumed the usual field breakfast of fried bacon, black coffee, and sourdough biscuits in Dutch ovens over coals.

We woke up in the hunting shack with anticipations of the same meal steaming in our minds. The owner of this ranch, Tom Christian, retains a chuck wagon cook to prepare regular breakfasts for tourists and civic groups. Arriving on a bus chartered by the Amarillo Chamber of Commerce, they ride out to the canyon rim in horse-drawn wagons and absorb a bit of Palo Duro lore from ranch hands who show up for the occasion, which Christian calls Old Cowboy Morning. He had invited us to join the party. As we rode out across the floor, some of the rancher's Herefords scattered before us with inquisitive bawls and clattering hooves. Selden, in tune with his origins, blames farmers for the deterioration of the grassland plains. He says they based their hopes and dreams on the good years of rain, not the insufficient average. But the stark floor of Palo Duro lends testimony to the damage done by cattlemen as well. As we crossed one particularly barren patch of red soil, Selden said he wished that the ranchers could find a way to let the canyon rest four or five years—at least see if it's capable of ever coming back.

Drawing on my reading, I observed that when Charles Goodnight turned Palo Duro into the Panhandle's first cattle ranch, the grassy dells were luxuriant enough to support ten thousand buffalo. Goodnight said that with the help of rifle shots ricocheted off the cliffs, he and two cowboys drove the bison herd fifteen miles up the canyon to make room for the cattle, creating a cloud of red dust that rose a thousand feet in the air. Selden squinted at the

high draws and spectacularly broken terrain, speculating on the difficulty of the drovers' task. "I never quite knew whether to believe that story," he said.

Charles Goodnight was a rigid moralist. Yet in staking his claim to Palo Duro, he negotiated a non-aggression pact with the notorious highwayman Dutch Henry. He cut a similar deal with Mexican sheepherders, some of them former Comancheros, dividing the entire Panhandle approximately in half. The very scale of Goodnight's life strains contemporary imagination. Migrating with his family from Illinois the year before Texas joined the Union, he rode eight hundred miles bareback at the age of nine. In 1860, while raiding a Comanche encampment, he recognized Cynthia Ann Parker as a white woman and saved her from the Rangers' undiscriminating fire. During the cattle-market glut that afflicted Texas after the Civil War, Goodnight hatched the idea of driving Longhorns to the nearest rail depots. While blazing four cattle-drive trails, he designed the first chuck wagon, lost a partner (Oliver Loving) to the Indians, and once yielded right-of-way to a buffalo herd that he estimated was 125 miles long and 25 miles across. (The story of Goodnight and Loving, first told well by historian J. Evetts Hailey, inspired Larry McMurtry's Pulitzer Prize-winning epic novel, *Lonesome Dove*.)

Nearing forty, Goodnight anticipated a life of genteel returns on that investment. Dug in and prosperous, he irrigated crops, planted apple orchards, and owned stock in the opera house of Pueblo, Colorado. But the bank panic of 1873 wiped him out. With sixteen hundred Longhorns left to his name, Goodnight sensed the enormity of the power vacuum left by the Comanches' demise. When he found the old Comanche trail into Palo Duro and packed disassembled wagons and the first winter's provisions down on mules in 1875, his closest neighbor was a hundred miles away, the nearest store two hundred fifty. It's a measure of Goodnight's character that he could be that far down on his luck and simultaneously determine that he was just the man to fill that vacuum. He seized Palo Duro because of its water, sheltered pastures, and those sheer rock walls. With the end of the free range already in sight, think of all the fence-building labor he saved.

To certify his vast homestead claim, Goodnight persuaded John Adair, an English investor, to secure the deeds to twelve thousand acres the first year. Paying money its due, Goodnight named his dream ranch the JA. Adair drove a hard bargain: On a salary of twenty-five hundred dollars a year, the famous trailblazer had to return his haughty partner's investment at the end of five years, plus interest and two-thirds of the profit. Goodnight assembled the Panhandle's first great cattle ranch by snookering the speculators who held the paper title to Palo Duro. With other buyers in view, they accepted his

offers of twenty cents to seventy-five cents an acre. By 1882 Goodnight held 82,000 acres and went right on buying. As a cattle king he functioned like a stern Baptist overlord. Decreeing prohibition forty years before the idea caught on nationwide, he fired or blacklisted any cowhand caught drinking, gambling, or fighting. At the same time, he rewarded employees such as Tom Christian's grandfather with bargain-price homesteads of their own. Goodnight asserted that during the years of his management, the JA books showed a seventy-two percent profit. But the 1880s brought another depression, and Goodnight foresaw the demise of the huge cattle ranches. In 1887 he sold his share of the JA to Adair's widow and settled on a smaller ranch a few miles out from Palo Duro.

On that ranch Goodnight participated in a poignant ritual: paunchy and winded Comanche horsemen, whose absence from the reservation no longer threatened anybody, visited so they could run down a few head of his buffalo in the old way. Goodnight became the friend of Quanah Parker, by then a celebrity who partied with cattlemen in Fort Worth and hunted with Theodore Roosevelt and shipped a horse to Washington to ride in one of his inaugural parades. An amateur naturalist, Goodnight maintained one of the country's largest herds of buffalo, which he shared with the national parks and zoos. He devoted his last years to the breeding of cattalo, a cross of Polled Angus cattle and American bison that he ballyhooed, to a rather skeptical audience, as the solution to world hunger. Late in life Goodnight allowed a photographer to juxtapose his white-haired and goateed profile against that of a buffalo. Except for the darker figure's horns, the resemblance was uncanny. Visionary and throwback, Goodnight died in 1929.

Oil, of course, was the industry that could have changed Palo Duro forever. A sign in the state park recalls the 1919 drilling project that reached a depth of 26,000 feet. With a roar of Pleistocene repudiation, an air pocket blew the bit and drill stem up through the derrick with such violence that the ruckus could be heard nine miles away. The wildcatters scrapped that project fast. Palo Duro has a way of taking care of itself. Human claimants tend to be incidental.

There is little danger of cul-de-sacs and ranchette subdivisions finding their way here. Still, leaving the canyon in the hands of private ranchers exacts a price beyond the stubborn overgrazing. Despite its recreational potential, only the ranchers' hunting clients and lucky acquaintances really get to enjoy it in the wild. Acquired in 1933, the state park is large, handsome, and tastefully designed. But the Panhandle's shortage of public nature retreats is so extreme that in the summer, Palo Duro State Park resembles Coney Is-

land. Also, the state's designers may have erred on the side of restraint. After a drive through the park, I came away a bit disgruntled. It needs to be more than a place to throw a Frisbee under the cottonwood trees.

So what am I suggesting? The park offers two state historical markers, a replica of Goodnight's dugout, a tour-guide train, and the amphitheater musical *Texas,* which in saccharine fashion dramatizes much of the narrative related here. I just wish the state had posted beneath the best example of the Spanish Skirts—called, for quite literal reasons, the Devil's Slide—something other than a marker directing attention to the nearest latrine. Besides, the state park is confined to the mouth of the canyon. The creeks have converged, and the Prairie Dog Town Fork is actually the headwaters of the Red River. Though the cliffs are impressive, within the park Palo Duro is more broad river valley than broken canyon. History makes the best distinction. Goodnight used what was probably the Panhandle's first barbed wire to separate the present parkland from the rest of the canyon. He reserved the lush grass along the river for John Adair's herd of purebred English cattle. Beyond the wire, back up in the maze of rockslides and hoodoos, Goodnight turned his Longhorns loose.

From the hunting shack's cottonwood grove we had climbed several hundred feet of jumbled plateaus. Seldon pointed out a V-shaped line etched on the rock wall's shadowed face. That, he said, was our destination—the scenic route. Dorothy slid me one of her patented frank looks. We dismounted and rested on the last grassy level. Putting up pencils, tightening saddle straps, swigging water from our plastic canteens, we chatted with a calm I could not have imagined twenty-four hours earlier. The black mule lowered his head meanwhile and, with shy insistence, began to nudge my leather chink with his snout.

"Awww," said our guide, grinning sentimentally. "Stagger Lee's in love." Considering the fright we'd given each other the previous day, I could have thrown my arms around the big thing's neck.

As we started up, Dorothy peeked at the distant treetops below and grimly shook her head. The path was wide, scraped, and regular enough to qualify as more than a livestock trail, but in comparison, yesterday's bulldozed switchbacks were a country club boulevard. I rocked forward in the saddle and placed as much weight as I could directly above Stagger Lee's shoulders. Wedged below in recesses of the eastward cliffs, high shaded dells glistened with dew. It would take an agile and determined cow to overgraze that grass. I have never felt more suspended between the easy, mundane present and a

far more difficult but colorful past. As often as it seemed safe, I craned my neck and stared. Motionless on one of the low mesas, a big dark brown steer watched us climb.

A friend who is an academic historian tells me, without meaning to offend, that Texas is almost ahistoric. He implies that our habitation of this terrain has been too sporadic and recent to make much difference in the world scheme of things. Driving through ugly shopping centers and desolate small towns, I find it hard to argue with him, but for me Palo Duro belies that allegation of impoverished human experience. I know. Our insignificant little adventure had lasted not quite one full day—it was silly and presumptuous of me to insert that passage in a drama that's gone on for thousands of years. I suspect that participants in an archaeological dig feel just as dwarfed and stirred. It's not just what you find. It's what the resonance of that hole in the ground makes you think.

Selden pulled up and tightened his grip on the pack mule's halter rope. Before us the red clay turned into a stratum of dusty white caliche, roughly three hundred yards across, that looked very loose in composition and angled up the cliff at a grade of about forty-five degrees. The ledge on the right pitched straight down, out of sight. "One at a time," Selden told us. "When I reach the end of that dirt, then you start." Letting Pumpkin trail behind, he spurred Reddy's flank and rode ahead.

"I'm next," my wife announced, without a hint of compromise. I knew her game. If she came off backward, I was to play shortstop to her rolling ball. She hung on fine, but Fat Mule paid for his gluttony and girth. Twice during that climb, the mule had to stop and rest. Dorothy endured those delays with a petrified stoicism, though in acknowledgment of the rightward chasm she directed her gaze slightly to the left. I wouldn't have been much help if needed. I was yanking reins, jerking Stagger Lee's head, yelling, "Whoa!" Mules desire nothing as much as the company of other mules. Witnessing the departure of his mates, Stagger Lee was snorting and stomping and dying to go.

At last I called off the fight and let him have his head. Raising my knees and clamping them tight, I hunkered over his neck and found that sure spot of rhythmic balance. Though I may have resembled a hybrid of Willie Shoemaker and Ichabod Crane, I didn't have to grab the saddle horn once. In retrospect, that may have been a show of dumb bravado, but my confidence in that beast of burden was absolute. The slobber of Stagger Lee's exertion foamed over the bridle bit and hung in a light green string from his chin. With his head down, he thrust with his hindquarters, drove with his shoulders, and sent waves of brute strength right through me. We cleared the dan-

gerous caliche and reached a gate, the end of our climb. With exhilarated hoots we burst over the canyon rim, fresh upon the placid scene of Old Cowboy Morning. What status! Tom Christian's cowhands raised jovial halloos at the sight of Selden, their favorite criminal lawyer. The guests, members of a Young Leadership group in Amarillo, gaped at us from the picnic tables, some with aluminum forks raised. Sex, maybe . . . I'm sure that's better.

Walking somewhat bowlegged in our thorn-scraped chinks, we carried our blue metal coffee cups and plates to an unoccupied table. Dorothy and I laid our gimme caps aside and made a mild show of ordering our dirty, matted hair. Such are the powers of human recovery; it's amazing how one night's saddle-sore dudes can turn into the new day's grizzled hands. Baked over mesquite coals in large Dutch ovens, in the manner of Ranald Mackenzie's troopers, those biscuits may have been the best ever soaked in gravy. A bank president and former state legislator, Tom Christian wore a hat that looked like a cross between a bowler and a Stetson. Telling stories about his grandfather's employment by Old Man Goodnight, he tried to make sure everybody was entertained and had plenty to eat. Sartorially, Amarillo's young leaders ran to starched jeans, shined boots, silk scarves tied like bandannas. Pleasant folks.

With peals of glee, a couple of women were throwing cow chips. After each Frisbee-like toss, they brushed and clapped their hands fastidiously. A larger group of women hung on the words of the volunteer cowhands, particularly Roger Johnson, the one with the clipped moustache, nice shoulders, and gleaming white shirt. With just the right amount of courtly restraint, he sidled against the posterior of an attractive woman and showed her how to twirl his lariat. Excusing himself with a forefinger touched to his hat, Roger walked over to our table and took a seat on the bench. "Who are these people?" asked Selden, shoving his plate away. "They're from Amarillo? I don't know a one."

Roger grinned and flicked cigarette ash into Selden's gravy. "Hell, no," he quipped, reminding our guide of his law practice back in town. "There ain't no murderers."

Everyone seemed to recall the work day at once. Tom's cook soaped dishes and used suds to douse the fire. Our mules appeared to know that within the hour they'd be back in their paddock, rolling in the delicious dirt. They picked their way through the flatland's mesquites in a fast walk. Sighting Selden's pickup and gooseneck trailer, they broke into that god-awful jouncing trot and finally achieved an ungainly canter.

To our right, the team of blindered horses hitched to the tourist wagon

overtook us on the road. The young leaders stared at us through a great billow of dust. Choosing not to eat that dirt, Roger spurred ahead on a well-bred chestnut quarter horse. It stretched out easily with arched neck and tail, a flash of white stockings. No doubt about it—the horse is the lovelier beast. Roger cupped his hand beside his mouth and shouted, "What are you going to *plant* with those things? Go get yourself a plow!"

Historic snobberies. Selden grinned and turned up his nose, having none of it. We knew what our animals were good for. With pressing appointments in the civilized present—airplanes taking off, clients in jail—we galloped our mules in the fair morning sun.

JANUARY, 1985

THE FORGOTTEN PEOPLE

*In the rich panoply of the Texan experience, no participants have shown
more courage than the Kickapoo Indians. Since the first French fur
traders entered the Great Lakes region in the seventeenth century, the
Kickapoo have fought and run and endured incredible misfortune in
order to preserve their religion and culture. Colonists of Texas under
Mexican rule gave them land in exchange for their protection against
raids by Comanches, Kiowas, and Apaches. Ordered out by leaders of the
Republic of Texas, the Kickapoo departed—some north to the Indian
Territory, more of them south to Mexico, where they were again welcomed
and valued as protectors. I was aware of none of that a century later. I
knew the Kickapoo only as a pariah band of squatters who ended up
living under the Rio Grande bridge at Eagle Pass. My wife, who worked
in the administration of Governor Ann Richards, one day told me an
intriguing tale about a state substance abuse worker, trained as a
cultural anthropologist, who was applying those methods to his field work
with Eagle Pass Kickapoo who were addicted to paint fumes. Thus began
a magazine story that took two years to complete. Fate for the Kickapoo
has been an unjust master. They possess an indomitable spirit. But the
odyssey that brought them to the borderlands of Texas and Mexico is
valiant and sad.*

The Kickapoo Indians live in a world that only resembles yours and mine. I
began to understand this one day in April, 1994, on the parking lot of a shopping center in Eagle Pass. Eric Fredlund, an anthropologist who had befriended
the Kickapoo, was taking me to Nacimiento, the Mexican reservation and
adopted holy land of the small border tribe. First he went inside a store to
buy some sunglasses and cigarettes, leaving me in a Chevy Blazer with Joe
Hernandez, our driver, guide, and translator. Joe, whose Kickapoo name is
Ta-Pe-A-ah, was twenty-three then, five feet ten with thick, broad shoulders, a

laborer's build. He wore boots, jeans, a cap, and sunshades that masked a large shy face. There is a Lake Kickapoo in the part of Texas where I grew up, and, just to break the silence, I asked Joe if he knew the place. He looked back over the seat and replied quietly, "No. We're kind of allergic to lakes."

I blinked and asked him what he meant. "When I was a kid," he said, "I used to drive up to Del Rio a lot, to that big lake there, Amistad. But my dad told me he didn't want me going up there. That lake, it makes big rains."

I mused on that cryptic remark as we crossed the Rio Grande and drove south from Piedras Negras into the Coahuilan chaparral. Allergic to lakes? The Kickapoo came from the Great Lakes; they speak Algonquian and still tell stories of French explorers who found them around Lake Michigan in the early 1600s. Their migration to the borderlands of Texas and Mexico—which made them citizens of two nations—is one of the most remarkable odysseys in North American history, and they undertook it to sustain a religion and way of life that abounds with supernatural beings and events.

Yet Texans know the Kickapoo—if they know them at all—as a poverty-stricken people who for decades lived as squatters under the international bridge at Eagle Pass. (Since 1987 they have occupied a bleak 123-acre reservation on the outskirts of town.) They are seldom mentioned in a Texas frontier lore dominated by Comanches, Apaches, and Cherokees; it is a common belief today that Texas has just two tribes, the Alabama-Coushatta of the Big Thicket and the Tigua in El Paso. Yet the Kickapoo have played a lively role in Texas history, and their culture is arguably more intact than that of the better-known tribes. In anthropological circles, the Kickapoo have a reputation as the most unassimilated tribe in the contiguous United States. Along the border one sees them driving pickups, wearing shades, listening to country or rap music, but even in those moments they perceive a spiritual world to which most of us are blind.

I had been reading a monograph Fredlund was drafting about his work with the Kickapoo. "One informant told me of an incident," he wrote, "that occurred when he was traveling in the Midwest in a pickup truck with an elderly male relative. In the distance they saw a tornado heading in their direction at a high rate of speed. The man instructed him to stop the truck and get out quickly. The old man then said a prayer to the 'grandfather' who *was* the tornado. The funnel cloud rose off the ground and passed over their heads, returning to earth a half mile beyond where they stood, and resumed its path of destruction. The older man explained that there is no reason for a Kickapoo man to fear a tornado provided one is in harmony with the nature and spirits of the grandfathers and knows how to get the latter's attention."

The troubles of contemporary Kickapoo are legion, but in the view of tribal elders and administrators, two in particular imperil their existence as a distinct culture. Deer hunting is a sacrament among the Kickapoo; in their religion a father cannot baptize and bestow a tribal name on an infant unless he can contribute to the rite four slain deer. The animals are scarce at Nacimiento, their Mexican preserve, and rare as polar bears on their United States reservation, downriver from Eagle Pass. Mexican law tries to accommodate their need, though game regulations and posting of private property there have recently grown more restrictive, and in Texas the dual constraints are unrelenting. Few Kickapoo earn more than seven thousand dollars a year, and even if they could afford a private hunting lease, babies are born year-round, not just in the state's autumn hunting season. They get caught poaching and are fined $500, to them an impossible sum, so they work it off on county road gangs. What else are they going to do? Let their children go nameless?

The second crisis, addiction, threatens to do what 350 years of hardship could not: extinguish the traditional Kickapoo way of life from the earth. Like many Native Americans, the Kickapoo seem incapable of moderate social drinking; their elected council forbids consumption of alcohol on both reservations, though of course that doesn't solve the problem. But the intoxicant that terrifies the elders is common spray paint. About 450 people are enrolled as legal members of the Texas Kickapoo tribe. At least eighty, most of them adults, are addicted to paint fumes. Fredlund worked for the state, but part of his assignment was to write a grant proposal on the Kickapoo's behalf to the federal Center for Substance Abuse Treatment. His proposal had won a five-year, $2.6-million grant that made Eric a celebrated figure among the Kickapoo.

As we drove by power plants and coal mines and the Sierra Madres came into view, Joe Hernandez readily shared his experience with the anthropologist. He told us of his own addiction when he was twelve and thirteen. Nothing mattered to him but the visions of paint. He once saw his father looming tall as a giant. He likened other hallucinations to the flickering, jerky effect of dancers under a strobe light, and there were sounds as well—he could hear his blood racing, his heart was a drum. "Every day, every day," he said with a sigh. "You don't want to do nothing else. I wouldn't eat, and I kept getting caught by my parents. Even now when I smell paint, I still want to do it. But I had to quit. I didn't want to lose my dad."

On the rough gravel road that leads to Nacimiento, solvent abuse seemed even more of an aberration, something absurd and far away. The air was very clear, and above the light green mesquite and huisache foliage, the Sierra

Madres rose in subtly varied shades of cobalt blue. They spread in an arc around us, but the succeeding wedges looked almost equidistant, packed into a vertical plane. I had never seen mountains quite like them. Joe spoke happily of going off horseback on hunts of several weeks' duration and bringing back bear, turkey, and the deer that granted him the favor of naming his two small children. I remarked on a striking arrangement of peaks toward the west. Joe glanced at them and mystified me again. "We can't go over there," he said. "There's lots of big cats." Later I read in an anthropology book about the Kickapoo that large wild cats carry a strong taboo. Joe's explanation was less esoteric. "They make bad winds."

At Nacimiento a Kickapoo spiritual leader who is in his eighties relates in droll fashion the encounter that changed Kickapoo life forever: "The first white people we met were French. We traded them deer hides and they said, 'Ah, these are very good hides.' Then they asked us for a small place to sleep."

For the next two hundred years the Kickapoo were constantly at war. They fought the French and simultaneously fought their tribal enemies, the Iroquois, who came at them from the east, and the Sioux, who attacked from the west. The made peace with the French and helped them fight the English. After the American Revolution, they fought the settlers and soldiers of the United States. As a warring people they once besieged Detroit, were ferocious allies of the Ottawa chief Pontiac, and were among the losers of the Battle of Tippecanoe. Exhausted, they signed a peace treaty in 1819 and consented to forced removal from their northern homeland to a reservation in southeast Missouri. But they didn't like that place, and for most of the nineteenth century they resisted the swallowing giant called America by fleeing it southward. They left bands of themselves in Kansas and Oklahoma, but they were gypsies of the plains. They were unlike the Comanches, Kiowas, and Cheyenne they moved among. They greatly preferred deer to buffalo as prey, and though they value horses as an improvement over walking, they never made horsemanship into a martial and material culture. Nor did they fear the fierce tribes of buffalo hunters. Around Nacogdoches, Spain (and later Mexico) set up the Kickapoo as a military buffer against "wild tribes." Forced out of the Republic of Texas, Kickapoo once more were enlisted as protectors from the raids of Comanches and Mescalero Apaches, and in gratitude Mexico gave them seventeen thousand acres at the foot of the Sierra Madres in 1852.

The antipathy between the Kickapoo and Texans continued to be mutual and brutal. In 1865 a troop of Texas Rangers and Confederate soldiers attacked a Mexico-bound party of Kickapoo at Dove Creek, near present-day

San Angelo, and got themselves roundly thrashed. Still, fifteen Kickapoo deaths in that battle triggered a war of vengeance against Texans that lasted until 1873. United States General Phil Sheridan temporarily pulled away Colonel Ranald Mackenzie and his cavalry troops from their pursuit of the Comanches and Kiowas in North Texas. Without consulting Mexico on the matter, Sheridan sent the troops across the Rio Grande against the Kickapoo with the alleged orders: "Let it be a campaign of annihilation, obliteration, and complete destruction." After that bloodshed more Kickapoo were co-erced into Oklahoma residence; they agreed to go as long as the route by-passed Texas.

The next generation of Kickapoo living in Mexico suffered at the hands of Pancho Villa and other Mexican revolutionaries. Still, at long last they were where they wanted to be. Kickapoo might have never again intruded much on Texas if not for a calamitous drought that began in 1944 and lasted seven years. At Nacimiento they had no water except for barely trickling springs. Their wheat crops failed, their cattle starved, and the mountains nearby were largely hunted out. Though Mexico had been generous with loyalty and land, it offered neither jobs nor government assistance. So the Kickapoo became migrant farm workers—and the lowly and despised of Eagle Pass.

In a way they lived as they always had. They clung to their language, re-turned to Nacimiento for the spring holy season, celebrated ultra-secretive rites of spring renewal, then divided into kinship groups for the year's eco-nomic production. But instead of hunting, now the young and able-bodied weeded sugar beet fields in Montana and Wyoming, and picked cherries in Utah, and harvested apples and onions in Colorado. Later they found the approach could be applied to work caused by spring storms; they are able roofers. Until they moved to their reservation in 1987, the staging ground for the annual treks was the long flood plain under the Rio Grande bridge at Eagle Pass, where they built wickiups, but not with the cattail reeds and finely detailed craft of their ceremonial houses at Nacimiento. As if to acknowledge their transience and diminished state, they cobbled the domed structures together with plywood and tarp. They had no water, sewage, or privacy. People hurled down insults and trash.

About ten miles off the paved road that winds from the foot of the Sierra Madres to Big Bend, Joe Hernandez steered his Blazer through a tiny, wan village. The Kickapoo preserve lay across a tree-lined Rio Grande tributary called the Sabinas, which could only be crossed at a rocky ford. Nacimiento, which in Spanish means birthplace, was several hundred yards beyond the

crossing. There were some houses of gray cinderblock in the Kickapoo enclave, but the dominant architecture was the traditional loaf-shaped wickiups
made of the cattail reeds. People were strolling, chatting in groups, sitting on
straw cots under the shade of their summer porches—a scene of leisure. As
the day wore on, I could understand how the Kickapoo hold such land holy.
Under oak-forested mountains cut with dramatic rock cliffs, the village sat
beside the clear-running stream we had forded. Its fountainhead emerged
from a jumble of smooth white rocks amid thick and towering trees. As Joe
and I strolled through the bottom a tanager swooped past us. I asked him if
they had a name for their sacred stream. "No," he said. "We just call it River."

Like many in the tribe, Joe has had no formal schooling, yet he has learned
to read and write a little, and is fluent in three languages (he is least confident
in English.) "I was always with my dad, learning the tradition," he told me.
"But then I found out about money. I know now I was supposed to be going
to school."

Nacimiento had no water pipes or sewage systems, though Mexican officials were encouraging the tribe to start selling water meters. A clock and
small refrigerator in the Hernandez family's flat-roofed concrete house testified
to the arrival of electricity that year. Joe said that his dad was a boy when the
lines and poles were first promised. "I respect them for doing it," he said
nonetheless. The walls were decorated with family photos and a wanted poster
of a woman accused of defrauding the Kickapoo. Joe showed us his family's
most prized material possession, an 1894 model lever-action .30-30 Winches-
ter rifle. Outside, we examined their wickiup, and in a small fenced pasture
walked among gaunt horses and a mule. Joe affectionately rubbed the neck of
a palomino gelding named Flaco, which means Skinny. He asked if I wanted
to ride his hunting horse. I told him it would be a pleasure.

But we never got the tack out because Joe's dad drove up in an old red
Ford pickup. Eric had been trying to acquaint me with the mysteries of tribal
kinship and had told me to watch for the change in Joe's manner when he
was around his father. He grew quiet and seemed wary of looking at his dad
closely and directly, even as they talked. Jose Hernandez had an immense
head and a thick shock of gray hair. He spoke only Kickapoo and Spanish.

Jose was a member of the Traditional Council of elected leaders, and as we
talked in Spanish with our forearms resting on the rails of his pickup, he
picked up a can of processed meat in the truck bed and revolved it in his
hands. After a while he chuckled, handed it to me, and gestured for me to
read the label. Canned in Denmark, it was sent toward northern Mexico by
a hunger relief agency of the United Nations. For the Kickapoo, he said he

worried most about the hunting. "We have no books," he said. "Our customs are all in our heads." All the negotiations and entreaties he described were directed at Mexican officials; I asked him if the tribe had tried to communicate with anyone public or private in Texas, where over-populations of white-tailed deer are a widespread problem. He looked skeptical and said he wouldn't know how to begin. As we left, I told Jose that I hoped I saw him again. "*Ojalá!*" he replied: May God grant.

It seemed that my first exposure to the Kickapoo and their home in the Sierra Madres would end on that tranquil note—but it was not to be. The next morning, Eric and I emerged from our motel rooms in Múzquiz, a pleasant town on the main highway not far from Nacimiento, and found Joe waiting in the car. With him now was a strapping young man named Fernando, his friend since childhood. Fernando prefaced his replies to almost all our remarks with a soft, musically phrased, "Well, I don' know." Fernando was drinking beer and soon passed out in the front seat. We left him there and went into a roadside cantina, where we bought soft drinks. Inside, some Mexican men in ranching attire greeted Joe warmly, inquired about his father, and invited us to join them at their table. One of the men was a former mayor of Múzquiz. When Joe brought up the problem with deer hunting, the man replied carefully, with a politician's aplomb. "This is a matter of law, just like in the United States." As we stood to leave, the man suggested gently to Joe that he might want to check on some Kickapoo who were up the road a way.

About a dozen men were passing the time and bottles of sugarcane liquor in a shaded bar ditch; they had a nice view of the Sierra Madres. As Fernando dozed on and Joe grinned at their jests—they took pleasure in reminding him of a Comanche in his bloodline—Eric and I took seats on the ground among them and discreetly tried to decline the quart bottle making the rounds. But it wasn't easy: Refusing to drink with them was deemed a pejorative act. Finally I relented and took a swallow. The stuff was sweet and terrifically strong. The man next to me was not appeased. He had a dark pitted face, and his eyes kept coming back to mine. "My name is Dave," he said, with apparent reference to some past slight. "Don't call me Chief."

"Pleased to meet you, Dave."

"Dave," he emphasized. "Don't ever call me Chief."

Most of the men lived among the Oklahoma Kickapoo. They hold Nacimiento sacred, too, and often move back and forth between McCloud and Eagle Pass. "These are my uncles," Joe explained, turning up the bottle for the first time.

From Eric's briefing on kinship, I remembered that for the convenience of outsiders, they lump a great number of male relatives into the term "uncle." If an uncle asks you for a gift, you can't refuse him. I recalled this with a sinking sensation when they asked Joe to drive into Múzquiz and fetch them several more bottles of cane liquor. Fernando's head fell back as Joe lurched away in the Blazer. His *uncles* made him do it.

A little old man whom they called Coni eased forward and went to sleep with his head on the shin of a younger fellow. As if in a slow-motion topple of dominos, that man turned and slumped until his cheek was lying in the dirt. A string of drool leaked from his mouth and in time formed a small cone of mud. As my gaze fastened on this, another man sought to reassure us, or perhaps himself. "I just do this ever' once in a while," he said. "For the good times."

One whose name was Fidel wasn't buying that. Fidel fixed on me a stare of immense sadness and said: "I been doing this since 1975. I lost my house, I lost my wife. I lost everything. I gotta get straight."

As the bottle continued round, Eric leaned over and murmured a witticism of substance abuse treatment-speak: "This is a novel kind of needs assessment."

I expect my smile was a little tight. We were deep in a foreign country, and we were starting off the day in a ditch full of drunk Indians!

Joe rolled up then, flung the door open, and strode toward us with two paper sacks filled with quart bottles. Joe turned the first one up and held it skyward for a long time. "I love these peoples," he said, and almost fell.

Eric finally convinced Joe that we had to go, and coaxed the keys away from him. He navigated Múzquiz, but on the way down we hadn't paid much attention to landmarks. There were no highway signs in the towns, and soon we were lost. I asked some kids on the road if they knew the way to Texas; they shrieked with laughter.

We parked in front of a store, trying to regain our composure. Fernando woke up with a jerk, shook his head, slapped his face, and took command of the situation. "I don' wan' you to think we drink like this all the time," he said in his soft sing-song accent, and set out for home at eighty miles an hour. Joe was aware enough to feel badly about what had happened. In apology he offered Eric the gift of his dog, and dug in his wallet until he found its vaccination papers. Fernando firmly gripped the wheel and hardly spoke as trucks on the narrow highway soughed past. Eric looked at me with a wild grin. "They can really drive, can't they!"

When the federal government accepted Eric's grant proposal for the treatment program, his role was essentially over. But tribal administrators and elders still called him for advice, and six months of field work had affected him deeply; on days off he often came back to Eagle Pass. One night that summer I went with him to the tribe's first graduation ceremony. For people whose children seldom last in school as long as junior high, five completions of the state's GED requirements were indeed a signal event. The graduates wore caps and gowns, the families were all dressed up, and the Eagle Pass school superintendent delivered the commencement. Eric's friends asked him to make a speech, too. He stood before them frozen, then performed an unwitting, dead-on take on TV's Mr. Rogers. "Graduations," he began, "are special."

An hour later I followed him as, coattails flapping, he skidded down a slope into the netherworld of Kickapoo paint sniffers. They assembled under bridges, in a city park, along a railroad track, and next to a paved arroyo that winds through town. We found a woman seated barefoot on a piece of cardboard. She clasped his hand, asked him how he'd been, and after a few minutes began to cry. "I ain't got no shoes. My feet, they're sick." He gave her a couple of dollars and made her promise not to spend them on beer or paint. He found several pariahs digging in a dumpster outside a fried chicken place downtown and bought them a hamburger. When they were high they would rant crazily, incoherently, and sometimes they got in knife fights in which the point was to leave a scar, not to maim or kill. Yet he never seemed to fear them. Nor did a Hispanic man whose river bottom dry goods store they often camped behind: "No, no, these are good people," the man told us one blistering day. "They just got this terrible habit, and it's a shame to see what they're doing to themselves."

Eric sat amid the squalor of cans and rotted mattresses, looked them in the eye, gained their confidence, and got them to talk to him. He kept dwelling on the horror that all Kickapoo, including the paint addicts, expressed over the fate of a twenty-six-year-old woman who passed out from the fumes on the railroad tracks one night in 1992 and was cut in two by a locomotive. "According to the tradition of her people," a poignant item in a small local paper put it, "her soul will remain at the point of her death because she was not in grace and harmony with nature. She had chosen to alter her state of mind with the use of the spirits of the can. Her soul will remain at that site, seventy-two feet north of El Indio Highway on the road of steel, until judgment day."

Tribal elders and traditionalists hoped that Nacimiento was off-limits to

such degradation. "Texas is where we work," one of the elders had explained to Eric. "Nacimiento is where we go to live our lives as Kickapoo people." But I found on my trip to Nacimiento that you don't have to walk far into the brush to kick up one of the distinctive blue cans.

Solvent abuse is usually encountered among youths, and the clinical assumption has long been that if they keep it up, they either wind up dead or brain damaged. But some of the Kickapoo had been sniffing paint for more than a decade, and when they weren't high, they could carry on a perfectly lucid social conversation. The treatment program was being designed largely by the Tri-Ethnic Center for Prevention Research, which is affiliated with Colorado State University. It would rely heavily on medical testing, on Kickapoo translators, on an elderly spiritual leader named Alfonso, and eventually, on trained and licensed Kickapoo counselors. Nobody promised a miracle cure. Toluene and other solvent compounds attach themselves to fatty tissues, of which the brain has many: Detoxification could take months. Withdrawal symptoms might range from irascible anxiety to suicidal despair. Except for a few court-ordered commitments, participation among the addicts was voluntary. The therapists said themselves that a high relapse rate was preordained.

The treatment program called for a site removed from the Eagle Pass reservation, and tribal administrators—who are appointed by the federal government—finally settled on Quemado, a farm town of 426 residents seventeen miles north of Eagle Pass. A resident named Rod Bunsen had declared bankruptcy and was scrambling to keep his spacious house and spread, described on a highway sign as a quarter horse farm, out of bank foreclosure. Bunsen sold ninety acres and offered to lease the remaining property to the Kickapoo for the five-year term of the pilot project.

Neighbors in Quemado were outraged. Led by an Hispanic family named Moses, nearly three hundred residents signed a petition with a timeworn theme—not in my back yard. Lilia Moses is a diminutive math teacher in Eagle Pass. "This is not about the Kickapoo," she insisted. "If you remove their name from the project we'd be just as opposed—because it's a drug rehabilitation center. Why wasn't the community consulted? We're a twenty-minute drive from Eagle Pass, and the county can't provide us adequate law enforcement or EMS protection now."

Eight months into the five-year term of the grant, the project was stalled. "First we gotta pay property taxes," sighed tribal administrator Julio Fausto, an Eagle Pass native and retired Air Force officer. "And we're still up to our ears in tigers."

I thought it was a metaphor.

With few close neighbors, the Bunsen house sat on a rise surrounded by maize fields, the onetime horse show arena and an irrigation ditch at the rear. At the edge of the front yard, a brook trickled attractively through a stand of blooming cannas. Peacocks strolled about with their air of lordly fops. Inside, I found a broad expanse of Saltillo tile, a heavy Mexican-style chandelier, a long bar and kitchen designed for entertaining, and an upstairs hot tub. But the greater attraction lay out back: In pens and cages that did not look altogether escape-proof were African lions, Bengal tigers, a leopard, a black panther, a mountain lion, and several black bears. As back yards in Quemado go, evidently this was preferable to a band of Kickapoo paint sniffers. The heat-stricken animals lay panting while a work crew from the reservation prepared the place for occupancy. A black-maned male lion took exception to the shrill whine of a weed-eater put near the wire by an edgy young man named Roger Gonzales. The lion stood up and voiced a grumble that sent Roger and me stepping smartly to the rear.

Two men drove up and unlocked one of the sheds; I walked out and met Rod Bunsen and his son, Rod Junior. Rod Junior had written a letter published in the *Eagle Pass News-Guide* that accused the neighbors of bigotry and racism: "The Anglos in Quemado want everyone to be white and Protestant and the Hispanics dislike the possibility of Native American neighbors due to their (Hispanics') continual denial of their own ancestry." Rod Senior said that if the lease was voided and he lost his homestead because of it, he would sue everyone who signed that petition. "Ah, these rednecks," he said of his former neighbors. "They haven't liked anything I've done for twenty-two years."

As I drove home to Austin I kept thinking about Joe Hernandez's comment about the forbidden range of big cats in the Sierra Madres, and then I found the anthropological reference to them as taboo animals. I called Eric Fredlund and asked him if this stratum of the bizarreness might cloud the treatment skies over Quemado. There was a pause on the other end.

"Well! Words will have to be said."

All through the summer of 1994 the Kickapoo found themselves in battle with hostile Texans, though on more formally polite terms than a century ago. In June there was a face-to-face confrontation with the Quemado residents. Tribal administrators and defenders of the treatment program sat at a table facing the sullen crowd. Margie Salazar, Joe's wife, read a statement. She was the assistant tribal administrator—the highest position any Kickapoo had attained in the management of their own affairs. Visibly nervous, she re-

counted the tribe's history and asked for Quemado's support. "We were a self-sufficient and proud people. We maintained our culture, our tradition, and language over the years. But in 1944 a drought set in over all of northern Mexico. To survive, we had to resort to migratory work. As a child, I remember traveling with my parents on long difficult journeys. I worked in the fields, and we all chipped in to survive, but I knew there would be a better life. I worked very hard between trips to get my education and complete my GED. I did not want to keep working with my hands and never know the things that other citizens enjoy. You see, I am an American citizen, too."

There was a polite round of applause, but then the residents had their say, and within minutes other Kickapoo women walked out of the hall, weeping. One of the three Moses sisters voiced concern that the center would become permanent, would take in addicts from Dallas and Houston, and eventually would be "open to blacks, greens, yellows, browns, anybody who wants to come in." Fredlund made an attempt at humor. "Well, yes, they could come from Houston—as long as they speak the Kickapoo language." No one laughed. Another Moses sister went after him with an air of hostile cross-examination: "*What* is a research analyst?" An Anglo man with reading glasses and a graying crewcut had a chair at the front. As the jeers and shouts grew louder, he stood up, waved his arms, and loomed over the table. "I want to understand this young lady," he said, pointing a sheaf of papers at Margie Salazar, "and the tradition of the Kickapoo tribe. But this community has pride, also. And we're the ones who have to protect this place. The ones who live here. And we don't appreciate this business of you people—*outsiders*—using our taxpayer money, coming in here, without even consulting us, and telling us, 'This is the way it's gonna be! Whether you like it or not!'"

The other dispute between the Kickapoo and Texas is over gambling. Like the Tigua of the El Paso vicinity, the Kickapoo were trying to parlay their special federal status into revenue from gaming. The thrust of the argument was that by instituting the lottery, the state had already legalized gambling. The Kickapoo had contracted with a Nevada firm called Southwest Casinos, which had commissioned a set of architectural plans for a glassy, Lake Tahoe-like edifice that would have looked like an extraterrestrial shipwreck on the reservation at Eagle Pass. The Kickapoo met with state officials in Austin that September to discuss bingo and other gaming, and Joe's father, Jose, made the drive with his son and son-in-law. He attended the meetings and ate the consultants' barbecue, but he seemed to dislike the whole business. At the hotel, he didn't want to talk about it.

Jose had heard enough of my Spanish not to put much stock in it, so he spoke Kickapoo and asked Margie to translate what he said into English. Algonquian is a plosive and consonantal language; the Kickapoo dialect is spoken slowly. While Joe sat on the bed, quiet and receding in the presence of his father, Jose reposed in an easy chair and reflected on their spiritual life. "God made the deer. God put them on the earth—not man. If you go hunting and see that a deer is someplace very difficult, at the top of a mountain, you will probably let it go. But a Kickapoo will do anything, go anywhere, climb the highest mountain to get the deer. Because to us, the deer is sacred. If you kill a deer, it has one life. But if a Kickapoo kills a deer, it has four lives. That is how God made the earth—so there will never be a shortage of game. There is a story of a Kickapoo man who lived as a deer for one year. That is the reason the deer and Kickapoo know how each other think."

He went on: "Our traditions cannot be written down. They're told by fathers, passed down by sons and grandsons. A Kickapoo does not pray for himself alone. He prays for all people. And if Kickapoo are not allowed to practice their traditions, this will be borne out in wars, disease, natural disasters. Kickapoo always wanted peace. We would move on to avoid conflict and maintain the traditions. And that is how we arrived in Mexico." Joe applied a Kickapoo slant to Mexican presidents and history. Benito Juárez, himself an Indian, asked them to help fight the Comanches and Apaches, and they did. In return Juárez offered them money, but they turned that down in favor of Nacimiento, their treasured place, which was akin to an autonomous region. They could go armed, like soldiers. In 1939 Lázaro Cárdenas amended their agreement so that in perpetuity they could hunt in the Sierra Madres nine months out of the year, and carry on the ritual naming and baptizing of their children. But the wilderness had turned into *ejidos*, or "communal lands," and ranches whose owners did not respect historic rights of Kickapoo. Mexican president Carlos Salinas, he said, just ignored them.

I asked Jose what he thought would happen. He said the tribe was trying to arrange a meeting with the new president, Ernesto Zedillo. "We will tell him our story, perform a dance, and hope he responds to the story." But he wasn't sanguine about their prospects. "*Es perdido*," he told me wearily. It's lost.

More than a year passed before I saw Joe again. Margie gave birth to their third child in April of 1995. The little girl was properly named and baptized; Joe would only say that the deer were taken in Texas. Unable to find work as a roofer, he went north again as a field hand. In a pickup with Montana plates, he came home to a bitter summer. His dad was briefly hospitalized with heart

pains, and in Nacimiento the drought was so severe that the grass died and the spring almost dried up. Hay was either non-existent or priced off the market. Most of the Hernandez family's cattle survived, but in desperation the horses browsed a plant that Kickapoo believe is poison. The only one of Joe's five horses that survived was the favorite palomino gelding he called Flaco. Late in the summer I called the tribal office and was heartened when Margie said he was in Laredo, going to some kind of school. He told her when he came home that in truth he had checked into a treatment clinic to get help with his drinking. With leather, paint, and feathers, he made a sign that hangs in the tribal office. "*Nekotenoe Nakoti Wodii,*" it says in Kickapoo: One Day at a Time.

In November, 1995, I returned to Eagle Pass to see Joe. He worked now for the public housing agency in town, and on the reservation I found him standing proudly beside the home that had replaced the cramped travel trailer. It was precisely half a nicely painted frame house; from the peak of the roof, the rear wall dropped straight down. He had built it himself, and he figured he would pour the rest of the concrete slab when he had the money.

We set out the next day for Nacimiento in a cold, gray rain. It was still falling at twilight, when Joe forded the river and steered through a maze of bogs. We were unloading our bedrolls and gear at the cinderblock house when a man in coveralls and a wool cap walked by with a flashlight and a jambox radio slung across his shoulder, like a rifle. He and Joe spoke Kickapoo for a long time, and in time I recognized the man. His street name in Eagle Pass was Kisco, and he was one of the paint sniffers befriended by Eric Fredlund. Though Kisco had been living like that for years and had lost many of his teeth, he had a reputation as a lady's man. His favorite hangout was an arroyo bridge right beside the police station.

Joe and I spread our sleeping bags that night on the ground inside the wickiup, which smelled like clean straw. We lay on our backs talking in the light of a kerosene lantern and watched water drip through the ceiling vent. We spoke of language—and my admiration that he could manage three. "Sometimes I get them mixed up," he said. "And it's not just that the words are different. My dad and I don't speak nothing but Kickapoo, and there's some things that Kickapoo don't say. I can't tell my dad I love him."

I told him I had met Kisco in Eagle Pass. Joe said he was his mother's cousin, and had just spent several months at Quemado. Joe spoke with obvious respect for the man; in Nacimiento, the paint sniffer and pariah of Eagle Pass had the reputation of a great hunter. "We come to a hard mountain and ride all day to get to the top. He leads a pack horse and just walks right over it."

Joe and I had become close and confiding friends, and we talked late into the night. "In your religion," Joe asked me, "what's the difference between prayer and ceremony?" I thought about it and said prayer is when you speak to God or address him in your thoughts; ceremony implies an activity and place. Joe nodded thoughtfully. "I suppose that for Kickapoo peoples, ceremony is the prayer. I remember hearing the sound of it early in the morning, almost every day. It has to be done a certain way, exactly. My generation is losing it because we haven't had the chance to practice." I asked him if he could perform the ceremony, if he had to. "I don't know," he said. "And, you know, it's dangerous if you get it wrong."

Kickapoo believe that we are living in the last of four worlds. The first three were destroyed by air, rot, and water; this one will be consumed by fire. But their faith seems to be largely free of apocalyptic fret and doom. As long as they observe the tradition and conduct their lives honorably, at peace with nature, they will have an eternal reward somewhere in the western sky. In early spring the helper spirits of nature convey two signals—the second thunderstorm of the season and the leafing out of a certain kind of tree. The tribe's spiritual leader summons the people, and at Nacimiento the holy season begins. For several weeks Nacimiento is closed to anyone who is not Kickapoo. Near the end of the season, a few friends of the tribe are invited to join them. Last April I received such a call.

I arrived near sundown at a clearing among the wickiups and cinder block houses. Joe urged me to get something to eat—fried chicken, beans, bread, and venison—but it wasn't a time for talk. It was the night of the women's dances.

Wearing brightly colored frocks sewn with pennants, the women formed a row, pressed closely against each other. They were aligned by age, from the lead dancer, who must have been in her nineties, down to the little girls, some of whom were wearing modernity's running shoes with blinking reflectors under tradition's long skirts. As male elders in ordinary attire sang to the accompaniment of a drum beat, the women performed a shuffling dance around a fire, above which four cast-iron pots hung from a pole. It went on like that for hours. I had no idea what I was witnessing. Nor, had I known, would I have fully understood the spiritual significance, at least not like the Kickapoo. The sky was moonless over the Sierra Madres: flares of meteorites, and the first time I had seen a comet. The music was monotonous, mesmerizing. At the end of each dance the tribal elders raised a shrill cry: *Ki ki ki ki ki.*

A month later, back in Texas, the residents of Quemado got their way. What finally shut down the treatment center was budget pressure in Washington. Roberto de la Garza, an Eagle Pass resident who succeeded an ailing Julio Frausto as tribal administrator, enlisted Eric Fredlund as a consultant to salvage the program. The state came up with enough money to keep it going, on the condition that the center move to the reservation in Eagle Pass. Not far away from the two portable buildings that house the treatment center is the bingo parlor and a plain modular building called the Lucky Eagle where there are slot machines and blackjack tables. The local crowds have not generated much revenue for the Kickapoo, and the issue of whether the operation violates state gaming laws has yet to be resolved. But as it so often happens on Indian reservations, the competition for jobs and money would drive a deep schism within the tribe.

Last summer Eric Fredlund became the director of the treatment staff. Joe Hernandez works on the staff and is training to be a counselor. "It's no silver bullet," Eric told me. "I still have friends living under those bridges. People relapse, then try again. But solvent-exposed births have decreased sixty percent. And the arrest rate in Eagle Pass is down forty percent."

The modern world is neither arranged nor disposed to accommodate the Kickapoo way of life. Perhaps the only haven left to them is high in the Sierra Madres. Many times Joe and I had talked about my going with him on a horseback ride into the high country. As a gesture of friendship and hospitality, he kept asking me if I wanted to ride Flaco, his treasured hunting companion, but I think he also wanted to gauge my experience and skill in the saddle. Once, we even entered the tack shed, but we never mounted up. Instead, we climbed on a hill and sat on a rock ledge over the river. Joe pointed out cliffs and contours that marked the hunters' way up into the higher mountains. He described sudden snowstorms and fearing he was lost in the forest and the time a friend's horse fell off a cliff to its death and almost took his friend along. He said that I could go along on the next ride, perhaps on Flaco, but the more stories Joe told, the more that sounded like a young man's adventure. I explained that in my culture and family, the next week was Thanksgiving. The ride would have to wait.

He gave an embarrassed and respectful nod and said he had forgotten. But he would go anyway. For the next several days I thought of him often up in those mountains, practicing his religion, doing what he loves. I called Margie at the tribal office and asked her to have him call me and tell me the whole story as soon as he got back. When he called, he said four of them had gone for five days and brought back four deer. It was cold but beautiful up there.

They saw a lot of deer and quite a few bear tracks. The deer he killed, he said, was a small buck. It ran from him and he ran, too, then the deer stopped and looked back, about one hundred yards away.

On the phone then there was a long pause. "But you know Flaco? Skinny?" Joe's voice broke. "When we got home, Flaco died. I didn't ride him too hard, and he didn't act sick at all. But the minute we got to Nacimiento, he started shaking and couldn't breathe. He just died."

When he told me that I had to sit down. What more misfortune could happen to these people?

"My dad told me not to feel too bad," Joe said philosophically. "He told me, 'You know, sometimes horses know things. See things that are about to happen. And sometimes horses choose to die, to keep something bad from happening to you.'"

FEBRUARY, 1997

THE BEAT

The assignment was to find some ordinary street cops and view a Texas city through their eyes. I chose Dallas because Houston's police department was then embroiled in a scandal—killing prisoners and trying to cover it up. I explained my needs to a deputy chief in Dallas who now dressed in stylish tweeds but had roamed those streets in uniform for many years himself. Because of the temper of that time, I wouldn't have been surprised if he turned me down flat. But the officer looked me over, played a hunch, and decided I was all right.

The beat cops he placed me with were wary at first. But as the streets and shifts rolled by they relaxed and warmed up to me. When the action burst on us I kept my mouth shut but stayed right on their heels; they thought I was game. Both cops wanted me to meet their families, have a meal with them, see them in their suburban homes. And I did. But our common fascination was a Dallas I had not known to exist. I had thought the city was a sterile, rather uninteresting place, for all its millionaires. But the poor and lower middle-class neighborhoods that the cops cruised were alive with a humor and richness that had nothing to do with wealth.

Midnight is a peak hour in police work; sometimes the distinctions of shift, beat, and even patrol division evaporate in an emergency. That was how Ron Cawthon came to answer a backup call from Dennis Cozby, who works a different beat, one midnight three years ago. Cozby was training a female recruit fresh from the police academy when they caught a burglar inside a building. Through a window Cozby saw the burglar run toward the door guarded by the recruit. Unsure how she would react, he made the snap decision to fire, and the burglar died where he fell.

In the aftermath, Cozby was calm—he'd been there before. Cawthon stayed with him that night, even observed the autopsy. Cozby's .38-caliber bullet

had struck the burglar in the middle of the back, ricocheted down the length of his torso, then emerged low in the abdomen. Cawthon remembers thinking it must have rung that spine like a xylophone. This kind of thing doesn't happen every night, but then again it isn't that unusual for Cozby and Cawthon. They work beats in the toughest parts of Dallas.

Twelve years ago, when Ron Cawthon finished his rookie training and joined the Central Patrol Division, he answered a call to send a corpse to the morgue on each of his first four shifts. "My Lord," he thought, "is every day gonna be like this?" Cawthon is forty-two now, a grandfather. His forearms are blue with Navy tattoos, and he resembles a young Red Skelton when he smiles. His style of working the street is low-key. He listens to the small-time crooks with skeptical amusement, entangles them in their lies, and ushers them downtown to jail.

Compared to Cawthon, Dennis Cozby is a flamboyant character. On infantry patrol with the Third Marines in the Quang Tri province of Vietnam, Cozby was hit three times by enemy fire—in the leg, in the chest, and then by a bit of shrapnel that almost scalped him. Back home at the age of twenty, he joined the Dallas police and requested assignment to the tough Central Patrol Division. Cozby is now thirty. He still likes to talk about fighting in the Golden Gloves, riding bulls in the rodeo, playing semipro football; he often chews bubble gum while smoking a long, foul cigar. He's a man who is feared on the street. Fellow cops call him Mad Dog.

After completing training, all Dallas cops spend at least two years on the street. Most pursue rank and reassignment—or seek more staid employment. But Cawthon and Cozby have chosen to remain street cops. They have trouble counting the times they've required emergency treatment at Parkland Hospital. They've been shot at repeatedly but, so far, not hit. Both live with the knowledge that their gunfire has killed other men. Police work has cost each of them a marriage involving children. But their deepest common bond is the street itself.

Patrol cops are "charged" by the superiors with the murders, rapes, robberies, and even car wrecks on their beats. These statistics don't reflect the cops' energy and abilities; the numbers show what they're up against. In 1979 the three shifts on Cawthon's and Cozby's beats—six patrol units—responded to 12 murders, 14 rapes, 70 robberies, 122 car thefts, 164 aggravated assaults, 281 burglaries, and 538 simple larcenies.

Cawthon and Cozby don't "solve" many crimes. Mostly they talk to victims. They fill out the initial paperwork and phone the complaint downtown, where it becomes the responsibility of investigators elsewhere in the depart-

ment. They spend their shifts driving around, being seen—essentially, looking for trouble. Other patrol cops may merely answer the calls on their own beats, never ranging beyond those boundaries, but Cawthon and Cozby look for the action. They race to answer calls throughout the patrol division.

People on these Dallas streets fear the collective power of the police, but they talk back to individual cops and often fight back. If Cawthon or Cozby take them to jail, most make bond or post bail within hours. The next evening they're back on the street, nodding hello to the same cops, who nod back. Cawthon and Cozby are creatures of the street as much as the pimps, hookers, and winos they move among. They have to think like street people and learn their language, for they face a barrier of racial resentment. In this section of the city where forty percent of the residents are nonwhite, 212 of 234 beat cops are Anglo males.

Of all the streets worked by Dallas cops, Cozby's and Cawthon's beats in the Central Patrol Division are among the meanest and most dangerous. But though Cawthon and Cozby talk fondly of retirement and sometimes bemoan the futility of their efforts, they harbor no ambitions to be or do anything else. For five eight-hour shifts a week they confront the gruesome vitality of the streets, then drive home to the middle-class concerns of quiet households in the suburbs. It's a strange, schizophrenic way to live, but it's the life they know and want.

The R. L. Thornton and Central Expressways divide the Central Patrol Division into three distinct sections. North and west of the freeway interchange lie the downtown hotels and office towers, the restaurants and boutiques along McKinney and Lemmon, the mansions and azaleas of Turtle Creek, the pleasant hodgepodge of Oak Lawn. The heaviest action seen by patrolmen in this section is the revelry on the Friday of Texas-Oklahoma weekend.

North and east of the freeways, in the second and largest section, a dozen intersections of Carol Avenue attests to its polyglot diversity. Ross Avenue houses a Tradin' Hoss used-car lot and a string of others that offer "Se Habla Español." Bryan teems with white hookers near bars renowned as the stomping grounds of the Indians who live in that neighborhood. Four blocks away lies the inner city's restoration showcase, Swiss Avenue. At Columbia a custard-cone sign announces the building's new tenant, the Egg Roll Hut, while another sign identifies the Mex-Mex (Double-Mex) Lounge. Around the corner sits an Elm Street honky-tonk called It'll Do.

A four-block stretch of Hall Street between Central Expressway and Ross is dominated by the Roseland housing project—red-brick apartments that

might look ordinary but for the plywood nailed over a third of the windows. Except for Paisano motorcyclists who frequent a bar called Little David's, the faces here are black. Cozby has shot and killed two black residents of this Hall Street neighborhood, his former beat. The first was an old man who went berserk and started shooting at children in the project. The other ran from a botched heroin deal around the corner of Roseland into the Empire Grill, turned on Cozby, jammed a pistol in his midriff, and yanked the trigger three times as the surprised cop grabbed for his own revolver. The black's cheaper gun misfired.

Cozby's Beat 141, on the eastern end of Central's territory, is thinly populated and quiet until the bikers, truckers, cowboys, ex-cons, and street fighters crank up the bars along Tenison Park. The bars are uniformly low-ceilinged, windowless, and loud. North of the arrowhead-shaped park, at East Grand and Shadyside, is a disco called KC's. Samuell Boulevard borders the south end of the park. Cozby knows from experience that if he doesn't hit every bar in the 3500 block every night, the fights soon start. The names here are Kim's Place, Connie's Corner Lounge, the Gator Club, Monty's Lounge, and the Nineteenth Hole. Around the corner is another disco called the Lamp Post Club. Not long ago Cozby roared into the Lamp Post's parking lot with his siren whooping and yanked a van door open on bikers who had dragged a woman off the sidewalk with the apparent intention of raping her. Cozby had to let the bikers go; the distraught victim, married but slipping around on her husband, was afraid to press charges.

South of R. L. Thornton, the boundaries of Central's third section are Grand Avenue and East Grand, the Santa Fe railroad yards, and the Trinity River. There's little diversity here; the two-story houses that remain are beyond restoration. Most were torn down in a hustle of speculative apartment construction during the fifties and sixties. Constantly being passed from owner to owner, the yellow-brick complexes profit no one, least of all the tenants. Ron Cawthon recently answered the complaint of an apartment manager in "Grand City," as the drab units southwest of Fair Park are known. "They'd been without hot water for weeks, the wiring was blowing fire out of the plugs, and roaches were falling off the ceiling," Cawthon recalled. "She thought I could do something about the landlord. I said, 'Lady, why don't you move?'" He shrugged as she had shrugged. "Because I'm poor."

Cawthon doesn't range as far afield as Cozby because his Beat 135, along Grand Avenue, requires more constant attention. Scattered through these slums are inventive and successful businesses—a repair service for broken-down buses, a garage specializing in the exquisite restoration and sale of an-

tique automobiles. Though the Minyard's supermarket requires an off-duty police officer at all times, the other businesses along Grand Avenue report surprisingly few crimes against property—probably because most try to hire residents of the area. The frustrations of Grand City are turned inward, and the toll is human. In 1979 Cawthon's beat reported 116 aggravated assaults, and that figure only reflects the mayhem on one side of Grand Avenue; offenses across the narrow street show up in Southeast Division statistics. In 1979 the apartments along six blocks of Grand Avenue were the site of twenty-two homicides—making that area the deadliest neighborhood in Dallas. Of those twenty-two, five occurred in the Park South Apartments—346 units inhabited by more than a thousand people. In one nine-day period there were four shootings and one stabbing; all involved friends, lovers, or neighbors. Cawthon drives through Park South about once an hour.

Coordinating the officers' movement through this tangled landscape of thievery and violence is the job of the dispatcher on Central's radio channel one. Entrenched deep inside "Pei Palace," as the new city hall designed by I. M. Pei is known among the ranks, the police and fire departments' communications center has its own emergency water and power supply and would allegedly withstand a nuclear explosion. Telephone operators feed the information from their calls into a computer that delivers a print-out to the dispatcher for the appropriate channel. Some dispatchers are civilians, others are uniformed officers. They hunch over their boards with an air of harried vigilance; during peak activity on the night shift they're on for an hour, off for thirty minutes. A huge reel-to-reel multi-channel tape machine records all telephone calls and dispatches. A special telephone can establish direct radio contact between Dallas officers and those in Fort Worth and the outlying suburban areas—a handy device in case of a high-speed chase. One dispatcher monitors a screen that shows green sectors of his division with red dots denoting police calls in progress. Squad cars are represented on the map by automated brackets. If the brackets start flashing red and white, it means the patrol unit needs help.

This advanced technology is the only direct connection between street cops and city hall. The work of Ron Cawthon and Dennis Cozby seldom involves contact with any rank higher than the sector sergeant, who supervises several beats in the division. Cawthon and Cozby are "good cops" by the definitions of their superiors. But their own standards of performance are those of their peers. Their attitude toward rank isn't insubordinate—it's more like the mercenary's aversion to close-order drill. However sporadic, the major reward of their work is the action, and in the police department, promotion

usually involves removal from the action. Patrolmen become sergeants by passing a test drawn from a reading list of titles like *Fundamentals of Police Administration and Supervision: The Direction of People at Work.* Too often, they wind up tied to desks at the substation, trading recipes with the secretaries and answering the phone.

The Central Division substation at the east end of Hall Street, crowded by an R. L. Thornton overpass and the Southern Pacific railroad yards, was once a cotton gin. Now sparrows flutter among the disconnected blow chutes. Ron Cawthon's business at the substation is generally limited to drive-through errands and exchanges of cars, so the old building suits him fine.

The police department's day is divided into three eight-hour watches: midnight to morning, morning to afternoon, and afternoon to midnight. The last Thursday morning in December, Cawthon stood by the Xerox machine in the detail room at the substation, drinking coffee and waking up as other officers chatted about real estate transactions. In the adjoining classroom the second-watch cops who went out at 7:30 A.M.—they would be followed by Cawthon and the rest of the shift half an hour later—had assembled for firearms inspection. They stood in loose formation, talking and handling their guns.

A reverberating *boom!* sent Cawthon plunging toward the coffee machine. The bitter smell of discharged powder filled the detail room. "Man down!" somebody cried from inside the classroom.

An officer had been wiping his .45-caliber automatic with a handkerchief when two rounds went off—though Cawthon thought he had heard a single explosion. One bullet struck the .45's handler in the foot; the other hit a fellow officer in the groin and emerged from the back of his leg. Both officers were white with shock, but with help they were able to walk past Cawthon to a car. After they were gone, Cawthon fumbled the coins while shoving another fifteen cents into the coffee machine. His heart was still pounding.

"Lord, the paperwork," he grumbled a moment later. "Everybody in that room is gonna have to write a letter."

The substation now swarmed with plainclothes investigators from Internal Affairs. Hands in his pockets, Central's deputy chief, Robert Dixon, walked through the classroom in a stylish sport coat. He stepped gingerly, as if through a bomb site.

"That's all those automatics are good for," said Cawthon, who uses a .357-magnum revolver. "For a while we were having the same problem around here with shotguns. That was when we carried them in vertical racks behind the driver's seat. A lot of squad cars were coming in with holes blown in the roof."

The Deep Nights patrolman (Deep Nights is the midnight-to-morning watch) on Beat 135 was late coming off the shift, so Cawthon, working alone because of a death in his partner's family, was waiting for a car to drive. He leaned glumly against a fender in the asphalt floor of the onetime cotton gin for another half hour before Deep Nights 135 drove into the garage in a car that Cawthon didn't recognize. "What happened to ours?" he asked the cop, who also turned over to him the beat's walkie-talkie.

"They sent it back to the factory because the oil light kept coming on," said the cop. "Didn't you know that?"

Cawthon's mouth stretched in disgust. "Nobody told me."

Acquainting himself with the unfamiliar dash and steering wheel of the relief car, Cawthon drove out of the substation and slowly circled the ruins of the Pearlstone grain elevator. As usual, he headed first for Grand City. At the Park South Apartments black kids out of school on Christmas vacation were kicking a soccer ball across the asphalt lot. It rolled up against an old Rambler with four flat tires. The Rambler has occupied the same parking slot for nearly two years; Cawthon can't send a city wrecker after the abandoned junker because it's on private property. Younger black kids sifted the dirt in the bare yards between the stark building. One of them pedaled up to Cawthon on a bicycle and asked, "You got any Cowboy cards?" The trading cards, instituted by the Kiwanis Club as a police community relations program, bear likenesses of Dallas Cowboys Tony Dorsett, Harvey Martin, and other local heroes, along with a National Football League rule and a crime prevention tip.

"Sure do, sugar man," said Cawthon, reaching for a packet on the dash. "How about a Tom Landry?"

Leaving Park South, he nodded at a walking security guard carrying a shotgun, then turned up a side street. He pointed out a small frame house with a heel-pocked, muddy front yard and a volleyball net. "Two brothers live by themselves in there," he said. "Both minors. We catch them stealing cars in here all the time. Just joyriding—take 'em out and tear 'em up. Big old figure eights on a vacant lot around the corner. But the oldest one's sixteen now, so he's getting pretty close to the jailhouse."

He drove on through the empty apartment complexes off Grand Avenue, looking for winos and kids, who inhabit the building shells and often start fires. All the glass, doors, and plumbing had been crowbarred from the walls of one single-row complex. "As soon as they hear about the foreclosure they hit it fast," explained Cawthon. "They sell the stuff to salvage yards. And if we catch anybody, the owners of the building *know* that if they press charges, the vandal's friends are gonna burn it to the ground." He stopped beside a

ten-foot security fence erected by the bank that had repossessed a quadrangle complex. "You know what'll happen next?" he chuckled. "Somebody's gonna steal that fence."

One of the wounded patrolmen had been scheduled to work the next beat south of 135. Drifting over to cover for him, Cawthon sought out the chilled streetwalkers along Ervay. Most were black. When Cawthon joined the department the police could arrest known prostitutes—or anyone with a police record—and jail them for up to three days on mere suspicion. But the appeals courts took exception to unwarranted 72-hour holds; now Cawthon can't run prostitutes in unless he catches them breaking the law. Knowing that, the streetwalkers stand their ground. They know the street cops, and the cops know them. Both try to get along as best they can.

Cawthon was looking for a young hooker who'd run off with a white trick's wallet and trousers from a nearby motel rendezvous. The man had gotten them back and, leery of publicity, declined to press charges. Cawthon found the hooker huddled with two colleagues on a corner. She had a pretty fur coat, rouged cheeks, the eyes of a born heartbreaker. Cawthon rolled down his window. "Come here, Tyra."

Her gaze was apprehensive but direct. Cawthon said, "What's this I hear about you taking off with a trick's blue jeans?"

Tyra's face fell. She said nothing.

"Peddling your sweet little ol' wares is one thing, but if you go to ripping off tricks, I'll be down on you like ugly on an ape."

"I'm sorry," she said. "I apologized to him. I won't do it again, I promise. I was disappointed in myself, doing that. My husband whipped the fuck outa me."

Suppressing a laugh, Cawthon drove on. "Most of them live in Oak Cliff," he said. "And this is where they come to work. It hasn't been long since prostitutes were afraid to go outside in Dallas. If nothing else, we could run 'em downtown for violating the loitering ordinance. But there's really not much we can do about the hookers anymore. If they gang up, we can run 'em in for blocking a public sidewalk or roadway, but those are eighteen-dollar fines. That's just an occupational hazard; they carry enough to cover that in the hems of their skirts. The vice squad works the hotels, not the street. The only way we can make a prostitution arrest is if the girl propositions a cop, and you know she's not gonna do that to one in uniform."

Circling back toward Fair Park, he passed a residence where a domestic quarrel had recently ended in homicide. "When I got there the man was face down in the yard—nothing I could do for him," Cawthon recalled. "The

woman hollered, 'Here I am, I'm the one you're looking for.' The cheap little gun was inside on the bed. When I read her the statement she started crying, and I asked her why she did it. 'Because he called me dog bitch.' I said, 'That's all?' She said, 'I'm *tired* of that man calling me names.'"

After that, the conversation drifted to Cawthon's divorce from his first wife. In those days Dallas patrolmen worked rotating shifts—one month on each of the three watches. Since he had low seniority, Cawthon's days off were in the middle of the week. As the children reached school age, his family adapted to other schedules. They occupied the same house, greeted each other in passing. Cawthon excelled at his work, but the hours and strain of that work ruined his home life. After fifteen years of marriage and four kids, Cawthon agreed to a divorce.

"She was raising the kids by herself," he explained. "She never knew what to expect from one day to the next. She got tired of seeing me come in with my clothes torn off, my face stitched up. Of course, there were other things that we failed to work out, but essentially she gave me a choice of her or the police department." He shrugged, turning another corner, "I'm still here."

More out of concern for the officers' efficiency than for their home lives, in 1973 the police department adopted a schedule of fixed watches—the theory being that cops could know the streets and street people best if they were there at the same time every day. Enjoying the freedom of unanticipated bachelorhood, Cawthon chose the midnight-to-morning first watch. Washed in strange pale colors by neon and mercury vapor, Deep Nights in East Dallas provided meaningful police work—mayhem as the bars closed, burglars and car thieves caught in the act—while sparing him the drudgery of traffic patrol.

But at the twentieth reunion of his Samuell High graduating class he re-encountered a handsome divorcée named Barbara; they had once, while going steady with each other's best friends, double-dated at the drive-ins of Pleasant Grove. They married and consolidated families. They bought a house on Lake Ray Hubbard, a boat, and water skis. In the mornings, while he was on his way home, she commuted on Interstate 30 to her job as an office supervisor in a refrigerated warehouse not far from the Central substation. At night, he left for work not long after the supper table was cleared. Cawthon worked Deep Nights for four and a half years and gained a reputation as the department's model street cop, receiving thirty-seven official commendations and only four citizen complaints. But he recognized the symptoms at home. He could see it coming again.

He applied for a transfer and tried working as a corporal in the claustro-phobic jail. But he missed the street and soon surrendered his stripe of rank to return to East Dallas as a patrolman on the second watch. Seniority enabled him to claim Sundays and Mondays off. His hours now complement the sched-ules of his family, but day-shift police work can get awfully boring. When the action's hot on the third watch, Mad Dog Cozby may work twenty calls before getting off at midnight. Cawthon's busy on the second if he answers ten.

Seven hours of his shift had passed, and Cawthon had answered only three calls. The last was actually a few blocks inside Southeast Patrol territory. In the Texas and Pacific railroad yards, two blacks had climbed up and squeezed onto a railroad car that contained new Plymouths, then broken into a few of the autos' windows and trunks to steal the accessories shipped inside. When Cawthon drove up, three Southeast units were already there. They had one of the blacks handcuffed in a squad car; the other had gotten away. Cawthon found some floor mats and tires in a nearby vacant lot. A uniformed sergeant assigned the jail trip to one of his patrolmen, the paperwork to another. Cawthon volun-teered to wait beside the tracks for the officer from the fingerprint section. The dispatcher told him that the officer would arrive in about thirty minutes.

Cawthon had finished the day. He stretched an arm across the back of the seat and yawned. He reminisced about the time in the early seventies he and the Southeast sergeant had been involved in a shooting: a raging old black man had run out of his house on Hall Street firing at cops, who promptly riddled him. I asked if there'd been other shootings.

He stared at the gray distance of the railroad yards. "I was training a rookie one night and we got a disturbance call. When we got there we could hear the commotion in the back of a house, and a woman on the porch pointed us around a hedge. A black woman was being raped by her best friend's hus-band. 'God, help,' she was yelling, 'can't you see he's killing me?' The rookie and I threw down on him and told him he'd better hold what he had. But he jammed his thumbs in her throat and started trying to twist her around be-tween him and us. She was making strangling noises, so I let it go. The bullet hit him in the middle of the back and went right through—it must have parted her hair. Needless to say, she was hysterical. All she wanted was to be some-where else, so it turned into a wrestling match with her. She was my only civilian witness. The rookie came over and said, 'Ron, Ron, he's dead.' I said, 'That's unfortunate. Could you please give me a hand?'"

Cawthon was quiet for a moment. "At the hospital they took a handful of dirt and gravel out of her. He had savaged her like an animal. She told me she

had no doubt he would have killed her, because he knew she wouldn't let him get away with it. I've come awake in the middle of the night dreaming about that man, but I don't give him too much conscious thought. It's the people close to him who bother me. Everybody's got somebody who cares about him. By killing him, I hurt some people who didn't have anything to do with that."

I asked Cawthon why he no longer trains rookies.

"It just got old. If I drew a bad one, I'd finish the shift wanting to punch a hole in the wall. You ever spent eight hours saying, 'Turn left, turn right'? There are people in this department who have no business being police officers. Luckily, most get weeded out before they hurt somebody or get themselves in trouble. They come out of the academy and just want to experience it all, right at the start. I call them burn-'em-ups. They think people will look up to them because of that uniform. Why, bullshit, nobody really wants a cop around.

"You have to love this work to put up with it. And I do, but I don't try to set the world on fire anymore. There's more to life than that."

After showing the fingerprint man the damaged Plymouths, Cawthon headed for the substation. He turned the relief car and walkie-talkie over to the partners who worked the beat's third watch. Then he drove home to Mesquite still in uniform and parked his new Cheyenne pickup in front of his new brick home. His twelve-year-old son, Donnie, was throwing his Christmas football across the dormant Saint Augustine lawn. When Cawthon opened the front door, he walked into a wave of heat from the brick fireplace recently added to the living room. He kissed his wife, Barbara, and kidded her about the inferno in the fireplace. She asked about his attempt to quit smoking. "No cigarettes," he told her, "but I've got a hole in my cheek from the snuff."

Cawthon showered and changed into navy denims and a T-shirt. His sixteen-year-old daughter, Joanna, set the table while Barbara called Donnie inside. His eighteen-year-old stepson, Robert, was away at his part-time job at the Seagoville Gibson's. We ate the supper of fried pork chops, biscuits, gravy, vegetables, and iced tea, then sat with cups of coffee on the sofa. The wall behind Barbara's chair was decorated with her husband's professional plaques and certificates—Officer of the Year, the Life Saving Award, and one of the department's highest honors, the Police Commendation.

I asked Barbara if she'd had any exposure to police work before she married Ron. She smiled. "Not unless you count my traffic tickets. It took some getting used to. I still freeze up every time policemen come in the office where I work."

"And that's my fault," he said. "I told her not to worry about the phone's ringing—if anything ever happened to me they'd send somebody to tell her

in person." He noted her grimace. "I wish I could say I leave all that back there when I get off, but it has a way of running together. I catch myself talking to my family the way I talk to people on the street."

En route to the phone, Joanna walked through the living room. "Say *what*?" she quipped, affecting the ghetto jargon.

Cawthon watched his burning fireplace with an air of contentment. He was where he wanted to be; the hard streets of Central were somebody else's problem now. As we talked, the third police watch in Dallas was reaching the midpoint. On one of the streets walked by Tyra and the other hookers from Oak Cliff, two blacks triggered the burglar alarm in an electrical supply house while stealing aluminum conduits from a truck. Watching the suspects flee on foot, the partners on Beat 135 tried to drive after them, but the relief car's engine stalled. Walkie-talkie in one hand, .357 magnum in the other, the passenger cop chased one thief through a vacant lot, then attempted to follow him over a chain-link fence into the alley.

Central's second accidental *boom!* of the day blew the officer's thumb off and destroyed the beat's two thousand dollar walkie-talkie. Meanwhile, the relief car stalled again. Trying to run to his injured partner, the driver slipped and sprained his ankle. Another Central cop in a squad car a few blocks away responded to their call for assistance. At Ervay and Beaumont he ran into a fifty-three-year-old pedestrian and broke the man's leg.

The next day, December 28, Dennis Cozby arrived at the substation wearing blue jeans, Adidas running shoes, and a shirt with the tail out. Just back from a vacation he'd taken to help his wife with their new baby, he drove up to the station in a blue Monte Carlo. In the locker room he rediscovered with displeasure that he'd split the seat of his uniform trousers while frisking a prisoner. His mood wasn't lightened by the fact that while he was off, a Dallas businessman had lodged the eighth citizen complaint in his personnel file, which also contains fourteen commendations. Though a polygraph supported Cozby's innocence, he was still indignant—he begrudged the paperwork required by Internal Affairs.

All of that, plus the previous day's accidental bloodshed, had left Cozby in no mood for a slow night. At the intersection of Bryan and Carroll several young white women lounged in a parking lot. The arrival of Cozby's squad car sent them scuttling like quail. Rounding the corner, the hookers feigned interest in the newspaper racks in front of Pedigo's, sashayed past the liquor store, then, aplomb dissolving, jostled each other shoving through the door of the Kwik-Wash laundromat. "Move along, darlings," said Cozby. Then he laughed.

Idling through the lot, he stared brave hookers down with an expression of amused contempt. Resuming his patrol of Carroll, on impulse he turned into a broken concrete driveway between two nondescript apartment buildings. There he encountered a dented Pontiac occupied by a tall black man and a white woman; the drive was too narrow for both cars to pass. The Pontiac jerked unceremoniously as the black hit the brakes and tried to find reverse. Cozby grinned and turned on his red and blue lights.

As Cozby emerged from the Dodge he hitched up his pants and adjusted his belt, chewing on a fresh cigar. Black kids congregated and clamored for Cowboy cards. He dismissed them with a curt "Don't have any."

The tall black wore a gauze shirt and a hat with the brim rolled low. He carried himself with a measure of justified vanity, but his hands trembled in search of his ID. "How come you so nervous, Bimbo?" said Cozby. "Whose car is this?"

"It belongs to a friend."

Cozby stopped to look inside the Pontiac. The horse-faced girl wore jeans and a T-shirt; her arms bore ugly needle tracks.

"What you got in here, bub?"

Surrounded by brick walls, a tall fence, a Dempster Dumpster, and unamused black faces, Cozby radioed in for a backup, lit the cigar, and ordered the hooker out of the car. She observed her pimp's bust with glum resignation. On the Pontiac's dash Cozby found a knife and scabbard that he tapped against his palm. "Wonder how long this is, Bimbo."

"Aw, man, you don't hear what I'm telling you," wailed the pimp. "This ain't my car. That ain't my blade!"

Cozby mused, "If it's five and three quarters inches I'm gonna have to take you downtown. Sure wish I had a ruler."

"Aw, *man!* It ain't been an hour since I was at the store; another police walked out and looked right *at* that blade. He didn't say a word! You ain't about to lay that on me."

Riding downtown, Bimbo slouched beside Cozby in a gangly coil, hands cuffed behind him. "Tell you what," offered Cozby. "If the blade's over five and three quarters I'm gonna file on you because it's a prohibited weapon. But if your friend'll come down and sign a statement that it's his property, I'll drop the charges."

"Then you file on him?"

Cozby smiled. "Probably."

"Yeah, you know he gonna do that." Bimbo complained that being a black man—rather than the knife in question—accounted for his predicament.

Cozby asked if he really believed that. "Hell, yeah, I really believe it," snapped the prisoner. "Whose hands are free?"

From Mail Street Cozby drove into a basement garage marked by civil defense and private parking signs; only a few recognize it as the famous city jail ramp where Jack Ruby shot Lee Harvey Oswald. Cozby opened the metal door for Bimbo, then grabbed the suspect's arm when he started to turn right into the jail elevator entry from force of habit. In an office around the corner, Cozby asked a woman if he could borrow her ruler.

With theatrical precision he laid the ruler flush against the blade's hilt. The knifepoint touched the mark of five and one-fourth inches. Bimbo gasped relief and laid his forehead on the counter.

Cozby clapped him on the shoulder and escorted him back out to the Dodge. But when he tried to unlock the handcuffs, Bimbo shied away; in a world populated by lawbreakers and police informants, no pimp wants to look too chummy with a cop. Eyes narrowing, Cozby said, "Now, Bimbo, I can't keep a man in cuffs unless he's a prisoner, and you're not a prisoner anymore. That's regulations."

At the traffic light on Gaston and Caroll, Bimbo said, "You can just let me out here."

"Uh-uh," replied Cozby. "We're going right back where you were."

Familiar black faces, still unamused, stared from the porches of the apartments on Carroll. "Man, why you doing this to me?" muttered Bimbo, opening the door.

Cozby walked around the car to hand over the knife. "Here go, Bimbo," he said loudly. "*Thanks for your help.*"

It was not yet sundown. Cozby drifted on over to Hall Street and circled through the Roseland projects. While they look more livable than Grand City, they are bleak enough. A new Cadillac with blue California tags and Christmas presents visible through the back window turned in front of us. Cozby called in a stolen-car check on the license number, but it came back clean. I asked him what made him suspect the Cadillac.

"If people can afford a car like that, are they gonna drive fifteen hundred miles to visit folks who live in a place like this?" he answered.

About ten o'clock Cozby struck out for the bars on Samuell Boulevard. On the way he teamed up with another Central squad car, driven by one of his former rookies, a fellow from Michigan. Cozby seemed to thrive on the bravado of walking the bars—the hostile glances, the force of his presence in the territory where it's most unwelcome.

Inside Kim's Place, Cozby greeted the bouncer, then walked into the bar, looking for people drunk enough to send home. He grinned but moved on through the small fuss made over him by a young woman he called Fancy Nancy. ("Fender lizards," he calls the bar friendlies. "They'll crawl all over the car if you let 'em.")

As Cozby walked out, Fancy Nancy confided to me, "He's such a shit."

The Gator Club was a country hangout with a live band. Approaching it, Cozby noticed two Anglo men of about thirty who stood under the light outside the bar's door, foreheads almost touching. One had a flattened nose and a crumpled straw cowboy hat; the other had short dark hair and a beard. Cozby's stride lengthened. "What are we doing here... smoking a little *dope*?"

The one in the cowboy hat just sagged, but the eyes of the bearded one flashed wide in recognition. With impressive reflexes he flung the door open and headed for the bar's alley exit. Cozby bellowed and sprinted after him; the cop from Michigan spread-eagled the one in the cowboy hat against the nearest fender. The bouncer stepped outside and smiled gamely at a couple who were lingering on the sidewalk, uncertain that this was the right place to go dancing after all.

In a moment, the bearded one came hurtling back out in Cozby's grasp. Tossing him against the hood, Cozby frisked him roughly, then fumbled for his handcuffs. "What the hell you mean, Worley, running from a cop?" he demanded. "Resisting arrest—that's two grand and a year in jail."

A few days earlier Worley had gone to jail on a misdemeanor pot bust. As he adjusted to the prospect of going back, his expression became a mixture of long-suffering patience and passive defiance. He was mad at himself, madder at Cozby. "I didn't run that far!"

Cozby hurried back inside and began a flashlight search of the carpet around the pinball machine, hopeful that Worley had ditched a lid during his brief flight. Cozby doesn't bother with making marijuana busts unless he recovers a "usable quantity," and the roach shared by Worley and his friend didn't qualify. The commotion of Cozby's search drew a resentful look from a young two-hundred-pounder at a nearby table. "You're drunk," Cozby announced. "Get outa here."

The large young man scowled and glanced at a friend. "What did you say?"

Cozby leaned closer. "I said you're too drunk to be in here. And if you don't go home right this minute, I'm gonna take you to jail."

The young man clenched his jaw, stood reluctantly, and walked out. When Cozby rejoined the others, he asked, "Where'd you hide the rest of it, Worley?"

"The rest of what, Cozby?" the prisoner sneered.

As we walked the handcuffed pair toward the squad cars, Cozby noticed the two-hundred-pound youth, who had only retreated down the sidewalk, waiting for the cops to leave. "I don't think that boy believed me."

He brought the kid in handcuffs to the car. Because of the number of prisoners, Worley rode downtown in another cop car. He sat on cuffed hands in the back seat as his date approached the window. "I'm sorry," he told her.

"So am I, honey. I'll come get you out."

In the basement of the old city hall, the cops left their guns in a locker before riding the elevator up to the jail. Though Cozby had decided to charge the other two with nothing more than drunk and disorderly—a $78.50 fine— he was going to charge Worley with evading arrest—punishable by a maximum $1,000 fine and six months in the county jail. "Nobody'd ever bother you if you'd smoke your dope at home," he ragged Worley. "If you keep messing up on Samuell Boulevard, I'm gonna keep on throwing your ass in jail."

"Aw, Cozby, you'd bust a man for standing on the sidewalk," jeered Worley. "You'd bust him if he was standing there reading the Bible. That's just the way you are." Worley turned the conversation to the complaint filed against Cozby. "What about your suspension, Cozby? Let's talk about that."

"Ain't nobody suspended me, puke."

As the elevator door opened to the booking area, Worley taunted, "You sure would like to hit me, wouldn't you?"

"Come on, Worley. How many times have I hit you? Name me a time."

Worley's pause conceded the point. "Yeah, but you want to, I can tell by the way you're acting."

When Cozby got off work at midnight he changed back into his civilian clothes at the substation, then drove the Monte Carlo toward far North Dallas. As he turned off the LBJ Freeway, he noticed a fight in progress on a restaurant lot—serious enough that the losers were about to get hurt. Cozby thought for a moment, shook his head, and detoured back into the restaurant lot. He broke up the fight, shouted a couple of the combatants down, and kept them apart until Northwest Patrol cops answered the call. It was nearly two o'clock in the morning when he finally parked the Month Carlo in front of his two-year-old house in the Colony, an incorporated subdivision between Lewisville and Plano.

Inside the house, lights were on, music was playing. His wife, Debbie, greeted him as though it were early evening. He hugged her and hefted his blonde three-year-old daughter, Tonda, high over his head. She squealed and

giggled. Also waiting up for him was Tammy, the younger of two daughters from his first marriage. Slender, freckled, and pretty, Tammy lives with her mother and goes to elementary school in Hurst; she'd spent a week of her holiday vacation with her father. He and Debbie looked in for a moment on the three-week-old infant, Brandon, asleep between nursings. For the Cozby's it was a normal family evening at home.

They slept till early afternoon on Saturday. Cozby's family keeps nightclub musicians' hours because that's the only way they can spend any time with him during the week. Weekends are more conventional, since he has enough seniority to claim Saturdays and Sundays off. On Sunday I drove out to Cozby's house in the Colony. We talked about the conflicts created by his work.

"I wish they'd go back to rotating shifts," he said. "I can arrange my home life this way now, but when Tonda and Brandon start to school it won't work. I'll have a make a decision then. I've got enough seniority to go on days now, but I'm not ready to retire from police work yet—and that's what the second watch amounts to. I've thought about asking for Deep Nights. At least I'd be at home in the afternoons and early evenings, and I'd have a little more to do at work."

Debbie disagreed pleasantly. "No, if you're here I want you up talking to us and being with us. I don't want to have to tiptoe and keep them quiet all day while you sleep."

Later Cozby's father, mother, and younger brother drove over from Arlington to watch the televised play-off game between the Dallas Cowboys and the Los Angeles Rams. Afterward, his parents would take Tammy back to her mother's house.

Cozby started off watching the game on the floor beside Brandon, who wriggled around on his stomach on a blanket. After Debbie and the girls took the baby into the bedroom for his afternoon nap, Cozby moved to the sofa and opened a can of beer. It became apparent that the Cowboys were struggling through a sluggish performance. "If they get beat, this time I'm not gonna let it bother me," he said at the half. "Something's been wrong with them all year."

At the end, as Staubach tried to pull out the game and season on the last play, Cozby shook his head and radiated how much Dallas's failure bothered him. "Third and everything," he sneered, "and he throws it to the guard."

Worse than that, the desperation blunder turned out to be the football legend's last forward pass. Staubach retired after that season.

"Well, Houston's still in it," I said of Bum Phillips' team, trying to lighten Cozby's mood.

"I hate the Oilers," he replied.

The next day was Monday, New Year's Eve. Cozby had Tuesday off, which was also his mother's birthday, so his parents were driving back out to the Colony to celebrate, eat black-eyed peas, and watch the college bowl games on TV.

Still pale but recovered from the flu, Cozby's rookie was waiting for him at the substation. Baby-faced and single, Steve Talbott had given up his seniority in the De Soto police force for the high pay and faster nights in Dallas. This was no ordinary Monday shift: New Year's Eve is a guaranteed fast night for police work anywhere in Dallas, particularly in the neighborhoods patrolled by Cozby. Also, the 1980 beat realignments would take effect on Thursday, and Cozby was returning to his old territory around Hall and Munger Streets. This was his last night to walk the bars on Samuell Boulevard, which gave added meaning to the occasion. There was even a full moon.

Cozby and Talbott ate an early supper, then drove to a nearby bakery, where Cozby picked up his mother's birthday cake. They returned to the substation and Cozby locked the cake in the trunk of his Monte Carlo. In a jovial mood, he made a swing though Grand City about eight o'clock. With a playful little whoop in the mike of his bull horn, he startled some partygoers standing on a curb on Grand Avenue.

Cozby drifted on over to Hall Street and drove through the Roseland projects. Back on the 1800 block of Hall, his headlights fell on a dark brick wall painted to read BLACK GAIL'S DOMINO PARLOR. He turned left of Roseland and parked along the curb next to the closed Empire Grill, where the heroin dealer had tried to shoot him. Cozby opened the door and told the rookie, "If I'm not out in two minutes, come in after me."

The time passed. Talbott adjusted the bill of his cap and followed his boss inside the domino parlor. In a moment he hurried back out, looking worried until he satisfied himself that the squad car was still there. He pointed to the ignition and said, "Get the car keys. Come on in."

The first room contained a jukebox and pool table, but no people. Cozby moved into view in the back room. "Come on back," he invited with a grin. Between the john and the gas space heater sat a card table surrounded by six black men who had been playing draw poker for a pot of $167. The one who had the best cards was in his forties. Cozby had busted him so many times for gambling in here that he was comfortable with the process. Cozby told me that the man now owned the domino parlor; the previous owner was in the joint, having murdered a man here.

"Just get your ID's out for me and keep your hands on the table," Cozby said pleasantly. Talbott compiled a list of the players while Cozby wrote the

citations he considered sufficient if none of the men were wanted downtown. The players had been drinking beer, and a couple moved from their chairs toward the john. Cozby told them to stay put until he was through with them. They protested that, but most were good-natured about the bust. After they accepted their tickets, Cozby let them retrieve their money from the pot, use the john, and move around. One hobbled like Fred Sanford to lock the parlor's Hall Street door. But the gaunt face of one old man remained stony. His yellow eyes blazed.

"I know you," Cozby told him. "I wrote you a ticket in here about two months ago, didn't I?" The old-timer crossed his legs, said nothing, and looked away. "Scared the hell outa me," Cozby told me. "I told 'em to empty their pockets on the table, and up he comes waving a big old gun. Born in '02 and he's carrying a hogleg. That old man's crazy."

"You just do what you got to do," the old man shot back. "I ain't got nothin' to say to you."

Talbott came back inside and said that only one player had an outstanding warrant. He'd been one of the most agreeable, the warrant was for an unpaid traffic ticket, and unlike most people Cozby busts, he carried an ID with his picture on it—even had a Master Charge card in his pocket. Cozby let him ride downtown with his hands uncuffed. The poker player explained that he was a hog farmer. He talked knowledgeably about the pork market in Omaha.

After turning the poker player over to the booking sergeant, we rode the jail elevator back down to the basement. By now it was time to head for Samuell Boulevard. Cozby took the fast route east on R. L. Thornton, chose the exit at the end of Tenison Park, and cruised to the stoplight. The bars on Beat 141 were back to the left, under the expressway, but as he started to turn, a '68 Chevrolet fishtailed wildly and sped north on Ferguson Road. Ferguson is the territory of the Northeast Division, but the affront was too blatant to ignore. "Hey, hot rod," said Cozby, gunning the Dodge up Ferguson.

The Chevy's driver, a high school kid from Garland, had an adolescent complexion, a shock of frizzy hair under an auto-parts store cap, and the flabby bulk of a 220-pound Baby Huey. He handed over his month-old driver's license and steadied himself by touching the car. Cozby looked in on his teen-aged date and returned to the squad car for a warrant check, which was slow coming back because of the heightened police activity all over town. He wanted to chase the drunk kid home and get on with the night's work on Samuell Boulevard. Meanwhile, Baby Huey had a squabble with his girlfriend. He emerged from the Chevrolet, slammed the door, and started digging for something in his trunk.

Cozby turned on the mike of his bull horn. "Hey, get back in your car until we're through with you." Baby Huey gave him a sullen look but obeyed the order, slamming his door again. When the warrant check came back clean, Cozby told Talbott to write a ticket for Exhibition of Acceleration.

Baby Huey refused to sign the citation. He wanted to tell the officers about the wet pavement. As Talbott followed with the clipboard, he tried to walk away from the ticket and for unspecified reasons started cursing his date. Cozby intervened sharply: "If you don't sign that ticket you're going to jail."

Baby Huey bellowed, "You won't . . . let me . . . *explain!*" and unleashed a vertical roundhouse that left a two-inch dent in the Chevrolet's trunk.

Eyes wide, Cozby leaped on him from behind and applied a "choke-down" hammerlock. Baby Huey staggered under the cop's weight, tried to throw him over his shoulders, and at last fell sobbing against the squad car's hood. Alarmed by the kid's strength, Cozby slapped the cuffs on him and threw him into the back seat of the patrol car. "Once they start beating on that car, you're next," he explained.

Despite the girl's protests that she didn't know how to drive, Cozby left her sitting in the Chevrolet. Baby Huey raved in the back seat, "Oh, please don't take me to jail! *Please* don't. My folks are gonna *kill* me."

"Shut up," said Cozby, listening to a radio report of a westbound high-speed chase on R. L. Thornton. It ended before it got to us. Baby Huey pitched and heaved, fighting the handcuffs. "These things . . . won't let . . . my blood . . . *circulate!*" I was glad Talbott was in the back seat. "You gonna hit me?" raged the kid, in tears again. "*Go ahead!*"

"We don't wanta warp our sticks," said Cozby.

"I'm sorry," cried Baby Huey. "I *beg your pardon.* I was just trying to explain what happened. Please let me sign the ticket. I don't know how to act around Dallas cops—I just moved here from Virginia. I ain't ever *been* to jail before."

"Well, you're breaking in with style," said Cozby.

At the jail, the booking sergeant read Cozby's report and said he couldn't charge the kid with a moving traffic violation and drunk and disorderly without giving him a DWI. Cozby shook his head, dropped the traffic charge, and filled out the paperwork again. He was exasperated. The incident with Baby Huey had killed more than an hour—it was eleven o'clock by the time we got away from the jail. Cozby was missing all the action on Samuell Boulevard. "Slowest New Year's Eve I can remember," he apologized.

As it happened, the bars were almost mellow, by East Dallas standards. The same Friday-night regulars had come back to their favorite night spots

to see the new year in. They'd dressed up more and paid a higher cover charge for the cheap champagne and party hats and the privilege of getting drunk and sad together. Inside the Gator Club we saw the man with the flattened nose whom Cozby had busted for pot on Friday; instead of the battered cowboy hat, he wore a sport coat and a plastic lei. He turned his back rigidly as Cozby and Talbott passed. On the dance floor Cozby said hello to Worley, who looked up dreamily, managed a smile, and then snuggled his beard back against his partner's cheek. With an air of sheepish but genuine hospitality the barmaid inside the Nineteenth Hole invited us to help ourselves to the spread of dips, deviled eggs, and stuffed celery on the pool table. The only action came when a young man ran around the corner outside Kim's as he saw the cops approaching him. Cozby shouted him to a halt, frisked him, then let him go. The kid had been trying to disassociate himself from a teen-aged girl who was throwing up in the alley.

We finished the night chasing phantoms. As midnight approached, the Black Cat and cherry bomb firecrackers started going off. Or was that a .22 pistol—or a .357 magnum—or a twelve-gauge shotgun? The cacophony of explosions must have taken Cozby back to Vietnam. He turned corners frenetically, zoomed between rows of restored houses off Columbia and Munger. Adrenaline pumped in anticipation, but his expectations went unfulfilled. Cozby found nobody else to take to jail.

I observed that one winds up *wanting* the action—which is dependent on something bad happening to somebody.

Cozby shrugged. "Yeah, but it sure makes the time go faster, doesn't it?"

But police work is not the infantry Marines. It's just a way of making a living. Cozby drew a breath, calmed down, and headed for the substation. The cops on first watch would catch most of the hell of this night. It was two minutes past twelve and Cozby was working overtime. His mother's birthday cake was in the trunk of his Monte Carlo. Debbie and Tonda were waiting up for him at home.

As we neared the substation, the Central dispatcher advised Cozby to switch to Channel 10, reserved for direct communication between cops on patrol. A colleague requested some favor, to which Cozby agreed.

Following a pause, another cop spoke up. "Is Mad Dog still on the air?"

"Hyo," he acknowledged through the mike.

"Happy New Year, Dennis."

Moved, he cocked his head and smiled. "How about that? Somebody's still looking out for the kid."

MAY, 1980

OUT OF ACTION

I seldom write about the same person twice. Mostly that's just the nature of the business. For a short period of time I get deeply involved in others' lives, then the piece comes out and I move on. Unfortunately, more often than not, acquaintances that might have been friendships fade.

When the news of an explosive killing of a young black by a Dallas cop broke, I hadn't spoken to Dennis Cozby in four years. One of the sustaining mysteries of Dallas is why an American city of such crackling racial tension has never blown up in the way of Detroit, Los Angeles, Miami, and so many others. Dallas activists and the press were saying this killing of a black by a white cop might have lit the fuse at last. Cozby was bottled up tight, saying nothing to the press. Ignoring City Hall and the police department, I found out when his shift began and called him at the division station. At first he said he had no interest in talking to any reporter. "It's not you," he said, acknowledging that I'd treated him all right the first time. "Come up here and ride with me," he finally offered. "No promises. But we'll talk about it." So an outsider got the story that no reporter in Dallas could. I think Dennis used me, just as I used him. He thought that by going along with me, he could get his side of the story out. And he did.

Still it was a troubling story. If you wanted to find a modern semblance of frontier Texas, when wild young men carried guns and killed and got killed over nothing, the place to look was not the dusty plains or small towns. It was the rock-hard innards of our biggest cities. Those could be terrifying environs for the peaceable and law-abiding, and a scarred cynic like Cozby, handy with a gun, was a welcome sight to see. But if you happened to share the world view of Michael Frost, the man with the big cigar was a cold-hearted enforcer of a ruling system's cruelty and oppression—a violent man legitimized by his badge.

Dallas did not blow up because of the incident; for more than a decade

I again lost track of Cozby. If the paper-pushing jobs that resulted from the shooting were permanent, I knew he would eventually quit the force. But one day in 1997 when I was in Dallas fishing for leads in another story, I caught him by phone on his lunch break in the Central Patrol Division. He told me to look him up some time and pull a shift with him, for old times' sake. He was back on the streets he loved, riding herd, taking the bad guys to jail.

Last November 7, a slow Monday, Dennis Cozby worked alone on his partner's regular day off. Just after 8:00 P.M., the Dallas patrolman made a routine swing down Grand Avenue. For years this black ghetto southwest of Fair Park has exceeded all other sections of Dallas in violent crime. The windows and doors of liquor stores wear braces of thick iron bars. Armed guards walk the aisles of supermarkets. Vacant lots are a sea of broken glass, discarded furniture, rained-on trash. Near Grand's intersection with Lamar, the ramshackle houses yield to squalid apartment complexes. Boarded up in foreclosure, one sits behind a security fence erected to keep out arsonists and thieves. The vacancy sign of another emphasizes a wall in which every window is broken out. Still, these streets and parking lots throb with laughter and music at night. A fourteen-year veteran, Cozby has used his seniority to win this inner-city beat; its appeal to him was "activity." Cozby, who often lit up a fresh Grenadier stogie while making an interrogation or a bust, had a nickname in the ghetto. The black residents called him Cigar.

When the white cop turned onto Cleveland, he actually entered the beat of other officers. But the beats are so small and heavily patrolled that the police territories lose all but bureaucratic distinction. He saw a thick-necked, muscular young black man saunter down the sidewalk of a suspected "drug house"—or sales outlet—and mosey away from the curb in a 1976 Cadillac Seville. Cozby doesn't assign traffic control the highest priority; taking the time to work a car wreck sets his teeth on edge. But random street busts often rely on the well-played hunch. By driving on the wrong side of the street, the man behind the wheel of the Cadillac handed the cop his probable cause. Cozby turned on the lights, and anything slow and ordinary about that Monday shift evaporated in the cool night air. The Cadillac zoomed through a stop sign and careened around the corner on South Boulevard. The chase was on.

Michael Frost, twenty, had a street name of his own. People called him

Fleabag. He had a police reputation as a juvenile gang leader, drug dealer, and burglar. At fourteen he shot and wounded a girl named Twinkie, perhaps accidentally, though certain officers doubt it. A year later he was a suspect in the murder of a newspaper truck driver. In 1981, after witnesses picked him out of a photo lineup, he was charged with the much-publicized robbery and murder of a white insurance auditor and urban pioneer named Scott Woods. Later a grand jury no-billed him, and another man confessed to the crime. The same year, Frost was charged with shooting another black man and then pitching the gun to a friend, who for good measure shot the victim again. Prosecutors dismissed the attempted-murder charge when the victim subsequently died in another gunfight.

Then, in 1982, the grand jury indicted Frost for aggravated robbery. In the plea bargain, the young man acknowledged that with the help of an accomplice he had battered a nearby apartment dweller with a shotgun and relieved the man of his pistol, ten dollars, and a bag of marijuana. For that he got ten years' probation. He neglected to keep appointments with the probation officer and to make restitution and to pay his court-appointed lawyer's fees. He failed to attend his court hearing on a misdemeanor charge of evading arrest. If Michael Frost had made the drug buy that Cozby suspected, the search that came later failed to produce any evidence. But Frost had good reason to dread his next police interrogation. Just three weeks before Cozby turned on the lights of his car, the state had filed a motion to revoke Frost's probation and the city had filed another warrant for his arrest. Fleabag was on his way to the joint.

Frost had a seventeen-year-old passenger, Lonnie Leyuas, in his car that night; apparently he clung to the door, catatonic with disbelief and fear. After a two-block run Frost wheeled around the corner on Parnell. Cozby briefly bumped the siren. Two Dallas County deputies who were serving warrants in the area saw the lights and joined the chase, but they were on a different radio frequency; Cozby thought he was on his own. He saw the Cadillac shoot up the drive between the stained plaster walls of the KK apartments. A less aggressive cop might have acknowledged the danger of being alone and waited on reinforcements before risking the hostile potential of that enclosed lot. But caution and passivity have never been part of Cozby's style. Though he requested a backup, he had to rely on a series of snap judgments. From the time his call hit the air, his contest of wills with Frost lasted just thirty seconds.

The following is Cozby's hotly disputed account of what happened next. "The way the guy was acting," he told me, "I thought the car was stolen. I

expected him to take off on foot. He angled the car into the lot, and I pulled up right behind him. I came out with my gun drawn. Frost stood up on the ledge of the door. He never said a word. I told him, 'Hit the ground, face down, hit the ground.' No response. I told him to get up against the fender with his hands on the hood. He just stared at me.

"Standing up there, he had the height advantage, and he had leverage. When I got close to him, he jumped off the car and grabbed the gun with both hands. I controlled the trigger and never lost my grip, but he was lashing it back and forth, from side to side. He kept trying to get the barrel aimed at me. All the time, he butted me in the face with his forehead. Bang, bang, bang. I've never been up against anybody that strong. He drove me backward like a football player shoving a blocking sled. We hit a parked car, which knocked the wind out of me, and he bent me back over the trunk. My vision was blurred. I thought I was going to black out. I was losing the fight, and he wasn't going to let me walk away from it. He meant to kill me with my own gun.

"I was able to wrestle the muzzle back toward him and get off a shot. I thought I'd missed him, because if anything, he just got stronger. He drove me backward another fifteen or twenty feet. We hit the patrol car so hard it caved in the front quarter panel. I twisted the gun back around and fired again. This time, he crumpled and hit the ground on his hip. The deputies ran up then. We couldn't see any blood on Frost. He was conscious and still moving around, so one of the deputies handcuffed the guy. It wasn't me, I was in a fog. In fourteen years I've never been in a fight that violent. My uniform was torn. I was hurt and sore and thinking, 'Thank God I'm not dead.'"

We'll never get to hear Michael Frost's side of that story. He died at Parkland Hospital two and a half hours later, during surgery for two point-blank gunshot wounds. But the parking lot was filled with apartment tenants, among them members of the victim's family. Frost's last run from the Dallas law had carried him home. The black crowd raged around the white officers at once. "You didn't have to shoot him!" somebody cried. Then the flash-point accusation: "They shot him while he was handcuffed." Rocks and bottles started flying. With guns drawn, Cozby and the two deputies yelled warnings at the crowd to stay back. Though more squad cars and an ambulance arrived quickly, the situation was already out of hand. Police regulations prohibited Frost's mother and siblings from trying to comfort the dying youth. Investigators worked fast, stretching their tape measures, while other cops clung to the harness leashes of agitated, barking German shepherds. Grim and ner-

vous patrolmen stood guard with the stocks of their twelve-gauge shotguns propped on their hips, barrels pointed at the sky.

Under a flood of TV lights, the crowd clamored around the Channel 8 reporter with wildly differing eyewitness accounts. "I had no way of assessing their credibility," Byron Harris of WFAA-TV later said, "and I had fifteen minutes to decide how to play the story. We were afraid that whole side of town would go up in flames." In the report that aired at ten o'clock, a police spokesman recounted Cozby's version of the episode. A black teenager said he saw the cop fire the gun while Frost was defenseless, falling down. Byron Harris couldn't put the fury of the crowd out of his mind that night, or the certainty of its condemning chant: "*Seeeegar! Seeeegar! Seeeegar!*"

In the days that followed, sixteen-year-old Brenda Frost told the *Morning News* that she saw Cozby hit her brother with a nightstick. "Michael fell into him. That's when he shot him," she said. "Michael landed on his chest. He handcuffed him. Then he kicked him over and shot him again." At a packed meeting in the Martin Luther King Civic Center, Errol Sabbath, twelve, described the same sequence for more than a hundred angry people, adding that Frost jumped out of the car with his hands up. Yet Edward Frost, fourteen, told the same gathering that he watched Cozby beat his brother with a club, then handcuff him, then shoot him twice in the back. Lonnie Leyuas, who from inside the Cadillac had the closest view of the struggle, had given an account the night of the shooting that matched Cozby's in detail. The pathologist reported that Frost died from two bullets fired from within six to twelve inches of his abdomen. There was no evidence of any blows to the victim's head. He had powder residue on both hands, which suggests that they were very near the gun.

The conflicting testimony didn't stop Dallas city council member Elsie Faye Heggins from demanding Cozby's immediate dismissal. Heggins called for an inquest by a black coroner and discredited the independence and authority of the Citizens/Police Relations Board, which reviews controversies and makes non-binding recommendations to the city council. Later Heggins tempered her assessment of the particular incident but continued to raise the specter of the ghetto riots in Watts and Detroit two decades ago. Yelled at by black activists while making a public appearance in support of minority recruitment, police chief Billy Prince called the Heggins statements irresponsible but heeded demands to transfer Cozby and his partner to another beat. Prince called Cozby into his office and told him to keep on doing his job. But within the Patrol Division, assistant chief Leslie Sweet kept wondering if Cozby could ever again respond to an emergency with the same speed and

decisiveness. He recommended a transfer to the Criminal Investigation Division, a move that Cozby turned down. Expressing fears for Cozby's safety, Sweet wanted his veteran off the street.

Chief Prince had some good news for Dallas at the end of the year. The city's crime rate fell off seven percent in 1983, the largest decrease since 1971, and violent crime was down by twelve percent. Arrests were up by eleven percent. But at what cost, and through what means, was this law and order maintained? The most alarming statistic at year's end was the seventy percent increase in the police use of deadly force. During 1983 Dallas cops shot twenty-eight civilians and killed fifteen, a death toll exceeded only in New York, with thirty-one; Los Angeles, twenty-five; and Chicago and Houston, both sixteen. The carnage in Dallas wasn't entirely one-sided. Two cops were shot and killed and two others critically wounded that year.

Police officers are a free society's hired guns. In return for that dangerous service, we grant them windows of legal and moral exemption. Their definitions of self-defense and standards of civilized restraint aren't quite the same as ours. When cops' lives are even remotely threatened, they receive the benefits of every doubt. Some drunk and depressed old man fires a despairing shot from a .22 at the crowd of officers telling him to put the gun down; a fusillade from Magnums and riot shotguns ensues. Sad but justifiable, the grand jury concurs. Society's protection against the miscreant cop supposedly lies in the screening of police candidates, the individual discipline instilled by training and experience, the diligence and good faith of department superiors, and, in the end, the process of indictment, trial, and conviction—the criminal justice system itself. The problem is, any system tends to take care of its own.

Whenever a police department's use of deadly force jumps up dramatically, as it did in Dallas during 1983, two broad conclusions are readily drawn. Either the cops have gone berserk or conditions on the street have deteriorated to the point of civil insurrection. And with public leaders likening the situation to the urban race riots of the sixties, in Dallas each of those prospects is equally troubling.

Many residents who recall the crackling tension in South and West Dallas during those years wonder why the city didn't blow up then. Because of the threat of brutal and wanton firepower, critics of the city and its police force reply. The emotional connection between police violence and social injustice toward black people is a price that history exacts from all American cities, especially in the South. We like to think that Dallas has changed for the better, that its politics have moderated, that its race relations have cooled down. But the bottom line of the 1983 figures has a way of standing out. *Nineteen of*

the twenty-eight victims of police gunfire were black, and in all but three of those cases, the cops were white. The department could argue that such figures are deceptive. Though only twenty-nine percent of the city's population is black, last year sixty-one percent of the people arrested for violent crimes were black. And with a police force that is eighty-five percent white, the numbers just naturally shake down. But as one of the activists put it, the city and its police department could devise all sorts of studies and statistical analyses; meanwhile, the black community had bodies in the ground.

The result was a beam of intense heat focused on Dennis Cozby's bald head. The controversial shooting happened late in an already tense and troubled year. In addition there were the matters of his individual statistics and flamboyant style. Police records revealed that he had fired his gun at more suspects than any other officer on the force. In fourteen years he had shot at eight people, wounded two, and now killed three. The previous killing had happened in 1976, when a burglar ran from Cozby toward a door guarded by a female rookie officer. Unsure of how the rookie would react, Cozby shot the burglar in the back and killed him. According to investigators, it was a clean, or justified, shooting—perhaps the most chilling expression in the law enforcement trade.

Cozby was no faceless blue suit never heard from before. Residents along Grand Avenue told stories of Cozby's cruising through the apartment parking lots with soul music blaring from his bullhorn. They said he gave children candy in exchange for information about the suspects whose mug shots were lined up on his dashboard. One cop who worked the area said that black suspects dropped the name of Cigar in the same way that lawyers detained for traffic violations might mention their social acquaintance with Chief Prince. In the police department Cozby had another nickname. His own colleagues called him Mad Dog.

Cozby's visibility hadn't been limited to his beat. Motivated by ego and occupational pride, he had never dodged the press before, and now he paid for his high profile. He insisted, for example, that on the night of November 7 he had engaged in mortal struggle with a man who was a total stranger to him. After it happened, he never went near Parnell Street again. But *Morning News* reporter Doug Swanson found tenants who said that Cozby had provoked and harassed Frost for years. "Residents of the KK apartments say Cozby still comes around, wearing sunglasses and a sneer," wrote Swanson. Cozby couldn't believe that reporters would even listen to those people. He wasn't the one with a criminal record. Once upon a time, a cop's word in Dallas was almost law.

I met Dennis Cozby four years ago while researching an article about tough inner-city police beats. Back then Cozby's beat centered on the redneck and biker hangouts of Samuell Boulevard, but since the bars didn't heat up until late in the evening, he was free to roam other Central Division trouble spots for most of the shift. He made regular forays through the Grand Avenue beat. By all counts, that was the scariest concrete I had ever seen. The apartments along one six-block stretch had accounted for twenty-two homicides the previous year; security guards walked the lot of the biggest complex with loaded shotguns. Chewing bubble gum while smoking his cigar, Cozby barged with calculated nonchalance into places and situations that tied my stomach in knots.

He rode herd on the white bar fighters and black pimps with evenhandedness and humor. I thought he was cynical and ornery as hell, but I never saw him do anything brutal. Unlike some of the Dallas cops I met, he didn't indulge in racist invective. Nor did he exhibit the preoccupation with firearms characteristic of his trade. In my presence he never threatened to bring his gun or even his nightstick into play, though I watched him fight burly and angry fellows one-on-one to make arrests. The revolver on his hip, a standard .38, was a mute and grim reminder. The fear that he aroused in suspects, especially black suspects, seemed largely symbolic. In a city whose cops for decades had maintained a tradition of the Iron Hand, he represented the collective power of the police.

Veterans of his particular chauffeur service hated Cozby's smart-guy attitude and dreaded his diligence. Yet the prisoners who knew him didn't seem to expect imminent bodily harm. They weren't afraid to talk back. Cozby hassled folks of bad reputation and suspicious behavior. He was in the business of taking people to jail. The dictum of cop-turned-novelist Joseph Wambaugh applied: You can beat the rap, but you can't beat the ride.

Now, four years later, we had barely gotten past the initial pleasantries when Cozby made a swing by a two-story drug house on Munger. I would see that structure many times during our re-acquaintance, and all through the bitter December cold snap, the door to the upstairs apartment stood wide open. A black guy on the porch saw the police car and unwisely bolted up the red stairs. Undeterred by his recent experience with blind chases after suspects of unknown crimes, Cozby leaped from the car and dashed openhanded across the lawn, up the stairs, three strides ahead of his partner. "Bring the flashlight," he called down after a while.

At the top of the stairs the perspiring fugitive stood with his palms propped against the wall, staring down and muttering grimly. In the same posture a

much larger black man wearing a crumpled fedora looked around with the wan interest of someone caught in the wrong place at the wrong time. Cozby searched the floor with the flashlight till he found a cellophane packet containing the latest craze in Dallas street drugs, Ts and blues. The Ts were an oblong yellow painkiller called Talwin; more often lavender in color, the round blues were an antihistamine called PBZ. Melted down in equal proportions and injected into the bloodstream, the prescription drugs combine to simulate heroin. The pills sell for fifteen dollars a pair, which is cheaper than a pop of real heroin.

"It's changed since you were here before," Cozby told me. "These aren't kids smoking dope out behind the honky-tonk. All we're seeing now is junkies, most of them ex-cons." He looked around at the large fellow in handcuffs beside me. "What did you do your time for?"

"Oh, ah, counterfeiting," said the man.

"Hah," said Cozby.

He has a way of carrying on mild conversations with prisoners one minute, then referring to them like tagged objects in the property room the next. At the Dallas County jail, he removed the big man's handcuffs and let him take his place in the booking line. Cozby grabbed the prisoner's forearm and showed me his scarred and swollen wrist. "Look at that," he said. "They shoot themselves in the arms till they can't find a vein, then they go to work on the wrists. Shoot themselves in the neck. The nuts." He laughed harshly.

In the stream of cops and deputies and jailers, he lightened the mood and revived our previous, more genteel conversation. "So you got married since I saw you last," he said. "What does your wife do? She a writer too?"

I almost blew the line. Life doesn't serve many opportunities to cause a little stutter in the heartbeats of everyone around you. But I paid him back for some of the shocks he had gleefully sent through me. I laughed and cleared my throat and clapped him on the shoulder. "No, Dennis," I said loudly. "She works for the American Civil Liberties Union."

Cozby's small brick home in East Dallas had a realtor's sign in the front yard. He and his second wife, Debbie, had separated. He didn't attribute their difficulty to the Frost killing and its attendant publicity. That trauma mostly affected his children. His wife had a career of her own now, he said, and her company had asked her to consider a transfer to another city. Dennis had five and a half years to go to qualify for a pension while he was still young enough to pursue a new career, so he refused to leave Dallas. Then again, maybe it was just time. The divorce rate in the police profession is fifty percent.

A small desk drawer in the living room contained the mementos of his career. A March, 1982, feature in the *Times Herald* rather glowed about the work along Grand Avenue of the "Mad Dog and Blondie" tandem, Cozby and his partner Bob Kamphouse. A child's comic cartoon of a rotund cop with a long cigar had come in the mail, before the Frost shooting, with a warm and grateful note from a woman who lived in the KK apartments. "I miss the good people in that neighborhood," he said now. "They don't want characters like Frost around. The old ones have it worst. They're ripped off constantly and scared to death. Kamphouse and I made a difference down there. When we took on that beat, it had the worst crime numbers in town. That's not true anymore." Cozby is proudest of a September, 1982, letter to Chief Prince in which narcotics investigators recommended Kamphouse and him for certificates of merit. Signed by every officer in that division, the letter cited 220 drug-related arrests between January 1 and August 31 that year—an average of one a night.

In announcing the city's improved crime statistics for 1982, Prince told the *Times Herald:* "The presence of the police is more highly felt when you make traffic stops. The increased traffic enforcement has not only cut deaths and injury accidents, but I think it's also a factor in the number of felony arrests. The burglars, thieves, and the people doing the robbing and stealing are not walking. They're in cars, and we're finding more of them." When Cozby connected that silver Cadillac in the wrong lane of Cleveland with his suspicions of drug traffic in the residence alongside, and then turned on his lights on the pretext of a traffic violation, he acted at the behest of his superiors. Under common law, a citizen's misdemeanor is never cause for a police officer's use of deadly force, but in running away from those lights, Frost tipped the legal balance to Cozby. And if, as alleged, Frost resisted legitimate arrest with violent and life-threatening force of his own, he laid issues of criminal law to rest. Under the Texas Penal Code, Frost's resistance would be justifiable only if Cozby initiated the violence by using greater force than necessary to make the arrest and if Frost could reasonably believe that self-protection demanded immediate use of counter force.

"So the crunch," I suggested to Cozby, "is whether you had any business getting out of that car with your gun drawn."

"No, you don't do that to John Q. Citizen on the street," he replied, with some heat. "But nothing indicated that what I had here was a run-of-the-mill traffic violation. There were two of them and one of me. What was I supposed to do: say 'Uh-oh, this looks bad,' throw the car in reverse, and back the hell out of there? Frost was a young guy. If he was all that afraid of being arrested,

he could have outrun me on foot. Or, like ninety-nine out of a hundred suspects in the same situation, he could have put his hands on the hood. But he
was out to kill himself a cop. Everything that happened, he set in motion. He
could be alive today. He might be doing time somewhere, but he wouldn't be
dead.

Cozby said he had received a lot of supportive mail since the episode. Some
of it, he added grimly, was worthy of the Ku Klux Klan. "I don't know if it's
the history or the economy or the social change or the liberal gun laws—
though every punk on the block can get his hands on something to shoot." I
found it odd and ironic that he would characterize gun laws in conservative
Texas as *liberal*. "But one of the facts of this profession is that Southern cities
are the most dangerous places to be a cop. People in Dallas know that twenty-
eight civilians were shot by police last year. That's all they hear and read
about in the news. They probably don't know that Dallas cops were shot *at*
fifty-two times in the same period. They forget that the last two cops killed in
the Dallas–Fort Worth area were shot with their own guns. It hurts to build a
reputation in the community for solid police work and have it torn down
overnight. Sells newspapers, I suppose. But I'd rather have people think I'm
some kind of vigilante gunslinger than have them come to my funeral."

One night I asked Cozby if, with the benefit of hindsight, he would change
anything about his handling of the Frost encounter. He threw back his head
and replied, "Not a thing." And during the evening he demonstrated how the
episode had left his approach to police work fundamentally unchanged. It
was Monday, and once again Kamphouse had the night off. At the intersection of Hall Street and Central Expressway are the Roseland projects, a sprawling red-brick complex inhabited by black tenants. Making a routine swing
past the projects on his new beat, Cozby turned off Hall onto Roseland and
saw an old Chevrolet parked along the left curb in front of a dim little hangout called the Empire Grill. The Chevrolet pulled away from the curb and
angled up the street before us. "Hmmmm," said Cozby, then he turned on
the lights. The probable cause? Driving on the wrong side of the street.

This time, no high-speed chase ensued. There were four people, all black,
in the car. Cozby radioed for a backup and told me, "You stay back here." He
saw the shoulders of one man squirm and hunch forward, as if he was stow-
ing something under the seat. Standing in the middle of the street, Cozby
stooped and talked to the driver with a broad smile on his face. He straight-
ened up and struck a match with a flourish, then applied the fire to the tip of
a fresh Grenadier. The backup squad car pulled alongside Cozby's, blocking

the street. To our rear, another driver honked his horn in aggravation and punctuated the necessary U-turn with a squall of tire rubber. Soon the four were standing out in the cold with their hands on the Chevrolet's trunk. One, a teenaged girl to whom the experience was a novelty, looked around with dazed affability and often raised her hands. The three men communicated grimly with their eyes and kept their hands firmly on the trunk.

The red and blue beacons roved the stark brick walls and caught glints of seasoned resentment in the staring faces of people on the sidewalk. Others ducked their heads and hurried on. I have seldom felt more depressed than I did as I watched Cozby search the car. Many years ago he made his first kill as a cop on the same block. Chasing one party of a botched heroin deal, he rounded the corner on Roseland and ran inside the Empire Grill, where the black man turned on him, jammed a pistol in his midriff, and yanked the trigger three times. The Saturday night special misfired. Slower on the draw, Cozby pulled his revolver and killed him cleanly, as the saying goes. It could have gone either way. I wondered now if the locale touched a particular nerve of history in him. Or, after so many years on the same streets, do the busts and blood and adrenaline all run together?

He emerged from the Chevrolet and walked toward the other cops wagging two cellophane packets of Ts and blues. "Knew he had something under there," he grinned, having satisfied his unofficial quota of one drug bust a night. Cozby knelt in front of the headlights and broke open a plastic cylinder; two syringes fell out. He recited Miranda to a gangling man in his mid-thirties while applying the handcuffs. After warrant checks on the others came back clear, he wrote the driver his traffic citation and prepared to let them go.

The two cops who had answered the backup call were both in their twenties. As they started to pull away, the rider rolled down his window and said, "Cozby? Sometime at the station I wish you'd sit down with me and catch me up on all these new drugs. Ts, blues, pills, hell, I hear about them. But I don't know what they're talking about." Cozby beamed. He might fear the censure of a troubled and changing city, but he still had the approval of his peers. They knew what kind of a cop he'd been.

Driving toward the county jail, he looked back over the seat at me with an air of affirmation. "Junkies. Ex-cons. Almost every one with a history of violence. If they're out of dope, they're desperate. And if they're high, they're fearless."

The prisoner frowned at the impersonal assessment. "Hey, I ain't no junkie."

"Oh," Cozby grinned. "You just shoot up for recreation."

"Well, yeah. Now and then."

As it often happens when an arrest proceeds without violence and unnecessary rancor, cop and prisoner warmed toward each other in that strange reflex of relief. They chatted cordially. "How much time did you do down there?" asked Cozby, referring to the joint.

"Eight and a half years. Didn't get in no trouble, either."

"You *did* eight and a half? My God. What was the original sentence?" It's a kind of shoptalk. They do have a certain bond.

The man twisted his shackled hands and said matter-of-factly: "Thirty-five years."

Cozby whistled. "Mercy. What for?"

"Aggravated robbery."

Cozby slid me a triumphant glance. "Actually," the prisoner reminisced, "it was my money, you see. I took it out on loan, and this other dude collected it for me, then wouldn't give it back. So I commenced to pistol-whipping the dude. And on reflection, I took *all* his money."

After hearing testimony from twenty witnesses, on February 6 a Dallas grand jury no-billed Cozby for the fatal shooting of Michael Frost. District attorney Henry Wade cited the coroner's report as the conclusive evidence verifying Cozby's account. The victim's mother, Maxine Frost, responded bitterly:

"There's going to be five or six more killings like this if they don't get that man off the street. What's it going to take to keep him from shooting any other young black man? We'll just let the good Lord take care of Cigar." Black activists promised a stormy confrontation with the Citizens Police Relations Board. Several witnesses, the activists promised, would condemn Cozby and refute the grand jury finding for the public record. An attorney for the Dallas Police Association said he didn't "want to chill anyone's right to speak," but he mentioned that notes would be taken with the possibility of slander suits in mind.

Chillier still, on February 28—the morning of the public hearing—the grand jury indicted three of Cozby's seventeen-year-old accusers for aggravated perjury, a felony punishable by up to ten years in prison and a five thousand dollar fine. Lonnie Leyuas, the passenger whose statement the night of the shooting had supported Cozby's version, was charged with lying to the grand jury when he changed his story and said that the cop shot the prisoner while he was handcuffed. Indicted for testifying that Cozby struck Frost with a nightstick were an apartment resident, Victor Franklin, and the victim's sister, Brenda Frost. After that, witnesses who would speak for the public record

became much harder to find. At the ballyhooed public hearing, only one ac-tivist had anything to say.

In a study commissioned during the furor over Cozby and Frost, the re-view board found "no pattern of abuse and no evidence of misconduct by officers" in the police department's use of deadly force. The report recom-mended an ordinance that would assign investigation of citizens' complaints to a more impartial authority than the department's Division of Internal Affairs. In the most daring proposal—this was, after all, Dallas—the board urged *a city and statewide ban on the sale of handguns!* The study also suggested that foot patrols and storefront substations could help defuse ethnic tension and promote cultural understanding and that along with emphasis on "strategic withdrawal" from life-threatening confrontations, officer training should in-clude more simulation drills of episodes that could lead to the use of deadly force. Out of the twenty-eight shootings, the city's analysis cited seven cases in which police errors had exacerbated the situation. Although the commis-sion found that Cozby failed to take cover and maintain an adequate distance from Frost, by the lights of the system, the shooting was perfectly clean. As for the jarring statistics, the report implied, 1983 was just one of those years.

To Chief Prince, the net result vindicated Cozby and, by extension, the entire force. To the angry and embittered black citizens of South Dallas, it represented one more squeeze of the old Iron Hand. The department's fierce support of one corporal on patrol was more than the fortress mentality ex-hibited by all police officers when they come under public and media siege. By the definitions of the Dallas Police Department, Cozby had been a model street cop. His pursuit of crime was aggressive—though that standard of officer behavior is subjective at best and dangerously ill-defined. He was a proven and grizzled veteran. Superiors trusted his judgment in the heat of the fight. Even so, with the appearance of opportune political concession, the same superiors granted the least of the black activists' demands. The same day that the perjury indictments came down, Chief Prince announced that Cozby had been pulled off the street.

Cozby now rides herd on a desk. His beat is seventy-five percent paper-work. He wears a coat and tie, not the uniform blues, and arrives at the office at seven-thirty in the morning. In the general assignments section of the Crimi-nal Investigation Division, he prepares, for court presentation, cases involv-ing criminal mischief, felons in the possession of a firearm, and the like. As a detective, he's starting at the bottom. To the chagrin of some in the office, he still smokes cheap cigars.

Cozby's second divorce is final now. With joint custody of three children,

he already felt the need to spend his evenings at home. As a patrolman on the day shift, he faced the workaday tedium of endless, uneventful driving around—stopping motorists with expired inspection stickers, for lack of anything else to do. "As day jobs go," he described his new assignment, "this one's a peach. It's taken some adaptation. For one thing, my body and brain resist the notion that they're supposed to sleep at night. I miss the excitement, sure. I miss the friends I made. Blacks that I *arrested* before have told me they're sorry about the way this whole thing came down. But times are changing. So are people's attitudes towards the police. If anything ever happened, no matter how clean and righteous, I'd have it all to go through again. I feel like I've done my time. My dues are paid."

A good deal of his bitterness, he reminded me, is directed at members of my profession. "Mad Dog," he muttered. "How catchy. Do you know the first time somebody called me that? It was in the peewee Golden Gloves. I was six years old."

I used to think that when Cozby, the son of a Fort Worth fireman, finished his infantry tour in Vietnam—where he was wounded three times—he chose to go into law enforcement because it was a socially commendable way of venting all that pent-up steam. He wanted to be on the world's hot and hardened edge. Whatever his motivations then, he's no trigger-happy redneck now. He comes to work every day with a sour and dogged professionalism. He perceives himself as a protector of the innocent and believes in the system that has taken care of him. "Righteous" is a word often heard from him. Because of those perjury indictments, he thinks the forces of good won out. They made it easier for him to come in off the street. As one spokesman for the department put it, he's a company man.

Like most people, I am sheltered from the environment he moved in daily, and I dearly hope to remain so. But all the sordidness and inhumanities have to add up. He has the bleakest world view, the grimmest sense of human nature, that I have encountered in someone of my background and generation. Time and again, I've seen his darkest instincts about people proved right. When Cozby watched that muscular black youth saunter down the sidewalk on Cleveland Street that night, he didn't know about the arrest warrant. But somehow he knew that here was another guilty party whom he could throw in jail. Cozby was twenty when he graduated from the police academy and took on his rookie Central Division beat—the same number of years that trouble-prone black kid had on this earth. I don't know if Cozby can even remember how he perceived life back then. If he could, maybe he would have

more compassion for the expended possibilities of Michael Frost. Cozby hurts. He bleeds. I found in his emotional makeup every possibility except remorse. Recounting the experience with Frost fills him with such strong feeling that it's hard for him to even say the kid's name. "That scumbag," he growled once, "who made me kill him."

MAY, 1984

BIG

Boxing is one of my vices. I know it's corrupt, it's brutal, and its athletes run constant risks of fatal injury or permanent impairment. I offer no intellectual defense of it. Yet I love it. I accept this weakness in myself and, like the cigarette smoker who loves the taste and jangle of tobacco, I'll take a fair amount of abuse over it. But I'm not likely to give it up.

I thought George Foreman was an awesome heavyweight in his first career, and I rather liked his persona. His effortless knockouts of Joe Frazier and Ken Norton—conquerors of Muhammad Ali—were astounding things to behold. Still I found myself screaming for his nemesis Muhammad Ali in a closed-circuit theater screening of their title fight in Zaire. I was just beginning to write by then, and study how professionals went about writing, and on numerous occasions I noticed that Foreman as a subject could bring magic to the page. Norman Mailer, George Plimpton, and other writers fell into his spell. As a fight fan I found myself pulling for George when he embarked on his second career. It was a fluke that I got to write this story about his regaining a world heavyweight title. My friend, colleague, and mentor Gary Cartwright had twice written sympathetically about George's comeback, and he certainly would have had exercised his first claim on the assignment. But the Cartwrights were vacationing in Europe when George knocked out young Michael Moorer, and I quickly spoke up.

The profile subsequently appeared in Best American Sportswriting *1996, and of all the distinguished words that have been written about the boxer, the piece was selected as the basis for a TV movie about him. George makes his money off violence, subsequent federal indictments would imply that members of his team were involved in payoffs for ratings, and yet there is no question that boxing rescued him from the street thuggery of his youth. I hoped that George would retire and go out on top, but he chose to continue fighting, and the erosion of his skills*

began to reflect his age. When a mediocre youngster named Shannon Briggs was awarded an outrageous decision over George, I was glad— and not because I feared for his health. It was a fight fan's reaction. I couldn't stand to see him with nothing left but his jab.

In a room off a narrow hallway on the forty-second floor of Manhattan's Four Seasons hotel, heavyweight boxing champion George Foreman is talking to Ben Kinchlow, the dapper and urbane host of *The 700 Club,* the religious news and talk show. They touch lightly on matters of faith and George's penchant for naming many of his children George, but mostly they talk about fighting. Like nearly everybody else, Kinchlow doesn't call him Champ or even Mr. Foreman. One handshake and he's "George"—at forty-six, he brings that out in people. From his homes in Houston and Marshall, George has come to New York this December to host *Saturday Night Live* and to move along an autobiography in rush production at Random House, but he's plenty in demand elsewhere. The National Father's Day Committee wants to declare him Father of the Year. *Gumbo* magazine wants him as its gumbo marshal. A magazine in France wants to interview him on the subject of poise. *Life* magazine wants him to pose with a ballerina from the New York City Ballet (the hook is fitness and weight control). Since his knockout of young Michael Moorer in early November, the world has beaten a path to his door.

Both George and Kinchlow have deep, rich voices. They laugh a lot. But it's hard to hear too much of their conversation because bedlam has broken loose in the hallway. Certain hotel guests are allowed to register their dogs, and at this moment three Labrador retrievers are baying, snarling, throwing themselves against a door. The dogs are vexed because their owners are out, and for half an hour a camera crew from a South Korean TV network has been muttering and moving gear around in the hall. A hotel security chief steps off an elevator with a look of polite, intense displeasure. He wants those cameras to disappear—now. The Koreans acknowledge that they understand him but stand their ground: Their boss, a correspondent whom George's handlers know only as Mr. Soo, is in there with George and Kinchlow, and he has just stuck his head outside and told them to be ready.

The door opens and George ambles out, grinning. He is nattily attired in a size fifty extra-long sport coat. The man is vast—six four, about 250 pounds— but it is not the bigness of obesity. He has an odd, slow gait, as if his feet hurt. Over his shoulder he remarks to his courtly publicist, Mort Sharnik, that

Kinchlow looks like a movie star. The grin vanishes when George hears the dogs and their hard thumps against the door. Then, to the horror of the hotel security chief, the hall is ablaze in TV lights. The Koreans crowd into an elevator with George, shooting all the way. Pressed into a corner, towering over six men, George goes stiff. Beads of sweat pop out on his shaved head. "Please," says Sharnik. "Sorry," replies Mr. Soo, and the lights go out.

Down on the seventh floor, in a room reserved by Mr. Soo, George takes a chair and offers a few pleasantries as the harsh lights reignite and the camera rolls. Mr. Soo suggests a prayer. Everyone bows his head. "Heavenly Father," Mr. Soo begins, "we thank you for the opportunity to interview Mr. Foreman," and the conversation warps off from there. Mr. Soo commends George for his missionary work and for his practice of fighting on Saturday night and flying back to Houston to preach the next morning. "Preaching is my profession," George responds, smiling. "I just moonlight as a boxer." Mr. Soo says that it has been reported in the North Korean press that George will fight next in that country against a prominent Japanese wrestler. "Oh, I don't know about that," says George, after a slight pause. "But I've always wanted to go to Korea."

"*Norss* Korea?" cries Mr. Soo.

One can tell that George would like to slip his publicist a pleading look. "I just know it's one big beautiful country," he says gamely. "Always wanted to go there. And the food! I just love the food."

Mr. Soo leans forward, greatly pleased, and in a torrent of Korean wants to know what delicacies have pleased his palate. George is running now, praying for the bell. "What's that soup?" he says. "Something about sparrows?"

"Sparrow?" says Mr. Soo. He reels off the names of several soups.

"Yeah," says George, trying to remember. "Like . . . saliva of the sparrow."

At the end of the interview, George shakes hands all around and strides through the door and down the hall with lights and a camera three feet from his shoulder. In the elevator he turns and faces the orb of yellow glare, and Mr. Soo takes a long lateral step, centering himself. Just before the doors shut, Mr. Soo's head plummets forward, and he bows at the waist.

On, then, to the thirty-fifth floor, where George is doing a public-service spot for Martin Luther King Day. George has been asked to join actor Edward James Olmos, singer Tony Bennett, and model Lauren Hutton in a campaign that will, at Coretta Scott King's urging, attempt to redefine the holiday as an occasion for public service. All George knows is that he's supposed to say something about the importance of doing good. But now a starched young federal bureaucrat is asking him a long line of complex questions about the value, message, and meaning of King's life.

Though the smile popularly associated with George's big round face comes to him easily, it's not his continuous pose. The casual look is not a glower either, but it suffers no fools, or anybody who might take him for one. George studies the bureaucrat a moment, then interrupts him. "Have you got a script?"

The man hands him a fact sheet. George reads it and hands it back. On camera he begins: "To me, Martin Luther King represented pure patriotism. And nonviolence. You actually can turn the other cheek. There would be forced change, but not through violence. It wouldn't happen with a fist, or a stick." Onlookers gasp with admiration. He never stammers or has to start over. He nails it. Knocks them dead.

The irony of George's celebrity, which is hardly lost on him, is that it's lavished on a prizefighter—one who deeply loves his game. Though the populace honors the king, it harbors deep misgivings and class disdain for his bloody realm. But the element that enthralls people who care nothing about boxing transcends a seemingly quixotic seven-year quest that ended with an unmatched athletic achievement. The greater comeback of George Foreman spans four decades, and it is a stirring tale of a human being's redemption.

He grew up effectively fatherless, first in Marshall and then in Houston's Fifth Ward, where his mother moved in search of work. When he was fourteen, she was hospitalized for an emotional collapse brought on in part by his bad behavior. She sent a letter home that contained forty-five dollars to pay for his sister's graduation ring. George, who soon after that dropped out of school, stole the cash and bought a hat, a sweater, and a bottle of Thunderbird wine. For the next two years he lived mostly on the street, sleeping in abandoned shells of houses, playing dice, and rolling winos. His chums called him Monkey. One night, after mugging somebody, he slid under a house, hiding from the police. He could smell himself and kept thinking that they were going to send dogs after him, and that the dogs would smell him, too.

A public-service TV spot by pro football star Jim Brown prompted him at seventeen to sign up for the federal Job Corps program. First in Oregon and then in northern California he learned how to lay bricks, and though he brawled and caused trouble in the camps, there were glints of maturity and conscience—every month he sent home fifty dollars to his mother. At the second camp a coach named Doc Broadus got him interested in boxing. Two years later, following a relapse among the Fifth Ward muggers and winos, George won the 1968 Olympics by clubbing several youths senseless in Mexico City. It was a year of political rage and black power; on the medalists'

stand United States sprinters ducked their heads and raised black-gloved fists of protest during the national anthem. By contrast, George captivated the nation (which had no idea he had recently been a base Houston thug) by waving a little two dollar American flag when he received his gold medal.

As a young pro, George spent ten thousand dollars of his first substantial payday to buy his mother a house in nicer northeast Houston. He disposed of two great heavyweights, Joe Frazier and Ken Norton, in such quick and savage fashion that he was deemed invincible. Frazier hit the canvas so many times it looked like George was dribbling him like a basketball. But he was an unpopular champion. The public found George surly, which he was—but in retrospect, who could blame him? He was the one who had waved Old Glory in Mexico City. During the Vietnam War, he was prepared to enlist in the Navy or Air Force, but he drew a high number in the draft lottery and, like countless others, chose to pursue civilian life. Yet it was Muhammad Ali, stripped of his title because he refused to be drafted, who emerged from Vietnam as a folk hero. In 1974 George played the dope, as he cheerfully puts it now, in Ali's rope-a-dope brainstorm in Zaire, which ended with George exhausted and being counted out in the eighth round.

He dealt with it by trying to sleep with a different woman every night and by walking around his Marshall ranch with a lion on a leash. In 1977, maneuvering for a return fight that Ali was none too eager to grant him, he lost a decision to a clever Philadelphian named Jimmy Young, and after the match, in the throes of heat prostration, thought he was dying and found God. At twenty-eight he walked away from boxing. He got fat and happy (except for a bitter divorce and child-custody battle) and became a street-corner preacher. He stopped hating Ali and realized the man was a friend. If George hadn't been the greatest, he could look back and know he had stepped high in history's most gifted peerage of heavyweight boxers. For ten years he seldom even shadowboxed. Then, at thirty-eight, after begging for money to keep a Houston youth recreation center open, he started fighting again in places so far from a major airport that TV crews couldn't find him. Unlike many old fighters who try to make another go of it, he hadn't abused himself since his teens—aside from overeating—and except for Ali, Young, and a Denver slugger named Ron Lyle, nobody was ever in the ring with him long enough to damage his brain cells much. During his comeback, George fought every six weeks, shed forty pounds, and got some skills back: first the left jab, which, in his prime, opponents likened to being thumped in the face with a telephone pole; then the straight right that comes behind the jab; then the left hook that sweeps in after the right. He could shoot the jab out, dip a knee, and follow

hard with a left uppercut—a difficult combination, yet critics said he was pon-
derously slow.

In twenty-four bouts, George fought and stopped four quasi-contenders;
the rest were targets. Boxing insiders were laughing at him, but he was a big
name, and all at once the public loved him. What a nice and funny guy he had
become! Such a pleasant contrast to bad Mike Tyson. Of course, few really
believed in the fantasy. But then, to the consternation of Tyson's only credible rival, Evander Holyfield, Tyson let himself get knocked out by journeyman Buster Douglas and then was doing time in Indiana on a rape conviction. Prizefighters stay in the business for the prizes, not the joy of getting
hammered; for poor Holyfield, George was the only big payday out there. At
forty-two George put up a splendid fight, but the younger and faster hands
prevailed. Public sentiment shifted: Give it up, old man. It's not funny anymore. You're going to get hurt. Yet George kept fighting, risking the sad fate
of his historic soul mate, Muhammad Ali. He lost a decision to mediocre
Tommy Morrison and took a turn in a short-lived TV sitcom, in which, for
religious and marital reasons, he declined to kiss his co-star on the mouth.
He claims that one day the actress stormed off in a huff: "Well, I never!"

Then, last April, chance and market conditions rose up again. The gallant
Holyfield—weakened by his fight with George and two epic bouts with
Riddick Bowe—lost a close decision to an undefeated but little-known Detroit fighter, Michael Moorer. Holyfield announced his retirement the next
day (like many it was short-lived). There were other able heavies, such as
Bowe and Tyson, who was nearing the end of his prison term, that Moorer
might choose to hazard down the road. But in the meantime, the new champ
desired a big, easy payday. Once more, George was the biggest draw out there,
and he was getting older every day. In fact, to force the World Boxing Association to heed Moorer's wishes and sanction the Las Vegas fight, George
and his Beverly Hills lawyer, Henry Holmes, had to go to court on the basis
of inconsistent rules enforcement and age discrimination. Only in America.
George, who had received $5 million for fighting relative nobodies, accepted
about $2 million to get one more title shot.

George's trainer and strategist for the Moorer fight was a portly man named
Charlie Shipes, who owns a small long-haul trucking firm in northeast Houston. In the late sixties George, Shipes, and Sonny Liston, who was still in the
game following his two losses to Ali, were stablemates in Oakland, California. Shipes was a flashy undefeated welterweight, billed by his handlers as
the uncrowned champion, until Dallas's Curtis Cokes, the crowned champ,

dismantled him in his one title fight. George's other guru was Bob Cook, who in the late seventies was a standout La Porte High School running back. When college football didn't work out for him, he first bulked up as a competitive bodybuilder, started working out at George's youth center, and had eight pro fights. George now relies on Cook for weight training and nutritional advice. (All that business about hamburgers in both hands is for show; George eats more sensibly than most people.)

Before the fight, the sports media couldn't get a fix on Moorer's personality and thus decided the star in his corner was his voluble trainer, Teddy Atlas. But the twenty-six-year-old champ was no soup can. Moorer carried his 222 pounds impressively, and after beating Holyfield, his record was thirty-five and zero with thirty knockouts. Moorer is a lefthander and the first one to hold a heavyweight title; that's because right-handers hate them, almost never see them, and as champions, seldom give them a shot. It's awkward, as the punches zoom in from angles right-handers are not used to seeing. After watching tapes of Moorer, Shipes and George came away even more devoted to an old axiom of how to fight southpaws: straight right hand every time he wiggles.

Of course, he had to be close enough to land it. Though analysts scoff at George, inside the ropes he incites real fear. According to *Sports Illustrated*, Don King once proposed a Foreman bout to Tyson, who replied, "You like him so much, you fight him. No!" Several observers thought they saw that fright in Holyfield. George knew he couldn't win a decision against Moorer if the young man punched in flurries and danced far away from him. So he feigned a personal animosity toward him, suggesting he was a coward. The message: Come on in here. Atlas knew what George was doing. At center ring for the referee's instructions, the trainer ordered his fighter to look at nothing but George's chest. At the end of the first round, when Moorer took the stool, Atlas told him, "The hardest part of this fight is over. He's just a guy. Our sparring partners were better. Am I right or wrong?"

Moorer basically fought a one-handed fight. With his right he threw multiple jabs, hooks, uppercuts. His left was little more than a guard against the threat of George's right. Gaining confidence, he bobbed and weaved and talked to George. "Pop! Pop! Pop!" he said, landing punches. Though George was staggered several times, he knew he couldn't let himself get knocked down. "They'd just say, 'Oh, no, George is old. Stop it,'" he later said, explaining his thinking. But his height and bulk were a problem for Moorer. He held his arms high and vertically, and he deflected punches with his gloves and forearms. Moorer wasn't eager to burrow inside, so he often found himself loop-

ing punches over George's arms. Though more than half of his blows landed, many glanced harmlessly off the top of George's head.

George relied on jabs and straight rights—some soft, some hard, but he just kept coming. At the end of the sixth round—a rousing toe-to-toe brawl—Shipes suggested, "Try moving over to the right a little. Get away from that right hand." He was concerned about the damage to George's left eye. A round later, Atlas nagged Moorer to keep up the pace. "Remember when I told you about an old car? This is an old car. Let him go slow, he can make it down the road. Make him go faster, he'll start to break down."

In George's view the eighth round was pivotal. He surprised and wobbled Moorer with three quick rights and a thumping left hook. Moorer gave him a curt nod of acknowledgment. "The only way anybody ever gets a title shot," George said afterward, "is to convince the other guy, 'Aw, he's just in it for the money.' Then he gets in there and realizes he's in a *fight*. But you don't want to communicate that too soon, 'cause he'll change his plans. Way he took that hook, I thought, 'Ah, now I got him. I questioned his courage. He's not gonna run.'"

Angelo Dundee, the seventy-something trainer who worked Ali's corner in Zaire, had joined George's team a week before the fight. He's a good luck charm, he has seen it all, and he's one of the best cut men in the business. After the eighth he asked George, "You all right?" George: "Yeah." Dundee: "You sure?" But in the ninth George was pooped. Later he said that his cornermen were voicing fears about the scorecards, and after the ninth he snapped at them, told them to shut up. Whatever was discussed, he walked out in the tenth and turned it up. After two left-right combinations, he again crossed Moorer up with a right lead and left hook. Another hook missed so wildly that George almost spun himself around in a circle. "Give him all the credit in the world," sympathized HBO commentator Gil Clancy, "but he's a forty-five-year-old man in a young man's game." Then George landed another jab and right. Stung, Moorer stayed put and dropped his hands slightly. George had been stepping to his right, which is difficult for a right-handed fighter. He did it, as Shipes said, to escape Moorer's punishment, but he was also looking for an angular lane. The last right hand George should throw in his life—the one he could never land against Ali—sloped downward about two feet. Moorer dropped like a sack of flour, flat on his back, struggling to raise his head, as blood pooled in his mouth.

Pandemonium. George was on his knees praying. His brother Roy fainted. HBO's Jim Lampley, who had ridiculed the contest before it began, shrieked, "It happens!" Moorer, who fought artfully and won seven of nine rounds on

points, found a likable persona as a loser. Seated on his stool with the gloves off, he looked up at the camera, nodded gamely, and raised a thumb. He gave it all he had. George, with sunshades hiding a badly swollen eye, spoke into a microphone. "When you wish upon a star . . . doesn't matter who you are . . ." Ali, who later sent George a congratulatory note with a hand-drawn happy face, no doubt admired the poetry.

Moorer leaned through the shoulders and gibberish and planted a kiss on George's bald held. Pops.

High in NBC's office tower in New York, I am parked on a sofa with Mort Sharnik and Terry Sparks, a pleasant young man who travels with George and is sometimes referred to as his bodyguard, though the boss outweighs him by forty pounds. This, in its entirety, is Foreman's entourage. Sue Leibman, a *Saturday Night Live* associate producer who ushers guest hosts through the drill each week, hurries out of a meeting with the writers and approaches us. "George's title," she says briskly. "He is the . . ."

After a second we reply in a chorus, "World heavyweight champion."

Oliver McCall, a journeyman who shocked the Englishman Lennox Lewis with an early knockout, actually holds one of the three major sanctioning bodies' titles, but Leibman doesn't need to get into that. She nods and hurries back to the writers.

From another office, where George is holed up, comedian Carl Reiner emerges and is instantly crowded by the young staff. Reiner, who seems to have been making a courtesy call, walks off happily, twirling a forefinger. "If George Foreman says you're a genius, you're a genius!" It's seven at night, eleven hours since George started his day with an hour on the hotel's exercise treadmill. Suddenly Leibman rushes out to Sharnik, this time with a greatly troubled look. The bear in George has finally gotten riled and spoken sharply: He's still here because they want to take him out to eat?

Ushered down the elevators, we walk to a limo provided by the network. A Christmas shopper gapes and exclaims, "That's George Foreman!" George wears a topcoat and muffler over his dress woolens and a short-billed cap pulled down toward his nose. In the car, he stretches out his legs as the lights and street steam of Manhattan glide by. "TV," George says moodily when Sharnik asks him how it's going. "They don't know it's about eyesight. About visual. They've got all these writers who know they got to be funny, so they think and think and all they can come up with is dirt. It's just a constant battle. And you know you're in trouble because not one of 'em has a gray hair."

The limo stops in front of a deli, and Sharnik goes inside to get George's favorite New York supper: a pastrami sandwich on whole wheat with mayonnaise, lettuce, and tomatoes. The order frequently draws a laugh or double take; Sharnik sheepishly explains that the guy's a Southerner. As we move again, the conversation turns to boxing. "How good was Charlie Shipes?" I ask George.

"Best I've ever seen," he replies, animated for the first time since we left NBC. "He could do everything. Moving left jabbing, moving right jabbing: He was precision. And he wore these red trunks and red headgear; he just looked like a boxer. I used to say, 'I don't want to turn pro yet. I want to learn to box like Charlie Shipes.' Sugar Ray Robinson was like that. Except he had bad habits. Archie Moore was the best at defense." George raises his arms horizontally and ducks his head behind them. "Like this, but Archie was throwing punches all the time. He never hit hard"—George snaps his fingers loudly—"but they *rained* on you. Joe Louis: They used to talk about his devastating combinations, but the only punch he threw hard was the last one. That was the hardest thing for me to learn. You don't have to hit hard just because you're able to." He thrusts a big soft hand toward my face. "That's how I did it with Michael. Just let him see the jab. If you hit him too hard with the left, he'll start to worry about the right. And it'll put him too far back. When the time comes, I won't be able to reach him."

He lowers his head and looks at a brightly lit toy store. The building is flanked by three ledge steps of white rock. "See that?" he says. "One time in Houston, I watched Sonny Liston balance on a ledge like that on the ball of one foot. He did a deep knee bend, picked up the other foot, and stretched his leg straight out. Then he held his arms straight out and just stayed there, like a statue." George smiles at the memory. "Never seen anything like it."

Before the New York trip, I had gone to Houston to meet Charlie Shipes, whose home and trucking yard is tucked away in the pines off U.S. 59. Charlie's affable wife, Barbara, told me he was out trying to find a truck part and then let me through the security fence; she advised me to keep an eye on the pit bull that walked along at my calf. The Shipeses live in a mobile home surrounded by several tractor-trailer rigs. The only evidence of Charlie's lofty position in boxing was a couple of heavy bags under a shed and some photographs on the mantel. Barbara said she had been a friend of one of George's cousins, who introduced her to Charlie at George's church. She said she'd never seen a pro fight. "I hope George'll quit now," she told me. "He's got his health and all those kids still at home."

Just then, Charlie walked through the door in coveralls and a soiled cap. Smoking a cigarette, he reminisced about his own fifty-three and five record and the time Doc Broadus delivered them a huge youngster from the Job Corps camp in Pleasanton, California. "Sonny was good to George," he said. "George would bloody his nose, and Sonny wouldn't unload on him like a lot of fighters will. He was just bringing him along. George got his puncher's reputation because of the way he took apart Joe Frazier. But, hell, he did it with jabs, hooks, rights, and uppercuts. The man can box."

We talked about George's second ring career. He talks about Tyson, who'll get out of prison this spring—a fight that promoter Bob Arum says could gross $200 million. "Whatever George decides to do," said Shipes, "he's got my blessing."

But . . . Tyson? To me, the thought was terrifying: an angry creature who believes himself wronged and has spent three years in a cage. "Well, yeah. Tyson's good," Shipes said, now on his feet and shadowboxing. "Great hand speed, and he's kind of a switch-hitter. He'll step to the left and double hook, high and low, then do the same thing to the right. Ain't ever seen anything like it. But if a man's still got his legs under him, and there ain't no *nerve damage,* I'll take the experience. See, George came up with Ali, Frazier, Kenny Norton, Jerry Quarry, George Chuvalo. That's like going to Harvard. This young crowd now, they just been to junior college."

The next morning, the Sunday night before the New York trip, my wife and I went to George's Church of the Lord Jesus Christ. It's in a poor and neatly kept neighborhood that looks forgotten. Just down the street is George's youth center. Inside, the church is well furnished but spare. George doesn't evangelize much, even in the neighborhood, for fear of turning his church into a circus. Many of the people who go there are related to each other. George's nephew Jody Steptoe, who is an assistant pastor, sat on a chair tuning an electric guitar. There were about sixty people, all but four of us black. Steptoe stood up and started playing the guitar. "Glory, glory, hallelujah," he sang slowly, "I'm gonna lay my burden down . . ." A few women were on their feet swaying, two or three with tambourines. "Softly and tenderly Jesus is calling," they sang.

When the music stopped, George walked in, resplendent in a camel blazer. Approaching the pulpit, he kissed a child on the top of her head. George doesn't write his sermons. He selects a passage of Scripture, reads it in segments, and reflects on whatever comes to mind. This day his text was Luke, chapter 12. He told stories about how badly he hurt his mother when he was

growing up and how he periodically resolved to stop stealing—at least from her. The congregation burst out laughing when he pulled down his lip and mimicked a man with no front teeth. "Wake up from being dead drunk and my best friend says, 'George, look what you did to me.' 'I did not do that!' 'Yeah, you did . . . but it's okay.'"

He read some more Scripture, then recalled a low point in one of his five marriages. "Sometimes they just don't want you. I mean: you. I went up to my ranch, and all I could think to do was cut grass. Mow and mow and mow. I ran my tractor over a stump. I was trying to fix my mower with a sledgehammer and come way up over the top. Whomp! Hit myself right on the knee." He danced across the church on one foot. "Thank you, baby Jesus, thank you for all this pain! Take my mind off the mess I have made of my life." He limped on as the laughter subsided. "Amazing grace," he said, shaking his head. "That saved a wretch like me."

George looked again at the Bible in his hand and read loudly, "Take heed, and beware of covetousness, for a man's life consisteth not in the abundance of the things which he possesseth." In the sermon he fashioned the parable of the rich fool into a biting comment on the temper of these times. George knocked out Moorer the Saturday before Election Day. Many comeback candidates invoked his name in their acceptance speeches, but politically George is a fish out of water. He endorsed one candidate: Ann Richards, who was trounced by George W. Bush. Foreman is the poster boy of the much-maligned Great Society; he has often said that LBJ saved his life by creating the Job Corps. He once reflected on his flag-waving impulse at the Olympics: "What I did in Mexico City wasn't no demonstration. I was just happy and proud to be an American. When I looked at America, I saw a compassionate society that didn't give up on its underclass."

On this day, he didn't sound so confident of that fundamental generosity. "I'll tell you about middle class," he said. "Their mommas and daddies used to be poor. Now they've had a job ten years and have a credit card. Hear 'em talking at the barbershop. 'Look at all those people getting rich on welfare. All that stuff they buy.' Why, there's people in this country that don't have fifteen cents."

"Amen. That's right," several people said. George chewed on his lower lip, and he did not look happy. "You don't have to reform 'em," he said sarcastically. "Just don't give 'em nothing. *Shut up!*"

George has nine kids, ages twenty-two to three. One son runs the ranch in Marshall, his eldest daughter is in college, and the rest live in a home in the

Houston suburb of Kingwood. On Thursday afternoon during his week in New York, in his *Saturday Night* dressing room, he picks up a phone and calls home. He talks to his wife, Joan, who was born on the Caribbean island of Saint Lucia—yet he makes no mention of glitzy things and famous people. The conversation dwells on antibiotics and the child who's running a fever.

When an intercom booms George's name, he goes out in the studio to tape some promotional spots that the producers and network officials will review and air before the show. "Watch *Saturday Night Live,*" he commands in one, "or I'll beat you up and eat all your food!" In the studio there is genuine laughter as he tries out various routines. Later, he is joined by the show's musical guest, the rock group Hole. Hole's lead singer is Courtney Love, a bleached-blond miniskirted young woman with a tattoo on her shoulder and runs in her hose. She is the aspiring empress of grunge rock and the widow of Kurt Cobain, a Seattle rock star who was depressed and had a heroin problem and dealt with it by putting a shotgun to his head. Courtney's shtick is Madonna to the max: All week she has been trying to prove that she's the baddest girl around. She and George shake hands, and the crew positions the band around him. As the cameramen line up the shot, Courtney stands below George. She primps by shoving her breasts with the palms of her hands. "Tits," she keeps saying. "Tits." George keeps his eyes on the cue cards.

In one promo, Courtney and George are supposed to begin by hyping the show and then get into a mild spat. On the first take, Courtney ad-libs. She turns and bangs her fists against his chest and then tries to jump and wrap her legs around his waist. George fends her off, and he leaves the studio laughing, but in his dressing room he plops on the sofa dejectedly. Sharnik asks him about the scripts. "So bad they can't be fixed," George says with a sigh. "Start trying to change this, cut that, it just gets worse. I'm not gonna say anything. I just never shoulda done this. No way. Not in this lifetime."

Leibman, the associate producer, knocks on the door, comes in, and rests a moment, waiting for the wardrobe man. Once more, talk of boxing revives George's spirits. He elaborates on his belief that tragedy is interwoven in all feats of athletic greatness. "In boxing we got this saying: 'I'm gonna put my head on your chest.' Means I'm gonna take the best you got and come right through all your defenses. The first fight against Muhammad, Joe Frazier *did that.* To a man as great as Muhammad Ali. After that, Joe never was quite the same. What else did he have to prove?"

I glance at Leibman. Her eyes have grown very wide.

As George tries on sport coats he talks about Tyson, whose imminent return to the sport will be watched as closely as Ali's was twenty years ago.

"Boxing is a matter of who can fill the tent," says George, unbothered by the circus analogy. "Mike Tyson doesn't need the title. The title needs Tyson. But what he had, he can't get back. Because it was all speed. Tyson is not a powerful puncher." George shadowboxes, demonstrating his point. "Hit you in the ribs, and you say, 'My, that hurts,' so you bring down your elbow, and he comes right up to the head. But it takes at least two years in the gym to get that going, and then you got to fight constantly. Title fights don't get arranged that fast. Tyson is Humpty Dumpty. All the king's horses, all the king's men. Everybody gonna be whipping him."

George fiddles with his cuffs and looks in the mirror. "But there's a young one out there. Nobody's even heard of him yet. One day he's just gonna loom among us. Be like Tyson, when he first came up. People be standing around saying, 'You want him?' 'No, I don't want him. You want him?' I hope it's somebody like Joe Louis."

The halls leading into the *Saturday Night Live* studio are lined with photos of great comedians and great comic moments, and the production is amazing to behold: seven complex activities unfolding at once. But the dress rehearsal is painfully unfunny. The closest thing to humor involving George has him propelled by time capsule to Germany in 1939, where he changes history by knocking out Hitler and becoming World Fuhrer. The producers have flown in ring announcer Michael Buffer to put on a Nazi uniform and do his basso "Let's get ready to rumble" routine. At George's request, bit parts in the sketch are played by fight promoter Bob Arum and Henry Holmes, the lawyer and agent who won the age-discrimination injunction and negotiated his book contract. ("Yeah, But Henry's stock is down," George grumbled at one point during the rehearsals. "He's the one who got me into this.")

The sight gags feature actors and crew members whose eyes are swollen shut. In a demeaning skit, George, cast as TV's Incredible Hulk, grunts and smashes things until finally he calls the show's writers out and observes correctly that nobody in the studio audience is laughing. They wrote that! But the joke's on him.

Finally the cast assembles to close out the show. All keep a wary eye on Courtney Love, who reportedly came of age with a trust fund and is now looking for somebody else to throw her legs around. The victim will be her guitar player; they'll fall in a heap, her panties bared to all. George isn't smiling as he waits for the camera light to come on. He towers above the others and has a pensive expression on his face. The champ. Earlier in the week he told one interviewer who pressed him about his plans in the ring and be-

yond: "Just don't tell me I'm too old. I'm blue-collar, and I've got nine kids. I've gotta work till I can't work anymore." He told another interviewer that he wanted to shake every hand, sign every autograph. But this is the longest time he has spent in New York since he was a young contender fighting in Madison Square Garden. He's a grown man now. In his mind he's already at the airport. It's time to go home.

FEBRUARY, 1995

Showdown at
Maverick Ranch

Courage and grit have outlets besides violence, thank God. For three sisters born to a historic clan of Texas populists and eccentrics, their challenge came when the family's small Hill Country ranch and their way of life were pronounced fair game by a daunting two-headed beast— economic boosters of the city of San Antonio, and the road-building machine of the Texas Department of Transportation.

Alleged "highways to nowhere" have long been built around the outskirts of Texas' large cities, especially during real estate booms. A freeway in the making can double or triple the value of "raw land," as developers often refer to small farms and ranches. During the boom of the early 1980s, developers found they could facilitate construction of these wealth-enhancing highways by donating the right-of-way to the state. For the Department of Transportation it was a great deal. In a state that draws high marks for the quality of its highway system, the road builders could forge ahead at a fraction of the cost to the taxpayers. And Highway 211, on the western outskirts of San Antonio, came with a worthy rationale—it would feed a biotechnical research park whose flagship enterprise was devoted to cancer research and therapy.

The three sisters had little money to fight the state. But the road builders tried to force their way through an intact frontier community as listed by the National Register of Historic Places. They also failed to read their Texas history; though the Mavericks were no longer pillars of the San Antonio establishment, their name had become a word in our language, a word synonymous with independence. The road builders seriously underestimated the fire, spunk, and organizational ability of the three sisters.

My story was not exactly a hot property when I turned it in. In fact,

applicants for an editor's position at the magazine were given the draft
as a reclamation project that would measure their editing skill. But in
the end the article was a testament to the power of the press. I'll never be
a favorite around the Texas Department of Transportation. For all the
reasons above, but also because of my story, the road to nowhere was
stopped in its tracks.

On the road to Bebe Fenstermaker's house, wild turkeys run unperturbed
before a visitor's car. The dirt trail dips through a clear, shallow creek with no
name, though downstream, a spring rising from a cave commemorates a small
tragedy. In Bebe's mother's time, a woman visited the place and brought her
dog along. A rabbit dashed into the cave's catacombs, and the pooch unwisely followed, never to emerge. The women could hear its cries of doom
through the stony ground under their feet: Lost Dog Spring.

Bebe occupies a metal-roofed limestone house of the Maverick Ranch, the
historic Bexar County spread named for her famous family, which has owned
it for four generations. When she isn't teaching art at San Antonio College,
Bebe tears around the nine-hundred-acre property in her gray pickup. She
has been on the ranch since 1970, when she decided she no longer wanted to
live in the city. Around the same time, her sister Mary, who is now a travel
agent, reached a similar conclusion. She makes her home in a cottage across
the creek. Another sister, Martha, a painter and an art professor at Laredo
Junior College, occasionally lives here during the summer. Each of the three
is in her forties and unmarried. It's quiet on the Maverick Ranch. It used to
be peaceful.

For the past three years, the approach of survey crews, bulldozers,
earthmovers, and asphalt trucks has shattered the Fenstermakers' equanim-
ity. The Texas highway department—officially known as the Texas Department of Transportation—is building a partial loop around west San Antonio.
To finish that project, highway workers can scarcely avoid destroying the
family's retreat.

From the air, the piecemeal construction of Texas Highway 211 looks
bizarre. Due west of downtown, past Sea World and Kelly Air Force Base, a
two-lane road with a disproportionate swath of cleared right-of-way starts at
U.S. 90 and curls 3.5 miles north through ranchland before dead-ending in
front of what appears to be a landscaped college campus or office park. Amid
small farms and scattered home sites, the route vanishes northward for more

than seven miles. Then, in a raw, white caliche scrape, it reappears, for nearly seven and a half miles, with long bridges, elaborate runoff culverts, and curves blasted deep through wooded hills. Beyond the burg of Helotes, it dead-ends again at Texas Highway 16. A proposed fourth segment of 211, once more unseen, arcs northeast for fourteen miles through ranches and small subdivisions to Interstate 10 and an intersecting farm-to-market road. As outer loops go, this one is way out. Its terminus could be twenty-five miles from downtown San Antonio. The Maverick Ranch lies almost at its northern end.

Highway 211 has the sanction of San Antonio's most dominant forces—corporate, government, military, and academic. While he was mayor, the city's political giant, Henry Cisneros, made an ardent plea for the roadway to the Texas Highway and Public Transportation Commission, which has since authorized all but the last segment. (On the subject of Maverick Ranch and 211, Cisneros refused to be interviewed.) The campus-like tract west of downtown is the site of the Texas Research Park—San Antonio's dream of a high-tech future. The park, it is hoped, will cure diseases, spawn new corporations, and employ thousands of doctors, scientists, and technicians—many of whom live northwest of the city and would benefit greatly from a direct route connecting home and work.

In most cases, the outcome of such a story would be preordained. The highway department is one of Texas' most esteemed institutions. Once the department has approved a state roadway, it is almost impossible to move or stop it. Anyway, if individual rights were not made to yield, roads would never get built. Many landowners surrender without much struggle, quickly understanding the government's ability to absorb legal costs and to enforce its wishes through the power of eminent domain. In fact, many see a new highway route through their property as a godsend. This real estate alchemy turns raw land into shopping centers and residential cul-de-sacs. Everybody gets a bright, shining office tower.

But this battle of ranch and road, of history and modernity, isn't over—not just yet. A number of factors make it different from most. The Fenstermakers are not part of just any Texas clan. The Maverick Ranch is no ordinary Hill Country retreat. And 211 is not just another freeway of the future. Its pending completion casts light on the policy that governs how roads get built in Texas. Depending on your perspective, the conflict over 211 is one in which a privileged few are pushing their interests over those of a needy many—or it's an outrageous taxpayer-funded scam that will benefit only a few real estate speculators.

Either way, the power struggle being played out in San Antonio has cru-

cial implications. It pits old wealth and influence against new and ascendant forces entranced by the word "visionary." It pits rural serenity against urban hustle, environmental protection against economic stimulation, aging firebrand liberals against neoconservative technocrats. It's a classic confrontation: An immovable object meets an irresistible force.

Helicopters foreshadowed the Fenstermaker's trouble with the state. In December, 1988, Bebe noticed a chopper hovering so close to the ranch that treetops swirled under its blades. "That's my airspace," she fumed, but she quickly forgot the incident. Then, in April, 1989, a neighbor called. He had just heard in Boerne that the highway department aimed to put a road through his back pasture, heading north for hers.

The following Monday, Bebe drove into San Antonio to the department's district headquarters. A courtly engineer named Jay Mills showed her an aerial photo map with a route of the proposed extension of 211. The initial construction would be confined to two lanes, but several football fields of cleared land signaled the long-range intent: a full-blown expressway. Bebe pointed to a wooded section within the wedge of 16 and I-10. "He said, 'That's just empty land there. There's just a bunch of old houses with rusty roofs.' I said, 'Well, that's my home.'"

Martha, who would become the angriest sister, was initially ambivalent about the state's plans. "I'd been living in Laredo for several years," she says, "and I couldn't use the ranch all that much. The choice seemed to be, at the end of my life, which would I rather have—a lot of money and no ranch or the ranch and no money?"

After some deliberation, though, the sisters decided to put up all the fight they could. They hired Dallas attorney Eddie Vasallo, a specialist in eminent domain, and Grand Prairie consultant Len Lenard, a former Environmental Protection Agency official who says he became an environmentalist after getting doused with Agent Orange in Vietnam. They also secured the help of a state legislator, Jeff Wentworth, who found out exactly where 211 would cross the ranch: between two gates and a small cemetery on its southeast side. Armed with this information, Lenard and Martha met with highway department officials in December, 1989.

The environment would be their principal line of defense. Limestone holes such as Lost Dog Spring reach the Glen Rose Aquifer, and the creek and gullies wash runoff into similar recharge features of the Edwards Aquifer—San Antonio's sole source of drinking water. The water level of a well in nearby Bandera had dropped from 54 feet in 1953 to 355 feet in 1989. To the sisters,

this meant that the Hill Country did not have enough water to accommodate urban sprawl. They would talk about the air, which would be polluted by vehicular emissions. They would cite a Nature Conservancy study ranking the Balcones Canyonlands among the top twelve natural oases on earth and evidence that black-capped vireos and golden-cheeked warblers—federally protected endangered species—nested on the ranch.

They would also make a cultural case. Arrowheads and other artifacts have been unearthed on the Maverick Ranch that go back four thousand years. The ranch contains two Hill Country German homesteads and the remains of rock holding pens used in early cattle drives. From fence line to fence line, it is listed on the National Register of Historic Places.

Lenard and Martha arrived at the district office on Loop 410 expecting to raise those points in a private chat with Richard Lockhart, the district engineer. Instead, they walked into a room filled with several engineers, as well as archaeological and environmental officials from highway department headquarters. The officials said they were merely trying to serve a concerned taxpayer. But to this particular taxpayer, it was an ambush—an intimidating show of force.

Lockhart opened the meeting by saying that the department was not insensitive to matters of preservation; his ancestor Byrd Lockhart, for whom the town of Lockhart was named, was a surveyor in the time of Stephen F. Austin. Lockhart then turned over the floor to design engineer John Kight. What happened next shocked Martha. While the first route her family had seen would have devoured only a pasture, Kight invited her comment on a second one clearly drawn within ten feet of Bebe's back door.

"They were taunting us," Martha says. "There was a woman, one of the department's top environmental officials. I kept pressing her about aquifers and endangered species. She finally said, 'Look, you have to understand, my job is to build roads.'"

In September, 1990, the Fenstermakers carried the fight to Austin. Bebe testified before the Sunset Advisory Commission, which was reviewing the highway department's performance. She directed her thrust at tax dollars. "Some of the road is already built," she said, "although the highway department to this day has not held a general public hearing on the whole road, nor engineered the road, nor acquired the right-of-way, nor even chosen a route! No business could hope to get a construction loan without demonstrating that all major contingencies had been resolved." A commission staffer offered to arrange a third conference later that month between the sisters and their lawyer and San Antonio officials. At the conclusion of that meeting, the staffer

asked what had been accomplished. "Nothing," said Vassallo. The engineers stared back across the table and agreed.

Around this time, the sisters uncovered other possible paths through their property. On the tallest hill of the Maverick Ranch sits a strange concrete house with the interior design of a yacht. Relatives had built it in 1913; a third highway route would bulldoze it. Then there was the Nineteenth Amendment Oak, under which suffragettes, led by the Fenstermakers' grandmother, plotted in 1919. Another route would uproot even that historic tree.

Fighting the highway department, the Fenstermakers found, is maddening—like throwing punches at wisps of smoke. Although the highway department maintains that it is cooperating with the sisters, its engineers, as Vassallo had told them, are not required to disclose construction plans until their crews are at the fence line. In the 1991 legislative session, Mary testified before a Senate committee: "We have seen perhaps ten routes, seven or eight of which would go through our home.... We have had tremendous difficulty obtaining even that information from them. At great expense we have had to retain an environmental consultant and an attorney to help us. Often the only information we got came from our state legislators, who asked the questions for us when we could not get the highway department to respond."

So the battle lines were drawn. Three middle-aged sisters couldn't begin to match the resources of the Texas highway department. But they weren't about to back down. It wasn't in their nature.

Martha, Bebe, and Mary Fenstermaker are heirs to a family tradition of sufficient independence that the binding surname, Maverick, has become an English noun with connotations of contrariness. The patriarch, Samuel Augustus Maverick, who arrived in San Antonio in 1835, guided Ben Milam's insurgents through the town when the rebel Texans captured the Alamo. The day the Alamo fell to Santa Anna, Samuel was representing its men at the people's convention in Washington-on-the-Brazos, where he signed the Texas Declaration of Independence. After the war, he married Mary Adams of Tuscaloosa, Alabama, who composed a spare ink sketch and watercolor of the Alamo with its bombed walls still in ruin—the first icon of its enshrinement. In 1840, Mary ran through the streets crying, "Here are Indians! Here are Indians!" when a courtroom summit with Comanche chiefs turned into the raging Council House Fight. During one of the Mexican invasions in 1842, Samuel traded rooftop gunshots with Santa Anna's soldiers. Consequently, he was imprisoned for a short time in Mexico, where he was forced to work on a road-building project.

But it was unbranded cattle that put the family name into the English language. Around 1845, Samuel failed to brand a herd of cattle he had received as payment for a debt. Since cattle roamed free on unfenced open range, nearby ranchers began identifying any unbranded cattle as Maverick's. By the end of the Civil War, the term "maverick" meant any unbranded calf that had strayed from a herd, and the word eventually became synonymous with "rebel."

In San Antonio society, the Mavericks carved their niche among clothiers and bankers, Joskes and Frosts. Charles Goodnights and Burk Burnetts these folks were not. Samuel's son George—the Fenstermaker's great-grandfather—was a lawyer and a land developer. In 1907, he bought a nine-hundred-acre ranch twenty-five miles up in the Balcones Canyonlands and made it the family's summer residence. His daughter Rena Maverick Green—the Fenstermaker's grandmother—led Texas' suffragettes; she also helped found the San Antonio Conservation Society. In the twenties, Rena fought city plans to pave over the San Antonio River and make its bed a sewer. Her first cousin, Maury Maverick Sr., a San Antonio congressman and mayor in the thirties, was a populist radical who talked Franklin Roosevelt into approving a beautification grant for the San Antonio River. Maury Junior carried on his father's civil libertarian tradition in the legislature and in his legal practice. In a recent column in the *San Antonio Express-News,* Maury Junior conversed with the ghost of a favorite bartender, who said: "You Mavericks brought the first black slaves to San Antonio after the fall of the Alamo. Is that why you are such a guilt-ridden lefty?"

Rena's daughter Rowena helped save old Fort Davis. In 1941 Rowena married Leslie Fenstermaker, who would become one of the clan's few genuine ranchers. They and their daughters—Martha, Bebe, and Mary—lived in far West Texas until 1958, when they returned to bustling San Antonio. There, the family's connections swung up like loose boards. In 1961, Billie Lee Brammer published *The Gay Place,* which featured an LBJ-like governor called Arthur "Goddam" Fenstemaker. The sisters had an uncle named Arthur Fenstermaker. Brammer may have dropped a consonant, but sheer coincidence seemed unlikely.

As young women, Martha, Bebe, and Mary cut their political teeth on the long, bitter, fruitless attempt to stop construction of the McAllister Freeway through Olmos Park. Because the Maverick heritage had not bestowed on them a great deal of money, they needed to work. But the legacy had left them control of that lovely nine-hundred-acre place up in the hills. They stocked it with Longhorns and sought help from Texas Parks and Wildlife Department officials in stabilizing the deer population. In 1979 they won a listing for the

place, as an intact frontier community, on the National Register of Historic Places.

Samuel Maverick had been an attorney, merchant, legislator, and mayor—and, with land going for a nickel or a dime an acre, an avid speculator in real estate. What goes around comes around. One hundred and twenty years after his death, the early eighties craze in Texas land speculation would aim the bulldozers of the highway department straight at his descendants' door.

By 1980, the Mavericks were symbols of a languid old San Antonio that believers in a new era of progress meant to leave in history's dust. No more should the families of a few old *patróns* approve the loans, dole out the opportunity, chart the city's course. The lead disciple of this new faith was General Robert McDermott, the retired founding academic dean of the United States Air Force Academy who had built his San Antonio-based insurance company, USAA, into a powerhouse. The political champion was Henry Cisneros, the charismatic Harvard graduate who would soon be mayor.

Through their initiative, San Antonio reached the final five in the 1982 wooing of MCC, a computer technology consortium headed by Bobby Ray Inman, a retired admiral and former Central Intelligence Agency director. Inman later told McDermott that San Antonio really hadn't come close. Unlike Austin, the winning suitor, the city didn't have a big university, with the engineers and Ph.D.'s to feed the new payrolls. Look to your natural assets, Inman said; then proceed.

San Antonio's assets were distinctly medical. There was the University of Texas Health Science Center, the Brooke Army Medical Center at Fort Sam Houston, the Air Force's largest hospital at Lackland, a medical research facility at Brooks Air Force Base, and the respected Southwest Foundation for Biomedical Research, known by most San Antonians for its controversial medical experiments involving a large colony of captive apes.

Cisneros was an ideal pitchman. While his speeches could resonate with feeling for *apachería* and *comanchería*, eras in Texas when the most common surgery involved scalps, he cared about modern medicine too. In a publication known as his *Orange Book*, Cisneros effused about gene splicing, pancreas-substituting pumps, and a computer-controlled prosthesis called the MIT Knee. A "Tiger Team" was sent to study biomedical research parks in Pennsylvania, California, and North Carolina. The idea for the Texas Research Park was the result, and it was a captivating dream: In the course of finding new ways to treat and cure disease, physicians and scientists would spin off companies that would employ tens of thousands of people.

Land was no problem. In 1983, during the height of the real estate boom, Concord Oil CEO Tom Pawel donated fifteen hundred of the company's eight thousand acres to the research park project, anticipating sixty-five hundred acres of related development that would profit Concord greatly. Money wasn't a problem either. In response to a delegation led by Cisneros and McDermott, Ross Perot had ponied up $15 million—three times the delegation's request.

Transportation, however, *was* a problem. The only access to Concord's acreage was a narrow county road; even an infant research park would require a full-blown highway. How could the park's boosters convince the state to build them one?

For nearly two years, the boosters pondered the question. Then, unexpectedly, a solution appeared in the form of another roadway whose planning would serve as the model for their own. A few miles closer to the city sat the tract of land where Texas Highway 151 would be built. Originally conceived to relieve west side traffic congestion, 151 attracted the Sea World entertainment park—a gold mine for landowners on either side of the road. The highway won the state's approval because one such landowner, a flamboyant developer named Marty Wender, and his urban planner friend, the equally flamboyant Ralph C. Bender, had hatched a novel scheme: To make sure the highway department couldn't pass up construction, they donated the right-of-way on Wender's acres, kicked in a few million dollars for frontage roads, and persuaded the city and other landowners to do the same.

The developers could afford such largess. At the height of San Antonio's boom, the value of raw land suddenly blessed with a freeway shot from two thousand dollars an acre to fifteen thousand dollars an acre. Cisneros' pitch of Highway 151 had dazzled the highway commission and its chairman, Houston developer Bob Lanier, who later became that city's mayor. The project was ballyhooed as a national model of public-and-private-sector partnership. In it, the department had found the tacit formula that now dominates Texas road-building policy: If you want to propel a highway far up on the list of priorities, come see the commissioners with donated right-of-way.

"At the ground-breaking ceremonies for 151," Wender recalls, "everybody was there. Henry, Bob Lanier, General McDermott. We're standing around talking about economic development. So we said, 'Look, we're trying to build a fifteen-thousand-acre biomedical research park a little farther out. If we're creating jobs, will the highway department help us build a road to it?' Bob Lanier said, 'Yes. We'll look at it.' He said, 'This is a great day. Not only are we celebrating saving money, we got a freeway that promotes economic growth.

We got cash from the developers. We got the right-of-way free of charge. Everybody wins.'"

The highway commission approved construction of the second highway, 211, in March, 1986. At a cost of $18.5 million, 211 would cut north eighteen and a half miles from U.S. 90 to Highway 16. The northward route carried the highway department into sensitive territory—especially a recharge zone of the Edwards Aquifer. But its four-page environmental assessment sounded an all-clear on water and air quality, soil erosion, endangered species, archaeological and historical sites. And it praised the potential benefits the road could bring. "Long-term economic effects," the document held, "are almost of a magnitude that is hard to imagine."

Initial construction of 211 was limited to its first four miles: a two-lane highway, adjoined by strips of land cleared and blasted through mesquite savanna. With quick access to U.S. 90, it seemed to be all the road the research park's bioscientists would need for a decade or two. But developers were anxious to get the next fifteen miles of 211 built as well. By 1986, the real estate boom was going bust. Without a freeway, investors in rural Bexar County would surely be struck with all that overvalued land. With a freeway, however, they could flip those boondocks at a healthy price—one calculated in square feet, not acres.

To expedite the construction of this second segment, the four developers with land along that stretch of 211 retained Ralph Bender, the urban planner involved in the 151 project. For his clients, Bender drew maps for the highway department that would get them every possible foot of frontage. The developers donated the right-of-way for their land, which amounted to about eighty percent of the total, and promised to bear the cost of buying or condemning the rest.

It was a sweet deal for the highway department. Even if it collapsed, Bexar and Medina counties—not the state—would have to pick up the easement tab. Evidently, it never dawned on the department's engineers that there might be an *ethical* problem. The engineers justified their case with population growth projections and a long-range transportation plan that had called for such a road as far back as 1968. Yet they essentially gave over control of the department to real estate speculators, who led them by their noses: The speculators drew the maps, arranged for rights-of-way to be donated, and greased the way with multimillion-dollar incentives. By making it too tantalizing a deal for the highway department to turn down, shareholders in four private development companies got the state to build them a freeway that they believed would make them rich.

But the push for 211 didn't stop there. Egged on by the same developers, who saw dollar signs in the prospect of an even longer road, the highway commission, in November, 1988, authorized pursuit of a fourteen-mile extension that would arc from 16 to I-10 and FM 3351. The mere possibility of an Austin-San Antonio corridor of development was enough reason for the highway department to get the ball rolling—despite the fact that north of 16, no funds were set aside for actual construction, and the state, not the counties, would have to bear ninety percent of land acquisition costs.

Luckily, the engineers had a hole card. Just beyond 16 was the thirty-five-hundred-acre spread of a trusted ally: John White, who had made his living in Uvalde, mining rock that is greatly esteemed in Texas highway construction. White had sold his company and wanted to make it easier and more profitable for his heirs to divide the family's rural retreat. He explored the terrain with his longtime friends, district engineers Raymond Stotzer and Richard Lockhart, and eventually decided to donate his right-of-way to the new highway.

Unfortunately, that route through the White Ranch sends 211 straight at the Fenstermakers. It's nothing personal. The Maverick Ranch lies between the highway department and its legal objectives, I-10 and FM 3351. In order to skirt small subdivisions—with their utility connections, mortgage balances, and tricycles in the driveway—the department can scarcely avoid taking on the sisters.

As it happens, the Fenstermakers are not the only ones who oppose the construction of 211—just the loudest. A few miles north of the research park, for example, there's a Milton Stolte, who raises grain on an irrigated 329-acre farm. Stolte doesn't want to lose twenty-two acres and have his land cut in half by a winding highway route. "I went to Austin for that big commission meeting in March of '86," Stolte recalls. "When I signed in, they asked me, 'Are you pro or con?' I said, 'Con, I'm against it.' They said, 'You can't testify.' I did get to see a highway department guy who told me, 'Don't worry, this is all preliminary.' But after lunch, after Henry Cisneros made his speech, Bob Lanier looked left, looked right, and they all said, 'Aye.' The state could condemn my land."

North of 16, other landowners are also up in arms. A retiree named James Bowman has been to see design engineer John Kight. Upon discovering a route drawn within a baseball throw of his front porch, Bowman traveled to the district office, where he yelled and poked a finger in Kight's chest. More important, however, is Myfe Moore, one of John White's three children. Be-

fore signing the deal giving the state a fifth large donation of right-of-way, John White had a fatal heart attack. After her father died, Myfe told the engineers that she had no intention of honoring his wish to grant the right-of-way; she would fight 211 tooth and nail. "Mr. Kight came to our office one day," she says, "and implied that we had better get along and work together with them on a route that was acceptable to everybody, or else they'd come in where they wanted to. He said, 'You really wouldn't want us coming right by your house, would you?' Last time I saw him, though, he was extremely polite. He said, 'Do you ever consider that you've got all that beautiful land, thirty-five hundred acres, to use whenever you want, while all those poor families in San Antonio can't come on it? You know, it's almost a kind of financial discrimination.'"

Highway 211 will have to make a neck-wrenching detour if it cannot cross the White Ranch. That's fine with Myfe Moore. In late June last year, she gathered neighbors opposed to 211 to her ranch house to discuss just such a prospect. Present were ranchers, a lawyer, an agriculture teacher, a retired air-traffic controller, and Bebe Fenstermaker. As a group, they control virtually every foot of possible frontage between 16 and the northernmost border of Maverick Ranch. Their objective has become not just sparing individual properties, but stopping the highway altogether.

Sandy Logan, a dark-haired cabinetmaker who lives on forty acres of a divided family estate, sums up their sentiments best. "The main issue here," he told the group at Myfe Moore's, "is not so much the bird habitat or the springs and the wells. My grandfather came over from Scotland and bought this piece of property. Three generations now have been raised on it. It's our way of life. It's the way we chose to live."

In the face of such opposition, the highway department is softening up—at least externally. Responding to growing dismay over 211, district engineer Richard Lockhart says that even though the department will not necessarily seek federal matching funds for its work on 211—a process that would require it to meet very specific environmental guidelines—it will compile all the qualifying impact statements and honor the federal statutes on the stretch affecting the Maverick Ranch.

Internally, however, the department has the same old attitude about the Fenstermakers. About a week after the meeting at Myfe Moore's, I spent a day with David Otwell, the San Antonio district's public affairs officer. Together, we drove all over the back roads of northwest Bexar County. As we stopped in front of the Maverick Ranch gate, he chuckled at the marker of an

organization called Defenders of Wildlife. "Is that all you have to do to be a wildlife refuge?" he asked. "Put up a sign?"

Nor was he terribly impressed, as we pulled away, with the ranch's listing on the National Register of Historic Places. "I mean, who grants it? Do they actually come out and inspect the place and see what you've got? Or do you just send in an application and get a coupon back in the mail?"

"They" are the federally funded National Trust for Historic Preservation, and the certification procedure is rigorous. In any case, because the department has not sought federal highway funds for 211, no law prevents the state from condemning such a place. Neither does pressure from other state agencies. San Antonian T. R. Fehrenbach, the chair of the Texas Historical Commission, signed a resolution in January, 1990, imploring the department to find a route around the Maverick Ranch. But the document has no binding authority.

As we drove, Otwell mentioned Ray Smith, whom he called "a self-styled preservationist." I didn't let on that I'd already interviewed him. A building contractor, Smith belongs to the avocational Southern Texas Archaeological Association; he monitors construction projects as a steward for the state archaeologist. On the seven-mile segment of 211 ending at 16, Smith told me he had found five archaeological features that the department's contractors had illegally blasted or bulldozed through. They were burned-rock middens— strategic watering sites where successive bands and tribes had camped and cooked for centuries. One site, Smith said, was strewn across two acres.

"Burnt rock!" Otwell said. He dug his elbow into my arm. "Do we really need to save every place where some Indian took a shit?"

A week later, I returned to San Antonio to see Richard Lockhart. Otwell sat in on our meeting. The mood was relaxed until the end, when I raised two sensitive questions about the department's conduct.

The first, I said, dealt with strategy. A source with detailed knowledge of the San Antonio district office had told me that it is a common negotiating ploy to draw a route straight toward the home of a landowner. "Don't like that route?" my source had said, explaining the procedure. "Then how about this one a little farther down?" Along the proposed extension of 211, the Fenstermakers, James Bowman, and Myfe Moore had complained of variations on that theme.

"No, sir," said Lockhart strongly. "That is not a tactic. I deny that."

It was clear that he wasn't going to give ground, so I moved on to the second question: environmental neglect. I handed Lockhart a copy of an

interoffice memorandum supplied by my source. Dated November 20, 1989, the memo from design engineer John Kight to Richard Lockhart described Kight's reaction to the barren scrape of land at the juncture of 211 and 16. Otwell hadn't seen the memo, but citing internal policy, he had denied my request for an interview with Kight, which turned out to be a smart move. If neither Otwell nor Lockhart was having second thoughts about 211, it seemed that Kight was.

Kight's memo read in part: "In defiance to the plans and specifications and with total contempt to our natural environmental heritage; we have raped, pillaged, and utterly destroyed a God given treasure of natural beauty in our trees and landscape. It is both disgusting and distressing to witness this type of contemptuous attitudes that we, as caretakers of the land, display towards our natural resources, our neighbors, the public trust and the irreplaceable beauty of age old trees."

Lockhart was silent as he read.

"Granted," I said, "he's talking just about trees. But if the crews are doing that to trees, what are they doing to water? What are they doing to archeological sites?"

"I feel," Lockhart said, "that this is an emotional reaction to one incident. It's not a wholesale condemnation of our procedures. The point of land he's talking about is very rugged terrain. If you know anything about live oak trees and rock, you know the root system is very shallow and fragile. Our plan called for selected undergrowth clearing. But because of the terrain, a hell of a lot of trees got knocked down. I discussed it with my construction engineer and resident engineer and said, 'Let's be damn careful this doesn't happen again.'

"I don't disagree, in general, that the department has been portrayed as having a black eye in terms of heavy-handedness and, in some areas, disregard for the environment. Some of those accusations have been unfounded. Some have been genuine attempts by those concerned with the environment to make the department more responsive. And there's a concerted effort to be more responsive. Not that we weren't before."

So where do things stand? At the south end of 211, the Texas Research Park is showing signs of real life. It has curbs, fire hydrants, wildflower landscaping, street signs for Lambda and Omicron Drives, and a single building: The UT Institute for Biotechnology. In 1991 the institute lured a world-renowned Taiwanese scientist, Wen-Hwa Lee, away from the University of California at San Diego. In laboratory experiments, Lee isolated a protein that suppresses

the growth of human cancer cells. Unfortunately, humans suffer severe allergic reactions to the protein. Lee was excited about coming to San Antonio because he'll work closely with the esteemed Daniel D. Von Hoff, of the Cancer Therapy and Research Center, which is associated with the UT Health Science Center. Von Hoff's field is cancer drugs. His team could help Lee's team find a way to make the protein safe for application.

The Cancer Therapy and Research Center will occupy the next building on the park site. The Institute for Drug Development will follow. McDermott's insurance company, USAA, has promised a $6.6 million research grant to IDD. The only strings, Von Hoff says, are that the institute must try to cut the average discovery-to-approval time of cancer drugs from fourteen to seven years—and also create local jobs. Somehow, finding cures for horrid diseases ought to be motivation enough, yet it's not. The driving force of the research park is economic development. The mantra of today's politicians is job creation.

But as long as cancer is the focus of the bioresearch, there won't be many jobs anytime soon. "There's not enough money in it," Von Hoff explains. "The big pharmaceutical companies put their chips on drugs that treat chronic conditions like ulcers or hypertension or depression. Cancer drugs make people well, or pretty soon they die. Either way, it's a short-term payback."

As for the Fenstermakers—well, they press on. The engineers could finish the first eighteen and a half miles of 211 by 1995. Then, perhaps, they'll build the next fourteen. The process creeps along with no indication that the highway department has decided to spare the Maverick Ranch or any other property. Still, the engineers say they're looking at several possible routes. The segment north of 16 might fall victim to the endangered species controversy that snags development throughout much of the Hill Country. Or it might keep right on coming.

Back on the ranch, Bebe seems to have kept up her level of energy. She continues to drive her pickup as aggressively as she organizes neighbors. Riding in the bed one afternoon last summer, Mary Fenstermaker and I bounced, hung on the sides, and ducked the slap and claw of limbs and foliage. Our jeans and the black-and-white face of Sue, their mongrel Border collie, were splotched yellow with pollen from a bumper crop of the wildflowers called Mexican hats. The dog entertained herself by leaping and snapping at the low-hanging branches. "Sue, quit," Mary said with a smile. "Sometimes she gets too firm a bite and flips herself right out of the truck."

Bebe's tour that day included a plunge through brush to the stony mouth

of Lost Dog Spring. "Last time I went down in there," Bebe said, squinting into the fissure, "some rattlesnakes sent me right back out." We walked through the stone ruins of holding pens and stood beside a deep, clear pool where the sisters used to swim and wade their horses.

Mary's limestone cottage sits on a nearby rise, near a stone barn with nooks for nesting chickens, a stone root cellar, a stone smokehouse, and a contoured fortress wall around the compound that today would stop a tank. This is her haven—where she makes her peace with the passing years. Among the songbirds, with the dog cooling her belly in the creek, the thought of dynamited hillsides and advancing earthmovers as big as houses seems more absurd than obscene.

"They're not going to do it," Mary says. "They just can't."

MARCH, 1992

LAST OF A BREED

In recent years I, like many people, have been intrigued by the notion of "political correctness." The premise is that a socio-political orthodoxy enforces its biases and constraints on all manner of activity and expression. In popular usage it has come to mean a fuzzy-headed liberal agenda—radical feminism, affirmative action, animal rights, secular humanism, and so on. But in Texas precisely the opposite is true. The politically correct in this state adhere just as insistently to a conservative agenda of tax cuts, school vouchers, family values, and so on. Our most popular politicians make long careers in government offering themselves to voters as rescuers from government.

That was never Bob Eckhardt's style, and long ago, his incorrectness caught up with him at the polls. He drank too much, he married and divorced three times, he was an unabashed liberal—all of that taboo for a contemporary Texas politician. Eckhardt believed in government, and loved the legislative craft of it. His forebears also fought in the battle of San Jacinto and helped build King Ranch. Eckhardt disarmed Texas adversaries with his heritage, his civility, and his humor, all of which made him wonderful material for a profile of a Texan with the lifelong courage to swim against the tides.

On the patio of a South Austin restaurant, a young waiter took one look at Bob Eckhardt as the eighty-year-old patriarch of Texas liberals shambled forth in grimy blue jeans, a red flannel shirt, hand-tooled Mexican sandals, and his signature fedora. Without a word of instruction, the waiter walked inside and returned to our table with a margarita on the rocks, which he placed at the hand of the former Houston congressman. "Would you like your menudo?" the young man asked with an air of habit befitting a grandson. Yes, Eckhardt indicated, and corn tortillas. He placed his hat on the table and

tasted his salted tequila and lime juice, which he seemed to find quite satisfactory. It was ten o'clock in the morning.

I had gone to see Eckhardt in need of contrast and with hope of illumina-
tion. Among lawmakers from Texas, he ranks in importance with Lyndon
Johnson, Sam Rayburn, Ralph Yarborough, Lloyd Bentsen, and Phil Gramm.
Yet a politician like Eckhardt could never get elected to high office today. Nor
could Sam Houston. Emphasis on "the character issue"—and the cynical
backbiting that it provokes—has just about chased the characters out of Texas
politics. Excess and eccentricity are out. Bland and boring are in. Messiness
of personal and property affairs will not be tolerated. Eckhardt uses tobacco,
he drinks too much, his three marriages have failed, he's a liberal, and he is
unabashed on all counts. In Texas his political incorrectness is off the chart.
During Eckhardt's time, polls on Capitol Hill consistently listed him as one
of the ten smartest members of Congress. He still has plenty of things to say,
but his counsel is unwanted, even by his beleaguered Texas Democratic Party.
There's an element of sadness in his life now, but also one of grandeur. He is
a lion in winter.

For twenty-two years, first in the Texas Legislature and then in Congress,
Eckhardt represented the blue-collar heart of Houston's industrial complex.
The Ronald Reagan tidal wave of 1980 slam-dunked Eckhardt and dissolved
his coalition, an experience that hurts and haunts him still—not so much because of the rejection and indignity (as a campaigner he was always a bit passive and aloof), but because he is a politician who loved the process of legislating. Defeat left him with a gift rendered useless, a trade he could no longer ply.

But life goes on, and Eckhardt is a man of sufficient wit that he can find
comedy even in the experience of a 1987 stroke that for a time robbed him of
his speech. Eloquence was as much a part of his persona as bow ties, wide-
brimmed hats, and rumpled white suits. Eckhardt established his political
domain on the wharves of the Houston Ship Channel and in the refinery
yards of Deer Park and Baytown, but it's fitting that he came back to Austin
for his years of twilight. He bought a small, two-story West Austin house
because of its sprawling back-yard live oak. With mismatched lumber and an
oblique eye for design, he built himself a tree house. He climbs up there of an
evening for his Scotch and cigar and the voices of children in the park across
the street. And the women. His gait falters and the rakish grin is missing a few
slats, but they still come around.

Like Nadine. Eckhardt's second ex-wife, Nadine looks in on him now and
then with the exasperation and fondness born of old battles, healed wounds,

and shared children. This morning she had joined us for breakfast. We had been talking about his years as a University of Texas politico during the thirties. His peers and rivals included John Connally, a Lyndon Johnson protégé who became Eckhardt's nemesis. Nadine, known for tartness of speech and sharpness of opinion even when she was the wife of a congressman, said, "The first time I ever saw John Connally was in Lyndon's office. He was up there lobbying for the 1955 natural gas bill. He was kind of handsome in a Dudley Doright way, but he was a slime ball. No kidding. He ran a lobbyist operation out of the office of the Democratic Policy Committee."

Somewhat more sympathetically than his ex-spouse, Eckhardt reflected on their late colleague: "Connally was poor. His father was a butcher."

Eckhardt's own roots go deep into Texas soil. His great-grandparents Rosa and Robert Justus Kleberg immigrated from Germany in 1834. Their ship broke up off Galveston Island; around a piano they dragged up on the beach, they danced a Viennese waltz. In 1836 Robert Kleberg fought with Sam Houston in the Battle of San Jacinto. His son and Eckhardt's great-uncle Robert Justus Kleberg was the Corpus Christi lawyer who honored the request of Captain Richard King's widow and gave up his practice to run and double the size of King Ranch.

The Eckhardt persona and pedigree startled East Coast liberals, and it disarmed Texas conservatives. This was the running dog and fellow traveler, the bane of oil and gas titans? He came on more like a character in a play by Tennessee Williams. Remembering those days, Eckhardt laughed and put the spoon to his menudo, thinking of a time when red-baiting United States Senator Joseph McCarthy was a role model of the Texas Legislature. Eckhardt was practicing law then, heaping scorn on the legislature's theatrics and wondering how a person of his views could get elected to any post in Texas. "I used to get the angriest calls, and my secretary would take them. She was about sixteen. She'd say, 'No, sir. He may be a sot and a shyster, but he's no communist.'"

Eckhardt had room in his beliefs and style for a comity that is all but extinct in the petty savagery of American politics today. He moved to Houston because he thought he might have a chance there, and the night in 1966 when he made his leap from the Texas Legislature to Congress, he and Nadine left his blue-collar celebration and drove to the Republican campaign headquarters in an adjoining district, where they crashed the victory party of another newly elected congressman, George Bush. The Bushes were delighted, couldn't believe it. That gesture led to one of the most unusual friendships of our time.

Former President Bush was taking a leave from the interview circuit, but when informed of this article, he promptly sent a dispatch to my fax machine: "When Texas A&M permitted partisan politicking for the first time, Bob and I were the first two to speak. We drove up together, and when I got out of the car, the Republicans looked at me as if I had sold out to the liberals. Bob received the same look of betrayal from his crowd. Barbara and I have had friendly relations with Bob Eckhardt, and though our paths have not crossed in some time, we continue to treasure it."

Eckhardt was born in 1913 in a Victorian house three blocks west of the University of Texas, where he resided for twenty-eight years, until the start of World War II. His father, a doctor, must have been a very patient man. Eckhardt rode his horse and roamed the campus neighborhood and fields beyond with a gang of pals that included John Henry Faulk, the late civil libertarian and comic who was blacklisted during the McCarthy frenzy. At an early age, in the doctor's parlor and in Driskill Hotel suites, Eckhardt was encouraged to sit among the elders as they discussed politics. Two favorite uncles, Rudolph Kleberg of DeWitt County and Harry Wurzbach of San Antonio, served in Congress in the first decades of the twentieth century. Sometimes they peered down through the whiskey fumes and cigar smoke and asked him his opinion. Eckhardt was always sketching, and he became one of Texas' best political cartoonists.

Fat cats were his specialty as a caricaturist, yet at a time when other Texans suffered through the Dust Bowl and the Depression, Eckhardt himself enjoyed a blithe youth of Austin privilege. "One time we found him passed out in a brand-new suit in the front yard of the Pi Phis," recalls his brother Joe, a psychiatrist. "Daddy was terribly upset." In Washington the New Deal was at its peak, and in Austin Jimmy Allred, the most liberal Texas governor of the century, set a tone that pervaded the university. Eckhardt managed to get himself elected editor of the *Ranger,* a magazine of student satire. When the legislature voiced concern about the Marxist agitation seven blocks north, Eckhardt published a bright cover bearing nothing but a hammer and sickle. "I wanted to get investigated so bad," he says.

During the war he taught the theory of flight to cadet pilots at an Army Air Corps base in Coleman, though he had never been higher off the ground than the back of a horse. He married his college sweetheart, Orissa Stevenson, the daughter of a wealthy Houston insurance executive. Back in Austin, they had two daughters, and he launched a law practice. Diffident during his campus heyday, the postwar legislature was dead serious about left-wing sedi-

tion. Eckhardt lobbied the sessions for the CIO (not yet merged with the AFL). Ronnie Dugger, then a reporter and later founding editor of the *Texas Observer,* first saw Eckhardt perform when he told an inflamed committee that banning the Communist party was a dangerous and un-American thing to do. Dugger, who published Eckhardt's cartoons in the *Observer* and became his best friend, encouraged him to run for office, but hardly anyone else did. Eckhardt was routed in his one hometown race for the legislature.

In 1950 Eckhardt moved his family to Houston and practiced labor law. He became a favorite of Frankie Randolph and her organization, the Harris County Democrats, and won a seat in the Texas House in 1958. As a freshman, he passed the Open Beaches Act, a law that kept developers from decimating the Gulf shore. He and most admirers still claim it is his most impressive piece of legislation. Ingeniously, Eckhardt argued that Spanish law and frontier use of the beaches as coastal roads constituted a presumption of public ownership of the beaches up to the vegetation line. El Paso attorney Malcolm McGregor, then a House colleague, says, "It's amazing that he preserved access to the beaches without having to resort to condemnation, which the state couldn't have possibly afforded."

Other House allies were Fort Worth's Don Kennard, Angleton's Neil Caldwell, Athens' Bill Kugle, and Port Arthur's Carl Parker. Eckhardt was already honing his style. "It was sort of overkill," Parker observes of Eckhardt's oratory. "Shakespeare and Voltaire were lost on the Texas Legislature." In those days legislators had no offices apart from their desks on the floor. Eckhardt crafted legislation behind a partition built out of whiskey boxes. One of his bills proposed to lower the taxes of ninety percent of the oil and gas producers, while increasing those of the remaining ten percent, which were the largest producers—resulting in a net revenue gain for the state. Though the graduated tax failed, it got enough votes to alarm the oil companies; a critical battle line was drawn. At night "the cell," as Parker termed their insurrectionist group, retired to Eckhardt's apartment for more drink and plotting.

The sessions contributed to the dissolution of his marriage. After his divorce from Orissa, in 1962 Eckhardt married Nadine; his third daughter was born two years later. Nadine had moved back to Austin with her three children following her divorce from Bill Brammer, who wrote a much-praised political novel, *The Gay Place,* while working with her on Lyndon Johnson's Senate staff. Everyone remarked on the debt of that book's fictional Texas governor to LBJ's outlandish character. Some readers also saw in its hero, a boozy, liberal state legislator, a resemblance to Eckhardt. "There's not much

of me in there," he demurs, "and I knew Brammer pretty well." But no one denies that Eckhardt surged as a politician with Nadine's hand in the small of his back.

He suffered a terrible jolt in 1965. Orissa committed suicide while one of their daughters was living with her. But 1966 saw Eckhardt elected to Congress, forming that strange bond with George Bush, and moving to Washington with four children to start a new life. He arrived one term too late to share the best of LBJ's presidency. The civil rights and Great Society legislation had already passed; now the dominant issue was Vietnam. Eckhardt was the first Texan in Congress to break with Johnson over the war. Later, he was one of the authors of the War Powers Act, which sought to re-involve Congress in its decisions to impose United States military force. With Johnson driven from office by the war and Ralph Yarborough ambushed by Lloyd Bentsen in a Senate primary two years later, Eckhardt was the preeminent Texas liberal throughout the seventies.

Along with the War Powers Act, his primary legacy in federal government is environmental protection. Among Texas politicians, on that issue he was twenty years ahead of his time. He helped create the structure and policy of regulations that are strongly enforced today. In 1974 he engineered final passage of the bill creating the Big Thicket National Preserve. He helped define the Occupational Safety and Health Administration's workplace safety standards, and with the aid of a young Tennessee congressman named Al Gore, he helped retain the Superfund program for toxic waste cleanups. In 1979 he called for compensation of Nevada cancer victims who were subjected to fallout from eighty-six atomic bomb tests. The federal government is just now owning up to what it did to those people.

In Washington he quickly became a favorite character. Who else wheeled through Georgetown traffic on a bicycle, wearing a white linen suit, a bow tie, and yellow socks? Teddy Kennedy and the *New York Times* loved him; *People* ran a feature about his sideline as a cartoonist. Nadine, for her part, soon discovered the patent impossibility of living with the man. She returned to Houston in 1979, hoping a commuter marriage might work. It didn't, and soon after their divorce, he married Celia Morris. Celia was an emerging feminist author (the subjects of her books range from Ann Richards to abolitionist Fanny Wright) and the ex-wife of Willie Morris. He was another *Texas Observer* alum, a friend of Bill Brammer's, the author of *North Toward Home* and other fine books, and the editor of *Harper's* in its sixties glory. It was all very inbred, if not incestuous. But they were the royalty of Texas liberals, and Eckhardt pedaled his bicycle at the head of the parade.

He would have hooted at any suggestion that he had lost touch with his Texas roots. But all along he sowed the seeds of his political demise. In league with Northerners, he crafted an amendment in 1975 that extended oil price controls to the end of the decade—saving consumers billions of dollars, he claimed, but costing the industry several hundred million. He danced back and forth on regulation of natural gas. Eckhardt always claimed that he was a friend of independent producers, but in the end they were all out to get him.

In 1980 Eckhardt raised about $350,000 to the $800,000 of Jack Fields, his handsome young Republican opponent, but money was not the problem. Eckhardt was essentially an old-style precinct campaigner, and the demographics of his district had changed. He didn't understand campaigns driven by TV and phone banks. Some friends said he spent too much time hobnobbing with the Georgetown elite when he should have been rubbing elbows in the rough bars and union halls along the Ship Channel. And the topside of the Democratic ticket was manned by President Jimmy Carter; Fields ran with Ronald Reagan. By five thousand votes, at sixty-seven, the liberal warhorse was put out to pasture.

As Eckhardt and I drove back to his house, the state capitol rose before us. I asked him what he thought of Ann Richards' performance as governor. "So-so," he replied. "Sooner or later, somebody in this state is going to have to own up to the fact that if the people want all these services from government— improve the schools, bring the crime rate down—there has to be a fair and reliable way of paying for it." He said he had last seen her at a wake for Athens' Bill Kugle. "I told her, 'Ann, you'll kiss me in a restaurant, but they won't let me in your office.'"

And President Clinton? "I'm concerned about him," he said. Bosnia had dominated the news that week. "There has to be a constitutional structure to decisions of war and peace. He's the least prepared of any recent president to conduct foreign policy. But instead of consulting Congress, he's allowing decisions to be made by some United Nations military commander."

After Eckhardt's defeat in 1980, he stayed on in Washington. He practiced some law and lobbied for a few interests on the Hill but no doubt found the latter demeaning. In 1987 he suffered the stroke that affected his speech, and then his marriage to Celia broke up. But he never lost the magnetism and humor. One friend, Joan Sanger, remembers him from those days. An Austin attorney and ethics advisor, she is the cousin of Democratic kingmaker Bob Strauss—another contemporary of Eckhardt's in his University of Texas days.

Friends kept telling her that she had to meet Eckhardt, so not long after his stroke and divorce she called him up when she was in Washington on business. He urged her to come right on over.

"His doctors told him he could have one drink a week," she says. "So he filled up an iced tea glass with Scotch. One look at the place and you could tell what his wives must have gone through. On another visit he put me up in the library, near the kitchen. Every night I could hear this scurrying. By the third night, there was a loaf of bread that a mouse had eaten a very large hole in. I said, 'Uh, Bob?' He said, 'That mouse isn't bothering me. Is it bothering you? You know, it's awful cold outside.' He used to take me bicycling. Not in some park. Right down the yellow stripe, six lanes, rush-hour traffic. A light turned red, and he just sailed right on through it. Another man on a bike yelled, 'Do you know that guy?' I said, 'Yeah.' He said, 'God must love him. I've been watching him do that for twenty years.'"

Eckhardt is close to his daughters—Orissa, Rosalind, and Sarah—but they all live far away from him. In 1989 he moved back to Austin and bought the little house in Clarksville. The back yard that we walked through was lived in, to say the least—tools, barbecue pit and accessories, a hammock, numerous bicycles, the dried flower stalk of a century plant. Though sturdy and wired for night use with Christmas lights, the live oak tree house was precariously served by a chair at the bottom, then you have to take a long step to secure a foothold in a tight nook of the branches, twist sideways, and pull yourself through. I suppose a man of Eckhardt's age and accomplishment is entitled to break his own leg.

The interior of his house was filled with scattered newspapers, Bibles, assorted hats, pots and spoons frozen in dry muck of forgotten meals, photographs of him with John Kennedy, Lyndon Johnson, Ralph Yarborough. I followed him upstairs to his office, where he gave me a copy of a polished essay he had written titled "War and Peace in the President's First Year." He showed me cartoons going back to the thirties *Ranger* and a caricature of Gerald Ford sketched on a *Congressional Record.* He told me about a book he has been writing about the role of his ancestors in the Texas Revolution. Behind his chair were cardboard boxes variously labeled "Antitrust Through Environment" and "Why Not Try the Constitution?" and, in an open closet, the famous white suit. It's a little yellowed at the elbows now and permanently rumpled because he washes it out in the bathtub by hand.

"Which marriage was the most fun?" I asked him.

He flinched slightly, then gave me a sideward glance. "They were all fun. While they lasted."

"Tell me about the stroke."

"Well, I had too much to drink that night," he said without hesitation. "I knew something was awry, but I didn't quite know what. I couldn't make the telephone work. I finally got through to someone, and they sent a young fireman out. We lurched and rambled for an hour. He couldn't tell if I was sick or just some old drunk."

He laughed and slapped his large hands on his thighs. "Afterward I couldn't talk, so I started drawing. It was the damndest thing. I found I could draw just as well with my left hand as my right! Unprecedented. Something was bothering me, and it wouldn't go away. So one day I was drawing, and the sketch became this man with a fierce beard and wild, glaring eyes. Knives and guns, bandoliers. I thought, 'Good Lord, who is that? Why, that's John Brown.' Then it came to me. Harpers Ferry!" He slapped his legs again. "Kennard has a house in Harpers Ferry. I was trying to get word to Don Kennard!"

He grew reflective. "And I must say, Celia was very good to me then. But we fell into a terrible dispute, and . . ." He gave me a helpless look, over the ages, man to man. "Well. You know."

Outside there was a sharp close crack of lightning, and we engaged in a scramble to shut down his computer (which he learned to use at age seventy-nine) and save his latest essay. Downstairs, I told him that when the weather improved, I'd come back, join him in the tree house, and absorb some of his knowledge of single malt Scotch. He grinned and propped his hand against the doorframe.

"In the morning?" he said.

MAY, 1994

PART II

TEXAS
IN THE RAW

The Battles and Joys of Nature

One of my first memories was watching a collie chase a coyote around and around a haystack in the barnyard of my grandparents' farm. The Sheltons had six children and a consequent throng of grandchildren. My grandmother kept a plate of her crisp baking powder biscuits on a counter for the kids running through the house. Order and authority were imposed by my grandfather's often-threatened but seldom-used razor strap that hung from a doorknob. Ignoring posted signs, my cousins and I roamed the surrounding fields and pastures for hours on end, blasting away with shotguns and .22s. I guess the neighbors were tolerant. Those holidays and summer vacations were my initiation into rural Texas and the countryside. I grew up a town kid, though, then made my move to cities. The military instilled in me a sharp dislike for sleeping on the ground. I was not a particular seeker of nature.

Then I won a writing fellowship that allowed me to live six months on J. Frank Dobie's treasured Hill Country retreat, Paisano. For years after that I couldn't get enough of living in the country. I dwelt alone in a Central Texas cabin that allowed the wind to blow whistling through the cracks. I chopped firewood for the meager warmth of a pot-bellied stove. And loved it. Then at thirty-seven, to the jarred surprise of one who had come to terms with being a bachelor, I married and started helping in the rearing of a young stepdaughter. I moved back to Austin and there have remained. In my work I found myself settling down as well. I wrote an essay about the pleasure and frustration of vegetable gardening. I wrote about coyotes, the ornery, serenading

canids that thrive in South and West Texas while wolves, their supposed bet-
ters in nature, have all but vanished in our wild. I explored the Red River, the
homely border stream whose freshets and quicksand terrified drovers and
horses and stalled the great cattle drives—and suddenly the river and story
swept me along in unexpected quest for the other side, an essence of Oklahoma. I canoed the crystal clear but aptly named Devils River, the last unpolluted stream in Texas, and walked away from it bone sore, skinned, and cowed
by the beating it gave me. There is always that duality in Texas nature. For
every enjoyment of a painted bunting or sky full of hawks, experience has
taught me to look out for a scorpion in the sink or a rattler in the garden.

Texas seems so vast, yet the countryside is terribly restricted. An unfortunate legacy of our brief history as a nation is the subsequent barn sales and
giveaways of public land that other states, as territories, turned over to the
federal government as their price of admission to the union. However well or
poorly managed, the federal public lands in the West are still public. Texans
can't just go off in the wild like people in California, Arizona, and Oregon
can. More than ninety percent of Texas is privately owned, which makes nature treks difficult for most people. The privilege and access I've been granted
as a writer have been my work's richest bonus.

THE MEANEST RIVER

Texas is one of the rare geographical entities with three border streams. Certainly the Rio Grande and perhaps the Sabine have more historic resonance to most Texans than the Red River. Yet the immigrants who would ultimately tear Texas loose from Mexico arrived by ferry across the Red River. I grew up in North Texas counties defined in part by their proximity to Oklahoma. The Red was my youth's border stream, and after my rich experience riding a mule along its headwater creeks in Palo Duro Canyon, I thought it was a natural progression to write about the river the Red became. It was a chance to write about cattle drives and quicksand and dam-building. But it had never occurred to me that the rule on territory imposed by the Red had created a long and wide swath where even today, cities hold no sway. The research for the story consumed several months, to the exasperation of my editors, and like the river it took an abrupt turn. The editors said my ending was almost a different story, they couldn't see the connection, and they declined to publish it. But to me that was like telling a joke without the punch line. After all, the significance of border streams is that their nature is shaped by one's perception of what is on the other side.

I've never heard of a swimming hole on Red River. No canoeists navigate its rapids, and no college revelers float by in cutoffs and inner tubes, towing coolers of beer. Through seasons wet and dry, with rare exceptions it runs the color of chocolate milk, and it smells bad. Unlike our sightlier streams, it never washes clean over beds of limestone, granite, or gravel. To love this body of water, you have to forgive its ugliness and work your way back from there.

Nevertheless, a richly layered mythology has grown up around this muddy and moody waterway that separates Texans from Oklahomans east of the Panhandle. Part of the romance of the great American West, the Red River has inspired cowboy ballads, scores of historical novels, and some choice

westerns. In Howard Hawks' 1948 classic, *Red River,* John Wayne drives nine thousand head of Texas cattle north toward the nearest railhead. He spurs his horse out into the shallows of this river of promise, of starting over. The big trail boss points at clear pools and warns the drovers of quicksand here, quicksand there. Earlier, Wayne had nodded in the general direction of the Rio Grande—a glance of six hundred miles—and declared that all the land between the two streams now belonged to him. "Someday that'll all be covered with good beef," he vowed. "Good beef for hungry people." At his signal, cattle crowd down the grassy slope and wade into the Red with scarcely a splash. They don't get their noses wet.

But the scene, which was filmed in Arizona, completely misses the power of its title stream. The Red was the bitch river—the moment of truth and the psychological point of departure. South of it, trail drivers endured the resentment of farmers who did not want a million hoof prints in their fields. North of it, they encountered bands of Comanches and Kiowas, who were openly hostile in the early years. Later, when theoretically pacified on the reservations, the Indians extorted beefs of tribute, which they called "wohaw." Trail bosses tried to give them cripples. And the river showed the cowboys what they were in for. If they caught the Red "on a rise," all the rivers north were apt to be "up and swimming," too. The Washita and the North Canadian ran just as fast, deadly, and cold.

The Red begins with intermittent creeks and flash-flood draws south of Tucumcari, New Mexico, but it becomes a flowing river in the Panhandle's geological showcase of soil erosion, Palo Duro Canyon. Between the 99th and 100th meridians, its forks and tributaries continue to cut through the buttes and mesas of a crumbling, calcareous clay formation called the Permian Redbeds. Farther east, Oklahoma creeks deepen the water's rusty shade with iron and other minerals washed down from the Wichita Mountains. From streams, gullies, and bar ditches above Lake Texoma, about 20 million tons of dirt erode toward Red River every year. Below the dam, loam banks slough off and hit the water with a startling sound effect: *Galoomp!* The loose banks stir more mud in the mixture all the way to Arkansas, where the river makes its big south bend, and on through Louisiana, where it broadens and eventually joins the Mississippi delta. The Red can't help its color.

In the North Texas counties where I grew up, soil conservationists and highway engineers have used junk cars to keep good dirt and bridges out of Red River. Against the caving banks, the Hudsons, Studebakers, and Olds 98s are planted side by side with the heavy engines down, windows broken

out, connected by strands of oilfield cable—a nostalgic kind of boondock pop art, I always thought.

The river's charm and value lies in the bottomland. Teenagers make sunning beaches of sand bars that can be as white and soft as any dunes on Padre Island. When I was in college, we sang, boozed, and kissed around blazing campfires on the Red. River bottom parties were high points of the year.

Other nights, we crossed the bridges and descended on latter-day juke joints that served up fried catfish, hush puppies, beer, mountain oysters, and yowling country-western, all under the same roof. A vestige of days when the majority of North Texans voted to keep their counties dry and sober, these service establishments are strung all along the southern Oklahoma border. Boundary streams are more than bodies of water; depending on the direction of travel, they stir feelings of safety and homecoming, peril and adventure. And in Oklahoma, that strangely foreign land, anything could happen. You might fall in love. You might get killed.

Between 1867 and 1895, nearly 10 million cattle and a million horses moved up the trails that crossed the Red. Unlike the movie cowboys, the men who drove the Longhorns north feared stampedes far less than they feared rivers. Stampedes frayed their nerves and kept them up all night; river crossings killed them.

The cowboys' tales are as hair-raising today as they were when told around the campfire. Drovers used drowned horses for pontoons to float wagons across. One cowboy risked his life to rescue a mule that desperately treaded water because a cracked willow limb had snagged hobbles tied around its neck. Another time, in a flooding Red, two drovers somehow unsaddled a panicked horse that refused to swim. Their motives were less humane. Tied to the saddle was a cowboy's watch and his three hundred dollar stash.

The Chisholm Trail, named after a half-breed Choctaw, Jesse Chisholm, crossed the Red near the mouth of Salt Creek, a tributary in Montague County. The crossing at Red River Station was marked by a store-saloon and a raft ferry. Due to the exigencies of grazing and market, the Longhorns usually came up the trail during the spring storm season. One cowboy described an 1871 flood that had thirty outfits and sixty thousand head backed up forty miles south of the Red. Another vividly remembered the Red's power: "We had some exciting times getting our herd across Red River, which was on a big rise, and nearly a mile wide, with all kinds of large trees floating down on big foam-capped waves that looked larger than a wagon sheet, but we had to

put our herd over to the other side. . . . Three herds crossed the river that day and one man was drowned, besides several cattle."

Even today the Chisholm Trail is at the heart of Red River folklore. To find the crossing, you take FM 103 north out of Nocona, wind off westward on Montague County roads (some unpaved), and finally ask a farmer, busy dosing his dirt with ammonia, if this is the right ploughed field. Next one over, he replies. Landscaped with yucca and wildflowers and protected by a chain-link fence, the state's monument to Red River Station explains that an abrupt bend in the river checked its flow and created the fording spot; at the peak of traffic on the Chisholm Trail, some days the cattle were so crowded that cowboys walked on their backs. A few yards away, almost hidden by brush, a bullet-dented metal sign denotes the Scenic Chisholm Trail Walking Tour. It slopes down about a hundred yards, but you wouldn't want to picnic on the bank. The shallows look creamy and stagnant. The air sings with mosquitoes and gnats.

Local people know a prettier spot not far downstream. As you come into its stretch of river bottom, the flatness negates any sense of decreased elevation. But all at once the pecans, sycamores, black walnuts, and cottonwoods shoot fifteen feet higher in the air. Sand bars on the Texas side offer a fine view of a sheer and pocketed sandstone cliff. A fallen concrete abutment lies in pieces in an adjoining pasture, and rusted steel cables hang in the water from the Oklahoma bluff: fishermen know the place as Burnt Out Bridge.

Spanish Fort, the nearest town, is about five miles downstream from Red River Station. On a punitive expedition against all Indians in 1789, Spanish soldiers attacked a large settlement of Comanches and Wichitas there and got themselves thrashed. The Spaniards said the Indians had constructed moats and swore the stockade flew a French flag. Today, fewer than a hundred people live in the historic town. The onetime grocery store and post office has a new name painted across the front: Spanish Fort Coon Hunters Association. Inside, an old-timer named Virgil Hutson lives with his wife Mary. He sells hunting clothes and dog collars and posts neighbors' bulletins on his wall. "Wanted," says one. "Broke mule—15 hands or taller." The Hutsons do some truck-farming. The fertility of the valley's alluvial soil enables Mary to brag on a seven-acre plot that yields twenty bushels of tomatoes a day. But the river also takes the bounty away. She tells me she's seen it twelve feet deep behind that white house at the end of the road. The actual bed, she goes on, is a mile and a half away.

The paved road runs out at Spanish Fort. On Texas highway maps the Red River's farm-to-market roads are often dead-end streets. The Mississippi's

southernmost major tributary, Red River flows twelve hundred miles from its headwaters on the dry plains of New Mexico to its mouth through reasonably populous country. But above Shreveport, Louisiana, no town or city is properly built upon it. *Not one.* The Red's uncontrollability has created one of the longest corridors of rural lifestyle to be found in this country. If rivers can be invested with human traits, this one chortles at our expense.

The land grabs associated with Red River were shameless from the start. When Thomas Jefferson purchased 800 million acres of wilderness from France for $15 million in 1803, Louisiana was very loosely defined. Because the French explorer Sieur de LaSalle had oversailed the mouth of the Mississippi 219 years earlier and camped for a few months on Galveston Island, Jefferson proposed a southern boundary of the Rio Grande. "Absurd reasoning!" replied a Spanish diplomat. Red River became the Americans' fall-back position.

The wrangling over the Louisiana Purchase continued until 1819, when John Quincy Adams, as Secretary of State in the administration of James Monroe, negotiated the treaty with Spain. When a river becomes an international boundary, ordinarily the territorial claims meet at the midpoint of the stream. Ensuring the Americans' navigation and water rights, this treaty defined the boundary as the Red's *south bank.* In turn, the treaty had to be honored, if renegotiated, by revolutionary Mexico, and then by the Republic of Texas.

The first Anglo-Americans were fugitives from justice; in 1811 about a dozen outlaws pitched camp in the woods near an ancient buffalo crossing of the Red. The name "Pecan Point" referred to both sides of the river, but along with Jonesborough, a ferry crossing and village just upstream, it was the first permanent Anglo settlement in Texas—and the busy crossings of the Red River foretold the end of Hispanic dominion. The migratory trail channeled Sam Houston and Davy Crockett, with other pioneer Texans, to that narrow stretch of river valley. On the Oklahoma side, the United States government settled Indians whom it had forced off their homelands. Land north of the Red River was ceded to the Choctaws. A village called Shawneetown existed for a time. The Trail of Tears led to the Red's north bank.

When Davy Crockett crossed the river two months before his death at the Alamo, he wrote home: "I expect to settle on Bodarka Choctaw Bayou of Red River that I have no doubt is the richest country in the world, good land and plenty of timber and the best springs and good mill streams, good range, clear water . . . game a plenty . . . I am rejoiced at my fate."

Crockett saw the virgin valley. Spotted with meadow prairies and cut with tributary brooks, the forest of red cedar and bald cypress teemed with buffalo, black bear, whooping cranes, ivory-billed woodpeckers, green and yellow Carolina parakeets. But the river itself raised a major objection to Crockett's vision of Eden. For 165 miles in northern Louisiana, the Red was a growing logjam called the Great Raft. Though the river opened up in pools, the islands of dead trees created thirty-foot dams of such compaction that shrubs and grass took root above the water line. Geologists have advanced a theory that the backwash from a huge Mississippi River flood about A.D. 1200 may have first jammed the logs on Red River. Whatever its origins, the Great Raft grew about one mile a year. The spring floods brought durable cypress and cedar trees that accumulated faster at one end than they rotted at the other, and the obstructed river spread laterally into lakes and bayous. The creator of Caddo Lake was probably the Great Raft—not the earthquake of popular legend. The Great Raft not only closed the Red to steamship navigation; it disqualified adjoining terrain from cotton plantation or much permanent settlement. But United States Army engineers said nothing could be done.

To the rescue steamed Henry Shreve in 1833. Piloting steam-ships called the *Heliopilis,* the *Archimedes,* and the *Eradicator,* Captain Shreve essentially used them as battering rams. Hindered by sick crews, mosquitoes, and unreliable federal funding, he would back off and whack forward again, jars of their neck vertebrae notwithstanding. It took him five years to clear the Great Raft; today the city of Shreveport proudly bears his name. Swamps drained, restoring the prairies. But even south of Shreveport, the Red was never navigable more than half the year. Upstream, one prospective navigator counted twenty-one hundred snags and fifty-four drift piles in a 222-mile stretch. Shreve died in 1851. The reassembled raft closed the river that year for thirteen miles. It took Alfred Nobel's invention of nitroglycerine, which facilitated underwater demolition, to free the natural flow.

Civilizing the upper Red posed an entirely different set of problems. The government could only theorize about its source, for the river cut through plains controlled by hostile Indians. In 1852 an Army captain named Randolph Marcy set out to find the Red's headwaters. In the granite Wichita Mountains, fifty miles north of Red River, Wichitas told Marcy that all tribes feared the ride that he proposed. Westward, the Red was a stream of foul-tasting water that could not be healthily swallowed. Marcy calculated that the surface gypsum belt that dosed area rivers with purgative salts was 50 to 100 miles wide and 350 miles long. Along with the water, the soldiers and animals suffered 104-degree heat and horseflies that Marcy claimed were as big as

hummingbirds. During that summer, the column was reported massacred by Comanches. The War Department passed on this report to Marcy's family, who donned clothes of mourning. A minister preached his funeral sermon.

Not yet informed of their demise, the explorers ventured up the Red's North Fork. Marcy wrote that Comanches and Kiowas favored that stream, which crosses southwest Oklahoma and heads in the eastern Texas Panhandle, because of its rich prairies and abundant cottonwoods. When snow buried the grass, the Indians fed the trees' sweet bark to their horses. But Marcy correctly read the North Fork as a tributary. Returning to the parent stream, the column resumed its westward march along the Prairie Dog Town Fork. Four months after receiving his orders, Marcy found headwater springs, if not the true source. For the first time, the water was clear and sweet. Above the cottonwoods were magnificent multi-colored cliffs.

Unknown to Americans of Marcy's time, Palo Duro Canyon drove the captain to the far reaches of his prose style: "Occasionally might be seen a good representation of the towering walls of a castle of the feudal ages. . . . Then, again, our fancy pictured a colossal specimen of sculpture, representing the human figure, with all the features of the face distinctly defined. This, standing upon its lofty pedestal, overlooks the valley, as if it had been designed and executed by the Almighty Artist as the presiding genius of these dismal solitudes."

Texans were not immune to Red River greed. Contradicting Marcy's definition of the headwater stream, in 1860 the state legislature claimed the North Fork as the boundary. Once the Civil War re-established federal authority, the United States sued Texas for seizing a large chunk of southwestern Oklahoma. Reminding all parties of the 1819 treaty and Marcy's authoritative pronouncement, in 1876 the Supreme Court defined the Texas-Oklahoma political boundary as the south banks of Red River and its southern, Prairie Dog Town Fork. But private property lines were a different matter, and the river never ceased revising its banks. The legal matter came to a head with the discovery of the Burkburnett oil field. Every inch of the river bottom was suddenly desired for its mineral rights.

In a Supreme Court case of 1923, Oklahoma sued Texas over bottomland in Wichita County. The federal government, which owned the median riverbed in trust for Indian tribes, joined the Oklahoma side of the fray. Texas won that bout. Relying on scientists and surveyors who had tromped up and down the bottom, the court decision swung on the ways the river changes its course: If the river moves its banks by gradual and natural means of erosion or accretion—silting—all parties have to live with the consequences. But if

the cause is avulsion—man-made interference or calamities such as a one-hundred-year flood—Oklahomans can legally redefine the south bank. The Court accepted the scientists' suggestion of the boundary as the south *cut bank:* "the more or less pronounced bank or declivity which borders the sand bank of the river and more or less limits the growth of vegetation toward the river."

More or less. If only John Quincy Adams had known, while he was negotiating with Spain, that Texas would someday be part of the Union, oh, the headaches that could have been spared.

Claude Zachry's picture window and patio overlook the bluffs of Red River in Clay County. From his back-yard Bermuda grass, the red clay drops off two hundred feet. Though the Burkburnett oilfield is just twenty miles upstream, I saw none of the nodding, horsehead pump jacks that enable other cattlemen to hedge against the price of beef. Zachry's land value is bolstered by orchards of pecan trees that are evenly spaced in fields of maroon dirt, which he keeps planted in wheat and rye. Because of the frequency of floods, Zachry doesn't try to grow that grain to harvest; fat Herefords eat the green shoots. About a mile away, the sand flats and cocoa-colored river make a hairpin curve back toward the house and then disappear in the trees, seeking the mouth of the Little Wichita. Morning sun was burning through the night's rain clouds.

Tall and long-legged, Claude Zachry has lived on this ranch since 1929. I kept thinking of the old-timers in Larry McMurtry's early novels.

"When the river floods, how fast does it rise?" I asked him.

"Depends on how much water there is down below," he said. "If they've had rain downstream, that holds the head rise up. But it's not always gradual. Flood of '35, I saw horses and cattle and logs all come down together. Parts of houses with chickens still sitting on the roof." He rose from his easy chair and stared at the bottom. "I drowned a horse in that flood. I was trying to get to some stranded cows and didn't know how bad it was. I swam him back toward the bluff, and he climbed up in tree branches and hung on. But it was too much for him. He just gave out and died."

Ranching the bottomland is not the same as running a place up on the plains. On grassland wooded with mesquite, cattlemen thank their stars for knee-high clumps of little bluestem. Down among the pecans, big bluestem and Indian grass rustle chest-high in the breeze. But while plains ranchers can leave tractors in a partially plowed hayfield, every night Zachary moves his machinery to high ground, for fear of losing it. Because the last big flood

in 1983 deposited so much sand, he needs a four-wheel-drive pickup in the bottom pastures.

In recent years, Zachry and other Texas ranchers on Red River have been sued for prime land by Oklahoma neighbors. "Now I know there's nice folks in Oklahoma," he told me. "But it's different over there. When people first settled this country, nobody but outlaws would live across the river because there were so many Indians and so few sheriffs. People say, 'Well, all those bad sorts have been killed off.' I say, 'Yeah, but now you got the ones that killed them.'"

The latest Red River land dispute began in 1975 when a crewcut Oklahoma rancher named Buck James sued Texans in Clay County for nine hundred acres. Represented by a former Oklahoma attorney general, Charles Nesbitt, James claimed neighbors in Texas had squatted on his family's bottomland since 1930. A federal district judge in Oklahoma awarded the acreage to James in 1981. Contradicting testimony in the Burkburnett oilfield case, the judge ruled that a 1908 flood met the legal definitions of natural calamity, and that construction of the Highway 79 bridge between Wichita Falls and Waurika had unnaturally changed the river's course. So avulsion, not accretion or erosion, had repositioned the south cut bank.

This stretch of river recently has tended to shift its streambed northward, which accrues acreage for the Texans. But since the 1981 ruling, Texas landowners as far downriver as Denison have been sued for bottom pastures and even sand bars, which are quarried for gravel. Complaining that the burden of proof lies with them, the Texans are bitter. They say they're at the mercy of contingency lawyers who solicit clients along the river and file suit in Oklahoma for a percentage of whatever they can get. In Austin, those suits have raised concern over local taxing authority and enforcement of Texas hunting and fishing laws. The federal Bureau of Land Management has been trying to mediate an agreement among Texas, Oklahoma, and the Indian tribes. But as long as ambiguities like avulsion and accretion determine case law, a permanent political boundary will not halt the contention over private property lines.

Riding away from the house in his pickup, Zachry told me he didn't count on much help from politicians, since he used to be one. He was a Clay County commissioner for many years. "When I first ran for office," he said, "I called on an old man who was supposed to be crazy. He asked me, 'Are you a pretty good sort of fellow?' I said, 'Sir, I like to think I am.' He said, 'Then I can't support you. I don't want to be the one to ruin you.' Many's the time I've thought of that old man."

He descended a steep graded road and cut through the ploughed fields of his pecan orchard. As we left the pickup, he glanced at my feet to see if I was properly shod. The grass was wet, and snakes were out. "This place can really grow the cottonwoods," I enthused.

Zachry followed my upward gaze with less rapture. "Yeah. If there was any market for 'em, we'd sure be set."

The red ground underfoot was broken up in triangles and trapezoids of half-inch crust. Short grass grew beyond the point where it looked solid. Along the bank, the cracks in the soil were wider, predicting the next collapse. Served by crude gullies and festooned with dead or dying shrubs and grass, the wet sand bars and silent river offered a sullen contrast to all this luxuriant green.

"You are standing," said Zachry, "on Red River's south cut bank."

"It just breaks off in the river, doesn't it?"

"Farmers lost half-acres of cotton, in the old days."

Quicksand, which pervades the Red's legends, is created by upward-flowing ground water that holds soil particles in suspension. But if you look for the cinematic gloop that has the consistency of Malt-O-Meal and slowly sucks you under, you won't find it. In dry seasons, the bed is laced with wind-arranged sand and alkaline grit. Near the dividing and intertwining streams, which may run no more than shin-deep, the ground looks damp but easily supports the weight of a horse. The mud makes squelching sounds under its hooves. The horse takes another step on ground that looks identical—and the bottom falls out. Plunging and pitching, it strikes for anything solid. If it topples and rolls, a rider can be crushed and buried.

"Some horses have a light step, and a sense of just where they can go," said Zachry. "We called them river horses, and needed them, because we were always digging out bogged cows. For some reason, the river's not as *quickie* now as it used to be. Cows wouldn't sink out of sight, but the stuff flowed in and set like concrete. If they got eighteen inches of a leg caught, it would hold them till they died."

He moved the truck and showed me a spot with a higher cut bank. Pointing at willows and salt cedar, he said the changing river had given that acreage to Oklahoma. "It used to be yours?" I asked.

"Oh, yeah. I've ridden those woods a thousand times."

He stared at the sand bars and reminisced. "In fact, when I was a young man we used to cross it here every Saturday night. The closest dances were over in Ryan. When the moon's up on it, I never have seen it when it didn't look half a mile wide."

The prettiest stretch of river valley lies due north of Dallas. Here the longest of the Oklahoma tributaries, the Washita, angles down through the eastern Cross Timbers. Fringing the rich tall-grass prairie, the narrow strip of oak and elm forest attracted settlers because it supplied fuel and lumber. Preston Road in Dallas was once the Butterfield stagecoach line to Oklahoma Territory. But the Red's history is least recognizable along this stretch of river. If downstream towns and thousands of acres of farmland were ever to be spared its floods, a dam had to stop the Washita, too. Planning of the dam at Denison, ten miles below the Washita's mouth, officially began in Congress in 1929.

Since Lake Texoma would back far up the tributary and remove 200,000 acres from cultivation and property tax rolls, an Oklahoma governor named "Alfalfa Bill" Murray called it "the biggest folly ever proposed." During the dam's construction, Oklahoma twice sought work-stop injunctions from the United States Supreme Court. But no Oklahoma politician wielded as much power in Washington as Sam Rayburn, the Texas congressman from downstream Bonham. Because it was a domestic priority of the Speaker of the House, the Red River dam was completed in 1944—one of the only public works projects allowed to continue during World War II.

With 585 miles of shoreline, Lake Texoma is now the country's tenth-largest reservoir. The four-state apportionment of water rights irrigates some farms, and two generators in the dam provide backup electricity for towns and rural cooperatives in Texas and Oklahoma. But the lake's primary purpose is flood control. When a flood crests near Wichita Falls, it takes about three days to reach the Denison dam. Gauges up and down the river beam signals to satellites, which relay them to computers of the United States Army Corps of Engineers in Tulsa. That data governs the release of water through the dam. A June flood in 1957 cleared the dam by three feet and made a beautiful and frightening waterfall of the spillway—the only time the system failed. Ordinarily, the deepness of the lake turns the river's homely brown water a pretty jade green.

More than eight million tourists visit Lake Texoma every year. Convenient to Dallas-Fort Worth and Oklahoma City, docks of yachts and sailboats and hillsides of condominiums have begun to appear. Urbanity encroaches, but the submerged cut bank and foibles won't go away. Anglers can fish with special Texoma permits or take their chances with different game wardens and laws on either side of an imaginary Texas-Oklahoma boundary in the middle of the lake. Authorities briefly tried to mark the state line with a thirty-mile string of bobbing floats, but they proved impractical and were soon removed.

Below the even grass lawn of the earthwork dam, the Red reemerges from twenty-foot tubes. Frothing and slowing the water is a grid of concrete bulwarks patterned like a waffle iron. A reinforced building at the foot of the dam contains the generators. Inside this structure I met Guy Beasley, chief engineer at Lake Texoma. A rawboned man of ruddy complexion, he said he had been a small-college football coach, a petroleum engineer, a civil engineer, and a missile engineer; he applied for this job so he could move back home to Madill, an attractively wooded little town north of Texoma. Since the computers in Tulsa effectively engineer the dam, most of Beasley's work concerns management of the parks and campsites.

Coming into the building, I had passed a photo lineup of military men who have ranked in Denison Dam's chain of command. "So where's the Army?" I asked him. "Do you ever see uniforms?"

"Hardly a one," he said. "The Corps of Engineers is mostly civil service."

The outdoorsman's workplace was a small windowless office with dim, unnatural light. Glad to take me for a drive, Beasley directed me to an elevator. We came out in a humming, ground-floor room that houses the generators; they looked like children's tops turned upside down. He pointed at the concrete floor between them. "Since Texas and Oklahoma share the electricity, we figure that the state line goes right through there."

Along the dam, we poked through a field of little bluestem. A small bridge over a gully marked an old driveway. Veiled by the prairie grass were the straight lines of razed buildings.

"This was a German prisoner-of-war camp," he said, stopping the car. "There were two more over in Oklahoma, at Powell and Tishomingo. They were Panzer troops who had been captured in North Africa, and they finished the work on Lake Texoma. It was the biggest clear-cutting project in the history of the United States. They didn't have chain-saws then, so it had to be hard labor, but we never heard of anybody trying to escape. When I was a boy, a forty-five piece orchestra of Germans played a concert at my grade school. They had one guard who wore a sidearm. They must have played Wagner or something like that. Prettiest music I'd ever heard."

Twenty miles downstream, near Bonham, a bored kid passed the time peeling out on the Highway 78 bridge. Driving a mud-splattered pickup, he raced to the end of the rusting steel bridge, turned around, and peeled out again. The truck had Oklahoma tags. On a gray Friday in early spring, I had set out for a long drive in the country—a nature trek. An old friend named Roy rode along. We crossed into Oklahoma wherever we could, but pavement over

there was scarce along the river, all the land was ploughed, and the farm houses looked like John Steinbeck's hard travelers had just gone down the road, feeling bad.

Back on the Texas side, we passed through lush meadows and hardwood forest. Though we seldom saw the river, we sensed its nearness in long spaces that opened up in the horizon of blue-green foliage. This country has long had a reputation for hideouts of criminals on the lam. But the Texas villages— Ivanhoe, Tulip, Telephone, Monkstown, Direct, Chocota—have an appearance of rustic contentment and prosperity. "Since 1883," boasted the sign of a small Baptist church. "Until Christ comes again."

On the shoulder of Highway 271, which connects Paris with Hugo, Oklahoma, we hammed and photographed each other beside the upright granite map of Texas that marks the state line. The boundary markers are strapping and friendly things; you want to stand up against the Sabine and throw an arm around the Panhandle. Across the bridge, we circled past a drive-in with a tersely worded sign—Bob's Beer—and left the car on the lot of a large dance hall. Red River Junction was painted across its front. The river here was a quarter mile wide. It rose against the bridge abutments and swelled around them with a sound of rapids you wouldn't want to swim. Brush and brown foam gyrated in whirlpools. Roy looked back at the empty dance hall and laughed, imagining its conversations. "Let's get drunk and go fall in the river," he said.

An hour later, we arrived in Idabel, Oklahoma. Over 350 years, the nexus of settlement has gradually shifted twenty miles away from the banks of Red River. On Idabel's west end, black people pitched grain to chickens in barren back yards. Downtown looked like a neutron bomb had gone off. Nobody walked the sidewalks. Few cars were parked along the curbs. The squat rows of stores seemed to have gone up in a single burst of optimism. Since then, shopkeepers had painted and repainted their sections of identical storefront: gray, olive, white, maroon, with yellow undercoats and bare red brick showing through—fresh starts that hadn't panned out. The backs of the buildings bled with rain-washed stain. "I feel like I'm in Yugoslavia," I told Roy.

On a side street, he considered a long, narrow, unmarked building; a small solitary window was filled with crumpled tinfoil and blue neon letters—Coors. "That's it," he announced. "That's the one."

He was referring to the essence of southern Oklahoma.

"Uh . . ." I said.

He looked at me and grinned. "Are you telling me you won't go in there?"

"I'd have to drive around the block and think about it."

Inside, we found a proprietor named Rosie. She weighed about 180 pounds.

She had a black, beehive hairdo and an ornate rose tattooed on her chest. On her forearm was a cruder piece of work—Mean Bitch. She was friendly, but her eyes were circumspect. Why would total strangers show up in her joint? She suspected, I later learned, that we were cops.

"We're making a movie," Roy explained.

"Well, give us another hour," she said. "Come five o'clock, this place'll be roaring. Let the people get off work. You'll see." A phone rang behind the bar. Rosie answered and said, "You girls hurry. I got two movie producers sitting at the bar."

Our beers were served by a taciturn blonde in her twenties. The establishment offered nothing but beer, cans or throwaway bottles, one dollar. Not even a sack of potato chips. When the blonde collected empty bottles, she raised them high over her head and smashed them in a fifty-gallon steel drum that sat beside the cash register. The next five hours of my life were punctuated by the sound of breaking glass. It grows on you, after a while.

The jukebox was programmed with rock and roll, not country-western, and Rosie kept it turned up loud. She stood beside a small pool table and reflected, "This thing's more trouble than it's worth. Men get to shooting pool, and all they want to do is fight. I won't stand for it. I get right out in the middle of 'em. See if they want to fight me. Now, women"—she shrugged—"I just let them go. House rules. An Indian girl got into it with the one we call Slab Jaw the other night. They fought all over the place."

Just before five, a woman dressed in blue jeans and a T-shirt came in pumping her arms and belting out a Tina Turner song. "*What's love got to do with it?*" She took the stool beside me, and we struck up a pleasant conversation. Her voice was low and raspy. "Are you really making a movie?" she said.

"Absolutely not. That guy is a college professor, and I'm a reporter for a magazine in Texas." I swiveled on my stool, inspecting the place. "We're just looking for the story."

"Oh, Lord," she said, resting her forehead in her hand. "Well. Can newsmen shoot pool?"

Not as well as she could, it turned out. Besides, by the time we played our tie-breaker, several of Rosie's male customers were looking me over, desiring the table, sizing up my stroke. The woman and I shook hands, liking each other, and I eased out of the pool tournament.

By then Roy shared a table with the two young women that Rosie had summoned on the phone. "Aw," said Jan, the dark-haired one, when I introduced myself.

"Yeah, right. We've got the same first name."

She may have thought of herself as Indian, Hispanic, or both—in the Oklahoma melting pot, she may not have thought about it much at all. She had a faint harelip scar, but her eyes melted men like butter. "You feel like dancing?" she said.

"Sure." We shuffled around on the dusty concrete, dodging rearward pokes of pool cues and inward swings of the door. She wore a white, long-sleeved shirt and blue jeans tucked in fringed moccasin boots. "I like your shoes," I offered.

She cut her eyes with droll suspicion. "You making fun of me?"

"No!" I said.

Afterward, I sat with my back to the door. Every time it opened, Jan tensed and jumped forward in her chair. "I sure wish you wouldn't do that," I said nervously, scooting my chair around. The door swung open again, and through it walked an older woman with jeans and a denim jacket. She had a prominent underbite and a nasty shiner.

"Hey, Slab Jaw," Jan's friend taunted. "What happened to your face?"

The woman leaned across the table. "I got this over a man," she said, "and that motherfucker *loves* me."

She climbed on a stool and ordered a beer. I connected the name with Rosie's story about the bar fight, but did not fully piece the tale together until Jan rose with an air of unfinished business, walked around the pool table, and knocked Slab Jaw off the stool with a resounding left hook. There were no slaps, no squeals, no pulls of hair. Jan threw punches like a boxer, straight from the legs and shoulders, and with Slab Jaw down beside a booth, the punishment continued. Nobody in the bar said a word. An old man in the booth watched them for a moment, then dignified his gaze and raised his beer can to his mouth. The loser suffered it with quiet, stoic, tragic patience. I looked at Roy; his eyes had lost their mirth. Finally Jan came back to our table. The older woman crawled to her feet and wobbled to the same bar stool. With a shaking hand, she reached for her half-empty bottle.

Jan looked like her heart was about to explode out of her shirt. She gasped, "Will you buy me a beer?" I looked at Rosie and raised two fingers. I could use one myself.

"Well, it happened," I tried to make conversation, after a time. "Don't let it ruin your whole day."

She looked at me like I was crazy. "Ruin my day?" she said. "It's the best thing that happened all week."

Jan's friend walked over. "Slab Jaw said to ask you," she drawled. "She just wants to know what that was all about."

Down the bar, three hours later, Roy was deep in thought and conversation with Rosie. Our sojourn had taken him far beyond a nameless joint in Oklahoma. He was back in off-limits bars at the edge of Saigon—places where Southern rednecks, ghetto blacks, and Viet Cong called it off and for a few hours drank together, accepting each other for what they were. "Roy, we need to get out of here," I kept telling him. I couldn't move without bumping a shoulder; the jukebox screeched; the barmaid's glass breakage was continuous. And the 250-pounder with a pool cue in his hands looked like he was one scratch of an eight-ball away from sending somebody to the hospital.

With a gimme cap perched askew on his head, he was drunk, fat, young, and unhappy. A nervous Hispanic laborer jerked his shots and tried to keep a table of distance between himself and the burly challenger, who stood by the bar, glowered, and rocked slightly, using his pool cue for support. A smaller man in a plaid jacket watched his big friend with worry. Jan occupied the adjacent barstool and murmured to herself. Her head dipped with weariness, she would reach for her beer and miss, but then she'd smile and perk back up.

Watching her, I happened to see the big pool player rock too far back on his heels. Nobody touched him, but with loops of his arms he fell against the barrel of broken glass and hit the floor with a loud crash. The Hispanic jumped far away in fright and gripped his cue like a baseball bat. Other men ran into each other trying to escape. The fallen player's bearded friend leaped off his stool with wild eyes and a right fist raised and cocked to clobber . . . well, whom, and for what?

"Put your hand down!" Jan ordered him. Then, gently and reasonably, "Just put your hand down. Go on. Put it down." He looked at his fist like he'd never seen it before, then slowly flexed his fingers. The crowd heaved a collective sigh. The crisis dissolved.

Though it was no comfort to Slab Jaw, violence had freed the woman in Jan. Since then, she had been the belle of our frontier ball—a pretty girl who kept her dance card filled. She made old men feel young again. She had us all thinking: She's everybody's baby but mine. Jan climbed on the stool next to me. At the end of the bar, a tall, gray-haired man in farmer's overalls watched her with an even and unamused stare. She caught his look and turned her back on him, frowning. "God, I wish he'd leave me alone," she said.

"Who is that?" I asked.

"My daddy."

We went out back for a breath of fresh air. It had rained that week, and the alley was filled with dark auburn puddles. Red River mud. I was nearly twice her age, and married. I was in danger, I sensed, of violating a dictum that had

served me well in my long bachelorhood: Never see the day of knowing that you've become an old fool. "Have you ever gone anywhere?" I asked Jan. "Traveled?"

She stiffened and shrugged defensively. "I been to Texas."

"You need to go somewhere."

At that moment, the big gray-haired farmer walked out the back door and took long strides across the mud puddles. He paused on the heel of one brogan and offered his opinion of me without turning his head.

"Best get home. Girl."

In the movie, John Wayne is nursing a love wound when he first crosses Red River into Texas. A flaming arrow sails over his head and ignites the wagon sheet of his prairie schooner; a bare-chested Indian leaps headlong out of the darkness, brandishing a knife. With an imagery of baptism, the big guy drowns him in the river. I did not feel like John Wayne, Sam Houston, or Davy Crockett that night in Idabel, though for many months I had tried to chart their crossings. Roy muttered resentfully but soon slept when I told him I was going to leave him unless he came on now. I had rounded a bend in my own life and henceforth would choose to swim in more predictable shallows. I was ready to put youth's Red River behind me. The boyish associations make me feel more provincial than I am. It's no River Jordan, and even with the moon shining on the sand bars, it's not half as pretty as the Seine. It's just a muddy border stream. But coming southward, I always breathe easier when I hear the clicks under my tires of the narrow two-lane bridge. I know I'm back where I belong.

JULY, 1988

THE COW'S IN THE CORN

My dad was born in a Lampasas County ranch house, and my mother grew up on tenant cotton farms in Clay County. But the cowboys and farmers in my families were all in the generations before me. Dad made his living as an oil refinery worker, and I was a city boy, born and raised. Like many young writers, I started out on a tear about the ugliness of my home country. But in my thirties I developed a taste for living on a pretty place in the country, and for several years I couldn't get enough of it. My new and chosen homeland was Central Texas. My estrangement from the land and waters of Texas dissolved in those years. Nature and the outdoors became my favorite writing pursuit. I've always considered myself a journalist, not an essayist, and I'm in no way proud enough of my wit to advertise myself as a humorist. But life throws some funny and frustrating things your way, wherever you happen to land.

Several years ago I received a literary fellowship that included six months' residence on J. Frank Dobie's old Paisano ranch west of Austin. I used the time to make some badly needed course adjustments. I started a book, disciplined my work habits, and regained control of some depletive vices. In the afternoons I ran two miles through the woods to the mailbox, then I snorkeled and fished the emerald pools of Barton Creek. I borrowed some binoculars, bought a copy of Peterson's *Field Guide to the Birds of Texas,* dutifully recorded my sightings of loggerhead shrikes and rufous-sided towhees. In a hammock on the old man's front porch, I even read a bit of J. Frank Dobie. All this was undertaken with a certain droll skepticism, a sense of temporary aberration. I was living out one of the fantasies of my generation, but my lease on Walden Pond expired August 1. After that, I would get back to the land of highline wires, neon signs, and freeway traffic jams.

Out behind the house was a neglected garden plot that a previous fellow had impressively fenced, at great cost in labor, to keep the deer out. I admired his prose (somewhat more than Dobie's), and since the idea of gardening

seemed philosophically consistent with my turning over of new leaves, I purchased my first gardening magazine and rented my first Roto-tiller. On the back cover of that periodical was a photograph that still amuses me: Standing between rows of blooming rose plants, a ravishing, braless gardener in tank top and fatigue pants smiled down over the handles of her newest purchase, a two-horsepower Ariens tiller. A more truthful ad would have shown her arms raked bloody by the rose thorns, her dungarees in shreds. Soon I would be bucked and yanked by my tiller, numb to the shoulders, coughing muddy phlegm. For the first time I could appreciate the toil of my grandfather, who until he was nearly sixty plowed behind the backsides of draft horses and mules. Turning the soil, working it deep, is the most important thing a gardener does, and there's no joy in it.

Friends who recall that first garden assure me it was a scene of great beauty and culinary bounty. I recollect the bone-headed style of my endeavor. My instincts were organic, of course, as are all gardeners'. Unfortunately, I failed to discern that if a century's overgrazing hadn't robbed the ranch of most of its topsoil, all those picturesque brows of limestone wouldn't have been peeking up through the pastures. The floor of a nearby pen was deep with manure patties from a neighbor's cattle that occasionally eased through disrepaired fences to munch Paisano's longer grass. I broke wheelbarrow loads of these chips in organic sacrament and spaded them into my garden. And at last I planted.

All the transplants withered. Only the zucchini seeds came up. The forces of Whole Earth hadn't told me that it takes roughly fifty pounds of dry manure to produce one pound of soil nutrient. And while the use of chemical fertilizers poses negligible health hazard for humans, it's a stopgap measure at best; the artificial nutrients decompose quickly and do nothing for the permanent condition of the soil. But circumstances demanded the fast fix, so I made the next typical mistake. When considering fertilizer, one tends to assume that more is better. Most chemical fertilizers come in fifty-pound sacks, and the instructions on the sack seldom state clearly enough that a hundred-square-foot garden requires two pounds of these chemicals at most. They never say, "Warning: This May Be a Lifetime Supply." Fried by the overdose, my next installment of nursery transplants gasped and disintegrated into leafy outlines of dry white dust.

Luckily, I had gotten off to an early start, and it rained a lot that spring. I made a garden, but only the zucchini truly thrived. Two fifty-foot rows of it. How was I supposed to know? My previous exposure to summer squash had been limited to a passing interest in the supermarket produce bins and an

occasional pot of ham-bone stew. I couldn't begin to keep up with the garden's mass production. On the first day of their existence, the finger-size squash were good to eat. On the second, they grew tough and reached the size of large cucumbers. By the third, they were monsters. Toward the end, I came to cheer the invasion of gray squash bugs that stung the beast plants into inactivity. In thick gloves and long-sleeved shirt—the unpleasantness of squash harvest is surpassed only by that of the prickly and caustic okra—I plunged into this jungle, and with grunts of exertion, heaved the rampant zucchini over my colleague's deer fence. Some had the heft and balance, if not the length, of a thirty-six-ounce Louisville Slugger.

I don't believe in green thumbs: Show me the dirt under the fingernails. A garden of any size requires long hours of stoop labor, and while I still had a lot to learn, I discovered that on a given day—calm down, son, your check's in the mail—I could be a demon with a long-handled hoe. The immediate reward of that hard and sweaty work was an odd meditative trance. The avocation guaranteed an element of calm and order in a sometimes chaotic routine. My office calendar might reflect harried scribblings of airline reservations, rescheduled interviews, emergency dental appointments, but there in the margin, in a much steadier hand, was the garden reminder. During that week in February, I should plant the beets, the cabbage, the English peas.

As it happened, my experiment in rural lifestyle was no passing fancy. I later found my own country place—a cedar log house on a hill overlooking a long valley that my neighbors, German farmers, called Rogues Hollow. Their tractors growled long into the night; in late June the slopes turned bright sorrel with their contoured fields of ripe maize. Black gumbo soil compacted with golf-ball-size rocks—there was no question of that soil's fertility, though I shudder thinking of the broken backs of those who had to plow it with mules.

I laid out my garden a few strides from my screened-in porch. One evening at twilight I heard the strangest flapping whisper overhead. En route to summer residence at the Great Salt Lake, interlocking Vs of migrating white pelicans, more than a mile's worth of them, looped in ponderous and stately procession toward the government watershed lake at the base of the valley. Another afternoon, while I was out for my daily jog, a rare black fox ran across the road in front of me. I raced in joy back to the house, where the radio informed me that the latest maniac had just fired a bullet at the president. I saw my first eagle in flight while I hoed weeds in that garden. It was a lovely, secluded, impoverished time in my life.

The worst money crunch always came in the summer, when I ceased teaching part-time at the nearby state college. There were periods when the garden had to feed me; weeks passed without an ounce of hamburger in the refrigerator. But I knew better than to run those economics through the calculator. Even though I wrote the labor off, if I had added together the water bill, the costs of fencing supplies and the latest necessary tool, and the expense of succumbing to the impulses that always seize me in a nursery greenhouse, frugality would have had me standing in the supermarket checkout line instead of in my garden plot. The quality of the temporary vegetarianism was my reason for gardening.

As long as the vegetables taste right, home gardeners don't particularly care what they look like. If the potato has a dark spot, that can usually be corrected with a paring knife. Wholesale buyers of produce know they won't get that break from consumers. Commercial growers thus rely on hybrid strains that attain, then hold their picture-perfect color and shape through the rigors of transcontinental shipping. So we buy gorgeous table grapes that won't spurt juice even if stepped on, tasteless tomatoes of papery texture offered with the euphemistic "Firm—for Slicing," and the creepiest of the showcase ruses, those cucumbers and rutabagas that come rubbed in wax. I'd just as soon handle the toe of a pickled cadaver. Through most of the year, with certain vegetables, I can make the earth do better than that.

Even at the height of such scorn, home gardeners rely on the knowledge and resources of commercial agriculture. Our own empirical data do not tell us to plant our autumn Swiss chard as early as twelve to sixteen weeks before the first frost. When I moved to Rogues Hollow, one of the first calls I made was to the county's agricultural extension agent. (Of the calls received in these offices—a service of Texas A&M University—eighty percent come from home gardeners; in most of the large urban counties, the staff includes a full-time horticulturist.) The agent said that on the average I could anticipate first and last frosts on November 10 and March 15, leaving a 240-day growing season. That's the luxury of gardening in Texas. With enough sun and very little extra effort, it's possible to grow and harvest three overlapping but distinct gardens in a single year.

But the Sunbelt exacts its own hungry price. Because most of the frosts are light, the ground seldom freezes, and more insects and larvae survive the winter. With the prolonged food supply, insect populations increase geometrically. We not only have more insects than the Frostbelt, we have more *generations* of insects. The spring broccoli in my garden at Rogues Hollow was a very pleasant surprise. I didn't think the nursery transplants would like the

coarse and poorly drained soil or be able to withstand the heat so long. I
steamed the young heads, buttered them, substituted the tender leaves in recipes that called for greens or cabbage. Then one morning I walked out and
found the leaves of every plant riddled with holes the size of buckshot. I never
would have dreamed that growing vegetables would challenge my sense of
social conscience. I was face to face with yet another loss of youth's ideals. If
I let that go on one more night, my broccoli plants would be reduced to gnawed
green stumps.

Organic gardeners contend that even EPA-approved garden poisons can
threaten the health of humans. More likely, they just make the gardener's situation worse. Insects combat chemical warfare by inbreeding resistance to the
poisons, and genetic superpests can result. In the garden, insects tend to attack weak and struggling plants. By using proven organic methods to enrich
the soil and strengthen root systems, the gardener enables his flourishing
plants to shrug off insects. The Organics observe that one Baltimore oriole
consumes seventeen caterpillars a minute; over a three-month period, one
toad devours ten thousand insects. Cardboard toilet-paper spools worked
into the soil around tomato plants hold cutworms at bay. Bothersome slugs
crawl happily into a pan of beer and promptly drown. And in dire emergen-
cies, there are natural, biodegradable alternatives to the industry that gave us
DDT: soapsuds, nicotine sulfate, the dust of a poisonous daisy called pyre-
thrum, and the newest panacea, trichogramma wasps, whose larvae devour
the eggs of insect pests in stupendous quantities.

On the other hand, I tend to seek practical advice from the state Agricultural Extension Service of Texas A&M. While concurring that healthy plants
are the most resistant to insects, the Aggies go their own way, dusting plants
with Sevin, the carbaryl that succeeded DDT: Those other folks can feed the
little buggers if they want. In the best example of this ideological tension,
Aggie horticulturists are particularly fond of debunking the Organics' rever-
ence for marigolds. While the pungent yellow flowers are alleged to repel
Mexican bean beetles and some varieties of tiny, root-stinging nematodes,
they also serve as host plants for Texas' most destructive garden pest, the
spider mite. Close relatives of the blood-sucking chigger, spider mites extract
their dietary juices from the plant tissues of tomatoes, beans, cucumbers, and
eggplants, among others. "Picture yourself with fifty thousand chigger bites,"
one extension agent told me. "You get the general idea."

But the Organics claim the moral imperative, and they never let up. The
prophets of Whole Earth are like the old Barry Goldwater campaign slogan:
In your heart, you know they're right. Still, something in the manner of these

latter-day saints always puts me off. All gardeners are know-it-alls, but the other side of that nature is amiable and inquisitive. Conventional gardeners think they can learn something from their neighbor's triumphs and catastrophes. They've heard of the Tigris and the Euphrates. They know they didn't invent the process. As for my own straying from the fold at Rogues Hollow, I claim the defense of relativity. Though I was delighted to learn I had left that slumlord, the squalid cockroach, behind in urban haunts, the sheer numbers of critters out there in the natural world staggered me.

The same spring that I saw the pelicans, the black fox, and the eagle, I also had to give up walking the woods because of the swarming ticks. I killed three rattlesnakes within a horseshoe toss of my front porch. I left the door open for my pets, and one night while I was gone a skunk ambled into the kitchen. My dog held her nose, bared her teeth, and did her duty. Sometimes a scorpion would lose its footing on the ceiling, and a little *plop* of terror would land on the quilt Granny Shelton had fashioned from my baby shirts. I drenched every crack and cornice of my abode with Diazinon. If that cost my garden a few pollinating honeybees, they should have stayed outside where they belonged. In that frame of mind, counterattacking the cabbage loopers on my broccoli leaves with five percent Sevin dust seemed no great shakes. I had developed a case of the gardener's peculiar and incessant paranoia: The entire chain of being was out to rob the fruits of my honest labor. Bugs were one thing, but my worst garden enemy was the ubiquitous Black Cow.

If you can't eat cattle or sell them, they're nothing but trouble. Breeders of Angus cattle dismiss the following as contemptible slander, but I have it on the authority of my own observation, verified by my North Texas brother-in-law. "Oh yeah," he told me, "black cows are death on gardens. They're known for that." The cattle and I lived in grudging partnership on those acres of sticky gumbo. The landlady lived in the city, I paid monthly rent, and a rancher leased the grazing rights. My contact point with the forces of animal husbandry was Ronina, the rancher's niece. I knew right away that I wanted to get along with Ronina; she had a loaded .22 pistol in her hip pocket. But I had increasing difficulty admiring the attributes of her minions. One hot summer day I was fishing in the stock tank. A cow came to the bank, waded far out to cool off, drank long and deep, threw back her horns, and with a moo of great satisfaction splashed urine into her own water supply.

Without question, I sowed the seeds of destruction in my garden by planting corn. No matter how good it looks in the supermarket, corn is truly fresh only if you break it off the stalk and carry it straight to the boiling water; the

kernels' chemical conversion of sugar to starch is almost immediate. But for most gardeners, corn consumes more space than its production is worth, and no matter how much mineral oil or Tabasco sauce I pour on the silks, in the end I always peel off the shucks to find the foul mush of a well-fed earworm. And cattle will walk through fire to get at corn. They turned my first two garden fences—tight barbed wire, corner posts set in concrete—inside out. I trained my dog to chase off any large animal that set hoof on our hill. That worked with the deer but not the cows. I fired my .410 into the air to scare them away. I lofted a few arcs of that buckshot, which, I hope, stung their withers. They stared dully and chewed their cuds, waiting.

One morning I awoke to find a Hereford calf gamboling in my garden, enjoying my offering of corn. The calf reacted to my bellow with the surprise and injury of a reprimanded child, then cleared the fence with a nimble kick of its heels. I could no more have exacted vengeance from that creature than I could have fried the backstrap of Bambi. But the black ones were devious, calculating, vile. At night when I drove up to the house, a very hoarse collie greeted me with great anxiety; I saw the evil shadow slip around the corner of the screened-in porch with a supremely contemptuous flip of the tail.

I thought I had solved the problem when I installed a single-strand electric fence. Once they get the juice, cows usually stampede forward, breaking the circuit and tearing down the fence. But the simple design and repair allow for that contingency, and few cows come back for a second helping. Now I faced only the menace of the cottontail rabbits that were in love with my English peas. That's easy, a friend suggested. Just lay out a stripe of bone meal all the way around the garden. "What do you mean, they won't cross bone meal," I scoffed. "They forget how to hop?" It worked because of the smell; this I established when my cat, one of the least olfactory of creatures, jumped back from the powder as if she had just taken a draft of ammonia. At last I could sit back and watch my garden grow.

But the rancher kept changing the herd on me. Every other week three more cows had to test the fence. If I happened to be gone at the time, that would just be too bad. Out dove hunting one afternoon, I walked up the slope and saw that particular black cow, my nemesis. Ignored by the dog, whose spirit on this issue was just about broken, the cow and her calf grazed the garden boundary of Johnson grass. With a clumsy—or deft—move of her hip, the cow bumped her own offspring into the wire. The calf thrashed wildly, bawled to blue heaven—and removed the only obstacle to those knee-high stalks of sweet corn. You take the volts, kid.

On the worst morning of my gardening experience, I fumbled at the latch

of my gate. I had a roiling stomach, bleary eyes, a bad head full of urban debauchery. As I drove up to the house, a red-tailed hawk passed before me with a soothing, reassuring cruise. But the scene in front of the house took my breath away. The fence was down, of course. The cow had razed the corn and finished off the English peas, but apparently nothing else had suited her appetite. So she had stripped my broccoli and tomato and bell pepper plants, stepped on them, broken them, splashed them with excrement. The current ascendant star in my fall garden was butternut squash. Though vines of winter squash cover a lot of ground, the infant fruit of the yellow-meated butternut surpasses any of the spring varieties in boiled flavor; then it matures into the light-bulb-shaped gourd, good for baking, that keeps through the winter. The cow had sampled each of these, then spat out the broken gourds. She had pulled down the tops of the okra plants and splintered the stalks. My garden was gone. Wiped out without a trace.

A few hundred yards down the fence line, the cattle milled about on the site of the weak and shallow waterline connection—which their weight broke with great regularity, running up my bill and testing my skill as a plumber, always in freezing weather, but that's another story. Out of ammunition, having used my last shotgun shell a few evenings before in a stirring twilight bout with a rattlesnake, I kicked the cat away from my ankles and yanked open the door of the tool shed. With the collie bounding at my side—this was great fun—I stalked down the slope with a ten-pound sledgehammer and murder in my soul. There's a line in a novel that I admire, *All the King's Men,* by Robert Penn Warren: "We were something slow happening inside the cold brain of a cow." But the black cow was smart enough to recognize a madman when she saw one coming. She left her calf to its fate without a glance. I had them trapped in a corner of the fence. As I worked through the crossbreeds and the Herefords, the black cow made a low, uneasy sound and cut her eyes in both directions. The drama of a bullfight, played out in reverse. Gripping the handle of the sledge, I cried out and made my move, but she looked one way and juked the other; the mighty swing and miss carried me headlong into the barbed-wire fence.

The time comes when pastoral idyll gives way to considerations of schools, commuting distance, career ambition. Last year I married, moved back into the city, and assumed I had left vegetable gardening behind, if for no other reason, because the property on Possum Trot—always that overweening rusticity of Texas subdivisions—was too heavily wooded. Sunlight is the one deficiency that gardeners can't overcome. But that spring when the weather

turned warm, my wife was out raking leaves and planting bulbs, and I found myself uprooting the grass and spading the soil of the one five-foot triangle, at the corner of the driveway and the curb, where I might have a chance.

I didn't want much. Three or four tomato plants, some basil and dill. Even at that, the odds were long. Tomatoes require at least sixty percent of the day's direct sunshine, and the shade of the tall cedar reached the tiny garden shortly after noon. My neighbor, whose ornamental shrubs and flowers are for me a source of great wonder and mystery, came across the street with a little sack of five-ten-ten tomato food that had gone to waste after her unsuccessful attempt. She came back in June when I was picking my tomatoes ripe off the vine. "Nobody in this neighborhood's *ever* been able to grow tomatoes," she smiled and cheered.

Nice of her to say it, but she's wrong. There's a great backyard garden over on Twelfth Street and another one on Norwalk—my favorite: It's laid out with a fine ironic view of the Safeway store. That yard even has a grape arbor and a purple martin house. One day I saw the woman who lives on Norwalk pushing her husband's wheelchair down the side street so he could see the garden. I know those people. They hark back to days when the most desirable property came equipped with a root cellar and a canning porch. They're contemporaries of my grandfather, Dad Shelton, who retired off the farm and lived out his last years tending a huge garden in Henrietta.

That old man was reason enough for me to take up gardening; for the first time since I was a kid, I had something to talk to him about. One day I gazed out his living room window at about half an acre of collard greens. There wasn't a weed anywhere. I asked him how he managed that without using mulch. "Why, I never let anything go to seed!" he proudly said.

He raised that garden the way his immediate forebears farmed the American West—long, straight rows; the more space, the better. Hours of labor were no object. And if you overproduced, you shared with the neighbors, then you canned those collards. They're still good! The urban gardener seeks new alternatives. The Organics promote a component of the French intensive method called double digging. Working the soil two feet down enables root systems to go deep instead of spreading out, which means more plants can be squeezed in. With this method, they contend, a three-foot-square garden is big enough to harvest a variety of desired vegetables. I've got more space than that, but this spring I think I'll try it. I understand now that I need to garden. It's the gentlest, most intelligent thing I know how to do with my hands.

In January I was under pressure to tear down those ragged old vines that had survived the heat of August and set quite a few blooms in the fall. The

tomatoes ripened too slowly because the sun had moved to the south and left the plants in almost total shade. Yet the mildness of the winter had been ridiculous, and with each predicted light frost I brought the ripest tomatoes in to finish on the window shelf and covered the rest with tarps and plastic. "They're mealy," said my wife. "I don't think it's worth it." This from a woman who once sent off for boxes of ladybugs and praying mantises, who walked into a feed store in Pasadena and asked the whittlers where they kept the borage, who insisted on space in my cramped garden for her stand of zinnias. Oh, well. I'm sure I can learn from her.

"Yuk," exclaimed my stepdaughter at the supper table. "These tomatoes are terrible. They *look* terrible." I suffered these indignities in genial silence. The kid was right. Because I had never gotten the hang of watering a garden, my tomatoes suffered from blossom-end rot. I was a lazy gardener last year. I can do much better; in my dream garden I already have.

In that ideal world, the sun, plants, and bugs behave the way the Organics say they should. The shade of a tree reaches one corner of my garden early in the afternoon. These cooler beds contain my De Cicco broccoli and a handsome shrub of French tarragon (available only as transplants; seed catalogs often push the fraudulent Russian variety, as flavorless as vodka). Aphids in search of my romaine lettuce—which best resists the Southern sun's urge to rush it to seed—recoil from the interspersed chives. Beyond the shade, my red onions reinforce this line of defense. Closely planted nearby are two more stars of my palate, speckled lima beans and Red Lasoda potatoes. These natural companions discourage each other's most pernicious enemies—Mexican bean beetles and Colorado potato beetles.

Alongside, a bed of eggplants invites the potato beetles to dine here and leave the less hardy vines alone. The "trap crop" is more expendable because of kitchen limitations; a little eggplant parmigiana goes a long way. But with their velvety leaves and drooping lavender flowers that produce the sensuous blue-black fruit, eggplants are the ornamental prima donna of my garden. A neutral barrier, they also stand here to appease the caged Burpee Pickler cucumbers planted with companion dill and more bushes of speckled limas. Vegetables, like humans, are terrific snobs. Cukes like beans but associate their fears of disease—phytophthora, or late blight—with the dastardly potato.

As for the surplus of speckled limas, there's no such thing. Though hard to shell, baby limas are simply the tastiest bean in cultivation. I won't bother to pick more green than I have time to shell. Left on the vine, they harden and

deepen in glossy brown color till the sun-bleached pods crack open. Soaked overnight, then cooked with a little bacon and tarragon, these speckled limas taste even better than the fresh variety. Hands down, they're the best dried beans for the winter cabinet.

On opposite ends of the cantaloupe beds are my green bell peppers and Long Red cayennes (whose taste and reliability I find superior to the region's more chauvinistic jalapeño). In the fullest sun, beyond the pepper and melon beds, is the hallowed shrine of my symbiotic masterpiece. While the parsley attracts the pollinator honeybees, the sweet basil repels mosquitoes and flies, and both herbs impart vigor to my tomatoes and asparagus. Solanine in the tomato's leaves and stems repels asparagus beetles. According to the Organics, asparagus protects tomato roots from nematodes. But flavor, not these minor conquests of nature, is the primary reason people garden. Our taste buds make basil the tomato's perfect herb companion. Substitute basil for lettuce in a sandwich with mayonnaise, crisp bacon, and sliced tomatoes; you'll never go back to the standard BLT.

For that pleasure I must await the ripening of my caged Better Boy and Bigset tomatoes, but meanwhile the first shoots of asparagus have stemmed up through the mulch. The existence of this bed implies ownership of the ground I have tilled. Asparagus was introduced to the country by the Puritans, for whom it was the perfect crop, and a well-maintained bed of it can produce for up to fifty years. Unfortunately, the maintenance starts with the digging of a trench a foot and a half deep and never gets much easier than that. And even if you start with year-old transplants, establishment of the perennial fern requires a wait of two years before the first harvest. As a renter with an unpuritan approach to manual labor and a reformed chain smoker's need of oral gratification, I never thought I'd be in one place long enough to justify the wear and tear on my spading fork. But finally the time has come. This gardener has paid his dues. I caress and pluck the first tender spear. Oh, go ahead. It's been two long years. I bite the raw asparagus just below the lovely tip. Ah!

MAY, 1983

BRING 'EM BACK ALIVE

*My first exposure to Calvin Bentsen and his friends took place at a
bizarre, wacky, good-hearted dinner party. The rich Texans were wholly
at ease in a mansion decorated with hides, heads, and ivory of leopards,
lions, elephants. Initially I placed them in a novel by Hemingway. But as
I came to know them better, I saw that they were carrying on a rich Texas
tradition. After the Indian wars were over, Texas cattlemen grew restive
in their daily pursuits and succumbed to nostalgia; they befriended and
championed former foes like the Comanche chief Quanah Parker. In 1903
Theodore Roosevelt came down and joined them all in a big wolf hunt—
their greyhounds probably chased coyotes—on a prairie just across the
Red River called Big Pasture. The president had a great time dueling a
rattlesnake with his quirt, riding with them in a wild gallop down
the main street of a little Oklahoma town. They were genuine
conservationists of the land and its wildlife. Henry David Thoreau
reflected poetically on the wonder of Walden Pond, but as an aggressive
political movement, conservation owes a great deal more to Roosevelt and
his rowdy crowd.*

*Unlike other members of the Bentsen clan—notably Lloyd, Texas'
longtime United States senator and, at the end of his career, a United
States treasury secretary—Calvin had remained in the Rio Grande
Valley. He was a banker, not a cattleman. His ranch was primarily a
personal refuge and place to hunt. In its dust and scents he could call
back to his mind his great safaris in Kenya. His homes were filled with
enough hides and fur to warm a tribe of Eskimos, but with his
conservationist friends he had taken on the considerable chore of rescuing
black rhinos from poachers' relentless hunt for their horn, in their native
range. Their hopes to breed the rhinos in Texas would not meet with
immediate success. The animals fell victim to strange fevers and suffered
the cold of our northers. But the sight of the animals in a pipe corral in*

his ranch filled Calvin with a deep and sad nostalgia. His world view was as dated as the fiction of Hemingway, who, of course, was his favorite writer. The days of the grand hunts were gone. But with enough money and grit, these rich Texans believed they could accomplish anything. They thought they could save a 60-million-year-old beast from extinction.

Camouflaged by the spotty shade and dusty chaparral, the black rhino lies with her massive jaw against the ground, flicking her fringed ears at the nagging flies in her one-acre pen in the Rio Grande Valley. Suddenly she hears or smells something she doesn't like. She comes to her feet in stages, using her front knees for support. She stands there droop-bellied, about as tall and broad as a Santa Gertrudis bull.

Her skin is a gray, wrinkled, baggy fit, and her short legs are as sturdy and big around as fire hydrants. The fearsome part of her anatomy begins with a neck of astounding bulk and muscularity, yet the lines that flow into the two horns on her nose have an alluring symmetry and grace. Set below the shorter horn, her dark, piggish eyes are enclosed by puffy and deeply wrinkled bags of skin. She strains with obvious difficulty to see, then snorts and bursts forward with tremendous speed and agility. Sapling mesquites crack and flatten beneath the force of her charge. She gallops with a smooth roll of her shoulders and carries the business end of her nose low to the ground.

Near downtown McAllen, remote-control gates swung open to admit the cars of guests arriving at a dinner party that Calvin and Marge Bentsen were giving to celebrate the arrival of rhinos in Texas. During the three months the rhinos had been in the state, they had sent tremors through the rarefied worlds of big-game hunters and wildlife conservationists, creating a near-scandal that had rocked bureaucracies all the way to Washington. But this was a party, and on this particular night the rhinos were the symbolic guests of honor.

Within the compound, which covered a city block, the vehicles followed a circular drive past palms and willows toward a sprawling, one-story Spanish Colonial mansion. Around the side of the mansion, smoke billowed from a large barbecue pit. It was a warm May night, and the party's host, Calvin Bentsen, had sweated the back out of his long-sleeved khaki shirt from his belt to his epaulets. Though several young Hispanic men in white servant's tunics moved around inside the mansion, taking shawls and carrying trays of

drinks, Calvin trusted the cooking of the fajitas to no one but himself. Squinting through the smoke at the brisket strips, he raised and poked them gingerly with a long-handled fork.

A tall, handsome, freckled man with sandy hair and an endearing gap between his front teeth, Calvin was a McAllen banker and a relative of United States Senator Lloyd Bentsen, and he had recently committed himself to breeding rhinos. Under the auspices of Game Conservation International (Game Coin), a small group of hunters and conservationists had managed to cut through scads of red tape and transport five endangered black rhinos halfway around the world. Calvin's guests had all participated in the half-million-dollar project, but Calvin was the member who had volunteered for the headache and responsibility of keeping the rhinos on his La Coma ranch.

The guest list included Martin Anderson, an urbane Honolulu and San Francisco lawyer who owned a 1.5-million-acre ranch in Kenya, and Alejandro Garza Laguera, the scion of a wealthy industrialist clan in Monterrey, Mexico. The party was dominated, however, by Texas oilmen and ranchers dressed in safari attire. They had flown to the Valley, many in their own private jets, to toast their newfound success and celebrity as conservationists, but as the organization's name implied, their first interest was game, not wildlife. Game Coin treasurer Ed Wroe, a squat, gravel-voiced Austin banker, had told me, "You'll notice most of these people are hard of hearing in one ear. Which ear depends on whether they shoot right- or left-handed. All that heavy artillery takes its toll."

Calvin's wife greeted the guests at a set of front doors that were half as wide as most living rooms. Marge Bentsen was pretty and petite; her blond coiffure added three or four inches to her height. She wore an off-white, high-waisted, floor-length dress with puffed sleeves.

A long central hall, paved with Saltillo tile, led toward distant wings of bedrooms. The sitting room that faced the foyer had a plush sofa, Victorian chairs, and a glass-walled view of landscaped grounds. There were ebony sculptures and paintings with African themes, but my primary impression on entering the house was that I had never seen so many dead animals in all my life. Horns, antlers, tusks, hides—all were artfully blended into the mansion's decor. Marge delivered us to the young man who was to take our drink orders, then she returned to the dining room and resumed wrapping silverware in white linen napkins, which she then slipped into ivory napkin rings and inserted in the slots of a white ceramic rhinoceros. The centerpiece of the forthcoming buffet was a hollowed-out watermelon that some enterprising

soul, with the help of a couple of strategically placed green bananas, had turned into yet another likeness of a rhino.

In a kitchen anteroom at the end of the hall, where the barman was mixing frozen margaritas, one of the guests spoke deferentially to Harry Tennison, the president and board chairman of Game Coin. From time to time Harry turned away from the bar and raised a finger to his right ear, as if he was having trouble hearing. In his mid-sixties, Harry was the kind of happy old-timer that we all aspire to be. A retired Coca-Cola magnate living in Fort Worth, he had passed wealth on to his children and grandchildren and had freed himself to do anything he wanted. With ruddy, lightly veined cheeks and eyes that positively jitterbugged, he wore a loose-pocketed safari jacket and a string tie over his khaki shirt. The tie's draw piece was a miniature head of a big-horn sheep, cast in gold.

When the barman behind him hit the switch of an electric blender, Harry abruptly danced on his toes and jerked a minute hearing aid from his left ear. "Godamighty!" he cried in response to the blender's shrill whine. "You think that doesn't ring my chime?"

What Harry wanted to do most these days was to hunt birds and fish for salmon, but in his day as a big-game hunter, he had contributed trophies to the walls of Indian maharajas and African heads of state. He dropped names such as "my good friend Prince Philip." On a recent tour of England, his Game Coin colleagues had mentioned the desirability of having an audience with the queen. Their British host doubted that that was quite possible, but Prince Philip showed up shortly afterward, shaking hands and saying howdy.

Harry prided himself on his ability to get things done, and from the start he had looked upon the black rhino project as his private dream and mission. He foresaw the day when perhaps a hundred black rhinos might be scattered on ranches throughout the American Southwest. Coordinating their program with those of the nation's zoos, the rhino breeders would swap bulls and pamper the pregnant cows in the manner of livestock. In time some of the offspring might even be returned to the South African bush.

Significantly, Game Coin pulled off the importation of the rhinos without help from environmental groups such as the Sierra Club. Harry had nothing but contempt for them; he called them tree huggers. He borrowed his con-servationist approach from Aldo Leopold, Theodore Roosevelt, and Euro-pean dukes, barons, and lords.

Harry and I carried our drinks through another sitting room, with walls of jungle-green, where we lifted our glasses and extended our stride to avoid

stepping on the zebra-skin rugs—tails and manes intact—that were strewn across the tile floor. (One does not walk on another's trophies.) At the end of the room, glass doors framed by matched elephant tusks opened onto a patio.

"I have hunted all over the world," Harry said, savoring his good fortune. "I've hunted on the backs of camels, on the backs of elephants. Have you ever ridden an elephant? Darn things will beat you to death. Bounce you till your teeth fall out. Elephants have the clumsiest natural gait on earth—three feet down while one foot is moving. They have no rhythm to their souls."

"What prey," I asked, "is, ah, bad enough that you need to be on top of an elephant?"

"Tigers!" Harry cried with an ecstatic blaze of those kindly eyes. Just as quickly, his eyes clouded with concern for the potential misunderstanding. "But it was legal then, you see."

We crossed the patio to a ground-level wine cellar that was as large as a corporate boardroom. Its chandelier was constructed from antlers. Finished with his barbecuing, Calvin joined a small group of friends gathered there. He chatted with Jean Waggoner of Fort Worth, an heiress to the historic cattle ranch in North Texas. With short hair tinted blond, animated brows, and a regal way of carrying her head that accentuated the line of her throat, she probably intimidated attractive women half her age. An avid hunter who had done most of her tracking on this continent, she wore a Mexican sundress with belt and bracelets of finely crafted Indian silver.

Calvin rested a large hand on Harry's shoulder. "I've gone on six African safaris," said Calvin. "Brag on yourself, Harry. How many times have you been over there?"

"Thirty-four," said the older man, grinning fiercely.

Forsaking the racked bottles in view, Calvin opened a cabinet and brought out a liter of white wine. He brandished it proudly. Cries of enthusiasm greeted the label, Zonnebloem Premier Grand Crû.

"Wherever did you find it?" asked Jean. "I've looked all over Fort Worth."

Calvin winked at her and filled all the glasses around. "I now buy it by the case," he said. Bottled in the Republic of South Africa, then better known for apartheid than for its vineyards, the wine was crackling dry and very good.

Harry quaffed his wine and immediately poured himself another glass. "God, I love this stuff."

We walked away from the others and took a seat on a small sofa. His eyes dewed with sentiment as he looked upon his friends. With an expansive wave of a crystal goblet, he said, "These are the very best people I know."

Harry and his friends represent one endangered species, the big-game hunter, trying to save another—the black rhinoceros. That might seem odd, but rhinos have always had a profound effect on the human imagination.

Rhinos walked the earth not long after dinosaurs died out. Other mammals of that era, such as mastodons and saber-toothed tigers, succeeded the great reptiles in extinction, but rhinos have survived 60 million years. One of the first records of man's fascination with rhinos is a European woodcut, carved in Augsburg in 1515, that features a small spiral horn on the hump of a rhino's neck, reflecting an ancient belief that rhinos have some connection with the mythical unicorn. A more persistent belief—that powdered rhino horn is a aphrodisiac—is thought to have originated in India, whose traders controlled exports from East Africa. Peddling the dual horns of Africa's rhinos, the Indians probably added that selling point to a long list already drawn up by the Chinese and Southeast Asians.

Irrational belief in the magic of rhino horns has not been limited to unwashed peasants. Chinese emperors customarily received a cup or bowl elaborately carved from rhino horns on each of their birthdays; the scenes on those vessels depicted Taoist visions of immortality. Chinese and Southwest Asian physicians and pharmacologists have traditionally prescribed shavings of rhino horn for a range of ailments that includes snakebite, hallucinations, typhoid, carbuncles, high fever, night blindness, and general lethargy (use by pregnant women not recommended). Today, the use of rhino horns as an aphrodisiac in India is largely confined to the city of Bombay and the northwestern province of Gujarat. Rhino horn is expensive, and other animal products such as monkey glands and goat bile are offered as substitutes. The Indian government has cracked down on the trade to protect its own rhino population, but pharmacists in Singapore still carve shavings from rhino horns and sell them by the gram as nonprescription medicines. In Peking the influence of Chairman Mao, who boosted the integration of traditional Chinese medicine with modern Western practice, has contributed heavily to the rhino's demise.

Still, the largest single exploiter today is North Yemen, a tiny country on the lower end of the Arabian peninsula, across the Red Sea from Ethiopia. Men there desire rhino horn handles on the daggers they start wearing in their belts at the age of twelve. Fifty thousand North Yemeni lads come of knife-carrying age every year, and rhino horn daggers in that country's shops bring from five hundred dollars to twelve thousand dollars. Smugglers of rhino horn sail dhows out of East African ports on the Indian Ocean. Their supplies come from poachers who shoot the nearsighted rhinos repeatedly with

small-caliber rifles and shotguns and wait for them to bleed to death. Then they saw off the horns and leave the carcasses to rot.

Wildlife conservationists estimate that the world rhino population declined by half during the seventies, and the decade's toll on black rhinos may have been as high as ninety percent.

After opening several bottles of Zonnebloem Premier Grand Crû, Calvin led us out of the wine cellar, back across the patio, through the door framed by the elephant tusks, and into the den, where everyone was trying to keep from standing on the zebra-skin rugs. Sometimes the person who is not invited to a party says as much about the gathering as the guests who are. Noteworthy by his absence here was Texas' other breeder of black rhinos, a thirty-eight-year-old natural gas entrepreneur named Tom Mantzel. Tall and personable, Tom had helped engineer the movement among American zoologists to sanction breeding of endangered wildlife on private ranches. His fifteen-hundred-acre retreat southwest of Fort Worth near Glen Rose was stocked with exotics that included sable antelope, wildebeests, European red stags, giraffes, Saharan addax antelope, and Grévy's zebras. A shipment of cheetahs would soon be on the way.

Tom's involvement with black rhinos began in late 1981, when he attended a posh New York fundraiser for endangered wildlife. With the help of Industrial Vehicles Corporation (IVECO), an Italian truck company eager for publicity in America, and the African Fund for Endangered Wildlife, Tom raised enough money to import his own rhinos. But his wildlife sources were in Zimbabwe. When his project fell victim to that country's internal politics, he realized he could get the rhinos only through Game Coin. Harry Tennison, because of his hunting connections, was able to get black rhinos from a state parks board in the Republic of South Africa, but his fundraising efforts had come up short. In August, 1983, Tom approached the Game Coin board, proposing a marriage of convenience. Harry was out of the country when the contract was signed, and he went through the roof when he found out about it. He didn't want to share his precious rhinos with anybody.

But the shaky marriage survived, and in March, 1984, five crated, sedated rhinos boarded a 747 freighter. Their South African handler carried a gun loaded with a lethal dart; if one of those crates came apart, an angry and desperate rhino was capable of taking the jumbo jet down. The rhinos shivered overnight in New York City, boarded another flight to Houston, then were split up and trucked to the two ranches. The crated rhinos were lowered into their pens by crane and then released. While TV cameras rolled, they whirled,

snorted, threw up dust, charged every sight and sound. Their collisions with the steel fence sounded like car wrecks.

Tom Mantzel and Calvin Bentsen got along fine, but relations between Tom and Harry were slow to warm up. Their chronic disagreement had elements of the tension between Fort Worth's old and new guards, and it was also a matter of style. The fundamental difference in their outlooks was reflected in the way they reacted to the rhinos. To Harry, rhinos would always be magnificent dangerous animals, beasts whose ferocity confirmed his view of the world. To Tom and his young wildlife specialists, black rhinos were an endangered species that required protection. They discovered that they could lull the animals at the Glen Rose ranch into a passive state simply by stroking their abdomens.

"I have nothing against hunters," said Tom the day I visited his ranch. "I used to hunt deer myself. But Harry still talks about the Big Five"—the grand slam of safaris, in which an elephant, a rhino, a Cape buffalo, a lion, and a leopard are collected on a single African trek. "That's like white rule in Rhodesia. Those days are gone."

As we circumnavigated the zebra skins en route to the dining room, Ed Wroe mentioned *Boone & Crockett* (Daniel and Davy, of course), which is the official record book of American trophy hunters. Harry and Ed spoke euphemistically of "collecting trophies"—not "killing animals." Africa swarms with all sorts of critters, but one that they didn't mention this night was ticks. Just a month before the party, the United States Department of Agriculture had discovered that Game Coin had imported not only rhinos but harmful parasites as well.

Bureaucracies tend to look askance at the transcontinental shipment of wild animals, particularly when the animals are dangerous. Most private applications die in the maze of regulations, but in this case the Bentsen name couldn't have hurt, nor could that of Ray Arnett, one of President Reagan's assistant secretaries of the Interior. Arnett ranked in unpopularity among environmentalists right up there with his former boss James Watt, but Arnett was also a member of Game Coin. With all that pull, Game Coin administrators obtained a permit from Interior. Ordinarily, to protect livestock, the USDA would examine all exotic hooved animals and quarantine them for sixty days in New Jersey, but because rhinos have three toes, Interior was able to wave them through New York on Game Coin's assurance that the South Africans had taken all the necessary precautions.

It was all whoops and champagne until Calvin's older rhino cow died two

months later. Summoned from the Gladys Porter Zoo in Brownsville, veterinarian Sherri Huntress performed the autopsy. The cow, sixteen or seventeen years old, had died from old age and liver disease, which prompted accusations that the South Africans should never have shipped her at all. But the revelation of that postmortem was Huntress' discovery of live African Bont ticks on the rhino's hide. She duly reported it to the Department of Agriculture. Pointing fingers of blame at the Interior Department, USDA officials swarmed around the Edinburg and Glen Rose ranches for the next few days.

Huntress disabled Calvin's surviving rhinos with a heavy tranquilizer so the USDA inspector could proceed with an inch-by-inch examination. At Tom's ranch they were astounded that the employees' trick of stroking the rhinos' tummies eliminated the need for the dangerous sedation. The head of the USDA crew told Tom that they were concerned about a disease called heartwater, which is carried by the African Bont.

As the story unfolded, the news got worse. African Bont ticks are of the dreaded three-host variety. They might attach themselves to feral hogs, certain birds, or even rabbits, all of which disregard fences. One female African Bont tick might disperse twenty thousand eggs in her life cycle, and the specter of an uncontrollable tick was feared in the Rio Grande Valley. The nine counties between Del Rio and Brownsville encompassed the permanently quarantined danger zone of Texas fever, a virulent blood disease carried by ticks and against which American cattle have no immunity. The last major outbreak of Texas fever had devastated the United States cattle industry in the late thirties. The government vets found no more live African Bont ticks on either of the Texas ranches, but they placed Calvin's La Coma under a year-long quarantine, which meant that any animal shipped from the ranch had to enter the trailer soaking wet with tick dip, in the presence of a government official.

The dinner guests plucked their linen-wrapped silverware from the ceramic rhino and passed by the carved-watermelon rhino. Calvin served us personally. Arranging the brisket strips on each plate's flour tortilla, he said helpfully, "Get you some guacamole there and some of that *pico del gallo*. There you go, put it right on top of the meat. But watch it, now. It's hot." On one of the sitting-room sofas, I balanced the plate on my knees and unfolded my napkin. It was the first time I'd eaten fajitas with a sterling silver fork that weighed two pounds.

Ed Wroe occupied a Victorian chair across the room. He was talking about the thousands of dollars people pay for a native trophy whose antlered points

and spread were certified by *Boone & Crockett.* "It's outrageous," said Jean Waggoner, who shared the sofa with me. "People who don't hunt at all. Interior decorators! I would never have a trophy in my home that I did not kill." The purity of hunting, they all seemed to agree, was easily despoiled.

When the party started to thin out, we moved up toward the front of the house, where, in a small den, there was a glassed-in gun rack containing many of the rifles Calvin had used on safari. On a shelf, sample bullets of those firearms stood on end. Calvin explained which of the cartridges was suited for what prey (the one used for elephants was the size of his forefinger), then excused himself briefly and returned with a battery-operated cassette player. La Coma is well known among Calvin's friends for its quail and dove hunts. Following one of those weekend hunts, Calvin said, a famous guest had returned to his piano in Palm Springs and composed a personalized ditty about the outing for his Texas hosts. Calvin said the cassette had arrived in the mail not long before the entertainer died. He played it now as the last of the dinner guests gathered round to listen to the scratchy recording, to the tune of "Old Man River":

> *But old Cal Bentsen showed him who was best,*
> *'Cause he's the fastest gun in the whole Southwest.*

"That really is Bing Crosby," said one of the guests.

"Of course it is," cried Jean. "Oh, it's priceless."

The morning after the party, I met Calvin at his ranch north of Edinburg to look at rhinos and to talk about breeding them. From the highway, La Coma differed from the neighboring brushy range only in its tall game fence and a sign warning trespassers of dangerous wildlife. The foreman, Andy McClellan, was a swarthy and wiry man who stuffed his jeans into the tops of his manure-splattered boots. Four years earlier Andy had been an ordinary working cowpoke. Now ostrich chicks about the size of geese ran around the yard of his mobile home. The fender of his pickup bore a jagged hole—the result of a kick by an impassioned male ostrich.

Andy labored on this particular morning in the loading pens under the supervision of a young man from the United States Department of Agriculture. They were spraying the cattle, as required by the quarantine, and it wasn't pleasant work. The sun was hot, and the poison kept blowing back in the cowboy's faces.

Andy took a break beside a large mesquite. Reflecting on the problems of breeding rhinos, he said that he was certain the cow at La Coma had been in heat at least once. Rhino cows ovulate in cycles of twenty to thirty-five days,

and the estrus lasts only twenty-four to forty-eight hours. Pregnancy lasts about sixteen months, and the cows mother their calves for at least two years. As a practical matter, the breeders have to hope for one fertile night of passion every three or four years. When the female comes into heat, she signals her ardor with musky sprays of urine that carry six to eight feet.

When they finally mate, rhinos make up for their solitary ways, years of celibacy, and stormy courtships. Sometimes they swoon over on their sides, but usually they keep their feet. The cow squeaks and pants from time to time. The bull bites at the air; his fringed ears flap continuously. The breeders have been told to expect the act to last at least half an hour. Two Indian rhinos hold the unofficial record of eighty-three minutes. To Westerners, the great mystery of the rhinos' plight has been how Asians could ever have come up with that absurd business of an aphrodisiac horn. Perhaps now we know.

Andy said that the cow at La Coma had commenced spraying and rubbing suggestively against the fence that separated her pen from the bull's. The male lumbered right over.

For the life of him, Andy couldn't make himself open the gate, though. "It's an awful responsibility," he told me. "All I'd been hearing was how they'd rage and fight. I was afraid they'd hurt themselves. Next time I reckon I'll be ready."

"Do you plan to watch?" I said.

"Why, sure. I have to! If they start fighting and one gets the other down... uh, well, I don't know what I'd do. Bounce BBs off their ass?"

The rhino pens were hidden in a stand of mesquites about a mile away. Each fence post consisted of three, two hundred-pound lengths of oil field pipe that were welded together and rooted in a yard of concrete. The responsibility of housing black rhinos cannot be taken lightly. As Ed Wroe had said at the dinner party, "I think we need to get old Calvin about five million in liability coverage. Sure would be a shame if one of these things winds up in downtown Matamoros."

Calvin shoved the sole of his boot against an unyielding rung. "A member of Game Coin donated the pipe," he said, "and the fence still cost $95,000. Zoologists think black rhinos really need more room than this to breed successfully—maybe a hundred acres to approximate their territories in the wild. You can calculate the cost of that. We're hoping that as they become more adjusted, they won't need quite so much fence. The next plan calls for larger pens with sectioned telephone poles and cross strands of elevator cable."

A shirtless employee named Pancho Olegin was whacking at brush with a machete and dragging it up to the pens. In the African wild, black rhinos ate

the leaves and branches of acacia trees. In South Texas, they selected huisache as the tastiest substitute. Huisache is a chaparral bramble with inch-long, needle-sharp thorns. The rhinos munched it thoughtfully. Pancho knew the rhinos better than anybody at La Coma did. He slept at night on a cot in a nearby metal shed, and it was he who had run up to Andy's trailer, tears streaming down his cheeks, when the old cow died. Calvin asked him in Spanish to rouse the male, who had arranged his lair in the thickest brush and did not venture out often in the heat of the day. With an offering of alfalfa, Pancho slipped between the pipe and walked bravely through the mesquites. "Hey, Bull," he called. "Come on, Bull." He looked back at Calvin and shrugged. "*No quiere.*"

Pancho selected a fist-size rock and zinged it through the brush. There was an alarming meaty *thunk.* Taking no offense, the bull finally rolled over, snapping a few saplings, and followed Pancho's trail of alfalfa. Almost twice the size of the cow, he weighed thirty-five hundred pounds. Pancho stood behind a safety barricade and fed him more hay on a pitchfork. The bull playfully hooked the lower rung of the concrete-rooted pipe, causing the ground to tremble.

Watching, I thought about how Tom Mantzel runs along an identical fence at the Glen Rose ranch, slapping his thighs and cavorting with his rhinos. Tom's young male tosses his head and performs a silly tiptoe dance in response. The rhinos on both of the ranches are potentially dangerous but no longer quite so fierce. The translocation has changed them, as it has the men. Even crusty old hunters like Calvin and Harry have come to think of the rhinos more as pets than prey. Tom and Harry buried the hatchet not long ago at a Fort Worth dinner party. Harry told Tom that he just didn't have the heart to hunt in Africa anymore.

After Pancho finished feeding the rhinos, Calvin took me to the ranch house, which made the McAllen mansion seem a model of subtlety and restraint in the use of animal decor. The walls at the ranch were jam-packed with mounted antelope heads; the floor was covered with skins of lions and grizzly bears arranged so that gaping mouths with bared teeth greeted anybody who entered the front door.

Calvin talked about how he'd gotten his rhino, as he thoughtfully stroked the mane of a lion's pelt. "We set out from Nairobi with three lorries, a professional hunter, and the usual assortment of trackers, gun bearers, skinners, cooks, and tire changers. It took us three days to find the rhino. At the end of the second day, we came in exhausted and slept hard. That night a male walked right through camp, fifty feet from the tents. In stalking rhino, you always

want to be downwind. If they smell you, they're either gone or charging. As we followed the tracks, we saw that this one had picked up a companion. We were in very thick brush. We walked or crawled a few feet at a time. We knew something was in there, because we saw a tickbird, which has a swooping flight like our woodpeckers. That meant we were on top of either the rhino or a Cape buffalo. I was about forty feet away when I saw the rhino bull. I shot him once through the neck with a Holland and Holland .460 double-barreled rifle. He went down, but the rhino he'd been traveling with didn't like that one bit. We could hear it snorting and stomping around. The pro hunter fired in the air and finally scared the other rhino off."

Calvin ran his fingers through the lion's mane. "That was an ideal kill," he said. "An old male, probably sterile, that was no longer of any use to the herd. But the great safaris are a thing of the past. Back then, the going price was a $114 a day, so you might stay out for a month. Now it costs eight hundred to a thousand dollars a day. The people in charge of those African governments have tried to put the blame for their endangered wildlife on foreign hunters, but you don't find us extinguishing a species for its horn. My hunting licenses helped finance their force of park rangers. Those are poor countries over there. Without that revenue, park rangers are a luxury item. Who stands to benefit? Why, the poachers!

"They won't let us hunt at all in Kenya anymore," he went on ruefully. "And I sorely miss Kenya. I'd wake up over there and swear I was in South Texas. The vegetation and climate are similar; even the water tastes the same—which is how, as a conservationist, I came to want those black rhinos on my ranch. In their native land they don't stand much chance." He smiled and looked around at the antelope trophies. "I am aware, of course, that some people think horns ought to be growing on my head. Some might enjoy seeing my head mounted on that wall."

He walked outside to his van. "You're my friend," he announced with solemn and atavistic formality, then he drove away. In my hand was a gift bottle of South African wine. He left me feeling oddly sentimental. Calvin is a true rhinoceros. He's the great white hunter, and like the strange creatures making hay of his huisache, that's a vanishing breed.

MARCH, 1985

RUNNING RABID

In Wichita Falls my high school teams were called the Coyotes. At night you could hear the teams' namesakes singing to each other in the mesquite savanna. Later, when I lived in the country in Central Texas, I loved to listen to their strange, chortling serenades and on occasions I would catch a glimpse of one. They didn't bother me or my pets. The folklore of the Native American tribes that once roamed Texas are filled with tales that invest coyotes with the human traits of an unreliable but sometimes helpful trickster. I love the rascals. Always have.

But for many Texans, coyotes are not benign creatures at all. I was shocked one time to round a highway curve and see a large post oak festooned with dead coyotes hung up by their heels to rot. That pasture was in cattle country, and cattle ranchers have little economic reason to despise the wild canids; though scattered incidents of calf-killing might be gruesome, coyotes inflict little harm on their herds. But in the sheep and goat-raising countryside of the Edwards Plateau, coyotes are hated, trapped, and killed with reason. Unchecked depredation by coyotes can put sheep and goat ranchers out of business. Ranchers have now lost the federal price supports that underwrote their investment in mohair goats. But the ranchers still have brush that goats help them control, and with the growing popularity of cabrito, a common sight now is a border collie circling up short-haired Spanish goats. Sheep and goat raisers on the Edwards Plateau are permanently besieged. They occupy an island in a sea of coyotes.

This assignment about coyotes took me to the chaparral of South Texas. The wild canids had gotten in serious trouble—for both their species and ours. They had caught the rabies virus from Mexican dogs, and the prospect of an outbreak of coyote rabies in Texas is terrifying and real. The piece won a public service award from the Texas Veterinary Medical Association. State health officials have since done their best to

vaccinate pets and keep the outbreak from spreading, but once the first coyotes caught it, others were sure to contract the disease. A veterinary scientist used a striking metaphor to describe the futility of trying to eliminate coyotes from the wild: It's like trying to bail water out of an ocean or stream.

The nature and nightmarish potential of the rabies outbreak dawned on South Texans in late 1988 and early 1989, when coyotes were seen trotting through the streets of Rio Grande City. The first of these wayward canids crossed U.S. 183, the town's busy main drag, and sat down in the yard of a highway patrolman. The officer promptly shot it.

The creature's docile behavior was not atypical. The image of the rabid beast—staggering, snarling, drooling—is accurate but only half true; not all rabies is the "furious" type. Just as often, infected canids exhibit the lethargic and treacherous symptoms known as "dumb" rabies. A few weeks after that first incident, another coyote sat watching cars go by a couple of blocks from the Starr County courthouse. It too was shot. In the brush north of town, a third coyote wandered into the house of an old man and plopped on the floor. Exasperated men circled the house with guns, shouting and beating the walls trying to shoo it out. Finally one drew a deep breath and walked inside to kill it.

Although rabies occurs regularly on the Mexican side of the river, the disease has been virtually unknown on the American side. As of September 3, 1988, eighteen years had passed since rabies had been detected in Starr and its adjacent counties in any species except bats. Since that date—when a coyote of sickly appearance entered a rural yard near the village of Rincon, menaced the owner, and fought with his two dogs while he ran for a gun—ninety-three cases of animal rabies have been confirmed in Starr County alone. In a twelve-county area of South Texas, the number of cases is approaching three hundred and shows no sign of slowing down.

The infected animals in Starr County have included a raccoon, a bobcat, a goat, and three domestic cats, but the overwhelming majority of the cases have involved canids—twenty-seven coyotes, sixty dogs. The brush country outbreak has spread in a consistent pattern. In tiny ranching hamlets, for months there will be no sign of it; then all at once the residents are besieged. Rabid coyotes show up first. Then, after a lull of a few days to several months, unvaccinated dogs start to come down with it. Scattered fifteen to forty miles

north of Rio Grande City are Starr County's principal ranching hamlets. Their names—El Sauz, La Gloria, Santa Elena, San Isidro, La Reforma—reflect the county's dominant ethnicity. They are friendly little places with tidy homes and well-kept churches, perhaps a store and a school, cemeteries always aglow with floral demonstrations of Hispanics' esteem for the dead.

In March of 1991, a wave of rabies passed through these enclaves in northern Starr County. The following August, on a ranch between El Sauz and La Gloria, a fifty-five-year-old Hispanic woman got sick of canine rabies and died. State health investigators could never prove her tragedy had anything to do with the outbreak among coyotes; incubation of the virus within humans can take more than a year, making cause and effect hard to pin down. But investigators became suspicious when they learned that the woman's unvaccinated dog had recently died of unknown causes. A puppy that had played with the dog had later gotten a bone caught in its throat, and the woman had stuck her finger in the pup's mouth, trying to dislodge the obstruction. The woman's husband swore that she was never bitten, but then, one doesn't have to be. The virus can enter through a minor cut or an open sore. It can be transmitted through the mucous membranes of the eyes.

Unlike most viruses, which are blood-borne, rabies travels through the nervous system, reaching the spinal cord and then inching toward the brain. The gruesome vaccination ordeal of dozens of painful shots in the abdomen is an obsolete procedure; a newer and quite effective vaccine requires just six shots in the arm. But doctors have to realize that the doses are required, and rabies is notoriously hard to diagnose. Symptoms can include mental depression and restlessness, sore throat, fever, nausea, and stomach pains; the profile is easily mistaken for appendicitis. By the time lab testing confirms the disease, it is almost always too late. The patient can suffer seizures, hallucinations, uncontrollable excitement, and excruciatingly painful spasms in the neck and jaws. The spasms can be triggered by the slightest irritation. As a result, the patient is unable to drink, even though he may be consumed with thirst. Death from asphyxiation, exhaustion, or general paralysis usually follows in three to ten days. Rabies is a ghastly way to go.

North of the Starr County hamlets, the chaparral stretches virtually unbroken for fifty miles before it divides again for the Jim Hogg county seat of Hebbronville. Late one afternoon in September, 1991, a month after the woman died in Starr County, a three-year-old child was playing on her porch in Hebbronville. Inside the house, her mother suddenly heard the child screaming. She ran outside and saw blood and a nasty bite on her daughter's back. This time the victim did not die, but the source of her infection was indisput-

able. In the yard was a rabid coyote that had come right up out of the brush.

Fortunately for humans and their domestic livestock and pets, the dozen or so known strains of rabies tend to be host-specific. Dogs have dog rabies; raccoons have raccoon rabies. A particular strain can be transmitted to another species of mammal but not as readily as to the same species. In Texas, skunks are the creatures most often afflicted, accounting about half of the more than four hundred positive tests recorded by the Texas Department of Health each year. Bats come in a far distant second. Like humans and cats, coyotes have not developed an endemic rabies strain and until now were rarely affected by rabies. The animal's behavioral traits may help to account for that. Nimble and canny creatures, coyotes are hard to corner and can run at great speed. Too, they might just have a keen eye for sick creatures acting crazy.

The first crossover infection may have occurred long before the fall of 1988 and scores of miles from Starr County. Whenever it was, and wherever, a coyote contracted the strain of the rabies that United States scientists named—with undiplomatic bluntness—Urban Mexican Dog. It is a particularly virulent strain of rabies, and once it jumped into the coyote population, a vicious cycle of coyote-to-dog transmission was established. In this part of the country, where vaccination of pets is not consistently practiced, the disease spread rapidly in populous areas.

Through 1990 the outbreak was confined to Starr and its downstream neighbor, Hidalgo County. In 1991 it abruptly leapt one hundred miles north of the Rio Grande. The outbreak has since spread through twelve of the state's southernmost counties—roughly following a line from Corpus Christi to Laredo. In those counties, state health officials have now confirmed a total of 130 rabid coyotes and 149 dogs, only two of which had been vaccinated. Recently, a rabid coyote was killed on the beach near Port Aransas. As conditions now stand, there is no reason to believe the spread will stop short of the city limits of Victoria and San Antonio.

The present epidemic did not happen in a vacuum. Over the last several decades, coyotes have proliferated throughout North America as wolves, their chief natural rivals, have been eradicated. No habitat suits them better than the brush country of South Texas, and as the incidence of rabies has grown, local residents have come to believe that the number of coyotes is way up. The past two years have brought unusually abundant rain and mild winters; many species are doing well, among them cottontail rabbits, the primary prey of coyotes in the chaparral. With more rabbits for the adults to eat, more pups are likely to survive. Females are fertile at seven months and give birth to litters of six to seven pups.

But whether the coyote population is up or down, the incidence of rabies is definitely up. At the Texas Department of Health in Austin, Keith Clark, a Marble Falls rancher and veterinarian who monitors the outbreak, has been calling for emergency vaccination drives. A widely recognized authority on rabies, Clark says of the situation in South Texas: "We're up against something that's entirely new. Rabies is established in coyotes now. It's not going to go away."

"Here. Hold this," says Rio Grande City veterinarian Roberto Margo, placing a white plastic-foam container in my hands. Margo turns to his paperwork with a slight smile. "It's the head of a rabid dog—probably."

Packed with ice, the mongrel pup's head will go by Greyhound bus freight to the Department of Health, where Carter's technicians will indeed confirm it as Starr County's first case of 1993.

In addition to operating a private practice, Margo serves as the Starr County veterinarian. His position sums up some of the problems facing the impoverished county. Rio Grande City (population: 9,900) is the seat of Starr County but is unincorporated. Because of that, the city cannot effectively enforce measures such as mandatory pet-vaccination drives. All services, from water and sewage lines to public health and animal control, are administered by the county. But the county itself is so poor that it has no money to pay the county vet. Therefore, Margo does not earn a salary for his work. His situation has been frustrating.

Except for his years in college and the Air Force, Margo has always lived in Starr County—proudly chosen to live there—and with an image already soiled by repeated drug busts involving public officials, he knows that the last thing his community needs is a reputation as the rabies capital of Texas. Margo is a part-time rancher, and his outlook harbors no great love for that folkloric trickster, the coyote. In addition to preying on rodents—which nobody minds—coyotes also kill the Spanish kid goats that thrive in the chaparral and are sold for meat as *cabrito*. The coyotes also sneak up on cows that are temporarily paralyzed by calving and kill their newborn. Starr County has a number of drip-irrigated farms; watermelons are a substantial cash crop. Coyotes are notorious for gnawing and prying open the rinds and eating out the juicy heart.

Margo remembers when ranchers could buy strychnine in pharmacies and administer their own predator control. Congress and Richard Nixon outlawed that in 1972, but now some people are saying it is time to reverse the ban. They want bring back strychnine or use the controversial and lethal

poison known as 1080—sodium monofluoroacetate. In order to gain permission to use 1080, the county would have to persuade the Environmental Protection Agency to certify the coyote rabies outbreak as a federal health emergency. In Margo's opinion, an emergency is precisely what the situation is. "We're talking about human lives," he says. "What are they waiting for?" He gazes out at the grayish green chaparral that stretches north to the horizon. "How do they think it got to Hebbronville? Dogs and cats?"

In a pasture across the road from a subdivision of brick homes on Rio Grande City's north side, that day an affable career civil servant named Martin Mendoza and his newly employed Starr County trapper, Rene Muñoz, are doing as much as the law allows to contain the rabies outbreak. Mendoza lives in Kingsville and is a regional supervisor for the Animal Damage Control Division of the United States Department of Agriculture. Muñoz is a part-time rancher.

Mendoza is no ghoul. His job requires that coyotes be killed, but he avoids the use of steel traps and fence-line snares when he has an alternative. To spare the animals unnecessary agony, federal regulations mandate that the traps have to be checked as often as possible. "Nature takes care of overpopulation through starvation and disease," Mendoza says. "Right now coyotes have lots to eat. Rabies is the bad luck of the draw."

Rene Muñoz pokes his Bronco along *senderos* ("trails") that have been cut through the brush. He is checking on M-44 sodium cyanide guns, the primary means of coyote control in the area. The device is highly lethal, consisting of a short metal cylinder with a spring-loaded plunger inside. On top is a nub baited with something the coyote finds irresistible—like a foul paste of carrion and urine. When the coyote gnaws on the nub and releases the spring, the plunger sends a spray of dry cyanide crystals into its mouth. The coyote is dead in a matter of seconds.

If landowners consent, federal trappers bury cyanide devices in the ground on their property, prominently marking them with red warning signs in English and Spanish. The M-44's design is canine-specific so it does not pose a threat to other wild animals. Raptors and vultures are unable to trigger the guns with their beaks, and raccoons worry at the devices with their paws, which usually keeps them out of the line of fire even if they happen to trip the device. Ocelots, jaguarundi, and other wild cats are spared by the advanced decomposition of the carrion bait. They only like fresh meat. Dogs, though, are easy victims, an incentive to owners to keep them penned up.

Stopping the Bronco to replenish a coyote gun's bait, Muñoz shows me

his pocket carton of amyl nitrate ampules—the antidote for the poison, just in case. He talks about reading wind patterns, and planting the M-44s just under a ridge, where coyotes like to sit and smell and watch. He smears on the paste with a Popsicle stick. "I like to use jackrabbit," he says, grinning. "That coyote can hardly ever run one down, so he really likes the taste."

Besides being a part-time rancher, Muñoz used to work as a landman, a scout of promising oil leases, but then the bust hit. He needed a job, and this one came open. He converses with his boss in the easy way of border Tejanos, switching back and forth from English to Spanish, changing languages in mid-sentence.

Nearby, the bells of goats clank and tinkle. The sky is full of caracaras and hawks. The time is mid-January, and the mesquites are already leafed out lime green. Soon the huisaches will burst aglow in delicate yellow flowers the size of a dime, and it won't be long before spring rain will ignite the cenizo's purple blossoms. "Some people look at this and say there's nothing here," Muñoz says. "Thorns and ugly old brush. But to me, this is beautiful."

The same week that Muñoz is placing coyote bait around the countryside, Martin Mendoza drives to Laredo, where the city-county health director, Jerry Robinson, has convened an informal but urgent session of the commissioners' court. From Hebbronville, rabies has spread twenty-five miles northwest into Webb County, creating another rash of cases around the hamlets of Bruni, Oilton, and Mirando City. And now, suddenly, fifteen miles north of Laredo, a rabid puppy has exposed nineteen humans to the disease. The city of more than 120,000 is almost surrounded by cases of rabies.

The commissioners and Robinson discuss bringing in a helicopter and a sharpshooter to hunt down coyotes from the air. Their aim is to create a coyote-free buffer zone in the brush outside of town and buy time. Eventually, though, they decide against it because the method not only is expensive but also has limited utility. "It's effective," says John Spruiell, one of the vets who sat in on the meeting, "but coyotes are too smart—it only works once." And Spruiell doubts that much will come of Robinson's demand for a strict city pet-licensing ordinance. "We've seen it all before," he says. "The judges here just tell people that if they'll go home and get their dogs vaccinated, they won't have to pay the fines."

Spruiell goes on to point out that dogs and coyotes are not the only species that need to be targeted. "I've got a client, a rancher, who was out working on a windmill," he says. "Some of his cows and calves had come up close around. A coyote jumped out of the brush and ran right at those cattle. The

mother cows went out to meet it and tromped it down real good. Because that rancher just happened to be on that windmill, he knew he had to get those cattle vaccinated. But what if he hadn't seen that? Those cows are trained to come up and eat out of his hand. The next time he gets out of his pickup, his gentle Santa Gertrudis is going to come at him like a fighting bull."

It is hard to say which is more daunting—the logistics of dealing with the massive rabies outbreak or the ethical and social issues it has raised. At the meeting in Laredo, two other local veterinarians question the notion that wild-life should be randomly sacrificed when humans can easily protect themselves by taking responsibility for vaccinating their pets. But how realistic is it to expect people to suddenly respond when they have never done so before? Similarly, veterinarian Phyllis Voltz-Creamer's proposal of an oral vaccine for coyotes is greeted with a few discreet sighs. Webb County alone has thirty-three hundred square miles of uninhabited land. Estimates of coyote numbers in the brush country range from five to sixteen per square mile. The truth is, nobody really has a clue how many animals are out there or how they would reach them even if they did know how.

Yet John Spruiell and Martin Mendoza both say an oral wildlife vaccine may be the only long-term solution to South Texas' unique problem. At Texas A&M's school of veterinary medicine, Leon Russell, the faculty's rabies expert, emphatically agrees. "An oral vaccine hasn't been tried yet with coy-otes," he says. "But we need to be looking at Europe. The problem over there is foxes—a very similar species. Ten years ago West Germany, about the size of Oregon, was having more rabies cases than we see in the entire country. They got on top of it with computer grids, baits put out by hand and helicop-ter. They used chicken heads at first; now the bait's a little more sophisti-cated. Switzerland also stopped fox rabies, and it didn't bankrupt the gov-ernment. If a vaccine can work in the Swiss Alps, open country is no reason not to try it in South Texas."

He questions whether the control measures now under way will be effec-tive. "Every experience we have with wildlife control suggests the way we're doing it now, trying to create these buffers, just won't work," Russell contin-ues. When hunters and trappers have eradicated coyotes from a given area, he says, "the other coyotes sense a vacuum in the habitat, and they come pouring back in to get the food. You can't shoot or poison enough of them. It's like trying to bail water out of a river."

In rural Starr County, on the road from Rio Grande City to El Sauz, there is a turnoff and a small sign that reads Mirasoles Ranch. The place is not far from

the house where the woman fell sick of rabies three years ago. A few hundred yards down the dirt road is the remains of a community where nobody lives anymore. Some abandoned homes are of forties frame construction; three others—roofless stone houses—were erected in a prior century. From them, coyote trapper Rene Muñoz salvaged hand-hewn mesquite windowsills put up in their stucco by his ancestors. His cattle graze nearby.

As the sunset fades, the foliage, dirt, and sky meld into a uniform gray. A great-horned owl leaves a tree in ponderous flight. A cottontail hops across the road. And, as if I had called them up, coyotes erupt in their yodeling stammer of howls, hoots, yips, and hollers. There are probably only two or three of them, but they sound like twenty. The sound is one of the most enchanting in nature, but things are different now. I smile that the creatures have noted my presence. But I stay safely in the car.

MARCH, 1993

SYMPATHY FOR THE DEVILS

I chanced upon the Devils River and its canyon lands about twenty years ago. I was in Del Rio covering a trial, and afterward I had to go to Big Spring. I thought I knew just about every inch of West Texas, but for a short time on the highway I was dazzled by desert mountains through which flowed a beautiful, clear-running stream. The Devils River country was a place of mystery; few people I knew had even heard of the Rio Grande tributary. I read that the Devils was the least tainted river in Texas. I didn't know what that meant, exactly, but I wanted to see it and write about it. So a time came when I hitched a canoe ride with an old friend, Andy Sansom, who was the executive director of the Texas Parks and Wildlife Department. All he had ever seen of the Devils was from that highway, too. But he was constantly embroiled in the controversies of the river, which pitted recreational use against private property rights. On that canoe ride I saw the most pristine nature in Texas—water of such clarity and color it reminded me of the Caribbean. But even on clear days, with the river at normal flow, the Devils could be treacherous, even terrifying. I never feared for my life, but several times I thought that force of water against rock was going to send me tumbling and break an arm or leg. Then where would I be? I had found Texas' most inspiring wilderness, but who would carry me out?

On a clear morning last June I set out to explore the Devils River, the last major unpolluted river in Texas. It begins on a ranch in Val Verde County and flows about fifty miles south into Lake Amistad on the Rio Grande. At first it follows a narrow, twisting course through dramatic bluffs and lush wooded bottoms. At its midpoint, a hillside of springs releases twenty-two thousand gallons a minute; just downstream is Dolan Falls, the state's most gorgeous cascade. The lower half of the river broadens out, its banks scoured clean of trees by the force of its floods, resulting in a more Spartan look—

water and stone. For all its beauty, though, the Devils has a forbidding reputation: "Not a river trip for beginners, small children, or pets," I read in one white-water guide. It winds through one of the state's least-populated regions. It's hard to make a living in the labyrinth of arid canyons; passable roads are few and far between. And the sheep and goat ranchers who own most of the frontage want to keep it inaccessible and remote. But canoeists in search of unspoiled wilderness know it's their river too. The conflict is partly urban-rural and partly public-private, and on occasion it has gotten nasty. I was running the Devils with state environmental officials who are caught in the middle.

The upper river's only legal access point—a fishing campground called Baker's Crossing—flanks a bridge on Texas Highway 163 between Juno and Comstock. We were met there by the campground's owners, Mary and Les Hughey, who log in the names of river travelers in case a search for them becomes necessary. My partner in the first canoe was Andy Goldbloom, a Texas Parks and Wildlife Department administrator who organized our expedition and has tried, with some success, to turn the Devils wrangle into a dialogue. In the second canoe were an outdoors writer from Houston and Andy Sansom, the department's executive director. All were experienced canoeists—except me. I've never been hurt canoeing or even capsized, but I don't risk it much. White water is not my athletic cup of tea.

"I'm in shape and I'm coachable," I apologized in advance to Goldbloom, who told me not to worry. He put me in the bow, where my role had more to do with recognizing hazards than steering around them. He said I should remember two things: to pull in with the paddle to send the canoe outward; and if a rock snagged us, to lean toward it, not away from it. Otherwise, the canoe would easily tip over and fill with water, and the current would bend it around the rock like a pretzel. I found neither of these instructions instinctive—quite the contrary. As for my skills navigating the river, at this hour it all looked like sun-dazzled water. "Not so panicky," Goldbloom called out as I pulled in hard with the paddle and still watched the bow cruise straight into a rock. Poor guy; he was saddled with a project.

Bearded and soft-spoken, Sansom had never seen much of the Devils, though lately he and his staff had started talking with landowners and their legislators about a management plan for the river's protection and use. The negotiations have been slow, though, and they were hardly helped by a pair of stories on the Devils in the February, 1993, issue of *Texas Parks & Wildlife* magazine, the department's colorful monthly journal. Though one story expressed landowner concerns, the other contained a photo of a tent pitched in

violation of trespass laws on land owned by a hard-line rancher named T. J. Jarrett. The locals were none too pleased.

Obviously, our white-water trek was going to be law-abiding. Photos of either Andy in handcuffs would not do. In case we considered straying, our passage into the Jarrett ranch was greeted by a profusion of black-and-white signs: "Private River Bank. Do Not Leave Water. Trespassers Will Be Prosecuted. Protect the River. Do Not Litter." We stopped in a shaded cove, tied the canoes to a low-hanging branch, and, standing waist-deep in the water, used the boats as lunch tables. Andy Sansom threw out a fishing line and immediately hooked a fine bass, which he released. When we set out again, alligator gar trailed after us. Along with flowing schools of carp were great numbers of sunfish, catfish, and bass. I'd never seen anything like it in Texas.

Depending on the depth of the bed's layered rock shelves, the water color ranged from emerald to almost pink. Startled deer galloped in the shallows, hooves popping on the stone. Close against the stream were sycamore and pecan bottoms I associate with the Hill Country. I saw showy glints of king-fishers, tanagers, hooded orioles, and a painted bunting. Above the trees towered limestone cliffs stained gray with manganite and festooned with desert vegetation: tasajillo cactus with pretty red berries and nasty barbed spines, and ocotillo, the strange thorned plant whose spindly branches sprout scarlet blossoms often but leaf out only when it rains. To the eye it was paradise—but not to the muscles.

The flow during our trip was the Devils' average flow and the minimum said to be required for canoeing: 250 cubic feet per second. But that rate produces a river that is about six inches too shallow to keep a canoe in consistent motion. I heard later that the high temperature that day was ninety-seven degrees, which surprised me. Heat didn't seem to be a problem, but then, we were constantly refreshed. Though I doubt my paddling and navigation improved much, I became pretty agile at stepping in and out of a canoe. In the rapids, almost without fail, both boats bottomed out and snagged. (Paint scrapes on the rocks suggested this was not uncommon.) I'd grab the rope and haul the canoe while Goldbloom shoved. Often, within a few steps, I was floundering in water up to my waist. Even at ankle-depth the rapids flowed with tremendous force. Soon I hated the sound of rapids ahead, and not because I feared risking them afloat. By mid-afternoon my legs were gone. The only thing I could take comfort in was my choice of footwear—thick-soled athletic shoes. Sansom wore a pair of sandals whose ads feature a muscular pair of legs engaged in rock climbing. I'm amazed he got back to Austin with any skin left on his feet.

We came out of a difficult stretch into a long turquoise pool, parked the canoes on a rock, and spent the better part of an hour in recovery. I arched my back and moved my hands and feet just enough to keep my chest and face out of the water. It was as close as I've come to sensory deprivation. Above me were drifting buzzards and a cliff pocked with numerous caves. In my somewhat altered state, I imagined a cowboy bouncing down the rock, with a rappelling rope under his blue-jeaned thigh, to post the signs: "Private River Bank. Do Not Leave Water. Trespassers Will Be . . ."

Sansom floated in the same posture nearby. T. J. Jarrett, I commented, runs a very large spread. The state natural area that borders his ranch was still five hours away. Sansom said he'd had very little direct contact with the man. "He called me and said that people out here have an agreement. When they're chasing a mountain lion, it's all right to cross a neighbor's fence to kill it. He wondered if we'd grant that courtesy to him. I told him I hoped he understood that as a matter of public wildlife policy, there might be a problem."

It was sundown, thirteen hours after we had left Baker's Crossing, when a park ranger waved us into the next legal access point. Not long afterward, in the natural area's old hunting cabin, one heard nothing but snores.

Before canoeing the Devils, I roamed the region by car, and I highly recommend the drive. From Ozona to Comstock you can watch the river and its canyonlands form and grow. There are mesas, hawks, scissortails. On a ranch road, I turned around and headed back for a closer look at a western diamondback that stretched far across the pavement. The consoling thing about rattlesnakes is that they're extremely limited, in both thought and movement. When the sensations finally got through, the snake didn't like the heat and noise from my idling motor. It herked and jerked and rushed off into the grass. I saw more wild turkeys that day than I'd seen in my life. Pairs of them shot their long necks out and soared across the road. I passed one in a bar ditch pecking like a chicken out for an afternoon stroll

Still, the Devils' nature is deceptive. The river's constant flow is brief, but the watershed is vast—four thousand square miles. In the mesquite savanna north of Ozona are numerous draws with names like Buckhorn, Buffalo, Wildcat. Grass, cactus, and wildflowers grow undisturbed in them; swallows flutter in the ones pronounced enough to rate a highway bridge. Yet within a few miles, the modest swales have turned into two tributary riverbeds that are remarkable for their breadth of clearance and the size of their parched white rocks. The Dry Devils River loops eastward, near Sonora, and joins the flowing stream twenty-two miles above its mouth in Lake Amistad. Johnson Draw

broadens out south of its passage through Ozona; in a more direct route it meets the Devils near Juno and the headwater springs.

On higher ground around Ozona, six rock dams have been piled across the draws, but they were built one cloudburst too late. In 1954 a ruinous drought was broken by the inland shove of Hurricane Alice. The night of June 28, a flash flood destroyed half of the buildings in Ozona and killed sixteen people. The Devils has experienced rises of as much as fifty feet— which is how the dry white boulders came to be neatly arranged. The water catches beavers patching their dams; a wild and desperate ride later, they find themselves swimming in Lake Amistad. The rampages pluck out grown trees like weeds—and worse. Nineteen miles north of Comstock is a flowered roadside cross marking the spot where several motorists were swept away. Suddenly the brown froth was up all around them, and they couldn't get out.

Above the streambed and bottoms, cave dwellings of aboriginal tribes date back to 9000 B.C.; many are decorated with pictographs. Cabeza de Vaca forded the river during his crazed adventure of the 1530s. There are several versions of how the Devils got its name. Spaniards and Mexicans called it the San Pedro, two versions of the story go, until a United States Army captain set out to scout a road from San Antonio to El Paso in 1847. The expedition ran afoul of one of the flash floods, or else the soldiers, horses, and mules got terribly lost in the river's maze of canyons, which bristle with thorns and teem with snakes. In either case, the captain was said to remark on his emergence: "San Pedro, hell. That's the devil's river."

The sedentary Indian cultures had disappeared by then, but to nomadic tribes the Devils' southward cut through the Edwards Plateau was a favorite trail to Mexico. In 1857 one of the frontier's most ferocious battles between the Comanches and the cavalry was fought near the headwater springs, amid an inferno of dry brush the Indians had set to panic the horses ridden by the badly outnumbered soldiers. An arrow pinned the hand of a lieutenant, Kentuckian John Hood, to his horse's bridle. Hood lived to become a Confederate general and Civil War hero because the smoke abruptly cleared and Comanche women raised a demoralizing howl on seeing the number of their own dead, ending the fight.

The first permanent settlers arrived in the 1880s. Among them was David Baker, who built a home overlooking the fording point of the San Antonio–El Paso road. Baker's stagecoach way station was rendered obsolete by the Southern Pacific Railroad, but in his mind, hospitality required that food and shelter be offered to anyone who showed up in such a remote and difficult place. Today the house sits on the east bank, above the only highway bridge

across the Devils. Though it has created some strain between his descendants and their neighbors, his premise of hospitable obligation has been carried down four generations.

Mary Hughey inherited the ranch at Baker's Crossing from her first husband, who was David Baker's great-grandson. Hughey charges canoeists a ten-dollar put-in fee, and she makes them listen to a polite lecture on the hazards of the river and the rights and outlook of the landowners. She is entitled to both conditions. River access law in Texas is a bizarre tangle, but the situation on the Devils is unique. Many land grants there go back to Spanish or Mexican jurisdiction. And though in Texas most private property lines stop at a river, with streambed rights reserved for the state, the lines were clearly drawn across the Devils on five plats of an 1859 survey. For the first two miles downstream from Baker's Crossing, both the banks and the streambed are privately owned. Canoeists on this gateway stretch technically break trespass laws if they step or fall out of the boat—a point often raised by those who want to stop or limit such traffic.

But ownership of the water is governed by the definition of a navigable stream: If it retains an average flowing width of thirty feet from the mouth up, the public owns it. Measure every foot of it? Rainy season or dry? On close calls the law is a riddle. Still, most Devils landowners now tolerate a 1993 General Land Office survey that found that the river well exceeds the thirty-foot standard. The survey shifts the standard to a trespass law based on the gradient boundary, which sets public-private demarcation as a line drawn midway between the low point of the flowing water and the higher plane of the cut bank. Got your sextant? Small wonder that in legal and legislative circles, an old saw defines a navigable stream in Texas as one holding enough water to float a Supreme Court opinion.

The Devils' privately owned streambed takes in the property of the Hugheys and two downstream neighbors, one of whom is a tall and forceful man named Todd Simpson. On a visit to his restored ranch house, my eyes had fallen on a pillow silk-screened "Nouveau riche is better than no riche at all." A Houston entrepreneur, Simpson lost money in feedlots and plant nurseries before rebounding with a retail cold-brew coffee business. He and his wife, Betty, bought their ranch in 1987 and started building separate retreats on it for their children. Now they spend little time elsewhere.

On a six-hour tour of his land, Simpson showed me a grave plot where an 1880s settler buried five family members in six months; damage inflicted on his pecan trees by gnawing porcupines; watercress billowing in a riverbank

spring; and a burned-rock midden where aborigines cooked and camped for centuries. Simpson has one of the keenest eyes on the river for its overlapping vegetation of South Texas chaparral, the Hill Country, and the Chihuahuan Desert. He pointed out fragrant white bush, deadly poisonous mountain laurel, sideoats grama, lead trees, hop trees, and persimmons, and noted how pine forests had covered the canyons in damper epochs. He described mountainsides transformed by spear-like flower stalks of sotol, and the pale lavender blush of the country when humidity triggers the blooms of cenizo, or purple sage.

Geological maps refer to the region as the Devils River Uplift, and it's no exaggeration to call its canyon walls mountainsides. Our pickup jaunt across Simpson's land was a slow, lurching roller coaster ride. Ranching that country must be hell on tires and transmissions, not to mention horses. The high ground angles away from the river in long, narrow meanders; sheer limestone cliffs drop 350 feet into canyons that are about a thousand feet across. "From the air it looks like the ridges and furrows of a walnut shell," Simpson said. He stopped on the summit of one ridge and counted out six progressively bluer canyons and ridges beyond. That was where his real estate stopped.

Simpson represents a rare element on the Devils—the accepted outsider and latecomer. On the matter of canoeists, he sides with the ranchers. He shoos away "herpers" who come around hoping to catch the rare and valuable gray-banded kingsnake. He is a conservationist who is leery of the Nature Conservancy of Texas, the custodian of Dolan Falls, and describes Parks and Wildlife as an unwieldy bureaucracy. But he loathes the United States Fish and Wildlife Service, which enforces the Endangered Species Act. "In the name of that legislation the federal government has perpetrated outrage on the rights of private landowners," Simpson told me, raising his voice. "Why, it's the stuff of revolution!"

And before the canoe ride I had met one of the Simpsons' downstream neighbors, T. J. Jarrett, in a Del Rio coffee shop. More than any other rancher, he is responsible for tales of extreme inhospitality along the Devils, but he doesn't look like Caligula. A thin man in his early fifties, he has a habit of punctuating his speech with small, quick smiles, and the effect is mannerly. He recalled a University of Texas geography professor who told him that during flash floods, the Devils is the fastest-moving river in North America. "It can be deadly," Jarrett said. "If canoeists get stranded by a rise over on the east bank, they're in trouble—especially if they lose their food. There's no way we can get to them; it would take a helicopter to get them out. It's a ten-mile walk back through those canyons, *if* they can find the way.

"Other times," he went on, "the river stops flowing completely. People who think that's a white-water river have been sold a piece of goods. They show up with their canoes and two big ice chests, which they wind up carrying a lot of the way. It's at least six days down the Devils, and most of them are not in shape for that. We haul them out with heat exhaustion, broken shins." Of course, Jarrett's concern is balanced by self-interest. "Canoeists have ruined the upper Guadalupe for the people who live on it. All you see now is beer cans and trash. We don't want that to happen here. It's the American dream: have a little piece of land, a place you can retire to." Fixing his gaze on me, he said, "You live in Austin. How'd you like it if somebody decided to camp in your front yard, come right up on the patio, and use your barbecue pit?"

I said I wouldn't, then asked him how many canoeists are a problem.

"Not many," he conceded. "Most of them are real nice. It's the ten percent. We catch them taking down signs, climbing way up in the caves, looking for pictographs. And then they get belligerent, and you have to get a deputy sheriff out there to arrest them. Who wants to spend their time doing that?"

Jarrett's little piece of land flanks about five miles of river, and his warnings about the river's difficulties, I would find, were a blend of truth and deception. For example, it *could* take six days to run the Devils from Baker's Crossing to Amistad, but the streambed has almost no islands, and most landowners avidly prosecute any travelers caught camping on the banks. Realistically, prudence requires canoeists to make the trip in three days, and the last twelve hours are on open lake water in the teeth of a strong head wind.

After meeting Jarrett, I had gone out to Creek Boat Rental to meet Punk Rehm. A garrulous oldtimer with sideburns and a gimme cap, Rehm doesn't care what Devils River ranchers think of him. Most of his trade relies on the vaunted fishing on Lake Amistad, but for twenty-five dollars a head plus gas he'll shuttle canoeists to Baker's Crossing. When the lake is high enough, he runs a deck boat back into the inlet and tows the canoes the last few miles. Rehm took me to a shed where he repairs the fiberglass canoes he rents. They were crumpled, patched, beaten all to hell. "Seventy-five percent of the folks I see had a great time and can't wait to come back," he said. "The others never want to see the Devils River again. Sometimes they're so tired they can't crawl up in the boat."

The morning after our first river ride, in the state natural area's hunting cabin, our movements were stiff and slow; there was a good deal of lingering over one more cup of coffee. But once again the weather was perfect. Goldbloom went off to manage the logistics of getting us off the Devils. My new partner

was park superintendent Bill Armstrong, and I took to him at once. The restricted use of the natural area is bolstered by the lack of any sign on U.S. 277 indicating its existence, and from the turnoff, it's a twenty-two-mile drive over a rough gravel road to the house, barn, and horse corrals that Armstrong and his wife call home. As a canoeist, he wasn't out to prove anything. Our philosophies were identical: Enjoy the view when the paddling's easy and get through the rough spots however you can.

A few hundred yards downstream, still on state property, the Dolan Springs come gushing out of the limestone. We parked the canoes and walked to a cave that has a wall bearing the inscription "E. K. Fawcett 1883." The scratches of other free-range herders who camped there have faded from legibility and local memory. Fawcett bore down on his mark like he meant to stay; soon his claim took in several ranches and tens of thousands of acres. In 1988 his heirs wept at a real estate closing when the last of his empire was sold off to Parks and Wildlife. Andy Sansom told me it was one of the most moving things he had ever been involved in.

Back in the canoes, we heard the muffled roar of Dolan Falls, so we got out again, feeling the strength of its pull in water that barely reached our ankles. Running the falls is considered suicidal—it's a twelve-foot drop through an obstacle course of jutting rock, and powerful currents churn back under—but sometimes canoeists are unable to avoid it. They don't know the river well enough to recognize the falls; most of its noise is projected downstream, and when they jump out of the boat, the streambed is slippery. We manhandled our canoes over large boulders on the right. The cascade parts and falls in two streams around a rock that looks like a Mayan throne. A great blue heron that had been sitting here leapt out over the spray and moved off in its ponderous but elegant flight. In a few minutes we were paddling in circles in water the color of sapphire, shouting and mugging for photos in the roar and spray. Every ache was worth it, I was thinking, just to see this.

As we again set out downstream, the effect of Dolan Springs was evident; the river broadened out, and there were more rapids. When we snagged, I noticed that the rocks underfoot were now dark and slick with moss. We came into a rapid that broke up in finger channels and veered off to the right through tall clumps of river grass and shrubby trees. No question we had to drag the canoe—but which route? Armstrong and I chose one that suddenly shot us into a Class III rapid known as Three Tier Waterfall. Now the canoe was pulling us. We held it back through the first tier, but the next swoop of white water took my feet out from under me. I came up tripping and skidding, hanging on to the rope with one hand, grabbing at rocks and an exposed tree

trunk with the other, all the while thinking of T. J. Jarrett's precise and vivid warning: broken shins. I lost my grip on the rope, certain the canoe was bound for ruin. Greatly impressed, I watched my partner stay with it, holding on to the stern. Armstrong told me later, "I just sort of water-skied through it." If that comparison is apt, I suppose my descent through the waterfall could be described as bodysurfing.

I'm not complaining; I enlisted for every minute of it. I badly wanted to see the Devils, a canoe was the only available mode of transportation, and no water and terrain in Texas have bewitched me more. But if you try it, come prepared—and don't assume that skill is a panacea. As Andy Sansom told me at the takeout, "That river is not for everyone."

We passed up the third day of wind-beset passage toward Lake Amistad—an option we couldn't have exercised a year earlier. Twenty-five miles south of Baker's Crossing is the first hint of urban sprawl, a half-formed batch of river-side homes called the Blue Sage Subdivision. A man named Sam Dandridge runs a shuttle service, which Goldbloom had engaged for us. A wiry and friendly man, Dandridge has occupied a concrete cliff-top abode since 1981, when canoeists were hardly ever seen on the river. "Some people around here say, 'Don't talk to 'em. Don't even look at 'em,'" he told me. "Why, hell, I'd always say hello. Take 'em a six-pack if I had one."

Dropping riders and canoes at various points, the shuttle covered half an hour of up-and-down, dust-choked road to U.S. 277, turned south toward Del Rio, northwest on U.S. 90 across the bridges of Lake Amistad toward Comstock, and north again on Texas Highway 163 to Baker's Crossing. For Dandridge, the shuttle typically consumes eight hours and entails a 182-mile round trip; he charges a minimum of one hundred dollars. I asked him why he does it. "I like talking to happy people," he said, grinning. "Either they had a great time or they're plumb miserable. Either way, they're always glad to see me."

I cleaned up in my Del Rio motel room, changed clothes, and drove back out to Baker's Crossing. The sun was going down, and a rain shower moved through the valley. Mary and Les Hughey and I sat by a window, gazing at the Devils. "It can seem so harmless," Mary said, "and then it's totally destructive. I think that's why the name stuck. I've seen it jerk pecan trees out by the roots. The roar is incredible. The waves get as tall as a house. There are tides. After a rise there's a new world—dunes of sand, what's left of the trees. That river's going to have its way, and its way is often violent. If you go off in there and get hurt, you can cry and scream all you want. No one's going to hear

you. Canoeists need to be told that. But I have an equal responsibility to land-owners downstream. Their homes are private property, and for generations that river has been their jewel. If it's going to be opened up, there has to be a system."

I said, "I think T. J. Jarrett's 'system' is doing a bang-up job of protecting the ecology of the Devils River." Les looked at me closely for a moment, then guffawed.

It was more than just a bone-sore quip. Among the possibilities discussed at Parks and Wildlife are canoe permits, which would regulate traffic, and the lease of a couple of campsites along the river. No doubt the legislature will take a hand in designing any river management plan. But canoeing pressure amounts to only one or two hundred boats a year, and the river has its own ways of discouraging an armada. Parks and Wildlife has imposed new size limits on smallmouth bass and has committed its local game wardens to pro-tecting the upper Devils' lavish fishery. Actually, the greatest threat to the river is residential construction, not recreational use. The pristineness of the Dev-ils is the benchmark against which the state measures the water quality of other rivers. Its water is the purest because there are no towns, no wastewater treatment plants, no discharges of effluent. Isolation is the key to its health.

As I drove back to Comstock, I decided that I hope the ranchers hang on. Few of them are getting rich doing it. I came out of the rain and stopped a while on a ridge where the sotol had sent up stalks of bloom. At dusk it was all emptiness and quiet. You'd never dream such a river was out there. I sat on the hood and watched the desert steam.

NOVEMBER, 1994

PART III

TORN FROM ANOTHER COUNTRY
Texas and Mexico

As a youth I never joined my peers when they sped off for a weekend of drinking and whoring in the closest Mexican border town, Ciudad Acuña. That is a rite of passage peculiar to Texas and the other border states, but by the time I came of age the red light districts had been moved out from the downtown bars to compounds that were patrolled by soldiers and, to me, had all the seductive appeal of a penal colony. Boys Town turned me off.

For me the fascination with Mexico began with a magazine assignment. In 1976 a Dallas con artist grieved for a son who had been caught down there smuggling marijuana and for that crime suffered a horrid existence in a packed, airless Piedras Negras jail, across the river from Eagle Pass. When pleas to the State Department and offers of bribes to Mexican officials failed to get the youth moved to a more tolerable prison, his father hired an overweight, battle-scarred Vietnam vet named Don Fielden and a tow truck driver named Mike Hill to bring his boy home. The harebrained commandos burst in with ski masks and shotguns and emptied the whole jail. Escapees went splashing across the Rio Grande. Shadowy groups claimed responsibility for the raid, diplomats in Washington and Mexico City stammered and bristled, and newspaper and magazine writers swarmed, trying to get to the bottom of it. Through a lucky break and connection with Mike Hill, who became a friend, I got the story. The Mexican jailbreak piece was the first time I felt I could step up and play with anybody in the game.

After that my interest was fueled by romance. I fell in love with Dorothy

Browne, the woman I would marry, on a trip in Mexico. We vacationed often down there. I spent two years driving back and forth to the borderlands, coming to know the Kickapoo Indians. Then I befriended a talented young boxer named Jesus Chavez who was deported to Mexico, where he hadn't lived since he was seven years old. I wrote a story about his plight and my friendship with him, and, on a lark, three colleagues and I flew to Mexico City to watch his first fight down there. The night after the bout we went to a mariachi bar and talked and laughed and told elaborate stories. Then we simply got into the wrong cab. The driver delivered us to two *pistoleros* who robbed and terrorized us in the course of a long, wild, surreal ride. They pulled into a poor barrio and ordered us out of the cab. An insurrection broke out; in the reflex-driven blur I threw a punch at the leader, trying to get away from him.

He looked me in the eye and shot to kill me.

When I was back in Texas, hospitalized in Houston, my friend Greg Curtis, who in 1973 had been the first magazine editor to respond to my writing, mused in a generous *Texas Monthly* column: "All this makes it odd that he should now be better known for a piece of bad luck that has become an international incident than for what he has done and believed for twenty-five years."

One day another friend called with his perspective. "From the start you were always writing about violence and Mexico," he said. "It's like all that converged on you—like you went down there looking for what you found." Apart from his unintended cruelty . . . could that be true?

Diagnosed as a paraplegic and initially given little chance of recovery, I plunged into the task of raising myself out of a wheelchair. And eventually I did. I'm proud of the strength I found in myself. Still I'm filled with loss and second-guessing. Some part of that experience is the logical end piece for this book.

I've come to measure my life by magazine stories. They are the signposts, where and when and sometimes why. They have taken me on a humbling trek across Texas in the last quarter of the twentieth century. But they are not just incidents and situations that involved me for a while. They are people who have stayed with me, too. When I got hurt a wave of human feeling lifted me up and carried me away from that hateful *pistolero*. In describing it I have been struck by the number of people who used the word prayer. Though I'm not religious, it's nothing I discount.

One day in the hospital, the phone rang and a quiet man said: "*Amigo.*" It was Joe Hernandez, my translator and guide in my long exploration of the history, culture, and desolation of the Kickapoo. Joe always greets me that way. He asked me once to explain the Christian concept of prayer to him. I

tried, and he nodded thoughtfully, then said that for his people, ritual is prayer. Though the Kickapoo have a small reservation in Texas, their adopted homeland surrounds a pretty wellspring of a river at the foot of the Sierra Madres, a river that flows north to the Rio Grande. Their holy season there begins in the spring, when signs of nature—a crack of lightning, a branch leafing out— tell them that it's time. Joe said that night when I almost lost my life, he too was in Mexico, taking part in the religious ceremonies of his clan; then he had a sudden, strong thought of me. Joe's father is a tribal elder and keeper of their faith and tradition. Joe reveres him. My friend recalled: "I told my dad, 'Something's happened to Jan.' And then I saw the newspapers when we got back to Eagle Pass. I told him, 'The doctors say he's never going to walk again.' My dad said, 'Yeah, but those doctors, they're not in control.'"

TEXAS IS LOST

Imagine the raw, physical bravery required to pull up stakes and journey by saddle and wagon to start a new life in a remote province of Mexico dominated by hostile Indians. Courage is the bedrock trait of the real and mythical Texan character. What was it about Texas that lured Americans to risk their lives in that dangerous wilderness and forsake United States citizenship and institutions for those of Mexico? Through its own revolution, Mexico had inherited vast, imperial claims of Spain—far more country than the new republic could effectively populate and rule. For Americans who were brave or desperate enough, rich prairie and woodlands were available in Texas for the price of settlement—and a pledge of allegiance to Mexico. Most colonists from the north took that oath rather lightly; when provoked, they promptly reneged. One Mexican army officer and explorer, Manuel de Mier y Terán, saw firsthand the value of Texas to Mexico. The agricultural riches could feed a growing nation that elsewhere lacked sufficient arable land. Mier y Terán foresaw the consequence of allowing Texas to slip into the rule of norteamericanos. The squabble over Texas ultimately cost Mexico half its territory and cast it in history as the poor, resentful neighbor of the United States. This short piece was about the voice of a prophet crying in the wilderness. His calls fell on deaf ears.

As Mexican insurgents overran Oaxaca in 1812, routed soldiers loyal to Spain holed up in a Carmelite convent protected by a moat. Twenty-three-year-old Manuel de Mier y Terán directed rebel cannon fire from a drawbridge. In a show of bravado, another young officer decided to swim the moat. The dark water was mostly mud and slime, he found out. Instead of throwing the man a rope, Mier y Terán watched from the bridge and guffawed.

In the fast careers of powerful men, small slights have lasting magnitude. Twelve years later, that day's floundering knucklehead, Guadalupe Victoria,

assumed the Mexican presidency. Even he recognized the indispensable talents of Mier y Terán. He was a brilliant, loyal, educated, politically astute general, and any president had need of those qualities. Still, Guadalupe Victoria desired nothing but miles between himself and the inherited minister of War and Navy. Senators blocked the general's diplomatic mission to England, so in 1827 the president sent him to survey Mexico's boundary with the United States. If there couldn't be an ocean of distance, the empty and remote province called Texas would do.

Loaded with scientific instruments and reference books, the general's caravan crossed the Rio Grande in early 1828. Mier y Terán found the military garrison in sad shape. A few hundred unsupplied soldiers hoarded rice and scavenged buffalo meat and venison. To communicate with other travelers, soldiers would kill a hawk, tie a message to its wing, and hang it in a tree. The expeditioners thought Texas was bizarre. They had never heard bullfrogs before. Illiterate frontiersmen located underground water with quivering forked sticks; the fascinated general wondered if North American scientists had explained these water witches.

Mier y Terán spent two weeks with Stephen F. Austin. Kindred spirits, they began a correspondence that remained warm even in adverse times. Austin's colonists bred mules for export to the British and French West Indies and raised astonishing crops in the Brazos River Valley. The farmers told him that because of the mild winters, they could work longer in Texas and thus not so frantically and hard. They pressed him for tariff concessions, a port at Galveston, and an exemption from Mexico's revolutionary ban of slavery.

During those thirteen months he didn't exactly fall in love with Texas. The ratio of lawyers, he noted, was awfully high. The climate nearly killed him. The feverish general couldn't believe the summer heat and ordered improved thermometers from New Orleans to verify his readings. He diligently mapped and recorded, but Spanish troops dispatched from Cuba cut the mission short when they invaded Tampico in mid-1829. The mapping would be completed three decades later by other scholarly gentleman soldiers—who wore the uniforms of the United States.

The Veracruz governor, Santa Anna, took credit for the Mexican victory over the Spaniards and became a national figure, but military analysts give more credit to the artillery siege of Mier y Terán. Aides said he directed the cannon fire with a sword in one hand, a cup of chocolate in the other. Based in Tamaulipas, he then completed his report on Texas.

The visionary general anticipated an overpopulated Mexico with insufficient arable land. Texas, he had seen, was an agricultural bounty—and a mat-

ter of national security. Politicians in Mexico were debating whether to let Nicaragua and Guatemala join the federation after the Spaniards' expulsion. Forget about Spain, he urged, and look north.

"The department of Texas is contiguous to the most avid nation on earth," he wrote. "The North Americans have conquered whatever territory adjoins them." If Mexico surrendered Texas, "it would degenerate from the most elevated class of the American powers to that of a contemptible mediocrity, reduced to the necessity of buying a precarious existence at the cost of many humiliations." Any Mexican citizen "who consents to and does not oppose the loss of Texas is an execrable traitor who ought to be punished with every kind of death."

He begged for more troops and influenced legislation in 1830 that restricted American immigration. Colonists such as Stephen F. Austin were welcome but had to be outnumbered three to one. He wanted to recruit German and Swiss settlers and send Mexican convicts to Texas. Every Mexican governor was supposed to recruit 450 families for Texas: A total of one family signed up.

Mier y Terán was only forty-three, but an illness that began in Texas had ruined his health. Weary of his depression and a bleak life on the frontier, his wife left him and returned to Mexico City. An abrasive garrison commander at Galveston Bay drove even Austin to civil disobedience. Fighting broke out when a subordinate jailed some settlers, including William B. Travis, without charges.

Trying to quell that disorder was the last straw for Mier y Terán. "I am an unhappy man, and unhappy people should not live on this earth," he wrote a friend while staying in the village of San Antonio de Padilla. "I have studied this situation for five years, and today I know nothing, nothing, for man is very despicable and small; and—let us put an end to these reflections, for they almost drive me mad. The revolution is about to break forth, and Texas is lost."

The next morning, July 3, 1832, he put on his dress uniform and added a gay silk scarf. He spoke to a sentry, walked behind a roofless church, propped his sword against a rock, and drove it through his broken heart.

JANUARY, 1986

BUSTING OUT OF MEXICO

"Hey boy. You wanna go to Mexico?" Across the generations, how many excursions of young, careless Texans have been set in motion by such a call to romance and risk south of the border? In most cases, the destinations are no more dangerous than the red-light districts in the Mexican border towns. But when an affable tough named Mike Hill heard those words from a pal leaning across the door of his truck at a Dallas drive-in 1976, he was propelled toward an act of crazy bravado that could easily have gotten him killed.

Mexico was under mounting pressure to restrict its supply of illegal drugs to eager markets in the United States. Then as now, agents of our Drug Enforcement Agency were eager to help Mexican cops bust the drug runners, whatever their nationality. But the sixties had established a consensus in this country that smoking marijuana was not the worst of vices, and the laws against its use and supply were generally too harsh. At the same time, conditions in Mexican jails and prisons were squalid, in some cases life-threatening. Mike Hill became the partner of a Vietnam ex-Marine who had an offer of payment from a Dallas man if they could free his son, a small-time smuggler of marijuana, from a jail in Piedras Negras, across the Rio Grande from Eagle Pass. The success of the hair-raising assault in March, 1976, added one more indignity to the long list of perceived humiliations of Mexican authorities by Americans, and it set off a scramble of journalists in the Southwest. One of them was me. The story appeared in The Best of Texas Monthly with an apt subhead: "It couldn't happen this way in a million years. But it did." The story was an important breakthrough for me: I came away confident my reporting skills had caught up with my writing.

As it often happens, I broke the hotly contested story by means of a lucky break. I happened to strike up a conversation with Hill at a moment when he felt he was being dealt out of any glory and profit by his

partner, and he didn't have the money or car to get from Dallas to Del Rio, where he was being arraigned in federal court. I drove him down there, and after that the story opened up like a spring flower. Unlike his partner, who turned state's evidence against him, Mike never served a day in prison. Gerald Goldstein, a San Antonio lawyer who also became my friend, got his sentence overturned on appeal. I stayed in touch with Mike for many years, but eventually I stopped hearing from him. His encounter with fame had come and gone. Mike was no angel, and innocent Mexicans could have died because of his daredevil escapade. But in his mind the jailbreak was a mission of mercy. I miss his company and wish him well.

When the American inmates at Piedras Negras talked to Blake Davis, they sometimes caught themselves staring at the jagged, reddened scar that underlined the ridge of his jaw. Blake Davis, whose nickname was Cooter, was ebullient, powerfully built, well liked by the other Americans. Even in moments of discouragement he somehow managed a rueful smile. "Next week" was always the time of Blake's anticipated departure from the Piedras Negras jail. He always had a scam. Blake did not mind talking about his scar. He said he'd been arrested near Saltillo and charged with transporting 175 pounds of marijuana. For three weeks, Blake said, he was strapped naked to a bed while *federales* interrogated him, until finally he signed a Spanish confession he could not read. While he was in prison at Saltillo, Blake claimed he bribed a warden for two thousand dollars, but when the tunneling started the warden alerted the guards. Blake said he unwisely cried foul; the warden referred the matter to Mexican inmates who set upon Blake with crude knives and razor blades. Hence the scar. Blake's tale of horror did not rate him special privileges in the Piedras Negras seniority system. When he was transferred there in August, 1975, like all other new arrivals he took a seat on the floor.

When a Mexican attorney arranged his transfer from Saltillo, Blake thought he was destined for a federal prison in Piedras Negras called Penal. But Mexican officials claimed Penal was overcrowded, and they blamed America for a November, 1974, breakout in which twenty-four prisoners tunneled to freedom. Blake Davis was thus assigned to the Piedras Negras municipal jail. Inside the jail were five cells for men, one cell for women, and a drunk tank, each of which measured eight feet by nine feet. The windowless cells con-

tained four bunks, a toilet, a water faucet, and from six to twelve sweating, panting, claustrophobic prisoners. Mexican national inmates were eventually transferred to Penal, but the Americans waited for enough seniority to occupy one of the bunks. When they moved around their cells they shuffled. They never breathed fresh air, never saw the sky. The lights of the jail were never turned off, so their only concept of day and night came from the jail kitchen, which provided gruel in the morning, soup at noon, beans and tortillas at dinner. The Americans depended upon friends to bring them vitamins and food. After a few months their teeth began to decay and their hair began to thin. They passed the time playing scrabble and backgammon, studying Spanish. Two or three performed yoga and isometric exercises. Though the Americans hated and feared Mexican cops, they had a certain empathy for the jail guards, who were poor men working for five or six dollars a day and were helpless to do anything about the crowded conditions of the jail. The guards also seemed to understand that the Americans were under severe mental and emotional stress, prisoners of a foreign government and a foreign system of justice. Certain liberties were in order. Hard drugs could be smuggled past the guards, and the Mexican fink assigned to each cell containing Americans often operated a marijuana concession. Sometimes the guards allowed women to join the men in their bunks or in the privacy of the shower room. But now and then the powder-keg tension of the jail would explode. Some American would faint, his skin would turn the shade of alabaster, and the other Americans would start shouting angry demands for medical attention.

Except for weekenders in the drunk tank, all the American inmates were alleged narcotics violators. Mexico's judicial system is rooted in the Napoleonic Code, in which, essentially, suspects of a crime are guilty until proven innocent. Any felony suspect caught red-handed, *in flagrante delicto,* can be held, interrogated, and denied access to an attorney for three days. If, after six days, a magistrate concludes that evidence warrants a trial, and the maximum sentence of the alleged offense is more than two years, a suspect can be held up to a year before he is tried. Even if a suspect proves in a court of grievance that his Mexican constitutional rights have been violated, the charges against him still stand. In January, 1975, the Mexican government enacted a law that denied narcotics suspects any kind of release on bond. From the standpoint of the Americans in the Piedras Negras jail, Mexican law was a stacked deck. Only Davis had actually been convicted, but the rest of the Americans never talked about waiting for trial. They always said they were waiting for sentencing.

Blake Davis and the other Americans knew that a California congressman

named Pete Stark was spearheading a House subcommittee hearing on the fate of six hundred Americans in Mexican jails, but they placed very little trust in the United States government. The United States Drug Enforcement Agency (DEA) trains Mexican narcotics agents, analyzes Mexican confiscations in its Dallas laboratories, and stuffs American dollars into the Mexican control agencies at the rate of $14 million per year. Operation Cooperation, American officials like to say, is designed to disrupt the guns-for-drugs trade. But the American inmates claimed the barber-shirted federales busted any American they possibly could, by whatever methods, while their DEA benefactors applauded. It was no longer easy for American prisoners to bribe their way out of Mexican jail. One of the American inmates at Piedras Negras theorized that nothing had really changed: the favors of Mexican *mordida* still went to the highest bidder—the United States government.

Once a month United States consular officials came to the jail; one of those callers was Leonard Walentynowicz, the administrator who represented the State Department at the congressional hearings. But the American inmates were in no mood to wait on Washington. Every prisoner had a plan. One considered smuggling hydrochloric acid on visitors' day to weaken the bars of the shower room. Another wanted to blow a small hole in the roof. Another pinned his hopes on a brother-in-law who worked for the CIA. The most dubious scheme involved advance payments to the Mexican secret police, who would then assist the escapees through a shower room window.

Cooter Davis was king of the freedom schemers. For six months his father in Dallas had been trying to finance a Piedras Negras jailbreak. Every twelve hours, at six o'clock, the inmates were taken from their cells into the corridor for a *lista*. While the guards called roll, counted heads, and inspected the cells for signs of tunneling, the American inmates exchanged notes. They slept with their clothes easily accessible and tried to raise money through friends on the outside. Tuesday and Wednesday were the most likely nights, for there was less drunk traffic at the jail. Inevitably, the rumors reached the ears of the Mexican guards. One day in January an American tough recruited by Blake's father signed the visitors' register, submitted to a frisk by the guards, and came back to Blake's cell. The American whispered through the bars that the jailbreak was on. Some of the American inmates altered their sleeping habits so they would always be awake in the hours after midnight. But when the American returned to Piedras Negras, he passed word the next visitors' day that the break was no longer possible: Armed guards were now circling the block and maintaining a lookout on the roof of the jail. Some of the inmates grew tired of the constant anticipation. Every time the Coke ma-

chine noisily dispensed a ten-ounce bottle they wondered if commandos had broken down the door. After two months of breakout rumors, the guards also tired of hearing them. A new *comandante* ordered a search of the prisoners' possessions, but told the warden that the guard on the roof was no longer necessary.

Blake Davis remained optimistic, for the alternative to optimism was exceedingly grim. He had lost twenty-five pounds during his incarceration. His body was covered with boils, and a cyst at the base of his spine was seeping pus. Poison from an abscessed tooth descended with his saliva and gave him a stomach ache. Cooter had served only two years of a ten-year sentence. He did not think he could survive eight more years in a Mexican jail.

In the late forties, Sterling Blake Davis, Sr., introduced the limp-wristed flair of Liberace to the macho world of pro wrestling. While his old Houston crony, Gorgeous George Wagner, made a fortune with the routine on California TV, Dizzy Davis sported colorful, hand-sewn robes and dispensed flowers in the smoky arenas of Texas and Mexico. Sometimes called Gardenia Davis, he was often considered a better wrestler than Wagner.

Davis' luck since those days had been a carousel ride. By 1972 he owned a large home on the east shore of Dallas' Lake Ray Hubbard. But his health was failing, and he was only fifty-eight. One of his sons seemed to be adjusting nicely to middle-class adulthood. The other, Sterling Blake, Jr., was doing time in a federal penitentiary for possessing 770 pounds of marijuana in Arizona.

The old man would soon be in a heap of trouble himself. In November, 1973, he was named in a thirteen-count federal fraud indictment and was tried in February, 1974, in the Dallas courtroom of Judge Sarah T. Hughes, the much-respected magistrate made famous the sad day John F. Kennedy was killed and she had to swear in Lyndon Johnson as president. Testimony in the trial portrayed Davis as a shuck and jive artist who convinced seventy customers that bullfrog farming was the wave of the future. One investor testified that Davis falsely claimed to own a 650-acre frog farm in Arkansas, from which in a single year Rice University research scientists bought nine thousand bullfrogs—at sixteen dollars a frog. Frog distributors came from as far as Iowa and Florida to testify that Davis and two other men sold them a three thousand dollar bill of goods that included two portable swimming pools with inefficient filters, a few frogs, an instruction manual, and a piece of vibrating sheet metal called an automatic feeder. The instruction manual said bullfrogs could be taught to feed in captivity if they were offered a fare of

bouncing maggots, and then rabbit food, on the vibrating sheet metal. One distributor said he hung a rotting armadillo over the feeder to keep the frogs supplied with maggots. Another testified that his wife watched for signs of progress with binoculars from a nearby tree. Most said they eventually set the starving frogs free.

At the trial Davis contended the feeder worked perfectly for some of his clients, but the court remained unconvinced. "Now I heard the evidence and I don't think the feeder is working," Judge Hughes replied. After the jury found Davis guilty on ten counts, Hughes told him, "You are one of the best con artists that has appeared before me." She ordered him to make restitution to his former customers, fined him ten thousand dollars, and sentenced him to five years, followed by five more years probation.

Davis, who carries the scar of open-heart surgery, pled ill health. After studying the doctors' affidavits, in May, 1974, Hughes probated the remainder of Davis' five-year sentence. But that very same month Davis' son Blake, paroled by then on his Arizona pot conviction, was arrested 150 miles deep in Mexico and charged with possession of marijuana. Sterling Davis felt like a man accursed.

To pay his legal fees Davis had to sell most of the acres he owned on Lake Ray Hubbard. His probation officer vetoed a couple of ideas for new employment. Finally Davis offered his services to the administrator of a non-credit educational institute in Dallas, explaining that in the frog farm episode he had been a mere management consultant deceived by the two salesmen. Davis convinced the administrator he had valid degrees in psychology and experience as an industrial psychologist. At the institute Davis tutored night students on meditation techniques allegedly developed by long-lived Andean Indians. To avoid incurring the legal wrath of the TM organization, Davis called his course Transcendental Relaxation. In January, 1975, he applied for a state license to practice clinical psychology. The board of examiners informed him that before he could take the qualifying exam, two years of experience supervised by a licensed psychologist were required. Davis found a psychologist who would sponsor him. Extremely secretive about his personal finances, Davis put his hands on enough money to furnish an office on Northwest Highway with a fifteen hundred dollar stereo that played soothing music and a vibrating chair that gave the person sitting in it a massage.

At the same time, Davis was trying to get his son out of jail. He pursued embassy channels to no avail and developed a very low regard for Mexican attorneys. To his surprise, however, he learned that if nobody got hurt, and

no property was damaged, there was no law against jailbreak in Mexico. After Blake was transferred to Piedras Negras, Davis started looking for ways to raise money, including efforts to involve friends and families of the inmates. He put out a feeler that moved through an underground of Dallas bars, drive-ins, and all-night restaurants. It was not a very attractive offer. The jailbreakers stood an excellent chance of getting killed, and if they were captured by the Mexicans, they were as good as dead. And if they killed any Mexicans, the American government would probably extradite them. The money Davis offered was insufficient to attract professionals. Davis thus interviewed a long line of maniacs and scoundrels. One group Davis rejected wanted to storm across with enough explosives to start a war. He advanced money to another gang of small-time heavies who bought guns and an El Camino pickup, then partied until the money ran out in San Antonio. Davis had high hopes for the assault team that approached his son inside the jail, but they were frightened off at the last moment by the beefed-up security. He had begun to wonder if jailbreaks happened only in the movies.

At his Northwest Highway office on Monday, February 16, Davis gazed across the desk at another prospective jailbreaker. The man did not look like much of a commando. He had an enormous belly, and when he opened his mouth there was a dark gap where his two front teeth should have been.

Don Fielden was a Marine without a mission, a truckdriver without a rig. After moving to Dallas from the northeast Texas town of Gladewater, Fielden had dropped out of Woodrow Wilson High School and joined the Marine Corps in 1966. Assigned to the infantry during boot camp at San Diego, he underwent more training at Camp Pendleton and drew orders to join the First Marine Division in Vietnam. "They'd been telling us all along that this was a police action," he recalled much later. "They instilled that thought so deep in my mind I expected to go over there and use a .45 and a nightstick. Patrol the streets. The first night I was in Da Nang, they shelled the hell out of us. I thought, man, I ain't never seen a cop go through this shit."

Fielden explored the Vietnamese countryside by helicopter and combat patrol. "I was able to condition my mind to where it was like I was back home squirrel hunting," he said. "Except these squirrels were shooting back. I don't have bad dreams about killing people over there. I'm not ashamed of it. It was a job my country told me to do." Fielden helped ward off enemy attacks during construction of the air base at Phu Bai, then took his R&R leave in Japan. Nineteen days before he was scheduled to rotate back to the States, he was pulling radio watch in a sandbagged bunker near the DMZ. After finishing

his watch, Fielden stood at the door of an unfortified wall and gazed longingly at the two-man privy positioned a few yards away. How bad, he tried to decide, did he need to go? He paused in the doorway to monitor a radio message; at that moment a stray communist rocket scored a direct hit on the two-holer. Shrapnel gouged a chunk out of Fielden's shoulder and nearly severed his right leg below the knee.

At the United States Naval Hospital in Corpus Christi, Fielden worked in the Marine liaison office and extended his enlistment for a year. He soon learned that antiwar sentiment back home was running deep; even some of the sailors at Corpus Christi treated him like a murderer of children. On leave he found that things were no better in Dallas. Fielden's favorite times during that period were spent in the company of other convalescent Marines at a bar called the Town Pump. But there was scant future in the Marine Corps for a sergeant with a chronically aching leg. Fielden was severed from active duty in 1970 with a Purple Heart but no disability pension. In 1972 he received his honorable discharge in the mail.

Back in Dallas, Fielden sometimes told people that the hideous scar on his calf was the result of a motorcycle accident. He bought a Corvette and entertained new acquaintances with his jovial banter. But he was drinking heavily, and his weight pushed far past two hundred pounds. The father of two children, he soon would go through his third divorce.

Fielden was becoming a tough character in a tough town. The Marines had trained him to function in a world of total violence, where the ethic of work was survival. No civilian experience matched the overcharged excitement of Vietnam, but he didn't stop looking. He drove a truck and moonlighted for a heavy-handed collection agency that fronted as a nightclub janitorial service.

On the night of March 3, 1975, the freeway driving habits of a Dallas municipal employee so outraged Fielden that he fired off a couple of shots from his pistol—clean misses—while Dallas Cowboy flanker Golden Richards witnessed the incident driving in an adjacent lane. The grand jury no-billed Fielden when nobody chose to testify.

Fielden was relatively happy as a long-haul truckdriver. He liked his life on the road: trading truckstop stories reminded him of the masculine camaraderie in the Marine Corps' geedunk beer halls. But then on December 23, 1975, Fielden returned from a trip and parked his truck on the lot of his Dallas employer. When he returned the next day his boss told him, "We can't use you anymore. You're fired."

"Merry Christmas," Fielden said to himself.

Fielden was not making it on the outside; he remained a casualty of the Vietnam War. As a teenaged recruit Fielden never questioned the Marine Corps line. He labored torturously for abusive drill instructors who told him he would "never make a pimple on a Marine's ass." Fielden had proved himself a Marine at home in the barracks and overseas under fire. Now he was failing in a world that did not care if he had made the Marines. Out of work, out of family, running out of money, Fielden was desperate for drastic changes in his life. During the day he wasn't doing much of anything. At night he hung out in north Dallas trucker bars and discos—the world in which Sterling Davis' jailbreak offer was circulating. A friend explained the situation and gave him the doctor's phone number. On February 16, Fielden met Davis in the blue and silver office building on Northwest Highway.

Fielden had a very stone-faced way of listening to people. His chin jutted out and his mouth turned down. In the office Fielden listened as Sterling Davis recounted the story of his troubled efforts to free his son. Davis said that he'd studied in Mexico; a diploma on the office wall indicated he earned his Ph.D. from the University of Mexico in 1951. Fielden did not speak Spanish, and he asked Davis to provide him with the Spanish equivalent of "get your hands up" and other key phrases. The doctor stammered and changed the subject.

Fielden earned his high school equivalency certificate during his tour in the Marines. He respected men with superior education. He did not respect men who feigned academic credentials. Fielden pegged the man as a con, and he had scant compassion for busted dope dealers. But he said he would free the doctor's son for five thousand dollars and expenses, reimbursed afterward. It was a job, a mission, almost like the Marines. In a dull civilian world, where he did not quite fit, it was a chance to rejoin the action.

Fielden spent most of the third week of February in Eagle Pass, reconnoitering his combat patrol into Mexico. Fielden was pleased by some of the things he saw. The Piedras Negras jail was only three blocks from the Mexican tollgates at the International Bridge. On visitors' day he took Blake Davis some food and called him by the family nickname Cooter. Blake knew immediately why Fielden was there. Fielden thought the jail looked like the set of an Old West movie. The cells were locked with hasps and chains that could be cut with heavy-duty bolt cutters. But the jail sat far back on its lot, adjoined on both sides by the walls of buildings that extended to the street. When Fielden stepped out of the Piedras Negras jail, he was looking at the rectangular dimensions of a trap. Reluctantly, Fielden concluded he would need another man.

Mike Hill was broke and looking for trouble, if trouble would get him out of Dallas. Hill had been scraping a living off the streets of Dallas since he was thirteen years old, and at thirty-two all he had to show for it was a Chevy Step-Van painted reflective silver. He spent part of the winter of 1976 sleeping in his van.

The son of alcoholic parents, Hill stopped going to school when he started living alone in a deserted fire station. He subsisted at first on a diet of soda pop and bread, then stole a bicycle so he could take a delivery job. During the rest of his teens Hill's residence alternated between the homes of friends and the state reformatory at Gatesville. Hill always ran away from the juvenile prison. He couldn't stand the feeling of confinement. In 1965 Hill was convicted of burglary but his sentence was probated. Over the next decade he was jailed and hauled before grand juries on an assortment of charges but was never indicted. A marriage produced two daughters before it ended in divorce. He bought used cars wholesale, then sold them through the classifieds. He ran a wrecker service that rousted him out of bed at all times of the night.

Then in 1972 Hill discovered marijuana. When it wasn't feeding his paranoia, a marijuana high dulled the sharp edges of Mike Hill's world. He sold his business, motorcycled to Florida, and returned to exploit the Dallas towaway ordinance. A fleet of independent wrecker operators hauled cars away from private property posted with warning signs, then delivered the cars to a lot leased by Hill. Hill paid the drivers twenty-five dollars, then charged the owners of the impounded autos forty-three dollars in cash. Perfectly legal. Ensuring order at Hill's lot were snarling dogs and a gang of shotgun-toting cronies.

A *Dallas Morning News* story about the towaways placed Hill in the center of a storm of bad publicity, but worse news was yet to come. Hill's drivers towed away the car of Dallas Mayor Pro Tem Adlene Harrison. One driver tried to remove the car of Dallas undercover narcotics agents who were parked at a closed filling station observing a nightclub on Cedar Springs. The narcs ordered the wrecker driver away, and the driver called Hill. When Hill arrived at the site in his van, the narcs radioed a vice-squad officer for assistance. The ensuing argument ended, inevitably, in Hill's arrest. In Hill's van, Dallas officers told reporters after the incident, were a loaded derringer, a loaded pistol, a dagger, an unloaded shotgun, and two baseball bats. Adlene Harrison proposed a new tow-away ordinance to the city council, and a misdemeanor gun conviction was added to Mike Hill's growing record.

Yet through it all, Hill remained eminently likable. A blond mustache concealed a beer-bottle scar, the bridge of his nose was enlarged by numerous

fractures, and there was something tense and hard about his eyes, but when Hill laughed he was handsome. He was a good storyteller, and women found him attractive. He stood nearly six feet and was muscular, with only a little flab above his belt. He had an odd, slouching stride, shoulders hulking forward as he walked. Mike Hill was a familiar Texas character: the tough guy good old boy. When he drove his van into the lot of a favorite hangout the last week of February, he wasn't necessarily up to no good. He was just passing through. A friend who also knew Don Fielden stuck his head in Hill's van and grinned. "Hey boy. You wanna go to Mexico?"

Hill was intrigued; the whole idea seemed so *cinematic.* Besides, he needed money badly and an expense-paid trip to Mexico sounded like a vacation. The two men arranged to meet on Saturday night, February 28, at the Denny's on Industrial Boulevard. By this time Fielden was desperate for a partner. Few men had been interested in the deal before Hill: The risks were mortal and the take-home pay was only twenty-five hundred dollars. That night Hill listened to Fielden's story and studied his plans for the breakout while Fielden drew pencil sketches on paper napkins. Fielden kept emphasizing, "It's not against the law, as long as you don't hurt anybody it's not against the law." Hill avoided making a commitment for a while, but when Fielden said he wanted to leave on Monday, Hill replied, "What's wrong with tonight?" Fielden said he had to get some traveling money together and agreed to leave the next day.

Driving south in Fielden's Ford they quickly got on each other's nerves. Hill was a coffee freak, so every few miles Fielden had to stop at a cafe. Hill's legs were numb from the frigid gale of Fielden's air conditioner. Fielden wanted to talk about the break; Hill wanted to watch the passing countryside and think about getting laid in Mexico. Hill asked Fielden how much money he had raised, and his partner muttered, "A hundred dollars." Hill thought: a hundred dollars? I thought I was getting in on a big-time deal.

In the car were Fielden's sawed-off shotgun and Hill's twelve-gauge pump. As they drove farther south it became more apparent that Fielden intended to stage the raid without any further delay.

"Uh," Hill said. "I thought we were just gonna go down there and kinda look at it."

The next morning, March 1, Fielden and Hill paid nickel tolls at Eagle Pass and walked the International Bridge across the Rio Grande, on that day a shallow, muddy stream that swirled against the steep bank on the Mexican side. Hill had always been enchanted by the culture of Mexico. He liked the food,

the music, the brown-eyed raven-haired women. Hill was excited as he passed the Mexican customs inspector and the sign that read *TERMINANTEMENTE PROHIBIDA: La importación de armas y cartuchos . . .*

Hill's stomach convulsed with fear when he saw the jail. It was too well guarded, too far back from the street. Back in the Eagle Pass motel room, they considered diverting the Mexican cops' attention with fires or explosions, but whenever Fielden started talking too intently about the break, Hill rolled a joint and smoked it. On Tuesday, March 2, they watched the jail from a tamale stand and inspected the streets in the vicinity, attracting a following of shine-boys, pimps, and guides. Everything still looked wrong to Hill. The street in front of the jail ran one way in the right direction, but the road was extremely narrow. Cops stood in front of the jail. Hill and Fielden weren't even sure Blake Davis was still in the Piedras Negras jail.

Returning to the motel, Hill talked by phone to Sterling Davis for the first time. The doctor in Dallas "sounded real positive about not sending anybody any money," and he only presumed that his son had not been moved. Fielden wanted to stage the break while he still had money to pay the motel bill. At midnight Hill put on his gloves and drove the Ford across the bridge, but as Fielden inspected the sawed-off double-barrel, Hill continued to argue strenuously against going through with it. Hill said he didn't even know what Blake Davis looked like. If Fielden got killed, was Hill supposed to run in the jail yelling, "Which one of you guys did we come after?"

The argument was interrupted when a Piedras Negras patrol unit pulled up behind the Ford and turned its flashing lights on. Twisting around to see if the cops got out with pistols drawn, Fielden reached for the door handle and growled, "We're gonna have to take 'em out . . ."

"Wait a minute," Hill cried, grabbing for Fielden's arm as one of the cops got out of the car. "Let's see what he wants, and then we'll kill him."

As the Mexican cop approached, Hill extended a hand toward him and said, "*Señor*, which way to Boys Town?"

The cop's gaze focused on Hill's grimy glove, "Ah, *señor*," he said. "Follow me."

Trailing the patrol unit, Hill fell far enough back so that Fielden was able to ditch the guns in some bushes. In the bordello Hill and Fielden thanked the cops and went into one of the bars. Hill only had twenty dollars, but he was so happy he bought one of the whores several drinks.

The next day, Wednesday, was visitors' day at the Piedras Negras jail. A guard frisked Fielden and Hill and unlocked the door that led back to the prisoners. A stocky man with curly hair greeted Fielden from the first cell.

Fielden stood shoulder-to-shoulder with other visitors outside the bars as he whispered instructions to Blake Davis. Hoping to gain some insight into the man he was going to rescue, Hill spoke briefly with Blake, but he wanted badly to get out of that jail. Hill was convinced that the purpose of their visit was transparently obvious to the guards; compared to the other visitors, they looked like gangsters. And Hill had spent enough time in American jails to react emotionally to the horror of this one. The odor in the jail was appalling. The visitors were panting and drenched with sweat. Recalling the expressions of the prisoners' faces, Hill later remarked, "Have you ever seen a drowning dog?"

In the motel room Hill and Fielden argued again. Hill wanted a third man in the car with a walkie-talkie. "I've got to get this deal done," Fielden finally exploded. "I never took a deal that I didn't do. All I want is somebody to watch my back. I'll do it."

"Your back!" Hill cried. "I'm thinking about my butt, I'm thinking about my whole damn body!"

Fielden drove when they crossed the bridge after midnight As they headed for the brush where they had stashed the guns, Hill was talking fast and furiously. They'd been hanging around the jail for three days; the Mexican cops had to know something was up. They didn't have enough gasoline money to get back to Dallas. "I don't wanta do it tonight," Hill said. "My karma's not right."

Fielden was disgusted, but their lack of money worried him. Fielden knew from his combat training that in an operation like this, both men needed conviction, if not total confidence. Hill's reluctance could get them both killed. After they retrieved the guns from the bushes they came upon the same cops who had stopped them the night before. This time Fielden got out of the car. "Well, we're through in Boys Town," he told the cops. "How do we get out of here?"

The next morning a friend wired Fielden fifty dollars. They paid the motel bill, gassed up the Ford, and headed back to Dallas. On the way they had a flat. Fielden was uncertain he could ever count on Hill. But he had no other partner in mind; in hiring Hill he felt he'd already scraped the bottom of the barrel. Hill told Fielden he would proceed with the breakout only if they could recruit a third man and if they had enough money for their expenses. Fielden assigned Hill the task of finding the third man. As a token of good faith, Hill said he could probably raise the money if Fielden could not.

Saturday, March 6, Hill met Sterling Davis for the first time in the office on Northwest Highway. Hill was impressed by the verbal assurance of the craggy-

faced man, but something about the office made Hill think the doctor "hadn't been there too long." Davis showed Hill a photocopy of a check for five thousand dollars, but again refused to advance any expense money.

Hill proceeded with marked ambivalence. In the presence of Fielden, he offered the lookout job to a hulking friend. But something—perhaps affection, perhaps doubts about the man's reliability—made Hill ask his friend after Fielden was gone: "You remember those wetbacks you took on with a ball bat? They paid me two thousand dollars to get you across the border."

The friend quickly withdrew. With him removed from the picture, Hill next offered the job to Billy Blackwell, a stocky eighteen-year-old with shoulder-length hair who had previously worked for Hill in the wrecker business. Blackwell now mowed lawns for a living and said he could not read or write. Billy lived with a teenaged brother but he ran with a tough, older crowd. To Blackwell, Mike Hill was a figure to emulate. Hill often teased his young protégé. "Stick with me, Billy, and we'll go places," he joked. "Let's you and me rob a bank." Billy laughed at the banter and always tagged along; Mike hadn't gotten him in trouble yet. Hill was willing to trust his life to the eighteen-year-old. He knew that Billy Blackwell's loyalty was absolute.

Having fulfilled his responsibility of hiring a third man, Hill again stalled. By now both men had begun to feel some sense of personal obligation to Blake Davis, but Hill would have welcomed a development that took him off the hook. "I was trying to stay alive as long as I could," he later explained. He called Fielden and asked if he had been able to raise the money. Sounding dejected, Fielden said he had exhausted all his possibilities. Hill regretted his offer to raise the money himself. He considered telling Fielden that his monetary well had dried up too, but he hated to lie his way out of a commitment. He kept remembering his visit to the jail—the claustrophobic stench, the drowning-dog expression on the prisoners' faces. So instead he lied to raise the money. He told a business creditor that repossession of a tractor-trailer rig in Mexico was worth ten thousand dollars to himself and another man. With considerable misgivings, the creditor loaned Hill one thousand dollars, using the silver van for collateral, and said he was also willing to extend enough money on a separate loan to put Hill back in the used-car business. The offer provided Hill with a monetary out; he could pay his bills now without Sterling Davis' money. But Hill had become intrigued by another possibility. An electric-haired American in the cell next to Blake's had gotten word to Fielden that he would pay equal money if he came out, too. Fielden at first intended to bring out only those two men. Hill wanted to free all the prisoners. If every freed American voluntarily came up with five thousand dollars, they were

talking about a potential haul of more than fifty grand. Though Hill was more cautious than Fielden, he craved adventure, too. All those factors tipped the balance in favor of Hill's participation. He borrowed a spare for Fielden's Ford, walkie-talkies, new gloves, and blue ski masks with red insets on the faces. Hill was not an educated man, but he understood guerrilla psychology. They would go across in dark clothing, relying on the element of surprise. Mexican cops did not often encounter men with shotguns and ski masks.

On Wednesday morning, March 10, Hill phoned Blackwell and said, "Get your clothes together, Billy. We're going."

Hill smoked a joint as he waited for his partners, and when Fielden's Ford pulled up outside the metal prefab apartment Hill looked out and saw a man with sandy razor-cut hair. That's not Billy, he thought, then remembered that the youth had been instructed to wear a short-hair wig.

Hill had described the project to Billy in extremely vague terms. He suspected that his young friend thought they were actually going down to repossess a truck. As they drove south, Hill tried to impress Blackwell with the seriousness of the situation, "Billy, what it boils down to is we're going to war down there, actually."

Billy swallowed hard. "Well, Mike, don't you think I need a gun?"

In Waco Fielden bought a bottle of Scotch. Hill knew he had to be straight when he crossed the Rio Grande, but in the meantime he and Billy were passing joints. As darkness fell and they passed through San Antonio, tension in the Ford began to build. "Why don't you quit smoking?" Fielden finally said.

Hill thought about it for a minute and said, "Well, hell, you're drinking."

They checked into the Holly Inn in Eagle Pass and watched TV until it went off. Billy got extremely quiet when Hill and Fielden pulled out the guns and ski masks. Fielden briefed Blackwell on each of the five checkpoints, and shortly after 2 A.M., Thursday, March 11, Billy wrapped his jacket around the walkie-talkie and began his lonely walk across the International Bridge.

Hill and Fielden gassed up the Ford and returned to the motel, where Hill stashed the rest of his money, about four hundred dollars, in his shaving kit. He didn't want the Mexican cops to have it. Near the bridge again they tried to raise Billy, but a Mexican CB operator broke in over them. Finally Billy called from the vicinity of the jail: *"Ringo, this is Sam. There's a bunch of activity over here now. Cars coming in and out."*

"OK. We'll call you back in ten minutes."

Waiting at the border, Hill took a couple of swallows from Fielden's bottle

of Scotch. A few yards away two Eagle Pass patrolmen were conducting some kind of investigation. Hill and Fielden pretended to study a map, and the cops drove away after giving them a long look. The cops circled the block, circled the block again. Hill got out and went over to the patrol car. "We've been trying to read that map for an hour," he told the cops. "How do you get to Boys Town?"

The cops laughed, gave Hill directions, and drove away. In the car Hill and Fielden were unable to raise Blackwell. "They must've got Billy," Hill finally said. "Let's go on across." Crossing the bridge, Hill swallowed a tablet of speed.

Fielden's intelligence report anticipated three Mexican cops at the border, one in the small park behind the tollgates and three at the jail. At the border Hill saw at least six uniformed officers, all impressively armed with chromed sidearms. After clearing Mexican customs, Hill turned off the plaza and tried to circle through the maze of narrow streets to the jail. Very quickly they were lost. A carload of Mexican youths pulled up beside them. Hill and Fielden knew that the street in front of the jail led to the bordello. "*Pinoche, pinoche,*" Hill cried. The Mexican youths laughed and motioned for the Ford to follow.

After tipping their guides a dollar, Hill and Fielden at last raised Billy. "*Six of the cops just left,*" he radioed. "*There shouldn't be but three in there now.*"

They picked up Billy a block from the jail, and Hill parked the Ford one parking space away from the jail lot. "If you have any second thoughts, if your karma's not right . . ." Fielden began, but Hill was pulling on his ski mask, too.

On the sidewalk Hill did a double take as he passed the car parked in front of the Ford. "Don't freak out," he whispered to Fielden, "but there's a cop asleep in that car."

Fielden froze.

"What? Where?"

Headlights fell upon them from behind. Fielden concealed the sawed-off with his bulk and turned his face away; Hill stuffed his pump in a long flower pot on a wall, ripped his mask off, and turned to face the approaching motor-ists. Just some horny American boys, Hill sighed to himself with relief. He put his ski mask back on and stared across the street. In the police auto pound he saw cars with all the doors flung open. Paranoid flash: They'd been set up, cops were lying down behind the seats! Fielden forged ahead with the tense determination of a Marine about to plant the flag at Iwo Jima. Hill followed at a trotting walk, searching the rooftops for soldiers with rifles. When Fielden grabbed the handle of the jail door, for the first time Hill was absolutely certain this deal was going down.

Fielden had been studying a Spanish dictionary, but he was still not certain how to say "get your hands up." "*Palmo asente!*" he yelled as he burst through the door; when he saw the inside of the jail, he thought god *damn*, we're gonna have to teach that boy to count. Through Hill's mind sped an image from a favorite movie: Newman and Redford, Cassidy and Sundance, running toward a lethal hail.

Behind two counters five guards and five police officers were interrogating an eighteen-year-old Mexican girl who'd been jailed on drug charges but claimed membership in *Liga 23 de Septiembre,* a group of cop-killing terrorists in the Sierra Madres. When Fielden and Hill ran through the door the disbelieving cops froze for an instant, then scattered in ten different directions.

"Freeze!" Fielden bellowed, and gave one cop a whack with the shotgun when he proved reluctant to surrender his pistol. Hill vaulted across the counter, and the Mexican stenographer fell out of his chair in front of him. Fielden looked up after relieving the first cop of his gun and saw that two more had their pistols drawn and aimed. "Huh uh," Fielden warned, and the force of the sawed-off twin barrels won out: two more pistols dropped to the floor. Staring at the bore of Hill's twelve-gauge, two cops raised their hands; as if he were bailing water, a third tried to dislodge his pistol from his holster. Then Hill saw the M-1 propped against the wall. Easing toward the rifle, Hill glimpsed the toe of a man's shoe just behind him. He yelled and wheeled his twelve-gauge around. The cop reeled back in terrified surrender. Mike Hill had come very, very close to committing murder.

The element of surprise had worked. They had subdued the cops without firing a shot. Fielden hurried to the barred door that led back to the cells and popped the chain with the bolt cutters. While Hill watched the cops, Fielden encountered the unarmed guard who tended the cells and a Mexican prisoner who was outside his cell when the shouting started. Fielden ran to the first cell and weighed down on the handles of the bolt cutters. But this chain broke the jaws of the bolt cutters. Fielden looked helplessly through the bars at Blake Davis. Davis groaned, "Oh, shit."

"Get the key," one of the inmates recommended.

"How do you say keys in Spanish?" Fielden snapped.

"*Llave,*" the inmates clamored. "*La llave.*"

What were they saying? Yobby? The Mexican inmate lashed the unarmed guard with the broken chain. The guard finally got the message when Fielden held the sawed-off to his head. Fielden walked the guard to a desk in the front office, then came back and unlocked Blake Davis' cell.

Hill started herding the cops down the corridor toward the cells. The eighteen-year-old girl and professed guerrilla looked at Hill and said, "Me too?"

For all Hill knew the girl was a cop or a snitch. "You too, baby. You better move."

"Me too?" the girl said again.

Hill raised the shotgun to the girl's eye level and she followed the cops down the hall. Blake came out front and Hill handed him the Mexican M-1. While Blake watched the cops, Fielden unlocked the two remaining cells containing American men. One imprisoned Frenchman opted for the security of his cell, but the Mexican nationals were extremely willing to share the fruits of American labor. One of the American inmates ran around to the back and pried a weakened bar until the women were able to wriggle free. At least two dozen inmates were soon milling the corridor, shushing each other and trying to contain their excitement. "Nobody goes out before us," Fielden ordered. "There's a man out there who'll cut you in two."

The Mexican who had attacked the guard broke for the front. Blake shouted a warning and leveled the M-1, but the Mexican reached Hill, who'd been pacing nervously and exhorting Fielden to hurry up. The Mexican asked Hill if he had any more guns. Hill noticed the man had blood on his head. He handed over a cop's pistol, and the Mexican kicked open an office door, revealing two *federales* who had been interrogating his wife before the jailbreak started. Since then they had been hiding quietly. The Mexican proceeded to pistol whip the *federales* noisily.

"Who was that?" Hill asked Blake, who had followed the Mexican up the hall.

"He's all right," Blake replied, then returned to the back. Suddenly Billy's voice came from the walkie-talkie: *'Mike, you got two coming through the door.'*

Heart pounding, Hill crouched behind the counter and waited. The Mexican cops never arrived; opening the door they'd seen an American inmate carrying a carbine. "Billy, where are they?" Hill finally blurted into his walkie-talkie.

"I don't know, man. They left."

Inside, Fielden herded the cops into a rear corridor but he couldn't get the dead-bolt lock to slide. He rounded up Blake and his hirsute friend who had promised money and led the procession out of the office. One of the American men asked Fielden to take the women but Fielden shook his head. Fielden told the Americans to turn right at the sidewalk, right again at the first corner. "When you hit water you know you're at the river."

Hill was jumping up and down, trying to let Fielden know he was caught

up in the crowd. One of the American girls grabbed Hill's arm but he pried her fingers loose and joined Fielden, Blake, and his hairy, monied friend in the front ranks. They ran to the Ford as the escapees sprinted. As the five men pulled away from the curb, the Mexican cops were already filtering back into the front office of the jail, and in the excitement Hill had forgotten to cut the telephone line. The driver of a garbage truck pulled out in front of them. "Punch it!" Fielden yelled. "They're trying to block us in."

"Calm down!" Hill yelled. "That guy's just trying to turn around."

Hill had been in Mexico eight minutes, and the blurring rush of his amphetamine was really coming on. After what seemed like an eternity, they circled the plaza and reached the tollgate. Hill groaned and kept his foot away from the accelerator as the driver of a red station wagon chatted amiably with the customs tolltaker. Finally the station wagon moved on. Hill grinned at the Mexican official and handed him a quarter. Twelve cents would have sufficed.

As they crossed the bridge Fielden leaned forward and Blake started heaving incriminating evidence toward the river. Hill thought one of the guns bounced off the bridge, and Fielden looked back and saw one of the ski masks lying on the walkway. Everybody in the car was jabbering. Looming above the roof of the United States customs station was the neon sign of Texaco, and beyond that, Sears. "We're home," Hill was saying. "We're clean, just stay calm, we're gonna make it, we're doing it, god damn, we're home . . ."

The United States customs inspector was an old man. "Are you all American citizens?" he asked routinely. "Did you bring anything back from Mexico?"

When his editor called, *Dallas Times Herald* reporter Robert Montemayor was dressed to play tennis. A Texas Tech graduate, Montemayor had joined the *Herald* staff in hopes of specializing in reporting Mexican-American news. Tennis could wait. After nine months, Montemayor finally had a South Texas assignment.

On Friday, March 12, at the Maverick County jail, Montemayor talked to a Piedras Negras escapee detained on an outstanding United States warrant. The man sent Montemayor to the motel room of one of five escapees who'd been arrested in Eagle Pass and then released. They talked for two hours at the motel, and after midnight the escapee urgently requested a ride out of Eagle Pass for himself and his wife. He told Montemayor that Maverick County officers had warned that *federales* were in town looking for escapees. On Saturday Montemayor interviewed the *comandante* of the jail, then picked up his photographer and passengers and headed north. On the road Montemayor pressed the escapee for information about the breakout team. "They'll be

reading your newspaper," the escapee finally hinted. In San Antonio Monte-mayor gave the escapee his Dallas phone number and reminded him, "You owe me a favor."

Montemayor's indebted passenger forwarded the reporter's phone num-ber to Blake, who was staying at a Dallas Rodeway Inn only one block from the Mexican consulate. On Sunday, March 14, Blake called Montemayor and said he was sitting beside the two men who had pulled off the Piedras Negras jailbreak. He answered a few of Montemayor's questions but did not name Fielden or Hill, then said he had to turn himself over to federal marshals and would get back in touch in three or four days. Sterling Davis came to the motel happily shaking hands. Davis said there might be some movie money in this; one of his patients would draft an outline. Enthused, Cooter men-tioned that he'd been thinking about feeding some information to a *Times Herald* reporter. Sterling Davis was aghast. He pointed out that he was still on probation from the fraud conviction. Moviemakers fictionalized. News-paper reporters named names.

Billy Blackwell took his five hundred dollars and went back to mowing lawns. Hill refitted his van with carpet, Naugahyde upholstery with a Lone Star flag motif, and a decorative American flag on the rear panel. Fielden, aware that Maverick County officers had found his sawed-off shotgun and the Mexican M-1 in weeds ten feet from the river, and suspicious of Davis' Hollywood nego-tiations, told his story to his Dallas lawyer, Ernie Kuehne.

Blake had served fourteen months of his three-year United States sentence on the Arizona pot conviction. Since then he had served twenty-three months behind Mexican bars. Surely the federal authorities would agree that was pun-ishment enough. When Blake turned himself over to the marshals, he con-fidently expected to be interrogated and freed after a few days. Instead the marshals charged him with parole violation and remanded him to the federal prison at El Reno, Oklahoma.

Robert Montemayor still did not know the name of the escapee who had called him. The escapee he'd driven to San Antonio came by for some clip-pings one day and asked Montemayor if Sterling had called him. Sterling? Montemayor thought. The Mexicans had first identified the escapee Blake Davis as Sterling Blake. Montemayor ran a check of area prisons and located Blake in the Dallas County jail, but it was a week before he was able to reach Blake at El Reno. Blake detailed his experiences by phone, then referred the reporter to his father for more information. At first Sterling Davis denied any knowledge of the matter. But twice during April, Davis granted Montemayor interviews in his office.

"I'm smiling at you, Robert," Davis told the young reporter. "You'll never know if a word of this is true." Davis claimed he had spent seventy thousand dollars trying to free his son from Mexican prison. Montemayor applied a pencil to the doctor's figures and observed they totaled only forty thousand dollars. By now the famed *Times Herald* investigative reporter Hugh Aynesworth was working with Montemayor on the jailbreak story. Up to this point Davis had not revealed Fielden's name, but two days before the article was to appear, he referred Montemayor to Kuehne, who in turn gave the reporters his client's name. Aynesworth, who had a huge list of sources, quickly gathered information on Fielden, and when he told Kuehne the story was about to go to press, the lawyer called his client and said it looked like now was the time to talk.

Mike Hill was flabbergasted when he saw the copyrighted story in the May 9 *Times Herald.* Hill had scarcely kept his role in the jailbreak secret; among friends he talked of little else. But glaring from the front page of the Sunday paper was a photograph of Fielden under the headline: DALLAS MAN EXECUTED JAIL BREAKOUT. Fielden was described in the lead paragraph as "a former Marine sergeant turned soldier of fortune." In the story Fielden, apparently caught up in the drama of his own role, referred to Hill as "the backup man" and called Billy "a west Dallas punk."

The next day Hill decided to share the spotlight; he appeared on the Channel 4 evening news wearing a ski mask and wielding a shotgun. In colorful detail he described the experience of standing down the Mexican guards. Sterling Davis confirmed his role in the break to UPI and consented to an interview by Montemayor and two television reporters. But the media party did not last long.

The same Monday Hill appeared on TV, United States customs officials were in Kuehne's office looking for Fielden. The next night at a north Dallas singles bar, Kuehne and Fielden charted a course of action. They would cooperate fully, cop the best possible plea, and peddle the story for all it was worth. On Thursday, May 13, Fielden was charged with illegal exportation of the sawed-off shotgun and released on bond. Hill, who was not part of the bargain and had not been consulted about it, underwent the same process the next day. The following Tuesday, Fielden, Hill, the elder Davis, and his problematic son Cooter were summoned before the federal grand jury in San Antonio.

The Piedras Negras jailbreak was flaring into an international incident. Mexican officials called Fielden and Hill common criminals and decried their heroes' reception by the American press. The Mexican government initiated extradition proceedings against the American escapees. Wary of more Ameri-

can raids, penal authorities busily transferred prisoners and tightened security at all Mexican jails. In the past, United States embassy and consular officials had fielded allegations of Mexican abuse of American prisoners. Now the issue graduated from their hands. Out of Secretary of State Henry Kissinger's mid-June negotiations with Mexican President Luis Echeverría came proposals for a United States-Mexico prisoner exchange. In late June President Gerald Ford signed a military assistance bill that Congress had amended to commit the force and authority of the presidency to the investigation of abuse of American citizens incarcerated in Mexico. Kissinger would later submit a personal report to Congress; Ford would negotiate directly with the Mexican president.

To Mike Hill it seemed the world was spinning on his axis. Heads of state were probably talking about him! Yet Hill was broke again, and he was in the worst trouble of his life. One June night at White Rock Lake Fielden told Hill that he'd already cut his deal: It was every man for himself. Hill had been told by his lawyer to keep his mouth shut, but everybody else was talking. Once again Hill likened his predicament to scenes from his favorite movies, *The Getaway, The Missouri Breaks.* Paranoia overwhelmed him. Maybe he was an unwitting pawn on a huge conspiratorial chessboard. He was absolutely certain his old comrades were dealing him out of the movie game. Hill fired his lawyer and consented to an interview by Dan Rather. *60 Minutes* wouldn't talk to him in Dallas; Hill had to go to Eagle Pass, where he nervously answered Rather's questions with his back to the Rio Grande and Piedras Negras. But the *60 Minutes* story never aired. Hill summoned a press conference the morning of June 28. He told reporters that he deserved equal blame or credit for the break, then he hitched a ride toward his arraignment in Del Rio, where he intended to plead not guilty.

I broke into the hotly contested story by offering to drive a man with no money and no car to his court date on the border of Mexico. In San Antonio that night Hill told me there would have been wholesale changes if he had commanded the Piedras Negras operation. "Namely, I wouldn't have used Chubby."

Examining his motives, Hill said, "I've got a whole lot of potential. I can make a lot of money. Five thousand dollars don't turn me on enough to make me wanta go die for it. I can make five thousand dollars in a little while, just working, doing what I do. I don't know why I did it. But in the end I don't think the money had anything to do with it. I'll say this: If I ran for president I know seventeen people who'd vote for me."

In Del Rio the federal indictments rained down. The original indictments

against Fielden and Hill were superseded by a new four-count bill that named Hill on all counts, Sterling Davis on three, Billy Blackwell on two. Mentioned on three counts but indicted only for conspiracy, Fielden copped his plea. When Hill arrived in Del Rio he was looking at a maximum sentence of two years; when he left he was looking at as many as twenty-two.

Hill bitterly contended he was being prosecuted under pressure from the Mexican government. "If we'd killed anybody, the Americans would have taken us right back across that border, and I wouldn't have blamed them a bit. We don't have the right to go over there and kill anybody. I'd feel the same way if they'd come over here and killed anybody. But it was a peaceful kind of deal"—*peaceful?* I thought—"and the Mexicans don't have any right to be mad, because nobody got hurt. They ought to be thankful for what they've got. That's the main mistake people make: They ain't never thankful for what they got left. They just cuss everybody for what happened to them. They don't think about how bad it could have been."

In Dallas Hill delivered Blackwell to United States marshals on June 30, then learned the judge in Del Rio wanted a $25,000 cash bond. Billy was in jail three days before the bond was reduced. When we talked over supper one night, Hill glumly said he had twenty cents to his name. "I'm not working because I can't keep my mind on it," he said. "And the way things are going, it looks like I oughta take a little vacation. It may be a long time before I get another chance."

Ernie Kuehne was hopeful that Fielden would serve no more than a year. Endeavors to capitalize on Fielden's exploit had proved taxing but fruitful. Fielden made a couple of promotional trips to Los Angeles and finally sold his story rights to Mustang Productions, a company owned in part by former Dallas City Councilman Charles Terrell. Kuehne said the deal might run well into six figures; of course, given the uncertainties of the movie business, it might amount to very little. On the advice of Kuehne, Fielden had declined a *Sixty Minutes* interview, but after the plea was copped in Del Rio, he went public with a new image. He bought a new suit and had his hair styled. Kuehne portrayed his client as a figure larger than life, a patriotic veteran who, except for one wild act of valor, had a clean criminal record.

"Let him shoot his best shot," Fielden said of Hill's erratic efforts to crowd into the limelight. Asked for a personal reading of his former partner-in-arms, Fielden told me, "I wouldn't go out partying with him, drinking or anything. I'm not saying I'm better than anybody else, but we're coming from two different places. I like to feel I have a little class. I basically hired the man to do a job. He did his job, and he was paid for it."

Fielden delved into his motives at the time of the break. "No one should be treated the way those prisoners were being treated. But the number-one reason was the money. If somebody had said, 'Well, I can't give you any money, but would you please do it,' I would have said, 'Up your ass.'

"I really didn't think I was doing anything wrong," he continued. "If I'd known, going in, that I was going to be breaking the laws of this country— Mexico I didn't care about—I wouldn't have done it. But since I found out that I did break the law, I'll have to pay for it. That's the American way, isn't it?"

But surely Fielden understood that even American federal prisons were no picnic grounds?

"Now I won't go in liking it," Fielden allowed. "But the last thing I want is to owe this country anything. This country's been good to me. If I owe it a year or two or five out of my life, well, I can't run away. I'd be losing too much."

Mike Hill was convinced that Fielden's view of Hill as a hireling rather than a partner was costing "the backup" money. Had Blake's electric-haired friend kept his promise to reward his rescuers? Had the other prisoners shown their gratitude to the man the *Times Herald* had portrayed as the leader of the jailbreak? If so, none of the money had found its way to Hill.

Billy Blackwell mowed his lawns in a daze, wide-eyed with fright. In El Reno, Blake Davis talked to nobody and hoped for an early release on parole. The world of Sterling Davis had been crumbling for some time. On May 12 he was forced to withdraw his application for a state psychologist's license. On July 9 the Mexican consul in Dallas, Javier Escobar, announced that the National University in Mexico City categorically denied ever having granted Sterling Davis a degree. On July 12 Judge Sarah T. Hughes scheduled a hearing to discuss revocation of the discredited doctor's probation.

Subpoenaed as a possible witness, but unaccompanied by Kuehne, Fielden sat on the rear bench of Hughes' courtroom in a new suit. "This pretrial release program is all right," he told me companionably. "They'll send you to trade school if you wanta go. They keep trying to get me a job, and I tell them, man, I've got a job." A job promoting Don Fielden. Hill came in wearing a cowboy hat, accompanied by an attorney who wore a cowboy hat. Then Sterling Davis entered the courtroom, walking slowly and carefully, a gaunt but broad-shouldered figure in a gray suit. He was old for his years.

Judge Hughes said they would not discuss particulars of the Piedras Negras jailbreak, since Davis was charged in connection with that in another federal court. However, United States attorneys charged that in November, 1975, and

February, 1976, Davis violated terms of his probation by leaving the country without permission. They claimed that at the time Davis was telling reporters he had spent seventy thousand dollars trying to free his son, he had paid only $225 of his sixteen thousand dollar restitution obligations and retired only two hundred dollars of his ten thousand dollar fine.

On the stand Davis said one of the violations was the result of a misunderstanding on his part. To him Eagle Pass and Piedras Negras were one and the same. On one occasion he asked his probation officer if he could go to Eagle Pass to take Thanksgiving leftovers to his son. He attributed the seventy thousand dollar figure to a misunderstanding by Montemayor: he had told the young reporter about a woman in California who claimed to have squandered seventy thousand dollars trying to free her son, but he never claimed that himself. When he quoted that figure to the television reporters, he was trying to enhance his movie negotiations; indeed, he had warned the reporters that he would not be telling the truth. In order to meet the monetary demands of his probation, Davis said that in the past few weeks he had borrowed three thousand dollars on his life insurance policy, two thousand dollars from his son, one thousand dollars from his mother-in-law. After the trial in Del Rio the twenty-five hundred dollars he had used to post bond would be forwarded. He was prepared to sign over his movie contract rights.

"What is this movie?" Judge Hughes interrupted. "I want to know more about it."

"When this came out in the newspapers," Davis explained in a soft, deep voice, "people descended from everywhere. Movie and book people. Most were, pardon the expression, fly-by-nighters. But Warner Brothers advanced me a thousand dollars on a movie contract. The Warner Brothers people were here in town last week. They're supposed to start shooting in September."

The movie, of course, never got made. Davis continued that he was not a rich man. A thousand-dollar advance is not much assurance in the movie business.

He said that after the frog farm trial he had trouble finding work. Just when he was getting on his feet, he had to hire a full-time nurse for his invalid mother-in-law.

"How much did you pay the nurse?" the United States attorney asked.

"Eleven dollars a day," Davis replied.

"How did you afford that?"

Davis started to answer, then winced and closed his eyes. If the long moment of silence was a con, it was a brilliant performance. "I was working then," Davis finally said, "teaching. Sometimes the students asked for counseling."

Davis' attorney reminded the court of the doctor's heart and diabetic conditions and then played his trump cards. The attorney entered as evidence two letters that indicated the five thousand dollars that financed the breakout was raised by friends of Blake and forwarded to the doctor by a Tucson attorney.

Judge Hughes recessed the hearing pending disposition of the September 21 trial in Del Rio, where the elder Davis, Hill, and Blackwell would face the federal gun charges. Fielden's sentencing was set the same day in the same courtroom. Kuehne insisted that the terms of Fielden's guilty plea did not include turning state's evidence, but with the plea Fielden had waived his Fifth Amendment rights. If subpoenaed, Fielden would have no choice but to testify against his former comrades. As things would turn out, Mike Hill would be convicted and sentenced to six years in prison, but the conviction would be overturned on appeal—he didn't have to serve a day. The federal jury would acquit young Billy Blackwell at the trial. But Fielden and the two Davises would have to do their time.

Hill cut Fielden a baleful look as he left the courtroom. As Sterling Davis moved slowly toward the elevators, he nodded to reporters and Fielden. The smile on his face was inscrutably kind. In the hallway Fielden stood talking to the United States customs agents who had conducted the Piedras Negras investigation. For a man bound for the penitentiary, Fielden looked remarkably happy. His rounded cheeks seemed on the verge of explosive laughter. As a part of some publicity hustle, he was going to Scotland to dive in search of the Loch Ness monster. Don Fielden, Soldier of Hollywood fortune.

Four hundred and twenty-five miles away the Rio Grande was raging. Rain had been falling at Eagle Pass and Piedras Negras for nearly two weeks: maddening rain, ten or fifteen brief showers a day. Residents of Eagle Pass claimed the American escapees had picked the worst spot to swim the river. As the river sweeps around the International Bridge abutments it deepens and forms strong undertows. When the American escapees splashed into the water the morning of March 11 the Rio Grande was running shallow. Four months later the flooding river churned violently and frothed with heavy debris; only the strongest swimmer could have stayed alive in that current beneath the bridge.

Across the river, the Piedras Negras municipal jail was now a bristling fortress braced for attack. More armed guards, more heavy steel bars. It was no place for gringos to go sightseeing. A khaki-uniformed officer gripped his carbine sling and glared at three American visitors who seemed excessively

interested in the barred door and corridor back to the cells. When the suspicious-looking Americans hurriedly drove away, three guards ran outside to record the license number. Mexicans had learned to be careful. And in the coffin-like cells of Piedras Negras jail, two new American prisoners waited for someone to rescue them.

SEPTEMBER, 1976

THE CONTENDER

*More and more, my gaze as a writer was turning southward, toward
Mexico. I found a language tutor, a young immigrant schoolteacher and
mother, and developed a proficiency in Spanish. I'd like to add that I am
a law-abiding person. I have spent exactly one night in a jail—drunk in
public in Graham, Texas, at the age of twenty, and the morning wakeup
was an experience I have never forgotten and do not intend to repeat. I
have written about criminals with some sympathy but take pains not to
romanticize them. But if they've done their time and they're trying to stay
out of trouble, I give them the benefit of the doubt.*

*All of that coalesced in my friendship with a young man named Jesus
Chavez. I met him at an Austin boxing gym, where with help from him I
worked myself into the best condition of my life. I watched him train and
win fight after fight, steadily climbing in the rankings. Jesus had gotten
in trouble when he was in his teens, and I thought I was witnessing a
remarkable life's turnaround. I gave little thought to writing about my
friend; I could hardly be objective, and in time I thought sportswriters
would take care of that. But just as he reached the point of contending for
a world title, he ran afoul of a massive new immigration law that for his
one youthful mistake ordered him out of the country—for life. So I wrote
about our friendship and his dilemma. And that would take me farther
and farther into the experience of Mexico.*

Jesus Chavez's ring nickname is "El Matador," but he came out of his corner
like a terrier trying to dismember a stork. Bone-gaunt at 128 pounds, his
crewcut opponent, Wilfredo Negron, was five inches taller and had a nine-
inch reach advantage. Jesus missed often and sometimes badly. But in the
second round alone he threw 108 punches, and about 40 of them were
haymakers that landed. Hooks to the ribs, swooping right uppercuts flush to
the chin, and, midway through the round, he led with a left hook—a danger-

ous move against a right-handed puncher—that momentarily poised Negron on his heels and then delivered him to gravity and the seat of his trunks. Jesus spun off with arm upraised in the strut of the matador.

Like a bullfighter, he was young, handsome, and relentless. He had a pro record of twenty and one, a North American super featherweight title, a world ranking in the top ten, and a contract with a major promoter who touted him as a future world champion. Inside the ropes on that August night in 1997, with the Austin crowd roaring and his blood racing, Jesus Chavez felt untouchable. But out beyond the fans and the noise, he was extremely vulnerable. Outside the ring he was fighting the government of the United States, the country he'd lived in since he was seven. And it was poised to kick him out—for the second time in his twenty-four years.

The first time had been after he helped rob a Chicago grocery store in 1990, when he was a teenager. He got caught, did time, and was deported to Mexico, the country of his birth. He reentered the United States illegally, settled in Austin in 1994, and started his life over. He stayed straight, got in shape, and started fighting again. He turned pro. He fell in love. He was trying to buy a house in Austin for his parents and younger brother so that they could escape the hardness and cold of Chicago. But in 1995 he got nabbed by the authorities, and because of that armed robbery, federal law defines him as an aggravated felon who must be deported. He got a lawyer, who started filing documents. I wrote a letter for him. So did a former FBI agent, a Harvard professor, and other friends he had made in Texas. But it didn't matter how Jesus had behaved since getting out of jail. Last July, while he was training for Negron, the Immigration and Naturalization Service summoned him to San Antonio and ordered him to leave the country three days after the Negron bout. His attorney told him that he needed new counsel licensed to practice in federal appeals court. A desperate search ensued in which one immigration lawyer turned him down because of his felony, another demanded ten thousand dollars up front, another said he didn't want to take Jesus' money and do nothing for him, and another warned that if Jesus even questioned the deportation, he could go back to prison.

It was no way to train for a fight. In sparring sessions he was distracted and got belted. Twelve of Negron's fifteen wins were knockouts, and it was immaterial to him if Jesus was an emotional wreck. Finally Jesus' promoter, Main Events, steered him to a top immigration firm in Washington, D. C. In a deal struck with the INS, he could stay in the United States for two more months and make his pay-for-view debut in Atlantic City. That is, if he beat Negron. Afterward he would voluntarily leave the country. His lawyers hoped he might

then qualify for a skilled-worker visa that would allow him to train in the United States and pursue his athletic career. Of course, there was no guarantee of that happening. And the only permanent solution to his problems seemed to lie in a pardon by the state of Illinois—a long shot at best.

"All that month I wanted to quit," Jesus told me later. "But I had to have the money if I was going to be living in Mexico. I couldn't sleep. I was getting up dead, going home dead. And they had me in against this gunner who was knocking everybody out. I was scared. But that night in the dressing room a heavyweight on the card let me use his CD player. I put on the headphones and listened to the Gipsy Kings—good music, and I got into the rhythm. Then I greased up and wrapped up, and before I knew it they brought in my gloves. I looked out and saw the ring and chairs and all those people, still coming in. There it is, man. Let's do it. And then there was nothing left to do but to do it."

Negron somehow survived Jesus' second-round assault. In the corner Jesus' trainer, Richard Lord, and Lou Duva, the memorably chiseled and joweled patriarch of Main Events, yelled at him to settle down. He slowed the pace, but two rounds later the Puerto Rican again wobbled to his stool. Negron was in such pain his seconds had to wrestle him to get his mouthpiece out, and he kept pitching his head and shoulders between his knees, gasping for air. He couldn't breathe, sit up straight, or answer another bell because one of Jesus' rights had fractured his sternum. It's a cruel game, boxing.

"If I don't win the fight," Jesus reflected, "that big promoter's not going to be so interested. If I'm a losing boxer, how much chance do I have to get that visa?" In his mind, he was fighting for his life.

His is the story of the golden boy, the promising kid who makes one terrible mistake and spends the rest of his days trying to overcome it. He was born in 1972 in Hidaldo de Parral, Chihuahua, the little town where Pancho Villa was gunned down and buried. His parents christened him Jesus Gabriel Chavez Sandoval and, as things worked out, he would have need of all those names. That region of Mexico was mining country—coal, gold, silver, copper, and lead. Both his grandfathers worked in the mines and, for eight years, so did his dad, Jesus Sandoval. His mother, Rosario, was a nurse. Jesus Sandoval feared the mines and didn't want that life for his son, whom they called Gabriel. The elder Sandoval left his family in Mexico and eventually followed the *norteños'* well-beaten path to Chicago. When he found work and a downtown tenement of Mexican families, he sent money for his family's plane tickets. Jesus was an illegal alien employed by the city of Chicago. He worked on maintenance crews who, at great risk, were assigned upkeep of some of the

most infamous and murderous public housing projects in the country. But it was better than those Chihuahuan mines.

One day when Gabriel was ten, his dad dropped him off for swimming lessons at a recreation center. Gabriel heard a bell ringing, and down a hall he found his gift. He won his first fight by technical knockout as a 105-pounder. One of the coaches was an immigrant Irishman, high school English teacher, and former Golden Gloves star named Tom O'Shea. Near the rec center, O'Shea later opened a boxing gym in a settlement house. He discouraged kids who talked about turning pro, but he was a romantic about the amateur sport. For inspiration he recited passages from Hemingway on bullfighting, courage, and struggle. Some kid quipped that they must be matadors, and that became the name of the team and gym. Gabriel also trained with two other colorful Irish trainers—Sean Curtin, an ex-pro fighter and one of O'Shea's best friends, and a truck driver named Tom Foley, both of whom coached youngsters at a southside Catholic Youth Organization gym. Gabriel rode buses all over the city to learn from his mentors. The trainers were crazy about this sweet-faced kid who fought with the relentlessness and zeal of his hero Roberto Duran. They loved to tell the story about a Golden Gloves regional tourney when he was barely fifteen and dismantled a prison-hardened brawler from St. Louis who was ten years older.

In 1987 Gabriel's dad took advantage of a federal amnesty program and embarked on the slow process of becoming a naturalized citizen; the family was granted status as resident legal aliens. He bought a small house in a northwest Chicago neighborhood of Hispanic, black, and Polish families. O'Shea taught at a public high school a few blocks from the Matador Gym, and he helped arrange a transfer for Gabriel so he wouldn't spend so many hours on the buses. Gabriel had a job at McDonald's, he helped his dad cater Mexican food on weekends, and in 1989 he was voted Chicago's Amateur Boxer of the Year. The next year Gabriel ran his record to ninety, five, and five and reached the semifinals of the Golden Gloves nationals in Miami. He couldn't compete for the Olympics because he wasn't a citizen, but O'Shea had him on track for a boxing scholarship at Northern Michigan University. That summer he sent Gabriel out on a casting call for a movie about boxers, and the filmmakers called back offering him the part. But by then—to everyone's stupefaction—he was in jail.

"I had five hundred dollars in my pocket," he described the day that changed the course of his life. "I'd just cashed my paycheck. I didn't have any business going off to rob a store." The streets around the gym and school were the turf of a gang called the Harrison Gents. "I wanted to be a part of

that action, too. 'Hey, these guys hang out and smoke weed and they got all the girls.' One day I walked out of school and this kid said, 'We got this thing to do. You want in?' There were three of us, and I was the oldest. They had a delivery van full of bread and a sawed-off shotgun. There were three of us. On the way, I kept thinking, 'Man, we got this getaway car that smells like a *bakery.*' We put on hooded sweatshirts, one stuck the shotgun in an umbrella, and we went in a supermarket. We made a lady empty the safe, then ran outside and got away. One minute I've got homework in my hand and the next I'm robbing somebody? I threw away my friends. I threw away my family. I threw away living in the United States."

As soon as Gabriel was arrested, he confessed. His devastated parents didn't have the seven thousand dollars needed to make his bond, and he told them not to borrow it: He had made the mistake and was the one who had to deal with it. For the next eighteen months his world was a savage Cook County Jail wing known as the Gladiator School. He participated in a Scared Straight-like program in which inmates counseled teens who were in danger of putting themselves in that madness. His court-appointed lawyer told him before his trial that he might be looking at thirty years, so he copped a plea for seven. He did three and a half. He was processed at Joliet then sent to medium-security Illinois River. He finished out his sentence at Stateville, the maximum-security prison where Oliver Stone filmed much of *Natural Born Killers.* "We did what any parents would," remembered his father. "When he was in prison, I'd get off work on Christmas Eve and we'd drive all night in ice and snow, then sleep in the car a couple of hours because we only had the money for one night's motel. We didn't want him to be alone in that place on Christmas."

Jesus and his parents were permanent legal residents, but because they were not citizens, now he found he had no rights. As his release neared, the INS initiated deportation proceedings against him. He had no money, so he had no lawyer. In April, 1994, he got out of prison and was immediately put on a plane to Mexico City. He had the fifty dollars given all discharged convicts by the State of Illinois.

At least he spoke Spanish. With the help of a sympathetic cabbie and a bus driver who cut him a deal on the fare, Gabriel made it to Chihuahua and his grandparents' home in the town of Delicias. He stayed only a few days— his dad had arranged for a plane ticket, if Gabriel could make it across the border. A United States guard on the bridge in El Paso heard his American accent and waved him through; Gabriel was soon on a Southwest Airlines flight to Chicago. Austin, a city he had never seen, was the first stop. But the

sun was shining brightly, and the plane came in over lush, green hills and the Colorado River's winding string of indigo lakes. He saw people water-skiing. What a pretty place, he thought. If I could just start my life over, it would be somewhere like that.

Back in Chicago he encountered friends who were still getting high, robbing people, on their way to prison or an early grave. "I can't do this," he said to his parents. "I can't be here." In passing, he told his mother about the longing he had felt staring out that airplane window at Austin. After a moment she reminded him they had some family there.

On North Lamar Boulevard, Richard Lord's Gym sits among a block of metal bins that other tenants use for storage and small industry. The musty little gym is cold in winter, and on summer afternoons a large thermometer often reminds us we're doing this to ourselves in 102-degree heat. My fiftieth birthday was a convenient excuse to give up sparring, but hitting something that can't hit back is a terrific way to get rid of a long work day.

Richard is a bow-legged man of forty-three with a long pedigree in boxing. His father, Doug, managed and trained a stellar welterweight world champion, Curtis Cokes of Dallas, in the sixties. After graduating from the University of Texas, Richard turned pro as a lightweight. He could punch, but the hallmark of his career was his outrageous conditioning. He lost just once and reached number eight in the world rankings, but the title shot never came, and he retired in the eighties.

His gym drew a lot of young men and women who could fight. I can't remember the first time I saw the new prospect, but I recall Richard's wary excitement the day he got a call from Tom O'Shea in Chicago. "He told me there was a tremendous talent who might come around. Said he got in some trouble up there, but he was a good kid. He just needed someone to give him another chance." Gabriel Sandoval walked in the gym the same day.

The kid had two amateur fights in Texas, then turned pro for a $350 payday in August, 1994. He told Richard, who didn't know how illegal he was, that he wanted to be known as Jesus Chavez. Good name for a young Hispanic fighter dodging the INS and reinventing himself—the Mexican hero and champion Julio Cesar Chavez was then at the top of the pro game. "That's how we got the fight," added Richard, laughing. "Lewis Wood had won thirty-five amateur fights and his first four as a pro. The only guy who'd ever beaten him was Oscar de la Hoya in the Olympic trials. Gabriel Sandoval, they would have found out about. But Jesus Chavez? He's got no record, he's from Austin. Sure, bring him on."

Jesus' parents flew down to Houston for the bout. As he walked toward the ring the emotion of the moment overwhelmed him—he was crying. From the outset, Jesus and Wood went toe-to-toe. The angles of Wood's attack were throwing Jesus off, and midway through the fight Jesus realized Wood was a converted left-hander. So Jesus started fighting left-handed himself, confusing Wood. Jesus won a rousing upset decision over a fighter who now holds a North American featherweight title.

Two weeks later, Jesus was again supposed to lose in San Antonio to Rudy Hernandez, a national Golden Gloves champion making his pro debut. Gale Van Hoy, a labor union official in Austin, was one of the ringside judges. "It was Rudy Hernandez Night," he said. "They were handing out flyers, had a mariachi band. This other kid comes out in ragged trunks, old shoes, with a towel over his head, and just destroys him. I didn't work the Carlos Gerena fight down there, but I saw it, and that decision was highway robbery."

The split-decision, eight-round loss to the Puerto Rican came in January, 1995, in Jesus' fifth pro fight. All of us at the gym shrugged it off: Gerena had boxed internationally and was on a track with well-greased skids. Our guy was living in the gym. Jesus had a tiny room with a bed, a beanbag chair, a stereo, and a TV that didn't work. He kept up with Richard's regimen, sparred, and pushed us through our wheezing workouts. A couple of times his goading made me angry, but I was fascinated by how much he knew. "Relax your hand," he told me once when I was trying to make my left uppercut more than a clumsy shove, "and raise your left heel just a little." The heavy bag popped loudly and bounced on the end of the chain. At the end of a day we often sat on the ring apron talking about things far removed from boxing. When he grinned his small teeth parted and his eyebrows shot up with an air of impish wonder. He was an optimistic soul.

One day I was trudging on a Stairmaster when he came in with a pretty young woman who had short brown hair. He introduced me to Terri Glanger with a formality that made me wish my hand wasn't so sweaty. She was studying photography at the University of Texas, had worked out at the gym a few times, and they shared a ride to a San Antonio amateur tournament, where she took pictures. Her Jewish parents, immigrants from South Africa, owned a bicycle shop in Dallas. Driving down he told her about himself, which took her aback. But now they were dating. She picked him up at the gym at night— he didn't have a car.

"We'd go out to a restaurant," he said, "and I'd ask her to order for me. 'Well, Gabriel, do it yourself.' But that's what prison does to you, man. I was too scared to tell a waitress what I wanted to eat. She told me I'd better start

to think beyond boxing, and she really stayed after me to get my GED. She helped me study for it, and it was okay that I was doing stuff at an eighth-grade level. Then I went to meet her parents, and driving up she said she'd told them everything." Jesus laughed. "'Let's see now. He's Catholic, he's Mexican, he's been in jail, and he lives in a boxing gym. Way to go, Terri. You can really pick 'em.'"

But the Glangers received him nonchalantly and warmly, and when the troubles over his immigration status came, they were tireless allies. I thought Jesus lived in the gym that year because he was poor and dedicated. But he also did it because he feared subjecting his relatives and their children, with whom he had lived, to the anguish of seeing him hauled off in handcuffs. When he called himself Jesus Chavez instead of Gabriel Sandoval, he wasn't lying—those are his names. But it's also a common Hispanic tactic of evading the INS. He got back on the radar screen in 1995 when he went to get a driver's license and his papers weren't in order. He was in a holding cell and would have been deported that day if Richard hadn't known someone in the system who was a boxing fan. Released on personal recognizance, Jesus hired the lawyer who pursued a strategy of hope and delay. For a while it worked.

In August, 1995, Richard started promoting fights in the downtown Austin Music Hall. The Brawls in the Hall had two attractions: the novelty of skilled women boxing and the furious pace of Jesus' main events. Politicians wanted to be seen with him, and law enforcement officials started bringing him kids in gangs. They were amazed at how he seemed to get through to them.

Jesus got a break in August, 1996, when promoters brought in Mexican featherweight champion Javier Jauregui, who was in line for a world title shot. After six rounds the fight was even, and it looked like Jesus had burned him-self out. But he got a second wind and seemed to mature as the bout wore on. He punished the Mexican veteran with left hooks to the body—his best punch—and the unanimous decision established him as a world-class talent. In March, 1997, Jesus made his TV debut as a main event against a smooth and gifted puncher, San Antonio's Louie Leija. He mauled Leija in the first round, but in the third he walked into a hook and almost got knocked out: The Austin crowd gasped as he staggered and groped like an alley drunk. Yet he was dominant again by the bell. He knocked Leija down twice and the ref stopped it in the sixth. Fox commentators burbled about him throughout the fight, and replays aired for weeks. The performance won him his contract with Main Events.

Terri had moved to New York, where she worked for a prominent photog-

rapher. He flew up after his fights and she took him to Broadway plays and art shows in SoHo. Strangers hailed him on the street. He walked in Central Park and gaped at the skyscrapers and splendor of this country. He was a rising star. An American success story.

But not to immigration officials. His advocates could argue all day that he was a legal resident when he got in trouble; that the dad who brought him here as a child was now a naturalized citizen; that he had paid for his crime; that he was deported without legal representation; and that he showed abundant signs of being a responsible adult of some value. None of the human nuance mattered. Under fire from Congress for letting too many aliens slip through the cracks, the INS had no legal authority to overlook that aggravated felony. Since the fall of 1996 the agency had increased the rate of deportation by fifty percent, and about seventy-five percent of those expelled were being sent to Mexico. This country was committed to a crackdown on illegal immigration, and it was just getting started.

In September, 1996, the House of Representatives passed a massive revision of immigration law by a vote of 370 to 37. The Senate concurred 84 to 15, and President Clinton signed it. Two weeks after the Leija fight, the new provisions went into effect. Under the new law, an alien who had only been convicted of a state misdemeanor could be defined and removed as an aggravated felon. Judicial review and political asylum were greatly restricted. Families were being separated, people who only came here to work and who never robbed anyone. One of the immigration lawyers who turned Jesus down asked him: "Where is your tragedy?" He had no answer.

The backside of Atlantic City has a seedy appeal, and the Boardwalk is amazing—miles of meticulously laid and unwarped parquet floor. But the casinos get old fast. The gaming floors sound like an asylum of berserk musicians all playing the vibes. Jesus, Richard, and I walked through Caesars' Atlantic City to a basement employees' cafeteria, where the fighters had meal tickets. Jesus filled his plate with roast chicken, salad, and fruit. When we stood to leave, an employee addressed us gruffly: "Hey, put up your own trays."

Jesus lit up and grinned. "Cool, man," he said, doing as he was told.

"Reminds him of prison," said Richard. "Except the food's better."

It was the biggest fight of Jesus' young career: Atlantic City, pay-per-view, and the undercard of the Lennox Lewis-Andrew Golota heavyweight title match. The fight was something of a family affair. Doug Lord was there to help work the corner, and his great champion, Curtis Cokes, now trained Jesus' opponent, former kickboxing champion Troy Dorsey of Dallas. Once,

years ago, Dorsey had pulled off an upset and won a world boxing title. Now, at thirty-four, he looked like his pleasure was running head-first into walls. Recently he had undergone surgery to file down his stony ridge of brow, an accumulation of calcium deposits and scar tissue that had caused him to lose several fights on cuts. His record had slipped to fifteen, nine, and four, but he was a far bigger name than Jesus. And he was supremely confident.

At the weigh-in—they both came in at 129—they raised their fists and faced off in the ritual pose; Dorsey glared and played the moment for all the advantage it might be worth. Jesus' mouth started working, his eyebrows shot up, and he broke into that innocent's grin. Then he pulled on his clothes and raced through the casino, bounding up a moving escalator, until he reached a pasta restaurant. "Hate being hungry," he said, busy with his fork. He giggled at the thought of the staring match. "I try to do it, but I never can."

That afternoon he loosened up in a makeshift gym, then did some radio interviews. It was dark as we walked toward the hotel. A fan recognized him, and in a torrent of Spanish he danced about the Boardwalk, demonstrating the combination of jabs and uppercuts he felt Jesus' task required. "Bip! Bip! Bip!" the guy effused. Jesus gripped the strap of his bag and grinned, loving it. "*Viva Mexico, hermano,*" the fan said, and they engaged in a complicated handshake. Farther down the strip, Jesus noticed a sparrow that had gotten inside a yogurt shop and was fluttering against the glass. He opened the doors and started trying to shoo the bird out. A youth at the cash register told him curtly the place was closed. "No, we've got to get this out of here," said Jesus, flapping his hand at the captive bird. The kid stared at him, then rolled his eyes.

Pre-fight jitters erupted the day of the fight, taking the form of age-old antagonism between trainer and wife or girlfriend. Terri arrived from New York that afternoon. Richard saw them on the Boardwalk and couldn't believe it. "I said, 'What are you doing?'" Richard told me, beside himself. "'You need to rest! Eat a steak.' 'Well, Terri wants to go shopping.' 'Shopping! What have you had to eat?' 'Tuna sandwich I had in my room.' 'Tuna *sandwich!*' So he clenches his jaw and says, 'I'm going shopping with Terri. I'll see you there at seven.'"

That night, as we made our way through the convention center, Richard said gloomily, "First time I've ever gone to a fight without my fighter." Then Jesus was late. This did not bode well. But at 7:15 P.M. he walked in the dressing room, dropped his bag of gear, and flung out his arms like Gene Kelly. "Gonna be a great night, bro's. I am *pumped,* and I just got here!"

The structure filled up because of his Main Events stable mate, Andrew

Golota, a resident of Chicago. Britain's Lennox Lewis was a narrow betting favorite in the heavyweight fight, but it was Polish Pride Night. In honor of Golota, who owed his fame and title shot to two brawls against Riddick Bowe in which he was disqualified for flagrant punches to the groin, the balconies were full of rowdies who waved red and white Polish flags, wore red and white face paint, and brought the floor crowd roaring to its feet as they brawled among themselves. "LOW BLOW! LOW BLOW!" they raised a merry cry.

Lewis's first-round knockout of the Pole would turn them into unhappy drunks stumbling meekly in the night. But in this air of bedlam, Jesus stepped through the ropes in a new robe and trunks trimmed in Mexico's red, green, and white. He embraced his dad then moved around snapping warm-up punches. At the bell Dorsey charged forward, scarcely moving his head, punctuating his punches with karate-like grunts. Jesus skirted Dorsey's rushes, working off his jab and throwing quick, fluid combinations. In the broadcast crew was light heavyweight champion Roy Jones, widely considered the best fighter in the sport today. "Chavez does throw some pretty punches," Jones said in the second round. "Textbook punches. Excellent form."

Dorsey buckled Jesus' knees with a booming right in the third, but by the end of the round Jones was comparing Jesus favorably to himself. Jesus was landing three punches to Dorsey's one. He hurt his left hand in this target practice, so instead of the hook he showcased the right uppercut. From the third round on, a doctor stuck his head through the ropes to check on Dorsey. "Doing fine! Thank you!" the game fighter barked. The surgical reconstruction held up, but he suffered a small cut high on his cheek, and both eyes were closing. After the seventh, the doctor stopped it. As the victor hugged and kissed his girlfriend, his performance was greeted at ringside with an approving hum. Behind me, George Foreman's brother, the promoter Roy Foreman, sat beside Bert Sugar, the legendary former editor of *Ring* magazine. Sugar's signature is an oversized fedora, an unlit cigar, and an air of having seen it all, often to his regret.

Foreman asked him what he thought of this new one.

Four-word reply: "Too nice a kid."

Eleven days later, Jesus left the country, taking little but clothes, his bag of gear, and his Dalmatian. He went to live with his grandparents in Delicias, Chihuahua. One day he returned to his birthplace, Parral; he met his ninety-six-year-old great-grandmother and saw the Pancho Villa tourist attractions. He found a gym of sorts in Delicias and a few capable sparring partners. His twenty-fifth birthday fell on the revered holiday of Mexican families, the Day

of the Dead. He helped his relatives make their preparations, and Terri and some friends from Austin flew down to Morelia to help him celebrate. "I think I'll be happy," he told me before he left. "Finally I get a chance to rest. Finally I get to kick back and, hell, enjoy a cold Corona."

But Jesus went to Mexico with the necessary patience of someone doing time. His lifeline is the telephone. In Atlantic City I had met Steve Farhood, a former editor of *Ring* who now provides boxing commentary for the CNN/ SI network. "The contract with Main Events was a major breakthrough for him," Farhood said. "Otherwise he wouldn't have gotten the exposure. He's an entertaining young offensive fighter, very exciting to watch. His big chance is going to come sometime in 1998."

Only not in Mexico. Trying to maintain his world ranking and chance at a title shot, Jesus accepted a fight in Mexico City this April against a journeyman opponent, but for less than five percent of the money he had made in Atlantic City. In Mexico's fight business, Jesus is an interloper, a foreigner. Jesus' talent and appeal have made him a commodity in America, and it may be that like a few athletes and show business professionals, he'll get a special visa and be allowed to pursue his opportunity in the United States. Among the criteria are the applicant's economic value and international standing. After the Dorsey fight, the alphabet soup of boxing organizations had him ranked as high as first, third, and fifth in the world super featherweight standings. But such a visa would only be good as long as he's practicing his skill. What happens in a few years when the prizefighter's taken all the punches he can?

"At the end of his career," the Irish trainer Tom O'Shea mused about Jesus, "I wonder where he'll be. Five percent of the boxers make eighty-five percent of the money. Those are lousy numbers, especially for the little guys. Boxing is experiencing its last gasp. All the grand heroes are gone. Ah, but Gabriel, my wife, and I talk of him still. He had this joy—the joy of the warrior. I read about great generals and battles and see ones like him marching in the ranks. None of us will ever understand how he got mixed up in that robbery."

The irony of Jesus' exile is that he represents the wan hope of the American criminal justice system—a male youth who commits an act of violence, accepts his punishment, grows up, and rehabilitates himself. But the law says that only citizens deserve a second chance. The old country, he finds, is not really his country. So he bangs on the bags and waits, a contender in no-man's-land.

APRIL, 1998

LEFT FOR DEAD

Months passed and the fast return and immediate title shot for my friend Jesus did not materialize. Opportunity was calling but reality failed to pay heed. Sensing a story that might tap into the vast Hispanic market, an independent producer and director had talked to me about developing Jesus' story into a movie script. I needed to talk to him about that possibility, but mostly I just wanted to see him. Meanwhile, Jesus' promoters had no interest in doing business in Mexico. He had realized that while he was in immigration limbo, the only continuing leverage he had in the fight game was his World Boxing Council ranking and his North American title. Jesus had to continue fighting, so for a few hundred dollars—on his last fight in the States he had made fifty thousand dollars—he returned to the ring in Mexico City. While working on my Texas Monthly *piece, my editor Mike Hall and fact-checker John Spong had fallen into the thrall of the character and story. Along with one of John's friends, David Courtney, they cooked up the idea of going down there to watch the fight. By the time the idea got to me they had a cheap airfare and a borrowed apartment in a nice part of town. Why not? We were unaware that the same month the United States State Department added Mexico City to its list of most dangerous foreign destinations.*

I never saw the taxi driver's face. I said hello to him as I slid across the back seat in the early-morning hours of April 20, 1998, but he stared straight ahead and offered nothing but a vague grunt. I didn't look to see if he had credentials and a mug shot pinned to his visor. I was fairly drunk, and so were my friends.

For the four of us it had been a fine Sunday wandering Mexico City. A night of swapping tales and chasing tequila with beer in the mariachis' mecca, Plaza Garibaldi, had seemed a fitting way to cap off our weekend. But we had already taken one cab ride from the plaza to our borrowed apartment, and we

knew landmarks along the well-lighted way. Now this driver made a sharp turn and raced through a dark barrio. "This doesn't look right," I said.

Why didn't I lock the doors, if my presentiment was so strong? Or just throw my arms around his neck? I could have easily overpowered the guy. But you want it *not* to happen; you want to be wrong. And so you fail to act.

We reemerged on the Paseo de la Reforma and breathed easier. But in the detour we had picked up a tail—a green and white Volkswagen Beetle cab. Riding in the front seat of our Japanese compact was Mike Hall, a thin, fortyish magazine writer and semiretired rock musician. The taxi carried us into the Polanco district, almost to the apartment—then the driver stopped abruptly in the middle of a block. Mike had noticed the VW, and he looked back and saw a nightmare. In disbelief's slow motion two men jumped out and ran toward us holding guns. "Go, go!" Mike cried, turning to the driver, but he was hunkered down, stonefaced. The deliveryman.

The pistoleers threw open the doors and vaulted inside; with a lurch our taxi sped off. Both men appeared to be in their thirties. Their guns were old, scarred .38 revolvers. The robber in the back seat was fat, doughy-faced, and nervous. He forced down the heads of John Spong and David Courtney and tried to hide his own face by burrowing into an absurd, rolling semblance of a football pileup. In the middle, pinned back by their weight, I sat face to face with the honcho in front. He had sharp, angular features and black hair combed Elvis-fashion. Possibly a ladies' man. "Shut up! Go to sleep!" he yelled. He sat on Mike's leg and stuck the gun's muzzle in his ear.

The last thing I needed was a lot of eye contact with this guy. But I could scarcely avoid it. Responding to my gaze, Honcho leaned over the seat and pistol-whipped me across the cheekbone. One whack, almost casual. He was asserting his dominance, controlling an animal. His English was good. He was used to handling a gun and ordering people around. Even odds, the robber was a cop.

Until I was close to forty all I knew of Mexico were the dusty and bleak border towns. In the Southwest, roaring off down there to get drunk and go whoring is a gringo rite of passage. Danger is part of the thrill. Long after I ceased to get any kick out of that, I married a woman who introduced me to Zihuatanejo, Cozumel, Oaxaca, Puerto Vallarta, the Sierra Madres—a Mexico I came to love. Mexico City, though, had never been my favorite destination. Friends told me about its bohemian enclave in the 1950s; they went to college there, living off their GI Bill payments, and danced the nights away in jazz clubs, reviving the Charleston, showing off the dirty bop. One recalled a club

whose patrons filled a table six inches deep in surrendered knives and guns, but even there he never felt menace. It snowed one time, he said, and for three days the vast, ancient lakebed lay cloaked in sootless white. If scenes like that still exist in Mexico's capital, I have never seen them. The first morning I awoke there, people walked to work with handkerchiefs pressed to watering eyes, because of the horrid air pollution. Political strategists of P.R.I. (Institutional Revolutionary Party), Mexico's embattled ruling party, are said to be delighted that Cuauhtémoc Cardenas, son of a revered president and the great hope of the P.R.D. (Party of the Democratic Revolution) the left-middle opposition alliance, was elected mayor of Mexico City in 1997: Trying to govern it will be his ruin.

On a cheap air fare and a whim, we had gone down there to watch a prizefight. I worked out at Richard Lord's Boxing Gym in Austin, and there had befriended a young pro in his stable, Jesus Chavez. A son of legal Mexican immigrants, Jesus was an amateur sensation in Chicago, but at seventeen he got mixed up with a gang and took part in a harebrained armed robbery. He did time in Illinois, moved to Texas, and completely turned his life around. But just as he gained a number-one world ranking as a super featherweight, the Immigration and Naturalization Service ordered him deported. Living with grandparents in Chihuahua, he had to continue fighting if he wanted to hold on to his ranking and hopes of a world title shot. For a pittance, he was making his Mexico debut.

I had written a *Texas Monthly* profile of the fighter. Mike Hall edited the piece, and John Spong was the fact-checker. David Courtney, a friend of John and a former intern at the magazine, was game to join us on the trip. I heard people talking about green cabs in the San Antonio airport and again behind me on the plane. Was the danger real? Or was it gringo paranoia? In Mexico City that night we dropped our bags at the apartment and went for a walk. An Explorer stopped, and a Mexican couple chewed us out for our lack of caution. "This place can be very dangerous for you," the woman said. I looked around and thought the lecture odd; the Polanco is a virtual country club.

The way to break into the taxi business in Mexico City is to buy a Volkswagen bug, remove the passenger's bucket seat, paint the car white with green stripes, and hit the streets. You see them by the thousands. But we were in little danger of getting highjacked in one of these unregulated gypsy cabs—our legs wouldn't fit in a VW. Later that night we hailed a regulated red Ford cab. The friendly driver took us to the Plaza Garibaldi, found a table for us in the Tenampa Bar, which has terrific mariachis, and he came back for us exactly when he said he would.

The next morning we met Jesus at his hotel and accompanied him to the weigh-in. A sportswriter asked him if his problems with United States authorities could be resolved. "*No sé*," I don't know, he answered. His opponent, Moi Rodriguez, was a thin, curly-haired Mexico City journeyman. Rodriguez pulled Jesus aside and told him: "Don't say that. You must believe that God is with you and that you'll get to go back to Texas and have the life you want."

Seven hours later they were trying to take each other's heads off.

After the weigh-in we boarded a subway with Wayne Harrison, a young man I had known at the gym in Austin. He lived in Mexico City now and marketed boxing equipment; he also kept a keen eye on Mexican fighters who might make suitable opponents on cards in the United States. Over lunch Wayne warned us that the Arena Coliseo was in a rough part of town. The last four times he had gone to the fights, he and his girlfriend had been attacked by muggers. I blinked and said, "What did you do?"

"Ran from them twice. Another time I sprayed them with some Mace. Other time I had these little scissors in my fist and I, uh, popped a guy one."

I made a mental note to send him a copy of my article, addressed to "Scissorhands."

The storied Arena Coliseo looked like a pit used for cockfights. The chairs at ringside were painted bright yellow, purple, and aqua; cheaper seats were arranged in circular balconies right above the ring. Chicken wire was put up to keep occupants of these seats from throwing things at the fighters. Jesus was rusty, and Rodriguez fought gamely, scoring with jabs and uppercuts. But in the third round Jesus landed a concussive right that wrenched Rodriguez's head far around on his shoulders. Rodriguez stayed on his feet but touched the canvas with his gloves—making it a knockdown—then wandered goofily, smiling. The referee started a count but then looked at Rodriguez's eyes and waved his arms, stopping it.

Outside we learned there weren't enough van and car seats for Wayne, his Mexican girlfriend, and me. Wayne said it would be folly to hail a cab here. Jesus' manager, Richard Lord, assigned us an affable young bruiser he had brought along for such contingencies. "Four blocks," said Wayne. "Straight ahead, don't stop." It was the spookiest short, quick walk of my life. Then we burst into a mass of light and noise, mariachis everywhere. The safe haven was Plaza Garibaldi.

Afterward, in the tony section called the Zona Rosa, we unwound with Jesus and his Texas cornermen. For me it was a bittersweet reunion, knowing I was going home and perhaps he never could. When Jesus trained me at the

gym in Austin, he pushed me hard, calling and catching punches with thick mitts on his hands. "How you gonna hit me standing way out there?" he ragged me, trying to instill a sense of range. "Step up in the pocket."

Those words came back to haunt me.

Whatever the causes, violence has engulfed Mexico. In Juárez, across the Rio Grande from El Paso, police claim that in the last five years at least ninety-five women have been murdered, many of them raped, while walking to work at *maquiladoras,* American-owned factories that take advantage of Mexico's cheap labor. "Lightning" kidnappings are the latest rage: People are snatched by men who have researched their finances and demand their liquid assets by the end of the day. The country's most notorious kidnapping ring was run by an ex-cop who specialized in cutting off victims' ears. In 1998 sixteen Mexico City cops were charged with gang-raping girls aged eighteen, fifteen, and thirteen in a police horse stable. In 1999 five Mexico City cops were charged in the killings of seventeen people. The victims had been pulled over and were then driven in police vehicles to remote areas, where they were robbed and shot with service revolvers. Affluent Mexicans hire bodyguards and consider the cops uniformed *rateros,* thieves.

Not since the Mexican Revolution has travel there seemed so dangerous. The State Department warns Americans to avoid six highways plagued by bandits. In 1998 American fishermen were murdered in Baja California; a Vermont artist and former Yale professor was raped then drowned in the surf at Puerto Escondido. A camera and sound crew from CNN was robbed at gunpoint while leaving the parking lot of Mexico's Foreign Secretariat. A Mexico City bandit jammed a pistol in the face of boxing promoter Don King and got away with a Rolex watch said to be worth one hundred thousand dollars.

But nothing got the attention of Americans like the December, 1997, shooting of a real estate broker named Peter Zarate. An ex-Navy Seal, Zarate caught a ride in one of the capital's green taxis, tried to fight his robbers, and they killed him. Five men confessed to the police, but a judge released them, calling the leader a "modern-day Robin Hood." Mayor Cárdenas sacked the Mexico City police chief he had earlier appointed and dozens of officers. A new federal police force is organized on the premise that only a completely fresh start can root out the criminals with badges. But in a perverse way the anti-corruption drive has added to the problem. Before, the bad cops got their money largely through extortion. Deprived of their uniforms, they still have guns, and in Mexico City the cab scam is the easiest way to make crime pay. Tourists aren't

the only prey: A Mexico City newspaper conducted a poll and proclaimed that a *fourth* of the city's residents have been robbed in that fashion.

The morning after the fight, my colleagues and I turned into resolute tourists. We went to the anthropology museum and roamed Chapúltepec Park amid Mexican families dressed in finery for Sunday mass. In tribal garb some Indians shinnied up steel poles, attached harnesses to their necks and heads, and against the gray sky assumed postures of flight as the poles whirled them round and round. We stopped and watched a mime. Stricken by the air pollution, leaves hung limply from trees that were centuries old. In another part of the city, that afternoon a man who had given us directions to an art fair reconsidered, called out, and hurried after us. Don't go off in those streets to the left, he warned us: *"Muy peligroso."* Danger.

But it was like some sly, subtle force pulled us along.

Above the Zócalo, the festive city square, we had our first drinks on a rooftop restaurant as a recording blared the Mexican national anthem and the sun and flag came down. I would have been happy to go to the apartment, pack for the airport, and read. But we walked on and plunged into a sidewalk market that was dim, crowded, confusing. At last we escaped that, and for the second night in a row I heaved a sigh of relief. Plaza Garibaldi.

We returned to the Tenampa Bar that had served us so well Friday night. Once more we laughed, talked, and drank to excess. I told them about the time I was falling in love with Dorothy; in a Puerto Vallarta cafe she got the mariachis to sing "Malageña Salarosa." Now a gleaming troupe with a horn section and spurs on their boots performed the Mexican love song with such melody and grace it brought tears to my eyes. David Courtney wore a ridiculous hat, a sort of brown straw derby that he had purchased on the Zócalo. At midnight he announced it was his thirty-second birthday. He grinned as we slapped him on the shoulder and bought another round. We had a great time.

After we called it a night John Spong walked out to the taxi stand and waved on the green VWs. A Japanese import pulled up next, and because it looked fairly new and costly, we thought it was safe. But the white car bore a green stripe.

When the robbers jumped in our cab, in an instant I went from drunk to sober. A gun in your face does that to you. They didn't rob us promptly; the leader took Mike Hall's watch, then seemed to get distracted. On and on we rode with the second gunman, this wordless, out-of-breath hooligan, in our laps. The ridiculousness magnified the terror. I watched Mike lean over until

his head touched the driver's shoulder. His expression was that of someone firmly bent on riding this out. For no reason I could determine, Honcho hit me with the gun again. I was astonished by my calm.

"Well, so much for not taking the green cabs," reflected John, a funny auburn-haired man who comes from a family of Episcopalian clerics. In the hassle and back talk of telling Honcho that he had spent his last peso on beer, John got his mouth bloodied by the gun. "I don't know, man," he said in high register, to no one in particular, "this has gone on a long time."

On my right, David was twisted like a pretzel under the second gunman's weight. Still he clung to the dumb straw hat. "I can't breathe, get him off me," he groaned at one point. Moments later David announced: "I'm gonna open the door and throw this fat fuck out of here."

That's interesting, we all thought. But watching Honcho's gun, which was aimed at Mike's head, John said, "You might hold up on that."

We careened onto a hellishly lit freeway that was black with soot and shreds of exploded truck tires. Then we were on an upper deck and could see nothing but distant lights on the mountainsides. As the ride carried us deeper into anxiety and unknown sections of the city, emotions ran wild. John and David discussed strategies of escape while I thought, Hasn't anybody noticed that one of these guys knows some English?

"Give us your money!" Honcho screamed at me.

"Well, let me get my hands free!" I yelled back. It was unfortunate and inevitable; we had a relationship now. I struggled and finally came out of the pile with my wallet. Honcho snatched it and tore my watch off my wrist.

Their take was about $150 and one of my credit cards—in the shattered Mexican economy, a fair night's work. I leaned forward and tried to reason with the guy. Others thought my pitch might have been too loudly stated. "We've given you everything! *Todo*. What more do you want? What's the point?"

Dismissively, Honcho turned his gaze away. As we came off the freeway into another barrio, he said they were going to separate us. If I had been more familiar with the cab scam, I might have thought they meant to take me and my credit card to an ATM machine—where with great displeasure they would have learned that I never set up PIN numbers for cash withdrawals. Whatever they intended, it sounded like a bad situation getting a lot worse. I thought they meant to kill us.

Mike breathed a prayer when the cab stopped near an intersection. Honcho got out first and ordered the rest of us to follow him. "Screw you, it's our cab," John rejoined. "We don't know where we are. We've got no money; we

can't get home." Mike climbed out, followed by the second gunman. But two men were trying to control four. As I came out behind David, Honcho grabbed my left arm roughly; John had the brass to step out on the driver's side.

"Run, run, scatter!" cried David. The fat robber clubbed him on the head with the gun and ripped his shirt, but David broke free and sprinted out into the street. I saw or heard none of that. I felt Honcho's grip loosen on my arm, and in reflex I threw his hand off me. After that it was all instinct and adrenaline.

The leader came after me with a look of fury. I didn't have the sense to turn and run. I weighed 195 pounds then, and in the gym I had learned to throw a hard left jab; I guess I thought I could stagger the smaller man, then make my escape. But I also felt the pleasure of anger—of striking back at the only real enemy I had ever had.

Except I failed to heed my young friend's advice: Step up in the pocket, Jesus said. If I was going to throw a punch at a man with a gun, I damn sure needed to land it. And by inches it fell short.

My friends said Honcho fired once at the ground, almost like he was seeing if the old gun worked. It's odd; I have no memory of that. With stone contempt and considered aim, he looked me in the eyes and pulled the trigger.

In the air between us a wan flash of lightning appeared, crackling from above his left shoulder to the ground. As the bullet's force threw me backward I swear I could feel its churning spin. The pain was instantaneous and absolute. I cried out to my friends a line that in movies always made me cringe.

"I'm killed."

The *rateros* and the taxi vanished from our lives. I was embarrassed by what I'd said. Mike thought it was so trite I must be joking; I had staged a comic pratfall to let them know everything was fine. But I knew at once that I was gravely hurt. I had turned and raised my arm at the gun. The slug broke both bones in my left arm at the wrist, entered my abdomen below my ribcage, and came to rest in my spine. I was in agony and furious at myself: You had a good life, a good marriage, and you come down here and get yourself wasted by some chickenshit thug.

As Mike held my head, John and David ran up and down the block, crying for assistance. The street was well-lighted, and I became aware of a circle of faces above me—expressions stricken, frightened, wondering how to help. A young paramedic who lived in the barrio kneeled beside me, checked my vital signs, shooed away a woman who tried to give me the water I craved, and sent the ambulance to the best hospital in the city.

In the ambulance I said, "Mike, I'd rather die than take this pain, but I want to see Dorothy again."

"Well," he said gently, "there's your reason why."

In the American British Cowdray emergency room I screamed with every breath. "*Plácido, plácido,*" a doctor said. Calm down. Mexican hospitals have little morphine; they use a synthetic substitute that's just not the same. Sometime during that endless night I was tired and scared to the limits of my being. "*Estoy muriendo?*" I asked a nurse. She talked me through that and persuaded me I wasn't dying, that I had to hang on.

At midday Dorothy arrived with my stepdaughter, Lila. Sick with fright and worry, they encountered a young surgeon, Roberto Castañeda, who had already operated on me. Bleeding internally, I had lost two and a half liters. He repaired the vessels and removed a few inches of my small intestine. Then he turned me over to the neurosurgeons, who carefully plucked the bullet from my spinal column. Having saved my life, Castañeda at once took my family into his emotional care. My wedding ring was fastened to his watch. He advised them not to put too much stock in the gloomy prognosis of the neurosurgeons, who indeed said I would be paralyzed from the waist down. Castañeda had seen me move my feet. Before we left Mexico in a rescue flight from Houston, he implored them: "Please don't hate my country."

The rescue jet was staffed by the team of a seventy-year-old Houston doctor named Red Duke. He is famous in Texas because of a folksy syndicated TV program of health tips that runs on the news of local stations, but behind the persona is a world-acclaimed trauma specialist.

Doctors in Texas had debated when and where I should be moved. The surgeons in Mexico said I was ready to go, but Dorothy and Lila were filled with apprehension. The jet was not allowed to use the international airport in Mexico City. Around 1:00 A.M. on Wednesday—just forty-eight hours since I had been singing with my friends and the mariachis of Plaza Garibaldi—an ambulance carrying my family and the medical personnel began a long, slow, bumpy climb to an airstrip in ancient Toluca. Our plane took off with me bound tightly to a stretcher. The technicians had brought plenty of morphine. The flight to Houston was short and smooth but nerve-wracking for Dorothy and Lila. I snored loudly with my eyes wide open. That's not a good sign, I have since learned. I was at the first tier of descent into a coma.

With the plane on the tarmac of the Hobby airport, the woman in charge of the rescue team strode up to Dorothy with her own eyes wide and her voice charged with tension. "Ms. Browne, we're having trouble waking him up."

Then, amid the scramble of nurses and paramedics, I stopped breathing. While Dorothy and Lila were quickly ushered off the plane, the technicians forced tubes down my throat and began to inflate my lungs.

"They OD'ed him!" Lila cried out in fear and accusation.

"Lila," Dorothy said with bitter despair, "don't ever put your life in my hands."

I resumed breathing and regained a degree of consciousness. Something was clamped over my mouth, and I struggled, fighting it. The face of the woman in charge appeared above me. "Mr. Reid," she said urgently, "you know me. You talked to me in Mexico City. You're in Houston now. And"— I'm pretty certain she said this—"you're blowing it!"

The nurses and technicians breathed easier and waited for an ambulance to arrive. But not for long. "Get a helicopter in here!" Dorothy screamed at them.

As the aircraft rose with me and veered north toward a hospital with the sprawling Houston Medical Center complex, Dorothy and Lila were the ones in a racing ambulance. For all they knew I was dead. Dorothy had been told that I would be under the care of a top neurosurgeon, Guy Clifton. When the ambulance reached the hospital emergency room, they ran inside. They encountered a tall, bony old fellow with a droopy mustache. He wore hospital greens and was scratching himself. When she burst upon him, blurting my name and demanding to see Dr. Clifton, the old-timer drawled, "I'm Red Duke. I'm gonna be your doctor, and I'm gonna be your mother."

At the end of my stay in Hermann's Hospital, the neurosurgeon Guy Clifton came in with the results of an MRI examination of my spine. He was delighted that the surgeons in Mexico had been so skillful and successful; he wouldn't have to operate on me again. "You may walk again and you may not," he told me. "It's going to take a year to eighteen months for this to play out. But nothing on here," the doctor went on, waving the test results, "says you *can't* walk."

After telling me about the MRI results, he said, "Now we're going to get you up." I laughed and thought, Right. Mexican doctors had said I survived partly because I was in such good shape. But now I had no strength at all. I could move my head, my hands and arms, and, with difficulty, my feet. Nurses put me on what looked like a stretcher, then one hit a switch and the device groaned, twisted, and turned into a chair that vaulted me upright. Drunk at once from the change in altitude, I glanced down and saw something pale flop like a salmon thrown on a bin of ice. Talk about a bottom line. It was my right foot.

For the next several weeks my home was a highly regarded rehabilitation hospital in Houston known by its acronym, T.I.R.R. (Pronounced "tear," as in weeping—the proper name is The Institute for Research and Rehabilitation.) For two hours each morning and afternoon, working with therapists I stretched, pushed, and tried to rouse my slumbering limbs. It didn't hurt my morale that nearly all the therapists in my year of rehab would be engaging, attractive young women. There was no bawdy talk or making passes, though I witnessed some of that. What we had to do was too important to screw up the chemistry. "Look at you!" Sherry would exclaim, grinning, as I made some small gain. Theresa was filling out a form for me one day. I watched her pause at a line and then write, "Paraplegic." My reaction was ludicrous. *Who, me?* But it was impossible to feel sorry for myself. Everywhere I looked someone bore up bravely under a condition far worse than mine.

I was extremely lucky. The bullet invaded my spinal column without injuring the cord and came to rest in a mass of nerves called the *cauda equina*. Unlike the spinal cord, those nerves are capable of healing and regenerating. I had what is known as an "incomplete" spine injury. That was the good news. But not so cheery was the condition of my left leg. While the right grew stronger each day and soon would support my standing weight, muscles in the left twitched and fired, trying to remember what to do. The knee buckled and the leg was numb. In a way I was grateful. After I was shot, "referred" pain from the spinal injury had burned in my shins and feet like the blazes of hell. Specialists brought this odd kind of pain under control with drugs normally prescribed for epileptic seizures and depression. But more weirdness followed. First the symptoms felt like a fluttering surge of electricity moving slowly down my left leg. Then the phantom pains turned nasty. Several times a day, they twisted me up with burning, lockdown cramps that first seized my left leg, then my right foot, and felt like I'd stuck them in an electric socket. And as time went by they got worse, not better. Doctors offered vague clinical explanations and prescribed more drugs; the head physical therapist at the rehab hospital hiked her shoulders and explained, "Aw, it's those funky gunshot wounds."

In the days following the shooting, an Austin newspaper had printed my remark to Mike Hall that I'd rather die than endure the pain, except I wanted to see Dorothy again. Suddenly friends and strangers back home were making us into Scotty and Zelda, Tracy and Hepburn. But life and love consume a lot more soap than opera. When I was in the hospital Dorothy took a leave from her job and assumed a manic gypsy life. Some days she lived in a borrowed

apartment near the Houston Medical Center, learning from the therapists what my condition required of her. Then she was on the highway back to Austin, where she enlisted an architect and builder to modify the house for my wheelchair. She acknowledged her obsessive behavior; one day, preparing to drive back to Houston, she raced around wondering how she could possibly leave our house-sitter with a spice rack devoid of peppercorns.

The strain took its toll, of course. At the rehab hospital therapists agreed with her that while I worked hard at my exercises, other times I demonstrated a strange, spacey passivity. Was it all the medication I was taking? Or was it having nurses attend to my every need? A few days before my discharge, the doctors insisted wisely that we spend a weekend away from the hospital. We checked into a nice hotel, drank and ate with friends, and once more enjoyed being in the same bed. But I forgot essential things related to my medical condition; she had to drive back and get them. On the hottest day of the year I insisted on keeping a social engagement; she had to haul the heavy chair in and out of the trunk.

"Are you depressed?" she said when we quarreled.

"I'm starting to be."

"I knew you were going to say that!"

The next week my head swirled in confusion and despair. Dorothy had panicked, telling staff that I wasn't ready to go home. But the day came anyway, and two months after my near death in Mexico City, I rode in a car on a highway in Texas, staring with amazement at the parched grassland.

"You'll have good days and bad days," doctors and therapists warned me. But they failed to say how often the good and bad would be rolled into one. At dinner one evening a pain outbreak began with a buzzing tightness in my left knee. By midnight the spasms came every eight minutes. My groaning and hissing drove my wife to the guest bedroom. It was a miserable night. Friends drove me to an Austin hospital for outpatient therapy three times a week. That morning I wheeled into the exercise room groggy and ill-tempered. My regular therapist said she had to evaluate a stroke victim, and she introduced me to a young blond woman who would fill in with me. Sarah was a contract therapist, working here and there as needed, and she apologized for being so green about spinal injuries. "Green?" I said, surprised, for she was very good. On the exercise mat skilled physical therapists kneel and roll and pivot around their patients with the grace of dancers. The leg lifts and stretching moved me into that zone of relaxed airiness I once knew as an athlete. For twenty minutes then I moved around the room on a walker. I

wobbled and jerked but in my mind I cruised. Outside, the day looked glorious. "Slow down, take shorter steps," said Sarah. "But you're doing great."

On insurance and other forms my doctors describe me as an incomplete paraplegic. It rattles me every time; I guess the element of disbelief will always be there. Paraplegia affects not just the legs. It impairs every function from the waist down. The bladder and bowels. Making love. I've soiled my pants and hated the smell of my urine. The ease and steadiness that can come with a long marriage has been stolen from us. My bedside table used to be piled with books and magazines; now it looks like a pharmacy shelf. I no longer go out in the world with the assurance I'm big and strong and can take care of myself.

But after six months of dogged effort and therapy, I sent the wheelchair back to the medical supplier. I didn't need it anymore. I got my legs back under me, and I'm proud of that. It has been the hardest work of my life. I used to get around with a walker, then progressed to two forearm crutches, then just one crutch. Now I'm able to walk with a cane. Indoors I often get from room to room without that, though I'd rate my gait as a Frankenstein lurch. Not long ago, something wondrous happened. At the end of a day I set out to walk my dog around the block. A few hundred feet from our gate, I wondered why I was so unsteady. Jake wasn't yanking the leash any harder than usual. Was I wearing the wrong shoes? Or was I just tired? Then it came to me. I forgot the cane!

I see some valor in what happened that night in Mexico City, but not much heroism. We all were looking out for ourselves; I'm just glad none of my friends got hurt. As for Honcho, let him have the hell he's in. A host of caring people, many of them strangers, many of them Mexicans, delivered me from the likes of him. I could forgive him if it mattered, but can't see how it does. I don't dwell on the *pistolero*. He has no presence in my dreams. I escaped him in the outpouring of friendship and rescue that began with a spill of letters across my bed that first morning I emerged from the cloud of morphine. From a past girlfriend came the best first line: "Jan—Never go to a gunfight without a gun." The notorious Don King sent me a warm note and five thousand dollars for my medical fund, and there were dozens more like him. But it bothers me that while my surgeon Roberto Castañeda found out how to call us in the States, and Oscar Espinosa, the nation's Secretary of Tourism, requested a meeting to express his regards and concern, not one law enforcement officer from Mexico has spoken to me.

I often talk to Jesus Chavez, my friend the banished fighter. He blamed

himself when I got shot. He has to accept the terms of Mexico City; it's the only place he can get the training he needs. But he's learned to dress in tattered clothes and closely watch the routes of cabdrivers. In August, 1998, he was preparing for a fight with Francisco Martinez Lagunas, a veteran battler and father of three. One day some *rateros* tried to carjack Lagunas. Like Peter Zarate and me, Lagunas tried to fight them. They got rid of Jesus' opponent, shot him dead.

I fell in love with my wife in Mexico. In a time-forsaken Pacific village called Yelapa, we rented gaunt horses and rode along a river rushing down from jungle mountainsides. We came to a ford that was running high, and the nags refused to cross. But that was fine, for all around us, caressing our arms and faces, was a storm of purple, blue, and gold butterflies. I hate to think we'll never see such loveliness again. I still haven't seen Zacatecas, Guanajuato, or Veracruz. But not Mexico City. A dark beast is loose on those streets, and I never aim to feel its breath on me again.

OCTOBER, 1999

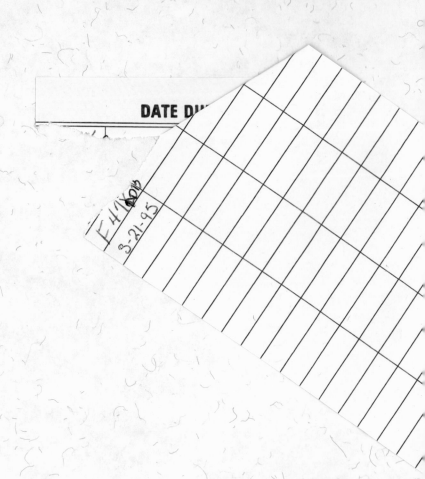

DATE DUE

E41/XOB
3-21-95